Winston S. Churchill

VOLUME II

Young Statesman

1901-1914

Also by Randolph S. Churchill

THE STORY OF THE CORONATION

THEY SERVE THE QUEEN

FIFTEEN FAMOUS ENGLISH HOMES

CHURCHILL, HIS LIFE IN PHOTOGRAPHS
(with Helmut Gernsheim)

WHAT I SAID ABOUT THE PRESS

THE RISE AND FALL OF SIR ANTHONY EDEN

LORD DERBY: ''KING OF LANCASHIRE''

THE FIGHT FOR THE TORY LEADERSHIP

TWENTY-ONE YEARS

THE SIX DAY WAR
(with Winston S. Churchill)

WINSTON SPENCER CHURCHILL IN 1904

RANDOLPH S. CHURCHILL

Winston S. Churchill

VOLUME II · 1901–1914

Young Statesman

ILLUSTRATED WITH PHOTOGRAPHS
AND MAPS

HOUGHTON MIFFLIN COMPANY BOSTON

1967

First Printing R

Theme of the Work

He shall be his own biographer
—*Lockhart*

Theme of Volume II

How a soldier of fortune
by diligence and high ambition
turned himself while in his thirties
into a parliamentarian
statesman and author
of the first order

Acknowledgements

THE AUTHOR WISHES first to acknowledge his indebtedness to Her Majesty the Queen, who graciously gave permission for him to have access to the Royal Archives and to use other documents which are her copyright. For guidance in the selection of this material, the author is grateful to Mr Robert Mackworth-Young, Librarian at Windsor Castle.

Thanks are also due to those who have kindly allowed the author access to their Archives: Sir Max Aitken (Bonar Law and Lloyd George Papers and for holograph material); the Marquess of Bath (Marsh Papers at Longleat); the Earl of Derby; the Duke of Devonshire; the Earl of Elgin; the Duke of Hamilton and Brandon (Fisher Papers at Lennoxlove); Sir Shane Leslie; Pamela, Countess of Lytton; Mrs Airlie Madden; Miss Judy Montagu; the Bodleian Library and the Warden of New College, Oxford (Milner Papers); Lord Ponsonby of Shulbrede; the Earl of Rosebery; the Marquess of Salisbury (Salisbury and Quickswood Papers at Hatfield); Baroness Spencer-Churchill. The Trustees of the Smuts Archive; the Bodleian Library, Oxford and Mr Mark Bonham-Carter (Asquith Papers); British Museum (Balfour and Cecil of Chelwood Papers); and the New York City Public Library (Cockran Papers); Mr Roy Jenkins (Home Office Papers).

The Crown copyright material included in this volume is reproduced with the permission of the Controller of Her Majesty's Stationery Office.

Copyright permission has also been kindly provided by Sir Max

Aitken (Beaverbrook, Bonar Law and Lloyd George); Mr Julian Amery; Mr Mark Bonham Carter (Asquith); the Earl of Balfour; the Earl Beatty; Lord Beauchamp; the Earl of Birkenhead; Mr Charles Blacque (Beresford); Sir Dudley Bowater; Lord Brassey; Viscount Brentford (Joynson-Hicks); the Honourable Edward Carson; the late Lady Crewe; the Earl of Elgin; Viscount Elibank; Viscount Esher; Viscount Harcourt; Lord Henderson; Sir Charles Hobhouse; the Marquess of Lansdowne; the Marquess of Londonderry; the late Viscount Long of Wraxall; Major-General Godfrey Wildman-Lushington; Mr Harold Macmillan; Mrs Airlie Madden (Hynes); the Duke of Marlborough; Mrs C. F. G. Masterman; Mrs Terence Maxwell (Chamberlain); the Earl of Midleton (Brodrick); Lord Mottistone (Seely); Mr James Pope-Hennessy; the Earl of Rosebery; the Marquess of Salisbury (Hatfield and Cecil of Chelwood); Viscount Scarsdale (Curzon); the Earl of Selborne; Baroness Spencer-Churchill; Mrs John Stevens (Hely-Hutchinson); the Duke of Westminster; the Viscount Wimborne and by Mr P. G. Agnew of *Punch* (Sir Henry Lucy).

And also to the following publishers and copyright holders: Ernest Benn (*Lord Curzon* by Lord Ronaldshay); Collins, Sons and Co (*Winston Churchill As I Knew Him* by Lady Violet Bonham Carter); Constable and Co (*Lord Crewe* by James Pope-Hennessy); Country Life (Lord Riddell's *Diaries*); Curtis Brown (*Memoirs* by Sir Almeric Fitzroy); the Syndics of the Fitzwilliam Museum, Cambridge (Wilfred Scawen Blunt's *Diaries*); Mrs E. H. Hassall and Mr N. E. Hassall (*A Number of People* by Edward Marsh); Hodder and Stoughton (*Richard Burdon Haldane, An Autobiography*); Hutchinson Publishing Group (*My Political Life* by Leo Amery); Methuen and Co (*Problems of Poverty* by J. A. Hobson); Odhams Press (*Great Contemporaries* by Winston S. Churchill); Charles Scribner's Sons (*The World Crisis* by Winston S. Churchill); the Trustees of the Passfield Trust (Beatrice Webb's *Diaries*); the Public Trustee (*King Edward VII* by Sir Sidney Lee).

The events recorded in these pages happened many years ago, and in some cases it has not been possible to trace the holders of copyright. Will any copyright holders who have been omitted please accept the author's apologies?

For reminiscences the author is indebted to Margaret, Lady Birkenhead; Group Captain Ivon Courtney; Baroness Spencer-Churchill and Mr James Wilson.

To the following the author expresses his thanks for reading the proofs and for tendering valuable advice: Mr R. A. Bevan, Admiral Sir Peter Gretton, Mr Cameron Hazlehurst of Nuffield College, Oxford, Mr Tom Hartman, Mr G. Norman Knight who has also compiled the index, Mr Robert Mackworth-Young, Mr Anthony Montague Browne, Baroness Spencer-Churchill and Mr Ivan Yates.

Finally the author desires to express his indebtedness to the following who have assisted in sorting, assembling and studying the material: Mr Michael Wolff, who, as in the first volume, has directed the research; Mr Andrew Kerr, who has prepared all the material for the press; Mr Martin Gilbert, Mr Martin Mauthner, Mr George Thayer, Mr Frank Gannon, Mr Alan Thompson and Mr Robert Taylor who have all contributed to various aspects of the research. Also to his secretarial staff: Miss Eileen Harryman, Archivist, and Miss Barbara Twigg, principal private secretary; Mrs Trevor Adams; Mrs Margaret Bentley and Miss Lynette Parker. And to Mrs R. A. Bevan, who assembled the illustrations and advised on their selection.

Contents

xiii

$\mathscr{L}$

Illustrations

xvii

MAPS

BY JOAN EMERSON

Preface

THE FIRST VOLUME of this work was a simple and unadorned tale. It was that of a boy's days in his nursery, at school and in the army. Except for his immediate family — his father, his mother, his brother and, above all, his nanny, the immortal Everest — few people impinged greatly upon his life. There were no more than fleeting glimpses of prominent people in the great world in which his father and mother lived. It was not only a simple tale, it was a straightforward tale. There was little need to explain or enlarge. The story told itself.

It will be very different in this and succeeding volumes. When Volume II opens, our hero — for such as he has become — is already world-famous and well equipped to tread the stage which his father had quit a decade before. The stage will now become richly peopled; new issues and controversies, often of great complexity, will emerge; life will become much more complicated as the pages are turned. He will cross the floor of the House of Commons, he will write his father's life, he will get married and become a father. The complexities of four great Government departments will have to be unravelled: much administration and legislation will be considered and explained. Many topics which have long lost their novelty and have fallen into desuetude will have to be brought alive. But this is not a history of the first half of the century; these events and issues must be strung upon the fragile cord of an individual life.

This volume covers not only Churchill's abandonment of the Tories for the Liberal Party; it also deals with the considerable social

revolution with which he and Lloyd George were principally concerned, which involved as its political climax the clipping of the
powers of the House of Lords in the Parliament Act. He then quits
these fields for war preparation at the Admiralty. Moreover, there
is much to tell of his part in Irish affairs while he was at the Home
Office and the Admiralty. Churchill will be seen to have played a
leading role in all the exciting and indeed frenzied events which
marked the first six years of Asquith's famous administration.

Although much will be drawn from the letters and papers of other
people, as in the first volume Churchill will continue to "be his own
biographer." That does not mean that we shall rely over-much upon
his published works, though, since he was a man who earned his
living by his pen, quotations from his books not only contribute to
the narrative but give some idea of his growing literary powers.
Considerable extracts from his speeches will often have to be given,
not only to show him in action but also to mark his style and power
of argument; for he was an orator not less than writer. But the field
in which he will still predominate as his own biographer will be in
the vast number of his own previously unpublished letters and
memoranda. Such letters give a true insight into a man's character
and often serve as a supplement and a corrective to what he may
do or say in public.

RANDOLPH S. CHURCHILL

Stour
East Bergholt
Suffolk
April 1967

Short Biographies
of the Principal Characters

TO BE BROUGHT BEFORE THE READER
IN THIS VOLUME

ASKWITH George Ranken, 1st Baron (1861–1942); Controller-General, commercial, labour and statistical department, Board of Trade 1909–11; Chief Industrial Commissioner 1911–19; KCB 1911; created Baron 1919.

ASQUITH Herbert Henry, 1st Earl of Oxford and Asquith (1852–1928); Prime Minister 1908–16. Liberal MP for East Fife 1886–1918, Paisley, 1920–24; Home Secretary 1892–5; Liberal Imperialist during Boer War; Chancellor of Exchequer 1905–8; displaced by Lloyd George 1916; resigned liberal leadership 1926. Created Earl 1925. Married first 1877 Helen, daughter of F. Melland, died 1891; 2nd 1894 Margaret (Margot), youngest daughter of Sir Charles Tennant, 1st baronet.

BALFOUR Arthur James 1st Earl (1848–1930); Conservative MP for Hertford 1874–85, for East Manchester 1885–1906, for City of London 1906–22; associated with Lord Randolph in the Fourth Party; entered Cabinet 1886; Conservative leader in Commons 1891–2, 1895–1902. As Prime Minister 1902–5 sought to keep Party together during tariff reform controversy; set up Committee of Imperial Defence 1902; inaugurated Anglo-French *entente* April 1904. Resigned Party leadership November 1911. Succeeded WSC as First Lord of the Admiralty 1915. Foreign Secretary 1916–19. KG 1922; Earl 1922. Died unmarried.

BECKETT Ernest William (1856–1917); Conservative MP for Whitby 1885–1905. Formerly a partner in the Banking firm of Beckett & Co in Leeds. Succeeded his uncle as 2nd Baron Grimthorpe in 1905.

BERESFORD Charles William de la Poer (1846–1919); 2nd son of 4th Marquess of Waterford. Rear-Admiral Mediterranean 1900–2; Conservative MP for York 1897–1900; for Woolwich 1902. Commanded Channel Squadron 1903–5; C-in-C Mediterranean Fleet 1905–7; Channel Fleet 1907–9; retired as Admiral 1911. Unionist MP for Portsmouth 1910–16. His younger brother William married 1895 Lilian, widow of the 8th Duke of Marlborough.

BIRKENHEAD Frederick Edwin Smith, 1st Earl (1872–1930); Conservative MP for Walton (Liverpool) 1906–19; a brilliant lawyer and debater, he formed a lasting friendship with WSC shortly after entering Parliament; Solicitor-General 1915; Attorney-General 1915–19; Lord Chancellor 1919–22; Secretary of State for India 1924–28; married Margaret Furneaux 1901.

BOTHA Louis (1862–1919); Commandant-General of Boer forces 1900; carried on guerrilla warfare 1900–2; surrendered May 1902; visited Britain 1902; founded Het Volk party which won first elections under responsible government 1907. As first Prime Minister of Union of South Africa 1910–19 supported Britain in World War.

BRODRICK William St John Fremantle, 1st Earl of Midleton (1856–1942); Conservative MP for Surrey 1880–1906; Secretary of State for India 1903–5; for War 1900–3. Succeeded as Viscount Midleton 1907; created 1st Earl 1920.

BURNS John Elliot (1858–1943); trade union leader and agitator; elected Independent Labour MP for Battersea 1892. President of local Government Board and Cabinet member 1905 (first artisan to reach that rank). Opposed the Webbs' plan to reform the Poor Law. Twice re-elected at Battersea as a Liberal in 1910 elections. President of Board of Trade 1914, resigning at outbreak of war.

CAMPBELL-BANNERMAN Sir Henry (1836–1908); Liberal MP for the Stirling Burghs 1868–1908; succeeded as Liberal leader in House of Commons 1899; denounced British "methods of barbarism" in South Africa. Prime Minister December 1905 to April 1908; established responsible government in Transvaal and Orange River Colony. His wife Charlotte died 1906.

CARSON Sir Edward Henry (1854–1935); Conservative MP for Dublin University 1892–1918, for Duncairn (Belfast) 1918–21; became leading advocate after Oscar Wilde's libel action against Marquess of Queensberry 1895. Solicitor-General 1900–5; as leader of Irish Unionists in Commons 1910–21 successfully ensured the exclusion of Ulster from Irish Home Rule. Attorney-General in Asquith's coalition government May 1915 to October 1916, First Lord of the Admiralty under Lloyd George December 1910 to July 1917, War Cabinet until January 1918. Lord of Appeal 1921–9. Knighted 1900. Created Life Baron 1921.

CASSEL Sir Ernest Joseph (1852–1921) ; naturalized international financier and philanthropist of German-Jewish origin. Racing enthusiast; close friend of King Edward VII, and of WSC, skilfully guiding both in their financial activities. Gave about £2 million to charities. Knighted 1899.

CECIL Hugh Richard Heathcote Gascoyne (1869–1956); 5th son of 3rd Marquess of Salisbury and brother of Lord Robert Cecil. Conservative MP for Greenwich 1895–1906, Oxford University 1910–37; Baron Quickswood 1941. Until WSC crossed the floor, Hugh Cecil was his closest political friend, giving his name to the "Hughligans," and fighting ardently in defence of the Church of England and against Joseph Chamberlain's tariff policy.

CHAMBERLAIN (Joseph) Austen (1865–1937); son of Joseph, and half-brother of Neville Chamberlain; Liberal Unionist MP for East Worcestershire 1892–1914; Financial Secretary to Treasury 1900–2; Postmaster-General 1902–3; Chancellor of Exchequer 1903–5 and

1919–21. Foreign Secretary 1924–29, First Lord of the Admiralty, very briefly in 1931; supported his father's views on tariff reform. After Balfour's resignation 1911 he and Walter Long, as rivals for Conservative Party leadership, stood down in favour of Bonar Law. KG 1925.

CHAMBERLAIN Joseph (1836–1914); member of Birmingham screw manufacturing firm; as mayor 1873–5 improved the city's housing and sanitation. MP for West Birmingham 1885–1914. Broke with Liberal Party over Home Rule 1886; joined Salisbury's third Cabinet as Colonial Secretary 1895 and sought to further the cause of British imperialism; resigned 1903 over tariff reform, for which he campaigned until 1906 when ill health forced him to withdraw from public life. Three times married; his sons included Austen and Neville. Despite their differences over the tariff issue, he and WSC remained good friends.

CURZON George Nathaniel, 1st and last Marquess Curzon of Kedleston (1859–1925); MP for Southport 1886–98; Viceroy and Governor-General of India 1898–1905. Lord Privy Seal 1915–16; Lord President of the Council 1916–19; Secretary of State for Foreign Affairs 1919–24; Leader of the House of Lords 1916–25. Created Baron Curzon 1898 (Irish peerage); Earl Curzon of Kedleston 1911; Marquess 1921. Succeeded as 5th Baron Scarsdale 1916. His first wife, Mary Victoria, died 18 July 1906.

DEVONSHIRE Spencer Compton, 8th Duke of (1833–1908). Conservative MP 1857–91. As Lord Hartington founded, with Chamberlain, Liberal Unionists which broke up Gladstone's administration in 1886; joined Lord Salisbury's coalition government as President of the Council 1895–1902; held same office under Balfour 1902–3. Strongly opposed Chamberlain's tariff schemes and resigned 1903 due to Balfour's equivocal pronouncements on tariff. Also a respected leader of Victorian society. Succeeded as 8th Duke 1891; married 1892 his inseparable companion Countess Louise Fredericke Auguste, widow of 7th Duke of Manchester.

ELGIN Victor Alexander Bruce, 9th Earl of (1849–1917); Colonial Secretary 1905–8 while WSC was Under-Secretary of State for Colonies. Married first in 1876 Constance Carnegie, daughter of the ninth Earl of Southesk by whom he had six sons and five daughters; she was ill for some years before her death in 1909. He married secondly in 1913 Gertrude Lilian, widow of Captain Frederick Charles Ashley Ogilvy.

FISHER John Arbuthnot, 1st Baron (1841–1920); entered Navy 1854; First Sea Lord 1904–10, he organized redistribution of fleet to meet growing German threat; advocated Dreadnought battleship and cruisers; issued programme of eight battleships 1909–10; reappointed First Sea Lord 1914, resigning over Dardanelles 1915. Knighted 1894; baron 7 December 1909.

GLADSTONE Herbert John 1st Viscount (1854–1930); youngest son of W. E. Gladstone; MP West Leeds 1880–1910; Liberal Chief Whip 1899–1905; Home Secretary 1905–10; first Governor-General of South Africa 1910–14; Viscount 1910.

GREY Sir Edward, third baronet (1862–1933). Liberal MP for Berwick on Tweed 1885–1916. Supported Boer War. Like Asquith vice-president of Liberal League led by Lord Rosebery. As Foreign Secretary, 1905–16 upheld Anglo-French *entente* against German pressure. Created Viscount Grey of Fallodon 1916. His first wife, Dorothy died after carriage accident 4 February 1906. Married widow of 1st Baron Glenconner 1922.

GUEST Frederick Edward (1875–1937); younger son of 1st Baron Wimborne, and WSC's cousin; Liberal MP 1910–22 and 1923–9; Conservative MP 1931–7. Helped promote aviation in Britain. Married, 28 June 1905, Amy Phipps of Pittsburgh, USA.

GUEST Ivor Churchill, 1st Viscount Wimborne (1873–1939) ; son of 1st Baron Wimborne and Lord Randolph's sister, Lady Cornelia; WSC's cousin; Conservative MP for Plymouth 1900–6; Liberal MP for Cardiff 1906–10; Paymaster-General 1910–12. Created Baron Ashby St Ledger 1910; succeeded 1914; created Viscount Wimborne 1918. Married, 10 February 1902, Hon Alice Katherine Sibell Grosvenor, daughter of 2nd Baron Ebury.

HAMILTON Sir Ian Standish Monteith (1853–1947); served as soldier in India where he met WSC; commanded mounted infantry division in advance on Pretoria 1900 (in which WSC took part). Military Secretary at War Office 1900–3; Quartermaster-General 1903–4; headed military mission with Japanese 1904–5; GO C-in-C Southern Command 1905–9; General 1907; Adjutant-General 1909–10; GO C-in-C, Mediterranean command 1910–14; commanded Anglo-French army at Dardanelles 1915. Knighted 1900.

HOPWOOD Sir Francis John Stephens (1860–1947). Appointed a member of the Commission to South Africa to advise on the Constitution for the Transvaal and Orange River Colonies. Permanent Secretary Board of Trade 1901–7; Permanent Under-Secretary of State for Colonies 1907–11; a Civil Lord of the Admiralty 1912–17. Knighted 1901; Privy Councillor 1912; created Baron Southborough 1917.

LAW Andrew Bonar (1858–1923); Conservative MP for Blackfriars (Glasgow) 1900–06, Dulwich 1906–10, Bootle 1911–18, Glasgow Central 1918–22; an iron merchant before entering politics, he rose rapidly to the front rank of the Conservative Party; as a compromise candidate with the skilful aid of Sir Max Aitken, succeeded Balfour as leader of the Conservatives in the House of Commons, 1911; Secretary of State for the Colonies in Asquith's coalition government; Chancellor of the Exchequer under Lloyd George 1916–18; Lord Privy Seal 1919–21; Leader of the House of Commons 1916–21; Prime Minister and First Lord of the Treasury 1922–23.

LLOYD GEORGE David, 1st Earl (1863–1945); Liberal MP for Carnarvon Boroughs 1890–1945. Opposed Boer War and Balfour's policy of rate-aid to voluntary schools. President of Board of Trade 1905–08 (when succeeded by WSC). As Chancellor of Exchequer

1908–14 introduced "People's" Budget 1909 which led to constitutional crisis over House of Lords' veto. With WSC responsible for introducing far-reaching social reforms on which welfare state based. Succeeded Asquith as Prime Minister 1916, resigning 1922. Created Earl 1945.

LOREBURN Robert Threshie Reid, 1st Earl (1846–1923); called to Bar 1871; entered Parliament as Liberal 1880; Solicitor-General and knighted 1894; Attorney-General 1895. Supported Boers during Boer War. As Lord Chancellor December 1905 to June 1912 established Court of Criminal Appeal 1907. Created Earl 1911. Died childless.

LYTTELTON Alfred (1857–1913); son of 4th Baron; barrister 1881–1903; Liberal Unionist MP 1895–1913. Succeeded Chamberlain as Colonial Secretary September 1903–5; introduced Chinese labourers on Rand goldfields 1904; drew up (abortive) plan for granting representative government to Transvaal 1905. Father of 1st Viscount Chandos.

McKENNA Reginald (1863–1943); Liberal MP Monmouthshire North 1895–1918; Financial Secretary to the Treasury 1905–9; President of Board of Education 1907–8; First Lord of the Admiralty 1908–11, when he exchanged offices with WSC; Home Secretary 1911–15; Chancellor of the Exchequer 1915–16; retired from politics in 1919 when he became Chairman of the Midland Bank.

MALCOLM Ian Zachary (1868–1944); one of the "Hooligans." Conservative MP Stowmarket 1895–1906; Croydon 1910–19; Parliamentary Private Secretary to Chief Secretary for Ireland, George Wyndham, 1901–3. Married, 30 June 1902, Jeanne Marie Langtry, daughter of Lady de Bathe (Lily Langtry, the famous actress).

MARSH Edward Howard (1872–1953); son of Professor Howard Marsh, Master of Downing College, Cambridge. 2nd Class Clerk, Colonial Office 1896; Assistant Private Secretary to Joseph Chamberlain 1900–3 and to Alfred Lyttelton 1903–5; 1st Class Clerk 1905.

Private Secretary to WSC 1905–15; 1917–22, 1924–9; accompanied WSC on tour of East Africa 1907–8; Private Secretary to J. H. Thomas 1924 and 1929–36; Malcolm Macdonald 1936–7. Trustee of the Tate Gallery 1937–44. Created CMG 1908; CB 1918; CVO 1922; KCVO 1937; WSC's lifelong companion. Art and Literary patron. Died unmarried.

MORLEY John, 1st Viscount (1838–1923) ; Liberal MP 1883–1908; Secretary of State for India 1905–10; Lord President of the Council 1910–14 when he resigned over British intervention. His official biography of Gladstone published 1903.

NORTHCLIFFE Alfred Charles William Harmsworth, 1st Viscount (1865–1922); largely self-educated; founded halfpenny *Daily Mail* 1896 which pioneered popular journalism; founded *Daily Mirror* 1903; chief proprietor of *The Times* on formation of company 1908. Amassed huge fortune. Created Baronet 1904, Baron 1905, Viscount 1918.

REDMOND John Edward (1851–1918); Irish Nationalist MP for New Ross 1881–85, Wexford North 1885–91, Waterford 1891–1918; a barrister; succeeded Parnell as leader of the Irish Nationalist Party at Westminster.

ROBINSON Joseph Benjamin, 1st Baronet (1840–1929); South African mining magnate who secured valuable diamond claims at Kimberley and sank first shaft on Rand. Sympathetic to Boer cause he quarrelled with other mine owners. After 1904 sought to show that supply of African mine labour was sufficient to dispense with Chinese coolies thus finding favour with WSC who was responsible for carrying out Liberal pledge to end Chinese experiment. Granted baronetcy 1908. In 1922 Robinson was recommended for a peerage. Vehement protests caused him to decline the honour.

ROSEBERY Archibald Philip Primrose, 5th Earl (1847–1929); Secretary of State for Foreign Affairs 1886 and 1892–4; Prime Minister 1894–5; a friend of both Lord Randolph and WSC. Always a reluctant politician, after 1901 he ploughed a lonely furrow away from his Liberal Imperialist supporters.

RUNCIMAN Walter (1870–1949); Liberal MP. Defeated WSC at Oldham 1899, but lost seat to him in 1900. Returned to Parliament 1902–18, 1924–31; as Liberal National 1931–37. Parliamentary Secretary to Local Government Board 1905–7; Financial Secretary to Treasury 1907–8; President Board of Education 1908–11; of Agriculture 1911–14; of Trade 1914–16, 1931–37. Sent to Czechoslovakia in 1938 by Lord Halifax as "independent mediator" between the Czechoslovak Government and Sudeten German Party. Lord President of the Council 1938–9. Shipowner: Walter Runciman & Co, Moor Line, Anchor Line. Created Baronet 1906; Privy Councillor 1908; succeeded father as 2nd Baron 1933; created Viscount Runciman of Doxford 1937.

SALISBURY Robert Arthur Talbot Gascoyne-Cecil, 3rd Marquess of (1830–1903); Conservative MP 1853–68; Prime Minister 1885–6 (unsuccessfully challenged for leadership by Lord Randolph 1886), 1886–92; 1895 to July 1902 when he resigned position to his nephew Balfour. Succeeded 1868. Married Georgiana Caroline, daughter of Sir Edward Hall Alderson 1857.

SEELY John Edward Bernard (1868–1947); fourth son of Sir Charles Seely, 1st Bart. While on service in South Africa (DSO) where he first met WSC, he was elected Conservative MP for Isle of Wight, 1900. Joined WSC in attacks on Mr Brodrick's Army; crossed the floor in March 1904 on the issues of Chinese labour and free trade and was re-elected unopposed as Liberal MP for Isle of Wight. Under-Secretary for the Colonies 1908–10; briefly Under-Secretary, then Secretary of State for War 1911–14, having to resign as result of his actions in Curragh mutiny. Served in France 1914–18, commanding Canadian Cavalry brigade under WSC; Parliamentary Under-Secretary Ministry of Munitions and Deputy Minister of Munitions 1918; Under-Secretary of State for Air and President of

Air Council 1919; PC 1909; Major General 1918; created 1st Baron Mottistone 1933.

SMUTS Jan Christian (1870–1950); led commando in closing stages of Boer War. After Liberals took office December 1905, Boer party Het Volk, sent him to London to plead for responsible government for Transvaal; met WSC while in England. Played important part in formation of Union of South Africa 1909–10; with Botha invaded German South-West Africa in 1914–18 war. Prime Minister of South Africa 1919–24, 1939–48.

SPENDER John Alfred (1862–1942); a contemporary at Balliol (under Jowett) of Curzon, Cosmo Lang and Edward Grey. Edited *Westminster Gazette* 1896–1921, which under him became an influential liberal evening paper. Intimate friend of many members of Campbell-Bannerman's cabinet, and later his official biographer.

STANLEY (Beatrice) Venetia (1887–1948); fifth daughter of 4th Baron Stanley of Alderly. Friend of the Asquith family. Married The Hon Edwin Samuel Montagu, second son of 1st Baron Swaythling in 1915. Cousin of CSC.

Winston S. Churchill

VOLUME II

Young Statesman

1901-1914

I

The Young Member

CHURCHILL TOOK his seat in the new Parliament on 14 February 1901. He was just twenty-six years old, but he had already equipped himself by his own exertions for the long parliamentary life which lay ahead. He owed little to anyone save his name and his family tradition; he had been a true soldier of fortune who had made his way to the front with his own sword and pen. He had gathered a modest fortune of £10,000 by unremitting toil. On this he could hope to support himself as a bachelor for the next four or five years.

His had been no automatic entry into Parliament such as was often found in those days for the connections of noble and powerful families. He had twice fought the overwhelmingly working-class constituency of Oldham in the Tory interest and had proved successful only at the second attempt. He had incomparably more experience of life and of the world than many of his parliamentary colleagues ten or twenty years older than himself. What he lacked in book learning and formal education he was to assimilate by his ambition and his growing powers of concentration as he ruthlessly thrust himself forward along the parliamentary path which he had long been determined to follow. Nearly fifty years later Bernard Shaw, at the age of ninety-four and a week or two before his death, sent Churchill a copy of his new book, *Sixteen Half Sketches,* in return for a gift of flowers he had received in hospital. Shaw wrote: "You need only read 'Am I an Educated Person' as you and I are officially classed as ignoramuses." Self-reliant, spurred by a burning sense of personal destiny as vivid as that of the young Bonaparte, Churchill faced his new opportunities with composure allied to a spirit of adventure.

Though his means for a parliamentary career were modest for those days, Churchill still found it possible to help his mother, who was as usual in financial difficulties. At the age of 47 she was now married to George Cornwallis-West, the handsome but impecunious subaltern in the Scots Guards who was hardly older than Churchill himself and whose marriage gave rise to the displeasure as well as the chaff of the social and military circle in which he moved. On the day Churchill took his seat in Parliament he wrote to his mother: "I enclose a cheque for £300. In a certain sense it belongs to you; for I could never have earned it had you not transmitted to me the wit and energy which are necessary." And towards the end of the year he felt able to relieve his mother of her obligation to pay the allowance of £500 a year to him. In a memorandum to the family lawyers, of which he sent her a copy, Churchill wrote:

WSC to Lumley & Lumley
EXTRACT

17 December 1901

Copy

. . . I recognise that it is difficult for her to make me or my brother any allowance, and I feel it my duty on the other hand to assist her in any manner possible without seriously prejudicing my reversionary interests. I therefore forego the allowance of £500 a year she and my father had always intended to give me. . . .

What I desire in my brother's interest as in my own is that there should be a clear understanding, necessarily not of a legal nature, that in the event of Mr George Cornwallis-West being at some future time in a superior financial position my mother will make suitable provision for her children out of her own income; in other words that she will reciprocate the attitude I am now adopting. . . .

*

The Parliament that was opened by King Edward VII on February 14 was the first of his reign. The war in South Africa was foremost in the Speech from the Throne, and was to dominate the subsequent session. Lord Roberts had handed over his command to

Lord Kitchener and had returned from the war at the beginning of January; the Queen had conferred an Earldom on him and had invested him with the Garter just twenty days before she died on January 23. But the hopes of an early victory and peace which the capture of Pretoria had engendered in the previous July, and which had largely contributed to the Tories' victory in the October "Khaki election," gradually diminished. By the beginning of 1901 the country was facing the prospect of an extended war of attrition. Now what mattered most was that the war should be conducted effectively and that the Army should be properly organized for that purpose.

The Liberal Opposition was divided now as it had been in October between the "Imperialists" like Rosebery, Asquith, Grey and R. B. Haldane, who supported the vigorous prosecution of the war and the so-called "pro-Boer" little Englanders like Campbell-Bannerman, Morley and Lloyd George. Opposition to the Government would merely serve to advertise their differences.

Within an hour of subscribing to the Oath, Churchill took part in his first division, on a motion by Mr Balfour to pass the sessional order forbidding peers from taking part in Parliamentary elections. Churchill was on the side of James Lowther, the Tory member for the Isle of Thanet, whose amendment opposing the motion was, however, defeated by 328 votes to 70. Although the Whips do not seem to have been "on," and voting somewhat cut across party lines, Churchill found himself in the same Lobby as most of the Irish and Radical members, and in a different lobby to that of Balfour and other leading members of the Tory Party.

The Chamber in which he had taken his seat was instinctively known to him. It was unchanged since the days of his father, one of the four or five greatest parliamentarians of the previous century. He had never heard him speak in the House, but he had read all his speeches and memorized many. His vivid visual imagination had made familiar to him, while still a schoolboy at Harrow and a cavalry subaltern in India, the historic arena where he was to live his life and fulfil his destiny. For a new member he was well-equipped with the traditional parliamentary vocabulary — "upstairs" for Committees: "another place" for the House of Lords: "out of doors" for speeches made away from Westminster: "my right honourable friend" for the leaders of his own Party: "the right honourable gentleman" for the chieftains of the opposite side: "the honourable and gallant member" for those who had held the King's Commission: "the honourable and learned member" for those who had some pretension to legal knowledge. He knew that in theory, though not in practice, speeches must not be read, that they must be addressed exclusively to the Speaker: that the Mace on the table was the symbol of the King in Parliament, which is where the legality of the state is vested: but that when money matters are discussed the Mace is put under the table, the Speaker leaves and the House goes into Committee under a Chairman so as to emphasize the Commons' power over the purse.

He knew about the Army Annual, the first Bill introduced each session, which begins "Whereas it is illegal for the King to keep a standing army in time of peace . . ." He knew these forms symbolized the cause for which the Commons had fought and decapitated Charles I, and that all this was enshrined in the doctrine that the Redress of Grievances must precede the voting of Supply. He knew that unbelievably harsh and wounding things could be said and should be said without rupturing cordial private relations. There was much else, some of it of an intricate character, but he had no difficulty in picking this up quickly since, to use a phrase favourite with him all his life, "he had the root of the matter in him."

More than forty years later, when Hitler's bombs had devastated the Chamber where he had spent his life, it fell to him, as the wartime Prime Minister to move:

"That a Select Committee be appointed to consider and report upon plans for the rebuilding of the House of Commons, and upon such alterations as may be considered desirable while preserving all its essential features."

He took good care, while he still had his wartime authority, to make sure that the Chamber should be rebuilt almost exactly as it had been before. Since it embodies the kernel of all he had learned about Parliamentary government, it may be convenient to quote here an extract from his speech on that occasion:

> There are two main characteristics of the House of Commons which will command the approval and the support of reflective and experienced members. They will, I have no doubt, sound odd to

foreign ears. The first is that its shape should be oblong and not semi-circular. Here is a very potent factor in our political life. The semi-circular assembly, which appeals to political theorists, enables every individual or every group to move round the centre, adopting various shades of pink according as the weather changes. I am a convinced supporter of the party system in preference to the group system. I have seen many earnest and ardent Parliaments destroyed by the group system. The party system is much favoured by the oblong form of Chamber. It is easy for an individual to move through those insensible gradations from Left to Right, but the act of crossing the Floor is one which requires serious consideration. I am well informed on this matter, for I have accomplished that difficult process, not only once but twice. Logic is a poor guide compared with custom. Logic, which has created in so many countries semi-circular assemblies with buildings that give to every member, not only a seat to sit in, but often a desk to write at, with a lid to bang, has proved fatal to Parliamentary Government as we know it here in its home and in the land of its birth.

The second characteristic of a Chamber formed on the lines of the House of Commons is that it should not be big enough to contain all its members at once without over-crowding, and that there should be no question of every member having a separate seat reserved for him. The reason for this has long been a puzzle to uninstructed outsiders, and has frequently excited the curiosity and even the criticism of new members. Yet it is not so difficult to understand if you look at it from a practical point of view. If the House is big enough to contain all its members, nine-tenths of its Debates will be conducted in the depressing atmosphere of an almost empty or half-empty Chamber. The essence of good House of Commons speaking is the conversational style, the facility for quick, informal interruptions and interchanges. Harangues from a rostrum would be a bad substitute for the conversational style in which so much of our business is done. But the conversational style requires a fairly small space, and there should be on great occasions a sense of crowd and urgency. There should be a sense of the importance of much that is said, and a sense that great matters are being decided, there and then, by the House.

Four days after his first division, on Monday, February 18, shortly before 10.30 p.m. Churchill rose from the corner seat of the second

Bench above the gangway immediately behind the Ministerial Front Bench to make his maiden speech. The word had gone round the dining-room and smoking-room that he intended to speak, and the House had begun to fill soon after dinner to be treated to a swash-buckling speech by the member for Carnarvon Boroughs, Mr David Lloyd George, who was emerging with a growing reputation after more than ten years in the House. In the Ladies' Gallery were Lady Randolph and four of Churchill's paternal aunts, Lady Wimborne, Lady Tweedmouth, Lady Howe and Lady de Ramsey, as well as Mrs Gully, the Speaker's wife, Lady Hilda Brodrick, Mrs Joseph Chamberlain, Lady Harcourt and Lady Cranborne. Balfour was there on the Government Benches, and so was Joseph Chamberlain. On the opposite side were Sir Henry Campbell-Bannerman, Sir William Harcourt and Mr Asquith. "He had an audience to listen to his maiden speech," noted the *Morning Post,* "which very few new members have commanded." "And in that packed assembly," added the *Yorkshire Post,* "everybody a critic, watching to see what sort of a start he would make in politics, Winston Churchill made his debut." His audience was not so much prompted by direct interest in himself as to judge how "Randolph's boy" would do. Even after Churchill had begun his speech members were still streaming into the Chamber.

Lloyd George had had an amendment to the Address on the King's Speech on the order paper, but when he rose to speak he announced straight away that he did not propose to move the amendment. Instead, he devoted himself to a bitter attack on the methods of warfare being practised by the Generals, and in particular by Kitchener, in South Africa. For Churchill, who had prepared every word of his speech with painstaking care, Lloyd George's failure to move his amendment was an unexpected reverse: he would now have to improvise, at any rate his opening remarks. Next to him sat Thomas Gibson Bowles, the member for King's Lynn, a colourful personality who had in his time been proprietor of *Vanity Fair.* Bowles now came to Churchill's rescue, and whispered to him that he might say, "Instead of making his violent speech without moving his moderate amendment he had better have moved his moderate amendment without making his violent speech." "Manna," recalled Churchill, "could not have been more welcome in the Wilderness." Churchill said:

When we compare the moderation of the amendment with the very bitter speech which the honourable member has just delivered, it is difficult to avoid the conclusion that the moderation of the amendment was the moderation of the honourable member's political friends and leaders, and that the bitterness of the speech was all his own.

Then with a graceful gesture and a generous acknowledgement to the benefactor by his side, Churchill went on:

It has been suggested to me that it might perhaps have been better, upon the whole, if the honourable member instead of making his speech without moving his amendment, had moved his amendment without making his speech.

Not that Lloyd George's words were to be invested with any significance:

I do not believe that the Boers would attach particular importance to the utterances of the honourable member. No people in the world received so much verbal sympathy and so little support. If I were a Boer fighting in the field — and if I were a Boer I hope I should be fighting in the field — I would not allow myself to be taken in by any message of sympathy, not even if it were signed by a hundred honourable members.

This sentence gave both sides something to cheer. When Churchill said "and if I were a Boer I hope I should be fighting in the field," the Irish members shouted their delight and Chamberlain was heard to turn to a neighbour and say: "That's the way to throw away seats." But when Churchill mentioned the message of sympathy "not even if it were signed by a hundred members" the Tories chuckled at the allusion to a telegram sent by one hundred Radical MPs to the King of Greece four years before, just a week or two before he was forced to sue for peace from the Turks.

Churchill went on to make some observations on the future of South Africa. He appealed for delay in implementing a new constitution for the Transvaal after the war until the British settlers had returned. "The interim," he said, "should be filled by a civilian not a military administration" — and here he went out of his way to pay tribute to Sir Alfred Milner. As he had done the previous year when still in South Africa, Churchill appealed for leniency towards the rebels and called for a promise to those willing to surrender that their security, their religion, their rights and "all the honours of war" should be guaranteed. He went on:

> Of course we can only promise, and it rests with the Boers whether they will accept our conditions. They may refuse the generous terms offered them, and stand or fall by their old cry, "death or independence."

Once again the Irish cheered. But this time Churchill turned on them: already he was showing an ability to lay traps in debate, to anticipate the reactions of the other side of the House.

> I do not see anything to rejoice at in that prospect, because if it be so, the war will enter upon a very sad and gloomy phase. If the Boers remain deaf to the voice of reason, and blind to the hand of friendship, if they refuse all overtures and disdain all terms, then, while we cannot help admiring their determination and endurance, we can only hope that our own race, in the pursuit of what they feel to be a righteous cause, will show determination as strong and endurance as lasting. It is wonderful that honourable members who form the Irish party should find it in their hearts to speak and act as they do in regard to a war in which so much has been accomplished by the courage, the sacrifices, and, above all, by the military capacity of Irishmen. There is a practical reason, which I trust honourable members will not think it presumptuous in me to bring to their notice: it is that they would be well advised cordially to co-operate with His Majesty's Government in bringing the war to a speedy conclusion, because they must know that no Irish question or agitation can possibly take any hold on the imagination of the people of Great Britain so long as all our thoughts are with the soldiers who are fighting in South Africa.

Turning to the war itself, Churchill welcomed the decision to send new reinforcements, and pressed for more. He could not forbear to give a word of praise to his old friend and military patron, Sir Bindon Blood. Nor did he forget to take a swipe at the persistent

and venomous critic of his subaltern days, Henry Labouchere, the
editor of *Truth* and one of the members for Northampton.

> Some honourable members have seen fit, either in this place or else-
> where, to stigmatise this as a war of greed. . . . If as the honourable
> member for Northampton has several times suggested, certain capi-
> talists spent money in bringing on this war in the hope that it would
> increase the value of their mining properties, they know now that
> they made an uncommonly bad bargain. With the mass of the na-
> tion, with the whole people of the country, this war from beginning
> to end has only been a war of duty.

And so he went on to his peroration:

> I think if any honourable members are feeling unhappy about the
> state of affairs in South Africa I would recommend them a receipt
> from which I myself derived much exhilaration. Let them look to
> the other great dependencies and colonies of the British Empire and
> see what the effect of the war has been there. Whatever we have lost
> in doubtful friends in Cape Colony we have gained ten times, or
> perhaps twenty times, over in Canada and Australia, where the
> people — down to the humblest farmer in the most distant provinces
> — have by their effective participation in the conflict been able to
> realise, as they never could realise before, that they belong to the
> Empire, and that the Empire belongs to them.

One final word remained:

> I cannot sit down without saying how very grateful I am for the
> kindness and patience with which the House has heard me, and
> which has been extended to me, I well know, not on my own account,
> but because of a certain splendid memory which many honourable
> members still preserve.

Churchill received many compliments on his speech in the House,
and not only when what he called "the usual restoratives" were being
applied. Sir Robert Reid, the Liberal member for Dumfries Burghs,
later to be a colleague of Churchill's when, as Lord Loreburn, he
became Lord Chancellor in the Liberal Government of 1905, followed him: "I am sure," he said, "the House is glad to recognise that
the honourable member who has just sat down possesses the same

courage which so distinguished Lord Randolph Churchill during his short and brilliant career in this House." Joseph Chamberlain, who wound up that night, spoke of a "very admirable speech, a speech I am sure that those who were friends and intimates of his father will have welcomed with the utmost satisfaction in the hope that we may see the father repeated in the son."

Two of those who congratulated Churchill on the floor of the House were evidently so moved that they forgot normal parliamentary usage: Mr Asquith referred to him as "my honourable friend" as if they already belonged to the same party, while Mr Broderick went so far as to refer to him as "my right honourable friend," thereby suggesting that he had already been sworn of the Privy Council.

Churchill got a "good press" the next day, though naturally the Radical papers tended to carp. The Parliamentary sketch writer of the Tory *Daily Telegraph* wrote: "He had a great opportunity, and he satisfied the highest expectations. He held a modest page of notes in his hand, but rarely referred to it. Perfectly at home, with lively gestures that pointed his sparkling sentences, he instantly caught the tone and the ear of a House crowded in every part." The Tory *Morning Post,* for which Churchill only recently had been a correspondent in South Africa, wrote: "The general opinion was that he had fully justified the expectations which had been formed — based as they were on the recollections of his father's great achievements and on his own career as a writer and speaker. . . . Both in form and substance [the speech] was worthy of the traditions of the House and of those personal traditions to which Mr Churchill in concluding made the touching reference."

The *Daily Express* — the half-penny paper owned by the Tory, Mr C. Arthur Pearson — referred to "Mr Churchill's spell binding." "A very successful first appearance it was. For more than half an hour he held a crowded House spellbound. It was not only the facility of his phrases, and the clearness of his views, but a certain youthful breeziness, a rare unaffectedness which fascinated his hearers." The Tory paper the *Standard* wrote: "He spoke with great self possession, modestly, and with a restraint of manner, and with no trace of a desire to be rhetorical."

The reaction of the Radical Press was mixed. H. W. Massingham, perhaps the most powerful of the political journalists of that decade, wrote in the Liberal *Daily News:*

> Mr Churchill does not inherit his father's voice — save for a slight lisp — or his father's manner. Address, accent, appearance do not help him.
>
> But he has one quality — intellect. He has an eye — and he can judge and think for himself. Parts of his speech were faulty enough — there was claptrap with the wisdom and insight. But such remarks as the impossibility of the country returning to prosperity under military government . . . showed that this young man has kept his critical faculty through the glamour of association with our arms.

The Liberal *Daily Chronicle* commented:

> Mr Churchill is a medium-sized, undistinguished, young man, with an unfortunate lisp in his voice. His style, too, is not very literary, and he lacks force. All the qualities which made his father the most daring and dauntless of recent parliamentarians have been missed out in his son, or else they have exhibited themselves in the restless spirit of the soldier and adventurer, but he has some inherited qualities, candour and independence.

J. B. Atkins, Churchill's former colleague as a war correspondent, took a contrary view in his sketch for the *Manchester Guardian*:

> His was a carefully turned speech, filled with antitheses of a literary flavour. His father, with all his power, had little literary sense, and this possession is all in favour of the young member who started so well tonight. He was wise to stick as he obviously did to his prepared speech and not to be drawn away by tempting interruptions.

Only a few letters of congratulations sent to Churchill survive. Doubtless many of the good wishes that followed the maiden speech were expressed verbally. Campbell-Bannerman, the Leader of the Opposition, wrote to say "with how much pleasure I listened to your speech."

Churchill himself wrote a highly revealing comment to his distant relation by marriage, Murray Guthrie, when thanking him for his congratulations on the maiden speech. "It was a terrible, thrilling yet delicious experience."

After the speech the phrase "if I were a Boer I hope I should be fighting in the field" aroused persistent comment, and while it found general acceptance it was also criticized by correspondents in the Liberal evening newspaper the *Westminster Gazette*. A month later, on March 18, Churchill wrote the following letter to the editor explaining his position:

WSC to the Editor of the Westminster Gazette

18 March 1901

Sir,

Your correspondents vary in their opinions, but pay me an equal honour by noticing my observations. My justification of the phrase and idea in question is briefly this. Every man owes a duty to his country, and is under a high moral obligation to bear his part in sustaining its fortunes. Again, in all great controversies the number of just and fair arguments on either side is large enough to enable most honest men to find complete conviction. Neither side has a monopoly of right or reason. Therefore, although there may be a balance of moral right on one side of the quarrel, that balance is rarely sufficient to outweigh the great patriotic consideration first mentioned. From this I argue that while the Boer cause is certainly wrong, the Boer who fights for it is certainly right. Much more so then, is the Boer who fights bravely for it. If I were so unfortunate as to be a Boer, I should certainly prefer to be the best kind of Boer. Hence the original proposition.

Your correspondent who thinks that such an argument would also justify the conduct of certain Chinese in their course of massacre, treachery, and torture displays an astonishing ignorance alike of South Africa, of China, and, let me add, of reasoning, for it is evident that no patriotic obligation could justify such acts.

I am, Sir, your obedient servant
WINSTON S. CHURCHILL

*

Most young members, when they have made their maiden speech, do not trouble the House again for some weeks, or even months. Not so Churchill: he was in a hurry. Twice again in the following week, on both occasions on matters concerning South Africa, he thought it useful to intervene. But his next really effective speech came on March 12, when the Government were awkwardly placed over the treatment of Major-General Sir Henry Colville, and he sought to extricate them. Colville had been appointed Commander-in-Chief in Gibraltar after holding a command in South Africa. But subsequent official enquiries into incidents in the South African war had shown his conduct in an unfavourable light; twice, at Sanna's Post and at Lindley, he had failed, though in a position to do so, to attempt the relief of troops who were in difficulties. The War Office had called on Colville to resign his command at Gibraltar; Colville refused, whereupon he was dismissed and the aggrieved General wrote an injudicious letter to the press appealing, in effect, for the support of public opinion against the decision of the War Office.

Now the House was debating an all-party amendment calling for an enquiry into the Colville case, and the Government was hard-pressed to resist it. Churchill came to its aid with an effective debating speech. First he established his credentials: "Those who have not themselves had any actual experience of war may have some difficulty in understanding . . . from the little I have seen of it; . . . having personally collected information on the spot. . . ." Then he seemed to give the supporters of the amendment something to cheer:

> If it be true that General Colville made a fault, why was it that the official despatch, published since, did not make any reference to that fault or point out the blame he incurred? Perhaps it will not be entirely agreeable to many of my friends on this side of the House if I say that I have noticed in the last three wars in which we have been engaged a tendency among military officers — arising partly from good nature towards their comrades, partly from the dislike of public scrutiny — to hush everything up, to make everything look as fair as possible, to tell what is called the official truth, to present a version of the truth which contains about seventy-five per cent of the actual article. So long as a force gets a victory somehow, all the

ugly facts are smoothed and varnished over, rotten reputations are
propped up, and officers known as incapable are allowed to hang on
and linger in their commands in the hope that at the end of the war
they may be shunted into private life without a scandal.

But scarcely had the Opposition cheers been raised when Churchill
turned on them:

> On whom does the responsibility for the continuance of the system
> rest? When Lord Roberts went out to South Africa he struck out
> a new and true line. The truth, the whole truth, was to be told to
> the country frankly and fairly. The House will remember the publi-
> cation of the Spion Kop despatches and the reception that the publi-
> cation met with from honourable and right honourable gentlemen
> opposite. That settled the policy of candour in military matters, for
> some months to come at any rate. That is why the despatches con-
> tained no incriminating matter in regard to General Colville.

But he left to the end his most decisive point — "unanswerable" said
the usually impassive *Annual Register,* "that the right to select, to
promote and dismiss" must be left with the military authorities:

> Selection is the only hope for increased efficiency in the army, it is
> the only way in which we can prevent the upper ranks being clogged
> with incapable men. The principle of selection is challenged, and
> would be destroyed if a Commission were appointed in this case.
> I have been told by a distinguished general officer that, in conse-
> quence of the outcry which has occurred, already several persons
> against whom it had been proposed to take steps have been screwed
> back into their places. In regard to the selection of officers, the
> House ought not to interfere in any particular instance except for
> grievous reason. Personally, I have no hesitation in expressing my
> firm support of the attitude of the Secretary of State for War, and I
> exhort the right honourable Gentleman, not only for the sake of the
> army, but also in the interest of the House, not to budge an inch
> from the position he has taken up.

The Secretary of State for War, St John Brodrick, was much
relieved and expressed his gratitude. The note he passed to Churchill
at the end of this speech survives:

That is so! May I say you will never make a better speech than you made tonight. Of course you will speak on better subjects — but you filled the House & held it — & got the debate back on to big lines. It was a great success and universally recognised.

St J. B.

The amendment was defeated by 262 votes to 148, there being some cross-voting among parties in the lobbies. Churchill wrote to his mother the next day:

WSC to Lady Randolph

13 March 1901   105 Mount Street

EXTRACT

. . . There is no doubt that the speech turned votes and shifted opinion at the time when the current was running very strongly against the Government. George Wyndham and all my friends think that as a Parliamentary coup it is far better than I have ever done. I know of several cases where people who were going to vote against the Government decided to vote the other way, and if you read the *Daily News* or *Daily Chronicle* you will see that my intervention was by no means ineffective. . . .

It must have been this speech that impelled Lord Curzon to write the following letter from India:

Lord Curzon to WSC

Viceregal Lodge
Simla

13 May 1901

My dear Churchill,

Just a line to congratulate you upon the successful inauguration of your Parliamentary career. I did not write to congratulate you upon your maiden speech because I have never known a case in which a young member who was expected to make a good maiden speech, has not been described as having done so. I remember in my own case making a maiden speech (I think that I ran a tilt at your father in it) which *The Times* next morning described as brilliant and which was plastered with amiable but uncritical praise. All the while I knew well enough that it was execrable. I therefore never compliment maiden speeches, because with three exceptions (Disraeli's, Drage and my own) I have never heard [of] a really bad one.

I have however been very pleased to see the manner in which you have not merely won but retained the ear of the House.

There is no more difficult position than being on the benches behind a Government. It is so hard to strike the mean between independence & loyalty.

The great thing is to impress the House with earnestness. They will forgive anything but flippancy.

Yours sincerely
CURZON

*

A few days before Churchill had made this highly successful intervention in the Colville debate, Brodrick had outlined a scheme for Army Reform. This involved the creation of six army corps, three composed of regular forces and the other three of militia and volunteers. This was largely regarded as a "paper transaction," though it was to involve the recruiting of some 50,000 extra militiamen. The additional cost was £3 million, bringing the total of the Army Estimates for ordinary services, that is, excluding estimates for war services in South Africa and China, to £29,685,000, an increase of more than £5 million on the previous year. Churchill made no immediate comment. He studied Brodrick's plan in the course of the next month. The first two weeks in April he went to Spain, visiting Madrid, Seville, Granada and Cordoba, as well as Gibraltar. On his return to England he gave a lecture to the United Institution on technical aspects of the war in South Africa, particularly on the role of the Cavalry — a notable distinction for one who, though he had seen a great deal of war, was still only a subaltern.

Then, in Liverpool on April 23, he made the first of many speeches spread over the next three years attacking Brodrick's scheme. He concentrated on three criticisms: that it would be ineffective and would not in fact make the army stronger; that it was bad value for money; and that if anything deserved increased expenditure it was the navy and not the army. In his speech to the Liverpool Conservative Association, as published in the *Liverpool Daily Echo,* he gave some hint of the line along which his argument was to develop:

> There has been a great demand for army reform and I am pledged to it up to the hilt. Either it means a bigger army for the same money or the same army and less money. What I pledged myself to at the last election was a better, not a bigger army, value for our money not more of the same old bad bargain. Any danger that comes to Britain would not be on land; it would come on the sea. With regard to our military system we must be prepared to deal with all the little wars which occur continually on the frontiers of the Empire. We cannot expect to meet great wars; we can only assure ourselves that ultimately we shall be able to realise the entire forces of the Empire. . . . I cannot help regretting that we have plunged into this course of extreme army expenditure, for I think our game essentially is to be a naval and commercial power. I cannot look upon the army as anything but an adjunct to the navy and I look upon the navy as the force which in the hour of difficulty is going to turn, if necessary, every city into an arsenal, and the entire male population of the countryside into an armed camp. I hope that in considering the lessons of the South African war we shall not be drawn from our true policy, which is to preserve the command of markets and of the seas.

Two days later he followed the same line of argument in a speech to the Stafford Club at Oxford. At the same time, when Brodrick had placed on the order paper a motion asking the House of Commons to approve his scheme, Churchill tabled an amendment. This was to be debated in the House on May 13. Sir William Harcourt, the former Liberal leader in the House of Commons who, seven years before, had fought bitterly against Rosebery for the leadership of the Liberal Party and lost, wrote to tell Churchill that the amendment was much to his liking. The Vice-President and Secretary of the Army League, on the other hand, wrote to *The Times* to say that it was not to their liking and *The Times,* in a leading article on May 2, seemed to agree. Churchill, for his part, stoutly defended his position in two

letters to *The Times,* in which he denied that there was any incon-
sistency between earlier pleas for a strong army and reinforcements
for South Africa and his present attitude:

> No one who has pledged himself to army reform need accept any
> scheme which may be suggested without discussing the details or
> counting the cost. Still less is he under any obligation to support
> schemes of army increase. A better army does not necessarily mean a
> bigger army. There ought to be ways of reforming a business, other
> than by merely putting more money into it.

But all this was mere preliminary sparring. The battle itself was
joined in the debate on the army scheme that opened on May 13.
That evening, at 11 p.m. in a crowded House (members had to stay
on anyway for a division on another topic that was to take place at
midnight) Churchill rose to make his speech criticizing "Mr. Brodrick's Army." Churchill himself admitted: "I took six weeks to
prepare this speech, and learnt it so thoroughly off by heart that it
hardly mattered where I began it or how I turned it."

Churchill began by criticizing the mounting costs of the Army,
from £17 million in 1894 to nearly £30 million in 1901–2, and he
congratulated Brodrick on his success in getting so much money out
of the Treasury. He went on to contrast the present situation with
his father's stand against military expenditure — "if I may revive a
half forgotten episode." Lord Randolph had "gone down for ever,
and with him, it seems, there fell also the cause of retrenchment and
economy, so that the very memory thereof seems to have perished,
and the words themselves have the curiously old-fashioned ring about
them. I suppose that was a lesson Chancellors of the Exchequer were
not likely to forget in a hurry." He opened a book from which to
read — though in fact he had learnt it by heart and was able to close
it dramatically when only half-way through — his father's letter of
resignation to Lord Salisbury on 22 December 1886. "I decline to be
a party to encouraging the military and militant circle of the War
Office and Admiralty to join the high and desperate stakes which
other nations seem to be forced to risk," he recited. And then Churchill added: "Wise words, sir, stand the test of time, and I am very

glad the House has allowed me after an interval of fifteen years, to lift again the tattered flag I found lying on a stricken field." It was time, he said, that a voice was raised from the Conservative benches to plead the cause of economy. "If such a one is to stand forward in such a cause, then I say it humbly, but with I hope becoming pride, no one has a better right than I have, for this is a cause I have inherited, and a cause for which the late Lord Randolph Churchill made the greatest sacrifice of any Minister of modern times."

As to the army scheme itself, it left most of the great questions connected with army reform almost untouched. Why three army corps? One was "quite enough to fight savages, and three not enough even to begin to fight Europeans." Britain's military system should be adapted to dealing with minor emergencies smoothly and conveniently. "But we must not expect to meet the great civilised powers in this fashion . . . a European war cannot be anything but a cruel, heart-rending struggle, which, if we are ever to enjoy the bitter fruits of victory, must demand, perhaps for several years, the whole manhood of the nation, the entire suspension of peaceful industries, and the concentration to one end of every vital energy in the community."

In days when wars had arisen from the policy of a minister or the passion of a king, when a comparatively few professional soldiers were involved, one could talk of European war, "but now, when mighty populations are impelled against each other, each individual severally embittered and inflamed — when the resources of science and civilisation sweep away everything that might mitigate their fury, a European war can only end in the ruin of the vanquished and the scarcely less fatal dislocation and exhaustion of the conquerors. Democracy is more vindictive than cabinets. The wars of peoples will be more terrible than the wars of kings."

What, then, was to be Britain's weapon? "The only weapon with which we can expect to cope with great nations is the Navy." The tremendous new expenditure on the Army, Churchill claimed, directly challenged the principle that the superiority of Britain's Navy was vital to her existence. "Why should we sacrifice a game in which we are sure to win; to play a game we are bound to lose? The whole course of our history, the geography of our country, all the evidences of the present situation, proclaimed beyond a doubt that Britain's power and prosperity depended on the economic command of markets and the Navy's command of the seas." But there was a higher reason still: "It is known, alike by peoples and by rulers, that upon the whole . . . British influence is a healthy and kindly influence. . . . We shall make a fatal bargain if we allow the moral force which this country has so long exerted to become diminished, or perhaps destroyed, for the sake of the costly, trumpery, military playthings on which the Secretary of State for War has set his heart."

In reply from the Government benches, Mr Arthur Lee (later Lord Lee of Fareham, who was to give Chequers to the nation for the use of Prime Ministers as a country residence) told Churchill not to confuse filial piety with public duty. Brodrick, who had been Under-Secretary of State at the War Office when Lord Randolph had battled with W. H. Smith, the Secretary of State, over the Army Estimates in 1886, mocked: "I confidently expect that Parliament, which was not afraid to part company with the brilliant statesman in 1886, will not sleep the less soundly because of the financial heroics of my honourable friend the member for Oldham." Brodrick accused Churchill of harbouring "a hereditary desire to run imperialism on the cheap." He said he could never subscribe to Lord Randolph's theory that the Treasury should dictate to all other departments, turning a blind eye to the progress of science and a deaf ear to the arguments of responsible ministers. As to the possession of a sharp sword leading to its use, he thought the country had been in a more perilous position when the sword was not sharp enough.

Churchill's speech was fully reported in the *Morning Post*. He had taken the precaution of sending it off before it was delivered, as Lord Randolph used to do. It is also available in *Mr Brodrick's Army*, the slim volume of speeches on army matters which Churchill published in 1903. It was warmly cheered by the Opposition, many of whom also wrote of their delight. "I cannot resist," wrote Sir William Harcourt, "the pleasure of joining my congratulations to the host which you must have received on the brilliant success of your speech which has established your future in the House of Commons on a foundation which cannot be shaken." The Radical editor of *The Review of Reviews*, W. T. Stead, wrote: "Just a line to thank you with all my heart for your speech last night. It confirms

the hopes raised by your admirable letters from South Africa." John
Burns, the veteran Radical, wrote to Lady Randolph:

John Burns to Lady Randolph

14 May 1901   House of Commons

Dear Madam,

Years before your son secured the position he now occupies I expressed to you a kindly hope for his future.

His excellent speech of last night is by far his best effort and I
write you to congratulate him, through you, on his success and to
share with his mother the hope that he will go further in the
career he has chosen and on the excellent lines of his courageous
speech of last evening.

Yours sincerely
JOHN BURNS

Lord James of Hereford, Lord and Lady Randolph's old friend, a
staunch Liberal Unionist and a member of the Cabinet as Chancellor
of the Duchy of Lancaster, wrote: "Although I cannot agree with the
views expressed in your speech I must sincerely congratulate you
upon its merits. It has given you a great Parliamentary position —
and with the restraining influences of moderation and discretion I
feel sure that you have a very broad path leading to great success
before you."

But for Churchill the speech of May 13 meant more than the gaining of a Parliamentary reputation. Writing in *My Early Life* he
commented: "It marked a definite divergence of thought and sympathy from nearly all those who thronged the benches around me."
Already at the end of March Churchill had been complaining to his
mother that there was a good deal of dissatisfaction in the Party, and
a shocking lack of cohesion. "The Government is not very strong . . .
The whole Treasury bench appears to me to be sleepy and exhausted
and played out" — this after just one month of the new session of
Parliament. Churchill and a few friends decided to enliven the
proceedings. He had become associated with a small group of dis-
sident young Tory members, which included Ian Malcolm, a friend

of the family, who had recently married the daughter of Lily Langtry; Lord Percy, the eldest son of the seventh Duke of Northumberland; Arthur Stanley, a younger son of the sixteenth Earl of Derby; and Lord Hugh Cecil, a younger son of the Prime Minister, Lord Salisbury. Later they were on occasion to be outrageous in their Parliamentary manners and the critics dubbed them the Hughligans, or Hooligans.

It was a modest attempt at a latter-day Fourth Party. They began to meet for dinner on Thursday evenings; occasionally they asked leading political personalities of the day — maybe a Tory, maybe a Liberal — to join them at dinner.

In Ronaldshay's *Life of Lord Curzon* a letter dated 21 July 1901 from Lady Curzon to her husband in India is quoted:

> Some of those foolish hooligans (who exist to entertain lions at dinner) invited Sir W. Harcourt to dinner last Thursday, and as Winston did not know he had been asked, *he* invited Lord Rosebery! Both accepted, and for the first time the Hooligan Party was confronted with a crisis. . . . They didn't know what to do. Lord Rosebery was put off and asked to come another night, unless he desired the pleasure of meeting Sir William. Awkward, to say the least! *Later.* Have just heard that night of dinner arrived, Lord Rosebery had been put off and Harcourt forgot to come!

WSC to Lord Rosebery
(*Rosebery Papers*)

EXTRACT

24 July 1901   105 Mount Street

. . . We were vy disappointed that you could not dine with the "Hooligans," but I trust you will consider yourself pledged to come next session on some Thursday. . . .

Lord Rosebery to WSC

24 July 1901   38 Berkeley Square

My Dear Winston,
    Many thanks for your kind note.

I have an idea. If I cannot go to the Hooligans why should they not come to me on Saturday Aug 3 to spend Sunday?

Vy sincrly

A R

WSC to Lord Rosebery
(Rosebery Papers)

2 August 1901   105 Mount Street

My dear Lord Rosebery,

I will come down in my motor car in time for dinner tonight. The others feel they ought not to miss the Colonial Office vote; and they will telegraph to you the train they will come by tomorrow.

It is vy good of you to have us down and we are all looking forward to our visit exceedingly.

Yours vy sincerely

WINSTON S. CHURCHILL

The Hooligans to Lord Rosebery
(Rosebery Papers)

6 August [1901]

Dear Lord Rosebery,

We who do not agree always, are united in thinking that the Sunday we spent in your company was among the pleasantest we can remember; and we wish most sincerely to thank you for your kindness and hospitality.

Yours vy truly

HUGH CECIL: WINSTON S. CHURCHILL: PERCY:

IAN MALCOLM: ARTHUR STANLEY

PS This has taken us a great deal of trouble to make up. My colleagues behave very badly I am sorry to say. H.C. [next phrase scratched out and illegible] (stopped by the censor).

Lord Rosebery to WSC

[handwritten letter]

6 August 1901   Mentmore

My dear Winston,
  I cannot tell you how much I enjoyed the Hooligan visit. It rejuvenated me. If they or any of them wish for moral repose while Parliament sits they will find it here.

Yours

A R

Lord Rosebery to WSC

9 August 1901   Mentmore

My dear Winston,
  The Hooligans will be very welcome on Wednesday. The Hoplites [*Ancient Greek heavy infantry*], I used to read in ancient history, were accompanied by shoals of light infantry. If you wish to bring any light infantry let me know. There is lots of room.

Yours

A R

Thirty-five years later Stanley Baldwin was to attack some left-wing members of the Tory Party, such as Harold Macmillan and Robert Boothby, when they were associating rather closely with Lloyd George, for "hunting with packs other than their own." The Hooligans could have been attacked on similar grounds. Such records as survive seem to suggest that they spent far more of their time with the right wing of the Liberal Party than they did with their Tory colleagues.

Sir Edward Grey to WSC

16 August 1901   House of Commons

Dear Churchill,
   Will you dine at Brooks' with me at 8 tonight? I have been trying to get all that is left of the hooligans, but have only so far succeeded in getting one. Asquith is coming and we could join you both.
                                            Yours sincerely
                                            E. GREY

During his summer visit to Scotland, Churchill mixed predominantly with Liberals; for after staying at Dunrobin with the Tory Duke of Sutherland he went on to Guisachan to stay with his uncle Lord Tweedmouth, who had been a Minister in the previous Liberal Government. "I have seen a lot of the Liberal Imperialists lately," he wrote to Rosebery on 20 September 1901. "Haldane and Edward Grey were at Guisachan where I passed a pleasant week; and Asquith very kindly took the chair for me at St. Andrews [at a lecture]."

When he came south again, Churchill delivered major attacks on the Government's handling of the South African war which was still dragging wearily on, and on the chief ministers of the Government itself. At the end of a long speech at Saddleworth, Yorkshire, in which he had made detailed criticisms of the handling of the war, Churchill set out to apportion the blame.

Is it the Chancellor of the Exchequer? [Sir Michael Hicks-Beach] . . . I myself would think it a monstrous thing if persons who were spending such vast sums of money — not in the best way — were to excuse their own blunders and mistakes by trying to lay the blame on the Treasury and on the Chancellor of the Exchequer, whose special function it is, while providing necessary monies for the war, to guard against waste. . . .

Where shall we look? The War Office? Well of course in a certain sense Mr Brodrick is responsible for every matter connected with the war. He would be the last man to shrink from, and indeed I think he would be the first to court that or any other responsibility. But I say it with the utmost deliberation, the country will be most unwise to allow such an assumption to be made. Nothing can be more dangerous to the public and Imperial welfare than that [the] prosecution of the war in South Africa should come to be regarded as a departmental affair under the sole and peculiar care of a single over-burdened Secretary of State. The country looks to Mr Balfour and Mr Chamberlain, the one the Leader of the House of Commons and the apparent successor of Lord Salisbury; the other *fons et origo* of the policy we are fighting for, and, as everyone knows, the most prominent member of the Government; and — if my voice can carry so far — I warn those two distinguished men, the mainguard of the Unionist Party, they cannot devolve the weight and burden of this tremendous enterprise — the greatest we have set our hands to since the times of Napoleon — on any subordinate Minister, or any particular department, but that it rests on their shoulders, and that with its successful conclusion is bound up their political fame and their personal honour.

Churchill wrote to Rosebery asking for approval. At Oldham, he said, he had addressed some twenty meetings "and I find everywhere the same feeling: absolute determination to force the war through: perplexity and disappointment at its prolongation (not perhaps quite so keen as one would have expected, because people are afraid that to doubt may be unpatriotic): and I must add a good deal of calm patience more likely to flash into anger than to fade into apathy, but not yet to the point of either." Rosebery replied: "I got your speech out of the *Morning Post* and liked it very much. It came at a most opportune time — but as usual things have settled down again to relative calm."

Just in case his voice did not "carry so far" Churchill wrote to Joseph Chamberlain drawing attention to his speeches. In this letter, dated 14 October 1901, he said: "It is not enough for the Government to say 'we have handed the war over to the military: they must settle

it: all we can do is to supply them as they require!' I protest against
the view. Nothing can relieve the Government of their responsibility.
If Kitchener cannot settle the question you will have to interfere."

Chamberlain replied: "As you invite my opinion, which I certainly
should not otherwise have intruded, I am bound to say that while I
value your suggestions, and have in the past endeavoured to profit by
them, I do not think the public discussion of them in the form of a
criticism upon the Government and the military authorities is profitable; and I think you must see yourself that its first result is to encourage the enemy to blaspheme, both at home and abroad." After
this unpromising start, however, Chamberlain admitted the justice
of many of Churchill's remarks and the wisdom of some of his proposals. "Speaking generally, I agree with much that you say, and as
far as my influence goes, I am working in the same direction." On
the other hand, he could not see how far it was possible for the executive to intervene in the actions of the military. "It is possible that, if
the country were prepared to revert to the Roman system of appoint-
ing a Dictator, we should be more successful, but he would have to be
given a free hand for a couple of years, at the end of which he might
be hanged or crowned, according to the results. For a Government
to take the matter entirely into its own hands, and without considering the personal feelings of those engaged, and without their assent,
to make all the changes you suggest, would be to bring about wholesale resignations and a state of anarchy which would be worse than
anything which we have yet known."

*

Churchill was now comfortably installed in his bachelor rooms at
105 Mount Street where he was to remain for nearly five years,
although he had expected to stay only for the unexpired two years
of his cousin Marlborough's lease.

Churchill's engagement book for 1901 survives, and it is possible
to give some details of the varied political, social and sporting life he
led at the time. In the remaining two weeks of February after taking
his seat in the House of Commons he dined with Marlborough:
Lady Wenlock: Mrs Alfred Lyttelton: Brodrick: Lee and R. B.

Haldane who was to become War Secretary; and with Colonel Sir James Willcocks, the newly acclaimed hero of Kumasi. He lunched with his mother at Great Cumberland Place, and stayed with the Grenfells at Taplow. He also found time to attend a Cotton Trade Conference in London, to have a talk with his father's old colleague, Sir Henry Drummond Wolff, and to call on the Prime Minister, Lord Salisbury, at the Foreign Office. Besides making three speeches in the House, he went up to Manchester to speak in the Stratford by-election in which the Tory candidate was successful. All this in two weeks.

The engagement diary shows that during March Churchill dined with Lady Ribblesdale, lunched with Mrs Cholmondeley, Lady Londonderry and Lady Granby (later the Duchess of Rutland) and with Marlborough with whom he also spent a few days at Melton for the hunting. He also went to stay with Ernest Beckett at Virginia Water. He lectured in Nottingham, Exeter, Plymouth, Torquay, Hastings, Bournemouth, Southampton, Portsmouth, Folkestone, Dover and Chester (total takings £586. 3. 9d); and he spoke at Finsbury Town Hall on behalf of Sidney Low during the London County Council elections (Low was defeated and became an Alderman).

Altogether in the eleven months of 1901 he made nine speeches in the House, some thirty speeches in the country and lectured in twenty towns. He gave up twelve afternoons to polo, fourteen days to hunting and two days to shooting, and spent eighteen days on holiday abroad.

He continued to be concerned about his lisp, though his frequent public speaking in the House of Commons and in the country and on the lecture platform was beginning to cure him of this lingering impediment and at the same time to rid him of any inhibition which it had caused him. Those who heard him talk in middle and old age may conclude that he mastered the inhibition better than he did the impediment. Indeed, he may have unconsciously exploited the residual impediment to advantage in order to achieve a wholly individual style of public oratory.

At this time John Morley seems to have exercised a peculiar fascination upon Churchill. Philosopher and free-thinker, Morley was the disciple and biographer of Gladstone, and had been his Chief Secretary for Ireland. J. B. Atkins says that at about this time Churchill had told him, after a Hooligan dinner at which Morley had been the guest of honour: "Morley is the true sort of Liberal. The Liberal Imperialists are not true Liberals. I like one thing or the other, not something, fading into something else. If I were a Liberal I should be with John Morley." This was a passing mood. After Churchill had crossed the floor and joined the Liberal party he continued his close friendship with Morley, but certainly from 1911 onwards, though the phrase had by then lost its political significance, he would have been classed as a Liberal Imperialist himself. At heart Morley was a pacifist, and he demonstrated this by his resignation from the Government in 1914: Churchill never was.

In December 1901 Churchill was Morley's guest at dinner. Among those present were Buckle of *The Times,* and Spender of the *Westminster Gazette,* as well as Lord Goschen, who had succeeded Lord Randolph as Chancellor after his resignation in 1886. "Everybody most kind and caressing," wrote Churchill to his mother on December 13, "particularly the host who like so many of these Liberals commands my affection at once."

It was at this dinner that Morley commended to Churchill a book recently published, *Poverty: A Study of Town Life* by Seebohm Rowntree. Morley's own copy had been lent, but when he wrote to Churchill about it he added with whimsical intent: "'Tis sure to be on the table at the Carlton." Churchill went out and bought a copy of this classic study of the poor of the city of York, and was greatly moved by it. He set out to bring it to the attention of those whom it might otherwise have passed by, writing an article for a Service journal on the rather thin pretext that the condition of the poor affected the quality of men recruited for the Army and Navy. There is no record that the review was ever published, but Churchill's manuscript survives. After giving a long, detailed summary of Rowntree's investigation into the plight of the poor of York and his conclusions, Churchill writes with bitter irony:

> Consider the peculiar case of these poor, and the consequences. Although the British Empire is so large, they cannot find room to live in it; although it is so magnificent, they would have had a better chance of happiness, if they had been born cannibal islanders of

the Southern seas; although its science is so profound, they would have been more healthy if they had been subjects of Hardicanute. But it would be absurd to trust to such arguments, impudent to urge them upon a Parliament busy with matters so many thousands of miles from home. There is a more important consideration. Not the duty of a man to man, nor the doctrines that honest effort in a wealthy community should involve certain minimum rights, nor that this festering life at home makes world-wide power a mockery, and defaces the image of God upon earth. It is a serious hindrance to recruiting.

At Blackpool on 9 January 1902 he said:

I have been reading a book which has fairly made my hair stand on end, written by a Mr Rowntree who deals with poverty in the town of York. It is found that the poverty of the people of that city extends to nearly one-fifth of the population; nearly one-fifth had something between one and a half and three-fourths as much food to eat as the paupers in the York Union. That I call a terrible and shocking thing, people who have only the workhouse or prison as the only avenues to change from their present situation.

To Mr J. Moore Bayley of the Midland Conservative Association he had written on December 23:

WSC to F. Moore Bayley

EXTRACT

23 December 1901   105 Mount Street

. . . I have lately been reading a book by Mr Rowntree called "Poverty" which has impressed me very much, and which I strongly recommend you to read. It is quite evident from the figures which he adduces that the American labourer is a stronger, larger, healthier, better fed, and consequently more efficient animal than a large proportion of our population, and this is surely a fact which our unbridled Imperialists, who have no thought but to pile up armaments, taxation and territory, should not lose sight of. For my own part, I see little glory in an Empire which can rule the waves and is unable to flush its sewers. The difficulty has been so far that the people who

have looked abroad have paid no attention to domestic matters, and
those who are centred on domestic matters regard the Empire merely
as an encumbrance. What is wanted is a well-balanced policy midway
between the Hotel Cecil and Exeter Hall, something that will co-
ordinate development and expansion with the progress of social comfort and health. But I suppose the Party machinery will carry
everything before it, and, as heretofore, the Extremists on both sides,
whether progressive or reactionary, will set the tune and collar the
organisation, and all we wretched, unorganised middle-thinkers will
either be destroyed between the contending forces, or compelled to
serve in support of one disproportionate cause or the other. But I
shall watch the Chesterfield experiment with interest. . . .

Already we see, as we shall later, Churchill seeking a central position within the parties, and even stumbling towards the idea of a
party of the centre, which would exclude the extremists of both parties from the political spectrum. It was with these ideas jostling in
his mind that he addressed himself to Rosebery's famous Chesterfield
speech. This was delivered on 16 December 1901 in the presence,
among others on the platform, of both Asquith and Grey, who lent
their tacit and later their explicit approval to what the former Prime
Minister had to say. On the war, Rosebery maintained the old
Liberal Imperialist position that it should be prosecuted to a successful conclusion with the utmost vigour. But when it came to making
the peace, he succeeded in taking up the middle position between the
two extremes of his own party. On the one hand, he favoured a
negotiated peace rather than unconditional surrender; on the other
hand, he thought that it was not fair for Britain to go cap-in-hand
suing for peace, and that, however unpalatable it might be for them,
the Boers would have to negotiate with their arch-enemies Chamberlain and Milner.
    All this was much to Churchill's taste. Even more so — and a
source of great annoyance to the traditional Liberals — was Rosebery's attitude to the old-fashioned Liberal domestic policy. In a
speech in the City of London five months before, in July, Rosebery
had called on the Liberals to wipe their slate clean: this time, at
Chesterfield he urged them to put away their "fly-blown phylac-
teries"; it needed little time to confirm that by this Rosebery meant

a large chunk of Gladstonian Liberalism, and Home Rule for Ireland in particular.

What remained in doubt was Rosebery's own position. Would he rest on one or two speeches, and then return to the retirement from which he had emerged during this year in so startling a fashion? Or would he remain on the scene, prepared to lead a Middle Party that could include some of the brightest hopes of the Liberals, including Asquith, Grey and Haldane, and some of the most promising of the young Tories? On this vital question Rosebery vouchsafed no elucidation. In July he had said: "For the present, at any rate . . . I must plough my lonely furrow . . . but before I get to the end of that furrow it is possible that I may find myself not alone." At Chesterfield he had concluded: "What I can do to further [my policy] I will do, for my services are, as they have always been . . . at the disposal of my country. . . . It is not to Party that I appeal. . . . I appeal unto Caesar from Parliament . . . to the silent but supreme tribunal which shares and controls, in the long run, the destinies of our people. I mean the tribunal of public opinion, that of commonsense."

Once more we see Rosebery as ever seeking the palm without the dust. Unless a crown were served up to him on a gold platter he shrank from exposing himself to the rough and tumble not only of political intrigue but also of political combinations and public disputations. It is fruitless to speculate on what might have happened if he had been of different mettle: the historian must deal with men as they have shown themselves and as he has found them.

Rosebery had taken good care to announce well in advance that he was going to make an important speech at Chesterfield. A month before, on November 15, Churchill wrote to him:

WSC to Lord Rosebery
(Rosebery Papers)

EXTRACT

15 November 1901

. . . I am so glad you are going to speak next month; and I think you ought to do so. People are restless and anxious, and they look to you for guidance. When they see you only speak about unimportant matters, they are disappointed and misunderstand your real feelings about national affairs.

John Bull is a stupid creature, but faithful. My own idea is that it does not matter how many mistakes one makes in politics, so long as one keeps on making them. It is like throwing babies to the wolves: once you stop, the pack overtakes the sleigh. This explains why it is the present administration prospers. . . .

A few days before the Chesterfield speech, Churchill, about to leave London for Oldham, had tried to see Rosebery.

WSC to Lord Rosebery
(*Rosebery Papers*)

12 December 1901   In the train

My dear Lord Rosebery,

I enquired at Berkeley Square last night, only to learn that you were at the Durdans — I presume in travail. So as I shall not see you again before you speak at Chesterfield, I send you this line to wish you from my heart all good fortune and success on public & personal grounds alike. But I hope you will not be content with one speech.

Yours vy sincerely
WINSTON S. CHURCHILL

As might have been expected, Churchill must have reacted enthusiastically to the Chesterfield speech, for Hugh Cecil found it necessary to utter a timely word of caution.

Lord Hugh Cecil to WSC

28 December 1901   Hatfield

. . . As to the Imperialist [Rosebery] & his Middle Party, I will send
you in a week or so a full statement of my views about negotiations:
shortly they amount to this — unconditional surrender is best but
may be too costly to attain. But as to joining a Middle Party, that
may be a very proper course when there is a Middle Party to join.
Now there is none. And the Imperialist's best friends cannot deny
that his aspirations are not always realised. So that whatever it might
be wise to do if for instance you were offered office in a Rosebery
administration, now it be madness not to remain unequivocally
Unionist.

That of course does not in the least preclude honest criticism of
the Govt. But it means that it should be clear to the audience that
you are criticising not for the sake of finding fault (in the manner
of Tommy Bowles) but because you believe the criticism to be a
just one. It also means that the criticisms should be moderately &
courteously expressed & that fair opportunities should be taken for
criticizing the opposition including the Lib Imp tho' there too
urbanity would be wise in view of possibilities of future co-operation.

In short as we agreed at Blenheim it is wise to play a waiting game
& not to respond to the Imperialist's invitations until he has built
himself a house to entertain you in. Now he has only a share in a
dilapidated umbrella!

Of course all these tactical considerations ought to be subordinated
to the duty of honestly pressing views you believe to be sound. As
long as one is conscious of acting for a principle or cause I shouldn't
bother myself about parties, Unionist or Middle — they are only
instruments after all. But in so far as tactics may rightly be considered I am sure the part of wisdom is to keep both feet securely
planted on Unionist terra firma until there is equally firm land,
Middle or otherwise, to step on to. . . .

On 9 January 1902 Churchill went to speak at Blackpool. This had
been the scene of Lord Randolph's great "chips" speech in 1884 —

"the finest and most famous speech which he ever delivered in this country," as Churchill described it on this occasion. Churchill permitted himself a profusion of lighthearted sallies at the expense of the divided Liberal Party — the followers of Campbell-Bannerman and the Liberal Imperialists alike. Of the Chesterfield speech he had this to say:

> The recent speech of Lord Rosebery has attracted a great deal of attention, and has been found not altogether disappointing to those who have listened to it. I welcome that speech as a Conservative standing on a Conservative platform — and I shall tell you why. Because it breathes a spirit of patriotism, a spirit of patriotism which some of the speeches of the leaders of the Opposition have conspicuously been lacking in. I welcome it because it is a great contribution to public knowledge of the questions which are agitating the country at the present moment. . . .
>
> I welcome Lord Rosebery's speech because he is the only man amongst the opposition who has a patriotic mind, and who is in a position to offer responsible criticism. Lord Rosebery possesses the three requirements an English Prime Minister should have. He must have a great position in Parliament, popularity in the country, he must have rank and prestige.

His criticisms of Rosebery were of the mildest, centring as they did on the disparagement of the House of Commons in which Lord Rosebery was wont to indulge.

The Liberal Imperialist Council was transformed at the beginning of March, into the Liberal League, with the object of promoting the old Liberal Imperialist ideas and of "cleaning the slate." Rosebery was president, and Asquith, Grey and Sir Henry Fowler were vice-presidents. Campbell-Bannerman quickly made it clear that if the League put up candidates of its own this would signal a formal breach in the party. Rosebery had, for his part, already separated himself from the party's official leadership, for when Campbell-Bannerman had announced at Leicester on February 19 that the "old policy" of Home Rule remained as "the sole remedy for the condition of Ireland" Rosebery promptly repudiated his views. "I remain," he wrote in a letter to *The Times,* "outside his Tabernacle, but not, I think, in solitude." And he referred to "this moment of definite separation."

Asquith, when faced with Campbell-Bannerman's challenge over independent candidates for the Liberal League, was not prepared to court a rupture. The forces Rosebery might have rallied after Chesterfield grew dispirited and returned to their varying allegiances until the march of events restored to them a natural harmony.

*

At the same time as Lord Rosebery was engaged in his impotent struggle with himself, Churchill neglected no means to promote his own views in Parliament and in the country and to make his presence felt on the political.scene. The first three months of 1902 were fully taken up with speeches on the prosecution and conduct of the South African war, some criticism of aspects of War Office organization, and with one of his now periodical and eagerly awaited attacks on Mr Brodrick's army corps scheme. An enquiry into the supply of re-mounts for the cavalry in South Africa, had, early in the year, re-vealed gross carelessness and mismanagement. Allegations of corrup-tion were easily refuted; but the charges as to the condition and quality of the remounts — many of which had died or proved un-serviceable on arrival in South Africa — and as to the price paid, which was declared to be too high by up to £10 a horse, had to be admitted. Churchill, who had had first-hand experience of these remounts, was listened to with considerable respect when he spoke on the subject; and he joined in the general demand that an enquiry into the remount department as a whole should be held immediately, and not "after the war," on the ground that after the war it would be too late to do any good.

As to the war itself Churchill supported the Government in its desire to prosecute it vigorously; indeed, he on several occasions expressed doubt whether the forces available to Kitchener for this purpose were adequate, and he called for reinforcements. At the same time he expressed the hope that peace should be effected by negotia-tion rather than by force, provided that the Boers gave up their claims for independence. In the debate on the Army Estimates in March, Churchill made a vigorous attack on the insufficient sums credited to the Intelligence Department of the War Office — to which his friend

Captain Haldane had by now been posted — and its consequent inability to carry out its duties properly. But probably his best speech was once again on Brodrick's army scheme. This speech was notable for an attack on the concept of conscription and universal service, which, he claimed, he had discerned in Brodrick's original proposals but which he now professed to see had disappeared from the plans of the Secretary of State. He hoped that

> his right honourable friend had finally and thoroughly abandoned the fatal and foolish theory of conscription, which no doubt would be still of some use providing occupation for members in another place [the House of Lords] who had not got too much to do, but which never seriously entered into the practical politics of the country. His right honourable friend, in a very eloquent passage in his speech, said that conscript soldiers did not fight at Alma, Waterloo, or Delhi. He thought his right honourable friend might have said with equal force that it was not conscript soldiers who had fought the long weary war in South Africa so steadily and unflinchingly. He did not wish to say anything uncomplimentary to any foreign nation in view of their extremely delicate susceptibilities [*a reference to the offence taken by the German Reichstag to a speech of Mr Chamberlain's earlier that year*] but he should like to see the conscript soldiers who would do what the British soldiers had done in South Africa.

Once again, he called for a strengthening of the Navy at the expense, if need be, of the Army. He expressed himself happy to see that the Navy Estimates had been increased and the Army Estimates reduced so that fears that the Army Estimates would exceed those for the navy had been falsified.

> If he might presume to lay down any principle at all he would say that the first and main principle which should animate British statecraft in the realm of imperial defence was the promotion of a steady transfer of expenditure from military to marine; and the high ideal which should be held up before the eyes of the present or any other government was that in times of peace the ratio of expenditure between the Navy and the Army Estimates ought to be, quite irrespective of the scale of the estimates, something like two to one on the side of the Navy.

Churchill continued to make a name for himself attacking the mismanagement, or what he regarded as the misapplication, of funds voted in the estimates. At the same time he felt disturbed at the lack of Parliamentary control over Government expenditure. Balfour, who had sensed that there was a general feeling of inquietude about this in the House, proposed that a select committee should study by what means Parliament might have stricter control over Government expenditure. At this time Churchill made proposals to Balfour for a new committee of the House that would take a more detached overall view of the merits of public expenditure. In a long letter dated May 15 Balfour pointed out that no committee of the House could really pass judgement on the merits of, say, Army and Navy expenditure without examining closely related aspects of foreign, colonial and Indian affairs. Nor could any one such committee be expected to have enough expertise to adjudicate between the merits of, say, armed services expenditure and spending on the social services. Did Churchill really think that a committee of the House would behave very differently in its attitude to public expenditure than the whole House did at present?

Churchill spoke in favour of Balfour's proposal for a select committee to study the problem of Parliamentary control, and was himself appointed a member. From July 15 onwards he attended a number of the Committee's meetings, and assiduously questioned the witnesses. One of Churchill's main concerns was to discover the fact that the principal control over expenditure of a technical nature lay in the hands of Treasury clerks who themselves had no specialized technical knowledge.

Before the Committee reported, Churchill set down in a lengthy memorandum his views of how Parliamentary control over expenditure could be improved. He put his finger on what he considered the most glaring defect:

Public expenditure may be considered in three aspects: policy, merit, and audit. To take a hypothetical instance: whether the standard of professional skill in the Royal Army Medical Corps should be improved or not is *Policy;* whether this result should be sought by building a special hospital for army surgeons, or whether arrangements should be made with existing civil hospitals to afford them opportunities of practice and study; whether in the one case the contracts for the hospital are the best that can be made, or in the other the arrangements are economical and efficient — all this may be called *Merit*; and whether in fact the money provided is expended faithfully and with proper authority is *Audit*. In other words — What should be done is a question of *policy:* in what way it should be done is a question of *merit:* and whether it is honestly done is a question of *audit*.

He proposed to fill this "lacuna" with an Estimates Committee which should sit in addition to the Public Accounts Committee — which would now simply be called the Accounts Committee and charged only with audit. This new Estimates Committee would hold a kind of post-mortem examination on the merit of the estimates after they had been presented and perhaps even voted on in the House. Churchill pointed out that even if it were too late to prevent errors of judgement in the current year the report of the Estimates Committee would be able to prevent further damage being done in future estimates. Although Churchill's suggestion for a third committee was not adopted, the Public Accounts Committee in later years has successfully fulfilled many of the objects for which Churchill pleaded in his memorandum. Over the years much waste of public money has been exposed and, although it could not be retrieved, these transactions have served as warnings against profligate expenditure in the future.

During 1902 Churchill made considerably fewer speeches in the country than he had in the year before. He was obviously finding it increasingly difficult to serve up the sort of party pap which Tory audiences required. "I cannot make speeches in the country with any satisfaction now," he wrote to Rosebery on January 10. "I cannot work up the least enthusiasm on the Govts behalf: and yet popular audiences seem to gape for party clap-trap." Later in the year he began to find it easier to mount the platform: he became interested in the Government's Education Bill and made a number of speeches expounding its provisions and commending its objects — at the Oxford Union, in Accrington, at Oldham and at Preston. The Education Bill, introduced by Balfour on March 24, took all secondary and primary education out of the hands of school boards and placed them under the care of county and county borough councils. At the same time, it brought under the control of the local authorities not only the board schools but also the "voluntary schools" — principally Church schools — whose managers were, however, allowed to retain rights over the appointment of teachers while undertaking to maintain the fabric of the schools. The measure infuriated the nonconformists; for one thing, they had been active and influential on the old school boards; for another, they regarded it as iniquitous that religious teaching — in effect, Church of England or Roman Catholic teaching — should be paid for out of the rates; and in single school districts, particularly in Wales, Church of England schools which at one time had seemed to be literally crumbling away were now to be buttressed by the ratepayers against their wishes and religious inclinations.

For the Liberal Party, with its powerful Nonconformist influence, the Bill provided an opportunity to heal the wounds which the Boer War had caused in their ranks. For Joseph Chamberlain, with his Unitarian and Radical background, the Bill also presented problems of conscience which he allayed with ill grace; but he wrestled with his conscience and his final decision to bring the nonconformist Midlands over to the Government side in support of the Education Bill persuaded him that a new demon in political controversy now needed to be raised.

Churchill did not profess to be an expert on the subject. "Some people," he told the House in Committee in July, "profess to be experts on all subjects, but I am quite ready to admit that Education is not my strong point." It was, however, Lord Hugh Cecil's strong point. His speech on the Second Reading was described by the *Annual Register* as "the most striking speech of the Debate," and "recognised by the best judges as bringing him within the front rank of Parliamentary orators." Throughout the long debates, Cecil gave the Bill, from his High Church vantage point, uncompromising support — so uncompromising that he felt impelled to vote against the Government when compromises were in fact made. Churchill believed that he had a duty to explain the Bill to his chapel-going constituents, and did so in blunt terms to his Tory chairman.

WSC to F. Travis-Clegg

EXTRACT

21 July 1902   House of Commons

... There is, I understand, a very general agreement throughout the
party in Oldham, and even in some quarters beyond it, that the Education Bill now before Parliament will in fact effect a real and substantial improvement in the existing system, that it will increase the
volume and improve the quality of education, that it gives to Voluntary schools a long-delayed, urgently needed measure of justice, and
that for all these reasons it deserves consistent support....

The Hooligans, and in particular Churchill with Cecil, acted in
unison on numerous occasions throughout the year. Perhaps their
most spectacular coup was in connection with the Deceased Wife's
Sister Bill. This perennial measure, designed to permit a man to
marry the sister of his deceased wife, had been introduced again the
previous year, 1901. As had come to be expected, there was a large
majority in favour of it, but Hugh Cecil argued passionately against
it, claiming that it threatened the sanctity of marriage and the purity
of family life. Five years before, when he was reading the *Annual
Register* and contemplating the subject in the abstract, Churchill had
raised no objection to the Bill. But he could claim that he had
inherited opposition to this measure not only from his father but
from the Marlborough family as a whole: three Dukes in succession
had voted against the measure. Churchill was not overly impressed
by Lord Hugh's theological arguments. Indeed he must have viewed
them with tolerant amusement in so far as he understood them: but
with Cecilian craft Lord Hugh produced a secular argument which
carried more practical weight. Among the working classes and lower
middle classes it was very much the custom that when a wife died her
unmarried sister might move in to attend the wants of the bereaved
husband and children. This was a humane and sensible arrangement.
If, however, marriage between the man and the deceased wife's sister
were permitted, the finger of scorn might be pointed at those who did
not avail themselves of the opportunity which the new law would
provide. Anyway it was a good parliamentary lark. Together with

the other Hooligans (they were all then bachelors) Churchill and
Cecil plotted to kill the Bill, at any rate for this Session. The Bill
came up for the Second Reading on Wednesday, February 8. Under
Standing Orders at that time, opposed business could not be proceeded with after 5.30 p.m. Being a Private Member's Bill, it was
necessary for the remaining stages of it to be taken "upstairs" in the
Standing Committee for Law, unless, which was unlikely, the Government gave time for it to be debated clause by clause by the whole
House.

Thus on that Wednesday the House would have to vote before
5.30 p.m., on an Amendment by Lord Hugh Cecil on the Second
Reading, and on the motion to send the Bill "upstairs" to the Committee. The division on the Amendment had been completed, and
the division on the Second Reading was called shortly after 5 p.m.
Normally there would have been plenty of time for the further division on the Committee Stage — provided, which was in itself doubtful, that no debate was allowed on that motion. But just in case there
was time for the further division, the Hooligans loitered so long in
the "No" Lobby that by the time the result of the division on the
Second Reading was announced — a clear majority in favour 249 to
124 — it was already half past five and no further progress could be
made. The Government, as expected, declared that they could find
no time for the Bill to be discussed by a Committee of the whole
House during the current Session, so the Bill lapsed.

Many members were gravely offended by these proceedings, and the
Speaker expressed his regret that they should have taken place. "A
good deal of indignation was felt" recorded the *Annual Register*;
the loitering manoeuvre was generally recognized as being altogether
at variance with the best Parliamentary traditions, and as opening up
alarming new possibilities of obstruction. Members and Parliamentary correspondents were quick to recall the way in which the
Fourth Party had upset Mr Gladstone's Government by astute use of
House of Commons procedure.

In April Churchill took the lead in a revolt of Tory back-benchers
against the Government over the case of Mr Cartwright, who was
being held in South Africa under the authority of martial law and
was prevented from visiting England. Cartwright had just finished

serving a sentence of twelve months' imprisonment for a libel on Kitchener which had appeared in a paper he edited, *South African News*. On expressing a wish to visit England "for private reasons," he had been forbidden to do so on the grounds that "it seemed inexpedient to increase the number of persons in this country who disseminated anti-British propaganda." Morley, who had raised the matter by moving the adjournment of the House, described this answer, given by Lord Stanley, the Financial Secretary to the War Office, as the most outrageous and indefensible ever given to the House. Churchill blamed the incompetence of the military authorities in South Africa for abusing their powers under martial law, and for the worst of reasons, because where could the dissemination of anti-British views do less harm than in Britain itself? The debate became heated, the Motion was pressed to a division, and Churchill and seven other Tories, including all the available Hooligans, voted with the Liberals; notwithstanding, Morley's motion was defeated by 279 votes to 182. Churchill recounts in *My Early Life* how that night the Hooligans entertained Chamberlain to dinner, and how they taxed him with the ineptness of the Government's handling of the case.

"What is the use," Chamberlain demanded, "of supporting your own Government only when it is right? It is just when it is in this sort of pickle that you ought to have come to our aid."

A few weeks later Churchill took up another case of administrative injustice, this time with rather more success. During the early summer a number of fires had broken out at the Royal Military College, Sandhurst; they were evidently the work of an incendiary. When, on June 25, the fifth fire broke out, the Commander-in-Chief, Lord Roberts, ordered that all cadets in "C" Company — where the fire had occurred — who could not prove that they were not in the College at the time of the outbreak, would be rusticated, and that all servants who did not have an alibi would be dismissed, unless within forty-eight hours the instigators of the fire came forward. No incendiary was found, and twenty-nine cadets were rusticated and three aged servants were dismissed.

From July 7 onwards Churchill, together with Hugh Cecil, bombarded *The Times* with lengthy letters citing individual cases of hardship and unfairness — for the rustication would mean a loss of six months' seniority and an extra term to be paid for by parents who in some cases could not afford it. But what most animated Churchill was the sheer unfairness of "this travesty of justice" which violated three cardinal principles of equity: "that suspicion is not evidence; that accused persons should be heard in their own defence [there was no charge, no trial, not even enquiry]; and that it is for the accuser to prove his charge, not for the defendant to prove his innocence."

Churchill tried to move the adjournment of the House, but the motion was not accepted. Balfour refused to allow time for the discussion of the affair. The headmaster of Sherborne, the Reverend Frederick Westcott, wrote to *The Times*: "The innocent, doubtless, suffer with the guilty; but then they always do. The world has been so arranged," exposing himself to the withering retort from Churchill: "Has it.indeed? No doubt he has taken care that the little world over which he presides is arranged on that admirable plan, but it is necessary to tell him that elsewhere the punishment of innocent people is regarded as a crime or as a calamity to be prevented by unstinted exertion. So long as the delinquencies of a schoolmaster are within the ordinary law the House of Commons has no right to intervene; but when a Commander-in-Chief and a Secretary of State are encouraged to imitate him, it is time to take notice. Does Mr Westcott flog his boys in their corporate capacity?" Being an old Harrovian, Churchill had probably not heard of the famous Eton headmaster, Dr Keate, who in 1832 birched more than eighty boys in the course of a single day.

Other writers to *The Times* declared that it was in the interests of discipline that the decision of the Commander-in-Chief should be upheld. But Lord Carrington and Lord Rosebery, egged on by the Hooligans, raised the matter in the House of Lords. The War Office's action was defended by the Foreign Secretary (Lord Lansdowne), the Lord President of the Council (the Duke of Devonshire) and the Under-Secretary of State for War (Lord Raglan).

But the most startling intervention came from the Commander-in-Chief himself, Lord Roberts, who promised that each individual case would be investigated again and that the innocent would be allowed to take their examinations at such a time as not to lose a term. This was no more than the justice Churchill had been seeking, and *The Times,* which for once had espoused his cause, gave him some credit as "an effective advocate." The three servants and all but two of the cadets w̧ere eventually reinstated, and the Commandant of Sandhurst was replaced following the report of an enquiry by the War Office Committee on Military Education which disclosed "a grave state of things" at the College.

Throughout 1902 the Hooligans continued to maintain close and friendly relations with the leading Liberals. In the month of May alone they invited to dine with them, at different times, the leaders of the two wings of the Party, Rosebery and Morley, as well as the Leader of the Party itself, Sir Henry Campbell-Bannerman. But it was with Rosebery that Churchill himself remained in the closest contact. The year, whose early months had excited Churchill's political expectations, was limping, so far as new party alliances were concerned, to a somewhat drab conclusion. Yet he still did not despair that Rosebery might possess the key which could open the way to a new departure.

WSC to Lord Rosebery
(*Rosebery Papers*)
EXTRACT

10 October 1902   105 Mount Street

... If by an "evolutionary process" we could create a wing of the Tory party wh could either infuse vigour into the parent body or join a central coalition, *my plan* would become most important as an incident in or possibly as the herald of the movement. But the risk & peril of it would be vy great, & it would carry consequences to me wh I cannot foresee; & only the conviction that you are upholding the flag for which my father fought so long & so disastrously would nerve me to the plunge. The Government of the Middle — the party wh shall be free at once from the sordid selfishness & callousness of Toryism on the one hand & the blind appetites of the Radical masses on the other — may be an ideal wh we perhaps shall never attain, wh could in any case only be possessed for a time, but which is nevertheless worth working for; & I for my part, see no reason to despair of that "good state."

But I should like to bring you & Beach together. There lies the
chance of a central coalition. "Tory-Liberal" is a much better name
than "Tory Democrat" or "Liberal Imperialist": & certainly neither
paradoxical nor unprecedented. The one real difficulty I have to
encounter is the suspicion that I am moved by mere restless ambition:
& if some issue — such as Tariff — were to arise — that difficulty
would disappear. . . .

2

Crossing the Floor

ON 14 APRIL 1902 the Chancellor of the Exchequer, Sir Michael Hicks-Beach had reintroduced, as part of his Budget, a registration duty of threepence a hundred-weight on imported corn and grain, and a duty of fivepence a hundred-weight on imported flour and meal. Hicks-Beach said that in view of the continuing demands being made on the Exchequer, especially by the service departments, it was necessary to enlarge the existing basis of taxation. At the same time, however, he denied that the tax on imported corn was the precursor of a protectionist policy, maintaining that registration duty, which had survived Peel's repeal of the Corn Laws, had been abolished by Gladstone's Chancellor, Lowe, only in 1868, and that this must have been a mistake.

The Corn Tax was expected to raise £2,650,000. Hicks-Beach had to meet an actual deficit of £27 million and a total deficit of some £45 million, about £18 million being put by for emergencies in connection with the war. Seven months before, in September 1901, Hicks-Beach had circulated two memoranda to his Cabinet colleagues which showed that Government expenditure since the Salisbury administration took office in 1895 had risen by forty per cent, not including any expenditure on the war; that direct taxation — at 1s. 2d. in the pound — had just about reached its limit; and that unless retrenchment and economy were pursued "the only possible new indirect taxes which could produce any important amount, without a complete return to a protectionist policy which be corn or meat or petroleum, on the political objections to which I need not dwell."

Predictably, the announcement of the Corn Tax led to cries from the Liberal opposition that it was a tax on the people's food. Equally predictably but more ominously, it was greeted with a shout of "Well done! Well done!" from the leader of the militant protectionist wing of the Tory Party, Sir Howard Vincent. It was to his view that Churchill reacted immediately; in a prophetic passage in the speech he made only a few hours after the Chancellor had sat down on 14 April 1902, and more than a year before Chamberlain was to raise the cry of Tariff Reform in Birmingham on 15 May 1903, Churchill said:

And so it comes to this: here is the corner into which we are being driven. After the war is over we shall have to meet increased demands for ordinary expenditure, with a revenue which will be less than the present revenue by the revival of the Sinking Fund and the reduction of the income tax; and we shall have to do this without the patriotic stimulus due to the war, and perhaps without the prosperous conditions of the present time. The result is plain and evident. The basis of taxation will have to be enlarged — further enlarged — and it is just as well to face the fact that further expenditure means the serious taxation of bread and meat and other necessaries in the food of the people. And that, Sir — I say — is going to raise two gigantic issues. First of all, I am persuaded that it will raise the whole question of fair trade. Taxation, imposed no doubt sincerely to begin with solely for revenue purposes, will under the influence of the hon and gallant member for Sheffield [Sir Howard Vincent] — not less gallant in the field of economics than on the field of war — assume a protective character. For why, it will be said, should we not kill three birds at one stone — collect our revenue, support British industries, and consolidate the Empire?

I wonder, Sir, what will happen in this country if the fair trade issue is boldly raised by some responsible person of eminence and authority. We shall find ourselves once again on an old battlefield. Around will be the broken weapons, the grass-grown trenches and neglected graves — reviving former memories — and party bitterness, such as this generation has not known. How is it going to split existing political organizations — now so artificially serene? These are the questions of the future; but, Sir, when I think of this budget, I would say, of the near future, and when they arise they will have to be answered, by timid men as well as by bold men. . . .

Churchill's prognosis seems in retrospect unbelievably prescient. Indeed, reading the above passage carefully one is almost inclined to think that he was luring the Tories to their doom so that he might have an honourable pretext for leaving them and joining the Liberals, whom he was finding increasingly sympathetic to his rapidly maturing political conceptions. We have seen in the previous chapter how six months later, in October 1902 he was to write to Rosebery almost yearning for the emergence of a policy of Tariff Reform. A week after his speech on Budget day, Churchill and the other Hooligans entertained Chamberlain to dinner. It was the night of the Cartwright debate. After dinner, Chamberlain turned to the Hooligans as he was leaving and said to them: "You young gentlemen have entertained me royally, and in return I will give you a priceless secret. Tariffs! There are the politics of the future, and of the near future. Study them closely and make yourselves masters of them, and you will not regret your hospitality to me."

Despite the misgivings he expressed in the House, Churchill found himself able to vote in favour of the Budget. This may have been because he knew that his father's old friend Hicks-Beach was at heart a staunch Free Trader, and also that he was under the safe Treasury chaperonage of two eminent civil servants, Sir Francis Mowatt and Sir Edward Hamilton, both notable and articulate Free Traders. Churchill was able to explain away his support of the tax to his constituents by saying that it was "the most convenient method of raising money for purposes of which the electorate have approved," adding that unless the whole community bore a share in the burden of taxation, "what check is there upon expenditure?"

And a few weeks later he repeated, in a letter to the Newcastle Anti-Bread Tax Committee dated June 5, that while he strongly desired that the reduction of national expenditure might make the removal of the tax possible, "as a fiscal measure the corn tax is the best practical method of raising the money needed under the present Budget, and all who have confidence in the present Government are bound in ordinary common sense to support it."

In fact, the issue of Protection was raised in a different form, and sooner than Hicks-Beach or Churchill seem to have expected. On May 12, in the course of a debate in the Canadian Parliament, Robert

Borden, the leader of the Opposition, proposed that the House should pass a resolution in favour of the establishment of reciprocal tariff preferences within the Empire, and Sir Wilfrid Laurier, the Canadian Liberal Prime Minister, accepted the idea and referred to the corn tax in England as a "step . . . which would make it possible to obtain preference for Canadian goods." On the following day, in the course of the debate on the Finance Bill, Campbell-Bannerman at once drew attention to the statement made in Ottawa as evidence that the corn duty was the first step in a system of preferential tariffs. Balfour refused to accept this interpretation; but this did not deter the Canadian Prime Minister at the Colonial Conference in London a few weeks later from using the corn tax as a lever to advance the case for Imperial Preference.

The Colonial Conference was spread over ten meetings which lasted from June 30 to August 11. In the middle, on July 11, Lord Salisbury resigned: with him went Hicks-Beach, who seized the moment to sever himself, with as little fuss as possible, from colleagues with whose views on economy and taxation he was growing increasingly out of sympathy.

Balfour became Prime Minister and C. T. Ritchie moved from the Home Office to take Hicks-Beach's place as Chancellor. Balfour did not, as had been expected, make a major reconstruction of the Government; although he did find room for Percy, the mystical member of the Hooligans who was an expert on Persia and things oriental, as Under-Secretary of State for India. Balfour did not avail himself of this opportunity to offer Churchill any Ministerial office. So high was Churchill's opinion of his own merits and so considerable had been his early parliamentary success that, whatever others might have thought, we may be sure that he would have been in no way surprised by inclusion in the ministry. Once in the Government he might have found it difficult to leave and would have had to fight tariff reform from the inside: his easy and swift transition to the Liberal benches would not have been possible. Another opportunity to cross the Floor might never have arisen and he would have gone down to defeat with the Tories in 1906. His whole life would have assumed a different pattern.

A week later Churchill was writing to the Chairman of the Oldham

Tories, Travis-Clegg, a lengthy account of the session and "of the general course of public affairs" for the annual report of the Oldham Conservative Association. After a number of loyal and optimistic remarks concerning the Party's fortunes and new leadership, Churchill wrote:

> I hope to have an opportunity when I come before my constituents at the General meeting [in October] . . . of dealing with another formidable question towards which the increase of expenditure is steadily drawing us — the question of what is called Fair Trade. Time is, I think, coming near when men will have to make up their minds on this great issue, to formulate their opinions, and set them forth without hesitation or doubt.

As in the previous year Churchill was spending the late summer and early autumn in Scotland, interspersing his social and sporting activities in the houses of Scottish noblemen with political talk. Once again he stayed with the Duke of Sutherland at Dunrobin and with Lord Rosebery at Dalmeny; but this year he was also commanded to Balmoral.

WSC to Lady Randolph

EXTRACT

27 September 1902   Balmoral

Dearest Mamma,

I have been vy kindly treated here by the King, who has gone out of his way to be nice to me. It has been most pleasant & easy going & today the stalking was excellent, tho I missed my stags.

You will see the King on Weds when he comes to Invercauld; mind you gush to him about my having written to you saying how much etc etc I had enjoyed myself here.

This visit was a signal honour for a young member of 27 who had been less than two years in the House of Commons.

By the end of the year, Churchill was quite clear what his attitude was to be on the tariff question; he set it out in a letter to a constituent:

WSC to Ernest Fletcher

EXTRACT

14 November 1902   105 Mount Street

Dear Sir,

I have never described myself as an "ardent Free Trader" but as a "sober admirer of Free Trade principles" which is not quite the same thing. . . . As to the question of "a protected Empire," I could not pretend to put any arguments at length before you but it would seem to me a fantastic policy to endeavour to shut the British Empire up in a ringed fence. It is very large, and there are a good many things which can be produced in it, but the world is larger & produces some better things than can be found in the British Empire. Why should we deny ourselves the good and varied merchandise which the traffic of the world offers, more especially since the more we trade with others, the more they must trade with us; for it is quite clear that we give them something else back for everything they give to us. Our planet is not a very big one compared with the other celestial bodies, and I see no particular reason why we should endeavour to make inside our planet a smaller planet called the British Empire, cut off by impassable space from everything else. The idea does not attract me as an idea, because, although it may be worth while as circumstances arise, to make commercial treaties in special cases, either with our Colonies or with foreign countries, I for one, should scrutinize these projects very carefully. . . .

On November 19 the Cabinet, after "long and elaborate discussions" finally resolved, according to Balfour's letter of that date to the King, "that, as presently advised, they would maintain the corn tax but that a preferential remission of it should be made in favour of the British Empire."

Chamberlain left on a trip to South Africa confident that Imperial Preference had been agreed in principle. Meanwhile Churchill went to Egypt as the guest of Sir Ernest and Lady Cassel for a trip up the Nile on a *dahabiah* with such varied companions as his Aunt Leonie, the Duke and Duchess of Connaught, and Mrs Keppel, the friend of King Edward VII. But he derived the greatest benefit from the presence of Sir Michael Hicks-Beach and of Sir John Gorst, another of Lord Randolph's old friends:

WSC to Lady Randolph

EXTRACT

19 December 1902   Savoy Hotel
                                                   Cairo

... Beach & the Beach family were really quite an accession. I rejoiced in my talks with him. He is such a good and true friend; &
we agree in almost everything political. I only wish he were going
to be back in Parliament during the early part of the session for I
foresee many possibilities of co-operation: & in regard to the book
[Life of Lord Randolph] he has been vy diligent & ready to help.
Gorst *père* is also here: I think he will have to advise the new "group"
on questions of procedure next session. . . .

In this letter Churchill recorded that he had "learned 'Bridge' and
we now play every day at least four rubbers. It amuses me." In fact,
he never prospered at this game and he abandoned it after a few
years. It is a curious fact that politicians do not usually make good
bridge players. Churchill, Asquith and Birkenhead were all duffers
and consistent losers. It may be that politicians, who tend to be wilful
men of action, always want to play the hand and overbid. They like
one-man shows rather than partnerships. Of course, there have been
exceptions. Bonar Law was competent if pedestrian, Duff Cooper
good but erratic. In our own day and age we have the brilliant
exception of Mr Iain Macleod, who is one of the four or five best
bridge players in the country and has even written a book entitled
Bridge Is An Easy Game. Mr Christopher Soames, a latecomer to the
bridge table, has shown an exceptional flair for the game.
     While he was in South Africa, Chamberlain had told Milner about
his plans for Tariff Reform and Imperial Preference. Milner had
listened enthralled. Thus encouraged Chamberlain soon after his
return to England set forth his proposal first to the Prime Minister,
Balfour, and later to the public. Chamberlain publicly declared for
Tariff Reform and Imperial Preference in his political stronghold of
Birmingham on 15 May 1903. Towards the end of his speech Chamberlain defined the issue which he was raising with unexceptionable
clarity and force:

The people of this Empire have two alternatives before them. They may maintain if they like in all its severity the interpretation — in my mind an entirely artificial and wrong interpretation — which has been placed on the doctrines of Free Trade by a small remnant of Little Englanders, of the Manchester school, who now profess to be the sole repositories of the doctrines of Mr Cobden and Mr Bright. They may maintain that policy in all its severity, though it is repudiated by every other nation and by all your own Colonies. In that case they will be absolutely precluded either from giving any kind of Preference or favour to any of their Colonies abroad, or even protecting their Colonies abroad when they offer to favour us. That is the first alternative. The second alternative is that we should insist that we will not be bound by any purely technical definition of Free Trade, that, while we seek as one chief object free interchange of trade, between ourselves and all the nations of the world, we will, nevertheless, recover our freedom, resume that power of negotiation and, if necessary, retaliation whenever our own interests or our relations between our Colonies and ourselves are threatened by other people.

Churchill saw his opportunity and answered Chamberlain six days later at Hoxton:

Mr Chamberlain is hardly the man to have made such a declaration unless he had behind it a very carefully-thought-out scheme in principle and in detail which he was prepared at the proper time to launch and to support, not only by facts and figures, but by those moral and sentimental arguments which are always needed to start the great movements of an enlightened people. I think he will need all his weighty arguments, all his eloquence, and his unexampled dialectical skill, and all his reputation and authority if he is to persuade the British people to abandon that system of free trade and cheap food under which they have thriven so long and have advanced from the depth of woe and poverty to the first position among the nations of the world.

Do not let us lose our sense of political proportion. The policy which the Unionist Party ought to pursue must be a policy of Imperialism, but not of one-sided Imperialism. It must not be a policy which looks only abroad or only at home. While we cherish the loyalty, the help, and the comradeship of our colonies we must be careful not to disregard the urgent needs of our great population at home or do anything to injure that elaborate machinery by which the great wealth of England is produced. The far-seeing eye of Lord Beaconsfield ranged widely across the waters to the most distant colonies and possessions of the Crown, but at the same time he was able to set first and foremost in his mind the virtue and prosperity of the people of Great Britain. It will be by following his example as closely as possible in that respect that we shall best serve the interests of the Unionist Party and the country in which we are so proud to live.

Throughout the summer the Government and the Tory Party were bedevilled by the fierce animosity which Chamberlain's policy, wholly unauthorized by the Cabinet, had let loose. Chamberlain had already with the help of Devonshire wrecked the Liberal Party by his opposition to Home Rule for Ireland. Was the erstwhile Radical leader now to destroy the Tory Party on his own?

Balfour reacted to this unwelcome and unwonted division with typically Balfourian finesse which was the negation of leadership. If he had enthusiastically espoused either of the two causes that were tearing his party into pieces, he might have prevailed; but he had a genius and a weakness for seeing both sides of the question and for failing to be convinced by either. Throughout the summer Balfour took the sophisticated urbane line that his colleagues should be permitted to differ, expound their views and discover how the party reacted. The result was inevitable: the lesions in the party grew.

The day before Churchill had spoken at Hoxton he had written to Moore Bayley who was one of the few Tory Free Traders in Birmingham:

WSC to F. Moore Bayley

EXTRACT

20 May 1903   105 Mount Street

... The almost insuperable difficulties of framing any scheme which would satisfy all the Colonies, & the certainty of future bickerings and hagglings are alone enough to discourage any but old men in a hurry! The only way in which we can help the Colonies is by paying duties on raw materials and foodstuffs — the very commodities taxation of which cannot be of the slightest use or value to the manufacturer.

Is it conceivable that the manufacturer will be content to bear this burden all by himself and let both English agriculturists and Colonial producers gain the benefit? No, he will infallibly demand a *quid pro quo;* and as surely as we embark upon the slippery path of protection, we shall finish up amid a tangle of high protective tariffs of all kinds. If that be so, exit for ever the banking, broking, warehousing predominance of Great Britain.

I do not want a self-contained Empire. It is very much better that the great nations of the world should be interdependent one upon the other than that they should be independent of each other. That makes powerfully for peace and it is chiefly through the cause of the great traffic of one great nation with another during the last twenty-five years, that the peace of Europe has been preserved through so many crises.

And even if it comes to an European war, do you not think it very much better that the United States should be vitally interested in keeping the English market open, than that they should be utterly careless of what happens to their present principal customer? I deprecate very much the raising of this controversy, it is premature, it is ill considered, it is unsound. It is far more sensible to try to get the Colonials gradually to adopt our free trade system, than that we should try their vicious policy of protection. If, as I fear may be the case, this question is raised as a vital issue, great harm will be done to Imperial sentiment by the language which will be used about the Colonies and their share in the burdens of the State; and most certainly it will split and tear the Unionist party from one end to the other. I earnestly hope you will practise the greatest caution. . . .

This last paragraph must have been one of the earliest recognitions of where America's true interests in Europe lay and earliest anticipations that America might be drawn into an European war on the British side. All his life this was to be a persistent and growing theme. On May 25 Churchill wrote to Balfour about Chamberlain's speech at Birmingham:

WSC to A. F. Balfour
(Balfour Papers)

25 May 1903
Most Private

Dear Mr. Balfour,

You have shown me so much kindness in the past that I am encouraged to write to you frankly now about Mr Chamberlain's recent statements; & indeed the matter seems to me so important that it is my duty to do so.

At Birmingham he advocated Preferential Tariffs with the Colonies; in his letter of Monday to a Mr Loveday he revealed plain Protectionist intentions; & in the House on Friday last he showed himself prepared to use Old Age Pensions as a lever to attain these ends. Now I see it stated by Mr Bonar Law that you are agreed with him in all this.

I earnestly hope this is not true & that you have not taken an irrevocable decision. Hence this letter.

I am utterly opposed to anything which will alter the Free Trade character of this country; & I consider such an issue superior in importance to any other now before us. Preferential Tariffs, even in respect of articles wh we are bound to tax for revenue purposes, are dangerous & objectionable. But of course it is quite impossible to stop there and I am persuaded that once this policy is begun it must lead to the establishment of a complete Protective system, involving commercial disaster, & the Americanisation of English politics. I do not now attempt to argue all this. But I submit these two points to you.

1. From a national point of view there is no case for a fiscal resolution: not in the Trade Returns, nor Income Tax receipts, nor in a colonial demand, nor in a popular movement.

2. From a party point of view: the government is probably less unpopular than any which has ruled 8 years in England. Their record — army & expenditure apart — will make a fine page in history. They have no reason to dread an appeal to the constituencies; & even if a general election should result in a transference of power, the conservative party would be in a strong minority quite able to protect those causes & institutions which they cherish. In five or six years a healthy operation of opinion would recall them once more to power. Why is it necessary to play such desperate stakes?

I feel perhaps that I may have sometimes been the cause of embarrassment to the government. It is difficult to write about such things because of obvious rejoinders, but I should like to tell you that an attempt on your part to preserve the Free Trade policy & character of the Tory party would command my absolute loyalty. I would even swallow six army corps — if it would make any difference & sink all minor differences. But if on the other hand you have made up your mind & there is no going back, I must reconsider my position in politics. Please do not consider this letter disrespectful or anything but a statement of fact. I should be very sorry to cause you annoyance of any kind. But after all you ought to know how seriously some of us regard this great question.

Yours vy sincerely
WINSTON S. CHURCHILL

Balfour in reply said:

A. F. Balfour to WSC

26 May 1903   10 Downing Street
Private Dictated

My dear Winston,

I am very much obliged to you for your letter.

I have not seen Chamberlain's letter, and am mildly surprised that Bonar Law should have taken us under his aegis, as you tell me he has done.

I have never understood that Chamberlain advocated protection, though, no doubt, he is ready and, indeed, anxious — for a duty on food-stuffs, which may incidentally be protective in its character, but whose main object is to provide an instrument for fiscal union with the Colonies. This is a very different thing from protection, both in theory and in practice. But undoubtedly the matter is one of difficulty, and requires the most wary walking.

Yours sincerely
A. J. BALFOUR

Balfour's answer made it plain that he was no more ready to show his hand in private than he was in public.

The extent to which Churchill was already prepared to operate with the Liberals on the Tariff issue is well illustrated by an exchange of letters between himself and Campbell-Bannerman at this time:

WSC to Sir Henry Campbell-Bannerman

29 May 1903   105 Mount Street
Copy
Most Private

Dear Sir Henry Campbell-Bannerman,

I am anxious about your amendment to the Finance Bill, which seems to me to court a decision of first importance upon a false issue. After all we like the Finance Bill, and refusing to proceed with it will unite the whole Conservative party: protectionists who will be glad to triumph over you: free traders who are bound to support Ritchie and the repeal of the corn tax. The result can only be a disastrous division and an immense victory for Chamberlain. This is Sir Michael Hicks-Beach's opinion as well as that of my friends.

Is it not possible for the discussion, for which we are all anxious, to be raised in some other way? You are quite justified in asking the Government to put down a resolution, or in moving a vote of want of confidence on the ground that their public utterances conflict with their declared fiscal policy — and Mr Balfour would be bound to give full opportunity. But let us at any rate have a discussion which can be terminated by a division on a fair issue.

You will of course understand that the position of those Conservatives who are unalterably opposed to the impending fiscal change is one of great difficulty and danger; and I earnestly hope you will consider us in the course you take.

Believe me, yours sincerely
WINSTON S. CHURCHILL

Sir Henry Campbell-Bannerman to WSC

[handwritten letter reproduction]

31 May 1903   6 Grosvenor Place
Private

Dear Mr Churchill,
    I am much obliged for your letter.
    The debate on Thursday and the statement of policy made on the part of the Government, have of course rendered my amendment inappropriate and therefore superfluous, and it will not be moved. There is still much to learn as to their plans, but we have ascertained enough for the basis of a general discussion.
    I should think this must be generally obvious, but I have taken means to make it publicly known.

Yours very truly
H. CAMPBELL-BANNERMAN

In the course of the summer the tariff reform dispute led to the establishment of two rival organizations who competed with each other to impose their fiscal policy on the Tory Party and the Government. Churchill was a prime mover in what was ultimately to be named the Free Food League: this was established on July 13.

In the course of forming the Free Food League Churchill encountered a rebuff. In June he had invited Archibald Salvidge, who was already a power in Liverpool politics, to a small dinner in the House of Commons to meet other Unionist Free Traders including Lord Hugh Cecil, Goschen, St Loe Strachey, Editor of the *Spectator*, and Sir Michael Hicks-Beach. At the end of the dinner it was intended that everyone should express their opinions, and then Salvidge speaking for the Industrial North should express his own. But Salvidge was a staunch party man. He gathered from the conversation at dinner that the company were all opposed to Joseph Chamberlain. When it was suggested that everyone should express their views in turn, with Salvidge speaking last, he interrupted according to his biographer, his son Stanley Salvidge:

> "I am afraid," said Salvidge, "that, with all respect, I had better give my views first. I have come here under some misapprehension as to the nature of the gathering. I look upon it as little short of a cave or plot against one of the leaders of our party — a leader who means more to the masses of the Industrial Midlands and North than all of us put together. I am sorry to make such a poor return for hospitality, but I think it would facilitate the business in hand if I now withdrew from this table."
>
> He then went off to report what he regarded as a plot to Chamberlain. Salvidge forthwith invited Chamberlain to speak to the Liverpool working-men's Association on tariff reform. Despite this inauspicious occasion, Salvidge ultimately threw in his lot with the Free Trade wing of the Tory Party, and he joined Lord Derby in early 1913 when the latter compelled the newly elected Tory leader Bonar Law to abandon Food Taxes.

When the League was launched, no fewer than sixty Unionist Free Traders in the House of Commons joined. These included Hicks-Beach as Chairman, Churchill, Lord Hugh Cecil, Sir Ernest Beckett, Sir Edgar Vincent (brother of the Protectionist Sir Howard), Sir J. Dickson-Poynder, Jack Seely, Sir John Gorst, Gibson Bowles, Ivor

Guest, Arthur Stanley Wilson, Henry Hobhouse, William Galloway, Lord Richard Cavendish and Sir Samuel Hoare, whose son of the same name was later to acquire notoriety in 1935. A number of peers were also listed, notably Goschen, Cowper and James of Hereford. After his resignation in October the Duke of Devonshire was also to join the League.

Compared with the Free Food League, the rival Tariff Reform League could only bring thirty members of the House of Commons into the field, half the strength which the Free Food League had rallied. However, they had twice as many Dukes. Apart from the Duke of Sutherland, who was elected Chairman, they had enrolled the Duke of Westminster. The MPs included Griffith-Boscawen, Evelyn Cecil, Edward Goulding, Arthur Lee, J. T. Middlemore, Parker Smith, Sir Herbert Maxwell, Sir A. Henderson, Sir Gilbert Parker and Sir Thomas Wrightson.

Churchill continued his exposition of the free trade cause through-out the summer — still inside the ranks of the Tory party. As early as May 28 he made an attack on the leadership of his own party such as had seldom come from an aspiring back-bencher of less than three years standing. On the motion for adjournment over the Whitsun recess Chamberlain replied to an amendment moved by Sir Charles Dilke. Churchill spoke immediately afterwards:

> It is an economic absurdity to say that Protection means a greater development of wealth; and to say that it means a fairer distribution of wealth is a "downright lie."
> ... This idea means a change, not only in historic English parties, but in the conditions of our public life. The old Conservative Party, with its religious convictions and constitutional principles, will dis-appear, and a new party will arise, rich, materialist, and secular, whose opinions will turn on tariffs and who will cause the lobbies to be crowded with the touts of protected industries. What is the cause of this change? Never was the wealth of the country greater, or the trade returns higher, or the loyalty of the Colonies more pronounced. Is it that we are tired of these good old days?

On July 16 Churchill attacked Balfour for attempting to muzzle the Unionist Free Traders.

WSC to the Editor of The Times

EXTRACT

16 July 1903

. . . While Mr Balfour silences his followers in the House of Commons Mr Chamberlain is busy with their constituencies. Within the
last few days circulars have been sent to local Conservative agents
inviting them, irrespective of the opinions of their members, to
disseminate protectionist propaganda. Leaflets are to be supplied
gratis. They are to report what free trade arguments are producing
an "effect," so that "if necessary" leaflets can be "specially prepared"
to answer them. The cost of "house-to-house distribution" is, where
desired, to be defrayed. These circulars emanate from a Mr Vince,
of Birmingham, whose name is already familiar to us in connexion
with Mr Chamberlain's correspondence, and who has long been one
of his most trusted agents. But still we must be loyal to the policy
of impartial inquiry and the open mind. . . .

While the Tory party under the supine leadership or masterly
inactivity of Balfour — the reader must decide for himself — was
tearing itself to pieces in public the traditional urbanities and
amenities of English political life continued to be maintained in
private. Sir Edward Hamilton wrote in his diary on 26 July 1903:

> W.C. is taking a very devoted line against C. [Chamberlain]. He
> is thoroughly in earnest about it and it does him credit, for it is
> doubtful whether he is playing the card best for himself — now that
> Marlborough has been bagged by C for his Under-Secretary. It is the
> fashion to run him down — but I think there is a great deal in him
> and that he is bound to win in the long run.

WSC to Lady Randolph

EXTRACT

12 August 1903   105 Mount Street

. . . Last night Jack Seely and I gave a dinner at the House of Commons which "A.J.B.," Austen Chamberlain, George Wyndham, St
John Brodrick, [Hugh] Cecil and Ivor Guest with some others at-

tended. We had a pleasant evening. A.B. was most amiable and good humoured in spite of the fact that Cecil and I had been very rude to him in the House of Commons in the afternoon, as you will see if you read this debate. He chaffed and chatted in the best of spirits.... After dinner A.B. made us go into his room where we sat and talked a long time — Jack (our Jack) [Churchill] was there too — and when I came out of his room to go to a Division, of course I ran straight into J.C. who gave me an extraordinary look of reproach as much as to say "How could you desert me" and I confess I felt very sorry for him indeed. I have far more respect for him than for those time-servers who have been waiting to see which way the cat will jump and who, although perhaps only a week ago were ready to shout down people like Cecil for daring to question Chamberlain's policy, may easily in the near future be occupying themselves with destroying his [Chamberlain's] influences.

I cannot help admiring Chamberlain's courage. I do not believe he means to give way an inch, and I think he is quite prepared to sacrifice his whole political position and Austen's [his son's] as well, for the cause in which he is so wrapped up. Of course the Unionist Free Traders will support Mr Balfour with great determination if Chamberlain should leave the Government....

In September a remarkable and probably unique series of events took place. On September 9 Chamberlain offered to resign. Balfour gave a dubious response. But at the Cabinet on September 14 he took occasion to force the resignations of Ritchie, his Chancellor of the Exchequer, and Lord Balfour of Burleigh, his Secretary for Scotland. Neither of these two important ministers — nor indeed the rest of the Cabinet apart from Chamberlain himself — knew that Balfour already had Chamberlain's resignation in his pocket.

The next day Lord George Hamilton, Secretary for India, still unaware of Chamberlain's impending departure, resigned in sympathy with the virtual dismissal of his two Free Trade colleagues. On September 16 Balfour accepted Chamberlain's resignation but persuaded him to agree that no announcement should be made for two days. He had already procured a similar stipulation from Ritchie and Balfour of Burleigh. On September 18 all four resignations, Chamberlain, Ritchie, Balfour of Burleigh and Lord George Hamilton were announced. The public was considerably mystified by these strange transactions by which Balfour had with some disingenuity succeeded in shedding both the Protectionist and the Free Trade wings of his Government simultaneously. Even more muddled than the public was the Duke of Devonshire, Lord President of the Council, who, through his own slipshod habits, did not know that Chamberlain had resigned. He therefore sent in his resignation. When the next day he learned through his stepson-in-law, Edward Stanley (later 17th Earl of Derby), that Chamberlain had resigned, he authorized Stanley to tell Balfour in the circumstances he would withdraw his resignation. It seems as if Balfour would have liked to have let him go, but he agreed to let him stay. However, an angry letter from Ritchie to Devonshire suggesting that he had betrayed his friends led the Duke to embrace the first opportunity of resignation on October 6.

It was a slender occasion. Balfour made a speech at Sheffield on October 2 along the lines of his usual middle-of-the-road technique. Devonshire seized the opportunity to resign on the grounds that the Prime Minister had not declared himself ardently for Free Trade. Readers who seek a fuller account of this strange political episode will find it in the author's *Lord Derby, King of Lancashire* and in the new study of A. J. Balfour by A. M. Gollin who takes a different view.

Churchill was as mystified as was everyone else. He was agog:

WSC to Lady Randolph

18 September 1903   Invercauld

Dearest Mamma,

I am indeed sorry to miss you here: but we shall see each other often in the autumn, & I may need your assistance in Oldham, if you have time & inclination.

The situation is most interesting & I fancy a smash must come in a few days. Mr Balfour is coming to Balmoral on Saturday. Is he going to resign or reconstruct? If he resigns will the King send for Spencer or Devonshire? If for either will he succeed in forming a govt & what kind of Government? If he reconstructs — will it be a protectionist reconstruction of a cabinet wh does not contain the free trade Ministers, or a free trade reconstruction of a Cabinet from which J.C. has resigned? All these things are possible.

I go to Dalmeny tomorrow. Write to me there. I have put my name down at Balmoral — but I fear I am still in disgrace.

Your loving son
WINSTON S. C.

The Free Traders were naturally anxious to obtain the support of the Duke of Devonshire.

WSC to Duke of Devonshire
(*Chatsworth Papers*)

13 July 1903   House of Commons

...I want to urge you, that the conditions of fairness and impartiality in this controversy will be altogether destroyed if procedure is construed and used to prevent all unprejudiced debate in the House of Commons ... inactivity and silence would most certainly be interpreted in the country as weakness and indecision. ...

With all the information now available — and it is unlikely that much new evidence will emerge — it is still very hard to penetrate and reconstruct what was in Balfour's mind at this time. He may have thought that he had pulled off a Machiavellian coup by ridding himself simultaneously of the leading tariff reformer in his Government and of the ardent Free Traders. Perhaps he thought that he would have a more tranquil life and could go on governing the country in his usual ruthless and efficient fashion. But he may have misjudged events. The grandson of the great Lord Salisbury was to remark in the early 1960s that Iain Macleod was "too clever by half." Maybe the same can be said of Balfour. The underlings could be spared: the almost concurrent departure from the Government of Chamberlain and Devonshire was a tremendous weakening of his administration. Chamberlain was the hero of the hour, the most exciting figure on the political scene and the darling of the Tory Party. Devonshire was a Duke in days when Dukes still counted. He controlled a number of county boroughs and carried a considerable weight and opinion with him. Moreover, though he sometimes failed to have the key to his personal Cabinet box on his person and neglected to read Government despatches, at the same time he was no fool. And his wife, the German-born former Duchess of Manchester, the celebrated "double-duchess," was a highly intelligent woman animated by a proud ambition to make her second Duke Prime Minister. She scarcely could have aspired to make the Duke of Manchester ("silly but not dull" was Disraeli's description) Prime Minister.

There were not lacking responsible friends and relations to urge Churchill upon the course which was clearly forming in his mind. His aunt, Cornelia, wife of the first Lord Wimborne, ardently sought to woo and seduce Churchill from the Tory Party. She was a bigoted Protestant and founded an Institution (to which she gave considerable sums of her husband's money) called Lady Wimborne's Protestant League. She financed and organized a number of branches all over the country. In Liverpool she was a little unlucky. She employed an unknown and impecunious young lawyer, F. E. Smith, as the secretary of the local branch and authorized him to take and furnish an office. One day she let Smith know that she was coming to Liverpool to inspect the premises which he had acquired on her behalf. Smith felt that his office was rather bleak and bare and, not at that time being fully conversant with the religious controversies involved or with the real objectives his patroness was seeking, went out and for a knock-down price bought twelve somewhat inferior reproductions in colour of the Virgin Mary. These he caused to be hung as gracefully as he could contrive on the walls of the office of the Protestant League. When Lady Wimborne surveyed Smith's handiwork she dismissed him instantly. She was a highly intelligent old battle-axe. Smith probably embroidered this story against himself.

Lady Wimborne to WSC

15 October 1903   Wimborne House
                                                   Arlington Street

Dearest Winston,
    You know, I am sure, how deeply interested I am in your career & dear Ivor's. I feel the present moment is such a critical one for your

fortunes & his that I should so like to see you & have a chat. Do come round & see me anytime before I go away on Saturday afternoon. I thought your letter quite excellent & it reminded me of your Father's way of going straight to the point. Of one thing I think there is no doubt & that is that Balfour & Chamberlain are one, and that there is no future for Free Traders in the Conservative party. Why tarry!

Yrs affecly
CORNELIA WIMBORNE

Churchill's unusual personality was beginning to make an impact on a wide variety of people. Some were repelled, some fascinated by the growing compulsion and brilliance of his conversation. Among those who put down their earliest recollections was Wilfrid Scawen Blunt, the poet and writer, who always championed the nationalism of countries other than his own. He recorded in his diary on 31 October 1903:

I stopped to luncheon with Victor and Pamela [Lytton] and met there for the first time young Winston Churchill. He is a little, square headed fellow of no very striking appearance, but of wit, intelligence, and originality. In mind and manner he is a strange replica of his father, with all his father's suddenness and assurance, and I should say more than his father's ability. There is just the same gaminerie and contempt of the conventional and the same engaging plain-spokenness and readiness to understand. As I listened to him recounting conversations he had had with Chamberlain I seemed once more to be listening to Randolph on the subject of Northcote and Salisbury. About Chamberlain he was especially amusing, his attitude being one of mingled contempt and admiration, contempt for the man and admiration for his astuteness and audacity. In opposition Winston I expect to see playing precisely his father's game, and I should not be surprised if he had his father's success. He has a power of writing Randolph never had, who was a schoolboy with his pen, and he has education and political tradition. He interested me immensely.

Churchill had by now decided after much heart-searching that his destiny lay with the Liberal Party. In a letter of outstanding candour to Lord Hugh Cecil he explained his situation, aspirations and plans. As with many other important letters it was, for some reason, never sent. Fortunately, unlike many other important letters in history, it has survived. The background to this letter was Balfour's famous speech at Sheffield on October 2 where, to some extent, he came off the fence and declared for retaliatory tariffs.

WSC to Lord Hugh Cecil

24 October 1903   105 Mount Street
[*Note on letter*] Not sent
Most private

My Dear Linky,

I want to impress upon you that I am absolutely in earnest in what I said to you yesterday & I do not think that anything is likely to happen to turn me.

I understand your plan vy clearly; and it is not mine. I do not want to be enrolled in a narrow sect of latter day Peelites austerely unbending in economics, more Tory than the Tories in other things. I do not intend to be a "loyal supporter" of the Unionist party or of this present administration, & I object to be so labelled. These old ministers who have come forward to help us on free trade are involved in varying degrees — but all vy deeply — in the blunders and follies of the last four years. They all feel — as I cannot feel — identity with the earlier glories of the Unionist party. It seems to me certain that the Duke [of Devonshire] will be a paralysing influence. He is, according to Victor Cavendish, to be "a drag" on the fiscal policy of the Government; & no doubt he will also be their defender in all other things. This is all vy well for a peer; but for a member dependent upon the vote of a constituency the position is quite untenable. No one will know better how to profit from it than Joe. I do not object to fighting against heavy odds. I do object to being compelled to choose bad ground to fight on. Much may be done by even a few men whose position is clear and logical. But to proceed making perfervid protestations of loyalty to the "party" & yet to trample on the dearest aspirations of the party & thwart its most popular champions is to court utter ruin.

You like this sort of thing. You derive a melancholy satisfaction from the idea of being driven out of politics nursing your wrongs. And when I think that no one will be more mercilessly outspoken than you I think you will have your martyrdom as you wish.

But I do not share this view. I am an English Liberal. I hate the
Tory party, their men, their words & their methods. I feel no sort of
sympathy with them — except to my own people at Oldham. I want
to take up a clear practical position which masses of people can
understand. I do not want to stay splitting hairs upon retaliation
and contracting all sorts of embarrassing obligations. Already I have
freely against my inclination taken a backward step in subscribing
to A. Balfour's policy. I have done this simply & solely because I
want to cover the formation of your League & it was the only way of
staving off the crisis. I feel vy uncomfortable about what I have
said, & am not sure even of its honesty. To go on like this wavering
between opposite courses, feigning friendship to a party where no
friendship exists, & loyalty to leaders whose downfall is desired,
sickens me. Moreover from a tactical point of view it is the surest
road to destruction.

I entirely dissent from your doctrine that no forethought should
be exercised. It is madness when dealing with such antagonists as
we have to face. The Tory party would show me no mercy, & I do
not expect it or desire it. But upon the other hand I want to be
free to defend myself — and I mean to be. It is therefore my intention that before Parliament meets my separation from the Tory
party and the Government shall be complete & irrevocable; & during
the next session I propose to act consistently with the Liberal party.
This will no doubt necessitate re-election which I shall not hesitate
to face with all its chances.

It troubles me much to write all this; but I am convinced that the
position you wish to take up is neither practical nor consistent. Free
trade is so essentially Liberal in its sympathies & tendencies that
those who fight for it must become Liberals. The duty of those
who mean to maintain it is not to remain a snarling band on the
flank of a government who mean to betray it, but boldly & honestly
to range themselves in the ranks of that great party without whose
instrumentality it cannot be preserved.

Nothing need happen until December at any rate, unless Oldham
explodes: but I cannot leave you longer in doubt as to my intentions,
& you will of course have to steer accordingly. It would be far better
for the country in the long run if you were to face the real facts of
the case and help to preserve a reconstituted Liberal party against
the twin assaults of capital & Labour. And wherever you go you can
only do your best for those religious causes which you care about —

and your efforts would be more effective on the Liberal side than on these Tory materialists. But you must choose, as I have done, for yourself.

Yours ever
W.

I should like you to show this letter to Jack Seely and talk to him on the subject.

Towards the end of the year Churchill wrote a full account of the political situation, as he saw it, to his American friend, Bourke Cockran:

WSC to Bourke Cockran
(*Cockran Papers*)

12 December 1903   105 Mount Street
Private

My dear Bourke,

I was glad to get your letter and also to read in the "Democratic Campaign Guide of Massachusetts" your excellent Free Trade speech.

We are fighting very hard here, but I think on the whole, the outlook is encouraging. I believe that Chamberlain will be defeated at the General Election by an overwhelming majority. What will happen to the Free Trade Unionists by whose exertions this result will have been largely attained is quite another matter for I regret to say that the Liberal party think a great deal more of winning a seat here and there by destroying a Unionist Free Trader than for the principles of which we are fighting in common.

I do not think people like Lord Hugh Cecil and myself will be shut out of Parliament. The freedom which we possess here of standing in any constituency enables those who are well known and looked upon as prominent politicians to find another road back [to] the House of Commons when one particular constituency rejects them. But I fear the rank and file of our small party will suffer terribly — many of them being altogether extinguished and ending their public life once and for all.

I can quite understand your being perplexed by the attitude of Sir Michael Hicks-Beach, but he is an old Tory, has lived all his life high in the councils of that party, and although he is a staunch Free

Trader, he cannot bear the idea of severing himself in his old age from all those other causes for which he has fought. Consequently he tries to run with the hare and hunt with the hounds in perfect good faith though not I fear without some loss of public credit.

I think when the Address comes on, there will be a very bitter and protracted Debate culminating in a decisive decision. Those Unionists who fought against the Government will move steadily forward and endeavour to obtain Liberal support, those whose courage fails them will probably be engulfed in the Chamberlain abyss.

It is more and more plain that there is no real collusion between Mr Balfour's government and Mr Chamberlain, but their weak position is untenable. Nobody trusts them, nobody wants to fight for them; and now that the Duke of Devonshire, who is moving with more determination every day, has taken the decisive step of advising Unionist Free Traders to vote against Protectionist candidates irrespective of party considerations, I would not be at all surprised if the Government, to save their lives, are not obliged to throw themselves into Mr Chamberlain's arms. Once they do this, the line between the parties will be very sharply drawn. Feeling is getting much more bitter on both sides than when you were here last and I think there are very stormy times ahead. The accession of the Duke is a matter of enormous importance to us, not only because he commands immense weight in the country, but he has so much social influence that leaving the Conservative party with him does not mean going out in the wilderness as it would have done a year or two ago. That perhaps is a small consideration compared to the great issues with which we are dealing; but it is a small consideration which counts for a good deal with many people. I have had all sorts of rows and troubles in my own constituency and I am thinking of trying my luck in pastures new. After all, Oldham will most certainly return a Liberal and Labour member at the next election, both staunch Free Traders, so that I do not feel that I shall be losing a counter in the game if I look elsewhere.

I have never received a copy of your speech at the Liberal Club. I wish I had been able to get hold of it. It would be very useful. I should not be surprised if the General Election took place between Easter & Whitsuntide but I think the Government have bargained successfully for the Irish support so that they will not go out unless they want to.

I am sorry you are not going to run Bryan for the Democratic presidency. He has made a very good impression over here and his

oratory was considered very remarkable. Surely it cannot be true that
Mr Hearst of the *New York Journal* will be the democratic nominee.

I wish you would send me some good free trade speeches that have
been made in America, and some facts about corruption, lobbying,
and so forth.

If all is quiet in this country, I shall certainly come over to see
the Presidential Election next autumn and very likely Lord Hugh
Cecil will come with me. It is rather an inspiring reflection to think
that so many of us on both sides of the Atlantic are fighting in a
common cause — you to attack protection, we to defend Free Trade.
I think what the double victory would mean for the wealth and
welfare of the world.

Yours vy sincerely
WINSTON S. CHURCHILL

PS Moreton [Frewen] is stumping the country for Chamberlain.
What fools these Bimetallists are!

Later in the following year Churchill had to explain that the
political situation in England prevented him visiting the Democratic
Convention to which Bourke Cockran had invited him.

Churchill had not yet decided to join the Liberal Party. As so
often in his life he sought a central position among the moderates of
both parties. Churchill in the winter of 1903–4 supported the idea of
some understanding being reached between the Duke of Devonshire
and Lord Rosebery. He sought a compromise on the question of
denominational education which would reconcile Lord Hugh Cecil
and Lloyd George and so pave the way for a Rosebery-Devonshire
both parties. Churchill in the winter of 1903–4 supported the idea of
government. Lord Rosebery remained aloof from such intrigue.

Churchill went ahead making arrangements with the Liberals in
the form of an electoral pact with the Unionist Free Traders. He
wrote to Devonshire about it.

WSC to Duke of Devonshire
EXTRACT

13 January 1904   105 Mount Street

. . . While staying with Ivor Guest in Northamptonshire I went over
to see Lord Spencer, and had a long talk with him. He thinks that
time will be a great factor in an educational concordat; and he said

that already in many parts of the country settlements were being effected. He seemed very unhappy about Rosebery, who will not play. . . .

Lord Spencer was most friendly to me, and would like to help our people, but he dwells a great deal on the obvious difficulties; some people could be arranged for, others no. I said we should certainly stand together; and then quite suddenly came across me the explanation of Lord Rosebery's attitude. He said to me at Mentmore that he could be more useful in bringing people together if he were independent. I thought this a mistake then — but if he were making his co-operation contingent on a suitable combination of Whigs and Unionist free traders, his plan would have a different complexion. At any rate it is certain that his aloofness causes the Liberal leaders the utmost anxiety and disgust.

I lunched with Herbert Gladstone yesterday, and talked to him a great deal about seats. There is no doubt that he will try his very best to save the seats of Unionist free traders who are sincere. About fifteen could be settled quite easily; but there are some very hard cases which would require more pressure. Several Liberal constituencies have approached me, and I think I could make my own terms as a Unionist. . . .

Churchill's apprehensions that he might run into trouble in Oldham were shortly to be fulfilled, though not quite in the form in which he had expected. On December 23 the General Purposes Committee of the Oldham Conservative Registration Association met and passed the following resolution: "That this meeting intimates to Mr Winston S. Churchill, MP, that he has forfeited their confidence in him as Unionist member for Oldham, and in the event of an election taking place he must no longer rely on the Conservative Organisation being used on his behalf." This resolution was to be submitted to a meeting of the General Executive on 8 January 1904.

Churchill, in a long, reasoned reply to his local chairman, J. Travis-Clegg, wrote a few days later pointing out that he had no intention of "relying upon" the support of the Oldham Conservative Association or for that matter on any organization of a protectionist character. If necessary, he added, he would form his own Unionist Free Trade Association to help him fight elections. He pointed out that, in the past, the Conservative Party had been a Free Trade party, the principles of which Mr Balfour had endorsed upon becoming Prime Minister; but that in his Sheffield speech of 2 October 1903 Balfour had declared for a fundamental reversal of the policy of the last fifty years. Therefore, wrote Churchill, "it is not against me that any charge of breaking pledges can be preferred." He argued that his own pronouncements against protectionism preceding Balfour's Sheffield speech had been endorsed by the Association. He also noted that his criticism of Brodrick's army scheme of 1901 — a policy endorsed in principle by the Conservative Party — had also been praised by his constituents. Churchill placed the blame for the split in the party on Chamberlain (whose protectionist candidates, he predicted, would all be defeated) — "as the result of the unrestrained ambition of a single man."

Churchill felt that he had no obligation to resign his seat if the resolution of December 23 were passed against him; but, he wrote, he would give the wishes of the Association — as he had done in the past — his most earnest consideration. Towards the end of this long letter he pleaded for a full and open discussion of the issue so that the electors, nearly 13,000 of whom had voted for him in 1900, could make up their own minds. Until that time, he concluded, he would continue "to do his best to oppose all protectionist manoeuvres in Parliament and to explain to the electors of Oldham how closely Free Trade and cheap food [were] interwoven with the welfare of the Lancashire artisan."

This powerfully argued letter was plainly intended to forestall the meeting of the Association which was to be held on January 8. It made no difference. J. Travis-Clegg wrote to him after the meeting: "The resolution was carried against you last night with only one vote to the contrary, and that was a Chamberlainite who wished to confine the resolution to the fiscal question merely and not to say that you had forfeited confidence as Unionist member. There were perhaps half a dozen who did not vote at all. I hope the Association will let the matter rest where it is and pass no more resolutions. I think it is their intention undoubtedly that you should continue as member during the present Parliament."

The penultimate stage in Churchill's transformation from a Tory to a Liberal took place on March 29. During the debate in the House of Commons on the Easter adjournment, Churchill rose to speak immediately after Lloyd George who had followed Balfour. Either by design or accident Balfour rose at the same time and left the Chamber. Churchill immediately protested to the Speaker that Balfour's exit showed "lack of deference and respect" to the House. At this, all the front-bench ministers rose and repaired to the Smoking Room. They were followed almost immediately by the Tory back-benchers, some of whom lingered at the door to jeer at Churchill who stood alone, silent, with only a handful of Tory Free Traders at his side.

Eventually Churchill spoke. He had tried in vain, he said, for a number of months to discover Balfour's opinions of Chamberlain's ideas. He felt that the country had a right to know where the Prime Minister stood. In his efforts to find out, he declared, he, Churchill, had passed from a position of an independent supporter to that of a declared opponent. If his constituents wished him to resign, he added, he would do so.

So spontaneous was the action of the Tory back-benchers in following their front bench out of the House that few observers doubted that this was a deliberate and organized insult to Churchill. Sir John Gorst, Lord Randolph's old colleague in the Fourth Party and now a Unionist Free Trader, spoke shortly after Churchill and attacked his own party for treating Churchill "with the most marked discourtesy which I think I have ever seen." And he reminded the House that Churchill was the son of an old colleague of his, "an old Leader of the House of Commons, who of all men in the world, deserves well of his Party, who was the ornament and leader of that Party in the House of Commons at one period of his life and I think if every other consideration of fair play failed the hereditary right of the honourable member for Oldham to the respect and consideration of the House ought to have preserved him from such treatment as he received at the hands of his party this afternoon."

On April 3 Churchill wrote to his Tory Chairman at Oldham reminding him of his speech in the House of Commons on March 29 in which he declared himself ready to resign and to submit himself for re-election. He would, he added, leave the decision of holding

such an election in the hands of the Oldham Conservative Association. Churchill was playing a crafty game. He offered to resign and
let Oldham have a by-election. He indicated that he might stand at
this by-election but did not commit himself to do so. If he had forced
the issue and the Tory Association had accepted it, one thing was
certain: the Tory Party would have lost the seat — either through
Churchill splitting the vote and letting the Liberal in or probably
through the Liberal, under pressure from headquarters, withdrawing
and throwing his support behind Churchill. It is clear that on both
sides it was shadow-boxing.

The members of the Association, realizing that a General Election
had to take place within the next eighteen months and being reluctant to mobilize their supporters in the interim, did not force Churchill's hand. At a meeting, on April 13, they resolved not to accept
Churchill's offer; they were content to stand by their resolution of
January 8. Thus a by-election was averted and Churchill continued
to sit as the Member for Oldham until the General Election without
further interference from them.

On April 22, Churchill spoke for three-quarters of an hour during
the debate on the Trades Union Trades Disputes Bill. It was one of
the most radical of his early speeches. In it he argued, in part,
that the rights of Trade Unions should be clearly defined. According
to the *Daily Mail*, his words betrayed "Radicalism of the reddest
type."

However, the impact of his speech was lost at the end. His memory
temporarily collapsed and his imaginative powers for once deserted
him. "It lies with the Government," he said, "to satisfy the working
classes that there is no justification . . ." At this point he hesitated,
having lost the thread of his argument, and stopped speaking. He
seemed confused and began to fumble through his pocket for notes
which might prompt him. Having not found what he wanted he
abruptly sat down and covered his face with his hands, muttering, "I
thank honourable members for having listened to me."

Some of the younger Tories were tempted to jeer at Churchill; but
most of the contemporary accounts dwell on the murmur of sympathy
amid which Churchill sat down. It was not ten years since Lord
Randolph's death and the memory of his last few halting speeches in

the House, painful to friend and foe alike, was still vivid in the minds
of older members of the House. Was Churchill, they wondered, to
succumb in the same way? Friends hastened to reassure him. Sir
Shane Leslie has told the author how on the following day he visited
Churchill at Mount Street. His brother Jack and Sir Alfred Harmsworth were there sympathizing. Churchill enquired if there was any
way in which he could train his memory, and asked Shane Leslie to
investigate Mr Pelman's system. In fact, as we have already shown,
and as will continue to emerge throughout these volumes, Churchill's
memory was capacious. This was one of those lapses that occasionally
occur to even the most practised speaker if he does not have the aid
of fairly full notes. Until then Churchill's speeches had indeed been
most thoroughly prepared; but he tried to deliver many of them in
the House of Commons by learning them by heart beforehand. Churchill hardly ever again ventured to make a public speech without the
fullest, almost verbatim, notes to guide him.

A month or so later he took the ultimate step and crossed the floor.
On May 31, the first Parliamentary day after the Whitsun recess,
Churchill entered the Chamber of the House of Commons, stood for
a moment at the Bar, looked briefly at both the Government and
Opposition benches and strode swiftly up the aisle. He bowed to the
Speaker and turned sharply to his right to the Liberal benches. He sat
down next to Lloyd George in a seat that his father had occupied
when in opposition — indeed, the same seat on which Lord Ran-
dolph had stood waving his handkerchief to cheer the downfall of
Gladstone in 1885.

When Churchill crossed the floor Henry Lucy wrote in his Diary:

> Winston Churchill this afternoon abandoning the Unionist camp
> seated himself among the Radicals below the gangway opposite. The
> move as affecting his future career is frankly discussed in the smoking-
> room and other social resorts of members. On the whole, regarding
> the matter strictly from that point of view, it is agreed that he has
> made a mistake. As Mr Chamberlain recently demonstrated, a man
> who has established a weighty position in political life may with
> personal advantage go over to the ancient enemy. The member for
> Oldham has not yet reached that position. He is still a skirmisher

in the political field, and carries only the weight of his sharp-shooting rifle to the aid of his new comrades. . . .

Winston Churchill may be safely counted upon to make himself quite as disagreeable on the Liberal side as he did on the Unionist. But he will be handicapped by the aversion that always pertains to a man who, in whatsoever honourable circumstances, has turned his coat. In running for the prize of office he will, moreover, be brought in competition with many able men of his own age who, having been loyal to Liberalism throughout, will resent being set aside in favour of a late-comer to the vineyard.

3

The Young Liberal

CHURCHILL realized that his future did not lie with Oldham, and he had for some time been on the look out for a constituency which he could fight in the Liberal interest. Unofficial feelers were put out by the Liberals in the North-West Division of Manchester. Manchester was the perfect staging-post for him and he was the perfect candidate for a Manchester seat. Manchester was the citadel of doctrinaire Free Trade and Churchill had proved his credentials by intimating that he was about to break with the Tories on this very issue and by his capacity for expounding the Free Trade argument in the liveliest and most up-to-date fashion. He was now to make himself highly acceptable to the powerful Jewish community in Manchester. It is not without significance that many of his leading supporters in Manchester were Jews. The names of Nathan Laski, Chaim Weizmann, Israel Zangwill, Joseph Dulberg and Barrow I. Belisha stand out among his early adherents and supporters. No wonder that he so early was indoctrinated in the cause of Zion, long before it became fashionable.

In March 1902 a Royal Commission on Alien Immigration, presided over by Sir Kenelm Digby, the Permanent Under-Secretary at the Home Office, was set up by the Government. It reported a year later and its recommendations were the basis for the Aliens Bill of 1904, introduced by the Home Secretary, Aretas Akers-Douglas on March 29. A series of pogroms in Tsarist Russia over the previous twenty-five years had brought to England a large and increasing number of Jews, most of them poor, ill-educated and unskilled. In order to check the number of aliens — in Stepney alone there were

54,000 all told, Akers-Douglas said — and to alleviate conditions of overcrowding, the Bill gave the Home Secretary considerable powers of discretion and control.

WSC to Nathan Laski

EXTRACT

30 May 1904   105 Mount Street

... What has surprised me most in studying the papers you have been good enough to forward me is how few aliens there are in Great Britain. To judge by the talk there has been, one would have imagined we were being overrun by the swarming invasion and "ousted" from our island through neglect of precautions which every foreign nation has adopted. But it now appears from the Board of Trade statistics that all the aliens of Great Britain do not amount to a one-hundred-and-fortieth part of the total population, that they are increasing only 7,000 a year on the average, and that, according to the report of the Alien Commission, Germany has twice as large and France four times as large a proportion of foreigners as we have. . . .

Churchill went on to refer to the old system of asylum from which the country had so often gained; the dangers of entrusting powers of exclusion to the police and to the customs authorities. He quoted Lord Rothschild, who was a supporter of the Government, as having said: "The Bill introduced into the House of Commons proposes to establish in this country a loathsome system of police interference and espionage, of passports and arbitrary power, exercised by police officers who in all probability will not understand the language of those upon whom they are called to sit in judgment. This is all contrary to the recommendations of the Royal Commission." Churchill concluded by saying that "the simple immigrant, the political refugee, the helpless and the poor — these are the folk who will be caught in the trammels of the Bill and may be harassed and hustled at the pleasure of petty officials without the smallest right of appeal to the broad justice of the English courts"; and that "the whole Bill looks like an attempt, on the part of the Government to gratify a small but noisy section of their own supporters and to purchase a little popularity in the constituencies by dealing harshly with a number of unfortunate aliens who have no votes. It will commend itself to those who like patriotism at other people's expense. . . . It is expected to appeal to insular prejudice against foreigners, to racial prejudice against Jews, and to labour prejudice against competition. . . ."

Churchill sent this letter to the *Manchester Guardian;* it gratified the Manchester Jews.

On June 8 the Government announced that they were going to send the Aliens Bill to Grand Committee instead of discussing it on the floor of the House, since they did not think it was of a contentious nature. This led to an animated debate in which Churchill took the opportunity of making his first speech from the Opposition benches. Others who spoke in opposition to the proposal were Campbell-Bannerman and Asquith.

In his speech Churchill contrasted the decision to send the Aliens Bill to Grand Committee with that concerning the Deceased Wife's Sister Bill the year before. The Government had opposed sending this Bill upstairs because of its controversial nature. Churchill contended that the Aliens Bill was even more controversial, and that Grand Committees were not designed for debating such measures. He said: "Does the Home Secretary really imagine that he is facilitating the passage of this Bill by sending it to a Grand Committee, the machinery of which is unfitted to the conduct of controversial subjects? . . . The proposal shows that the Government are not in earnest."

The Government had their way, the Bill was sent to the Standing Committee on Law, and Churchill was one of those selected by the Opposition to serve upon it. He seems to have taken every advantage of putting his views before the Committee and at one time he provoked great indignation by speaking seven times on one amendment. The Committee became so smothered with amendments that on July 7 the Government was forced to announce the Bill's abandonment. The Liberal Members who had served on the Standing Committee carried a resolution on July 11 proclaiming that the Government had never intended to pass the Bill: it was merely a piece of electioneering: and that the Government should have persevered with the Bill with the proposed amendment. This last was somewhat disingenuous since the withdrawal of the Bill was a considerable blow to the Government as it showed that it was not in charge of the work of the session.

The following week Churchill received good news from Manchester.

Nathan Laski to WSC

EXTRACT

14 July 1904   54 Princess Street
                                                        Manchester

Dear Mr Churchill,

Though I have not written you ere this, yet my thanks are not less hearty & sincere for the splendid victory you have won for freedom & religious tolerance.

You will doubtless be interested to know that I have got a body of splendid workers together for you & as far as our district is concerned — victory is assured.

Doubtless also, you would have learnt that Dr Dreyfus — one of the principal supporters of Mr Balfour — will support your candidature — & as he is a likely Lord Mayor — I know he refused the honour last year — he will prove a valuable ally. . . .

I have had over 20 years' experience in elections in Manchester — & without flattery I tell you candidly — there has not been a single man able to arouse the interest that you have already done — thus I am sure of your future success.

Believe me, yours sincerely
N. LASKI

The dead Bill continued to be a topic of interest. In a letter to *The Sun* of December 17 Churchill answered some questions which the paper had put to him on November 29.

WSC to the Editor of The Sun

EXTRACT

17 December 1904   105 Mount Street

. . . With regard to your third question "Is it good for the men of England that bad foreign women should flood our land?" my answer is, of course, "No"; but you would be rendering a service to the cause with which you are associated if you explained clearly the process of examination or inspection by which women of immoral character are to be distinguished from among the numbers of passengers who are landed annually at British ports.

The position of those who resisted last year's Bill is simple. We say, "Shut out the alien; if diseased — always; if immoral — when you can find out; if criminal — after you have convicted; but do not shut out persons merely because they are poor, and do not thrust upon police and Customs House officers duties which they cannot properly discharge. . . ."

Churchill's opposition to the Aliens Bill established his reputation as a leading champion of the rights of minorities, which also served, no doubt, to consolidate his position in Manchester. None the less, he had to acquiesce when the Liberal administration of which he was to become a member had to enact a similar Bill, although in more modified form, in 1906.

*

Mr Brodrick's proposal for six army corps had meanwhile hung fire. Under the pretext of awaiting the reports of various committees on reorganization, time passed and as it passed many of the original proposals were eroded or abandoned. The original plan which Churchill had so much opposed when it was introduced in 1901 had involved the creation of three army corps overseas and three embryonic ones at home. In October 1903 St John Brodrick was moved to the India Office and replaced at the War Office by H. O. Arnold-Forster.

Eventually on July 14 Arnold-Forster introduced new proposals for the army. They differed markedly from those which had been put forward by Brodrick in 1901; the six army corps were to be disbanded, the number of men needed cut from 680,000 to 200,000, and the Cardwell linked-battalion system, which had been continued by Brodrick, was now to be abolished. In fact, this last was not carried out. Although more money would be spent on the Volunteer Army it would be a smaller, more efficient force. The estimates would not be reduced very much during the first year but in the following years there would be a substantial reduction.

There was not much criticism of the Bill during its passage

through Parliament and it was passed on August 8. However, the new Act did not seem to work smoothly and in December Churchill wrote three articles in the *Daily Mail* in which he pointed out the defects of the new system. He first traced the history of the British Army and of its management under St John Brodrick. He wrote on 17 December 1904:

> The Army is not like a limited liability company, to be reconstructed, remodelled, liquidated, and refloated from week to week as the money market fluctuates. It is not an inanimate thing, like a house, to be pulled down or enlarged or structurally altered at the caprice of the tenant or the owner; it is a living thing. If it is bullied, it sulks; if it is unhappy, it pines; if it is harried, it gets feverish; if it is sufficiently disturbed, it will wither and dwindle and almost die; and when it comes to this last serious condition, it is only to be revived by lots of time and lots of money.

In the last article on December 19 he plainly showed that he did not think much more highly of Arnold-Forster's scheme than he had of Brodrick's.

> Undaunted by his predecessor's fate, with even more than his predecessor's self-satisfaction, and even less than his predecessor's prudence, Mr Arnold-Forster now desires once again finally to reform the Army from top to bottom upon a plan of his own.
>
> It is not within the power of a minority to arrest this course any more than it was in our power to prevent Mr Brodrick from breaking his neck.
>
> Time alone and bitter facts will bring their proof. It is enough to say that this new scheme of Mr Arnold-Forster's is not endorsed by a single military man of eminence in the land, has been proved utterly unworkable by some of the most experienced and distinguished of public servants that the War Office has ever produced, and that it is commended to the public upon no authority but his own. How far will he carry it? How much evil will he do? That is a question I cannot answer. It depends upon the date of the general election.

Concurrently with the dispute over the Aliens Bill there was some degree of controversy over the Licensing Bill which the Government had introduced on April 20. We need not concern ourselves with the details of this somewhat unimportant Bill. As so often Churchill managed to become involved in a lively disturbance. On a Government motion for the closure of the debate before the Bill was remitted to Committee, a concerted attempt was made to howl him down. Churchill alleged that this action had been organized by Chamberlain, who indignantly refuted the charge. At the Speaker's behest Churchill withdrew it. So great was the uproar that he found it impossible to conclude his speech.

On August 2 Balfour had to ask the House to pass a resolution to enable the Government to proceed with business after midnight on four days of the week and after 5.30 p.m. on Fridays. Only in this way could the Government's business be completed by August 15 or 16, the date it was planned to end the session. As it was, no fewer than ten Bills could not be completed within the session and would therefore have to be dropped. The Government was chid by the Opposition for the barrenness of the session, and Churchill seized the opportunity to make a sharp attack on the Prime Minister himself.

> There is one thing on which we may congratulate the Prime Minister. After all, we are nearly at the end of the session, and here is the Prime Minister still! The procedure of the House of Commons has been mutilated. Never mind! A great quantity of money has been expended. Never mind! No legislation of any value has been passed. Never mind! But here is the Prime Minister, at the end of the session, a great deal more than many people could have expected or hoped for. I offer to the right honourable gentleman, most sincerely, my most humble congratulations on his achievement.

Balfour dismissed this as "an occasional seasoning of the ordinary elaborately prepared personalities of the member for Oldham."

Unlike the Aliens Bill, the Licensing Bill became law. However, the discussions were somewhat protracted and it took some extra days to pass the Lords. Thus it was not until August 15, three days after the opening of the grouse-shooting season, that Parliament was prorogued. The "sacred bird," as Churchill had referred to it, flew without even being winged by any Parliamentary shot-gun for three days.

On July 21 Churchill had learned that his aunt, Lady Tweed-mouth, was dying. Her husband wrote: "My darling is very ill, cannot get better — must more or less quickly get worse day by day till the end comes and all we can do is to make her comfortable and save her such trouble & sorrow as we can." A week later he wrote of her interest in Winston. "Both your letters have given very great pleasure to poor Fanny. She bids me tell you that she is very fond of you and takes the greatest interest in your career and hopes you will make a great name for yourself and your family." She was to die a few days later.

Churchill spent part of the summer in Switzerland, with Sir Ernest Cassel at his remarkable villa perched high in the Swiss Valais near Brigue, overlooking the Italian frontier.

WSC to Lady Randolph

22 August 1904   Villa Cassel
                                                                Moerel, Valais

Dearest Mamma,

I have waited a week so as to write with certainty about the effect wh this place produces. It is wholly good. I sleep like a top & have not ever felt in better health. Really it is a wonderful situation. A large comfortable 4 storied house — complete with baths, a French cook & private land & every luxury that would be expected in England, is perched on a gigantic mountain spur 7,000 feet high, and is the centre of a circle of the most glorious snow mountains in Switzerland. The air is buoyant and the weather has been delightful. Nearly every day clear and cool and bright, so that we can sleep with windows wide open & breakfast & lunch on the verandah. There are all kinds of beautiful walks and climbs from the modest 20 minutes on the flat to a very formidable scramble and exercises. Far below in the valleys which drop on both sides of the house, the clouds are drifting, & beneath and through these, green plains and tiny toy churches and towns. . . .

The days pass pleasantly & very rapidly. I am astonished to think I have been here a week. It seems three days since we cleared the duckweed from the Elizabethan moat [at Salisbury Hall]. I divide them into three parts. The mornings when I read and write: the afternoons when I walk — real long walks and climbs about these

hills or across the glacier: the evenings, of course 4 rubbers of bridge
— then bed. I shall stay here till Septr 1 & then to meet Sunny at
Mont d'Or.

I thought a good deal over all you said to me about yourself & I
feel sure you are right to concentrate on and take pains with the few
people you really care about. But I have no doubt that when papa
W. [Cornwallis-West] is at length gathered to Abraham you will be
able to renew your youth like the eagle. Cassel & the Colebrookes
asked a great deal after you. The newspaper cuttings are very civil
about my recent performances & have seen them in quite the right
light.

Ever your loving son
WINSTON

In October, Churchill went on a speaking tour of North Wales,
and it was at Carnarvon on October 18 that he spoke for the first
time on the same platform as David Lloyd George, the Radical member for the borough. In November he went to Glasgow where he
fulfilled a number of speaking engagements. The most important of
these was at St Andrew's Hall on November 10. In this he indicted
Balfour's government for increasing the power of the executive and
diminishing the authority of Parliament. "The House of Commons
has lost power altogether to shape legislation. Even the largest details
of great Bills are no longer discussed. And it has lost the power to
talk about what it likes." Next he alleged that the executive was
daily becoming "more and more subservient to the capitalistic interests in the country." He was, he said, a great deal more afraid of the
Independent Capitalist Party than of the Independent Labour Party.
"No one seems to care anything but about money today. Nothing is
held of account except the bank accounts. Quality, education, civic
distinction, public virtue seem each year to be valued less and less.
Riches unadorned seem each year to be valued more and more.

"We have in London an important section of people who go about
preaching the gospel of Mammon advocating the 10 per cent com-
mandments — who raise each day the inspiring prayer 'Give cash
in our time, O Lord.' " The last Liberal Government had made it a
rule not to allow any Minister to be a director of a public company.
Churchill calculated that 31 out of 55 present Ministers were direc-

tors, holding between them 68 directorships. "That laxity of principle is a sign of the degeneration of the day." He lamented the recent purchase of the Free Trade London newspaper *The Standard,* by the protectionist Arthur Pearson. "What shall we say of those who use vast wealth to poison the fountains of public information?" He seemed to be anticipating the attitude of the Monopolies Commission of our own times on the proprietorship of newspapers.

Lady Randolph, who was in the Royal party at Sandringham at the time, seemed to have taken more note of the Chairman's opening remarks — he had said that the Prime Minister's temporary illness had come in the very nick of time to save him from political disaster —than of her son's immensely popular and successful speech.

Lady Randolph to WSC

12 November [1904]   Sandringham

My dearest Winston,

I read your speech at Glasgow with such interest — I did not discuss it with the King, you will be surprised to hear. I think it was rather a pity your Chairman attacked A.B. the way he did. I see the audience resented it — at least so the papers make out. Henri de Breteuil tells me that in France they look upon you as the coming man. Here I am in a hot bed of protectionists. You have probably seen the party in the papers. We have been asked to stay on till Monday. It has been most pleasant nice weather — pleasant people & excellent sport. George shot very well & are both in good favour — so that is all right. Where shall you be next week? Salisbury Hall is at your disposal if you want to come. By the way, I have been so ill ever since I ate those oysters with you — I had to see the doctor here, & he told me I had been poisoned. I am all right now — we are thinking of going to Paris for Xmas. Why don't you come? The Breteuils would put you up — now goodbye.

Yr loving
MOTHER

The guests had been assembled to celebrate the King's 63rd birthday on November 9. The party included, beside members of the Royal

Family and courtiers, the Austrian Ambassador (Count Mensdorff), the Duke of Richmond, the Marquis and Marquise de Breteuil, the Marquis au Lau, Lady Cadogan, Lady Maud Warrender, Mr and Mrs George Keppel, Henry Chaplin, Sir Donald Mackenzie Wallace and General Sir Albert Williams — as well as Lady Randolph and George Cornwallis-West.

Churchill replied giving details of his successful speech at the St Andrew's Hall where at the end the audience had all stood up and applauded. He accepted her invitation to go to Salisbury Hall.

The Duke of Devonshire had recently made an important speech in favour of Free Trade at Rawtenstall. Churchill went on in his letter: "Fancy *The Times* boycotting the old Duke's speech. What blackguards the Protectionist Press are." He was a little naïve at this time about the habits of the Press from *The Times* downwards. In later life he used often to remark on "The Power of the Press — and of the Suppress." This evil course has been preserved until very recently whenever it has suited the mandarins of Printing House Square.

At this time he became involved in a misunderstanding with Lord Salisbury, who had succeeded his father, the great Prime Minister, in August 1903, and who at this time sat in the Cabinet as Lord Privy Seal.

The correspondence gives some idea of the hostility Churchill was encountering as a result of his change of party, and the delicacy of his position in relation to his father's and his own friends.

Lord Salisbury to WSC

EXTRACT

17 November 1904　　　　　　　　　　　　20 Arlington Street

... Bother politics! But you will forgive me for saying that — though may we always remain personal friends — in politics as distinguished from personal matters I have to do, not with the people who have left us, but with those whom we still retain.

Yours ever
SALISBURY

WSC to Lord Salisbury
(*Hatfield Papers*)

19 November 1904   105 Mount Street
Private

My dear Lord,
    I am told that the Russians & the Japanese have agreed not to
fire upon each other when they draw water from the Shaks. My remarks on politics were in character detached musings — neither serious nor calculated, & like the chaff we may imagine the water parties
of those fierce armies exchanging on their patch of quasi-neutral
ground, across their street of necessary river. If you have found this
presumptuous — forgive me. Next time I draw water I will talk
only about the weather — & all questions concerning the defence or
the relief of Port Arthur shall be strictly avoided.

Yours sincerely
WINSTON S. CHURCHILL

Lord Salisbury to WSC

EXTRACT

20 November 1904   Windsor Castle

My dear Winston,
    My letter was impertinent and in its implied rebuke not very just
— for a man is right to change his Party if it does not suit his opinions. And I do not doubt that this was your case in many respects.
So I am sorry. And yet in my heart I think it was not your act but
your demeanour in so acting which led me to be rude. . . .

WSC to Lord Salisbury
(*Hatfield Papers*)

EXTRACT

21 November 1904   105 Mount Street
Private

. . . Believe me I recognise & understand the antagonisms wh must
exist between politicians; & I should be vy sorry to transgress that
line of half-chaffing half-candid intercourse which prevails between

people who know each other though on opposite sides, in this country almost alone of modern countries.

I readily admit that my conduct is open to criticism — not — thank heaven — on the score of its sincerity, but from the point of view of taste. I had to choose between fighting & standing aside. No doubt the latter was the more decorous. But I wanted to fight — I felt I could fight with my whole heart and soul — so there it is. Linky understands. Of course politics is a form of tournament in wh mudslinging and invectives are recognised weapons. But taking part in such an ugly brawl — does not in my mind prejudice relations. . . .

A comical event occurred at this time. Churchill, with what justice it is hard to estimate, referred to one of the Preston members, Sir W. E. M. Tomlinson, as a "miserable old man." A friend of Tomlinson's thereupon wrote to Churchill challenging him to a bout of fisticuffs. Churchill found a dignified and honourable escape from what might have been a tiresome imbroglio:

WSC to E. Clarkson

24 January 1905   105 Mount Street
Copy

Sir,

I beg to acknowledge the receipt of your letter of the 18th instant. I cannot consent to recognise you as a principal in a matter which obviously concerns Sir William Tomlinson and myself. The advantages of settling political differences by the methods you suggest are not immediately apparent; but I feel that it would in any case be highly irregular for one of the principals to be represented in person, and the other by a champion. Such combats even if desirable should invariably be conducted either between principals on both sides or between champions on both sides. Several gentlemen whose qualifications seem unimpeachable have written to me offering their services in the latter capacity. I should not be unwilling to put you in communication with them on the chance of their being able to afford you the active exercise you desire.

Yours faithfully
[WINSTON S. CHURCHILL]

That seems to have been the end of the matter.

*

The King opened Parliament on 14 February 1905. It was a dying Parliament; no one bothered to express surprise that no major legislation was introduced. The Opposition naturally made great play with the fact that the Tory party was split and that the Prime Minister seemed unable to say yes or no to the simplest question.

Except for a speech on the Supplementary Army Estimates (in which he referred to "those gorgeous & gilded functionaries with brass hats and ornamental duties who multiply so luxuriously on the plains of Aldershot & Salisbury," which led the King to comment "What good words for a recent subaltern of Hussars!") Churchill did not play much part until March 8 when he introduced a subtle motion on Imperial Preference calculated to put both Balfour and Chamberlain in the most awkward position in his power. It was only a short debate, but he managed to draw into it both Balfour and Chamberlain. Lord George Hamilton and Asquith both supported Churchill's motion.

In August Lord Curzon, Viceroy of India, resigned as a result of a dispute between him on the one hand and the home government and the Commander-in-Chief, Kitchener, on the other, as to whether or not the Commander-in-Chief should have the exclusive control of the military aspect of army administration and should be the sole voice on this subject in the Viceroy's Council. Curzon wished to maintain the existing powers of the Viceroy in these matters, but he was overruled and Kitchener triumphed over him. On August 26 and 28 the somewhat acrimonious correspondence of these two incompatible personalities was published in London. Churchill was very much on Curzon's side.

WSC to Lady Randolph

EXTRACT

31 August 1905   Ashby St Ledgers
                                                              Rugby

. . . Of course I am all for Curzon as against Kitchener, and for Constitutional Authority against military power. I cannot believe a Liberal Government will allow the Commander-in-Chief in India to engross to himself so much power. I am thinking of breaking into print upon the subject in the course of the next few days. I hope you found John Morley sound on this question. I should be greatly disconcerted if I thought the Liberal party were prepared to acquiesce in the handing over of the Indian Empire to an ambitious and indocile soldier. The military member in India is really in the same position as the Secretary of State for War in England. What has happened is that the Commander-in-Chief has not merely swallowed up his own War Minister but the Viceroy as well.

The appointment of Minto, poor dear thing, is another piece of Arthurism *in excelsis*. For cynical disdain of public interests and contempt of public opinion, it exactly matches Brodrick's appointment to the India Office. . . .

His fears about Lord Minto proved groundless. Under the Liberal Government he was to be responsible, with the new Secretary of State for India, for the much admired Morley-Minto reforms.

*

In May 1903 the young member for Oldham had rhetorically summed up the protectionist argument — then masquerading as Fair Trade — which he had already opposed. Why "should we not kill three birds at one stone — collect our revenue, support British industries, and consolidate the Empire?" they asked. But that, Churchill said, wasn't the way it worked out.

One year later, but before he crossed the floor, he addressed the inaugural meeting of the Free Trade League, on 19 February 1904. The Unionist Party was itself divided into three by the Free Trade issue, he said. There were the "whole hoggers" who were for taxing everything except bacon. Then the Unionist Free Traders who wished to tax nothing except for revenue. And lastly there was the largest part, "consisting of gentlemen who say, from various reasons, that they are loyal to the great policy of Sheffield, whatever that may be. I think we may call these people the 'Sheffield Shufflers' — because it is quite clear that they are ready to support any policy, and to fight and shout for any formula, however meaningless, however dishonest, which they think will put off a general election." He spoke of the effects of protection on the shipbuilding industry:

How will the shipping and shipbuilding trades be affected by the proposed tariff? They cannot fail to be injured, and they will be injured in two ways. First, the cost of all the materials used in the construction of ships will be increased, and consequently we shall be less able to compete with foreign nations both in respect of the ships we sell and the freights we carry; secondly, they will be injured by the restriction of ocean traffic generally, and by its diversion from our shores to other countries. After all, why should so many ships come to British ports? Why should we carry on an extensive entrepôt trade? Why should sixty millions' worth of manufactured goods be sent into the United Kingdom, unloaded there, warehoused there, made up into fresh cargoes, loaded into ships again, and distributed at a profit all over the world? Other harbours are as wide and deep as ours; other climates are quite as genial — other skies are just as blue. Why should the world's shipping labour in the chops of the Bristol Channel, or crowd up the dreary reaches of the Mersey? It is because our harbours are more nearly as nature made them; because the perverted ingenuity of man has not been occupied in obstructing them with fiscal stake nets and tariff mud bars. That is why they come. That is our one great advantage; and when we have thrown it away, what shall we have to put in its place? . . .

But the theory of Protection is either right or wrong. The doctrines that by keeping out foreign goods more wealth, and consequently more employment, will be created at home, are either true or they are not true. We contend that for a nation to try to tax itself into prosperity is like a man standing in a bucket and trying to lift himself up by the handle. But if the theory is true, what a curious position we should be in. What a mistake it would have been to have built the Manchester Ship Canal. Here is a great work, built what for? To facilitate dumping — to pour a stream of foreign imports into the heart of industrial Britain. But that is not the only curious reflection that would occur to one if the Protectionists were right in their theory. If it be true that imports are an evil, and that by shutting them out you could acquire great wealth, then I say that it is true everywhere. It is just as true for Ireland as for Australia. It is just as true for India as for Canada.

On the effects of protection on the cotton industry he said, "Tariff duties, whether Retaliatory, Preferential, or Protective, would not make the cotton fields larger, would not ensure good harvests, would not promote cheap transit, would not destroy the ravages of cotton insects, American speculators, or other pestiferous vermin."

His argument was easily summarized: "When things are cheap, people will buy them who will not buy them when they are dear. When things are cheap, people can buy them who cannot buy them at all when they are dear. And people will buy more of everything. If prices are raised, everyone will have to pay more. As they pay more, so they will buy less. This is true always everywhere; but most of all is it true about the trades which depend on foreign export, which have to compete with other nations in foreign or neutral markets."

On June 4 Churchill addressed the Cobden Club in the Midland Club, Manchester, at its dinner to celebrate the centenary of the birth of that Free Trader. After paying tribute to Richard Cobden as one of the founders of Free Trade, Churchill turned to attack the Government and the Prime Minister in particular for his policy of retaliation and his determination to stay in office:

> I think we are entitled to congratulate the Prime Minister upon the remarkable achievement that after a year of controversy, very severe controversy, no one has ever been able to find out whether he believes or does not believe that a 10 per cent *ad valorem* duty on foreign imported manufactured articles would be a good thing for this country or a bad thing. No one has ever been able to find out what he means by the terms "fiscal reform" and "retaliation." Apparently all that is necessary to be considered a loyal member of the Protectionist party is to anathematise the shade of Cobden and vote with the Government Whips. And yet on this simple pro- gramme the Prime Minister has ridden serenely on to power; has reconstructed the Cabinet with a freedom of selection which Lord Salisbury and Mr Gladstone hardly ever enjoyed. He has imposed upon his colleagues a rigid assent to a formula which they none of them understand and which with no power to understand they dis- sent from. He has organised his Cabinet through the operation of what is rather a religious test than a political opinion — an act of faith rather than an exercise of reason. I have listened to many de- bates in the House of Commons lately, and have been much re- minded of a story I have heard of Oliver Cromwell. There was a time when he was responsible for the conduct of business in the

House of Commons, and it happened that the business he had to carry through for the Government justified a very indefensible action. A very worthy and venerable member of his party came and complained and said he was obviously wrong. "Never mind," said Cromwell, "I am going to do it." "Oh," said the member, "if you do I shall have to take the sense of the House upon it." "All right," said Cromwell, "you shall have the sense of the House and I will have the nonsense, and we will see who has the best of it." And the Government had a larger majority than ever. While the Government goes on its path, supported by the votes of Protectionists and of Free-Traders and even of those unfortunate members of the Unionist party who are going to lose their seats through the exertions of the Tariff Reform League — which is hunting the Free-Traders remorselessly and steadily down — some of us are retiring, many may go down, some, like myself, have formally associated themselves with the Opposition. Others have actually joined the Liberal party. After the election hardly half a dozen determined men — determined Free-Traders — will remain in the ranks of one of the great political parties of this country to mar the symmetry of a party which will undoubtedly, whatever the course of the next few months may be, be a party of what is called fiscal reform.

Mr Balfour tells us that his method is different from the method employed by Sir Robert Peel and by Mr Gladstone in introducing great quest[ions to the notice] of the country. No one — certainly no one who reveres the memory of [these] two distinguished statesmen — would challenge his right to do so. The matter is certainly different, and it would be more successful but for one fact which seems to be overlooked — that there are such things, such very inconvenient things, as general elections. And I venture to say that when a general election comes a far heavier price will be paid for all this shifting and dodging than would ever have been paid even if a wrong policy and an unwise policy had been honestly placed before the country.

On May 13 Churchill spoke at Manchester alongside John Morley. He gave a succinct account of what he regarded as being the policies of the Unionist Party:

The great leader of the Protectionist party, whatever else you may or may not think about him, has at any rate left me in no doubt as to what use he will make of his victory if he should win it. We know perfectly well what to expect — a party of great vested interests, banded together in a formidable confederation, corruption at home, aggression to cover it up abroad, the trickery of tariff juggles, the tyranny of a party machine; sentiment by the bucketful, patriotism by the imperial pint, the open hand at the public exchequer, the open door at the public-house, dear food for the million, cheap labour for the millionaire.

Balfour's long-awaited declaration of policy, at Sheffield in October 1903, had produced the rather nebulous concept of retaliation. On 15 June 1904 Churchill poured scorn upon it. "Retaliation," he said in a speech at the Midland Hall, Manchester, "is the declared policy of His Majesty's Government. The Cabinet are agreed upon it. Mr Balfour has declared it at Sheffield in the great speech which he made, announcing to all the world and to his followers a policy which neither he nor they nor any one else has ever been able to understand . . . We know that retaliation, whatever it may mean, is the party test."

Over the next ten months Churchill proceeded to develop these arguments in a crescendo of closely knit statistics and invective. By the time of the Election, it is no exaggeration to say that he had become the Opposition's most popular and effective exponent of the Free Trade case. While Churchill reserved his invective largely for the public platform, he gave the House of Commons the best fruit of his thought and the most reasoned arguments in his power. Often in later years he would say: "The House of Commons is a jealous mistress: you must give her the cream of your thought." His speech on his own motion which he moved in the House of Commons on 8 March 1905, "That, in the opinion of this House, the permanent unity of the British Empire will not be secured through a system of preferential duties based upon the protective taxation of food," was among the finest he made at this time; in a letter the next day "Loulou" Harcourt described it as "the best you have ever made."

First he sought to expose the falseness of Chamberlain's claim that a scheme of preferential tariffs need not include raw materials. "There is no logical or scientific distinction between the raw material of manufacture and food, which is the raw material of human life. No scheme of Colonial preferences could be a scientific scheme unless it applies equally to food and to raw material. That is equally true whether the question is argued from a Free Trade or a protectionist point of view. Every argument, moral or material, that can be advanced in favour of the preferential taxation of corn, meat and dairy produce holds good, even in a stronger degree, in favour of the preferential taxation of timber, leather and wool. Any system of Imperial Preference which includes the one and excludes the other must be lop-sided and illogical in its conception, and whimsical and unfair in its operation." He complained that Chamberlain had, in all his proposals for Imperial Preference, forgotten India — "that most truly bright and precious gem of the Crown," as Lord Randolph had called it — simply because the proposals had originated at the Colonial Office while Chamberlain had been Secretary of State there.

Of course, Chamberlain's scheme would mean higher prices. But this, said Churchill, was not the main argument against it. And here Churchill went on to deploy the classical argument against protection and for Free Trade:

> The main argument against these taxes is based on a great principle, which is that this country should be free to purchase its supplies of food wherever it chooses and whenever it chooses in the open markets of the world. That is a principle greatly valued in the House of Commons, for which on this side every member is prepared to make the greatest exertions, and for which on the other side of the House some members have already made, and are still prepared to make, sacrifices, for which, I believe, their countrymen will not be ungrateful. It is a principle of special importance to Lancashire members, who, travelling from one great city to another, see in every valley of that undulating region towns and townships which are the homes of a vast thriving population living on a soil which could not support in decent comfort a twentieth of their number. I have been told that within thirty miles of the Manchester Exchange — I might say of the Free Trade Hall — there is gathered together the greatest concentration of human beings on the surface of the globe. This mass of people are absolutely dependent for the food they eat and the material they employ upon supplies which reach them mainly from foreign lands. They are dependent on the condition of a crop at one end of the world, and the state of a market at the other; and yet, upon this artificial foundation, through the inestimable advan-

tages of unfettered enterprise, and of unrestricted sea communication, they have been able to build up a vast industrial fabric, which,
it is no exaggeration to say, is the economic marvel of the world.
They have had lately rather an unpleasant experience in Lancashire,
a shortage of cotton and a "corner" following thereon. The right
honourable member for West Birmingham has reminded us piously
that that shortage was due to the act of God; it is not, like the Sugar
Bounties Convention, due to the wisdom of a paternal Government.
But what is the remedy proposed for that state of things? It is to vary
and multiply the sources of cotton supply, so that, when there is a bad
harvest in one place, good crops in another may repair the deficiency.
But if your preference is effective, and in so far as it is effective, it
must tend to limit and localise the sources of supply, and to make
them more and more dependent upon a single source of supply.

At present we stand on very firm ground in respect of food. With
the telegraph and with steamships there is hardly a food-exporting
country in the world that is more than sixty days from Liverpool.
The harvests of the world are at our disposal, and, by a system which
averages climatic risks, we secure not merely a low but a fairly stable
price. With that marvellous operation by which the crowded population of this island is fed, we cannot take the responsibility of interfering. There will be good years and there will be bad years. Great
fluctuations must necessarily occur from time to time in all commodities which depend upon climatic conditions. . . . There are
many factors in prices — harvests, freights, speculations — which do
not recognise the authority of the House of Commons. Taxes alone
are absolutely in our hand. These fluctuations have occurred in the
past; no one can doubt that they will occur in the future. Whatever
rise may take place in the future the preferential duties, if imposed
— although, perhaps only a small contributory factor to the rise —
will have to bear the brunt of public indignation. It is upon these
very links of Empire so laboriously and expensively forged that the
direct impact of public displeasure in times of scarcity must inevitably descend. If there is an unpopular tax to-day we are in no
great difficulty. If public opinion is sufficiently incensed a pliant
Chancellor of the Exchequer, or, failing that, a vote in the House of
Commons, will remove the cause of offence and gratify the national
will. But these preferential duties, if they are imposed, will not be
taxes which the House can remove at its pleasure. They will be fixed
by treaty with every self-governing colony scattered all over the surface of the world. In consideration of these taxes this country will

have received concessions — though that is not a part of the argument we hear much about — with regard, say to certain classes of manufactured goods. Upon the basis of these mutual concessions industries will have grown up, and, however fierce the demand, you will not be able to alter your preferential duties without the consent of the other party to the bargain. In that day there will, indeed, be a shock to the permanent unity of the Empire which may well excite the concern of those who care about it. In that day, when a British Ministry with taxes which it cannot remove without a long delay, is confronted by the imperious demand of a hungry and an angry electorate, you will realise the truth — perhaps to be denied to-night — that it is a grand and cardinal error in Imperial statecraft to lay the foundations of a democratic Empire upon the protective taxation of food.

It is a sober fact that the British Empire produces within its limits every commodity which luxury can imagine or industry require. I do not wonder that many honourable gentlemen have been captivated by the idea of creating a self-supporting and self-contained Empire. I frankly admit myself the fascination of the idea — until you look into it. Then it is apparent — though this, of course, is disputable — that it rests on no moral, logical, or scientific foundation. It does not make for prosperity, it does not make for international peace. The dangers which threaten the tranquillity of the modern world come not from those powers that have become interdependent upon others, interwoven by commerce with other States; they come from those powers which are more or less detached, which stand more or less aloof from the general intercourse of mankind, and are comparatively independent and self-supporting. Quite apart from the economic argument, which on this side we regard as sanctioned, we do not want to see the British Empire degenerate into a sullen confederacy, walled off, like a mediaeval town, from the surrounding country; victualled for a siege, and containing within the circle of its battlements all that is necessary for war. We want this country and the States associated with it to take their parts freely and fairly in the general intercourse of commercial nations. We do not mind even if we become dependent on foreign nations, because we know that by that very fact we make foreign nations dependent upon us.

There had been factions within the Tory Party, notably Chamberlain's, which had pressed Balfour to resign and go to the country as early as February 1905. Chamberlain thought that should the Government lose the election, their defeat would not be as great as it would be later, when the splits inside the party became more apparent to the public. In the event of Balfour agreeing, Chamberlain said that he would soft-pedal on Tariff Reform. Since Balfour did not accept Chamberlain's proposal, Chamberlain renewed his attack on the Unionist Free Traders with increased vehemence. Balfour felt it was his duty to carry on with his Administration as he considered that the Liberals were unfit for Government.

His two successive War Ministers, Brodrick and Arnold-Forster, were both thought to have been failures but he was determined to complete the reorganization of the War Office. The Committee of Imperial Defence had been in existence since before the Boer War, but it was Balfour who was making it into an effective body. He had shown a great interest in the development of the 18-pounder gun, with which he intended to equip the Army. Although he gave the order for it to go into production in December 1904, certain technical difficulties were not overcome until the middle of 1905. He would not resign until he had seen that it was to be a success.

In the last year of his administration he had not only renovated the Imperial Defence Committee; he had, with Lord Lansdowne, cemented the foundations of the *entente cordiale* with France. All these measures were ones to which he attached the greatest importance. But there was another side to the coin. Partisan tactics may not have been the cause of Balfour's undignified clinging to office; but they certainly played a part in the decision to resign rather than dissolve Parliament. There are good grounds for believing that the Tories felt that the Liberals were so disunited that they would be unable to form a Government. But nothing brings quarrelling colleagues together more quickly after nearly twenty years in Opposition than the thought of office and power.

On December 4 Balfour, without his Government suffering a further defeat, resigned and the King sent for Sir Henry Campbell-Bannerman to form a new administration. Balfour, in what was generally thought to be a rather weak explanation of his action, explained that the habit of "mutual criticism" in the Unionist Party would have made the Government's position well-nigh impossible regarding the Redistribution Bill which would have come up. In

these circumstances he said he felt an obligation to hand over a task
which he admitted his Government to be incapable of carrying out to
his confident opponents.

Until the King sent for Campbell-Bannerman it was far from certain that he would be the new Prime Minister. Three months before,
Haldane and Asquith, staying with Grey at his fishing lodge at Relugas, had entered into a compact that they would only serve under
Campbell-Bannerman on condition that he went to the Lords. It was
further agreed that Haldane should be Lord Chancellor, Grey Foreign Secretary and Asquith Chancellor of the Exchequer with the
Leadership of the House of Commons. This Relugas compact took
on even more importance when a month later, on October 13, Lord
Spencer, the Liberal leader in the House of Lords, and the only real
possible alternative to Campbell-Bannerman, suffered a sudden cere-
bral attack while shooting at North Creake, his Norfolk estate. He
was the Red Earl whom Mr Gladstone had wished to foist on the
Queen when he resigned ten years before. But the Queen never
sought Gladstone's advice and, confronted with the choice of Rosebery or Harcourt, opted for the former. Although Spencer soon
rallied, he was for ever out of the running; he died in 1910.

Balfour and many Tories had favoured resignation rather than dissolution because they felt that either the Liberals could not form a
Government or that if they did it would be a very weak one, as many
of their outstanding leaders would refuse to serve. In the event, of
course, only Rosebery could not be reconciled to the Liberals, and
it was Balfour's own party that was a shambles of disorganization and
disunion. Haldane had told the King of the Relugas agreement and
the news must have got around and doubtless formed part of the information on which Balfour based his calculations.

For many years Campbell-Bannerman had been accustomed to take
his wife, who was an invalid, to Marienbad in Bohemia for the month
of July. At the turn of the century the King had started going there
too. He had been somewhat doubtful of Campbell-Bannerman's
qualities, particularly because in the Boer War Campbell-Bannerman
held Gladstonian views on foreign policy and had denounced Kitchener's conduct of the war as based upon "methods of barbarism."
The King first began to see the point of Campbell-Bannerman when

Lord Carrington succeeded in bringing them together at a private dinner. It was a capital success. Later in July when the King and Campbell-Bannerman were both in Marienbad they had numerous talks and the King became satisfied that he would be a suitable successor to Balfour, whose Government he knew was doomed.

It was not only some of his colleagues who were anxious that Campbell-Bannerman should go to the Lords. Even after the matter had been disposed of, Dr Ott, his Marienbad physician, wrote begging him not to stay in the House of Commons. Actually the two people who were most keen that Campbell-Bannerman should go to No 10 and stay in the Commons were himself and his invalid wife: she arrived in London from Scotland proclaiming "no surrender."

Campbell-Bannerman, with the King's approval, first offered the Foreign Office to Cromer, who was still High Commissioner in Egypt. On Cromer's refusal on the grounds of ill health, he offered it to Grey and the Exchequer to Asquith. Haldane wanted to be Lord Chancellor but had to make do with the War Office, where he was to shine. The new Prime Minister wanted to give the Woolsack to his old Scottish friend Sir Robert Reid who, on accepting it, became Lord Loreburn. Grey proved the difficult one, but Haldane and Asquith persuaded him to join the Government as Foreign Secretary. It was explained that the Relugas agreement was no longer in effect since it had been predicated on the assumption that the Liberals would not take office until they had won the election. The need to bring the Party together on the eve of the election dominated all. Balfour had grievously miscalculated. If he had dissolved instead of resigning, the Liberals might have found themselves in disarray: jockeying for position might have continued all through the campaign.

Churchill was approached quite early in the day and was offered the Financial Secretaryship to the Treasury which is ordinarily considered the stepping-stone to the Cabinet. But he may have calculated that he would have little chance to shine in the House with so experienced and formidable a chief as Asquith sitting at his side. On the other hand, as Under-Secretary to the Colonies he would have as his chief Lord Elgin in the House of Lords. He thus would have the management of parliamentary business, and since Elgin liked to spend as much time as possible in Scotland he would be to a large extent put in charge of this important department. It was also the post held by his friend and cousin Marlborough in the outgoing government. Churchill managed to persuade the Prime Minister to make him Under-Secretary for the Colonies. He wrote to Lord Hugh Cecil on December 16 that "I had some difficulty in securing my wish as it involved considerable alteration in other minor offices." Thus though he was assured of the Colonial Office on December 9 it was not announced until four days later.

Campbell-Bannerman took six days to complete a rather swollen Cabinet and there were rumours of difficulties: but all went well and within a few days the Government was complete down to the last Under-Secretary and Whip. Room had been tardily found for Mr Walter Runciman who for several days had expressed himself in lively perturbation at the prospect of exclusion. His letter to Churchill is too long to be quoted here, but its risibility alone justifies its inclusion in the Companion Volume where it may be read with relish.

The King let Campbell-Bannerman have a free hand with his appointments and only intervened in the choice of the political members of the Royal Household and Lords Lieutenant. For instance, as Sir Sidney Lee records in his admirable Life of King Edward VII, "the King also demurred to the appointment of Lord Wimborne [husband of Churchill's aunt Cornelia] as Lord Lieutenant of Dorset, preferring Lord Portman for the post." According to the King (28 March 1906) Lord Portman was "the right man in every way," and the King disliked his being passed over in favour of a "political turn-coat." However, he acquiesced, "but unwillingly," to the appointment of the Government's nominee. Apparently there were no royal objections to a turncoat like Churchill becoming Under-Secretary.

Sir Sidney states that in his "personal relations with the new ministers" the King "showed every sign of amiability." However, "the King did not conceal his lack of sympathy" with the extreme views of some of his new ministers. Mr John Burns, President of the Local Government Board, in his election address had advocated the abolition of the House of Lords. The King was to point out:

As Sir Henry Campbell-Bannerman has so recently recommended several prominent members of the House of Commons to be peers, the King is somewhat surprised that a member of the Cabinet should have made this declaration.

The Prime Minister in reply was quite conciliatory:

That is the worst of the abrupt appointment of men to the Cabinet without serving an apprenticeship in subordinate office. I have had two or three cases of want of discretion already from the *novi homines* including the Secretary of State for War [Haldane].

Before long one of the newest newcomers of all, Mr Lloyd George, was to rouse even more drastic protest from the King.

Before Churchill's appointment had been announced he had reported with punctilio for duty to his Secretary of State.

WSC to Lord Elgin
(*Elgin Papers*)

My dear Lord,

The Prime Minister has invited me to join his Government as Under-Secretary of State for the

9 December 1905   105 Mount Street

My dear Lord,

    The Prime Minister has invited me to join his Government as Under-Secretary of State for the Colonies, & I learned from him that this was agreeable to you. In case you wish to see me I shall be in London on Monday during the middle part of the day & I would like vy much to call upon you, if you find a moment to receive me.

I had intended to go out of London for a day or two; but of course I can put this off if you wish it.

Believe me, Yours vy faithfully
WINSTON S. CHURCHILL

Lord Elgin to WSC

10 December 1905   29 Hyde Park Gate

Dear Mr Churchill,

Many thanks for your letter — I am sorry I missed your message — but my family is scattered about London at present.

We have rather a tough job before us — but with your assistance I hope & believe the Colonial Office will make a good show.

I shall be at 95 Eaton Terrace at 12 o'clock to-morrow and if quite convenient for you I should be very glad to have a few moments conversation. Of course I know nothing yet which renders this necessary.

I have to go to Scotland on Tuesday but am told I must be back on Thursday, and may put in a day or two then at the office to study a few details. I mention this simply to help your plans.

Yours sincerely
ELGIN

The easy-going nature of the Secretary of State augured well for his relationship with his new Under-Secretary. Among numerous congratulatory messages he received on his appointment was one from Sir Walter Hely-Hutchinson, Governor of the Cape, who wrote from Capetown "A line to congratulate you on your first step on the ladder to the Cabinet. You will find the work at the C.O. interesting, especially as regards S. Africa, your knowledge of which will be of great use to you."

His old headmaster, Welldon, who was now a Canon of Westminster, wrote:

Dr. J. E. C. Welldon to WSC

13 December 1905   Little Cloisters
                                          Westminster Abbey

My dear Churchill,

You will, I am sure, let me, as an old friend, congratulate you with
all my heart upon your happy entrance into official life. When I
think of the last words in which your father asked me, at my own
door in Harrow, to keep an interest in your future, it is with something of a pathetic feeling that I look forward, in full confidence, to
your making a noble use of the responsibility now laid upon you.

Believe me with all good wishes, Sincerely yours

J. E. C. WELLDON

Among others who wrote were his old friend from the South
African war days J. B. Atkins, who had now transferred his allegiance
from the *Manchester Guardian* to *The Standard,* and was reporting
in Paris. His cousin Marlborough wrote: "I am truly glad. Henceforth you will be the most formidable of those whose duty it will be
to defend the Colonial policy of your party. You don't realize yet
what a position is now offered to you. Your speeches will be read
throughout the Colonies and you alone will be the mouthpiece of the
Govt in this particular policy."

*

Churchill wasted no time in selecting a Private Secretary at the
Colonial Office. His choice fell on an obscure clerk in the West
African Department, two years older than himself — Edward Marsh.
This appointment was to become the basis of a lifelong friendship.
In his Memoirs Marsh recorded:

On December 13 I got a note from Lady Granby [later Duchess of
Rutland] asking me to a party on the following evening to meet
"Lots of my own especial friends." One of the first people I met was
Winston Churchill. "How do you do?" said I, "which I must now
say with great respect." "Why" he pounced, "why with great re-
spect?" "Because you're coming to rule over me at the Colonial
Office." A little later I saw him on a sofa with his aunt, Mrs Leslie,

who was one of the "especial friends," looking in my direction and as it seemed discussing me; but I thought no more about it.

Marsh had met Churchill twice before, and had not formed an entirely favourable impression of him. The next morning, Churchill's first day at the Colonial Office, he asked for Marsh to be appointed his Private Secretary, although Marsh was no longer in the class of "Juniors" to whom such posts, with their extra pay, were a perquisite. Marsh continued in his Memoirs:

> I was a little afraid of him. I had still not imagined that we could ever have anything in common. . . . Late in the afternoon I betook myself to Lady Lytton [Miss Pamela Plowden who had married the Earl of Lytton in 1902]. (I learnt afterwards that she had taken a hand in the boosting of me at the party) and poured out my misgivings. Her answer was one of the nicest things that can ever have been said about anybody. "The first time you meet Winston you see all his faults, and the rest of your life you spend in discovering his virtues"; and so it proved. That night I dined alone with him in his flat in Mount Street, and so far as he was concerned all my doubts were dispelled — he was the man for me, though I could still hardly see myself as the man for him.

That night he wrote to Churchill's aunt, Mrs. Leslie.

Edward Marsh to Mrs Jack Leslie

(*Leslie Papers*)

EXTRACT

[13 December 1905]
[Copy]

. . . Such an excitement. I *must* tell you. Your nephew has asked me to be his private secretary for 6 months or so. It will be the most interesting thing I've ever done but I'm most terribly afraid of not being the right person and turning out a failure. I'm sure it's your doing. When you come back in May I'll tell you whether I bless you or curse you! You'll find me a grey-haired skeleton in either case as he means to work me to death. It's funny that just after we were discussing the problem of what I should do to age myself this easy solution should have dashed [?] forth. I've just dined alone with

Winston. He was most perfectly charming to me but made it quite clear what he would expect in the way of help and I almost *know* I can't do it — its awful! . . .

Henceforward until his retirement thirty years later Marsh was to accompany Churchill to every Government department he occupied: to the Board of Trade, the Home Office, the Admiralty, the Duchy of Lancaster, the Ministry of Munitions, the War Office, back to his original Colonial Office and the Treasury. They were inseparable. Whenever Churchill was out of office, Marsh reverted to the Colonial Office, serving under, among others, the 9th Duke of Devonshire and J. H. Thomas. These peregrinations with Churchill inevitably interrupted what would have been Marsh's normal promotion. But whether Churchill was in or out of office their friendship persisted; indeed, he became a great family friend and was a constant visitor to Chartwell even in the bleak thirties. After Marsh had left the Civil Service in 1937, he frequently, as he would have said, "corrected the orthography" of Churchill's books.

*

By the end of 1905 dissolution was imminent, but the election campaign was already under way before it had been announced. The King dissolved Parliament on Monday, January 8, and the new Parliament was to assemble on February 13. It was no wonder that everyone was already campaigning: for in those days of staggered elections the first constituencies were to poll as soon as January 12. Churchill's seat in North-West Manchester, indeed the whole of Manchester, was among the earliest to vote, on January 13. Four days before the dissolution the Under-Secretary of State for the Colonies travelled north and took up his action station for his first contest as a Liberal.

4

The 1906 Election

EDDIE MARSH records that when he and Churchill arrived at Manchester on 4 January 1906, they installed themselves in the Midland Hotel and walked out to take the air. They soon found themselves in the slums:

> Winston looked about him, and his sympathetic imagination was stirred. "Fancy," he said, "living in one of these streets — never seeing anything beautiful — never eating anything savoury — *never saying anything clever!*" (the italics were his — it would be impossible to give a better rendering of italics in the spoken word).

Manchester in 1906 was the greatest manufacturing city in Lancashire with a population of nearly 640,000. It was divided into six parliamentary constituencies, while the contiguous though independent borough of Salford had three Parliamentary divisions. Of these nine constituencies only Manchester North, represented by Mr Charles E. Schwann, had returned a Liberal to the previous Parliament, and then by a bare majority of twenty-six. All the other eight seats in Manchester and Salford were held by the Unionists, among them Manchester East represented by Balfour.

North-West Manchester, for which Churchill had been adopted as Liberal candidate, had 11,411 voters on the register. The division comprised the greater part of the financial and commercial centre of the city, and also the prosperous residential area of Cheetham Hill, in which there were 470 of the constituency's estimated 740 Jewish voters. North-West Manchester had been represented, since the formation of the constituency in 1884, by an eminent Tory business-man, Sir William Houldsworth, a powerful figure in Lancashire politics who had taken Churchill under his protection when he was Conservative candidate at Oldham six years before. So powerful was Sir William and so strongly entrenched were the Unionists in North-West Manchester that in the elections of 1892 and 1900 the Liberals did not even trouble to contest the seat. So when in April 1904 Churchill had accepted the offer in principle of the North-West Manchester Liberals to become their candidate there were many who felt he had entered a fight in which the odds were exceptionally heavy against him. But then, just three months later in July 1904, Sir William Houldsworth announced that he did not intend to stand again "owing to his health and various other considerations." This created a pro-found change in the situation. Sir William was, it is true, nearly seventy years old, but neither in the House of Commons then nor later did he show signs of flagging, and he lived to the age of eighty-two. Nor can it be said that he did not relish the prospect of a fight with Churchill: on the contrary, he threw himself into the 1906 cam-paign so heartily that it was observed that he was completely over-shadowing the Conservative candidate on whose behalf he was work-ing. This poses an enigma as to why he did not stand.

The North-West Manchester Tories had chosen as their candidate a forty-year-old solicitor from London, William Joynson-Hicks. He was not a Chamberlain protectionist but a Balfourite "retaliator," and then somewhat half-hearted about it. Indeed, the only things he seemed to feel strongly about were sabbatarianism and temperance which were in the course of the election to embarrass him. Whatever he did, Joynson-Hicks did with great earnestness.

He and Churchill were later to serve as Cabinet colleagues in Baldwin's Government of 1924-9. In 1932 Churchill wrote of "Jix," as he had come to be nicknamed, in *Thoughts and Adventures*: "The worst that can be said about him is that he runs the risk of being most humourous when he wishes to be most serious."

Churchill had already published his Election Address from the Colonial Office on January 1. It was a sober and realistic statement of the Government case and of the general failure of the Tories in

the previous Parliament. His strongest arguments turned on the case
for Free Trade:

> Whatever may be the precise relations, personal or fiscal, between
> Mr Balfour and Mr Chamberlain, it is certain that the victory of
> one is the victory of the other; that the victory of either is the victory
> of both; and that victory of both involves the erection in one form
> or another, upon one pretext or another, of a retaliatory, preferential
> or protective tariff. Of all such plans I am the enemy. I do not
> accept a policy of Retaliation; for I believe with Sir Robert Peel
> "in fighting hostile tariffs by free imports." I am opposed to all de-
> vices to entangle the Empire in a net of differential duties; for I
> will not consent to hamper our freedom to purchase food and raw
> material in the markets of the world, and I do not believe in buying
> loyalty for cash. Most of all, I will resist any attempt to protect
> Home Industries from foreign competition: for I believe that such a
> system would prove a fertile source of national impoverishment and
> of political corruption, and far from relieving traders from their
> present embarrassments, or removing the evils of unemployment,
> would only aggravate both.
>
> Being convinced that all or any of these plans are founded upon es-
> sential fallacies, and would prove in practice injurious to the pros-
> perity and honour of the British Empire, of the United Kingdom,
> and in particular of Lancashire, I think it right to declare my hostil-
> ity to them with the utmost plainness, in order that no man may
> support me under any misconception.

Although Manchester had for nearly fifty years been a Tory stronghold it was, after all, the city of Cobden and Bright (John Bright was
for ten years its MP) and the Free Trade Hall stood — still stands for
that matter — as a witness and reminder in the North-West division
of Manchester to the enthusiasm that their anti-corn law league, anti-
tariff policies aroused there. Now, in 1906, the Manchester business-
men and the cotton magnates again showed little sympathy for tariffs;
and so it was that Churchill received the powerful backing of tradi-
tionally Tory business groups for his passionate defence of Free
Trade. The Manchester Guardian Society for the Protection of
Trade, The British Cotton Growing Association, and the Free Trade
League all endorsed his candidature. Perhaps the most dramatic

demonstration of solidarity for the Free Trade cause was that at the Memorial Hall on January 10. The meeting, held under the chairmanship of one of the leading Manchester cotton manufacturers, Mr Tootal Broadhurst, was remarkable for the fact that all the speakers (other than Churchill) and most of the dignitaries on the platform were Conservatives, many of whom had until the Free Trade controversy held office in their local Conservative associations.

For once, Churchill's speech was of less interest than the Chairman's. Said Mr Tootal Broadhurst, in a speech that was promptly printed and circulated throughout the constituency:

> For Free Trade or against it! There is no halfway house for timid retaliators to shelter in. . . . This North-West division of Manchester . . . is mainly Unionist rather than Liberal, and it is only by the absolutely straight voting of every Free Trade Unionist that the election of the Free Trade candidate, Mr Winston Churchill, can be assured. This, no doubt, means some sacrifices. We do not agree with Mr Churchill on all points; we do not approve of everything he has said — but I hope no Free Trade Unionist will allow any personal feeling on such points to prevent him from supporting in this election the great cause of Free Trade, of which Mr Churchill is a most able and courageous champion.

Churchill for his part extended a sympathetic welcome to those who had changed sides on this issue alone. He had led the way in a speech to a similar audience at a meeting of the Free Trade League at Cheetham Town Hall on January 8.

> I do not think that a public man ought to change his party lightly. I do not think he ought to be let off easily; his action ought to be scrutinised; his motives ought to be canvassed and examined, justly, it is true, but carefully. He must justify his action not only at the moment but by the course he takes in the years that follow on. I do not think this argument applies to the ordinary citizen. The regular voter who does not wish to take a prominent part in politics is not subject to any of that criticism which is naturally directed against a leader or a prominent man. He has a perfect right to make up his mind on the merits of the issue presented. It is more than a right, it is a duty, and I am proud to stand on this platform tonight with

gentlemen of position and influence in Manchester who have chosen rather to face the obloquy of leaving their former party than abandon the principle which they hold dear. It may be that the Liberal Government does things of which they may disapprove. But their influence would not be less; it would be more, because they would be among the supporters of the Government they helped to bring into being; and further, in the end it would be open to them to go back and rejoin the party from which for the time being they had severed themselves. These gentlemen, I venture to say, are not exposing themselves to any reproach whatever. On the contrary, I feel that their action will be endorsed by public opinion.

Free Trade had to be Churchill's prime issue. While other Liberal candidates attempted to worship at other altars it will be noticed that Churchill made none save nominal oblations on the issue of Chinese labour in the Transvaal, partly because he understood the difficulties, and partly because he realized that if he was going to win it was going to be on Free Trade. On the issue of Chinese labour he confined himself to saying in his election address:

My opinions on the subject of Chinese labour are unchanged, except that having had access to official information I hold them more strongly than ever. A Liberal Government, while it is forced to bear any part of the responsibility, is bound to do its utmost to restrict such a system, and to put down its abuses.

Having already acquainted himself at his new Office with some of the difficulties inherent in the situation, he did not even go as far as the Prime Minister, Campbell-Bannerman, had gone in his speech at the Albert Hall on December 21 where he had said that he would stop forthwith the recruitment and embarkation of coolies.

The trouble was that nearly 14,000 licences for the further importation of coolies had been issued in November. To cancel them would require new legislation which could not be carried until the Parliament had met and might involve the Government in considerable expense in indemnifying the mine-owners who had indentures for this labour and were making their plans on the basis that it would be available. Asquith, the new Chancellor of the Exchequer, and the law officers were quick to spot this and at a Cabinet on January 3 they persuaded the Prime Minister to modify his plan and to say that there would be no further recruitment but to drop the pledge about embarkation. This question of Chinese labour was not only to bedevil the election and obscure the issue of Free Trade and protection: it was also later to cause acrimony between the two parties.

Churchill, though he was sincerely committed to the withdrawal of the Chinese, did not allow himself the same extravagance of language as that of many of his fellow candidates. A year before, he had received a letter from his father's old friend Abe Bailey in Johannesburg which, though it may have painted an over-rosy picture of conditions on the Rand, must certainly have been present in his mind and have enabled him to take a more balanced view of this difficult problem.

Abe Bailey to WSC

EXTRACT

16 January 1905   Johannesburg

... The Chinaman has in so many unexpected ways justified his position that all local agitation is dead and the leaders of the anti-Chinese party have publicly withdrawn from any further opposition. Instead of hoarding his wages the Chinaman is spending them far more freely and extravagantly than the Kaffir. I have been over their quarters and it is amazing to see the trinkets, clocks, crockery etc that they have purchased for themselves — and being free from any western associations they use for feeding purposes those articles of crockery which we use in the intimate recesses of our bedrooms — at one mine they have purchased bicycles, and at another have put up £100 for a theatre. Everyone is struck with their healthy contented appearance; and they have completely adapted themselves to European food — and very excellent food it is too — as I have seen for myself meat and vegetable stews — beautifully cooked rice — tea *ad libitum* — to say nothing of the tinned food, milk and jam which they purchase for themselves. They walk in and out of the compounds to the stores — or sit outside smoking and chatting either with themselves or the Kaffirs. They are in fact very much like the Kaffir, and the two seem to have quite fraternised.

And again on February 12:

Abe Bailey to WSC

12 February 1905   Johannesburg

. . . The Chinese are working quietly and fairly satisfactorily — and the steady increase of native labour is a very hopeful sign. I do not think there is any danger of the Chinaman ultimately supplanting the native as a worker in the mines — but of course it will take some time — several years in fact before the supply of native labour is really adequate to our wants. . . .

Churchill had also made the acquaintance of a Mr Frederick Cresswell, a mine manager from South Africa, who urged that more white labour and better equipment would be more efficient than imported coolies, and would cause fewer problems. With ready access to the Colonial Office files on the one hand, and advice from trusted friends on the other, Churchill was probably as well briefed on the question of Chinese labour as anyone fighting the election. This enabled him to take up a position of which he had no need to be ashamed after the election; moreover, it enabled him to deal with Chinese labour on an altogether more knowledgeable level than most of his colleagues and opponents. On 11 January 1906 Charles E. Hands, who was covering the Manchester election for the *Daily Mail*, wrote:

The forlorn hope appeals to the instincts of the fighting MP, so the difficulty of making a lucid and effective statement on Chinese labour seems to have appealed to Winston Churchill. He had watched one after another of his opponents endeavour unsuccessfully to achieve the feat, and then confidently and joyously stepped forward and accomplished it himself. He not only proved clearly in a few words that coolie labour on the Rand is not slavery, but he succeeded in getting a crowded audience to listen to him while he proved it, which is more than any other politician has so far succeeded in doing.

What had excited Hand's admiration was the speech Churchill had delivered at Lever Street Schools on January 9:

There was no reason or right for making this grizzly experiment. At the same time, if it had not been made, I believe it is true to say that the revival in South Africa would not have been so rapid. . . .

The experiment of Chinese labour was made in defiance of the wishes of the Liberal party, and 45,000 Chinamen were set to work upon the mines of South Africa. But now that they are there the whole of the industries of the country have adapted themselves to this labour, and if you suddenly repatriated these Chinese it would undoubtedly cause a great relapse in South Africa and many thousands of English workmen would be thrown out of employment. We do not approve of this system, but we think that if the serious step of repatriating the Chinese at once is to be taken that step must be taken upon the authority of a representative South African government, because it is a matter which affects South Africa much more than our own interests in this country. Only six days before the late Government went out of office they issued 12,000 more licences to import Chinese. These licences are, however, lawful documents, carrying with them the weight and authority of the British Government. The moment Lord Elgin obtained power his first act was to say "No more."

I have to say this. The new government is a government of law and order. And has to obey as well as administer the law, and where people have definite legal claims against the Government to which we have been committed by our predecessors we cannot get away from them. It would mean that heavy compensation claims would be sustained in the courts. We decline to allow the system of Chinese labour to be extended; we intend to submit the whole matter to a really representative South African assembly.

Mr Balfour has contended that we have termed this labour slavery, and that we ought to use force of arms to end it. I have never called it slavery, because I think there are conditions which do not constitute slavery. For instance, a labourer cannot be bought or sold. On the other hand it is certainly servile and improper labour.

Manchester was the home of the suffragette movement, and indeed of the Pankhursts, the remarkable mother and daughters who founded and sustained the cause. A plaque was put up in 1960 to commemorate their first demonstration at a meeting at the Free Trade Hall addressed by Grey and Churchill three months before the 1906 Election. A good account is given in the *Manchester Guardian* of a typical meeting interrupted by suffragettes. This one was held at St John's Schools, Gartside, on January 9:

While he was answering the third or fourth question he broke off abruptly, and, to the surprise of the audience, uttered the words, "You have got it the wrong way round." Following the direction of Mr Churchill's eyes, the audience saw a woman holding up the white and black flag, which has become so familiar an object at Mr Churchill's meetings. The flag, which bears the words "Votes for Women," was held wrong side up. The woman was at the side of the room farthest away from the one narrow door by which the densely packed audience had entered. It is believed that when she began to speak, the audience showed the liveliest indignation, and utterly refused to hear her. The Chairman, in a loud voice, said: "If that lady interrupts again she is to be carried out." Mr Churchill appealed to the audience to assist the course of order and in a moment or two was able to resume his replies. He had, however, only spoken a few more words when the woman cried out "Will you give us a vote?"

At this there was a great uproar. Mr Churchill asked that the woman should come to the platform, and this she proceeded to do. The audience hissed her vigorously, and the complacent smile with which she regarded them in return appeared to cause still more irritation. The Chairman made her sit down on a vacant chair and Mr Churchill appealed again for order. "Will everybody," he said, "be quiet. Let us hear what she has to say."

The woman then stood up and said: "Men and women ——" Cries of "We want to hear Churchill" (Cheers) — "I should like to ask Mr Churchill as a member of the Liberal Government whether he will or will not give a vote to the women of this country?" — (Loud cries of "Never.")

It was noticeable that the women of all classes of society, who were among the audience in considerable numbers, joined heartily in the cries of "No" "Never," which followed upon the question. A woman's voice said "You are disgracing us," and still another said "Leave it to the men."

Mr Churchill said: "This lady has asked me a question. She has a perfect right to ask it, but I don't know why she didn't send up a notice of it on paper like everyone else has done." (Cheers.)

The woman said she had done that before. (A voice: "And you have had your answer.")

Mr Churchill: "We should be fair and chivalrous to ladies. They come here asking us to treat them like men." (Laughter) "That is what I particularly want to avoid. We must observe courtesy and chivalry to the weaker sex dependent upon us." (Hear hear.) "The only time I have voted in the House of Commons on this question I have voted in favour of woman's suffrage, but having regard of the perpetual disturbance at public meetings at this election, I utterly decline to pledge myself. . . ."

On another occasion he remarked: "I am not going to be hen-pecked on a question of such grave importance." This word, which some people thought Churchill had coined, dates back at least to 1680. Swift used it in referring to the relationship between the great Duke of Marlborough and his duchess Sarah. The phrase also occurs in Byron's *Don Juan*. Churchill had long been familiar with his writing:

> "But — oh! ye lords and ladies intellectual
> Have they not henpecked you all?" (Book I, Canto xxii.)

Once, during the election when challenged for being a turncoat, and faced with contradictory statements he replied:

> I admit I did say so and I admit that it was a very stupid thing to have said. I said a lot of stupid things when I was in the Conservative Party, and I left them because I did not want to go on saying stupid things.

Another time he replied:

> I admit I have changed my party. I don't deny it. I am proud of it. When I think of all the labours Lord Randolph Churchill gave to the fortunes of the Conservative Party and the ungrateful way in which he was treated by them when they obtained the power they would never have had but for him, I am delighted that circumstances have enabled me to break with them while I am still young and still have the first energies of my life to give to the popular cause.

An unusual meeting for those days was held in a charitable school known as the "Charter Street Ragged School," where on Sunday mornings free meals were served to children and old people in Angel Meadow, just outside his constituency. The *Manchester Guardian* reported it:

The school is outside the North-West Manchester Division, and not even his strongest political opponents could accuse him of wishing to make capital out of this visit, which was in no sense political. . . . No member of a British Government has been ever before within its doors. It was the usual Sunday morning gathering; over 400 children received breakfast, and in another room over 400 men, the flotsam and jetsam of humanity, were also given a meal; nearly 100 more waiting outside in the street were given some food. The Manchester Sacred Song Association were present, and contributed some excellent music. . . .

Mr Churchill, before rising to speak, asked for the "Glory" song to be sung, and it was joined in most heartily. He then said that he had been very deeply touched by the singing. It made one feel very far removed from the ordinary, outside world, especially from the, at times, brutal details of politics and elections. He was quite disinclined to speech-making there, because he did not wish it to be thought that he was taking advantage of that occasion to push himself forward on matters in which he was greatly interested. Let them rather look at some of the larger courses in which life lay, and which perhaps, led us to the consideration of another life beyond. He quite agreed with Mr Johnson [*the Honorary Superintendent who had introduced him*]; and what had been said of the terrible sufferings and perplexities of life in these great cities of the present day. There had never been such great cities before where poverty and wealth and suffering jostled each other as they did today. The increased education had enabled people to appreciate the evils by which they were surrounded and to see the pleasures which dangled just beyond their reach. They saw on every hand evidence of great luxury, and he feared, of waste also.

It was a very grave and sad reflection that with all our advances and science and skill and wealth we did not seem nearer to solving the old unhappiness of the human heart, physical sufferings, than we were hundreds of years ago. It was a helpful work Mr Johnson and his friends were doing. Humanity could only be helped under the Providence of God by human beings. No Bill in Parliament, no code or system, could alone help them, although these would contribute in making conditions in which the world might grow brighter and happier.

It was not possible by any mechanical state system to adequately deal with this question. The Lifeboat Service of the world was manned by the arms of men, and rescue work was voluntary. It was the personal influence of man upon his brother man in difficulty which alone could lift him.

Throughout the short campaign, Churchill naturally directed most of his fire against Balfour. Balfour with his elevated though toppling position scarcely condescended to answer. At the outset of his campaign Churchill had said at Manchester on January 3:

Mr Balfour did not believe in Protection. As between Lord Hugh Cecil and Mr Chamberlain Mr Balfour was far more closely agreed with Lord Hugh Cecil, and he thought that the fiscal question, on the whole, was a matter of minor importance compared with other causes upon which Unionists were agreed. Indeed, Mr Balfour almost forgot to mention the fiscal question at the Queen's Hall the other night. He would not lift a finger to help his brilliant kinsman, and would they believe it, at the great meeting in London there sat on Mr Balfour's platform both Lord Hugh Cecil and his Protectionist opponent. Both sat there and supported their leader, though fighting each other to the death. One would have thought that a statesman would have made it clear which of these two gentlemen's supports was most agreeable to him. One would have thought a leader who meant to lead would at least inform his followers which of them was treading in his footsteps. The honour of leading a great Party was no doubt a worthy object of desire, but some would think that it might be too dearly purchased if it involved not merely the suppression of conviction, but the cold-blooded sacrifice of friends.

Mr Balfour and Mr Chamberlain are the twin brothers of extravagance — financial voluptuaries, such as we have never been able to afford before.

Polling took place in Manchester on Saturday, January 13, and the results were announced about half past nine that evening. Churchill had a spectacular victory. The figures were:

Churchill	5,639
Joynson-Hicks	4,398
Liberal Majority	1,241

89 per cent of the electorate had voted. But much more than this was bound up in Churchill's victory. He had led the fight in the whole

area. That morning, of the nine seats of Manchester and Salford only one was held by a Liberal, all the others by Tories. By ten o'clock that night there were seven Liberals, two Labour, and no Tories. And Balfour himself was out. It was a joyous harbinger of the seats which yet had to poll in the next days and weeks. After the count Churchill said to his supporters at the Manchester Reform Club that he had come to Manchester at a time of darkness for himself and in an hour when free trade seemed to be in danger of being swept away as an obsolete dogma. "We have put all that right now, and the Liberal army will march on without pause to complete triumph."

*

The extent of the Liberal victory was enormous. Liberals won 377 seats, Labour 53 and Irish Nationalists 83, a "Ministerialist" total of 513. Against them the Tory Opposition mustered only 157, of whom 11 were Unionist Free Traders, about 36 "Balfourites," and the rest Tariff Reform supporters of Chamberlain. For the first time in more than twenty years the Liberal Party enjoyed an overall majority.

5

The Life of Lord Randolph

CHURCHILL WAS always a man capable of operating on many fronts simultaneously. In 1902 he had, with the help of Lord Rosebery, persuaded his father's literary executors to entrust to him the writing of Lord Randolph's Life. Amidst the turbulence of his political activities he was able to complete his work within a period of three and a half years. The two-volume book was published by Macmillan & Co in January 1906 and has ever since been praised as one of the three or four outstanding political biographies in the language.

As was Lord Randolph's wish, the work was to be subject to the scrutiny of the executors. These were Lord Randolph's brother-in-law George Curzon who had sat as Tory MP for High Wycombe until he succeeded as fourth Earl Howe in 1900, and Lord Randolph's friend Ernest Beckett — a Yorkshire banker who was for twenty years Tory MP for Whitby until 1905, when he succeeded as second Baron Grimthorpe.

At first the executors seemed a little uncertain as to what were their powers and their responsibilities. They consulted Mr John Pemberton, a barrister and Parliamentary colleague, who foresaw all sorts of difficulties in the way of the trustees' exercising full control over the biography, and suggested a number of new clauses to a draft agreement between Churchill and the trustees to cover this and other points at issue. Another possible source of interference lay in the proviso that Rosebery, as Foreign Secretary at the time Lord Randolph executed this Trust, was to be given a copy so as to ensure that no improper use would be made of India Office and Foreign Office papers. Churchill answered the threat of interference from the trustees in magisterial fashion.

WSC to Ernest Beckett

EXTRACT

[September 1902]   105 Mount Street

My dear Ernest Beckett,

I incline strongly to the belief that the duty of the literary executors is discharged "when to the best of their judgement they have selected a suitable biographer." Questions of style, literary taste, of the scope of the work, of the proportion of various incidents in the work, are all matters of opinion, and matters upon which opinion will very often be divided. A syndicate may compile an encyclopaedia, only a man can write a book. Once the human element in a book is destroyed by unsympathetic or foreign alterations, it cannot be of any real literary excellence and its only value is to be found in the facts it records. Therefore I am of [the] opinion — and my opinion would be the same if I were an outside person advising you and not interested in any way myself — that the fullest discretion and liberty in the treatment of the subject must be accorded to the biographer; and I am quite certain that whatever arrangement my strong personal feeling both of desire to write this work and of friendship to you might lead me to acquiesce, no stranger, writer of any literary distinction and of financial independence would undertake the task if he were "liable to have the entire work or even a whole chapter objected to. . . ."

But Churchill then went on to agree that the literary executors should retain the right to withhold from publication documents that they might consider injurious to Lord Randolph's memory or disparaging to others; that they should be entitled to see the work before publication; that any unresolved dispute between trustees and author should go to Lord Rosebery, or, if he were dead, Sir Michael Hicks-Beach for arbitration; that the work should be completed if possible within five years; and that the biographer "shall take all financial liability and all profits." As far as can be ascertained, neither Howe nor Beckett interfered with Churchill's efforts. There is no record in the Chartwell Papers of any differences of opinion among them.

It is one of the merits of primogeniture that the money and amenities of a great family can be made available to gifted but impoverished members of a cadet branch. Thus it was that Churchill's cousin, Sunny Marlborough, placed a set of rooms at his disposal at Blenheim and mounted him on his fine hunters for three or four months during the years when he was writing his father's Life. He also made Churchill free of the muniment room at Blenheim and subsequently caused all of Lord Randolph's important political papers to be bound in thirty-two handsome blue morocco volumes, richly emblazoned back and front with the Marlborough arms in gold leaf. These were presented to Churchill by the 10th Duke of Marlborough, Sunny's heir. They are now in the possession of the author. In the same way, another cousin, Ivor Guest, later 1st Viscount Wimborne made available to him a room at Wimborne House, Arlington Street, next door to the Ritz Hotel.

Later, when he went abroad to stay with Sir Ernest Cassel in Switzerland he wrote to his mother:

WSC to Lady Randolph

EXTRACT

25 August 1904   Villa Cassel

. . . I have been working away at my book and am slowly getting into the stride. But the difficulty of the task impresses me as I proceed. What to leave out, how to work this in — what line to take in regard to a whole series of conflicting or contradictory letters? At present I am writing nearly everything. It will be easy to cut it down afterwards. . . .

*

Churchill had taken possession of his father's papers during the late summer of 1902 and immediately set about asking all his father's surviving contemporaries for the use of whatever relevant documents they had in their possession. He wrote, for instance, to Joseph Chamberlain. Chamberlain, with his usual zeal and interest, immediately sent the young biographer all the material he could find. Within two weeks Churchill had absorbed it all and had returned it. Two years later Chamberlain expanded these documents with his own reminiscences:

WSC to Lady Randolph

EXTRACT

24 September 1904   Blenheim

. . . You will laugh when I tell you that I spent last Thursday night at Highbury and had five or six hours most pleasant and interesting conversation with Joe about old letters and old politics. I suggested an interview in London and he replied by an invitation to dine and sleep. He is, of course, tremendously partisan in his views both on men and things, but it was quite clear to me that we understood each other on lots of questions, and that my company was not at all unpleasant to him.

He got out the cup which my father gave him on his third marriage and made great fuss about it and generally I preserve very pleasant recollections of a most interesting episode. . . .

Thirty years later Churchill's powerful memory enabled him to recall the evening in greater detail. In his essay on Joseph Chamberlain in *Great Contemporaries* he wrote:

We dined alone. With the dessert a bottle of '34 port was opened. Only the briefest reference was made to current controversies. "I think you are quite right," he said, "feeling as you do, to join the Liberals. You must expect to have the same sort of abuse flung at you as I have endured. But if a man is sure of himself, it only sharpens him and makes him more effective." Apart from this our talk lay in the controversies and personalities of twenty years before.

Chamberlain had also enjoyed the evening. "I am very glad," he wrote to Churchill from Highbury, Birmingham, on 29 September 1904, "that you were able to come and talk over the matter with me. It revived old times and the memories of my pleasant associations with your father. I hope the book will be a great success. I am sure that it will create a very great interest; but you must take care to keep the Government in until it is published, as the public cannot stand two sensations at the same time."

Balfour also promised to help; feeling confident, he wrote on 8 October 1902, that he had destroyed none of his documents. Yet two years were to pass — two years incidentally which saw Churchill change from a Tory to a Liberal — before Balfour admitted that the hunt for his papers had proved unsuccessful. "This is curious," he wrote Churchill on 29 August 1904, "for it is very unlikely that I should have thrown them away, and though our correspondence was not large in amount, partly because I am the worst of letter-writers, and partly because most of our communications were oral, yet some letters there must have been."

Churchill sent copies of his manuscript to various interested parties inviting their comments. Balfour, for one, objected to some passages concerning his part in acting as intermediary in an abortive exchange between his uncle Lord Salisbury and Mr Gladstone in 1885 over the possibility of granting some measure of self-government to Ireland. Balfour had played only a minor part in this affair and did not wish to be dragged into a potential controversy. He asked Churchill to delete the passage, but the substance of it has remained.

In pursuance of the terms imposed on him by Lord Randolph's literary settlement he consulted St John Brodrick, who was now Secretary of State for India. Brodrick in turn consulted Lansdowne at the Foreign Office. Brodrick, whom Churchill had bitterly assailed in the previous two years, proved more helpful than did Lansdowne, who was a trifle pernickety. Brodrick made some suggestions. He was particularly concerned that Churchill should get the permission of King Edward before he published letters which passed between Lord Randolph and Queen Victoria, and between Lord Randolph and the Duke of Connaught. Churchill sought and obtained this permission. Brodrick was also concerned about Churchill's references to Queen Victoria's personal likes and dislikes. "It is very interesting," he wrote in October 1905, "but is it fit for publication?" Churchill evidently thought so. Lord Randolph, he wrote in his book, had grievously offended the Queen by his premature disclosure of his resignation to *The Times;* "and in the mood that was abroad he found, like Macaulay before him, that to write on Windsor Castle paper may sometimes be accounted as a crime."

It was, however, Lord Rosebery upon whom Churchill relied the most for papers and for information, and who proved the most awkward. On 11 September 1902 Churchill wrote to him: "I will bring with me my fat box of papers — amid which I am now busy and I am sure there are some you would like to see, and also several points on which I want to ask your advice . . ." "Here are some proofs," Churchill wrote eventually to Roseberry in January 1905, "they are very rough and raw . . . I shall be very grateful for any comment or criticism. . . ." Rosebery gave much criticism, some of which was not accepted. He noted, for instance, on 28 October 1905, that he did not like the opening about Blenheim and felt that it should be left out. Churchill evidently disagreed with Roseberry upon this point. So does the author. The reader must judge for himself. He will find the relevant passage on page 4 of Volume I of the present work. A few days later, Rosebery wrote to Churchill: "Your father might speak a little more for himself in some chapters which contain more historical narration — good as it is in itself — than is necessary for the biography." Rosebery concluded by saying: "The biographer should be the unseen wire-puller." The author of the present work has been fortified in his own judgement by the first sentence but has rejected the second. He does not regard either his hero or other characters as puppets or marionettes. Neither Churchill nor his son accepted this meretricious advice.

Rosebery wrote down some recollections in 1905 of his association with Lord Randolph; Churchill was most anxious to use them in his book, particularly in the introduction. Churchill never received these recollections, Rosebery claiming in September of that year that they had been burnt in the fire. In the middle of October, Churchill wrote down all that he could recall of what Rosebery had told him and sent what he had written to him. On October 19 Rosebery wrote that he had found his notes "in an obscure drawer," adding "because I suppose there was no fire in June."

He concluded by saying "they might just as well have been in the fire, for they would be quite out of place in an introduction." The next day Churchill wrote back: "Please let me have those notes. I want them. If they will not make an introduction, I have another use for them. Let me quote them by extracts in the different places where they chronologically fit." Rosebery would have none of it. He wrote Churchill four days later:

Lord Rosebery to WSC

EXTRACT

24 October 1905   Madresfield Court
                                                   Malvern Link

. . . Do get that paper of mine out of your head. As I had told you I burned it I thought it only truthful to tell you when I found I had not. But it is theoretically burned, and if you allude to it again, into the fire it shall go. . . .

This episode reveals the extraordinarily ambivalent character of Rosebery. He first volunteers information; says he made a note and will send it to Churchill, later says he has burnt it; when Churchill puts down his own recollections of the conversation, Rosebery asks Churchill not to print it; admits he has not burnt his notes, declining to send them to Churchill, but says that if further badgered in the matter he will burn them. As an historical source he proved as difficult as Balfour. It is strange that writing thirty years later in *Great Contemporaries,* Churchill revived a recollection, unfortified by any documentation, which seems quite contrary to the account given here.

Lord Rosebery's interest was so strong and his desire to help delineate his friend so keen, that he took the trouble to write a considerable appreciation of Lord Randolph, which he suggested I should incorporate textually in my account. I was deeply touched, and at the same time embarrassed: for after all I had my own way of doing things, and the literary integrity of a work is capital. Moreover, his picture of Randolph Churchill's schooldays contained the word "scug," an Eton slang term which I considered derogatory and unsuited to a biography written by a son. . . . I therefore deferentially but obstinately resisted this expression. He stuck to it and explained

its harmless Etonian significance. In the end he wrote that I had
rejected his contribution and that it was withdrawn.

The notes which Rosebery "burned" or suppressed were to reach
the public in the form of a monograph. Concerning this, Churchill
in the same essay on Rosebery wrote: "A few years later it appeared
as the widely read and deeply interesting monograph on Lord Randolph and my book about him, in which Lord Rosebery drew with
admiration and affection the 'brilliant being' who had so compul-
sively cheered, charmed, directed, and startled his youth and prime."
When this monograph was published, actually within nine months of
Churchill's work, Rosebery sent it to him with a card:

Lord Rosebery to WSC

October 1906   Rosebery
                                                        Gorebridge
                                                        Midlothian

Dear Winston,
    I am sending you an advertisement of your book.

                                                            Yours
                                                              AR

Churchill had substantially completed his biography before he set
about selling it. When he did he chose an unusual and as it
proved a highly resourceful literary agent in Mr Frank Harris.
Harris was a brilliant journalist and successively the editor of the
Evening News, Fortnightly Review, Saturday Review and *Vanity
Fair*, and he had been among the first editors to publish articles by
George Bernard Shaw and H. G. Wells. He was to become notorious
because in his later poverty in Paris he published a scabrous work
called *My Life and Loves*. However, at the time Churchill was writing the biography of his father, Harris was regarded as a leading
literary figure, and having some acquaintance with Lord Randolph
he undertook to take over the sale of Churchill's book.
    Churchill wrote to Harris on 2 October 1905 outlining the agree-
ment between the two of them. "I authorise you as my friend to talk

in confidence and privacy to publishers about my book. I reserve to myself the right to decide freely on every offer — whether as regards whole world rights, or English, foreign or colonial rights — even to the extent of taking a lower one if I choose. But if as the result of your negotiations, I make a bargain, then I shall pay you 10 per cent of the excess net profit accruing to me from the bargain above £4,000 as such profit may be realized. Let me know if this is your agreement."

Harris telegraphed three days later: "Your letter perfectly correct. Have put all in train. Shall be ready meet you with rest of suggestions any time after next Monday." He had great hopes for the book, for he wrote to Churchill on October 7: "Properly worked this book should bring you in £10,000 or I'm a Dutchman! And it's cheap at the price." Harris then got in touch with a number of publishing houses, notably Longmans, Heinemann, Methuen, Hutchinson, Cassell, John Murray and Macmillan.

The best offer came from Macmillan & Co. George Macmillan, one of the Company Directors originally offered £7,000 for the entire copyright in Great Britain and the United States. Harris, however, was able to have this increased to £8,000.

WSC to Lady Randolph

EXTRACT

30 October 1905   105 Mount Street

. . . I settled this morning with Messrs Macmillan that they shall publish my book on the following terms:
£8,000 to be paid as follows:
£1,000 now
£1,000 when the proofs are corrected and
£6,000 on the day of publication.

In addition to this after Macmillans have earned £4,000 profit for themselves, we are to divide all further profits which may be realised during the period of legal copyright. I think you will agree that I was right to close with this. Tempting as it was to "run" the book myself,

I do not think anyone can say I have not sold it wisely and well. I have paid Frank Harris £400 being 10 per cent commission on the excess £4,000 he was able to get for me over and above the £4,000 which Longman had offered originally. I think he has earned it well. I could certainly never have made such a bargain for myself. . . .

*

Just as the election campaign began and eleven days before polling in Manchester, Churchill's *Lord Randolph Churchill* was published. Thus he achieved what Joseph Chamberlain had jocularly warned against.

The reviews were numerous and lengthy. The following extract from the *Times Literary Supplement* gives a representative opinion:

It is a pleasure to be able to say that a life so well worth writing has been admirably written. Sons have not always proved the most judicious of biographers, and Mr Winston Churchill's warmest admirers would not ask us to think him the most judicious of men. But here is a book which is certainly among the two or three most exciting political biographies in the language, and yet the young Achilles had done due honour to his Patroclus without sacrificing any slaughtered Trojans on the funeral pyre. The book is a son's book, of course, written from a particular point of view; and there are, of course, things which might be said against Lord Randolph Churchill but are not said here. That is inevitable; but the worst kind of biographer is not he who has a point of view, but he who has not — and certainly Mr Winston Churchill has not unduly obtruded his. One hears the son's voice in a good many places and hears it willingly; the voice of the politician one hardly ever hears. Good taste has not generally been considered the strong point either of the biographer or of his father; nor has either of them been conspicuous for self-restraint. But the severest critic will find very few lapses of taste in this book; and for those few it is not the writer's pen, but his subject's tongue, that is responsible. And as for self-restraint, who could have believed that Mr Winston Churchill could write a book that is full of Mr Chamberlain, and not altogether empty of Mr Balfour, and yet write it like an historian, and not at all like a man on a party platform? But he has. Even the temptation of the fair trade controversy, and Lord Randolph's conversion to economic orthodoxy, has not made him swerve from the path of virtue. Once, and once only, so far as we have noticed, does he indulge himself in the luxury of using the past to point the moral of the present. And then the allusion is as innocent as it is isolated. It occurs in the account of his father's resignation. "It is no doubt true that he rated his own power . . . too high. Like many a successful man before him — *and some since* he thought the forces he had directed in the past were resident in himself, whereas they were to some extent outside himself and independent." The italics are not in the original; and, even with their assistance, this single shaft shot at our existing political actualities can hardly be said to look very venomous.

But let there be no mistake. Virtue does not necessarily imply dullness. The book is, on the whole, a serious and fair-minded record of Lord Randolph's career. But its interest never flags for a moment. No one who cares for politics will willingly put it down when it is once in his hands. People who do not care for politics had better not touch it.

Most of the critics were struck, almost amazed, at the "maturity of judgement, levelheadedness and discretion" (*Sunday Times*) that Churchill had displayed in writing this Life. His style, too, pleased many — "He has chosen the grand manner . . . but the general effect is of dignity and ease" (*Spectator*). All the critics were curious to know whether the work would show a filial bias and whether his clashes with Balfour and Chamberlain would be revealed in his assessment of their roles in the life of his father. They were unanimous in pronouncing that Churchill had "to a remarkable extent avoided the pitfalls of the partisan" (*Spectator*). "Consanguinity," wrote Toby MP (Sir Henry Lucy) in *Punch,* "is by no means a recommendation for the post of biographer. The family circle is lacking in the opportunity of perspective indispensable to the formation of true judgment of character and conduct. Exceptions are found in Lockhart's life of his father-in-law, Scott and in Trevelyan's masterpiece the Memoir of his uncle, Lord Macaulay. Winston Churchill has established a third exception to the rule."

The book received almost universal acclaim in the Press; most of the reviewers particularly praised Churchill for having written a valuable addition to the history of the decade 1880–90 as well as an admirable biography of his father. However, there were two notable exceptions. First the *Sun:*

> Mr Churchill leaves the real life still to be written, because he leaves the curtain still to be lifted on the real man. In this book the dead statesman is a tabernacle without a key. Perhaps some future biographer will unlock the door and reveal the secret within — a strange, temperamental madness, a deep-seated defect in the organic material which left Lord Randolph at times something less than the master of himself or of his opportunities.

Then there was a virulent review in the *Daily Telegraph*:

> For all practical purposes that career came to an end with Lord Randolph's precipitate resignation of his office as Chancellor of the Exchequer in December, 1886, at which date Mr Winston Churchill was in his thirteenth year. We call attention to this fact because it palliates, if it does not altogether excuse, the lack of good taste and the malice of a very considerable portion of these two handsome volumes. Some other hand or hands must have been at work — hands which seem to have been trained in the worst school of American journalism. We hope, however, that the reader will not be deterred from following the narrative to an end by the repugnance which the earlier chapters are likely to create. . . .
>
> At Eton, to judge from Mr Churchill's own account, Lord Randolph could hardly have been a very attractive boy, for we are told that his father, the Duke of Marlborough, found it often necessary to reprove some schoolboy misdemeanour, pert speeches to masters, an overbearing manner, the unwarranted fagging of small companions, or the breaking of other people's windows. And the duke, who seems to have been gifted with fair insight into character, wrote to him on one occasion:
>
>> I fear that you yourself are very impatient and resentful of any control; while you stand upon some fancied right or injury, you fail to perceive what is your duty, and allow both your language and manners most improper scope.
>
> In this respect, at any rate, the boy was father to the man. One thing, however, must always be set down to Lord Randolph's credit

— the veneration and affection which he always displayed for his parents, which, in one respect, at any rate, he does not seem to have bequeathed to his successor, for there are passages in this book which most English sons would have hesitated to write about their fathers...

We pass over the incidents of Lord Randolph's courtship and marriage with the remark that they are told with a freedom from reserve not common in this country. We come to the point at which the work might well have begun. . . .

Mr Churchill winds up these two interesting volumes with a panegyric upon his father which it would be ungenerous to criticise. Fortunately, Lord Randolph Churchill has been allowed to tell his own story in his own words in these 1,000 pages. The record of his career, stripped of the glosses, suggestions, and inferences with which Mr Churchill naturally seeks to clothe it, is plain enough for the public to understand. . . .

His character, his temperament, and a certain intellectual obliquity of vision prevented him from making permanent and beneficial use of powers which were unquestionably very remarkable. Only those who knew him personally could describe the curious fascination which he exercised over those brought into contact with him, and they could not explain it. His treatment of his friends was often atrocious, sometimes even not honourable: he was very careless of the truth, and he did things for which other men would almost have been ostracised. Yet, however badly he may have behaved, however deeply he, may have wronged one, there was that mysterious attraction about him that if he came without apology or explanation, but with an open hand, it was practically impossible to refuse to grasp it. Those who had the strongest grounds for resenting his conduct were those who watched the failure of his career with the greatest sorrow and mourned most sincerely over his premature death.

One word must be said about the editing of this work. Mr. Churchill's part has been done with very considerable ability, but with occasional lapses into execrable taste, which have not been wanting in his own political career. There are passages which a judicious and reverent editor would have carefully excised. Perhaps he thought that the records of public debates and speeches contained so much that was offensive to political and private good taste that a few supplementary gems would not matter. But we let that pass, and add the remark that though these two volumes contain much calculated to set the reader's teeth on edge, they are quite indispensable to anyone who wishes to understand the checkered and eventful history of the last quarter of a century.

The review in the *Daily Telegraph* prompted the Duke of Marlborough to write to the Editor and complain:

The Duke of Marlborough to the Editor, the Daily Telegraph

3 January 1906   Blenheim

Sir,

I have read the article published in your paper on the life of the late Lord Randolph Churchill written by his son.

I do not desire to express an opinion on the review which you make of Mr Churchill's book.

I wish, however, to remind you that you have permitted yourself the use of the following sentence in giving your own impression of the character of the late Lord Randolph Churchill: "His treatment of his friends was often atrocious, sometimes even not honourable: he was very careless of truth." These are terms which you do not hesitate to employ against the character of a statesman who is dead, but which you would not have ventured to use if he had been alive.

I desire, therefore, to ask if you withdraw in unequivocal terms a statement which is unfounded in fact, and that you will offer an apology for the use of language which many will deplore.

In proportion to the frankness of your withdrawal and the extent of your apology, I shall recognise the good taste which you presumably possess yourself, since you censure so severely the lack of it in others.

Men in public life can defend themselves when their honour is impugned. But when the attack is delayed till after their demise they entrust the defence to those who share their name.

It is on behalf of Lord Randolph's family who loved him, his friends who esteemed him, and his political associates who honoured him that I desire to offer an uncompromising protest against an attack on the memory of a departed statesman the method of which appears to me to be essentially un-English.

I remain, Yours faithfully

MARLBOROUGH

The Duke also wrote to Churchill on the same day and explained that the word un-English referred to the Jewish ownership of the paper, and he hoped that the significance would not be lost. He further said that he "would take the first opportunity of offering Levi Lawson a public affront." The *Telegraph* made a withdrawal on January 5.

Having submitted the Duke of Marlborough's letter to our reviewer, we learn that he is not anxious to pursue the matter further. We consider, therefore, it our duty to express our deep regret that the particular passage complained of, which we unhesitatingly withdraw, should have appeared. For the rest we sincerely disclaim the intention of wounding the feeling of the members of the late Lord Randolph's family.

Churchill received a great many letters of appreciation. Among the first, and most valued, was one from Lord Rosebery.

Lord Rosebery to WSC

EXTRACT

15 January 1906   Dalmeny

... I have been solacing myself in my solitude at Rosebery with the Life of R.C. Of course I had seen a great deal of it in proof, but I now have read it as a whole, as a book; and I must congratulate you without qualification or reserve. I am I think naturally a cold-blooded critic. But here I can only dwell on one long monotonous note of praise. The plan was beset with difficulties. A son, who hardly knew his father as a public man or not at all, writing his father's life; the story only ten years old and full of delicacies & resentments; many survivors of those times, whose toes it was impossible to avoid treading upon, still in existence. Moreover the career to be written about was full not merely of dazzling successes, but of perturbances and infirmities. And the author had normal animosities by leaving his party, and had to write with delicacy about both parties in view of past and present connections. Well — there is the hideous nature of the task — under rather than over stated. And what is the result? Honestly, at the moment, I cannot find a fault. Good humoured, impartial, vivid, sympathetic, and written in an admirable style, with little refreshing ironies to flavour the whole composition, it is a book difficult to lay down. It presents too, a marvellous picture of a gifted, complicated ill-fated lovable being, written with the affection of a son but with a sympathetic impartiality; and of a career to which there is no parallel in our history. I wish we could have ten volumes of his letters, but I shall not live to see the day when they can honourably be published, so I must go without.

There are one or two little proof errors I have marked when you want them, e.g. the first Lord Aukland was never Governor-General of India. With this book and your remarkable position you seem to me at the moment to be at a crisis in your life so dazzling as to be dangerous. But I will not act the part of the moralising slave in the triumphant car, but heartily wish that the lustre may continue, even if there be a lurking and inseparable peril.

Yrs always

AR

Chamberlain also wrote:

Joseph Chamberlain to WSC

EXTRACT

10 February 1906   Torquay

. . . I have now nearly finished your book & must tell you that I think it is admirably done. It is extremely difficult for a son to write his father's life with sufficient impartiality & restraint, but you have succeeded & have allowed the facts & the letters to tell their own story while the necessary arguments are not open to any hostile criticism. . . .

J. A. Spender, who was to be the biographer of Campbell-Bannerman and Asquith, and was the editor of the Liberal *Westminster Gazette* wrote to Churchill:

J. A. Spender to WSC

EXTRACT

2 January 1906   45 Sloane Street

. . . I must add . . . a private word to say what a brilliant book I think it is, & how masterly in its grasp of forces &.characters. But apart from that you have done what you chiefly set out to do — the son's part to the father as very seldom it has been done before. May I offer you my very warm congratulations?

You need nothing to better your "situation," but a book of this kind does place you among the literary few — which is a great thing for a politician. . . .

W. F. Monypenny, who was at this time in the midst of his Life of Disraeli, later to be completed by G. E. Buckle, editor of *The Times,* also wrote:

W. F. Monypenny to WSC

EXTRACT

14 February 1906   2 Queen Anne's Gate

. . . I cannot refrain from telling you how much I have been delighted and from congratulating you on what seems to me a really great performance. Though I am not able to contemplate it from the summit of the mountain of achievement but only from half way up the slopes, still I am one of the small band of people who from practical experience can form some notion of the difficulties of such a task: and so you will perhaps not think it mere presumption if I say that alike in style and architecture and for its spirit, grasp and insight the book seems to me truly admirable. It might perhaps have gained in dramatic intensity by being a little shorter tho' I have not found a dull page in it. It has immensely clarified my views of the post-Dizzian epoch, and, what will probably please you most, immensely raised my conception of your father as a statesman. . . .

The book did well. In the first week it sold 2,306 copies and in the first seventeen weeks up to the end of April 5,827 copies, this not counting the American edition. In the following year a one-volume edition of 3,000 copies was printed and sold. Forty-five years later it was republished by Odhams Press with a new introduction and a hitherto unpublished memorandum by Sir Henry Drummond Wolff as an appendix. This new edition has already sold as many copies as the original edition.

6

The Conciliation of South Africa

THE NEW PARLIAMENT was opened by the King on 19 February 1906. Considering what the new Liberal Government was to achieve it is noteworthy how little was promised in either the Liberal election programme or in the speech from the Throne. The Liberals had been so long out of office, had been so divided and were so unprepared for their astonishing victory that they do not seem to have worked out any far-reaching plans. Indeed, they had fought the election on two negative issues — opposition to tariffs, opposition to Chinese labour. These had ensured their victory but hardly provided the material for new and constructive legislation. "The Bill of the Session," as Mr Augustine Birrell, its introducer, described it, concerned Education. It was aimed at placing all state-aided elementary education, including church schools of all denominations, under the local authority, and limiting religious instruction to readings from the Bible. Bills dealing with the law of trade disputes, reversing the Taff Vale judgement which had held that a union could be sued for the torts of its members, and with Workmen's Compensation were also promised in the King's Speech, but, apart from a vague reference to Ireland which caused a flurry on the Opposition benches among those eager to revive the bogey of Home Rule, the only other item of interest was the promise of an early grant of "responsible" instead of merely "representative" Government, as had been formerly mooted, to the Transvaal. It was not until Asquith and Lloyd George had cemented their radical alliance that the series of social and economic reforms was introduced which was to make Asquith's Government shine in history.

South Africa presented the Liberals with their most urgent Imperial problem. Even while Campbell-Bannerman was forming his administration there had for some time been agitation among the Boers for constitutional advance and against the importation of Chinese coolies for the Rand mines.

What the Liberal administration wanted to achieve in South Africa was succinctly put by Churchill: "We hope to build upon the reconciliation and not upon the rivalry of races!" To effect this reconciliation Campbell-Bannerman chose the men most qualified: Elgin and Churchill. Elgin, though he had no personal experience of southern Africa, had served as Viceroy of India from 1894 to 1899. A more important consideration was that he had been chairman of the Royal Commission which had investigated Britain's military preparations for the Boer War. A third factor was that Elgin was descended from two notable colonial administrators. His father, the 8th Earl, had been Governor-General of Canada from 1846 to 1854. During his tenure of office he had adopted and introduced the principle of responsible government devised by the 1st Earl of Durham to pacify the "two nations warring in a single state" that he had found in Canada. Lord Durham was the 9th Earl's maternal grandfather. It was Elgin's grandfather the 7th Earl of Elgin who salvaged in 1801 the marble frieze of the Parthenon in Athens, later known as the Elgin Marbles and acquired by the British Museum.

Until his appointment in December 1905 as Under-Secretary for the Colonies, Churchill had had no administrative experience. There were compensating attributes, however. During the early stages of the Boer War he had travelled widely in South Africa. He had met numerous Boers and had conversed with them while he was among them as a prisoner. After his return to England and entry to Parliament he had continued to follow events in southern Africa closely. He had shown much goodwill towards the Boers, pleading for a lenient peace and magnanimity towards the defeated. He had kept up his correspondence with old friends there, such as Abe Bailey and Ian Hamilton. Whenever South African affairs were debated in the House he had spoken with authority. And though Churchill was not in the Cabinet, once appointed Under-Secretary his position was much enhanced in that the Colonial Secretary sat in the Lords.

It was common ground between the two parties that self-government should be granted. As far back as 1901, while war was still being waged, Chamberlain was telling the new King of his anxiety "to be able to accord free institutions" to the Boers. The question was, how and when.

Again, the clauses of the Treaty of Vereeniging which ended the war promised that "as soon as circumstances permit, representative institutions, leading up to full self-government, will be introduced." But did the circumstances of 1905 permit? The Transvaal, and the Orange River Colony, had since the end of the Boer War in 1902 been administered as crown colonies. Then, in March 1905, Alfred Lyttelton, Chamberlain's successor at the Colonial Office, announced that the Transvaal would be advanced to representative government. It was generally assumed that the Orange River Colony — which, unlike the Transvaal, had a homogeneous Boer population — would receive similar treatment. The Lyttelton constitution, as it came to be known, was a cautious but logical step forward; all other colonies had first enjoyed a period of representative government before passing to the next stage — responsible government in which the executive was responsible to an elected legislature. But this completely failed to satisfy the Boers who had already enjoyed complete independence only four years earlier.

Lyttelton proposed to give the legislative assembly a majority of elected members. The executive, however, would consist entirely of officials, would be able to veto any law passed by the legislature, and would retain full control of the colony's finances. It was not therefore surprising that the Boers should threaten to boycott the new constitution as they had already done with the existing legislative council. On the other hand, there were powerful voices, both in the Transvaal and in England, campaigning as forcefully against further political concessions to the Boers. For British settlers as well as mine-owners and shareholders the war — which had cost Britain 30,000 lives and £250 million — was still far too near. Even within the Liberal Party itself there were men of influence who were reluctant to hustle the Transvaal into premature self-government and possibly into the hands of the Boer majority. There were many who felt that the colony should first pass through a transitional period of representative government, a period which, it was hoped, would lead to a strengthening and consolidation of the now weak and divided British community.

Churchill took a large part in persuading the Government to renounce the Lyttelton constitution and to grant responsible self-government. Before the Cabinet finally made up its mind Churchill had drafted three powerful and well-reasoned memoranda arguing the case against the Lyttelton constitution and for responsible government. The first two of these expressed his own views; the third the views of the Cabinet Committee formed to study the question.

J. A. Spender, Campbell-Bannerman's biographer, maintains that Campbell-Bannerman never hesitated to reject the Conservative scheme. "He said flatly that one plan was right and the other wrong, and refused to be involved in any legal or constitutional argument which favoured the more cautious procedure." The Prime Minister, he affirms, was for "sweeping [the Lyttelton constitution] all away." But Churchill's account of how the initial doubts against the Lyttelton plan were raised is surely more plausible. "Just at the time that the Government changed in December two questions arose — the question of whether or not soldiers should be allowed to vote; and the question whether it would not be better to have sixty constituencies instead of thirty; and, as both questions involved necessary alterations in the Letters Patent, the time was ripe, quite apart from any differences which the change of the man at the helm might make, for a reconsideration and review of the whole form of the government which was to be given to the two colonies." Thus it was that a Cabinet Committee was set up to reconsider and review the question. Loreburn was appointed chairman; Elgin, Morley, Bryce, Ripon and Asquith were among its members. Churchill was not a member although he was permitted to take part in its deliberations.

Unlike the Colonial Office, whose memoranda to the committee advocated caution and delay, Churchill from the beginning took the initiative in urging the new Government to formulate a fresh constitution for the Transvaal. His memoranda, printed for circulation and discussion in the Colonial Office, in the Cabinet Committee and in the Cabinet itself, not only represent the personal views formed by him on the basis of his own enquiries but also are written in an individual style whose authorship is unmistakable. Thus in his Colonial

Office paper (South Africa No 804) printed on 3 January 1906, and written just as he was embarking on his election campaign, Churchill begins a demolition of the case for the Lyttelton constitution with imagery drawn from his own experience as a soldier:

> We have therefore abandoned one practical and defensible position, *viz*, Crown Colony Government. It will not be possible to return to it. We must now move on to another position which, while affording security to British interests, is capable of permanent defence. Mr Lyttelton's plan (despatch of the 31st March) does not appear to promise either permanence or stability. When one crest line is abandoned it is necessary to return to the next. Halting at a "halfway house" mid-way in the valley is fatal. What is the next defensible position? I submit that it will not now be possible to deny the Transvaal a representative Assembly with an Executive responsible thereto.

Churchill then enumerated, only to dismiss, the six principal reasons that lay behind Lyttelton's proposals. "The reasons set forth by Mr Lyttelton are hardly convincing even on paper," Churchill concludes. They "have been collected to make some show of defending a decision already arrived at by an odd mixture of venturesomeness and timidity."

Churchill argued simply but effectively that if the British Government implemented the Lyttelton constitution it risked provoking a deadlock between an elected assembly and a nominated administration. Moreover, he forecast accurately that the Home Government would be subject to growing pressure for responsible government from the Transvaal.

In fact, in the same month, January, that Churchill drafted his first memorandum on the Transvaal, the Boer political party, Het Volk, despatched the clever and guileful Smuts to England to try to persuade the Liberal ministry to renounce the Conservative proposals and grant immediate responsible government. On reaching London the former Boer commander immediately sought interviews with as many Liberal leaders as possible, as his forthright letter to Churchill shows:

J. C. Smuts to WSC

Horrex's Hotel
Strand

9 Jan. 1906

Dear Mr. Winston Churchill,

I have come from the Transvaal in the hope that I may have an opportunity to discuss

Dear Mr Winston Churchill,

I have come from the Transvaal in the hope that I may have an opportunity to discuss with you the situation in the Transvaal and South Africa generally. I have no desire to trouble you while you are busy with election matters, but shall esteem it a great favour and honour if thereafter you could find it convenient to receive me.

We Boers feel very deeply that, unless the main features of the Milner policy are discarded the Liberals will reap what their opponents have sown in South Africa. The continuance of the policy which has been pursued since the conclusion of hostilities can in our opinion only lead to an impossible situation sooner or later, while the reversal of that policy will clear the way for a great Liberal reconstruction of South Africa.

I am very anxious to discuss with you the various aspects of the whole question as they present themselves to us in the hope that the Government may see their way clear to the adoption of a policy which will not only heal old wounds but also pave the way to union and happiness in South Africa.

Whatever political knowledge or experience I have picked up in

South Africa which might assist in the furtherance of this object I
place unreservedly at your disposal.

I am, Yours very faithfully
J. C. SMUTS

A note by Churchill on this letter reads: "Ansd January 11 promising further letter." In fact, the two future Prime Ministers did not
meet until January 19 and on January 31 Smuts forwarded to Churchill — as to other members of the Government — a memorandum
in which he most skilfully urged the immediate grant of self-government to the Transvaal and to the Orange Free State. But Churchill
was already drafting a second "Note" on the Transvaal Constitution:
this Colonial Office paper (South Africa No 817) was printed on
January 30 and contained what he called "a few observations upon
the constructive aspect" of the proposals for the new Transvaal constitution. Naturally it must have owed something to the interview
with Smuts, and Churchill was able to incorporate some of the information he had gleaned on that occasion and acknowledge its source.
But again the ideas and their expression bear Churchill's own individual stamp, as in this paragraph, in which the plea for British
impartiality as between the Boers and the British-born settlers is an
echo of much that he had written in letters and despatches from
South Africa six years before (see Volume I, Chapter 15):

British authority in South Africa must stand on two legs. The inherent vice of Lord Milner's policy was that it stood on one leg. Of
Lord Milner's zeal and integrity in the public service, of his con-
stancy through years of heartbreaking perplexity and peril, of his
honourable poverty and voluntary self-effacement, it is not necessary
to speak. But these considerations should not blind us to the fact
that after the Peace of Vereeniging, no more unsuitable agent could
have been chosen to discharge the functions of the High Commissioner. Being regarded after the war as the inveterate enemy of the
Dutch and the prime author of all their miseries, he was condemned
to fall back entirely on the support of the British; and of the British
party the mining interest is, of course, the only formidable fighting
part. The mining interest were, therefore, the only friends upon
whom he could rely, and to preserve that allegiance scarcely any
expedient seemed too desperate. But His Majesty's Government,

coming fresh upon the scene, suffer from no such disability. They are at present independent, uncompromised, free to hold the scales even, cut off from neither race, able to work on terms of impartial justice with both. Let not that supreme advantage be thrown away. We cannot take either the one side or the other. We are free from the trammels of the mining interest. Do not let us throw ourselves into the arms of the Boers. Do not let us do anything which makes us the champion of one race, and consequently deprives us *for ever* of the confidence of the other.

In this memorandum Churchill shows that he regarded as virtually settled — with some justice, as it turned out, but with what at the time must have appeared to be considerable presumption — the issue of responsible as opposed to representative government, the denial of the right of some 800 British soldiers in South Africa to vote, the doubling of the size of the assembly (sixty constituencies as opposed to the thirty or so envisaged by Lyttelton) and "absolute equality of language" as between Dutch and English.

An important matter that still remained to be decided was whether the proposed sixty constituencies should be determined on a basis of adult male votes or on a basis of population (i.e. men, women and children). The latter proposal would have suited the Boers, who had large families, in contrast to the English settlers, who for the most part were unmarried or had not brought their families out because of the unsettled state of the country and the high cost of living. In short, it would require fewer voting Boers than voting Englishmen to elect a member. Thus a constituency of 20,000, predominantly Boer, might only include 3,000 or 4,000 voters, whereas a similar constituency predominantly English might have as many as 10,000 voters; but each constituency would be able to elect only one member. A further inequality would arise, since the English for the most part lived in the towns, where the mining and business was done, while the Boers mostly lived in the country. Thus, as Churchill argued, the English would be paying as much as nine-tenths of the taxes. "Although this may not prove that they should therefore have more voting power, it certainly does not prove that they should have less."

Racialism was confined to the quarrels and different interests of

Dutch and English. No one in South Africa proposed that the coloured man, African or Asian, should have the vote, and in England only a few. It was only to be in a later and more "progressive" age that coloured men irrespective of education or property were to be considered eligible for the franchise under the slogan: one man one vote. Churchill urged the plan which favoured the English under the somewhat obscure slogan: one vote one value. All voters were to have a property qualification of £100 per annum, but it was not proposed that the payment of greater taxation would give more representation. One vote one value was only intended to deal with the balance of the relative populations, thus eliminating the non-voting women and children as the foundation of the constitution.

On February 4, at the specific request of Asquith and with the concurrence of Elgin, Churchill circulated a Cabinet Paper which summarized the reasons that had influenced the decisions of the Cabinet Committee on the Transvaal Constitution. Churchill's summary emphasized the urgency of the matter, and pressed for an early decision and elections along the new lines, not only because the people of the Transvaal were getting increasingly impatient but also "because the difficulties of the House of Commons situation may be considerable, if His Majesty's Government are forced for a prolonged or indefinite period to be *responsible* for the day-to-day administration of the Chinese Labour Ordinance, with its various objectionable features and possible recurrence of improper incidents. Time is therefore a factor which must powerfully influence, if indeed it should not govern, Cabinet policy."

The Cabinet accepted this advice and decided on February 8 to grant the Transvaal self-government at an early date: this implied months, rather than years. Smuts sailed back to South Africa two days later and the Cabinet's decision was announced in the Speech from the Throne on February 19.

A legend has been fostered by Smuts and his biographers of the role he played in persuading the Liberal Government to reverse the Lyttelton constitution and to grant the Transvaal immediate responsible self-government, and, more especially, of the influence Smuts is said to have exercised over the Prime Minister. There is no doubt that Smuts conducted his campaign with skill, subtlety and pertinacity

— that was why Botha had sent him over — and that his arguments would certainly have appealed to the liberal, non-Imperialist sympathies of Campbell-Bannerman. Nevertheless, it would be disingenuous to suppose that the Cabinet's decision was arrived at without a close scrutiny of all the facts as marshalled for its benefit, in particular by Churchill who was the prime mover on the British side in this matter.

Although the principle of responsible government had now been accepted the Cabinet had still to decide on the details of the constitutions for the two colonies — no easy matter as far as the Transvaal was concerned. Suffrage, the size and number of constituencies and similar technicalities had created such controversy in the Transvaal that the Government decided to send out a committee of enquiry, under Sir Joseph West Ridgeway, a former soldier and administrator who had unsuccessfully stood as Liberal candidate for the City of London at the general election. The Committee left for South Africa in April 1906 and spent some two months in the country hearing the views of the different factions and seeking to secure compromises from them so that a constitution might be formulated which would be acceptable to Boer and Briton and yet ensure a British majority in the legislature.

Eager though he was for self-government in the Transvaal, Churchill also feared that, with a Boer majority, capital in South Africa would take flight and all the fruits of the war would be lost. Churchill's fears were now fortified by Lord Selborne, High Commissioner in the Transvaal:

Lord Selborne to WSC

EXTRACT

Government House
2 March 1906   Johannesburg

. . . I am in deep anxiety as regards the effect of the period of suspense. . . . What will happen in the interval heaven only knows?

The capitalists will suffer, but I do not care for them. But the population which I do care for and cherish, miners, artisans and trading and labouring classes, will suffer quite terribly. Already the

Banks are calling in all over-drawn accounts and are everywhere
pressing for money that is lent. Everywhere work is being shut down;
building operations are being stopped, and artisans and clerks are
every day being turned off. This is not a funny picture; it is one of
very real danger and distress. The reason is that capital is frightened;
the future is unsettled. . . .

Churchill was of the same opinion. He wrote a Colonial Office
minute on March 15 addressed to Lord Elgin:

I fear the effects of delay in deciding the fundamentals of the Transvaal Constitution. It causes uncertainty to pervade all classes and
both races, not only in the Transvaal, but throughout South Africa.
. . . The fact which glares me in the face is that a six months' delay
in settling the fundamentals of the Constitution will, through economic pressure and political uncertainty, drive many British voters
from the Transvaal, and alienate from the Mother Country the af-
fections of the rest.

The Ridgeway Committee presented its report in July and by and
large its recommendations were accepted by the British Government.
By July 31 Churchill was able to outline in a major speech to Parliament the constitution which was to be granted to the Transvaal. The
principle of one vote one value was to be upheld; but as a concession
to the Boers the property qualification was to be abolished and universal white male suffrage was to be instituted. Churchill refused to
speculate as to the result of the election that was to be held on the
basis of the new franchise early the following year; but he did express
the hope that it might lead to a coalition government under some
moderate leader. There was, he declared, no dispute between Government and Opposition as to whether responsible government should
be granted to the Transvaal (and to the Orange River Colony) but
only as to when. And he concluded by urging the Opposition
to end their wranglings over South African affairs:

We are prepared to make this settlement in the name of the Liberal
Party. That is sufficient authority for us; but there is a higher
authority which we should earnestly desire to obtain. I make no
appeal, but I address myself particularly to the right honourable

gentlemen who sit opposite, who are long versed in public affairs, and not able to escape all their lives from the heavy South African responsibility. They are the accepted guides of a party which, though in a minority in this House, nevertheless embodies nearly half the nation. I will ask them seriously whether they will not pause before they commit themselves to violent or rash denunciations of this great arrangement. I will ask them, further, whether they will not consider if they cannot join with us to invest the grant of a free Constitution to the Transvaal with something of a national sanction. With all our majority we can only make it the gift of a Party; they can make it the gift of England. And if that were so, I am quite sure that all those inestimable blessings which we confidently hope will flow from this decision will be gained more surely and much more speedily; and the first real step taken to withdraw South African affairs from the arena of British Party Politics, in which they have inflicted injury on both political Parties and in which they have suffered grievous injury themselves.

The Liberal Government proposals were, however, bitterly attacked by the Unionists. Balfour described them as "the most reckless experiment ever tried in the development of a great colonial policy," and predicted that the Dutch would only use their votes as a substitute for arms: his speech was characterized by Campbell-Bannerman as the most unworthy he had heard in his entire Parliamentary career.

Churchill's speech moved his old friend Ian Hamilton to write an appreciative and revealing letter:

General Ian Hamilton to WSC

EXTRACT

Headquarters
Southern Command

2 August 1906
Private

My dear Winston,

I cannot let you off a letter of congratulation (which however I beg you on no account to think of answering) on the occasion of your brilliant and moving speech on Tuesday night. No other thing that has happened lately has given me so much pleasure for, as a staunch upholder of your genius, I have, during the last two months had to begin again my arguments with numerous people supposed to be more or less your friends, as to the possibilities of your failure. I feel now that the last bad corner has been turned, and that those who a week ago were busy shaking their heads over your supposed decline will now be amongst the most eager to applaud. . . .

*

An unusual friend whom Churchill made at this time was Arnold Maurice de Forest, known as Tuty. He was born Bischoffsheim in 1879 and was the adopted son of the Austrian Jewish banker Baron Hirsch. He was educated at Eton and Christ Church. A hereditary baron of the Austrian Empire, he received the royal authority to use the title of Baron in the United Kingdom in 1900, and in that same year entered the Prince of Wales Militia as a 2nd Lieutenant, in which rank he served until 1906. In 1900 he married Ethel Catherine Hannah, the only daughter of the second Baron Gerard. Churchill had known her since she was a little girl and her father and mother were "great friends of his." In 1910 de Forest unsuccessfully contested Southport as a Liberal and in 1911 was elected for West Ham North, which he represented until 1918. He served as a temporary Lieutenant Commander in the RNVR attached to the Royal Naval Armoured Car Force in 1914. Churchill had also known the Baron since his childhood — they had played together as children at Newmarket, and Churchill had visited him at Baron Hirsch's house in Paris in 1880. He spent eight or nine days in the autumn of 1906 at de Forest's castle in Austria, and during Churchill's by-election at Manchester in 1908 de Forest and his wife stayed with Churchill at the Midland Hotel.

De Forest pursued a tenacious friendship with Lloyd George and Churchill. As well as being a visitor to de Forest's many houses, Churchill often cruised in his yacht *Honor*. He was pugnacious in his defence against the many calumnies to which de Forest was subjected. When in 1909 the Gerard family turned against de Forest and began to spread disagreeable rumours about him in Southport, de

Forest wished to withdraw his candidature, but Churchill persuaded him to stay. "I told him he would do himself a great deal of harm if he ran away and left the constituency to the Labour movement; that when a man embarked upon a fight he must go through with it to the end."

In 1911 de Forest's friends were embarrassed and his enemies amused when he sued his mother-in-law for slander. The sole witness he called against Lady Gerard was Lord Derby; and to get his evidence he had to subpoena him. Derby's memory seemed inadequate to support the Baron's allegations and although de Forest was represented in court by four KCs — Sir Edward Clarke, Mr Astbury, Mr Hemmerde and F. E. Smith — the case collapsed before luncheon. Lloyd George, Smith and Churchill were more than once disconcerted by having de Forest's candidature for clubs vigorously contested by other members.

In 1914, simultaneously with his being gazetted as a Lieutenant Commander, rumours were put about that de Forest had sneered at Britain's "little victory" off Heligoland, it being stated that his sympathies were "entirely with the Germans." This information was placed before the Public Prosecutor together with a statement that he held "vast estates" — about 44,000 acres — in Moravia. De Forest enlisted Churchill's help in this matter, pointing out that he had put his Austrian castle at the disposal of the Red Cross, that at the outbreak of war he had given £1000 "in response to a personal appeal from the Prince of Wales on the eve of the public opening of his fund," that he offered his new house at Coombe both to the Red Cross and the War Office, that he had offered his yacht as a hospital ship and his house at Stratford as a recruiting station, as well as sending his name to the War Office for active service "in spite of my not very robust health." Churchill helped de Forest to clear his name by writing to the Public Prosecutor on 29 September 1914: "I am satisfied of Baron de Forest's loyalty and sense of duty, tho' it is clear at times he has talked loosely and argumentatively. He has been ordered to join at Dunkirk on next Saturday." The charges against the Baron were dropped.

In 1932 de Forest was naturalized a citizen of Liechtenstein whose principal diplomatic counsellor he became four years later. He is now Count de Bendern and a Counsellor of State to the Principality of Liechtenstein.

While Churchill was having a much-needed holiday on de Forest's yacht off Deauville, and spending the afternoons playing polo he wrote to the King explaining how he intended that the Transvaal Constitution should work. So far as we know he had no secretary with him; but this did not deter him from setting down and drafting in his own hand a holograph letter of 35 octavo pages, of which he then made a fair copy. The whole business can hardly have taken him less than four or five hours. Both this, and a slightly shorter letter Churchill wrote to the King later in August from Sir Ernest Cassel's villa in Switzerland, are to be found in full in the appropriate Companion Volume. Reviewing the session, Churchill told the King:

WSC to the King
(Royal Archives)

EXTRACT

15 August 1906   Deauville

. . . I hope I may venture to say that the session that is now over has been full of difficulties to me. All S. African business in the House of Commons has been left entirely in my hands. I have had to speak more than any other minister except Mr Birrell [on the Education Bill] & to answer something like 500 questions, besides a great number of supplementary questions put & answered on the spur of the moment. I have had no previous experience in this kind of work. I have had a new & unfathomed House of Commons to deal with in respect of subjects upon which it is strangely excited; & at least four perfectly separate currents of opinion to consider. If therefore I have from time to time turned phrases awkwardly, or not judged quite the right time or tone, I feel certain that Your Majesty will have put the most favourable construction upon my words & will have credited me throughout with loyal & grave intentions. . . .

Churchill went on to recall how at the beginning of the Session in February the King had impressed upon him the importance of the principle of "One vote one value." "I have always felt," Churchill went on, "that the British population would have felt themselves deserted if that point had been abandoned. Yet the arguments against it were not easy to meet. When Parliament met certainly the prevailing opinion in the Liberal Party was for the population basis; and that opinion was reflected in the Cabinet. With Lord Elgin's permission, however, I took it upon myself to make a speech in May [actually that made on April 5] in the House of Commons affirming the principle of 'one vote one value' and explaining all the arguments in its favour; and this was very well received by the House and confirmed next day by the Prime Minister. The principle was never subsequently in dispute."

In order to obtain general acquiescence. for this principle, however, Churchill had to abandon the franchise of £100 annual value and replace it with white adult male suffrage. But he pointed out that the difference between £100 franchise and manhood suffrage was insignificant. "It looks ponderous. It is in fact a feather weight." Churchill estimated that the difference at election time would be perhaps a gain to the Boers of two doubtful constituencies. Churchill was conscious that the King's principal anxiety was that the Transvaal Constitution might result in a Boer victory at the elections and in the extinction of the British element in South Africa, and perhaps even in another war. On the elections, Churchill quoted the forecast made by Sir West Ridgeway, that there would be a British majority of possibly nine, and certainly five. He assumed that Sir Richard Solomon, the present Lieutenant Governor, would be the first Prime Minister. He did, however, go on to discuss the possibility of there being so narrow a majority for either the British or the Boer parties that there might have to be a Coalition; again he expected the pro-British Sir Richard Solomon to be the Prime Minister. "The third alternative — namely a clear racial Boer majority — is outside the bounds of possibility." Nevertheless he told the King that "even in that impossible contingency, there seems no reason to apprehend evil consequences. Such an administration would be subject to too many restraints from an opposition united and almost equal to it in strength, from the Second Chamber, from the general power of the High Commissioner, and from the powerful currents of public opinion in England to embark on any dangerous or revolutionary course."

Ponsonby, the King's assistant Private Secretary, wrote back on behalf of the King from Marienbad, where the King was taking the cure. The King it seems was less sanguine than Churchill as to the future of the Transvaal. "The King knows you will agree with him that it will be deplorable to run the risk of another war in South Africa or of losing this Colony when we have spent so much blood and money. . . . So long as you bear this in mind and are careful to maintain British preponderance" — in the typed draft in the Royal Archives the word was "supremacy" — "you may rest assured that any measures that his Government may take for the welfare of South Africa will receive his Majesty's approval." The King expressly added, in his own hand-writing, the words italicized here: "His Majesty is glad to see that you are becoming a *reliable* Minister and above all a serious politician, *which can only be obtained by putting country before Party.*"

*

It had been obvious from the earliest days after the end of the Boer War that one effective way of reinforcing the British position in South Africa would be to encourage British emigrants to settle there. After the war Milner had hoped to attract up to 10,000 British families, but in the event only some 1,500 had gone to the Transvaal and the Orange River Colony. "The Cabinet," as Churchill wrote to the King in his second letter, dated August 20, from the Villa Cassel in Switzerland, "had fully recognised their responsibility towards the settlers who are already planted." But they were not anxious to encourage new settlers, such colonization being against the declared principles of most Liberals. To help the existing settlers Churchill therefore proposed a Land Board under the High Commissioner, but quite independent of the local government — "as it were a private corporation" — a "screen" between mortgagor and mortgagee which would ensure for the settler "not only a sympathetic administration but full security for such administration."

Such a board, specifically designed to foster the settlement of people of one race might be expected to arouse "antagonism and resentments" in the other. To overcome this Churchill hit upon an ingenious plan, originally suggested to him by Smuts, which he caused to be placed before the Cabinet in a paper printed on 24 July 1906. The plan, as he explained to the King, was: "That we should forgive the 30 millions (of pounds) war contribution for which Mr Chamberlain obtained a sort of promise, in consideration of a new loan of a much smaller sum being raised to be spent not in relief of the British taxpayer but upon certain Colonial objects agreeable to both races in S. Africa, & in which the Imperial Government takes a lively interest — namely Land Settlement & rural development generally & also the payment of certain vy hard cases of war compensation for which the Boers have clamoured."

If, say, £3 million of new money (Land Settlement already had had £3 million, £2½ million of which had been spent) were to be devoted half to Land Settlement and half to compensating Boers for their claims for war losses, "Parity of advantage between the two races would be achieved. . . . One Colonial horse," he explained in his Cabinet paper, "will pull the other along, and the generous action of the Imperial Government will encourage both." But Churchill warned the King: "There are great difficulties in the way of this plan. . . . If it fails, we must be content with something more modest and less attractive."

So it turned out. In the end Churchill had to be content with a Land Board, set up under the Governor for five years only — and at the end of that period the Land Settlement administration was in fact quietly transferred to the Governments of the Transvaal and the Orange Free State. As for Churchill's plans for financing it, they too came to nothing: the war contribution was indeed remitted, but the settlers had to make do as best they could with the funds then available for Land Settlement.

*

On 6 December 1906 the new Transvaal constitution was promulgated by Letters Patent — an administrative device which avoided the need for a Bill and therefore for approval by the Lords. The general election took place in the Transvaal on 20 February 1907. The Boer party Het Volk emerged with a majority of five in a legislative assembly of 69, and Botha the party leader was invited to form a government. Churchill and most opinion in London were proved wrong.

The advance of the Orange River Colony followed swiftly. Letters Patent granting a constitution similar to the Transvaal's were issued on 5 June 1907 and in November of that year — in accordance with expectations — the Orangia Unie carried 30 out of 38 seats in the general election. Thus some five years after the two sovereign Boer republics, the Transvaal and the Orange River Colony, had surrendered, both had regained — not complete independence certainly, but virtual self-government. To add to the irony was the fact that the former Boer Commander-in-Chief, Louis Botha, was now Prime Minister of the Transvaal.

In long-term retrospect it seems strange that no one on either side, Boer or British, Liberal or Tory, foresaw any racial issue between black and white. The racial issue was limited to Boer and British. After all, George III and Lord North had made no provision for the Redskins of North America when General Burgoyne capitulated at Saratoga in 1776. It has only been in much later times that it has been thought desirable and profitable to accord the franchise to people who cannot read or write. And it is too early yet to say whether a democracy of illiterates will prosper.

In this context the views of Churchill, who by 1906 may be said to have approximated in most matters to those of the Radical wing of the Liberal Party, are of interest. He explained them fully in a debate held on 28 February 1906 in the House of Commons on a motion demanding the recognition of Britain's Imperial responsibility towards the native races:

> If there be added the perceptible hardening against the native which is characteristic of the Milner regime, while I say there is no reason for immediate apprehension, I am bound to add that this aspect of South African affairs contains elements which require stern and patient attention. In the presence of such an issue all the harsh discordance which divide the European population in South Africa vanish. Farmer and Capitalist, Randlord and miner, and Boer,

Briton and Afrikaaner forget their bitter feuds and are all united in the presence of what they regard as the greatest peril which they will ever have to face. Even during the worst stresses of the war it was regarded as a nameless crime on either side to set the black man on his fellow foe. I would ask the House to remember for one moment the figures of the South African census. . . . In the United States the proportion of white men to natives is 8 to 1 and even there I believe there is something sometimes approaching to racial difficulties but in South Africa the proportion is one white man to five natives. I ask the House to remember the gulf which separates the African negro from the immemorial civilisation of India and China. The House must remember these things in order to appreciate how the colonists feel towards that ever swelling sea of dark humanity upon which they with all they hate and all they love float somewhat uneasily. . . . This black peril, as it is called in the current discussion of the day, is surely as grim a problem as any mind could be forced to face. Yet it is the one bond of union between the European races who live in the country, the one possibility of making them forget the bitter and senseless feuds that have so long prevailed; and which may have led the people of South Africa to look with a real feeling of self-restraint and comfort to the armed forces of the British Crown.

But Churchill went on to promise the House:

We will endeavour as far as we can to advance the principle of equal rights of civilised men irrespective of colour. We will encourage as far as may be in our power a careful, patient discrimination between the different classes of coloured men. We will not — at least I will pledge myself — hesitate to speak out when necessary if any plain case of cruelty or exploitation of the native for the sordid profit of the white man can be proved. Above all, we will labour to secure as far as we can a proper status for our Indian fellow subjects, and to preserve those large reservations of good, well watered land where the African aboriginal, for whom civilisation has no chance, may dwell secluded and at peace.

It is, in fact, virtually certain that the Liberals could not have gone further than this without completely alienating the Boers. In any case, one must bear in mind that though South Africa is today no longer in the Commonwealth, the South African settlement was durable by most standards, and the reconciliation which the Liberals sought to establish was in fact achieved. Both the British and a majority of Boers were loyal to the Empire in two world wars. It is true that in 1914 their appetites were whetted by German South-West Africa; but in 1939 there were nothing but intangible bonds, a common Empire and throne, evoked by the prestige of Smuts, to bring them in.

The settlement paved the way for the unification of South Africa in 1910 and the inestimable economic advantages that that brought to the country. We may conclude therefore that Campbell-Bannerman was not exaggerating when he wrote to Churchill that the Transvaal Constitution represented "not only the greatest achievement of this government but the finest and noblest work of the British power in recent times."

There was, however, one unfortunate legacy. Churchill had incurred the deep hostility of the Tories because of some remarks he made about Milner. The events are almost forgotten today, but because they are essential to an understanding of Churchill's future career, they will here be recorded at some length.

*

To meet the demand for unskilled labour in the Rand goldmines the previous Government had in 1904 authorized the recruitment of coolies from China. By 1906 some 50,000 were employed in the mines. They were imported on a three-year contract without their families. They were not allowed to settle in the country, they were confined to compounds on the mine companies' land, and they were frequently subjected to corporal punishment. These harsh conditions led to vigorous protests from Radicals and humanitarian groups in Britain. The cry of "Chinese slavery" became a feature of the Liberal election campaign, Campbell-Bannerman pledging his party to end the system.

On February 19, on the address on the King's speech, Chamberlain held up posters which, he alleged, had been distributed by the Liberal Party in various constituencies during the election in which his party had been soundly trounced. The posters caricatured Chinamen, not only in a state of slavery but also being subjected to horrible torture.

> I do not think that in any case it would be in very good taste to circulate them in the course of a political fight, and I do not think it was in very good taste that gentlemen should have on their platforms men dressed as Chinese chained together. That is a matter of opinion; but I understand that the gentlemen who provided all this literature do not now feel inclined to justify it.

Whatever may have been the attitude of the electorate on the Chinese issue, there is no doubt that there were Radical spokesmen who felt more keenly about it than they did about anything else. Quoth Herbert Paul, the Radical member for Northampton — the ancient citadel of men like Bradlaugh and Labouchere:

> What excited such intense indignation about Chinese labour in this country was the fact that it was the sign and symbol of that gigantic swindle, that colossal fraud, the policy of the late Government in South Africa. Five and a half years ago the people of this country were humbugged and deceived. In Lord Milner's happy phrase, they were drenched with lies; but their eyes were open now to the fact that the policy of the late Government was engineered in South Africa by blood-thirsty money grubbers mostly of foreign extraction, without honour, without conscience, without country, without God.

The bitterness of Tory feeling in the matter, doubtless envenomed by speeches such as Paul's, persuaded them to move an amendment to the Address on the King's Speech which could be brought to a vote. The Opposition amendment, which was debated in the House on February 22, regretted "that your Majesty's ministers should have brought the reputation of this country into contempt by describing the employment of Chinese indentured labour as slavery, whilst it is manifest from the tenor of your Majesty's gracious Speech that they are contemplating no effectual method of bringing it to an end."

As Under-Secretary at the Colonial Office it fell to Churchill to resist the amendment. It was fortunate for him and the Government that he at least had been most scrupulous in his handling of the issue during the election campaign. Churchill said:

I took occasion during the election to say, and I repeat it now, that the conditions of the Transvaal Ordinance under which Chinese Labour is now being carried on do not, in my opinion, constitute a state of slavery. A labour contract into which men enter voluntarily for a limited and for a brief period, under which they are paid wages which they consider adequate, under which they are not bought or sold and from which they can obtain relief on payment of seventeen pounds ten shillings, the cost of their passage, may not be a healthy or proper contract, but it cannot in the opinion of His Majesty's Government be classified as slavery in the extreme acceptance of the word without some risk of terminological inexactitude.

This celebrated example of polysyllabic humour was always to be misunderstood and to be regarded as a mere substitute for "lie" which it plainly was not intended to be.

After summarizing in reasonably objective terms how the situation had arisen, Churchill proceeded to explain the Government's future policy. Abe Bailey, in a letter to Churchill, dated 8 January 1906 ("I wish you every success Winston and my prediction may come true that one day you will be Prime Minister of England") had warned him: "If you good people do stop Chinese in any way there will be a panic. This could extend through SA." Now Churchill told the House: "I cannot but doubt that the sudden and arbitrary deportation of a third of the labour supply of South Africa would produce an utter economic collapse. We need not waste our sympathy upon the Rand magnates ... but to thousands of small people ... there might come the harsh and unexpected pinch of poverty and suffering." The system was therefore to be ended gradually, and the Government had hopes that the Colony's inhabitants would themselves co-operate, first because the representative Transvaal Assembly which was to be set up as a result of the new Constitution was expected to decide against the extension and perhaps for the ending of the system, and secondly, because the mine-owners themselves were getting disenchanted with the use of Chinese labour and were likely to concentrate on developing methods of mechanization. Meanwhile, however, the Government would take steps to improve the lot of the Chinese labourer. It would in future prevent fines, collective punishments and criminal penalties being imposed for non-criminal offences, and all trials were to be held in open court. Above all, the Government would "undercut cruelty" by subsidizing repatriation. "The spectacle of the Chinaman wandering over the veldt, his hand against every man and every man's hand against him, with half the world between him and his home in China, is as degrading, hideous, and pathetic as any this civilised and Christian nation has made itself responsible for in modern years. At any rate, that spectacle is gone, and gone for ever. The Chinese are free to be free."

Lord Percy, Churchill's former fellow Hooligan, thought it must have been painful for Churchill to be driven to describing the oratorical efforts of some of his colleagues as "terminological in-exactitudes." But it was Chamberlain who, in winding up, clashed directly with Churchill. "How did the Under-Secretary for the Colonies begin his speech yesterday? 'The conditions do not in the opinion of His Majesty's Government' — it is the whole Government now — 'constitute a state of slavery.' What do they constitute? To call it slavery is 'a terminological inexactitude.' That is English as she is wrote at the Colonial Office. Eleven syllables, many of them of Latin or Greek derivation, when one good English word, a Saxon word of a single syllable, would do! But it is quite sufficient."

Then Chamberlain returned to his charge about Chinese slavery posters at the election. "Does anyone mean to tell me," he asked, "that the speech delivered by the Under-Secretary yesterday, or the speech delivered by the Chancellor of the Exchequer [Asquith] today would have gained seats?" (Cries of "certainly") "They would not have gained a single vote."

Hansard continued, reporting the debate of February 22:

> CHURCHILL retorted that the words he used in his speech were almost word for word those he had used in his election at Manchester.
>
> CHAMBERLAIN: And what you said under those circumstances in the election at Manchester did not gain you any votes. What did gain the honourable gentleman votes was the production of these posters and placards, and the parading of every street in his constituency by a gang of men dressed as Chinamen and accompanied by some agent got up as a slave-driver.
>
> CHURCHILL called this statement imaginative but untrue.
>
> CHAMBERLAIN: The incident owes nothing to my imagination. I

sympathise with the Under-Secretary because he had to make that speech yesterday. He had, in effect, to tell his followers that they had all been on the wrong line, that they had all been misinformed, that the charge they had made was only an inexactitude.

And then Chamberlain, speaking about the proposed repatriation of Chinese labour, introduced a new allegation.

When honourable gentlemen opposite speak of "Magnates" they always appear to think of some persons who are not creditable acquaintances, and who live in palaces, mostly in Park Lane. But when this change is to be made, whom do the Government consult? I am assured that the terms of this alteration were submitted to the magnates before they were submitted to the House of Commons.

This brought both Asquith and Campbell-Bannerman to their feet. "There is no truth in it whatsoever," said Asquith. And Campbell-Bannerman asked:

Do I understand that the right honourable gentleman makes the explicit statement that the details of the policy which the Government have, through the Under-Secretary and through the Chancellor of the Exchequer, explained to the House were first submitted to some unknown person or persons or "magnates" living more or less in Park Lane?

CHAMBERLAIN: You called them magnates. At the least the Chancellor of the Exchequer did so.

CAMPBELL-BANNERMAN: I quote the words of the right honourable gentleman — magnates living more or less in Park Lane. I may say at once that to my knowledge there is not a word of truth in it. I think we are entitled to ask the right honourable gentleman not so much for the particular names concerned, but what is his authority for a statement which has not the slightest foundation in truth.

CHAMBERLAIN: I shall be happy to make further enquiries. My statement is of course not that every single thing that has been said was communicated in writing to anybody. That is not my statement. But substantially they were made aware of the principal reforms or alterations intended by the Government, and I am also informed that they were quite content.

CAMPBELL-BANNERMAN: Who are they?

CHAMBERLAIN: The representatives of the mining interests on the Rand. I refuse to name.

CAMPBELL-BANNERMAN: I say there is not a word of truth in it.

In Churchill's papers may be found two interesting postscripts to this debate. First there is a memorandum prepared by Churchill, evidently for the benefit of the Prime Minister, dealing with Chamberlain's references to consultation with Park Lane magnates. Dated the day after, February 24, this memorandum begins by pointing out that since taking office he had, with Elgin's full consent, made it his business to see "persons representative of every class, section, and interest in South Africa," and that he had discussed the proposals to repatriate coolies with "two of the most prominent representatives on either side of the Chinese question, whom I knew personally"— Frederick Creswell, who had appeared on a platform with him at Manchester, and Alfred Beit, the great financier, who had formerly been a friend of his father's and whose London address was Park Lane. "I do not know," Churchill concluded his memorandum, "how the right honourable gentleman for West Birmingham was led to the belief that "the terms of this alteration were submitted to the magnates before they were submitted to the House of Commons." I presume he must have overheard some private conversation, and learned in confidence that I had made such an enquiry, or in some way caught the tail end of some drifting gossip about a plan for repatriation which was being considered by the Government; and that thereupon he thought it proper to assert that the Government had submitted their proposals to the Mining magnates; and that he hoped to gain some advantage by making the allegation on the verge of an important division."

The following day Churchill received a memorandum from his friend Jack Seely which sought to shed some light on how Chamberlain had obtained his information. Seely stated that at a chance meeting between Churchill, Lord Percy and himself about ten days before, Churchill, in the course of conversation about the repatriation of the Chinese, told Percy: "Well, it's true that the mine people don't seem particularly frightened at this proposal."

The Prime Minister took a detached and somewhat Olympian view of this little storm.

Sir Henry Campbell-Bannerman to WSC

25 February [1906]   10 Downing Street

Dear Churchill,

   I remain of opinion that it is better to leave this matter alone, unless the newspapers tomorrow revive it, or J.C. (or some one else of importance) attempts to raise it again. I do not think this likely.

   As it is, he stands badly before the public, & we may leave it there safely.

                                                        Yours
                                                        H C B

Churchill was perhaps even more concerned to rebut Chamberlain's charge that he had gained votes in North-West Manchester by putting up Chinese slavery posters and by parading in every street in his constituency a gang of men dressed up as Chinamen. Churchill, it will have been seen, had immediately denied the allegation, and he was reassured by a letter which Mr Birdsall, the chairman of his "Literature Committee," wrote the following day. This stated that *"not a poster or placard* having any reference whatever, either directly or indirectly, to Chinese Labour was issued by us in the North-West division of Manchester. We purposely and assuredly refrained from doing anything of the kind." Churchill wrote to Chamberlain on February 26: "I was sure at the moment that your statement was wholly without foundation, and I have confirmed my opinion by most careful enquiry at Manchester. In these circumstances I have no doubt you would wish to withdraw an assertion which is at once prejudicial and quite untrue."
   Chamberlain replied:

Joseph Chamberlain to WSC

1 March 1906   40 Prince's Gardens

Dear Winston,

   I have now received replies to the enquiries which I addressed to N.W. Manchester on the subject of your note of Feb 26.

   I find that I was mis-informed as to the action taken in your Division in reference to the question of Chinese Labour, and that no mock Chinamen paraded in your constituency although they appear to have been present in some neighbouring Divisions.

As regards posters, Mr Gibbons, Hon Secretary of the Conservative Club, Cheetham Hill Road, states that a large placard representing a gang of Chinamen manacled was posted outside the Tower Liberal Club, Cheetham, and also at the Committee Rooms Cheetham Hill Road. This, however, does not justify the statements previously made to me & I unhesitatingly withdraw the answer which I made to your interruption in the House of Commons, and regret that I should have repeated a statement which now turns out to be without foundation.

Believe me, Yours very truly

J. CHAMBERLAIN

This, however, was an insignificant skirmish compared with the parliamentary battle that soon followed — the "Milner censure debate."

After eight years as High Commissioner of South Africa and Governor of the Transvaal, Milner had returned to England in May 1905. He had been elevated to the peerage as long ago as 1901, but it was not until 26 February 1906 that he chose to make his maiden speech in the House of Lords.

Milner's long speech, though critical of many aspects of the new Government's South African policy, especially its decision to scrap the Lyttelton constitution and grant immediate self-government to the Transvaal, ended with a passionate disclaimer as to any partisanship: "I have wished not to make a party attack. My desire is to serve our position in South Africa, and not to do anything to injure, to discredit, or to hamper the Government. I am not much of a Party man anyway."

The following day Lord Portsmouth, the Under-Secretary of State for War, startled the House of Lords by inviting Milner to say whether it was true that he had condoned the unauthorized flogging of Chinese coolies. An exchange of correspondence between Milner and the preceding Tory government which led to this conclusion had been published, as a Blue Book, in the previous December but had been strangely ignored during the election campaign.

The documents revealed that towards the end of August 1905 the then Colonial Secretary, Alfred Lyttelton, had been surprised to learn that Chinese labourers had been subjected to corporal punishment in the mines without having been previously convicted by a magistrate or without the sentence having been confirmed by the Supreme Court. Such floggings were not only illegal but had been carried out contrary to undertakings expressly given by the British Government to the Chinese Government and to Parliament. An even more astonishing fact was brought to light: Mr Evans, the late superintendent of foreign labour in the Transvaal who had permitted these illegal floggings, had informed Milner of his action, and had received Milner's sanction for it.

Following Portsmouth's challenge Milner immediately rose and made a full and free confession:

> I fully recognise that I took upon myself the whole responsibility. I think, in the light of subsequent events, that I was wrong, because whatever the drawbacks might have been of not having prompt repression of such offences, abuses might arise from allowing the punishment in any case.

The Radical Press greeted Milner's admission with gusto. "Is it any wonder when an essentially German mind drives English policy that the result is not exactly what the English public look for?" commented the *Speaker*. H. W. Massingham wrote in the same paper: "It is good for a nation to see clearly who are the authors of its misfortunes. It is better still for those men to show themselves for what they are . . . what struck me chiefly about Milner was his essentially un-English character. He has hardly any English characteristics . . . he is a pure bureaucrat and a pure ideologue . . . Lord Milner is an extinct force in our politics; yesterday he spoke for authority, today he is in the wilderness, *bombinans in vacuo*." And the *Manchester Guardian* wrote: "He empties the stale dregs of his war vocabulary on to his public and never, apparently, suspects that what used to excite now merely disgusts." The next day, February 28, Churchill, replying to a debate on the rights of the native races in South Africa, contrasted Milner's "fine professions" with his performances, and remarked ominously: "I should not myself be anxious to be forward in attacking him; but I tell the House most frankly that certainly, as far as I am concerned — and I think I speak for others who sit here — I should not put myself to any undue or excessive exertion to defend Lord Milner from any attacks which might be made upon him." The matter was taken up at Question Time in the

House of Commons on March 14. Churchill, asked by Hilaire Belloc, one of the new Liberal MPs elected for Salford, whether there was any guarantee that Milner did anything illegal at all if they had no record, replied:

> I think my honourable friend will see that there is no doubt what- ever that in authorising illegal punishment of this character at the same time that his official superiors were denying that such punish- ment was being permitted Lord Milner committed a grave dereliction of public duty and at the same time an undoubted infringement of the law.

Belloc was the distinguished poet and satirist. He suffered from an urbane anti-semitism. His gravity as a politician had already been questioned as a result of a privately circulated poem which that literary magpie Margot Asquith was later to print in her Memoirs.

Verses to a Lord who, in the House of Lords, said that those who opposed the South African Adventure confused soldiers with money-grubbers.

> You thought because we held, my lord,
> An ancient cause and strong,
> That therefore we maligned the sword:
> My lord, you did us wrong.
>
> We also know the sacred height
> Upon Tugela Side,
> Where those three hundred fought with Beit
> And fair young Wernher died.
>
> The daybreak on the failing force,
> The final sabres drawn:
> Tall Goltman, silent on his horse,
> Superb against the dawn.
>
> The little mound where Eckstein stood
> And gallant Albu fell,
> And Oppenheim, half blind with blood
> Went fording through the rising flood —
> My Lord, we know them well.

> The little empty homes forlorn,
> The ruined synagogues that mourn,
> In Frankfurt and Berlin:
> We knew them when the peace was torn —
> We of a nobler lineage born —
> And now by all the gods of scorn
> We mean to rub them in.

His sense of fun also betrayed him shortly after the election into a lampoon which made many earnest Liberals feel that he was not a serious politician:

> The accursed power that stands on privilege
> And goes with women and champagne and bridge
> Broke, and democracy resumed her reign
> Which goes with bridge and women and champagne.

These lines seem to have been directed against Asquith.

On March 17 a number of Ministers met at 10 Downing Street to discuss the Government's attitude to the following motion by the Radical member for Salford North, William Byles: "That this House expresses its disapproval of the conduct of Lord Milner as High Commissioner of South Africa and Governor of the Transvaal, in authorising the flogging of Chinese labourers in breach of the law, in violation of treaty obligations, and without the knowledge or sanction of his Majesty's Secretary of State for the Colonies." Among those present at the meeting was Lord Loreburn, who as Sir Robert Reid had been one of the leading pro-Boers in Parliament six years before. It is clear from a letter Loreburn wrote the following day to Churchill that the desire to censure Milner was not confined to the few hot-headed Radical back-benchers.

Lord Loreburn to WSC

EXTRACT

18 March 1906   8 Eaton Square

. . . those whom Milner and his friends have habitually insulted and those who have suffered by the war in this country would be profoundly irritated by anything like *commendation* of Milner. I believe they will be quite willing to refrain from censure, but I am certain they would be restive if they were asked to endorse praise. It is one of the best features of our public life that we are disposed to be generous to opponents. On the other hand there are many of us who believe after close study that Milner has not only been rash but also deceitful and that the more the thing is investigated the more it will appear that he has engineered the war by forcing the hands of foolish ministers. If we lose South Africa it will be almost wholly his doing and his folly or worse that has led to the postponement of social reform for our own poor people at home. He has received honours and incense while ruining South Africa. . . .

Loreburn was writing because at the meeting Churchill had put forward the view that Britain was too great a country, that the Liberal Party's success at the election had been too overwhelming, and that the situation in South Africa was too critical to warrant the Government "engaging in the task of making martyrs." Loreburn accepted this but added that in his view — "and my view is widely held" — Milner would be very generously treated if he was simply exempted from attack. Churchill seems to have had considerable hopes that his moderating influence would prevail, for on the day of the Downing Street meeting he had written to Lord Selborne: "Perhaps before this reaches you something may have been said to allay the anxiety and I must say to improve the temper of our excitable British friends. Such an occasion may perhaps arise on Wednesday night when a motion is to be brought forward censuring Ld Milner for the sanction of illegal flogging. I have I believe persuaded the Govt to allow me to meet this resolution by an amendment deprecating any formal censure of individuals in the interests of peace and reconciliation in SA. It will be a difficult job to persuade the House but I hope I shall be allowed to try."

Evidently Churchill was successful in this project for on the morning of the debate on March 21 he tabled the following amendment:

That this House while recording its condemnation of the flogging of Chinese coolies in breach of the law, desires, in the interests of peace and conciliation in South Africa, to refrain from passing censure on individuals.

Byles's motion was debated in Private Members' time after dinner. This motion itself was well-calculated to excite the feelings of both sides of the House. The atmosphere, however, had already been exacerbated by the debate in the afternoon in which Chamberlain had sought to oppose the passage of the Consolidated Fund Bill until there had been an official enquiry into Chinese labour. This provoked Churchill into one of his most insolent replies to Chamberlain:

> If Chinese Labour is of such importance, what a pity it is that the right honourable gentleman treated it with such levity. Everyone knows that in the debate on the address the right honourable gentleman attacked the policy of the Government, not on the ground that the Government were going too far in what they were doing against Chinese Labour, but he endeavoured to excite censure against the Government on the part of their supporters by representing that they were not going far enough. And he even allowed himself to say that he knew — how he knew I do not investigate — that the mine owners had been consulted on the policy and were perfectly satisfied. Now the right honourable gentleman a member of the City of London [Balfour] has come back refreshed with the latest views of the Stock Exchange.

Balfour on his return to Parliament at a by-election in the City of London had assumed the leadership of the Opposition. Churchill's gibe about the Stock Exchange was a tit-for-tat for what Chamberlain had said about the magnates in Park Lane:

> The right honourable gentleman the member for West Birmingham is now what I believe he once called Lord Hartington, the "late" leader of the Opposition.

He taunted Chamberlain with using the Chinese labour question to inflame first the feelings of Government supporters and then those of the Colonies.

> The right honourable gentleman has contracted deep obligations to this country in respect of South Africa. At his bidding, and on the faith of his instincts and foresight as a statesman, and by the force of the appeals he addressed to the House and the country, this nation and the Empire have made unparalleled sacrifices for South Africa.

No sooner had the war come to an end, and while all the business of settlement was still upon hand, the right honourable gentleman was tired of the South African situation, pushed it away from him as a toy which had ceased to amuse, and embarked at once upon another venture which was as rash and as uncalculated as the first, and the only difference between the two was that whereas the first enterprise of the right honourable gentleman has had the effect of nearly ruining South Africa, the second enterprise has had the effect of politically ruining himself.

Churchill knew it was good tactics to take on the men at the top. First he had been almost as provocative to Balfour as his father had been to Gladstone: now he turned his guns on Chamberlain. It was a favourite adage of his that one should "never make scapegoats out of small fry . . . I have always preferred, like Tarquin, to cut off the heads of the tall poppies."

Balfour remarked during his winding-up speech for the Opposition that Churchill had complained of the shortness of notice Chamberlain had given of his amendment. "I presume that was the reason why he spent most of his speech in a personal attack upon my right honourable friend. That, I am aware, is a form of debate which requires no preparation on the part of the honourable gentleman, or on the part of many of those who sit near him. That is a beverage which is always on tap." And then, pointing to the Government Front Bench, he added: "These gentlemen cannot get accustomed to their places. The time will come when they will learn to put off the garb of opposition which they wore with so much grace for so many years, and to accustom themselves both to the power and to the courtesy which ought to accompany power, when they are put in the possession of a following of 500 — or is it 600? — faithful henchmen."

*

This debate concluded shortly before 7:30 in the evening when the House adjourned for dinner: the evening sitting began at nine o'clock. Byles moved his vote of censure on Milner, and Chamberlain spoke immediately after the motion had been moved and seconded.

Like many great orators, he had the power of cloaking himself in passion which he did not really feel; but there can be no doubt of the sincerity of his feelings in the matter of Milner, whom he regarded not only as a friend but also as one of his staunchest supporters. First he dealt with the motion:

> What, I say, could be more despicable than to attack such a man without the sanction of the highest motive, which the honourable gentleman claimed for himself, and to persecute him for a single error of judgment in a long course of public service? . . . For a single error of judgment, upon this single point, they ask the House to inflict this humiliation on a most distinguished member of our Civil Service. . . . The resolution is retrospective. It is vindictive. Sir, let us have no cant about this matter. We all know, the country knows, that the object of this motion is to inflict humiliation upon a person who is as honest and sincere as any member of this House, but of whose policy honourable members opposite happen to disapprove; and for that and for party reasons they pick up a single point in a long history of self-sacrifice and devotion.

And he quoted the words of Disraeli on a similar occasion in the House of Commons fifty years before: "Great services are not cancelled by one act, by one single error, however it may be regretted at the moment." Then Chamberlain turned his attention to the amendment Churchill had put down on behalf of the Government:

> Sir, it is a cowardly amendment. . . . It is an amendment which insults Lord Milner, and at the same time accepts the substantial part of the resolution of the honourable gentlemen opposite. They think to gain votes by distinctly pointing at Lord Milner, and at the same time withdrawing his name. That is Party tactics; Liberal policy. . . . This amendment is entrusted to the honourable gentleman the [Under-] Secretary for the Colonies. What is the history — I am speaking of recent events — of the connection of the honourable gentleman with this matter? The other day he was asked a question on this matter, and from that almost sacrosanct position which he now occupies he described this action of the High Commissioners as a grave dereliction of duty. Brave words! [*Ministerial cheers*] You

agree? [*Cries of "Entirely" "Yes"*] Why, do not you see that these brave words have very weak conclusions. There is a man in the very highest position in the public service. He has been guilty in your minds and in the minds of the government of grave dereliction of duty and you are going to be satisfied with an empty resolution which, if you succeed in passing it, will be treated with contempt by everyone who has the honour to appreciate the services of Lord Milner. You cannot condemn him in terms of this kind without admittedly laying yourselves open to the charge that you do not believe what you say, for if you do believe it you would impeach him.

CROOKS (Woolwich): I will vote for it if you will move it.

CHAMBERLAIN: I see honourable gentlemen below the gangway appreciate the force of my argument. They would impeach him. They have the right to do it. They would repeat the experiment as in the case of Warren Hastings at heaven knows what cost to the country. . . .

Finally Chamberlain sought to attack Churchill personally:

The honourable gentleman who said Lord Milner had been guilty of grave dereliction of duty said another thing which astonished me and is quite new in official procedure. He said Lord Milner had made a party speech in another place, and that relieved him of any obligation whatever to defend him. Well, I do not think Lord Milner has lost much. But what a statement! The obligation by honourable and long tradition of great offices to defend any public servant who cannot defend himself against unjust or excessive censure is an obligation independent altogether of all party considerations. . . . But even if it had been a party speech, I will say that the honourable gentleman cannot, without a great breach of tradition, absolve himself from the honourable necessity placed upon a political chief to say all that can be said in favour of those who serve the department with which he is concerned.

CHURCHILL: It is not so.

CHAMBERLAIN: It matters very little to such a man — to a man who entertains that view of his own obligations and of Lord Milner's services. I think it is regrettable that, on the present occasion, the representation of the Government should be committed to his hands. I say it is the duty of a head of a department, whoever he may be, to defend the servants of the department.

For the second time that day Churchill followed Chamberlain in debate. "But I hope I shall not be drawn by that association into imitating or attempting to imitate the protracted, superlative, and I think rather laboured exhibition of contempt with which he has occupied the attention of the House," said Churchill in his opening remarks. First he defended Byles's motion. "It embodies a proposition, the truth of which I venture to think very few on this side of the House would care to dispute. It has been moved with sincerity and good feeling in speeches of much ability, delivered under great restraint." And again later he said: "I do not disagree in any way with the terms of the motion as stated by my honourable friend. . . . I admit its truth and admire its moderation. . . . The government have no intention whatever of disparaging the motives which induced the honourable member to place it on the paper." Nor did Churchill retract a single thing that he had said before of Lord Milner's action. "I say that in face of the abuses that grew up from this wicked permission, there has arisen a state of things which makes it impossible to wonder that persons should have been carried away by honest indignation to use the strongest language of condemnation about such a system."

Churchill went on, none the less, to explain why it had been thought right to table the Government's more moderate amendment. He suggested that there was something of the flavour of retrospective retribution in a new House of Commons going back upon events which had occurred under the authority of its predecessor, and, moreover, that it was contrary to right feeling to censure a man unheard. As to Milner, Churchill said, he had worked strenuously, faithfully, and disinterestedly — according to his lights. "Still less can it be denied that during the long period covered by these events, he has played a part which must leave its imprint, for good or for ill, extensively upon the pages of history. I have carefully refrained from passing either censure or eulogy on all or any of these events, not because I am without opinions which at other times I may think or have thought it proper to express — I trust with sufficient clearness — but because I think it would be impossible for us to do justice to his conduct either in the one direction or the other within the compass of a three hours' debate."

And then there followed a passage which for some reason, despite its ostensible fairness to Milner, probably gave more offence to Milner's friends and supporters than anything Churchill had said or done before:

> Lord Milner has gone from South Africa, probably for ever. The public service knows him no more. Having exercised great authority he now exerts none. Having held high employment he now has no employment. Having disposed of events which have shaped the course of history, he is now unable to deflect in the smallest degree the policy of the day. Having been for many years, at any event for many months, the arbiter of the fortune of men who are "rich beyond the dreams of avarice" he is today poor, and I will add honourably poor. After twenty years of exhausting service under the Crown he is today a retired Civil Servant, without pension or gratuity of any kind whatever.

Once more he used the phrase "honourable poverty" which he had already used in his memorandum to the Cabinet on January 30, and which he must have been echoing from Macaulay's famous passage on Warren Hastings. Churchill went on:

> It is not worth while to pursue him any further. . . . This new House of Commons is full of earnest, purposeful and vehement men. Let them not overlook or underrate the vexation and mortification which must be experienced by any vehement and earnest man who sees the ideals, the principles, the policies for which he has toiled utterly discredited by the people of Great Britain and who knows that many of the arrangements in which he has consumed all the energies of his life are about to be reversed or dissolved. Lord Milner has ceased to be a factor in public events.

Churchill warned the House to beware of falling into the same error as the Parliament of 1886 when the Conservative Government "carried away by the exultation of victory" embarked on the persecution of Parnell and the establishment of the Parnell Commission to its own resultant confusion and shame. "The moral which I draw from the Parnell affair — a moral which I think may be drawn also from the conflict of the House of Commons with Mr Bradlaugh in

1880 — is that it is never worthwhile for a great Party to pursue a private person, and least of all when that private person happens also to be a political opponent." The Tories did not much like the mention of Milner and Parnell and Bradlaugh in the same context.

Finally Churchill deployed the arguments which he had put before the meeting of Ministers at 10 Downing Street the week before. He appealed to the Government benches behind him:

> When we have so many real things to do which must be done in the present and in the future, why cannot we leave the past alone? I feel it my duty to say to the House tonight that we believe, having some access to information of authority, that this motion, if accepted, would undoubtedly aggravate social and racial animosity in South Africa. . . . The House of Commons can send a message to South Africa which cannot be perverted, misrepresented, or misunderstood, a message of comfort to a troubled people, a message of tolerance and conciliation to warring races, a message indeed of good hope to the Cape.

Balfour, who followed, characterized Churchill's speech as an extraordinary utterance. He declared: "I think the Under-Secretary and I think the House, have rather forgotten that they are arrogating to themselves the position of an historical judge; they are not dealing with an official but with a man who is no longer an official. They are dealing with transactions that are over. They are attempting to record an historical judgment, and it is in the interests of the House itself certainly not in the interests of Lord Milner, that I would earnestly beg them to reject with equal contempt the original motion and the amendment of the Government by which the Government have attempted to make these proceedings palatable to Lord Milner's friends in South Africa." Although some attempt was made to talk the Debate out and thus to avoid a vote, this was unsuccessful. Byles's motion was negatived without a division and Churchill's amendment was carried by 355 votes to 135.

The Government's action in accepting the principles of Byles's motion without actually naming Milner, and Churchill's speech in particular, incurred the fury of the Tory Press and of influential men and women throughout the country. Sir William Anson, the Warden of All Souls and one of the members for Oxford University, wrote to his fellow University MP J. G. Talbot, from the South of France:

> What a wretched figure the Government made of the Milner debate. They ought surely not to have left the matter in the hands of Winston Churchill who seems to have been both pompous and impertinent.
>
> It is terrible to think what harm that young jackanapes may do with a big majority behind him and an incompetent Prime Minister to look after him.

The King received an angry letter from Churchill's kinswoman, Lady Londonderry, to which he replied from Biarritz: "I quite share your views concerning certain proceedings in the House of Commons, and the conduct of a certain relation of yours is simply scandalous. It is indeed hard on Lord Milner to be treated in such a manner. Alas! nowadays Party comes before country." The King also wrote to Churchill's colleague, Crewe, "It is a pity that Lord Elgin does not seem to be able to control the violent and objectionable language of his Parliamentary Under-Secretary. It has made a painful impression on most people."

Churchill himself thought he was much wronged. He wrote to Selborne on March 24:

WSC to Lord Selborne

EXTRACT

Copy

... I had an anxious day in the House on Wednesday but in the result no harm seems to have been done either to the markets or to the party. That at least is something. I think the South African papers are very ill-natured about the Govt. After all, no other course but the one adopted by me would have prevented Lord Milner from being censured formally by the House of Commons. We interfered to parry the blow and did parry it, much to the disgust of many of our supporters. Surely that fact ought to have received the recognition of South African observers: instead nothing appears but the [angry comments] of the (great) political organisation of the Metropolitan dailies. ...

Selborne replied:

Lord Selborne to WSC

EXTRACT

15 April 1906   In train near Mafeking

. . . As regards the Milner debate, I fully realised that your intention
was to parry the blow aimed at him by his enemies; but if you put
yourself in the place of the South African Britisher, as in your dis-
passionate critical nature you can, you will not be surprised at their
attitude towards HMG. It is true to say that the South African
British as a whole idolise Milner, and to them it is absolutely impossible to conceive how any man can propose any thing in the nature of a vote of censure on him unless he is a traitor. After all men's
minds are made by their own history, not by the history and experience of their relations 6,000 miles away. And the great misfortune
of HMG is that they have tied to their tail a tin can of the metal of
Byles and Herbert Paul, without sense and without taste. The South
African Englishman does not understand English party politics and
he resents the Herbert Pauls' and Byles' venom more than words can
say. . . .

What effect Churchill's speech had on general Boer opinion is not
clear, but in Smuts it aroused a sophisticated but tolerant amusement:

J. C. Smuts to Margaret Clark
(Copy: Smuts Archive)

EXTRACT

23 March 1906   Pretoria

. . . I see our friend Winston is occupying the stage under the full
limelight and that his pity for the Chinese-flogging Milner is no less
Olympian than for the benighted radical who thought the Chinese
indentures partook of the nature of slavery. . . .

In the House of Lords a week later Lord Halifax moved: "That this
House desires to place on record its high appreciation of the services

rendered by Lord Milner in South Africa to the Crown and to the Empire." Many of the great figures in the land, some of them ghosts from Lord Randolph's past, rose one after another to pay tribute to Milner: Goschen, Roberts, Halsbury, Londonderry, Lansdowne — even the Archbishop of Canterbury, Randall Davidson. Many of them could not resist the opportunity of attacking the presumptuous Under-Secretary and comparing his earlier sayings and writings about South Africa in general, and about Milner in particular, with those of the day. The peers ignored the solemn warning of Ripon, that a vote on the motion might provoke a clash with the Commons:

> I have been fifty years in this House, and I have never seen such an attack in language and in form, upon the other House as I have had the misfortune to witness tonight. I do not know what will follow on these proceedings. I hope that nothing will follow from them, but I do say that it is highly undesirable that you should do anything to promote the needless quarrel between the House of Lords and the House of Commons or that you should do anything which is calculated to create what is vulgarly called a "wrangle."

Nine dukes (though not Marlborough who does not seem to have been present) were among the 170 who voted for Halifax's motion. Only 35 peers voted against.

In the course of the next year a public address to Milner was got up and members of the public were invited in *The Times* and the *Morning Post* by a committee headed by the Duke of Somerset to subscribe their names to the address, whimsically, at any of the branches of Messrs W. H. Smith and Son, the monopolists of newspaper distribution in the country. In August the address signed by 370,000 people was presented to Milner and in September 25,000 Cape Colonists signed a similar address — "a fitting and satisfactory conclusion," commented *The Times*.

During the Milner affair Churchill conducted himself with considerable address. Despite the Tory anger which he provoked he had genuinely tried to confine Radical hostility to Milner within reasonable bounds. Though he handled the matter so effectively it would have been well if someone, perhaps Asquith, had taken a hand: not that Churchill ever sought to leave the firing line or pray for aid from his superiors. But in a sense he was ill-placed to make the general criticisms of Milner which circumstances dictated. He had, after all, served in the Boer War; had met Milner and had been much impressed by him; he had been elected as a Tory for Oldham in 1900 in the "khaki election"; Chamberlain had travelled specially from Birmingham to speak on his platform at that election; Churchill's only legitimate grounds for criticism arose from the flogging of the Chinese and from the policies which Milner had planned for South Africa after the war; yet he was forced to assume a much broader basis for criticism.

It is surprising that the Tories did not make more of these points. Yet the issue rankled with them for years. Leo Maxse, and after his death Maxse's sister Violet, who in 1921 had married Milner, pursued Churchill·with an enduring vendetta on all matters with which he was concerned in the columns of the *National Review*.

Primitive tribes need totems, and even the great civilizations of the West have periodically felt the need of heroes who could be elevated far above the ranks of ordinary criticism or clamour. It seems necessary for the salvation or preservation of some creed or cult or policy to grant quasi-royal or sacerdotal mysticism to some individual who enshrines the often half-expressed cravings of a cause. In recent times we have seen such men as Lord Roberts and Lord Kitchener regarded as sacrosanct from criticism, though each was to fail his hero-worshippers in the end. Such a man was Milner. He was cherished all the more by his idolizers because the straightforward Victorian imperialism for which he stood was passing with the turn of the century. The radical upsurge of 1906 seemed fraught with doom to the builders of Empire. Some sacrifice must be made to avenge the falling idol; and who would prove a more serviceable sacrifice than one who had betrayed his class and party and seemed for ever to be lost to the ranks of the levellers. It says much for Churchill's resilience that he survived these hatreds, that he later served in the same government as Milner, that he returned to the Tory fold of which he became the shepherd, that nearly all his life his kinswoman Lady Londonderry invited him to the numerous abodes which her beauty and grace adorned.

*

Campbell-Bannerman had promised to end the Chinese labour system, but this proved easier said than done. Meanwhile alarming stories of "unnatural vice" in the compounds were reaching London. On the last day before the long summer recess, August 4, the Radical member for Newbury, F. C. Mackarness, raised in the House of Commons for the second time in eight weeks what he described as "the horrible moral cancer" which had been introduced into the Transvaal by the "herding together of fifty thousand Chinese of the lowest class without women." He claimed that the population and settlers in the Transvaal were becoming "habituated to practices that had always been held in deepest detestation by our race." As long ago as February 1904, when the introduction of Chinese labour was first mooted, the famous churchman Charles Gore, at that time Bishop of Worcester, had warned of the moral dangers inherent in the scheme. Now Churchill, replying to Mackarness, promised on behalf of the Colonial Office an immediate enquiry into his allegations that unnatural vice was rampant and obvious.

It was not until November that the report of the enquiry by Mr Bucknill came into the hands of the Colonial Office. Parts of the report had leaked out in the Liberal Press, and it was clear that the report fulfilled the liveliest expectations of the most fastidious Liberal opponents of Chinese labour. A demand was made in both Houses of Parliament for the Bucknill report to be published. Churchill told the House of Commons that the Government could not publish the report because the evidence was confidential, markedly conflicting and in any event unprintable. He felt able to deny the allegation that the offences had been tolerated by the Government, the police or the mine leaders, and pointed out that it was very difficult to tell by looking at a Chinaman whether or not he was a catamite. This word, hitherto unknown to most members of the House — in the proofs of *Hansard* it was printed as "malachite" — was most serviceable in a debate in which many MPs felt inhibited in expressing themselves frankly, despite the withdrawal of the ladies from their gallery. This accidental censorship on the part of *Hansard* and the delicacy of the ladies in the gallery was very far removed from the climate of bland toleration towards sodomy and indeed its contemplated legalisation which prevails today.

One thing clearly emerged from the revelations; the pressure to end the use of Chinese labour was bound to increase. So far, despite their condemnation of the system, all that the Government had been able to promise was that no fresh licences would be issued and no more recruitment would be carried out after November 30; and that at the same time every encouragement would be given to repatriating those Chinese who wished to return home. By the end of 1907 over 14,000, many "of them undesirables," left South Africa for China; but the scheme fostered by Churchill for paying the passages of labourers who wanted repatriation ended in what he himself regarded as a "fiasco," only twelve seeking this assistance in the first month. The decision whether or not the system of Chinese labour was to continue on the Rand was to be left to the new Transvaal Assembly after the elections had been held in February.

By the end of November Churchill believed and asserted that no more coolies were coming to South Africa. Early in December it became known that the steamship *Cranley* had left Chin-wang-tao on November 27 with 1,000 coolies aboard. Churchill explained to an agitated House of Commons that this information, which he himself had only gleaned from newspapers, was to him "as unexpected as it was unwelcome." This was nothing to the discovery, on the arrival of the *Cranley* in Durban, that the ship contained not 1,000 but 2,129. Due to an administrative blunder made as long ago as July 1906 licences had been issued for all but 259 of these. Elgin and Churchill were vexed, and it was thought at one time that it would be necessary to repatriate these 259 at a cost, to the Transvaal Government, of at least £12,000. But Churchill — on whom, after all, fell the burden of explaining all this to a restive Radical House of Commons — consented that the coolies need not be repatriated. "I only hope that the guilty 259 will pass undetected," he wrote to Elgin. The incident gave Churchill an opportunity of expressing his view on the question in the course of a long letter to Selborne:

WSC to Lord Selborne

EXTRACT

12 January 1906 [1907]   [Colonial Office]

. . . There is one point upon which there will be no yielding . . . we will not allow any more Chinese coolies, under indenture, to enter

South Africa. Everyone is resolved on that, the most moderate members of the Government, equally with the most extreme members of their party and the resources of the Foreign Office, and if necessary, of the Admiralty will be ruthlessly used to enforce that determination.

Do not, I pray you, allow those people with whom you come in contact to nourish illusions on this subject. Of course it is conceivable that this Govt may be overthrown, but that will not happen for two or three years at least and when it does happen, do you suppose that the Conservative party are going to deprive themselves of all chance of regaining power by announcing their return to office means the renewal of Chinese importation? Already no Conservative speaker attempts to justify the policy.

It is absolutely discredited, it is outside the area of practical politics, even by those who care about it and have suffered most for it. Therefore it behoves the Rand industry to face facts as they are, and to fill the constantly widening gap which the Chinese shrinkage will produce, by a reorganisation of native labour and still more by those attractive Gordon drills [mining instruments] of which we are beginning to hear a good deal. . . .

All this time Churchill had never lost sight of the need to replace Chinese labour. He spoke much of increased mechanization, and for a short while he explored the possibilities of Indians — but quite apart from the shortage of suitable men from India, John Morley, the Secretary of State for India, was unlikely to support this idea. There remained therefore the reservoirs of labour available on the African continent. Churchill's friend Creswell had always believed that white miners could work alongside natives on the Rand, and begged to be given the chance to prove his theory. Churchill actively encouraged him and persuaded J. B. Robinson — one of the most far-sighted of the Rand mine-owners, though by all accounts an unlovable man — to put one of his mines at Creswell's disposal, where 40 per cent of the miners would be white. Robinson was also eager to play a much more important part in securing alternative labour for the mines. Churchill had not by any means been convinced that it was impossible to obtain more native (or kaffir, as it was called) labour in the South African colonies. He believed that part of the trouble lay in the fact that the Rand mine-owners, through the Witwatersrand Native Labour Association, enjoyed a monopoly in the recruitment of labour. Moreover, he felt that the search for native labour outside the colonies — in particular in Portuguese East Africa — might be prosecuted with greater vigour by an employer who was not dependent on the W.N.L.A. Again, Robinson was the man for Churchill, who gave him every sort of official encouragement, and Selborne, Elgin, even Campbell-Bannerman were persuaded to view Robinson's efforts with favour. But in the end nothing came of these schemes. Employment of white labour at the mines was always to be dependent on the recruitment of additional native labour. As to breaking the W.N.L.A. recruiting monopoly, Robinson found himself squeezed by the other Rand mine-owners who threatened to expel him from their Association and who proved more powerful than the British Government in persuading the Portuguese authorities to deny him adequate facilities for recruiting in Portuguese East Africa.

The Transvaal elections which took place on 20 February 1907 led, as we have seen, to the formation of a Boer government. The results astonished Churchill and most other people who had given the matter their attention. Instead of the British having, as Churchill had predicted, a minimum majority of five, it was the Boer Het Volk Party that had an overall majority of five. None the less, Churchill's prediction that in the event of this "quite impossible happening" taking place the British would be able to keep their heads above water was proved true. Henceforward the Transvaal Government, under General Botha, was responsible for the Chinese problem which proved progressively less vexatious. Of some 60,000 Chinese half were repatriated between June 1907 and June 1908, and the remainder by 1910. The difficulties of recruiting native labour did not prove as insuperable as many had supposed.

Thus, in the space of a year, Churchill had, so far as the British Government was concerned, disposed of two of its most difficult problems — the Transvaal constitution and Chinese labour. At the turn of the year he was only thirty-two; it was a sure-footed performance for one who heretofore had lacked all ministerial and administrative experience.

Churchill could indeed look back with satisfaction on his part in settling South Africa's political problem. The urgency and assiduity of his work, the cogency of his arguments, the extent to which, with the apparent approval of his chief Lord Elgin and of the Cabinet, he rapidly assumed mastery of the task and virtually command of its execution, must excite the envy of any latter-day Under-Secretary of State. Though with added experience his powers were to mature, it may be concluded that already at the age of thirty-two he was a fully equipped statesman. He knew how to get to the core of the matter, he knew how to express himself in lucid and compelling language, and he knew how to get things done. His over-mastering ambition and his prodigious powers of work and concentration seemed, although he was in a junior situation, to dominate everything he touched. His parliamentary stature had grown and he had proved that he was of Cabinet timbre. No limits could be now fixed to his ultimate success.

7

Colonial Office

FOR ALL HIS preoccupations at the Colonial Office Churchill made
it his business to acquaint himself with many aspects of government
and to express his views on them. He had retained his interest in
military matters, and Haldane, the new Secretary of State for War,
confided to him a series of four memoranda on the current state of the
army which he had drawn up. At the beginning of May 1906 Churchill wrote a lengthy paper on these memoranda, which was in turn
discussed by the War Office and by Colonel Repington, the distinguished military correspondent of *The Times*.

That summer Haldane was invited to go to Berlin to visit the
German War Office and to apprise himself of the organization of the
Kaiser's War Staff. He went there at the end of August.

At the same time Churchill sought an invitation to attend the
German Army manoeuvres which were to be held in Silesia early in
September; the German Ambassador in London, Count Metternich,
willingly made all the arrangements. Churchill was much exercised
as to what he should wear at the manoeuvres.

Lord Knollys to WSC

EXTRACT

11 August 1906   HM Yacht *Victoria and Albert*
                                                    Cannes

My dear Churchill,
     I have shown your letter to the King and he desires me to say that

he thinks you will be quite right to wear your Yeomanry at the German manoeuvres. . . .

At the same time the German Military Attaché in London, Count von der Schulenberg, wrote giving further particulars:

Count von der Schulenberg to WSC

EXTRACT

.11 August 1906   German Embassy

. . . You have been invited by the Emperor, and during the whole time of your stay at Breslau you will be his guest, and the Hofmarschallamt will provide accommodation for you. You have nothing to do but to write to the German Embassy here the exact time when you will arrive at Breslau on the afternoon of the 6th of September. You will be met at the station by an officer and will find everything arranged for you.

In my opinion it would not be suitable to wear your diplomatic uniform, for on these military occasions military uniform is always worn in Germany, even at dinner to which you will certainly be invited. From your military uniform you want the Levée Dress for the review at Breslau and for a State Dinner, which will be given, I believe, the same day.

During the manoeuvres you will have to wear Undress Field Service Uniform with the sword. . . .

Churchill, after a few days at Deauville, whence he wrote his first letter to the King on the Transvaal, wrote to Marsh to ask him to obtain for him Marlborough's plume and leopard skin of the Oxfordshire Hussars. On the same day his brother Jack wrote to say that he could not help as his plume was lost and his leopard skin had been a hearth-rug for six years. Marlborough proved more helpful and lent both items of attire.

Campbell-Bannerman, the Prime Minister, who was on holiday in Marienbad, wrote to Churchill to say that the King had told him that Churchill was going to the manoeuvres and had asked him to warn him "against being too communicative and frank with his nephew." From Paris Churchill went to Switzerland where he stayed with his

friend Cassel, climbing "about these wonderful mountains for a fortnight in perfectly glorious weather." Finally he reached Breslau
where he attended the great parade. The next day he wrote:

WSC to Edward Marsh
(*Longleat Papers*)

EXTRACT

8 September 1906   [Breslau]

. . . After all I did not wear the leopard — not even a whisker — as
the parade was changed to a sort of half-manoeuvre order. He [the
Kaiser] arrived, however, growling at the last minute. . . .

When the manoeuvres were over he went to Venice via Vienna,
where he wrote:

WSC to Lord Elgin
(*Elgin Papers*)

EXTRACT

14 September 1906   Vienna

. . . I went to Breslau for the manoeuvres wh were indeed impressive.
There is a massive simplicity & force about German military arrangements which grows upon the observer; and although I do not
think they have appreciated the terrible power of the weapons they
hold & modern fire conditions, and have in that & in minor respects
much to learn from our army, yet numbers, quality, discipline &
organisation are four good roads to victory. . . .

On returning to England he told his Aunt Leonie, according to
her son Shane, "I am very thankful there is a sea between that army
and England." Churchill continued to Elgin:

. . . I had about 20 minutes talk with H.I.M. at the Parade dinner.
He was vy friendly & is certainly a most fascinating personality. He
was pleased to be sarcastic about "his design of flying across the
deserts to seize Cape Town" wh he suggested we attributed to him; &
he said that if a native rising took place all over S.A. "those people
(in Cape Town) would be vy glad of my troops." He enlarged on the

fighting qualities of the Hereros, & I said in reply that in Natal on the contrary our chief difficulty had not been to kill the rebellious natives, but to prevent our Colonists (*who so thoroughly understood native war*) from killing too many of them.

The Emperor was referring to the rising of natives in German South-West Africa, as a result of which German troops and police had crossed into the Cape Colony in order to pursue the rebels. In the end the rebellious natives were rounded up by Cape police.

In Venice he spent a quiet week, having "luckily just missed Consuelo's yachting expedition," and then went on in Lionel Rothschild's motor-car with Lady Helen Vincent and Muriel Wilson "on what has been a very delightful tour." They travelled at forty miles an hour across Italy — Bologna, Ravenna, Rimini, Urbino, San Marino, Perugia, Siena. "Such a lot of churches we have seen and saints and pictures galore," he wrote to his mother *en route*. "Today [29 September 1906] is the *Atonement* and our Jehu is fasting in solitude. Tomorrow we return in one fell swoop of 330 kilometres to Venice and I go on by the night train to Vienna and Eichörn. It has been vy pleasant. Nothing could exceed the tranquil *banalité* of my relations with M [Muriel] but I am very glad I came. . . ."

Some time after his return to England Churchill wrote to the Emperor to thank him for signed photographs of the manoeuvres which the Emperor had sent to him. They will, he said, "remind me of the magnificent & formidable army whose operations I was enabled by YM kindness to study so pleasantly, & of that beautiful Silesia wh was well worth coming to see for its own sake — & so well worth fighting for."

In return he asked permission to present to the Emperor a copy of his Life of Lord Randolph. Eight weeks later Baron von Stum of the German Embassy in London signified the Imperial willingness to accept this present: a year later, in January 1908, the Kaiser caused Count Metternich, the German Ambassador in London, to acknowledge it and to send to Churchill, "as a token of His appreciation of your present the two accompanying works *Französische Kunstwerke des 18 Jahrhunderts im Besitze Seiner Majestät des Kaisers und Königs* and *Der Kaiser und die Kunst.*"

*

At this time Churchill was involved in a family matter in which he was called on to exercise a high degree of tact and delicate judgement. His mother's young husband, George Cornwallis-West, remained estranged from his family and continued to be financially embarrassed. To add to his difficulties he had, it seems, fallen into the hands of an unscrupulous solicitor and lost a good deal of money as a result. Quite unexpectedly Cornwallis-West's brother-in-law, the Duke of Westminster, wrote to Churchill from Bulawayo:

Duke of Westminster to WSC

EXTRACT

19 August 1906   [Bulawayo, Rhodesia]

. . . What I want to do now is to help in some small way the difficulties that have fallen to George West in losing £8,000. I hear you & your brother Jack have between you come to his aid. I would have helped before I left, if there hadn't been some misunderstanding between us. I send you enclosed cheque to be used on condition that George should not know of this transaction till I choose, if ever, to let him know. I think it very hard that you & Jack should bear the brunt, when it should have come on me, as his brother-in-law. I hope you will take this letter in all confidence. . . .

It was clearly a generous gesture on Westminster's part, for he too was not "on terms" with Cornwallis-West.

Westminster's letter only reached Churchill in Vienna after he had attended the manoeuvres in Breslau: thence he wrote to his mother asking what the full position was and indicating that he might be able to help. Lady Randolph wrote back in a reassuring tone, indicating that she did not know the entire facts but that Cornwallis-West seemed to be in no desperate straits. It seems that her optimism was misplaced, for not long after Churchill fulfilled Westminster's commission:

WSC to George Cornwallis-West

18 October 1906   12 Bolton Street
Copy
Private and confidential

My dear George,

I send you herewith a cheque for £3,000 to be devoted to the repayment of the sums by wh you were robbed by your solicitor, & wh I understand you have now borrowed from Cox's Bank. The transaction is personal between us & the money is a loan to be repaid at any time at three months notice on my request. Meanwhile you should pay interest at 2½% per annum into my account at Cox's. Perhaps you will write me a letter confirming this in precise detail.

Yours ever
WINSTON S. CHURCHILL

WSC to Duke of Westminster

18 October 1906
Copy
Private & Confidential

My dear Bendor,

I could not carry out your commission satisfactorily until I returned to England & cld see George personally & find out the exact state of affairs. I have now succeeded in doing what you wish. I have sent him the £3,000 at 2½% & out of it he has repaid me the smaller sum with wh I had been able to assist him. The interest will be paid into my Bankers each year & will be forwarded by them to you. The principal is of course a loan wh I can reclaim at any time on your behalf.

George knows perfectly well that £3,000 is a sum far greater than I could spare to help him out of any embarrassment however grave, so that I had to practise a pious fraud in order to prevent his guessing or inquiring too closely about the source whence this money was derived. I therefore impressed upon him that in no circumstances was he to speak to Sir Ernest Cassel about the matter; & I am satisfied that he is persuaded that in some sort of way Cassel has come to his assistance, & that he has no suspicions that you were in any way concerned. I have therefore I hope complied with your wishes in every respect. But will you let me say that I shall hope most sincerely that the day will come in the future when you will allow me to make the truth known to George; for then your £3,000 will not merely help him out of his pecuniary difficulties; but will do what is really more important, remove all clouds between two honest-hearted men who are so nearly connected by family ties.

Let me say in conclusion that it gave me a vy warm feeling of pleasure to read your generous letter, & I think it vy kind of you to express so much sympathy with my mother. I hope you are enjoying yourself in S.A., & that your Land Settlement schemes are prospering finely.

Yours most sincerely
WINSTON S. CHURCHILL

The introduction of Cassel's name was peculiarly plausible since Churchill had just been staying with him in Switzerland. Not long after Westminster wrote once more:

Duke of Westminster to WSC

EXTRACT

14 December 1906   Grosvenor House

My dear Winston,
    Would it be too much to ask you to write a line to George patching up matters? I honestly think that the whole thing is so absurd now. I must thank you for all you have already done in the matter. So no more about it. . . .

It is not clear whether Westminster authorized Churchill to let Cornwallis-West know of the origin of the loan. Two days later the latter wrote to Churchill:

George Cornwallis-West to WSC

16 December 1906   Salisbury Hall

My dear Winston,
    Many thanks for your letter. I at once rang up Bendor and we

made it up through the telephone, but of course have written as well.
I am very grateful to you for the part you have played in the matter.

Yours ever

GEORGE C-W

Another family matter which disturbed Churchill at this time was
the matrimonial dispute between his cousin Marlborough and Consuelo Vanderbilt, whom he had married eleven years before. Sunny
Marlborough was one of Churchill's dearest friends and Churchill
was also deeply attached to Consuelo. Churchill laboured hard to
bring them together. His true, natural family loyalty was with Sunny;
but he so contrived his interventions that despite the fierce bitterness
that arose he remained a lifelong friend of both.

A separation, however, took place that year. Many years later, in
1920, Consuelo divorced Marlborough and married a Frenchman,
Colonel Jacques Balsan, and shortly after Marlborough married Miss
Gladys Deacon of New York. Colonel Balsan's family, however, were
devout Roman Catholics and would not accept Consuelo as his wife;
she therefore applied for and obtained from the Roman Curia in
1926 a decree of nullity of her first marriage. This enabled her to
marry Colonel Balsan according to the rites of the Church; it also
made it possible for Marlborough to fulfil a long-felt desire to be
received into the Roman Catholic church.

*

At the Colonial Office South America's difficulties were Churchill's
main pre-occupation. But there were over sixty other Territories
whose fortunes were in his hands. There was hardly a week in
the year when some major or minor problem did not arise in at
least one of them. In January 1907 a serious yet comical affair took
place in Jamaica. There was an earthquake which destroyed part of
the town of Kingston and killed 800 people. Rear-Admiral Davis,
commanding a United States warship in the harbour, at once landed
sailors to help in clearing the streets, and then sent a letter to the
Governor, Sir Alexander Swettenham, offering to assist "out of common humanity." The Governor took offence and wrote a letter of
singular imbecility to Admiral Davis:

Sir Alexander Swettenham to Admiral Davis
(Annual Register)

EXTRACT

[Kingston]

Dear Admiral,

Thanks very much for your letter, for your kind call, and for all the assistance you have given and offered us. While I most heartily appreciate your very generous offers of assistance, I feel it my duty to ask you to re-embark the working party and all parties which your kindness prompted you to land. . . . I found that your working party this morning was helping Mr Crosswell to clean his store. Mr Crosswell is delighted that his work should be done free of cost and if your Excellency will remain long enough, I am sure all private owners would be glad of the services of the Navy to save them expense. It is no longer a question of humanity. All those who are dead died days ago and the work of giving men burial is merely one of convenience. I shall be glad to accept delivery of the safe which the alleged thieves took possession of. The American Vice-Consul has no knowledge of it. The store is close to a sentry post and the officer in charge of the post professes ignorance of the incident. I believe the police surveillance of the city is adequate for the protection of private property. I may remind your Excellency that not long ago it was discovered that thieves lodged in and pillaged the house of a New York millionaire during his absence in the summer. But this would not have justified a British admiral landing an armed party to assist the New York police. . . .

The American admiral at once communicated Swettenham's letter to the Press, where it caused some commotion.

WSC to Lord Elgin

TELEGRAM

January 1907   Colonial Office
Copy

Swettenham's letter to American Admiral published in today's papers: Hopwood & I both think letter plainly indefensible & wantonly insulting. We consider it of highest importance that your action in relation to Governor's conduct should precede any demand for apology from United States. Sir Charles Hardinge [Permanent Under-

Secretary at the Foreign Office] fully concurs and thinks that incident is especially unfortunate in view of Root's [US Secretary of State] mission to Canada. We have telegraphed to Governor asking for text of his letter & if verified hope you will authorise instructions being sent forthwith to him to withdraw letter & express regret for having written it. In event refusal we ought to recall him at once.

CHURCHILL

Elgin concurred. Under these pressures Swettenham apologized to the Americans and offered to resign. A month before Swettenham had involved himself in a controversy about the use of Jamaican labour in the building of the Panama Canal and had used offensive expressions to the American canal officials. This had come to the notice of President Theodore Roosevelt, who had told his friend Mr Arthur Lee, the Member of Parliament for Fareham, but had added that he wished no action should be taken. Lee had informed Churchill; in these circumstances it was not surprising that Swettenham's resignation was eventually accepted on April 1: he was never heard of again in official circles.

*

As Elgin was in the Lords the main parliamentary business fell upon Churchill. But Elgin had an ailing wife, and he liked going to Scotland where he had many local obligations. It thus came about that his ardent lieutenant should also conduct most of the business of the office. For an Under-Secretary Churchill had exceptional opportunities.

But there were a number of minor issues on which they clashed, and on which Elgin usually had his way. For instance, Elgin resented Churchill's habit of writing his comments on departmental minutes so that they could be read by others than the Secretary of State, and he suggested that these comments, though welcome, should be sent direct to the Secretary of State. Elgin proposed in particular that Churchill paste a piece of paper over those of his comments he had already scribbled in the margins of minutes. Churchill acquiesced in this process, as is seen in a note of 1 September 1907: "I wrote a sour minute on Gallway about the Zulu prisoners in St Helena; but knowing your views in these matters, I have had it pasted all over." Churchill's directions for drafting a despatch caused greater acerbity.

Lord Elgin to WSC

17 June 1907   Colonial Office

My dear Churchill,

I have passed the East Africa (Nairobi) draft without comment: as I see you want it early. But I notice that you gave directions for its preparation "at once" though the despatch to which it is a reply was marked by Hopwood, quite properly, to me as well as yourself. I do not think this is a convenient course and I notice it now because it might have been very inconvenient to me — since Hindlip is attacking me in the H. of L.

Yours v. truly
ELGIN

In this instance Elgin was clearly in the wrong as well as being hypersensitive. Churchill took the opportunity to expose his Minister's fancied grievance in a magisterial letter:

WSC to Lord Elgin
(*Elgin Papers*)

18 June 1907

Dear Lord Elgin,

The Nairobi papers raised no question of policy not obviously determined by you already. No new issue of any kind was presented — except the preparation of a Blue Book to wh a terminal despatch is the usual, recognized & almost inevitable conclusion. It seemed to me perfectly natural that the proposed Blue Book should be presented for your approval or disapproval as a whole: & I do not see how such a procedure can be said to infringe in the slightest possible manner — direct or indirect upon your authority & effective control. So much a matter of form did I regard the drafting of the despatch — so clearly marked were the lines upon wh it should proceed — & marked by your decisions — that I gave no instructions of any kind verbal or written as to its tenor; nor did I alter a single word. The only decision I took upon myself was to direct that a despatch should be drafted for your approval in accordance with what I understand are in fact your views. This practice is adopted every day in the office by Assistant Secretaries & even by junior clerks. Where the policy is clearly decided it is unquestionably convenient. It saves time to the public, & to yourself the labour of reading the same file on the same point twice; & your decision is awaited as to whether the draft shall be altered, amended, suppressed, or replaced; or whether no despatch at all should be written, or no publication made. Over & over again Davis, Lucas, Antrobus, Hopwood & others have adopted the course of sending on the draft for consideration with the minutes. But if you do not wish me to exercise such a discretion, I am most ready to defer to your instructions.

Let me only add that I am quite unable to understand how you could have been inconvenienced in any debate wh might have arisen in the Lords. You would have sent for the papers. You would have found a complete statement as well as the various telegrams & despatches. This I should have thought would have been a help & not a hindrance.

But in any case it could easily have been destroyed or put aside unread.

Yours vy truly
WINSTON S. CHURCHILL

In the face of this, Elgin was at a loss for an adequate response:

Lord Elgin to WSC

EXTRACT

20 June 1907   Colonial Office

My dear Churchill,

　I am sorry I gave you the trouble of writing at length about the Nairobi despatch. We had not been quite at one at one stage but I admit we were at the end — & I had nothing to object to in the despatch. The difficulty is that I sometimes don't see the papers & get out of date with my information if they go back for drafting from you. . . .

Elgin was twenty-five years older than Churchill: he had been Viceroy of India while Churchill was a subaltern there. Of course, he was at the end of his political life and he realized that Churchill was at the beginning of his. It was remarkable in the circumstances that he viewed his brilliant young subordinate with, on the whole, such amiability. In fact, they got on surprisingly well; they spoke to other people in terms of marked civility about each other. It was only when Elgin became embittered at his brusque dismissal from office by Asquith in 1908 that he revealed his anxieties in a letter to his successor, Crewe:

Lord Elgin to Lord Crewe
(*Elgin Papers*)

EXTRACT

[?] May 1908　　　　　　　　　　　　　[Dunphail, Morayshire]

. . . When I accepted Churchill as my Under-Secy I knew I had no easy task. I resolved to give him access to all business — but to keep control (& my temper). I think I may say I succeeded. Certainly we have had no quarrel during the 2½ years, on the contrary he has again and again thanked me for what he had learned and for our pleasant personal relations. I have taken a keen interest in his ability and in many ways attractive personality. But all the same I know that it has affected my position *outside* the *office* — and the strain has often been severe. . . .

*

The expansion of the British Empire had led to the institution of regular meetings in London at which British and Colonial political leaders could discuss problems of common interest. The first such Conference was held in 1887. Thereafter they took place at regular intervals, the sixth Colonial Conference being arranged to meet in April 1907. The initial arrangements had been made by the Unionist Government and it had been hoped that Imperial Preference would be the principal topic under discussion with Alfred Deakin of Australia and Dr Jameson of Cape Colony as its principal protagonists. But it was obvious that the new Liberal Government would not entertain such an idea. Other subjects, however, were also planned for discussion at the Conference, including Imperial defence, the establishment of an Imperial Court of Appeal and immigration into the Colonies.

The arrangements for the Conference were in the hands of the Colonial Office, and before the end of 1906 Churchill was already actively concerned with them. Immediately a small matter of disagreement arose between Churchill and Elgin. Partly prompted by Ramsay MacDonald, the newly elected leader of the fifty-three Labour MPs, who had recently been on a tour of Australia, Churchill inclined to the view that the State Prime Ministers of Australia should be invited as well as the Federal Prime Minister. MacDonald had seen them all before his return to Britain and reported that they would be offended if they were not invited. Churchill favoured inviting them, because he thought that they would be less keen on Imperial preference than Deakin. As he wrote to Elgin on January 8: "Deakin is the most hostile to our Government of all the Australians, and [the Conference] will simply be turned into a demonstration of the Tariff Reform League. The State Premiers would *ipso facto* have gone the other way. *Divide et impera!*" Campbell-Bannerman, in his correspondence with Churchill, indicated that if the Australian Premiers were to be invited it might be necessary to invite the provincial Prime Ministers of Canada as well, and Churchill willingly assented to this.

Eventually the seven Australian Premiers formally requested that they be invited; Churchill argued his point of view in a series of letters to Elgin and submitted a memorandum to be placed before the Cabinet. This Elgin refused to circulate, maintaining that the Premiers should not be invited — "they are in some cases by no means high class." But he did promise to put forward Churchill's case, which seems to have been favoured by the King as well as by the officials at the Colonial Office. It did not, however, prevail: the State Premiers were not invited.

All the Colonial Prime Ministers except Sir Robert Bond of Newfoundland, who was delayed by ice, were assembled in London in time for the opening of the Conference on April 15, and were accommodated by the Government at the Hotel Cecil in the Strand. Among them there was Alfred Deakin of Australia, a stubborn, determined politician and a great orator, who had attended the Colonial Conference twenty years before as the thirty-one-year-old Chief Secretary in the government of the State of Victoria. On that occasion he had refused a knighthood, just as in 1907 he was to refuse a Privy Councillorship.

Then there was Sir Wilfrid Laurier, who five years before had pressed Chamberlain into committing himself in favour of Imperial Preference; a French Canadian, who despite considerable opposition at home had sent Canadian contingents to the South African war and was later to encourage the growth of the Canadian Navy. From Cape Colony there came Dr Jameson of the Raid, who had succeeded Rhodes as leader of the Progressive Party at the Cape and was now devoting himself, as Cape Premier, to furthering the union of South Africa.

But outstanding among the delegates — "a lion" whose presence gave a "dramatic touch" to the Conference — was Louis Botha, only five years before the commander-in-chief of an enemy army and now Prime Minister of the Transvaal. Civil authorities went out of their way to give him a special welcome. So did Churchill; and the gossip columnists fastened on to the friendship and mutual esteem that had arisen between the young Under-Secretary and the Transvaal Prime Minister. Botha was accompanied by his daughter Helen, of whom Selborne had written to the King in March, that she was "a distinctly attractive young lady, pretty, lively, and well turned out. She was educated at Brussels and, although she has never been to England, speaks English perfectly. Her age is about nineteen." Her presence in England soon caused tongues to wag.

The Editor, Manchester Chronicle *to WSC*

TELEGRAM

27 April 1907

Editor presents his compliments. Speaking meeting Halifax Yorkshire Liberal Federation yesterday Mr Unwin said was reported
something interesting likely to happen between yourself and Miss
Botha. May we confirm?

CHRONICLE MANCHESTER

The rumours were evidently published, for Miss Muriel Wilson
wrote from the South of France:

Miss Muriel Wilson to WSC

[2 May 1907]   Maryland
                                                St Jean sur Mer
                                                Alpes Maritimes

My dear Winston,
    I hear you are engaged to Miss Botha — is this true? But this is
not the only matter of congratulation on which I am writing you.
I was so pleased to hear you had been made Privy Councillor &
meant to write to you the moment I heard it — & then this place

with its lotus-eating propensities prevented me — ah it is such a divine spot — & the roses & honeysuckle smell almost too strong when we sit out after dinner — it is a world of profusion of the most gorgeous flowers & I look forward to a peaceful old age here in the sun & surrounded by the blue sea, & *you* I hope — & Miss Botha, & all the little Bothas will come & see me & my garden (I shall be like Alice Rothschild) & I will have a luncheon party to meet you — other old crocks like ourselves — & the Prime Minister will write his name in our visitors' Book & we will talk of Wisteria in Lady Brougham's garden of prehistoric times. . . . Alas! Alas!

Yours ever
MURIEL WILSON

Churchill had been sworn of the Privy Council on May 1. This honour not only reflected his stature at the Colonial Office and the part he had played in organizing the Conference but also accorded with the feeling that he was growing into a "responsible politician" as the following letter from King Edward indicates:

King Edward VII to WSC

6 April 1907   HM Yacht *Victoria & Albert*
                                         Toulon

My dear Winston,

Many thanks for your kind letter which I received yesterday just before my departure from Biarritz.

I was very glad to have the oportunity of having several conversations with you on various interesting subjects.

It is quite true that we have known your parents for many years (even before their marriage) & you & your brother since your childhood. Knowing the great abilities which you possess — I am watching your political career with great interest. My one wish is that the great qualities you possess may be turned to good account & that your services to the State may be appreciated.

Believe me, Very sincerely yours
EDWARD R

Leo Amery, an ardent Imperialist, was writing a series of articles on the Conference for *The Times*. Before the Conference began he

had a meeting with Churchill which he recalled in his autobiography
My Political Life:

> I had an hour and a half of hammer and tongs talk with Churchill.
> ... I found him strongly opposed to any idea of consulting the Colo-
> nies on foreign affairs, seeing no point in doing so until they were
> military powers whose alliance could be of any real value to us. Nor,
> of course, could I make any impression on his dogmatic Free Trade
> views, even to the extent of being willing to consider the idea of a
> minimum surtax for naval defence. His own idea seemed to be that
> the Colonial Prime Ministers should be given a good time and sent
> away all banqueted, but empty-handed.

This was indeed a very perceptive summary of Churchill's views.
As far back as January 8, when it was still undecided whether or not
the State Premiers would attend, Churchill had written to Elgin:

> We ought soon to begin to consider vy carefully how to give these
> visitors, whoever they may be, a good show. Don't you think Haldane
> might review his Army at Aldershot, & N. L. [National Liberal] Club
> might give a grand "swarree!" Then I would, if you agree, ask the
> Duke of Westminster — or will you — better still — to give a garden
> party & an evening party at Grosvenor House. He will do it like a
> shot. I feel we have not got the plant that the Tories had for
> sprinkling champagne, & must take thought accordingly.

The Prime Ministers were entertained by the Duke of Sutherland,
not the Duke of Westminster, at Stafford House, not at Grosvenor
House, and Haldane was unable to show off his army at Aldershot on
the appointed day because of heavy rain. Otherwise the entertainments went much according to Churchill's plans.

On April 16 the Premiers received the Freedom of the City of
London — all, that is, except poor Sir Robert Bond, who was still
ice-bound and who had to wait until May 1 to receive his. They were
entertained in the evening by the Eighty Club — a club of Liberal
politicians formed to celebrate Mr Gladstone's great victory of 1880
— at the Holborn Restaurant. There followed a dinner with the
Prince and Princess of Wales at Marlborough House: a brilliant banquet given by the Tory 1900 Club at the Albert Hall, the floor being

carpeted with an immense Union Jack: a dinner given by the Prime
Minister at 10 Downing Street; and several other dinners. "The
series of activities," commented the Annual Register, "proved a severe
tax on their strength."

Churchill was in his element in the speech-making that accompanied these festivities. In his peroration to his speech at the Eighty
Club he compared the building of the British Empire with that of a
great cathedral:

> Don't let us be in too much of a hurry in that in which we set our
> hands to do. Let us remember that it is a great and solemn business
> we undertake. Cologne Cathedral took 600 years to build. Succes-
> sive generations of architects died during its erection. Some built
> what had to be unbuilt afterwards; some were occupied in rectifying
> what had previously been erected ill — but all laboured reverently
> and faithfully, in caring for the cause. The work went on until it was
> finished, and now stands forth the great monument to excite and
> evoke the inspiration and imagination of all who behold it. That is
> the kind of work upon which we are engaged. Let us remember that
> the British Empire is a far larger fabric than any that was ever
> planned by a man; and that the materials we have to use in its con-
> struction and its consolidation are materials at once more intangible
> and more untractable than that which masons and ordinary archi-
> tects of the world are concerned with.

He used the presence of Botha to illustrate his conception of the
Empire: "As I saw my friend General Botha and Dr Jameson, who
had never met each other before (except at about 1,200 yards!), sitting
side by side in friendly consultation I could not help thinking to
myself that after all we had got a good deal to be thankful for in this
world of 'sin and woe.' " Churchill went out of his way to pay
tribute to Botha:

> He was the first man into the war and he was the last man out of it.
> Nothing in the Conference is more dramatic and impressive than his
> presence amongst us. His visits and the speeches he has made have
> strangely touched the imagination of the British people, and I will
> tell him on their behalf that while we are slow to make a friend, yet
> once when we have made a friend we are slower still to throw him

over. To those who, like my honourable and gallant friend and myself, fought during the war such an event comes home.

Despite the wish of the Colonial Premiers that Campbell-Bannerman preside over the Conference, it was the Secretary of State for the Colonies, Elgin, who took the chair, and he and Churchill were present at most of the meetings. Campbell-Bannerman presided only at the opening; thereafter Ministers from the home government took a leading part in those deliberations which concerned them. Thus Haldane, Secretary of State for War, and Tweedmouth, First Lord of the Admiralty, attended discussions on defence in the course of which they had no difficulty in gaining agreement for their proposals for the work of the Committee of Imperial Defence and of the Imperial General Staff and for the contribution that the Colonies were to make to the strength of the Imperial Navy.

The Conference had been under way for a fortnight before the most critical discussion was embarked on — that on Imperial Preference. Laurier contented himself with standing by his comparatively modest demands of 1902 for acceptance of the principles of Imperial defence and extension of existing preferential treatment where possible. It was Deakin, as had been foreseen, who moved that the 1902 resolution should be amended to the effect that the preferential treatment granted by the Colonies to the United Kingdom should also be granted by the United Kingdom to the Colonies and that the United Kingdom should in any case grant preferential treatment to the Colonies. Deakin was backed by Jameson of the Cape and Sir Joseph Ward of New Zealand; but the two most powerful personalities at the Conference, Laurier and Botha, stood aside. Asquith put the case for the home government: he pointed out that Free Trade was in Britain's economic interest, that the British people had rejected decisively the doctrines of protection, and that the only tariff which would be effective and evenly distributed among the Colonies would be that on raw materials and food, and this it was believed would lead to higher prices in Britain. Lloyd George supported Asquith, and while agreeing that the Imperial ideal was worth some sacrifices, he did not believe that Imperial Preference should be one of them.

It fell to Churchill to present the political arguments. The pro-

posed system of preferences, he declared, would involve the discussion
of new taxes in the Budget every year. This would create in this
country an "anti-Colonial Party," "a deep hatred against the Colonies." Grants of preference might be made dependent on the Colony
adopting certain policies demanded by the home Parliament, as, for
instance, policies towards the natives, and fluctuations in the supply
and demand of certain commodities would have to be met by taxes or
their remittance.

All this, Churchill concluded, would expose the whole fabric of
the British Empire to "wrench and shock . . . which anyone who cares
about it cannot fail to hope that it need never sustain." Deakin
replied forcefully and effectively:

> It suggests the indulgence of a riotous imagination when we find the
> Under-Secretary pointing to the natural, the ordinary, the inevitable
> proceedings in any Legislature as ground for rejecting the new de-
> velopment of policy, because it must involve a clashing of interests,
> and the annual review of its incidence by Parliament. Is our Party
> system to destroy everything except itself? Are we to put aside great
> projects because they are debatable, or close the Empire to avoid fric-
> tion in the House of Commons? Free criticism is the breath of our
> Constitution. To shrink from great tasks or newer enterprises be-
> cause of the greater burden they impose upon representatives, and
> representative institutions, means simply shrinking from growth,
> and from the responsibilities of growth.

Deakin's resolution was adopted, subject to the overriding reserva-
tion on the part of Britain in so far as it might imply any alteration
to her fiscal system; and the Conference agreed rather lamely that
the self-governing Colonial Empire, including the Mother Country,
should retain an inalienable right to order its own fiscal policies, and
that the development of inter-Imperial trade could best be served by
leaving freedom of action to each part of the Empire.

*

On the day after the Conference ended the *Daily Mail* published
a sensational account of the close of proceedings, representing that

Sir Robert Bond, the Premier of Newfoundland, had pleaded with
Elgin for a revision of the Newfoundland Fishery Treaties, and that
on receiving the reply: "We can give you nothing," had jumped to
his feet, denounced Newfoundland's treatment as "a gross humiliation" and a deliberate neglect of the Colony for the sake of American
interests, and walked out of the Conference chamber. Bond denied
that such an incident had occurred, and in the House of Commons
Churchill described the report as "a baseless and impudent fabrica-
tion" that bore not the slightest resemblance in substance or form
to anything that had taken place at the Conference. Moreover, he
expressed his surprise that a "person lately created a Peer [Lord
Northcliffe] should allow newspapers under his control to employ
methods of such transparent mendacity for political ends." Churchill
carried on this attack on the Press at a meeting in Edinburgh on
May 18: "A mischief-making Press, eavesdropping, misrepresenting,
dealing in word-pictures and dissolving views, tale-bearing, not
shrinking from wilful and persistent falsehood, have done their best
to sow ill-will between the Mother Country and the Colonies, to
make ill-feeling between Colonial representatives and Ministers of
the Crown." He referred to their "machine-made, linotype calumny."

But it was in the same speech at Edinburgh that Churchill underlined the uncompromising attitude he, alongside his colleagues in the
Government, had adopted towards Imperial Preference at the Conference:

> I refer to the demand for preference which has been made at the
> Colonial Conference, which is repeated day by day with a strident
> clamour by the Tory Party and the "pothouse Press" which support
> them. We are told the Government has banged the door. Well, upon
> what have they banged the door? They have banged the door upon
> Imperial taxation of food. Yes, they have banged it, barred it, and
> bolted it. It is a good stout door of British oak, the largest Liberal,
> Radical, and Labour majority ever seen in the House of Commons
> have their backs firmly against it. That door shall never be opened,
> not a chink shall ever be opened so long as Sir Henry Campbell-
> Bannerman is made the National Hall Porter. The Liberal Party
> stands like a rock between the hard-working masses, and all who
> would exploit their food supply and squeeze some shameful little

profit out of the scanty pittance of the weak and poor. Popular or unpopular, in office or in opposition, that is the line on which we fight. We shall not concede one inch. We shall not give one farthing preference on a single peppercorn.

*

Despite the dire foreboding by the Tories of the consequences of Boer supremacy in the Transvaal, Botha remained loyal to the British crown and his determination to do so was well symbolized by the presentation of the Cullinan Diamond. The largest diamond ever discovered in the world, the Cullinan was found at the Premier Mine near Pretoria in January 1905, and named after Thomas Cullinan, the mine's owner. The stone caused a considerable sensation, and was brought to England to be shown to the King at Buckingham Palace. It was uncut, weighed 3025¾ carats, and was nearly five times as big as the Koh-i-Noor diamond which had been presented to Queen Victoria in 1850. After his return to the Transvaal from the Colonial Conference in London Botha proposed in the Transvaal Parliament that the diamond be acquired for presentation to King Edward as a token of loyalty of the people of the Transvaal. Botha's resolution was carried by 42 votes to 19. The minority against the proposal were the British, who may have been jealous of the prestige which Botha had already gained in London and who feared that the presentation of the diamond would further magnify his position. Despite the lack of unanimity, Selborne wrote to the King urging him to accept.

But while the High Commissioner was enthusiastic, Campbell-Bannerman was less certain. Botha had moved his proposal in the Transvaal Legislature on the very day that the £5,000,000 Transvaal loan was being fiercely debated in the House of Commons in London. Campbell-Bannerman wrote to the King on August 21: "The general feeling [in the Cabinet] was that it was a matter on which we were hardly entitled to offer any advice to your Majesty; the gift seems somewhat inopportune at the present moment when a loan was about to be negotiated, and the grace of the act is the less secured by the want of unanimity in the local Parliament. There can be no doubt whatever that the intention is respectful, loyal, and kindly; the ques-

tion will be best solved according to your Majesty's own instincts."
Selborne, however, reinforced his earlier views in a telegram to
Churchill:

Lord Selborne to WSC

TELEGRAM
EXTRACT

22 August 1907

. . . My opinion has throughout been in favour of gift of Diamond
to His Majesty. I am writing fully officially about it. . . .

And Churchill added, in forwarding this opinion to the King:

WSC to Lord Knollys
(Royal Archives)

22 August 1907
Private

My dear Lord Knollys,

I enclose you a telegram I have received from Lord Selborne. I
trust no final decision will be taken by His Majesty in regard to it
until the whole facts arrive officially together with the opinion of the
High Commissioner which is on its way. Believe me it is a genuine
& disinterested expression of loyalty & comes from the heart of this
strange & formidable people. The Cabinet takes a vy unimaginative
view wh in my opinion does not do full justice either to the significance or to the importance of the event. The feeling of loyalty to
the King & of gratitude for the liberties which have been restored to
them in His Majesty's name, are the strongest links between this
country & the Transvaal.

I write this to you privately; but pray do not hesitate to show the
letter to the King if you think that course would be proper.

Yours vy sincerely
WINSTON S. CHURCHILL

The King begged Elgin to inform him what the Cabinet wished.
Elgin merely replied that the Government were awaiting further

information, and Campbell-Bannerman was even less helpful than before: "The Cabinet did not really want to shirk the responsibility, but he thought that the King himself was so good in matters of this sort that they might safely leave it in his hands."

It was Churchill who once more brought the reasons for accepting the gift most forcibly before the King.

WSC to Lord Knollys
(Royal Archives)

27 August 1907
Private

My dear Lord Knollys,

Many thanks for your letter & I appreciate fully the force of all you say. But please read the enclosed from Selborne which expresses a vy strong opinion, I agree with every word of it; & I earnestly trust that it may commend itself to the King.

I understand the Cabinet this morning was inclined to think that the Diamond should after all be accepted, & that in any case His Majesty should be advised to await the full despatch of the High Commissioner & the formal offer of the Transvaal Government.

It is a great pity that Botha did not defer his presentation till he was sure of a unanimous vote: but the fact is that he did not, & if there are disadvantages in the King's accepting the gift, they must be pronounced altogether less serious & grave than those wh would result from a refusal however graciously expressed.

Believe me, my dear Lord Knollys, Yours sincerely
WINSTON S. CHURCHILL

On this the King noted in his own hand: "I agree with this letter and after High Commissioner's telegram feel bound to agree with his advice."

The Cabinet finally gave its approval in November and the diamond was eventually presented to the King on his birthday, November 9:

Sir Francis Hopwood to WSC

EXTRACT

15 November 1907   Colonial Office

. . . Last Saturday, the King's birthday, Solomon [*then Agent-General for the Transvaal in London*] and I went to Sandringham to present the Cullinan Diamond. We had received a hint, anonymous it is true, that our train or the carriage in which we were to drive from the station to the house, might be held up and the diamond taken from us! We were accompanied all the way by the two principal members of the detective staff from Scotland Yard, and also by other minor detectives. Fortunately, or unfortunately, nothing happened, and the presentation was duly made in the presence of the King and Queen, The Queen of Spain, the Queen of Norway and a large house party, including the Duke of Westminster and Revelstoke. We had an informal luncheon there after the presentation and then returned to town. The King and Queen were very much impressed with the diamond, and arrangements are now being made to have it cut, so that it may be used for the Royal Crown. Needless to say, His Majesty presented Solomon with a KCVO. . . .

The following year the diamond was sent to Amsterdam and cut into a number of smaller stones. The largest — a $516\frac{1}{2}$-carat drop-shaped brilliant known as the Star of Africa Number 1 — now forms part of the head of the royal sceptre with the cross. The next largest — $309\frac{3}{16}$-carat brilliant known as the Star of Africa Number 2 is set in the circlet of the Imperial State Crown. Two of the relatively smaller stones were later set in the crown of Queen Mary, while other smaller gems and ninety-six small brilliants went to Messrs Asscher and Company of Amsterdam in payment for the cutting; some were re-acquired by the Transvaal Government and presented to Queen Mary in 1910.

One postscript remains to be added. In recognition of his part in gaining acceptance of the diamond by the King the Transvaal authorities presented Churchill with a model of the diamond. He enjoyed showing the gem to his friends. Eddie Marsh recounts how one day, when Marlborough's elder sister Lady Lilian Grenfell came to luncheon, "the object was sent for. There was some delay, and

other topics had already supervened when the butler presented himself at Lady Lilian's elbow with a shapeless lump on a salver, looking
like a not-very-well-strained white jelly that had escaped from its
mould. She eyed it with distaste, and said: 'No thank you!' "

*

During the summer recess of 1907 Churchill decided to undertake
a long journey to East Africa. After his arduous work in the previous
session he was in need of a change and Campbell-Bannerman begged
him to "mind his health" and not to "overdo it." No one supposed
that the visit of the energetic young Under-Secretary to half a dozen
Crown colonies would be entirely devoted to mere holiday-making.

Before he embarked on his African journey Churchill spent a
month on the Continent. First he attended the French manoeuvres,
accompanied by his new friend F. E. Smith, and so was able to compare the French Army with that of Germany whose manoeuvres he
had witnessed at Breslau the year before. He sent to Ian Hamilton,
at this time General Officer commanding Southern Command, a
report which was greatly admired and which was forwarded to the
War Office. Churchill also wrote an account to Elgin, and on the
basis of what he had seen in manoeuvres was able to tell him what
advice he could give to Haldane on the size and strength of the artillery units in the newly formed South African Army.

The French only needed batteries of four quick-firing guns, and,
"if the first artillery nation in the world is to prepare to fight European artillery with four gun batteries such a system should surely be
good enough for our South African needs which happily exclude a
possibility of operations against forces armed with artillery."

Churchill had met F. E. Smith shortly after the latter was elected
to Parliament as the Member for the Walton Division of Liverpool
in 1906. Smith had been distrustful of Churchill because he had been
brought up as an admirer of Lord Randolph Churchill and was also
a keen protectionist. He resented the fact that Churchill had crossed
the floor and joined the Liberal Party. They quickly seem to have
been on most friendly terms. There is a record of Smith having taken
Churchill down to speak at the Oxford Union on 1 March 1907, the

two speaking on opposite sides of a motion of no confidence in the Government. There survives also a cheap pocket edition of the Odes of Horace, printed in Latin and English, inscribed by Smith on 16 September 1907, perhaps a memento of their trip to France. Smith already no doubt thought he ought to try and improve Churchill's neglected knowledge of the classics.

Of Smith, Churchill was to write in *Great Contemporaries*:

> . . . our friendship was perfect. It was one of my most precious possessions. It was never marred by the slightest personal difference or misunderstanding. It grew stronger as nearly a quarter of a century slipped by, and it lasted till his untimely death [in 1930]. The pleasure and instruction of his companionship were of the highest order. The world of affairs and the general public saw in F. E. Smith a robust, pugnacious personality, trampling his way across the battlefields of life, seizing its prizes as they fell, and exulting in his prowess. They saw his rollicking air. Acquaintances and opponents alike felt the sting of his taunts or retorts in the House of Commons and at the Bar. Many were prone to regard him as a mere demagogue whose wits had been sharpened upon the legal grindstone. It is a judgment which those who practise the popular arts before working-class audiences in times of faction are likely to incur. The qualities which lay behind were not understood by his fellow-countrymen till the last ten years of his life.

Churchill went on to acclaim Smith as:

> . . . a sincere patriot; a wise, grave, sober-minded statesman; a truly great jurist; a scholar of high attainments; and a gay, brilliant, loyal, lovable being. We made several considerable journeys together. We both served for many years in the Oxfordshire Hussars. We were repeatedly together at Blenheim. We met and talked on innumerable occasions: never did I separate from him without having learnt something, and enjoyed myself besides. He was always great fun; but more than that he had a massive common sense and a sagacious comprehension which made his counsel invaluable, in public broil or private embarrassment. He had all the canine virtues in a remarkable degree — courage, fidelity, vigilance, love of the chase. He had reached settled and somewhat sombre conclusions upon a large number of questions, about which many people are content to remain in placid suspense. Man of the world; man of affairs; master

of the law; adept at the written or spoken word; athlete; sportsman; book-lover — there were few topics in which he was not interested, and whatever attracted him, he could expound and embellish.

Churchill was eager for his friend's political advancement, although he was on the opposite side. On 3 November 1909, when the first of the two "Peers *v.* People" elections of 1910 was impending, Churchill was writing to his wife about Smith: "He is a vy good & generous man. He works for every penny he has, & his health is far from strong. I do hope those Tories will give him a good office if they come in — wh they won't if I can help it." Churchill had some hand in obtaining a Privy Councillorship for Smith in the Coronation Honours of 1911, having persuaded Asquith to urge this course upon Smith's party leader, Balfour. "F.E.," wrote Churchill, "was the only one of my contemporaries from conversation with whom I have derived the same pleasure and profit as I got from Balfour, Morley, Asquith, Rosebery and Lloyd George."

The intimacy between these two brilliant beings extended to their families. Churchill became the godfather of F. E.'s only son, now the 2nd Earl of Birkenhead, and F. E. Smith became the god-father of Churchill's only son Randolph. A brilliant lawyer, debater, and orator, a sagacious statesman, from the time of the first coalition government onwards he and Churchill were united on nearly every public issue, and they both learned much from each other. Indeed, they fascinated each other, and were often the object of much censorious criticism from more prosaic politicians. Convivial in their habits, they did not share the same amusements. Smith liked bridge, golf, tennis, hunting. Churchill early abandoned bridge, though later in life he was to while away some time at backgammon, six-pack bezique, and gin rummy. As a young man Churchill had hunted a great deal, principally from Blenheim, where his cousin Marlborough mounted him for three winters while he was writing the Life of Lord Randolph; but after his marriage he did not pursue this sport. He had toyed with golf and tennis, but he had put them away. Shooting, polo, and some salmon fishing in Scotland and boar hunting in Normandy with his lifelong friend the Duke of Westminster were his chief outdoor pursuits.

Churchill had a limited store of Latin quotations. One of these was *parcere subjectis et debellare superbos,* which F. E. translated for him: spare the conquered and war down the proud. This was always the spirit that informed him, in peace and war, and the words came to him after the First World War. Eddie Marsh recorded in his memoirs:

> He produced one day a lapidary epigram on the spirit proper to a great nation in war and peace: "In war, resolution; in defeat, defiance; in victory, magnanimity; in peace, good-will." (I wish the tones in which he spoke this could have been "recorded" — the first phrase a rattle of musketry, the second "grating harsh thunder," the third a ray of the sun through storm-clouds; the last, pure benediction.

It was once suggested as the inscription on some war memorial, so it is said, but was unanimously rejected by the committee, who had very different ideas as to how people should behave in war or peace. However, these noble words were not to be lost to the language, for Churchill used them as the legend of his memoirs of the Second World War.

Churchill was undeniably fascinated by the awesomeness of war and the disposition of great armies. He never missed an opportunity to visit some great manoeuvres — the French in 1907, the German in 1906 and again in 1909, the English on Salisbury Plain in 1908 and 1910. Despite his Ministerial preoccupations he retained his active interest in the Yeomanry, and was soon commanding a squadron as a Major in the Queen's Own Oxfordshire Hussars. In 1909, when he went to camp with them at Goring, he complained to his wife, in a letter dated May 30, of the wrong tactics employed by the military commanders in the handling of infantry and cavalry during a Field Day. And he went on to confide: "Do you know I would greatly like to have some practice in the handling of large forces. I have much confidence in my judgment on things, when I see clearly, but on nothing do I seem to *feel* the truth more than in tactical combinations. It is a vain and foolish thing to say — but *you* will not laugh at it. I am sure I have the root of the matter in me — but never I fear in this state of existence will it have a chance of flowering — in bright red blossom."

And yet he was appalled by the horror of war. He was to write to his wife during the German manoeuvres of 1909:

WSC to his wife

EXTRACT

15 September 1909   Kronprinz Hotel
                                                     Wurzburg

... This army is a terrible engine. It marches sometimes 35 miles in a day. It is in number as the sands of the sea — & with all the modern conveniences. There is a complete divorce between the two sides of German life — the Imperialists & the Socialists. Nothing unites them. They are two different nations. . . . Much as war attracts me & fascinates my mind with its tremendous situations — I feel more deeply every year — & can measure the feeling here in the midst of arms — what vile & wicked folly & barbarism it all is. . . .

The public were intuitively to sense his first mood, and thus the myth of the warmonger was fostered; he was seldom given credit for the second.

After the French manoeuvres Churchill and F. E. went on to Italy where they met Marlborough. They were travelling in the car lent to them by Churchill's cousin Freddie Guest, who had originally intended to be with them on the expedition — indeed to go with Churchill to East Africa — but who had dropped out at the last moment because his wife was expecting their first child, Winston. Churchill was to become the godfather. F. E. left Churchill and Marlborough in Italy, and the two cousins went on to de Forest's place Eichorn in Moravia, where they pursued the partridge and the hare.

Early in October Churchill made his way in easy stages, by Vienna and Syracuse, to Malta, where he met his travelling companions Eddie Marsh and Colonel Gordon Wilson, the husband of Churchill's aunt Sarah; he was coming out as a last-minute substitute for Freddie Guest. Churchill also had with him his servant Scrivings. He and his companions were "installed in much state" in the wonderful old palace of the Grand Masters of the Knights of Malta.

The cruiser *Venus,* which the Admiralty had placed at Churchill's disposal, was "lying obedient and attentive in the Roads."

In the course of his week's stay in Malta, Churchill visited batteries and dockyards and "the elementary schools — which are really admirable in every respect . . . the Lyceum and secondary schools, the hospitals, the poor house and the prison — all that I have seen seems very worthy of the British occupation." He met the Archbishop and remonstrated with him for his inopportune pronouncements on the Government's treatment of the Roman Catholics in Malta. And in a long letter to Elgin, in which he discussed Colonial Office business as well as his private tour, he wrote:

WSC to Lord Elgin
(*Elgin Papers*)

EXTRACT

4 October 1907   The Palace
                                               Malta

. . . But now of course the *"pièce de résistance"* has been my meeting with the elected members. On this point I will write to you at greater length than this letter will allow. Their demand for a reconsideration of the Constitutional position was supported by a deputation of the nobility, the Ch of Commerce, & the advocates: & I am bound to say that their complaint — viz that they were never conquered by England, but that now we spend their money without allowing the Maltese any sort of control — is a vy real & to me at least a vy painful one. . . .

From Malta the *Venus* took Churchill and his small party to Cyprus. On arrival in Famagusta, and later in Nicosia, they were greeted by a turbulent demonstration in favour of *Enosis,* or union with Greece. Speaking to the crowd in Nicosia, many of whom were carrying Greek flags, Churchill said that he would be more impressed by the sound of argument than by flag-waving. The weekly illustrated magazine *The Bystander* commented, under the heading "Winston the wise visits Cyprus": "Mr Churchill's colonial tour, though of [un] official character, is being taken very seriously by the

Under-Secretary. His speeches, in Cyprus particularly, were models of discretion. Mr Churchill received deputations galore, and assured the Cypriots of the Government's goodwill, emphasising its intention to 'respect the national sentiments of both races,' and resolutely repudiating any desire on the part of Britain to abandon the island." Fifty years later his speeches were held up by the supporters of *Enosis* as favouring their cause. But a study of the full reports in the Colonial Office archives does not lend confirmation to this view.

From Cyprus the *Venus,* as he was to write in a later account, "threaded the long red furrow of the Suez Canal" and "sweltered through the trough of the Red Sea," to Aden.

WSC to Lady Randolph

EXTRACT

19 October 1907   HMS *Venus*
                                                    at sea near Aden

Dearest Mamma,

... Of course the Red Sea in October — especially when rough as well as sultry — is not an ideal condition. But it is nearly over now, and certainly, apart from nature, nothing could be more comfortable or more ceremonious, than this method of travel. I have two beautiful cabins to myself — one of which is quite a large room with a delightful balcony at the end overlooking the waves. The Captain is unceasing in his efforts to promote our comfort, & all the officers are most civil & attentive. I spend a good deal of every day, and almost every dawn on the bridge; & am becoming quite a mariner.

The Admiralty instructions are to the effect that the Captain is to study my wishes in respect to visiting any other ports than those originally mentioned; & I have availed myself of this to include Berbera, Somaliland, in my tour. We shall reach Aden tonight & tomorrow we have to coal there. During the night of the 20th we shall cross the Gulf & I shall spend I think two days looking into the affairs of the Somaliland Protectorate — upon which we spend £76,000 a year with uncommonly little return.

At the end of October Churchill arrived in Mombasa — three days late, because of his diversion to Berbera. While he was in the Red

Sea, he had told his mother, he was writing several long reports "upon things I want to have done." This was not at all to the liking of Hopwood, the Permanent Under-Secretary at the Colonial Office, who complained to Elgin of the streams of long memoranda which were reaching not only the Colonial Office but also the Treasury and the Foreign Office:

Sir Francis Hopwood to Lord Elgin
(Elgin Papers)

EXTRACT

27 December 1907   Colonial Office

... He is most tiresome to deal with & will I fear give trouble — as his father did — in any position to which he may be called. The restless energy, uncontrollable desire for notoriety & the lack of moral perception make him an anxiety indeed!

Churchill should have reserved his points until he returned home — anybody else would have done so both out of caution or at the dictation of personal convenience. Marsh gives a vivid description of 14 hours work in one day upon these memoranda in the heat & discomfort of the Red Sea —

I am bound to say that in all my relations with him he fully respects your authority & judgement but he can never understand that there is a better way of enforcing an argument than by intrigue & by pugnaciously overstating a case. ...

Had I followed my own wishes I should not have sent you his letters, which are marked "private" because I felt that they would not either in style or substance be pleasing to you. But it is always better to have no secrets or reservations.

Though an experienced civil servant and a man of brilliant abilities — he had become the permanent head of the Board of Trade at the age of forty-one — Hopwood certainly had ideas above his station. It was perhaps natural that Hopwood, keeping office hours in London and "minding the shop," should have resented Churchill gallivanting around Africa and bombarding him and other departments with memoranda. It was wholly unsuitable on the part of a civil servant to seek to make mischief between two of his political superiors.

THE DUKE OF MARLBOROUGH, WSC
AND THE EARL OF LYTTON

GUISACHAN, 1901

Above: WSC, Mr Haldane, Sir Edward and Lady Grey,
Lord Tweedmouth. Below: WSC, Lord Tweedmouth

" *Yes, men of Oldham.*"

" *It never got over my escape.*"

" *The duties of confidential adviser to Lord Roberts are not light.*"

" *That's how I fetch Oldham.*"

Illustrations for an article in which the young member for Oldham was found in front of a mirror, rehearsing a speech for his constituents.

E. T. Reed, *Punch*, 10 September 1902

Lord Hugh Cecil

Lord Percy

Ian Malcolm

Arthur Stanley

THE HUGHLIGANS

ARTHUR
BALFOUR

JOSEPH
CHAMBERLAIN

St John Brodrick

The Earl of Rosebery

Above left:
SIR ALFRED MILNER

Right:
LOUIS BOTHA

THE EARL OF ELGIN

H. H. Asquith

Sir Henry
Campbell-Bannerman

MISS MURIEL
WILSON

Sketch by
John Singer Sargent

MISS ETHEL
BARRYMORE

Sketch by
John Singer Sargent

WSC AND JOHN MORLEY IN PRIVY COUNCILLOR'S UNIFORM

EDWARD MARSH AND WSC IN AFRICA

Daily Mirror

ASK FOR the Special Extra
BEAUTY NUMBER
of the "DAILY MIRROR."
PRICE ONE PENNY.

THE MORNING JOURNAL WITH THE SECOND LARGEST NET SALE.

NOW ON SALE.

No. 1,414.   Registered as for G. P. O. as a Newspaper.   MONDAY, MAY 11, 1908.   One Halfpenny.

MR. WINSTON CHURCHILL FINDS "A SAFE SEAT" AT LAST: REJECTED IN MANCHESTER, HE IS ELECTED M.P. FOR DUNDEE.

Amid scenes of tremendous excitement Mr. Winston Churchill was declared member for Dundee on Saturday night, having polled 2,709 more votes than Sir George Baxter, the Unionist candidate. The Liberal majority, however, is practically only half what it was at the general election, when Mr. E. Robertson polled 5,411 more votes than the Unionist. In the photograph Mr. Churchill is acknowledging the cheers of his supporters.—(Daily Mirror photograph.)

VICTORY AT DUNDEE

Miss Clementine Hozier before her engagement

THE QUEEN'S OWN OXFORDSHIRE HUSSARS
ENTERTAIN KING MANUEL OF PORTUGAL

Jack Churchill is fourth from left in the top row, Lady Gwendeline Churchill is third from the left in the second row. Miss Clementine Hozier is second from right in the third row and WSC is third from the right in the front row.

WSC accompanied by his best man, Lord Hugh Cecil, arrives at St Margaret's, Westminster, in an electric brougham

Churchill, however, seems to have been unaware of his hostility, even his malice, and was to be the victim of them again a few years later when they were both at the Admiralty.

*

While he was in Africa Churchill received an offer from the *Strand Magazine* for five articles about his travels for £150 each. Churchill gladly accepted, for this £750 would "definitely liquidate all possible expenses in this journey" and with a further £500 from the book rights Churchill's expedition would show an unexpected profit. The articles and the book, *My African Journey,* were duly published, and the book has been widely read and praised. It is still in print. Letters which he wrote to his mother and to his brother, however, deserve to be quoted here because of their spontaneity in describing these experiences.

WSC to Lady Randolph

6 November 1907   Camp Thika
                                   (half-way between Nairobi–Fort Hall)

Dearest Mamma,

I wish I cld find time to write to you full accounts of all this most interesting journey. But my days are occupied literally from sunrise till bed either in shooting and travelling or else in official work wh presses upon me — in state apt for decision — from every side. I must however tell you about the rhinoceros hunt, which was certainly in its way quite as vivid & tingling an experience as any ordinary skirmish with bullets.

We left Mombasa after two days of functions & inspections & speeches, & proceeded up country by the Uganda Railway. Everything moves on the smoothest of wheels for me — a special train with dining & sleeping cars was at my disposal all the way, wherever I wished to stop — it stopped. When it went on, we sat (Gordon & I) on a seat in front of the engine with our rifles & as soon as we saw anything to shoot at — a wave of the hand brought the train to a standstill & sometimes we tried at antelope without even getting down. From the railway one can see literally every animal in the Zoo. Zebras, lions, rhinoceros, antelopes of every kind, ostriches,

giraffes all on their day & often five or six different kinds are in sight
at the same moment. At Simba — about 200 miles from the coast —
we stayed in a siding for two days & made excursions into the country.
The first day I killed 1 zebra, 1 wildebeste, 2 hartebeste, 1 Gazelle,
1 bustard (a giant bird). The third day was the feast of the skins.
We all started at dawn Gordon, I, the Governor's son & Eddie Marsh,
& marched off into the bush. After about two hours walking we saw
some ibex — a vy fine kind of antelope with beautiful straight horns.
Gordon & I stalked these & I wounded one vy severely. But he made
off & we followed him up. Suddenly on turning round the corner
of a hill & coming into a great wide plain of dry grass — we saw,
almost 500 yards away a rhinoceros quietly grazing. I cannot describe
to you the impression produced on the mind by the sight of the grim
black silhouette of this mighty beast — a survival of prehistoric
times — roaming about the plain as he & his forerunners had done
since the dawn of the world. It was like being transported back into
the stone age.

After we had reunited our party we started to sally out against
Behemoth & do battle with him: and we started accordingly across
this wide plain. We had not gone more than a hundred yards when
by the greatest good luck we saw quite close to us under some little
trees on our right two more rhinoceros placidly resting from the heat.
If we had not noticed them & had gone on & fired at the others, they
would have charged up-wind at us and as we should have had one
wounded monster on our hands already — it might have been nasty.
We changed our plan at once, hurried back to the edge of the plain
& sneaked up under the brow of the plateau to within about 150
yards of the two new rhino. Then I fired at the big one with a
heavy 450 rifle & hit her plum in the chest. She swerved round &
came straight for us at that curious brisk trot which is nearly as fast
as a horse's gallop, & full of surprising activity. Everybody fired &
both the rhino turned off — much to our relief, and then in a few
more seconds down came the big one on the ground & the smaller one
managed to get away under a heavy fire — this one we followed up
& killed later in the day. I must say I found it exciting and also
anxious work. The vitality of these brutes is so tremendous that they
will come on like some large engine in spite of five or six heavy
bullets thumping in to them. You cannot resist a feeling that they
are invulnerable & will trample you under foot however well you
shoot. However all's well that ends well.

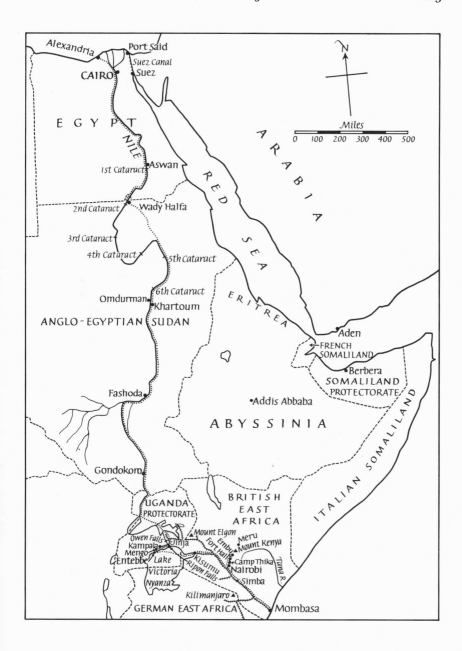

I began this letter four days ago at the Thika camp amid beautiful trees & waterfalls on my way to Fort Hall. I have not had *one quarter of an hour* to finish it till now 11th Nov back at Nairobi. All the time I have been moving about so fast, hunting lions, visiting stations, receiving native chiefs & riding through the country, and have been jolly glad to sleep in my clothes at the end of the day. The lion hunting was nervous work especially beforehand — till one had familiarised oneself with the idea. But of course I had several of the best shots in the country with me: & I don't think there was much danger. I only saw one lion & he escaped without being shot at. But he was a fine big yellow brute, plunging along through the high grass, & it was vy exciting wading along after him expecting to come upon him at any moment. Gordon however shot one, on the day when I was away at Embo & is delighted. He made a most excellent shot & killed the lion dead, but it leaped back into the reeds & no one could tell how much it was hurt. After waiting an hour & throwing stones etc, to make him move, our friends lost patience & vy daringly & vy rashly walked in to the reeds in time to finish him. This is supposed to be the most dangerous thing you can do; & had I been there I would not have allowed it. However after a few yards the royal vermin was discovered lying stiff & cold: & again all's well!

I could only spend the night of the 6th & the morning of the 7th at the Thika camp, as I had to get on to Fort Hall, wh I did by motor-car — about 8 miles an hour over unmetalled roads in the afternoon of the 7th. The 8th great Durbar of natives: 4000 — with all the chiefs stark naked in all essentials, — and in their full war toggery — they & women all dancing together & chanting in curious rhythms from daybreak on. I was presented by the various chiefs with 108 sheep, 7 Bulls, about £100 worth of ivory, an ostrich egg, many fowls & some vy good leopard skins. All these presents except the skins — wh I have kept — will be sold by Govt & in return presents of slightly greater value will be made to the chiefs. I have told them that each shall have a good bred ram to improve their stock. I also made them a speech wh comforted their anxious hearts.

After the pow-wow I had intended to ride to Tana river & then return by motor to Thika where our wild hunting party was assembled — & with that idea all arrangements had been made. But when I reached the lands of the Tana and looked out over the lovely &

delicious country that lies beyond stretching gently up by gradual slopes to the mighty snow-clad peak of Kenia — I could not bring myself· to turn back. So we chucked much kit and all other petty arrangements to the winds. I took Eddie Marsh, the Provincial Commissioner a young official named Dundas — who is a vy clever fellow & who amused me a great deal (he says he knows you — at the Whittakers!); & on we went without waiting even for the rest of our train. We rode through all this beautiful country and just got into the little port at Embo — 26 miles away — before it got dark — having nothing but what we stood up in & only a banana inside us. Embo is a new station opened only last year in a hitherto unpenetrated country. The two white officers there were properly astonished as you may imagine to see us swoop down upon them with the night. But they gave us a most excellent dinner & we all slept on floors & chairs & blankets utterly but naturally tired. What a difference to the fag of a London day. My health bounds up with every day I spend in the open air. At dawn we rode back to Fort Hall, where the motor car waited to take me back to Thika. There we hunted lions all yesterday — but without success — only finding great fierce wart-hogs which we killed — galloping one of them down & shooting him with my revolver & so in here (Nairobi) for dinner & delighted Governor who is just made KCMG.

Joyous times — you will say — & indeed it is true. The country across the Tana is much richer than anything I have seen in India or S. Africa. It is no exaggeration to say that in beauty, in verdure, in fertility, in the abundance of running water, in the delicious coolness of the air, in its rich red soil, it will bear a fair comparison with the valley of the Po. I have told the Governor he may now advance further into this country & establish a new station & post at Meru — fifty miles beyond Embo.

This will bring 150,000 more natives under our direct control & add several English counties to our administration area. There will not I think be any bloodshed, as the native chiefs want us to come — & about 100 soldiers will be sufficient. This will operate next month: & we do not propose to consult the Colonial Office till it is an accomplished fact! Thus the Empire grows under Radical Administration!

(margin note, bracketing the last paragraph: Secret)

Well my dear Mamma, goodbye now — I cannot write any more as today I have constant work at papers & with different departments & also we celebrate the King's birthday with a review & other festivities.

Perhaps Sunny would like to see this letter. But do not let any one
outside see it.

Your loving son
W

From Nairobi Churchill travelled west to Lake Victoria along the
railway whose development he had been championing at the Colonial
Office, just as his father had at the end of his life. He was agreeably
surprised at its efficiency. At Kisumu he embarked in a "large and
comfortable steamer" for Entebbe and Uganda. Churchill seems to
have been impressed by Uganda more than by any of the other
Colonies he had visited. He wrote to the King on 27 November 1907:
"The Beauty and intense fertility of the country are inspiring . . .
there is, however, a reverse to the medal . . . the worst of all is the
sleeping sickness . . . by which at least 200,000 persons have died
around the lake shores alone, and by which whole populous islands
have been swept clear." He was, however, charmed and delighted
by the Kabaka, the little King, at that time only eleven years old —
"exactly like Consuelo in his expression" he wrote to his mother on
November 23 — shy, graceful, distinguished looking, who was being
"most carefully educated" by an English tutor. Two months later
Churchill received the following letter from him:

King of Buganda to WSC

22 January 1908   Mengo
                                                   Uganda

Dear Mr Winston Churchill,

    I have sent the
pictures which you asked me to send them
to you. I have sent two pictures of me; and
the other ones are the men which you saw

Dear Mr. Winston Churchill,

I have sent the pictures which you asked me to send them to you. I have sent two pictures of me; and the others ones are the men which you saw the day when you came to see me. I am quite well, and I hope you are quite well too. Our football are going on very nicely, and the other day the Budu boys came to play football with my boys, and we beat them, but they are learning more. The words on the fortographs mean I am your friend.

I am your friend
DAUDI CHWA

From Kampala Churchill went to Jinja, and the astonishing sight of the Ripon Falls deeply impressed him, not only as a natural phenomenon but also as a potential source of power. It was not until 1954 that the dream became true and the waters of the falls near Jinja were harnessed to produce electric power. Queen Elizabeth II who inaugurated the Owen Falls Scheme as it was known, telegraphed to Churchill, who was Prime Minister at the time: "Your vision has become reality."

After twenty days' safari which carried Churchill and his party from Lake Victoria to Gondokoro, some 900 miles south of Khartoum — "sofari so goody" Churchill was wont to say at the end of each day of the march — they took train and steamer to Khartoum, where they arrived on December 23. That day Scrivings, Churchill's servant, fell ill: he was taken to hospital but died the following day of choleric diarrhoea. "Scriving's death," Churchill wrote to Jack on December 28, "was a great shock to me and has cast a gloom over all the memories of this pleasant and even wonderful journey . . . we passed a miserable day, and I had him buried in the evening with full military honours as he had been a Yeoman. The Dublin Fusiliers sent their band and a company of men, and we all walked in procession to the cemetery as mourners, while the sun sank over the desert, and the band played that beautiful funeral march you know so well." And with Omdurman in mind, he added in a letter to his mother that he always seemed to follow funerals at Khartoum.

"The remainder of our journey," Churchill concluded in his book, "lay in tourist lands, and the comfortable sleeping cars of the Desert Railway, and the pleasant passenger steamers of the Wadi Halfa and

Aswan reach soon carried us prosperously and uneventfully to Upper Egypt; and so to Cairo, London and the rest."

*

While Churchill was travelling in Africa he received a letter from his brother Jack telling him of his engagement to Lady Gwendeline Bertie, daughter of the 7th Earl of Abingdon. Both brothers had for some time been friends with Goonie, as she was known in the family. Jack and Goonie kept their secret well, for though they had declared their love for each other six months before, Goonie said nothing of it in the several charming letters she wrote to Churchill immediately before and after he left for Africa. She left it to Jack to break the news:

Jack to WSC

EXTRACT

14 November 1907   The Bath Club
                                                    34 Dover Street

My dear Winston,
    I am writing to tell you that a very wonderful thing has happened. Goonie loves me. I have loved her for a long time. . . .

*

Before he left on his journey Churchill had unsuccessfully attempted to let for six months or so his house at 12 Bolton Street. Jack had persevered and had found a tenant in Mr Robert Sievier at ten guineas a week. Sievier was a colourful character, well-connected, well-known on the Turf, in the cardroom and in the law courts. In the summer of 1908 he was to be tried and acquitted at the Old Bailey on a charge of blackmailing J. B. Noel, a South African millionaire. When the house had first been let to Sievier Churchill had expressed his "strong" misgivings about "dealing" with such a ruffian. "I trust *all* papers and personal effects have been secured." Now, however, Churchill was due to arrive back in London a month before the expiry of Sievier's lease. Lady Randolph, in one of her periodical fits of economy had planned to cut the exense of Salisbury Hall by £1,000 a year, and, if necessary, to let it and live at the Ritz Hotel instead.

WSC to Jack

EXTRACT

28 December [1907]   SS *Ambigol*
                                      Nile

... Please make some arrangements for me on my return. I leave Alexandria on the 9th by the *Heliopolis,* & either meet Sunny at Naples on the 11th or at Marseilles on the 12th, I hope the former. If Sunny comes out to meet me, ask him whether his servant can look after me as well, for I have masses of luggage, & no one. If Sunny cannot come, or perhaps in any case you might send your servant to meet me at Naples or Marseilles according as I shall telegraph.

On my return I think I shall go to the Ritz, & please ask Mamma to engage me a bedroom, a bathroom, & a comfortable sitting room, & to make the vy best terms she can with the Manager. She should tell them that if they make me comfortable & do not charge me too much I will in all probability stay a month, but if they overcharge me I will clear out at once & tell everybody what robbers they are. ...

In fact, he had no need to test the hospitality of the Ritz, nor did he have to take advantage of F. E. Smith's offer to share his house. Lord and Lady Ridley — she was a Guest and Churchill's cousin — placed the top floor of their house in Carlton House Terrace at his disposal.

Jack travelled back with Churchill from Paris to London, where they were met at Charing Cross Station by their mother: Churchill dined with her that night. On the following night, Saturday, January 18, he was the guest of honour at the National Liberal Club at a dinner to welcome him home after his five months abroad. "I come back into the fighting line," he declared to a cheering audience of about 250, "in the best of possible health, and with a wish to force the fighting up to the closest possible point."

8

Cabinet and Marriage

WHILE CHURCHILL was in East Africa, news reached him that Campbell-Bannerman's health had been deteriorating. Churchill was disturbed. "His removal from the scene," he wrote, "would lead to many changes; and I should be sorry to lose a good friend who has always shown me kindness." Six weeks before Churchill got home, the Prime Minister had a heart attack. He seemed to rally, and on 12 February 1908 he went to the House of Commons — one would judge somewhat unnecessarily — to introduce the special timetable for the Scottish Small Holdings & Land Valuation Bill. The effort, however, proved too great for him: he returned to Downing Street, where he died on April 22.

On March 3 the King, prior to his departure for Biarritz, had visited Campbell-Bannerman at Downing Street — a rare compliment from Sovereign to subject. The same day the King received the Chancellor of the Exchequer, Asquith, at Buckingham Palace. As Asquith wrote to his wife, Margot, the day after: "He said he had quite made up his mind to send for me at once in the event of anything happening to C-B or of his sending in his resignation." Thus, even before Campbell-Bannerman had resigned, Asquith was in a position to discuss the structure of his future Government.

Asquith went on to tell his wife about his audience with the King:

He had heard gossip that Winston was anxious to get into the Cabinet keeping his present office of Under-Secretary. He was opposed to this and said that Queen Victoria had vetoed a similar proposal by

Rosebery in favour of E. Grey when he was Under-Secretary for Foreign Affairs. I said that Winston had every claim to Cabinet rank and that he had behaved very well when twice passed over for Loulou [Harcourt] and McKenna, both of whom had inferior claims. The King agreed and was quite warm in his praise of Winston, but thought he must wait till some real Cabinet Office fell vacant.

In January 1907 McKenna had entered the Cabinet as President of the Board of Education, having been promoted from the post of Financial Secretary to the Treasury which Churchill had rejected at the end of 1905; and in March 1907, Harcourt, the First Commissioner of Works, had also been promoted to the Cabinet while retaining the same office. Though Churchill had viewed these promotions of his colleagues with apparent composure, he must have known that his claims to Cabinet status were being canvassed and could not be long denied. "But I do not see much prospect of a change at present," he had written to his mother from Aden on 19 October 1907. "The only thing that might happen would be for me to go into the Cabinet keeping my present office, when Ld Ripon goes. That would suit me vy well. But they are afraid that Elgin's position would become difficult, he being such an unassertive fellow." It would obviously have been undesirable for the Secretary of State and the Under-Secretary to be both in the Cabinet.

After his meeting with the King, Asquith felt free to discuss the construction of his Cabinet although Campbell-Bannerman, to the chagrin of some of his colleagues, could not be prevailed upon to resign. On 12 March 1908 Asquith had a full discussion with Churchill and two days later Churchill set down in a letter to Asquith his own views and feelings on what they had discussed at the meeting.

Three Cabinet offices were considered for Churchill: the Colonial Office, the Admiralty and the Local Government Board. Churchill expressed in his letter a preference for the Colonial Office, at which he had served for the past two years as Under-Secretary. "Practically all the constructive action and all the Parliamentary exposition has been mine. I have many threads in hand and many plans in movement." He thought that his return for North-West Manchester at the by-election consequential on his appointment to the Cabinet, would be made easier if he continued at the Colonial Office. For he intended to help the cotton industry by giving government encouragement to the construction of railway links in the cotton areas of East and West Africa — ideas which had been germinating for some time and which had been further developed during his African journey.

The Admiralty — "a contingency which I feel a personal difficulty in discussing," since his ailing uncle, Lord Tweedmouth, was still First Lord — he found the most glittering of all the posts. But if he had the choice he "should feel bound to stand by my own work here [at the Colonial Office] on purely public grounds." However, Churchill was most vehement in his refusal of the Local Government Board, which he said was "impossible."

> There is no place in the Government more laborious, more anxious, more thankless, more choked with petty & even squalid detail, more full of hopeless and insoluble difficulties: & I say deliberately that so far as the peace & comfort of my life are concerned, I would rather continue to serve under Lord Elgin at the Colonial Office without a seat in the Cabinet than go there.

He then went on to give a number of "public" reasons why he would be unsuitable for the post. He mentioned Bills that the Local Government Board would have to introduce concerned with social legislation with which he was not familiar. He pleaded lack of training in the detail of domestic politics; he claimed that he had never piloted a bill of any importance through Parliament — "that kind of thing exhausts me" — and he denied any acquaintance with those "basic subjects," the Poor Law and the law of rating. This was the first and probably the only time that Churchill excused himself from carrying out a job because of the labour and tedium involved.

In her interesting book *Winston Churchill as I Knew Him,* Lady Violet Bonham Carter gives an entirely different account of Churchill's attitude to the Local Government Board. She claims that "many years later he told me about it himself." According to this account Asquith offered Churchill the Admiralty, but he refused it and asked for the Local Government Board instead. Either Churchill's or Lady Violet's memory was at fault, because Churchill's letter, quoted above and written at the time, makes it quite plain that the Local Government Board was the last position he wanted. Lady Violet goes on to say that the same afternoon Churchill talked with Asquith (March 12) he met Sir John Fisher and told him that he had accepted the Board of Trade instead of the Admiralty: and that Fisher persuaded him to go back and ask for the Admiralty: but this was not possible as it had by that time been allotted to McKenna. This again cannot be entirely accurate. At the very least the events seem to have been telescoped together. Churchill's talk with Asquith was on March 12, before Campbell-Bannerman had resigned; his letter, which does not mention the Board of Trade, was written on March 14. It was not until more than three weeks later, on April 8, that Asquith, who had just been appointed Prime Minister, wrote to Churchill offering him the Board of Trade. This episode under-lines for the historian the superiority of documents over oral recollection, even when it is first-hand. Human memory is notori-ously fallible. In the nature of things no biography can be completely documented. The author has been exceptionally fortunate in the mass of documentation available to him; but as the work progresses he grows increasingly sceptical of oral reminiscences.

Churchill did not tell Asquith that since the beginning of the year he had been studying employment exchanges and unemployment insurance, particularly as operated in Germany, and that he was grow-ing increasingly interested in social problems. But he did warn Asquith in his letter:

> Dimly across gulfs of ignorance I see the outline of a policy wh I call the Minimum Standard. It is national rather than departmental. I am doubtful of my power to give it concrete expression. If I did, I expect before long I should find myself in collision with some of my best friends — like for instance John Morley, who at the end of a lifetime of study & thought has come to the conclusion that nothing can be done.

Churchill was closing no doors: "No condition personal to myself shall prevent me from serving you where you wish," he concluded; but he made it clear that if he did serve as President of the Local Government Board, he would expect the office and its salary to be on the level of that of a Secretaryship of State.

In the light of what was to happen in the next three years Churchill seems to have been a little disingenuous in his aversion to the *minutiae* of social legislation. He introduced many of the measures which he had found distasteful and of which he professed himself ignorant. Legislation on sweated labour, labour exchanges, unemployment insurance, shops and prison reform were either introduced by him or as a direct result of his efforts.

Eddie Marsh records in his memoirs that Churchill said to him at this time: "I refuse to be shut up in a soup kitchen with Mrs Sidney Webb." Churchill had known Sidney and Beatrice Webb, the great early Fabians, for about five years. Mrs Webb's first impression of him was "restless, egotistical, bumptious, shallow-minded and reactionary, but with a certain personal magnetism, great pluck and some originality not of intellect but of character." By early 1908, when Churchill had not only absorbed many of the Webbs' ideas but even seemed to be advocating some of them, Mrs Webb had revised her opinion: "He is brilliantly able — more than a phrase-monger, I think."

It is evident that Churchill's letter to Asquith had made little impact. Two weeks later when Margot Asquith wrote to him it was clear that the Colonial Office at least was out.

Mrs H. H. Asquith to WSC

EXTRACT

28 March 1908   20 Cavendish Square

Dear Winston,

There are a few moments in life when unwilling decisions seem forced on one. I know them well they make one feel sick & rebellious but I've had luck with mine. I knocked a great love out of my life to make room for a great character & do you suppose we ever regretted it? *Never.*

I was *very* touched by yr loyalty & sweetness when you said you wd give of yr best — I know you will & I believe it will be through you if we win in 2 or 3 years the Gen Election. It's being *in* the Cabinet that matters as the others need you badly.... Dull as it sounds no nation can be great that is not sound at core. This soundness largely depends on you & Henry. All Joe's [Chamberlain's] power started from municipal training — he wanted power far more than pomp — Curzon wrecks himself by confusing the 2. Power first & after that you can do what you like. . . .

Promotion for Churchill was imminent. "Some office must be found for Winston," Lord Esher wrote to Lord Knollys on March 15. Towards the end of March Campbell-Bannerman's doctors persuaded him to resign and on April 3 he formally submitted his resignation to the King. Asquith, as planned, travelled to Biarritz and waited on the King at the Hotel du Palais. On April 8 the King appointed him Prime Minister, "whereupon," Asquith wrote to his wife, "I knelt down and kissed his hand." It was the first and only time that a Prime Minister has had to go abroad for this purpose.

For an hour Asquith went over the ministerial appointments with the King who did not object to any of them, "and discussed the various men very freely and with a good deal of shrewdness."

That same day Asquith wrote to Churchill from Biarritz:

H. H. Asquith to WSC

8 April 1908   Hotel du Palais
Secret   Biarritz

My dear Winston,

    With the King's approval, I have the great pleasure of offering you the post of President of the Board of Trade in the new Administration.

    It is my intention to seek the consent of Parliament to placing the office on the same level, as regards salary & status, while retaining its present title, with the Secretaryships of State. But I am afraid that the change [of salary] cannot come into effect during the current year.

    I shall hail with much gratification your accession to the Cabinet, both on public & on personal grounds.

    I return to England tomorrow.

                                                    Yours always
                                                    H. H. ASQUITH

Parliament agreed in the following year to raise the status of the Presidency of the Board of Trade: but Churchill thought it prudent, in the atmosphere then prevailing, to offer to renounce the increased salary for himself, and his tactful and delicate gesture was, unfortunately for him, eagerly accepted by Asquith.

The Cabinet which Churchill was now to join has long been held up as the most glittering of modern times — perhaps of all times, since the *soi-disant* "Ministry of all the Talents" formed by Lord Grenville in 1806 on the death of the Younger Pitt was torn by faction and only lasted a year. The Asquith Government, on the other hand, apart from its brilliance, had real cohesion. In its seven years of life it had no resignations (other than that of Tweedmouth and Ripon) until 1914 when Morley and Burns as convinced pacifists were to leave the Cabinet.

In a letter to Miss Venetia Stanley, Asquith was later to describe Lord Crewe, who succeeded Elgin at the Colonial Office, as the ablest of his colleagues. Perhaps he was the steadiest; but there were others who were soon to show themselves worthy of a lasting place in any rollcall of English statesmen. Apart from Lloyd George, who became Chancellor and who was eventually to show himself, by intrigue and power of decision, the master of them all, there were, of the first mettle, Grey (Foreign Secretary), Haldane (War and later Lord Chancellor) and Morley (India); while in the second rank were men of much ability such as McKenna (Admiralty), Runciman (Education) and Birrell (Ireland). They were soon to be joined by men with the varying qualities of Herbert Samuel (Duchy of Lancaster) and Rufus Isaacs (Solicitor and later Attorney-General).

Churchill, at the early age of thirty-three, did not feel at all ill at ease in this company. Indeed he, together with Lloyd George, was the most scintillating in the Government, and they were soon to become known as the "heavenly twins of Social Reform." Of course Churchill had his critics, even among his colleagues. Haldane in his autobiography criticized both Campbell-Bannerman's and Asquith's Cabinets as being more like a meeting of delegates at which neither of the Prime Ministers succeeded in sufficiently controlling discussions. Churchill he described as being "as long winded as he was persistent." James Pope-Hennessy in his life of Crewe makes this perceptive comment of the relations between Crewe and Churchill:

It was an atmosphere in which impatient and emotional characters like Lloyd George or young Winston Churchill seemed especially noisy and disturbing. Churchill, in particular, would bombard
the new head of the Colonial Office with a shower of suggestions,
uninvited hints and scraps of unsolicited advice. "A typical missive,
born of froth out of foam," Asquith once wrote to Crewe of a letter
from a young Cabinet colleague [Churchill].

But Crewe's even temper was easily ruffled. In May Churchill was
asked by the Prime Minister to wind up on behalf of the Government
a debate on Natal. It seems that Asquith had not troubled to inform
Crewe of his wish and that the Colonial Secretary was under the
impression that his Under-Secretary of State, Jack Seely, was to make
the only speech from the Front Bench. When Crewe heard that
Churchill was to wind up he peremptorily had a verbal message sent
round to Churchill ordering him not to speak.

"I have not the faintest idea what your views are," he explained
later, "or what you would have said but I would have been bound by
them without any previous consultation with you. No department
can be conducted on such lines, and certainly none ever will by me."
Churchill, who notwithstanding had done as the Prime Minister
asked and wound up, made a dignified reply in which he pointed out
that he had gone to great inconvenience to make himself thoroughly
conversant with the subject of the debate though "the course was
indeed so obvious that there was hardly room for mistake, except
upon the assumption which you make so freely in your letter that my
personal clumsiness would upset so delicate a situation." And he
then castigated Crewe for sending a young gentleman along with a
verbal message — "a method openly discourteous to a colleague and
cruelly embarrassing to a young gentleman." Crewe, worsted in the
correspondence, begged that "we may now allow the matter to drop,
I trust with no ill feeling on either side." But the incident probably
left its impression on both men.

Mr Jock Colville recalls that his grandfather, Crewe, in the latter
part of his life, once told him that Asquith said to Crewe at this time,
"Lloyd George has no principles and Winston no convictions."

During the weekend in which Asquith's Cabinet was announced, Churchill spent the Sunday, April 12, at Salisbury Hall, his mother's house near St. Albans. Also there were Lady Blanche Hozier and her daughter Clementine, who was just twenty-three years old. Clementine was the eldest surviving daughter of the four children of Lady Blanche and the late Colonel Sir Henry Montagu Hozier. Lady Blanche was the daughter of the 10th Earl of Airlie and a granddaughter on her mother's side of the 2nd Baron Stanley of Alderley. Clementine's elder sister Kitty had died eight years before at the age of seventeen. Her brother Bill and her sister Nellie were twins and were three years younger than Clementine.

Sir Henry Hozier and Lady Blanche had become estranged — so much so that Sir Henry did not even list his marriage in *Who's Who*: there had been a separation between them and Lady Blanche was compelled to bring her children up in somewhat reduced circumstances; for economy's sake she had to spend a good deal of time at Seaford in Sussex or across the Channel in Dieppe. Sir Henry Hozier had cut a gay and flamboyant figure in the City of London. He had had a brilliant military career, being placed first in the examinations into and out of the Staff College, seeing service in Abyssinia, China and with the German Army in Austria and France, and he eventually held the rank of a Colonel in the 3rd Dragoon Guards. For a brief period he was a military correspondent of *The Times,* for whom he reported the Austro-Prussian War, before being appointed Secretary of the Corporation of Lloyds of London in 1874. During his thirty-two years with Lloyds he became known as an assiduous and effective lobbyist in Parliament and in the social and political circles of London. Among other things, he early promoted the use of radio telegraphy. He was created KCB in 1903 and died early in 1907.

Clementine was born on 1 April 1885 in London at her home, 75 Grosvenor Street. Her birth was sudden and took place in the drawing-room. She had been to school at Berkhamstead, where, besides becoming head girl, she extended a knowledge of French and German which she was able to perfect in the course of studies at the Sorbonne. She was a striking beauty, and one of the most admired girls of her generation. Beautiful but penniless she was befriended by Lady St Helier, who assisted her *début* in London society by buying her a coming-out gown. Lady St Helier was Clementine's great-aunt through her first marriage to Colonel John Stanley; it was she who ten years before, as Lady Jeune, had used her friendship with Sir Evelyn Wood to help Churchill when he wanted to go out to the Omdurman Campaign. Lady St Helier was not the only link between Churchill and Clementine, for Lady Blanche and Lady Randolph had been friends for many years. Twenty-six years before, as may be seen in Companion Volume I, Lady Randolph had entered in her diary on 4 January 1882: "Went out and breakfasted with Blanche Hozier." Lady Blanche was also a close friend of Churchill's aunt, Leonie Leslie, whose husband Jack was Clementine's godfather.

It was this link between Lady Randolph and Lady Blanche that indirectly led to the young couple being introduced to one another at a dance given by Lady Crewe in 1904. Churchill saw Clementine, then barely nineteen years old, and asked his mother who she was and if he could be introduced to her. Lady Randolph said she did not know the girl but would find out; and when she came back she said: "How very interesting: she is the daughter of a very old friend of mine, Blanche Hozier, whom I haven't seen for years." It was on the basis of this friendship that Lady Randolph came up to Clementine and asked to introduce her son.

Clementine said, "How do you do," and many years later she recounted the scene to the author: "Winston just stared. He never uttered one word and was very gauche — he never asked me for a dance, he never asked me to have supper with him. I had of course heard a great deal about him — nothing but ill. I had been told he was stuck-up, objectionable etcetera. And on this occasion he just stood and stared." She beckoned to one of her admirers, Charles Hoare, to rescue her.

All his life Churchill was always apt to be gauche when he met women for the first time. He had no small talk. He greatly preferred talking about himself. He could scarcely do this with strangers: hence the embarrassment he often caused. Miss Violet Asquith, as she then was, has described her own first meeting with Churchill two years before: "For a long time he remained sunk in abstraction. Then he appeared to become suddenly aware of my existence. He turned on me a lowering gaze and asked me abruptly how old I was.

I replied that I was nineteen. 'And I,' he said almost despairingly, 'am thirty-two already. Younger than anyone else who *counts,* though.' " After a long oration he suddenly ended with the immortal words: "We are all worms, but I do believe I am a glow-worm."

It was not until nearly four years later, in March 1908, that Churchill and Miss Hozier met again. This time it was at a dinner-party given by Lady St Helier. Again Clementine recollected in later life: "I had not wanted to go to the dinner at all. I had come home after giving French lessons at half-a-crown an hour, and was rather tired, when my mother said: 'Your Aunt Mary has just sent a message: she has been let down and is thirteen for dinner, and she would very much like you to go to dinner tonight.'

" 'I really can't,' I said. 'I don't want to go, I've got nothing to wear and have no clean gloves.'

" 'That is very ungrateful of you,' my mother scolded. 'Your aunt has been extremely kind to you. Let's have no more nonsense, go upstairs straight away and get dressed.' "

Meanwhile a similar drama was being enacted at 12 Bolton Street. Eddie Marsh found Churchill in his bath when he should already have left for Lady St Helier's. "What on earth are you doing, Winston?" Eddie asked. "You should be at dinner by now."

"I am not going," he replied. "It will be a great bore."

"But you can't do that — especially not to Lady Jeune. Remember how kind she was to you when she got Sir Evelyn Wood to get you to the Omdurman campaign."

Among others at the dinner-party were F. E. Smith and Lord Tweedmouth. Sir Henry Lucy, the parliamentary sketch writer (Toby MP of *Punch*) sat on one side of Clementine; Churchill was to sit on the other, but he was late and did not come in until the chicken. The dinner was in honour of Lady Lugard, wife of Sir Frederick Lugard, the great West African colonial administrator, and a considerable authority on colonial matters in her own right. As Flora Shaw she had been Colonial Editor of *The Times* when the Jameson Raid took place.

That she did not think highly of Churchill's capacities or of his methods at the Colonial Office is borne out in her correspondence with her husband. Miss Margery Perham in her Life of Lugard quotes her as writing of that "wild Winston" whose speech in the Milner debate was a disgrace to the Government; ". . . an ignorant boy, so obviously ignorant in regard to colonial affairs and at the same time so full of personal activity that the damage he may do appears to be colossal."

Churchill, who was still at this time Under-Secretary for the Colonies, appears to have ostentatiously ignored Lady Lugard in the course of the dinner-party and devoted all his attention to his beautiful young neighbour, much to the latter's embarrassment. He asked her whether she had read his Life of Lord Randolph. Lady Blanche, it seems, had repeatedly impressed upon Clementine the importance of this work, but she had not so far opened it. Boldly, she decided to be honest and admitted: "No." Churchill said: "If I send you the book tomorrow, will you read it?" Clementine assented, but he did not send the book. "That made a bad impression on me," she recalled.

But on the next occasion that they met, that Sunday in April at Salisbury Hall, he had evidently made a better impression upon her. Clementine and her mother were off to the Continent the following day for a six-week tour, though Lady St Helier had told Lady Blanche that she was mad to let Clementine disappear just when she thought Churchill was interested in her. Writing from Paris to thank Lady Randolph for her day at St Albans, Clementine referred to Churchill's "dominating charm and brilliancy."

Churchill himself was having a busy week following the appointment to the Board of Trade, but he took an early opportunity to write to Clementine.

WSC to Miss Clementine Hozier
(*CSC Papers*)

EXTRACT

16 April 1908   12 Bolton Street

. . . I am back here for a day and a night in order to "kiss hands" on appointment, & I seize this fleeting hour of leisure to write & tell you how much I liked our long talk on Sunday and what a comfort & pleasure it was to me to meet a girl with so much intellectual quality

& such strong reserves of noble sentiment. I hope we shall meet again and come to know each other better and like each other more: and I see no reason why this should not be so. Time passes quickly and the six weeks you are to be abroad will soon be over. Write therefore and tell me what your plans are, how your days are occupied, & above all when you are coming home. Meanwhile I will let you know from time to time how I am getting on here in the storm; and we may lay the foundations of a frank & clear-eyed friendship which I certainly should value and cherish with many serious feelings of respect. . . .

Churchill was now thirty-three; he seemed destined to rise; he felt in a serious mood for marriage. He had been in love before. He had been unofficially engaged to Miss Plowden and he had in his time proposed to Miss Muriel Wilson and to Miss Ethel Barrymore. In later life the famous actress confirmed to the author that she had been much attracted to Churchill, but that she had felt that she would not be able to cope with the great world of politics. He remained good friends with all of them. A telegram he sent to Miss Barrymore on her eightieth birthday survives. Now he was in earnest and he meant to see the matter through. But first there was business of a more pressing nature to be disposed of.

*

It was still necessary at this time for newly appointed Cabinet Ministers to have to seek re-election by their constituencies. This practice dated from the beginning of the eighteenth century. After the Restoration in 1660 the King had sought to "manage" the House of Commons by distributing offices and places of profit under the Crown. The Commons, bent on maintaining the power they had so recently acquired as a result of their successful struggle with King Charles I, were determined to make the holding of paid Crown Offices incompatible with membership of their House. However, it was realized that the complete separation between executive and legislature which would result from indiscriminate exclusion of office holders from the House of Commons might be undesirable. In a law of 1705, subsequently re-enacted in 1707, it was laid down that if any member of the House of Commons accepted an office of profit under the Crown his election was void, but he was entitled to seek re-election. Thus by 1908 Ministers in charge of Departments of State, but not the Under-Secretaries, had, on appointment, to vacate their seats and submit themselves for re-election. There were, of course, serious objections to the working of this principle in the modern twentieth-century state. The spectacle of Ministers hurrying off to go electioneering in the country as soon as they had been appointed, while the business of Parliament and the country might be held up, was unedifying.

Moreover, as the law stood the choice of new Ministers tended to be restricted by electoral considerations, those candidates for office with safe seats being clearly favoured, and in some cases, notably that of C. F. G. Masterman in 1914–15, a promising career was completely ruined by inability to obtain re-election. With this in mind the law of 1707 was modified by the Re-election of Ministers Act 1919 which made re-election unnecessary within nine months of a General Election, and in 1926 the principle was abolished altogether.

The necessity of by-elections when Government changes took place had, during the last decades of the nineteenth century and the first of the twentieth, been obviated by the opposition's readiness as a matter of courtesy in many cases not to contest the seats involved. But in 1908 the Tories were in no mood to allow the renegade and venomous Churchill to accept preferment to a Liberal Cabinet without a fight. Indeed, for some months previously the Tory press had been taunting Campbell-Bannerman for not promoting Churchill because the Liberals were afraid to face the electors of North-West Manchester. Joynson-Hicks and the Manchester Conservatives sought vengeance for the debacle of 1906, in which their leader Balfour with six other Tory notables had gone down.

"Well do I remember that fatal Saturday night," said Joynson-Hicks in one of the first speeches in this campaign, "when we went about with our leader practically slain, with our forces scattered in all directions, and the citadel of Conservatism in South-East Lancashire in the hands of a guerrilla chieftain who was once a Lieutenant of our party." Hostility to Churchill from his old party was continuous and vitriolic. Joynson-Hicks in his by-election manifesto marked the tone which was to be pursued for the rest of the campaign. He saw this as "the first occasion which South-East Lancashire has had of expressing its opinion of this government, who in the space of two short years have alienated our colonies, thrown away the fruits of the Transvaal war, attempted to gerrymander our Constitution, increased our taxation, flouted our religious convictions, let loose chaos and bloodshed in Ireland and are now setting out to attack every trade and institution not prepared to obey the rattle of the Radical drum."

Such was the animosity of the Tories that Lord Stanley, soon to succeed as 17th Earl of Derby, actually proposed to the Conservative Chief Whip, Sir Alexander Acland-Hood, that the Conservatives should replace Joynson-Hicks as their candidate with a Tory who, like Churchill, was opposed to the official Conservative policy of Tariff Reform. Prudently Acland-Hood rejected this idea on the grounds that it was too high a price to pay even to turn out Churchill. Those on the periphery of the Tory party were more bitter than those in control.

Joynson-Hicks' election manifesto averred that the recently proposed Education Bill "breathed enmity against the Church of England and Church of Rome," and he asserted that the Licensing Bill "embodied in naked form pure socialism." His manifesto ended with an appeal to the business community of North-West Manchester to declare for the maintenance of the House of Lords as a protection against "predatory and Socialistic legislation." Joynson-Hicks was less forthright over the tariff question. Despite Balfour's declaration at Birmingham, when he asserted that revision of tariffs was the "first great constructive work" of the Tory Party, Joynson-Hicks put his affirmation in what Churchill labelled an "obscure corner" of his manifesto, and merely said that he was in favour of a "revision of our fiscal policy on the Conservative lines laid down by Mr Balfour."

As President of the Board of Trade, Churchill saw his department as responsible for the direct defence of Free Trade. In his manifesto, however, he took a more extensive view of the purpose of his department than had his predecessors. The Board of Trade was, he said, to "foster the commercial interests of our country, within the limits of state intervention." Churchill clearly regarded the fact that, contrary to precedent, the Conservatives were contesting the election, as an irritable attack by the Opposition. "To delay and hamper the work of a great Department charged with important and complicated legislation of a purely non-party character betokens a keener zest for faction than for public interest." He believed that "machine-made calumnies of partisanship" would dissolve under the "honest examination of the people."

The principal difference between this election and that of 1906 was the appearance of a third candidate, Dan Irving of the Marxist Social Democratic Federation. Irving was a militant socialist who was later to become MP for Burnley. On this occasion, however, he did not enjoy the full support of the Labour Party. It had been feared that he would take votes from Churchill, but the balance was redressed by an Open Letter to Labour voters which H. G. Wells wrote on behalf of Churchill. Churchill had for some years been in lively and friendly correspondence with the famous author. That year, indeed, Wells presented his new book *New Worlds for Old* to Churchill with the accompanying note: "Here is the real Socialist case. . . . It isn't quite your Monster, much less is it [F. E.] Smith's monster." Although Wells was to campaign for Socialism and social reform for many years to come — his remarkable *Tono-Bungay* was to be published the following year — he was an independent rather than a party Socialist. Indeed, he was just breaking with the Webbs, Shaw and the Fabians of whom he had been an early supporter.

In his appeal to the Socialist voters of Manchester, Wells pointed out that Irving did not enjoy the support of any accredited or independent Labour Party. "He is representative not of Socialism as a whole . . . but of that extreme, old-fashioned and implacable type of Socialist theory — limited, doctrinaire and cantankerous, which has done so much to retard the development of a sound and statesmanlike propaganda in Great Britain." He praised Churchill: "We recognise in his active and still rapidly developing and broadening mind, in his fair and statesmanlike utterances and in particular in his recent assertion of the need of a national minimum wage, a spirit entirely in accordance with the spirit of our movement and one with which it is both our duty and intention to go, just as far as we can. . . ." And he contrasted Churchill's "brilliant career and vivid personality" with those of Joynson-Hicks who "represents absolutely the worst element in British political life at the present time . . . is an entirely undistinguished man . . . and an obscure and ineffectual nobody."

Among those taking part in the election campaign on Churchill's behalf was Lady Dorothy Howard, the third daughter of the 9th Earl of Carlisle, who was a cousin of Clementine's and who evidently possessed a powerful personality. Churchill had written to Clementine at the beginning of the campaign:

WSC to Miss Clementine Hozier

EXTRACT

16 April 1908   12 Bolton Street

. . . Lady Dorothy arrived of her own accord — alone & independent. I teased her by refusing to give a decided answer about women's votes, & she left at once for the North in a most obstinate temper. However on reading my answers given in public, back she came and is fighting away like Diana for the Greeks — a vy remarkable young lady in every respect. But my eye what a tyrant! Mind of marble — calm, unerring, precise, ruthless in its logic, devoid of flexibility — a thing to admire, but not bruise yourself against. Yet — a dear! . . .

Again, later:

WSC to Miss Clementine Hozier

EXTRACT

27 April [1908]   Taplow

. . . Lady Dorothy fought like Joan of Arc before Orleans. The dirtiest slum, the roughest crowd, the ugliest street corner. She is a wonderful woman — tireless, fearless, convinced, inflexible — yet preserving all her womanliness. . . .

The Chairman of the Liberal Election Committee was Alderman James Thewlis, the great uncle of a future Prime Minister, Mr Harold Wilson. The author is indebted to Mr Wilson's father, Mr James Wilson, for the following recollection. Thewlis and Churchill had been discussing the latter's Life of Lord Randolph. Churchill then said, "Thewlis, we Churchills die young, and I want to put something more on the slate."

In many ways the campaign appeared to be following the pattern of 1906. Liberal emphasis on Free Trade again won the support of Unionist Free Traders in the all-party Free Trade League, men like Tootal Broadhurst and F. Ashworth, President of the Chamber of Commerce. The *Manchester Guardian* enthusiastically reported that "Lancashire business men with unanimity, were ignoring old party lines, and coming forward to offer compliments to the President of the Board of Trade." The British Cotton Growing Association backed Churchill and praised his term at the Colonial Office for proposed measures like the Northern Nigeria Railway Bill, which was intended to facilitate the cheapening of communications to cotton-growing areas in Nigeria. A delegation from the important Jewish community at Cheetham Hill declared satisfaction with Churchill's replies to the issues of Sunday closing, the Aliens Act and the education question. Indeed, Dr Dulberg assured Churchill that 95 per cent of the Jewish votes were for him. It seemed that Churchill had maintained his support among the all-important cotton business and commercial community in Manchester. Joynson-Hicks attacked the "Mugwump Millionaires" of Unionism, who had deserted him. It looked as if the Tories were still as divided as in 1906. Right up to the close of poll on April 23 Churchill thought he would retain the seat. In the event Joynson-Hicks won with a small majority:

Joynson-Hicks	5,417
Churchill	4,988
Irving	276
Conservative majority	429

Swing to Conservatives 6.4 per cent

Among the enthusiastic Tory crowds a man was seen selling "Churchill memory cards," after the result had been announced. The *Manchester Guardian* reported a sorrowful Liberal supporter as prophesying: "It's a little too soon for that, my friend, you have not done with Mr Churchill yet. We have lost him for Manchester, like we lost John Bright before my time, but he will be a great figure in English politics all the same. Manchester will be sorry for what she has done today."

Austen Chamberlain wrote to his stepmother Mrs Mary Chamberlain, the third wife of his father Joe, with something less than his usual gentility: "Have you heard the Stock Exchange telegram to Winston on the morrow of his defeat? . . . It ran: 'To Winston Churchill, Manchester: What's the use of a W.C. without a seat?' Oh fie! . . ." However, Chamberlain added, "I am sorry for him. . . . Nothing in Winston's campaign became him like the leaving it. . . . He was dignified and courageous."

Frank Harris wrote and sympathised:

Frank Harris to WSC

EXTRACT

Vanity Fair
26 April 1908   33 Strand

My dear Winston Churchill,
   I did not congratulate you on your entrance into the Cabinet, because I thought the Cabinet ought to be congratulated; but now I cannot help writing to express sympathy with you over that wretched set-back in Manchester: the voice of the people is always the voice of the devil and has nothing to do with the voice of God. If the masses are saved it will be in spite of themselves, as one saves pigs from cutting their throats in a seaway, for higher reasons than the pig dreams of. . . .
   By the bye, I would have sent you the motor-car to Manchester; but to tell you the truth, a damned creditor got hold of it, and I have only just been able to get it out of his clutches. Huroo!
                                  Yours ever
                                  FRANK HARRIS

Many reasons were brought forward to explain the defeat. Churchill himself was a little later quite ready to place the blame on the "influence of money expended through half a dozen unauthorised associations and outside leagues, with the influence of the press dictated by the millionaire proprietors, who were rewarded by peerages for their privileges." When Northcliffe later remonstrated with him,

Churchill grudgingly absolved him from personal responsibility; but he was particularly incensed with the Harmsworth Press's *Manchester Courier,* against whom he initiated a libel action for suggesting that he had broken his parole while a prisoner of the Boers. The *Courier* apologized and withdrew its statement.

Churchill went on to complain that the "banding together of great vested interests threatened by radical legislation enabled pressure and force to be brought to bear on the particular constituency in which a by-election occurred." The Liberal Press also placed much of the blame for the loss on these pressure-group interests, though Runciman, who had been forced to fight a by-election on his appointment to the Presidency of the Board of Education, had held Dewsbury the day before, albeit with a greatly reduced majority.

There is little doubt that the result was a blow to the cause of Free Trade and that it gave a considerable impetus to the supporters of Tariff Reform when the citadel of Free Trade returned to the Unionist fold. The fact that the seat had been solidly Tory under Sir William Houldsworth from its formation in 1885 until 1906, and that it was clearly a marginal constituency which in a mid-election period was liable to swing back to the Conservatives should not be overlooked. Already the Liberals had lost three seats since the beginning of the year at by-elections. Swings of 5.0 per cent and 3.7 per cent produced Tory victories at Ashburton and Ross in January and an even greater swing of 6.6 per cent had resulted in the loss of Peckham in March.

But it is possible that the aggressiveness of Churchill's campaign upset some of the staid Tories who had gone over to his side two years before. Lloyd George came down for two days and made a series of brilliant speeches, but he scarcely trod softly on the susceptibilities of the Manchester business community. "Free Trade," he declared, "may be the Alpha but it is not the Omega of Liberal policy. It is a foundation on which to build."

Just as the Jews were regarded as decisive in 1906 — though their importance was perhaps exaggerated — so in 1908 the importance of the Catholic vote was stressed. There was some talk of the Irish vote being withheld from the Liberal candidate on the grounds that Asquith was a much less committed Home Ruler than Campbell-

Bannerman had been; but after receiving the usual assurances the leaders of the Irish party in the end urged their supporters to vote for Churchill. On the other hand, the ill-fated and much maligned Education Bill threatened the voluntary schools of the Roman Catholic Church as much as those of the Church of England and there was evidence that some of the 900 Catholic voters in the constituency were influenced not to support Churchill. It is strange that Churchill did not perceive the transcendent reason for his defeat. The Unionist Free Traders, who had flocked to his banner two years before when Free Trade seemed in danger from Joe Chamberlain's advocacy of Tariff Reform, were no longer disturbed by this issue. There was an overwhelming Liberal majority in the House of Commons and the Manchester Unionists, more concerned now about the possibility of Home Rule, naturally returned to their former allegiance.

To Clementine, who was staying in the Black Forest and had read the newspaper accounts of the election campaign with increasing excitement, Churchill wrote after it was all over in a letter from which an extract has already been quoted:

WSC to Miss Clementine Hozier
(CSC Papers)

EXTRACT

27 April [1908]   Taplow

... It was a real pleasure to me to get your letter & telegram. I am glad to think you watched the battle from afar with eye sympathetic to my fortunes. It was a vy hard contest & but for those sulky Irish Catholics changing sides at the last moment under priestly pressure, the result would have been different. Now I have to begin all over again — probably another long & exhausting election. Is it not provoking!

The Liberal party is I must say a good party to fight with. Such loyalty & kindness in misfortune I never saw. I might have won them a great victory from the way they treat me. Eight or nine safe seats have been placed at my disposal already. From my own point of view indeed the election may well prove a blessing in disguise. It is an awful hindrance to anyone in my position to be always forced to fight

for his life & always having to make his opinions on national politics
conform to local exigencies. If I had won Manchester now, I should
probably have lost it at the general election. Losing it now I shall I
hope get a seat wh will make me secure for many years. Still I don't
pretend not to be vexed. Defeat however consoled explained or discounted is odious. Such howls of triumph from the Tory Press; such
grief of my poor friends & helpers; such injury to many important
affairs. There is only one salve — everything in human power was
done. . . .

How I should have liked you to have been there. You would have
enjoyed it I think. We had a jolly party and it was a whirling week.
Life for all its incompleteness is rather fun sometimes.

Write to me again — I am a solitary creature in the midst of
crowds. Be kind to me. . . .

One of the safe seats placed at Churchill's disposal was Dundee.
In the course of the changes made by Asquith on becoming Prime
Minister, Mr Edmund Robertson, a distinguished constitutional
lawyer who had held junior office on several occasions and who had
been Liberal MP for Dundee since 1885, was elevated to the peerage
as Lord Lochee. Churchill decided to accept the invitation of the
Dundee Liberal Association to become their candidate. He did this,
he told his mother, on the strong advice of the Chief Whips in Scotland and England and with the recommendation of the Prime Minister. "They all seem to think it is a certainty — and even though a
3 cornered fight will end in a majority of 3,000. It is a life seat and
cheap and easy beyond all experience."

Churchill did not know when he wrote this letter on April 29 that
there would be a fourth candidate — Mr Edwin Scrymgeour, a local
Prohibitionist. Although Scrymgeour polled only a handful of votes
on this occasion, it was he who sixteen years later was to upset Churchill's prediction that Dundee would prove a "life seat."

The city of Dundee in 1908 was a bustling industrial and commercial centre. Jute, linen-making, shipbuilding, marmalade and
its well-known cake were the main sources of its wealth. With an
electorate of nearly 19,000 it was, like Oldham, a two-member,
primarily working-class, constituency. In 1906, it had, in fact, returned Alexander Wilkie as a Labour Member, along with the

Liberal Robertson. Churchill had clearly to persuade the class-conscious voters of Dundee that a Liberal Government had the interests of the working class at heart. A Labour candidate, George Stuart, was standing against Churchill with the backing of Keir Hardie and the Labour Party. He was regarded as a serious challenge to Churchill from the Left. Scrymgeour also stood as a candidate of the Left; while his main demand was for the prohibition of drink, he claimed to be a Christian Socialist, and also advocated payment of Members of Parliament, primary state education, and the state control of production, manufacture and exchange. Sir George Baxter, a local jute distributor and tariff reformer, was the Conservative candidate fighting under the slogan "Something must be done." The division of forces on the Left clearly appeared to be a threat to Churchill. He spoke of "the wanton division of the progressive forces" and "the false friends on our flank stabbing at us even while we fight for them." In the early stages of the campaign, it was felt that Baxter would be able to capitalize on the divisions and possibly gain the seat. Later on, the threat of Stuart, the Labour candidate, became more ominous, particularly when a national shipbuilding lock-out left 1,400 Dundee voters out of work. But Churchill was able to turn this to advantage by attracting favourable attention when, as President of the Board of Trade, he returned to London to initiate conciliatory talks which after the election were to end in a settlement.

In fact, Churchill, with characteristic dynamism and energy, was able to use the campaign both to display his formidable political ability and to explain and formulate his radical position more fully. Thousands flocked to hear his speeches at the Kinnaird Hall, and according to the *Manchester Guardian* memories of the great days of Gladstone were evoked.

Churchill's personal magnetism and spirited political leadership more than compensated for the ramshackle Liberal organization. He spoke of "unfurling the old flag of civil freedom and social justice under which your fathers conquered, under which you, in turn, will be unconquerable." A ferocious attack on the House of Lords and indirectly on the Conservative Party drew appreciative applause. "It is filled with old doddering peers, cute financial magnates, clever wirepullers, big brewers with bulbous noses. All the enemies of progress are there — weaklings, sleek, smug, comfortable self-important individuals." Churchill portrayed himself as being surrounded by "all the forces of reaction" and "every discontented irresponsible element in the community." He spoke of the new Liberalism and the social policy which he intended to pursue at the Board of Trade. He announced the old-age pension scheme for those over seventy, which would cost the Exchequer £6 million a year and would cover 500,000 people. The abolition of the sugar tax in the Budget was disclosed to an enthusiastic audience.

Churchill, however, felt that the Labour candidate was making sizeable inroads into the Liberal vote. His opposition to Ramsay MacDonald's "Right to Work" Bill in the Commons was used against him by hecklers and Labour speakers. Keir Hardie, in a letter of support to Stuart, spoke of Churchill's "shameless prevarication" on the question. The old-age pension scheme was greeted with derision by many who believed that few of the working class ever lived to reach the age of seventy. The challenge of Labour, in fact, provided Churchill with the opportunity to distinguish explicitly his radicalism from socialism. In a speech at the Kinnaird Hall he clearly marked out his brand of radicalism.

> Socialism wants to pull down wealth, Liberalism seeks to raise up poverty. Socialism would destroy private interests — Liberalism would preserve them in the only way they could justly be preserved, by reconciling them with public right. Socialism seeks to kill enterprise. Liberalism seeks to rescue enterprise from the trammels of privilege and preference. Socialism assails the maximum pre-eminence of the individual — Liberalism seeks to build up the minimum standard of the masses. Socialism attacks capital, Liberalism attacks monopoly.

Churchill believed there were "immense differences of principle, aim and political philosophy" between Liberals and Socialists. He asserted that the Socialists "had a creed of universal self-sacrifice, but preach it in the language of spite, envy, hatred and uncharitableness."

"They tell us to dwell together in unity and comradeship — but they are split into twenty obscure factions. They desire to reconstruct the world but leave out human nature." Churchill mused on the "barrenness of a philosophy whose creed was absolute collectivism." He saw it as "equality of reward irrespective of services rendered." Churchill regarded the slogan, "from each according to his ability, to each according to his need" as equalling "you shall work according to your fancy, you shall be paid according to your appetite."

Despite a Conservative scare in the *Dundee Courier* that the jute industry was on the brink of collapse because of American competition, Churchill was quite capable of scoring over his old enemies in the Tariff Reform League. Neither the priests, who sought support for the Conservatives among the 1,500 Catholic voters, nor the suffragettes made any impression on the electorate. On May 9 Churchill was returned by a sizeable majority:

Churchill	(L)	7,079
Baxter	(C)	4,370
Stuart	(Lab)	4,014
Scrymgeour	(Prohib)	655
Majority of Liberal over Conservative		2,709

Churchill collected 44 per cent of the total vote and with the progressive vote split three ways, it was clear that the Conservatives had made little impression, despite having a local and philanthropic manufacturer as candidate. The Liberal victory was also seen as a serious check to the hopes of Labour. Stuart had had many advantages with an overwhelmingly working-class electorate, a real and serviceable organization and fervent supporters. Churchill's aggressive radicalism and talk of social reconstruction paid handsome dividends. No doubt, his conciliatory intervention in the shipbuilding lockout dispute played some part in assuaging suspicions of his genuine concern for the working classes.

The joyous scenes in Dundee on election night testified to Churchill's attraction to an increasingly volatile electorate. The young Radical returned triumphantly to Westminster and was now eager to join Lloyd George in his "new departure in English politics." With the solid working-class constituency of Dundee as his base, Churchill was well-equipped for the Liberal Party's new policy of reform. His entry into the Cabinet had seemed long delayed. The campaigns of 1908 underlined his pugnacious political attitude, and marked his first real involvement in the politics of social reform.

*

On 4 August 1908 Churchill's younger brother Jack was married to Lady Gwendeline Bertie. Churchill, who had met Clementine at a few dances in the course of the summer, described the civil marriage at Abingdon — the religious service took place at Oxford the following day — in a letter to her on August 7. "We all swooped down in motor-cars upon the town of Abingdon and did the deed before the Registrar — for all the world as if it was an elopement — with irate parents panting on the path." The Berties were a Catholic family. "Afterwards we were shown over the Town Hall & its relics & treasures — quite considerable for so small a place — & then back go bride and bridegroom *to their respective homes* until tomorrow. Both were entirely composed & the business was despatched with a celerity & ease that was almost appalling." After the wedding, Churchill and a number of his friends, among them F. E. Smith, had stayed with his cousin Freddie Guest, younger brother of Ivor Guest, later Lord Wimborne, at Burley-on-the-Hill, a house near Oakham, which Guest and his American wife Amy Phipps had leased for a short while from the Finch family. On the night of August 6 a fire broke out. Eddie Marsh who was accompanying Churchill not only to the wedding but also on his other visits had packed his London clothes and, as he recalled in his book of reminiscences *A Number of People,* "all the country clothes I had, and took with me my Uncle Spencer's [Perceval] accurate gold watch on its massive chain, together with two or three valuable tie-pins which were the nearest I ever got to heirlooms." His lively account continues:

> In the middle of the night I was roused from the deep stupor which sometimes follows a specially good dinner, by my host pounding on the door. "Eddie, Eddie, get up at once, the house is on fire!" (It transpired later that the new heating apparatus installed by the Guests, which was in use for the first time, had been carried away by the zeal of the novice, and "heated" only too well.) I jumped out of bed, and like Satan "for the general safety despising my own" rushed downstairs in my pyjamas and slippers to what might be called "the pumps," without even thinking to put my more portable valuables in my jacket pocket, which wouldn't have taken a moment; but perhaps it was just as well, for my bedroom was exactly over the heart of the fire, and in a few minutes all was swallowed up.

I found grey darkness everywhere, for the first thing the fire had done was to derange the electric light. The large house-party assembled, dressed as might be, and soon we were joined by the fire-brigade and a concourse of neighbours. Winston commandeered a fireman's helmet and assumed the direction of operations, but he had nothing to go upon — the house was full of treasures, but nobody knew where they were. I devoted myself to the first room in which I found books, and threw them all out on the grass; but the light of day revealed them as the servants' library, and meanwhile all the priceless Elizabethan manuscripts etc had perished. My next futility was helping a band of willing workers to cut tapestries out of their panels in a part of the house which in the event the flames never reached.

Some time in the small hours they were got under, and we went out on the lawn, where it was a tragical sight to see the real owners of Burley (who had moved into a smaller house nearby) sitting in a gig and watching the destruction of their home, which had been their love and their pride, with tears pouring down their faces. But there was nothing more to be done, and in time for breakfast at the Rectory F. E. Smith and I, the only total losers, were rigged out in borrowed suits a world too wide for our shapely shanks. Thus "woefully arrayed" we returned to London, where there were still a few old clothes at the bottom of my chest of drawers — I have never since felt well-dressed or had everything handsome about me....

Churchill gave his own account at the time in the letter to Clementine part of which has already been quoted:

WSC to Miss Clementine Hozier

EXTRACT

7 August 1908   Nuneham Park

... The Fire was great fun & we all enjoyed it thoroughly. It is a pity such jolly entertainments are so costly. Alas for the archives. They roared to glory in about ten minutes. The pictures were of small value, & many, with all the tapestries & about ½ the good furniture were saved. I must tell you all about it when we meet. My eyes still smart & writing is tiring. It is a vy strange thing to be locked in deadly grapple with that cruel element. I had no conception — ex-

cept from reading — of the power & majesty of a great conflagration.
Whole rooms sprang into flame as by enchantment. Chairs & tables
burnt up like matches. Floors collapsed and ceilings crashed down.
The roof descended in a molten shower. Every window spouted fire,
& from the centre of the house a volcano roared skyward in a whirl-
wind of sparks. The Guests have no responsibility; & the Finches are
I hear well-insured. It is only the archives that must be mourned in-
consolably. Poor Eddie Marsh lost everything (including many of my
papers) through not packing up when I told him to. I saved all my
things by making Reynolds [the servant] throw them out of the
window. It was vy lucky that the fire was discovered before we had
all gone to sleep — or more life might have been lost — than one
canary bird; & even as it was there were moments of danger for
some. . . .

F. E. Smith's wife, Margaret, told the author later how she remembered Churchill on the roof trying to quench the fire with a
hose from the tiny fire-engine which had been brought from Oakham.
"He took charge of the whole operation. F. E. had been ill and was
not allowed to take part. When the cellar was brought out and laid
on the lawn, F. E. inspected it and said to me: 'There, I thought the
port was not what he said it was.'"

Clementine, who was staying in the Isle of Wight with the Godfrey
Barings at their house Nubia, had been much alarmed by the reports
of the fire and had written to Churchill to say how relieved she was
that no harm had come to him. At the same time, she received a
pressing invitation from the Duke of Marlborough to come to Blenheim, and Churchill reinforced his cousin's plea. "I want so much
to show you that beautiful place and in its gardens we shall find lots
of places to talk in and lots of things to talk about." Clementine
recalled that she was right down to her last clean cotton frock —
"everyone except me had a maid and I remember having to stand for
fear of getting it crumpled." But despite a "sudden access of shyness"
which had at first made her hesitate, she accepted the invitation and
arrived at Blenheim on Monday, August 10. Lady Blanche did not
accompany her daughter, so Lady Randolph acted as chaperon.

On Tuesday morning, August 11, Churchill, as was his wont, stayed
in bed late, which somewhat mortified Clementine, who was down in

good time. Marlborough, sensing this, sent a message to Churchill to bestir himself, and in the meantime took Clementine for a drive round the park. In the late afternoon Churchill took Clementine for a walk. It came on to rain, and they took shelter in the ornamental temple which stands some 200 yards to the west of the Palace and which overlooks the lake. There Churchill proposed to Clementine and was accepted. They agreed that nothing should be said until she had told her mother. But on their way back to the house they saw F. E. Smith. Churchill danced across the grass and, in full view of the servants, flung his arms around his neck and blurted out the news. That night, before going to bed, Clementine wrote him a loving note with a drawing of a heart, inside which was inscribed the word "Winston." The following morning Churchill came down to pick a bunch of roses for Clementine and wrote a letter to her mother, Lady Blanche, to ask her blessing and to invite her to come to Blenheim. Churchill accompanied Clementine meaning to return to Blenheim. Instead, he jumped on the London train and triumphantly brought them both back to Blenheim that evening.

"He is gentle and tender," wrote Lady Blanche to Wilfrid Scawen Blunt, an old family friend, "affectionate to those he loves, much hated by those who have not come under his personal charm."

Churchill made sure that his immediate family, his most intimate friends, his Cabinet colleagues and other important personages were apprised of his engagement before it was made public. To Pamela, by then Lady Lytton, he wrote:

WSC to Lady Lytton
(*Lytton Papers*)

12 August 1908   12 Bolton Street

Pamela,

   I am to marry Clementine & I say to you as you said to me when you married Victor — you must always be our best friend.

Yours ever

W

No reply from her is extant, but Muriel Wilson's is:

Miss Muriel Wilson to WSC

15 August 1908   Tranby

My dear Winston,

It was too nice of you to wire & I was most touched & I can't tell you [how] genuinely pleased I am at your happiness — I hope you are absolutely supremely contented — for you deserve everything of the nicest description. I watched you with Clemmie this year & wondered so much if you liked her. She is so extraordinarily beautiful I did not think you could help falling in love with her. I don't know her *very* well — but like her so much & I only hope she realises *how* lucky she is! I really mean this Winston dear — because I want you to be *so* happy & I want everything to go well with you always. I am awfully glad you are going to be married as I know how lonely you are at times & what a help a wife will be to you & I do think Clemmie *is* lucky!! Will you give her my love & tell her how much I congratulate her — & as to you I wish you every luck & happiness from all my heart. I hope I shan't lose a friend? if I thought this, I should be unhappy — but I feel we shall always like each other & remain real true friends — anyhow I shall always count you as such. Bless you dear Winston & I can't tell you how really delighted I was to get your wire.

Yours affectionately
MURIEL

Molly Hacket, by this time married to Muriel Wilson's brother, wrote very sweetly:

Mrs G. K. Wilson to WSC

19 August 1908

My dear Winston,

For the sake of old days, coupled with memories of a charming speech you made one night at supper when *my* engagement was announced (now, alas! over 13 years ago) I *must* bother you with this letter (which please do not trouble to answer) to congratulate you 1000 times and wish you every possible happiness in the world — I think Miss Hozier is very lucky, and am sure that anyone as beautiful and clever as she is will be an endless joy to spend the rest of one's life with.

Once more, endless good wishes . . . and endless happiness.

Yours very sincerely

MOLLY K. WILSON

The engagement was announced on Saturday, August 15, when the following announcement appeared on the court page of *The Times*:

MR CHURCHILL. A marriage has been arranged between Mr Churchill MP, and Miss Clementine Hozier, daughter of the late Sir Henry Hozier and Lady Blanche Hozier.

On the same day Churchill addressed a meeting of miners in Swansea, and made a speech on Anglo-German relations which gave notable pleasure to the Germans, as Lloyd George, telegraphing his congratulations from Hamburg, was to confirm. An account of this speech is given in the next chapter.

When news of the engagement reached Dieppe, a fishwife who was a friend of Lady Blanche and her daughter, ran through the streets crying: *"Ecoutez, écoutez! Voilà! La fille de la dame en bleu est fiancée avec un Anglais, ministre, millionaire, et decoré!"*

The King telegraphed his good wishes from Marienbad, and congratulations from friends and colleagues poured in by every post. Lloyd George wrote from Hamburg: "Your luck has followed you into the most important transaction of your life." Northcliffe, in congratulating Churchill, complained: "You kept your secret well or my young men were not in their usual anticipatory vein, which must be enquired into on my return to town."

Among the letters Churchill received was one from Lord Hugh Cecil. "Marriage," he said, "will be excellent for you mentally morally & politically. A bachelor is regarded as morally unprincipled." He added in a postscript: "Who is to be best man?" Churchill evidently did not feel he had to look any farther for someone to fill this post. Linky Cecil wrote two days later:

Lord Hugh Cecil to WSC

20 August 1908

21 Lewes Crescent
Brighton

My dear Winston,

I shall be charmed to be best man — tho' until just before the day absence & incompetence will make me inefficient I fear.

You can have two or three or even four clergy to do the ceremony. Are you going to be married by banns or licence? Unless you contemplate a special licence you ought to take steps soon. I fancy the Brd of Trade will make you a resident in St. Margaret's parish. But if not you shd take a room in the West Palace Hotel. After a fortnight's residence (I think) you can apply for an ordinary licence. A special licence costs a lot of money (£30?), so you had better go for an ordinary one or for banns.

What about music & hymns? Also seating arrangements etc: these things are properly for me to attend to subject to your directions but I am away. Probably you will be wise to go & see Henson [*then Rector of St Margaret's and later Dean and Bishop of Durham*] (or the curate in charge) & do whatever he tells you.

Yrs ever
HUGH CECIL

The marriage was arranged for September 12 at St Margaret's Westminster, the parish church of the House of Commons. A week before Lord Hugh Cecil delivered himself of the following homily: "I earnestly hope you will be both good & happy married; but remember that Xtian marriage is for Xtians & cannot be counted on to succeed save for those who are Xtians. And the marriage vow must be kept altogether — you cannot merely abstain from adultery & leave loving cherishing etc etc to go by the board."

It was only at the end of August that Dr Welldon returned from Newfoundland to the Deanery of Manchester where he was now installed. He wrote:

Dr J. E. C. Welldon to WSC

EXTRACT

28 August 1908

The Deanery
Manchester

... I do not think you need me to assure you how strong an interest I feel in an event so full of promise for your happiness in life as your marriage. For ever since your Father asked me to take you into my House at Harrow I have watched your life, both private & public, not of course with unchanging agreement but with that even closer sympathy which is born of the faith that a man will every year prove better & nobler than he was before. Now you will pass on to the loving care of one who will have a higher title to feel for you than I, yet the relation of a master for his pupils never really dies, & my regard for you has been specially deep & warm; so that every success which may assail you in the coming years will bring pleasure to me, even as the prospect of your marriage touches my heart with hope & joy. You will let me send you a little present this week as a sign of my good wishes.

Perhaps at such a time as this I may be permitted to call myself

Your affectionate friend
J. E. C. WELLDON

Churchill replied by asking Welldon to give the address at the marriage service.

A few days after the engagement Clementine began to have second thoughts. But her younger brother, who was just twenty, wrote and told her that she had already broken off at least one publicly announced engagement, and that although he was younger than she, he was head of the family and he could not allow her to make an exhibition of a public figure like Mr Churchill.

All went well and the wedding took place at St Margaret's as arranged, on Saturday, September 12, at 2 p.m. This would not have been possible but for the co-operation of a young couple who had already, before Churchill and Clementine had even become engaged, sent out their invitations for their wedding at the same time. Large crowds assembled outside the Church, among them the London "Pearlies" — the costermongers and their families to whom Churchill had, as President of the Board of Trade, restored some of their ancient rights of trading in the street.

Barely three weeks had elapsed between the announcement of the engagement and the wedding, and so most of Churchill's Cabinet colleagues found it impossible to alter their previous arrangements: it being the summer recess, most of them made their excuses one by one — a large proportion of them writing from Scotland — Asquith, Grey, Haldane, Morley, Crewe — all deeply regretting that they were unable to be present. The two families, however, were there in strength and Churchill's closest political colleague, Lloyd George, sat just behind him in the church. F. E. Smith, of course, was also present and so were old army friends like Sir Bindon Blood and Ian Hamilton and even his old mathematics master, Mr Mayo.

The bride wore a white ivory satin dress with flowing veil of soft white tulle, and carried a bouquet of white tuberoses and a prayer book bound in white parchment, the gift of Jack Leslie, her godfather. She was given away by her brother Bill and was attended by five bridesmaids, her sister Nellie, her cousins Venetia Stanley and Madeleine Whyte, Churchill's cousin Clare Frewen and Miss Horatia Seymour.

The opening sentences were read by The Venerable Basil Wilberforce, Archdeacon of Westminster. The marriage was solemnized by the Bishop of St Asaph, Dr A. G. Edwards. There is no clue as to why the leading divine in the Church of Wales — he later became the first Archbishop of Wales — was invited to perform his task; unless it was on account of the assistance he gave to Lord Randolph Churchill in 1893 when the latter made his last successful speech in the House of Commons on the Welsh Suspensory Bill. The prayers which followed the Blessing were recited by the Reverend Edgar Sheppard, Canon of St. George's Chapel Windsor Castle and father of the famous Dick Sheppard of St. Martin's-in-the-Field.

Bishop Welldon gave the address. "There must be in the statesman's life many times when he depends upon the love, the insight, the penetrating sympathy, and devotion of his wife. The influence which the wives of our statesmen have exercised for good upon their husbands' lives is an unwritten chapter of English history, too sacred perhaps to be written in full."

Lloyd George was among those who signed the register. The reception was held at Lady St Helier's house in Portland Place — where the Pearlies danced in the street. After the reception the bride and bridegroom left for Blenheim, where they spent the first two days of the honeymoon; the bride wearing a grey cloth costume with a deep black satin sash and a large black satin hat lined with velvet and adorned with a long sweeping ostrich feather. After Blenheim, Churchill and Clementine went to Churchill's bachelor flat at Bolton Street and then on to Baveno on Lake Maggiore and later to Venice.

The young couple received numerous presents. Among them a splendid scallop-edged silver tray presented by all his colleagues in the Government, with all their autographs engraved on the back; a gold-headed malacca cane from King Edward and a 10-volume edition of Jane Austen's collected works from the Prime Minister. Volume 3, which contains the first part of *Pride and Prejudice* is inscribed. "Winston Churchill — H. H. Asquith 12 September 1908 *nec aspera terrent.*"

This marriage, which was to survive until Churchill's death at the age of ninety in 1965, proved the sheet anchor of his career. The young couple were to move into an age of broken marriages and of divorce followed by remarriage, often several times over. Throughout the convulsions of political life and the waging of the two greatest wars in history, their love remained constant and abiding. As Churchill often remarked in other contexts: "Here firm, though all be drifting."

9

The Board of Trade

CHURCHILL'S COMMITMENT to a radical programme of social reform, made with such vigour and determination at the Dundee by-election, was not simply the result of a few weeks' acquaintance with the work of the Board of Trade. He had been brought up to believe that it was one of the primary tasks of Tory Democracy, of which his father had been the outstanding exponent, to pursue social reform. Indeed, he expressed the belief in an article in *The Nation* on 7 March 1908, "The Untrodden Field in Politics," that until Chamberlain had revived the issue of Tariff Reform "the whole enormous force of the Conservative Party had been continuously exerted in allaying discontent among the masses of the people." As a Conservative MP for the cotton town of Oldham Churchill had, immediately on his entry into Parliament, been brought into contact with the vast social problems which were becoming increasingly dominant in England at the turn of the century. It has been noted how as early as 1901 Seebohm Rowntree's study of poverty in York had made a deep impression upon him. "I see little glory in an Empire which can rule the waves and is unable to flush its sewers," Churchill had written. He was then well to the Left of his Party and it caused little surprise when he crossed the floor of the House and became closely associated with the progressive Radicals of the Liberal Party.

In 1906, in a speech at St Andrew's Hall, Glasgow, during the General Election campaign, Churchill had flirted with the idea of collectivism as a means of solving social problems. He saw it as the duty of the Liberal Party to embrace the cause of "the left-out millions." He spoke of the State "embarking on various novel and adventurous experiments," and his conclusion underlined his general support for increased social and economic intervention by the State

> I do not want to impair the vigour of competition, but we can do much to mitigate the consequences of failure. We want to draw a line below which we will not allow persons to live and labour yet above which they may compete with all the strength of their manhood. We do not want to pull down the structure of science and civilisation — but to spread a net over the abyss. And I am sure that if the vision of a fair Utopia which cheers and lights the imagination of the roving multitudes should ever break into reality, it will be by developments through, modifications in, and by improvements out of, the existing competitive organisation of society.

In the three months before going to the Board of Trade, Churchill spelled out more clearly the nature of his advanced views. In one of a series of public speeches on 22 January 1908 he spoke at Manchester of "the banding together of all the producing interests in the country to secure higher profits, not by their own merits or by improvements in their system, or the exertions of their talents or ability, but by procuring the arbitrary act of the state to aid them. That process inevitably results in a further impoverishment of the great left-out labour interest." In a speech in Birmingham on the following day, mainly devoted to a passionate defence of Free Trade, Churchill also gave his views on education, which transcended the religious obsessions which usually vitiated the arguments of either side. "Is it not a terrible thing," he asked, "that the whole of our educational system upon which so many millions are lavished, stops short at the age of 14, and that boys and girls, just at the age when they ought to receive training and discipline to make them good craftsmen and careful housekeepers, are allowed to slip away from all guidance and control and fritter away priceless years on odd jobs and idleness, and be awakened at 20 or 21 by the stern realities and harsh revenges of life?" He advocated, "the organisation by the state of the proper training and apprenticeship of any persons, even though it involves a very large new expenditure." And Churchill ended this speech by stating that the Liberal Party sought to "promote the cause of temperance, nationalise and extend our system of education, develop proper methods of technical instruction, to mitigate the sorrows of old age, in opening the land more freely to the millions, in adjusting more fairly the burden of taxation upon earned and unearned increment."

In his article "The Untrodden Field in Politics," Churchill reflected on the growing commitment of Liberalism to social reform. He believed that while "the Liberal Party has not abandoned in any respect its historic championship of liberty, in all its forms under the sky — it has become acutely conscious of the fact that political freedom, however precious, is utterly incomplete without a measure at least of social and economic independence." Churchill ruminated that divisions of opinion in politics were no longer confined to purely political questions. He spoke of the "lines of cleavage . . . becoming social and economic." He now argued that "science, physical and political alike, revolts at the disorganisation which glares at us in so many aspects of modern life." As he put it, "we see the riddles of employment and under-employment quite unsolved," and he advocated "a scientific treatment of the residuum," particularly in "the mighty trades which openly assert the necessity of labour surplus — on hand — in the streets and round the dock gates — for the ordinary commercial convenience of their business."

Churchill had no dogmatic inhibitions against government intervention to deal with the social and economic problems caused by a free market economy. In this article he advocated State acquisition of the railways and canals, and the development of certain national industries like afforestation, as a means of "counter-balancing the natural fluctuations of world trade." He went on to propose "an altogether unprecedented expansion in technical colleges and combination schools to train our youth in the skill of the hand, as well as in the arts and letters, and to give them a far greater degree of discipline in mind and body." He concluded: "From many quarters we may work towards the establishment of that National Minimum below which competition cannot be allowed, but above which it may continue healthy and free, to vivify and fertilise the world."

In 1908, in fact, there was an alteration in the Liberal Government's attitude to social questions. Little had been achieved in the first two years by either Burns at the Local Government Board or by

Lloyd George at the Board of Trade. Save for the measures to reverse the Taff Vale judgement, which had nothing to do with social reform, and the Provision of Meals for Children Act, the Liberal administration had not begun to grapple with the problems affecting the wage-earning classes. In part this was due to the intransigent attitude of a Tory House of Lords that was ready to obstruct any Bill involving new Government expenditure. But 1908 saw a marked change of tone on the part of the Government. Asquith's own accession, and the zeal, dynamism and determination of Churchill and Lloyd George gave the impetus necessary to overcome any obstacles in the way of this new departure. Speaking to the Birmingham Liberal Club on 13 January 1909 Churchill proclaimed:

> The social field lies open, there is no great country where the organisation of industrial conditions more urgently demands attention. Where the reformer casts his eye he is confronted with a mass of largely preventable and even curable suffering ... whilst our vanguard enjoys all the delights of all the ages, our rearguard struggles out into conditions which are crueller than barbarism.

No longer was a Liberal Government to be chiefly preoccupied with the troubles of the dissenting schoolmaster or preacher, or with those of the temperance reformer and frugal manufacturer. "The unemployed artisan, the casual labourer, the sweated or infirm worker, the worker's widow, the underfed child, the untrained, undisciplined and exploited boy labourer," these were henceforth to be the concern of Liberal politicians.

The apparent readiness with which the Asquith Government agreed to tackle these problems more resolutely than its predecessor was perhaps due in large measure to the depression of 1907–8 and the continued deterioration in the economic situation. Unemployment, which in the past ten years had averaged 4 per cent of the working population, suddenly began to rise dramatically. In the first six months of 1908 the rate had become nearly double that of the first six months of 1907. It stood at 7.2 per cent, which meant more than 800,000 unemployed out of the working population of 11,500,000. The hardest hit industries were engineering, shipbuilding and the metal trades: coal-mining and building were also badly affected.

Declining wages coupled with a rise in retail food prices accentuated the problem. It was the worst unemployment since the early 1890s. This economic depression also came at a time when Liberal supporters were feeling particularly frustrated by the obstructionist attitude of the House of Lords towards the numerous Liberal measures of 1906–7 and by the by-election defeats which their candidates were beginning to suffer.

It was clear that Tariff Reform was not as dead as many Liberals had supposed on the morrow of their great electoral triumph. The door had certainly not been "banged, barred and bolted" as Churchill so confidently asserted only a year before in the summer of 1907. There were many in the new Government who were convinced that the best way of countering the new protectionist propaganda was to find means to alleviate the increasing mass unemployment. To no one were these considerations more vivid than to Churchill. His passionate defence of Free Trade from the attacks of Tariff Reformers was coupled with a growing readiness to seek solutions to unemployment and poverty through an increased measure of state intervention into the field of labour and social policy. Free Trade was not a question which Churchill had superficially used as an excuse to leave the Conservatives. He believed in it intellectually and emotionally. He told the Liverpool Financial Reform Association at the Sun Hall on 12 April 1909: "In this Tariff Reform agitation we are confronted with the most formidable attempt to alter the social and economic balance of this country, to the prejudice of the wage-earner and the detriment of capital, that has ever been seen in English history since the Labourers Acts of the 14th Century and the Enclosure Acts of the 18th Century."

Churchill was seeking "a scientific solution" for the unemployment problem. To him Tariff Reform was an "impudent irrelevance." It was, he said in Birmingham, "a mere grimace of cynical mockery, for persons to pretend that the imposition of food taxes or of a tinpot ten per cent duty on foreign manufactured articles would have an effect on unemployment in England."

Churchill in his by-election campaigns of 1908 had also clearly defined his commitment to a form of Liberal collectivism. He believed "the truth lay midway between individualism and collectivism." He saw "the need for a greater collective element in the State and the municipalities." He named tramways and public works as fields of advance. He went on to praise Labour, shrewdly remarking that "the Trade Unions are the most respectable and most powerful element in the Labour world" and called them "the bulwarks of our industrial system." Yet he also repudiated Socialism as a constructive possibility. In its place he gave the people of Dundee a poetic vision of the new Liberalism, as a "quickening spirit, as immortal." He concluded that "it would live on through all the days, be they good days or be they evil days. I believe it will even burn stronger and brighter and more useful in evil days than in good — just like your harbour lights which shine out across the water, and which on a calm night shine with soft refulgence — but when in a storm flash a message of life to those who toil on the rough waters."

*

At this time, when he first came to the Board of Trade, Churchill took the radical position on every issue confronting his Party, not even excepting female suffrage. When it came to the old Liberal shibboleth of temperance, he gave his backing to the Licensing Bill of 1908. At a Hyde Park rally on 25 July 1908 before 100,000 people and flanked by Labour leaders such as Arthur Henderson and Will Crooks, he said: "The cause of temperance is closely involved with almost every great social cause in which democracy is interested. Unless progress is made in grappling with the evils of the drink traffic, much of our social legislation, much of our attempt to spread wider the circles of comfort among the masses of our land, will be brought to naught or long delayed."

On foreign policy he took the same wrong-headed position as other Radicals on the Left and in the Liberal Party. When speaking to the miners of South Wales in Swansea on 14 August 1908 he discounted any conflict as possible between Great Britain and Germany: "I think it is greatly to be deprecated that persons should try to spread the belief in this country that war between Great Britain and Germany is inevitable. It is all nonsense." He first pointed out that England's island position "freed us from the curses of Continental militarism"

and went on to say: "There was no collision of primary interests —
big, important interests — between Great Britain and Germany in
any quarter of the globe." In fact, he concluded, there was nothing
to fight about, "although there may be snapping and snarling in the
newspapers and in London Clubs."

Churchill was not then so early alerted to the dangers of German
militarism as he was to be twenty-five years later. Fortunately this
was only a momentary aberration into which he stumbled alongside
his new colleagues. Within three years he was fully convinced of the
German menace and was privileged on this occasion, as he was not
on the second, to take effective steps to arm the nation against the
dangers which he foresaw.

He had inherited a good deal of Lord Randolph's isolationism and
had not yet perceived the profound truth contained in Eyre Crowe's
famous Foreign Office Memorandum of 1907 that it was in the
interest of Britain to maintain the balance of power in Europe by
being the friend or the ally of the second strongest power on the
Continent. Once he had assimilated this thought he lived with it and
on it; and throughout his life he would point to the fact that Britain
had, albeit unconsciously and without promulgating this theory,
practised it; how under Queen Elizabeth I England had defeated
Philip II of Spain; how Marlborough under good Queen Anne had
defeated Louis XIV; how under George III and Pitt she had defied
and defeated Napoleon; and how in his own time under George V
and Lloyd George Britain had worsted the Kaiser. We may be sure
that the message was strongly in his bones all through the 1930s when
he sought to rouse his countrymen against Hitler and in the 1940s
when he was allowed to play a notable share in achieving the libera-
tion of Europe from a despotic tyranny.

In the shrinking of the old European world and in the growth of
the giant powers, the Soviet Union and the United States, Eyre
Crowe's doctrine may no longer be applicable; but it served us very
well five times over four centuries — a unique record of a consistent
and persevering foreign policy — always directed at the same end, no
matter whence the danger came, and always triumphant in the end.

The only shortfall in this record was that of Oliver Cromwell.
Harold Macmillan told the author in 1962 the following pregnant

anecdote. He described how in Cairo in 1943 Churchill suddenly said to him late one night: "Cromwell was a great man wasn't he?" "Yes, sir, a very great man." "Ah," he said, "but he made one terrible mistake. Obsessed in his youth by fear of the power of Spain, he failed to observe the rise of France. Will that be said of me?" He was, of course, thinking of Germany and Russia.

*

When Churchill arrived at the Board of Trade there were already a number of legislative measures in hand which it fell to him to see through Parliament. One was the Port of London Bill which Lloyd George had introduced only a few days before the Cabinet changes were announced. This Bill, setting up the Port of London Authority so as to make London more competitive in terms of both British ports and their subsidized rivals on the Continent, took the rest of the year to pass through Parliament. A new clause, introduced in December by Churchill to give the Board of Trade instead of Parliament power to acquire land and authorize work, was fiercely resisted, and had to be modified before the House of Lords assented to it.

As first chairman Churchill appointed his Parliamentary Secretary, Hudson Kearley, soon to become Lord Devonport, of whom Belloc was to sing so unkindly:

> The grocer Hudson Kearley, he
> When purchasing his barony,
> Considered, as we understand,
> The title of Lord Sugarsand,
> Or then again he could have been
> Lord Underweight of Margarine,
> But, being of the nobler sort,
> He took the name of Devonport.

The other Bill already before the House was the Coal Mines (Eight Hours) Bill which had in fact been introduced by the Home Secretary, Herbert Gladstone, who was nominally in charge. The object of the Bill was to improve safety conditions in the mines by reducing within eighteen months the number of hours worked daily under-

ground to eight. It was, however, Churchill who on July 6 wound up
the debate on the second reading. He used the occasion to make a
notable speech which aroused considerable enthusiasm among the
Liberal and Labour members.

> The general march of industrial democracy is not towards inade-
> quate hours of work, but towards sufficient hours of leisure. That is
> the movement among the working people all over the country. They
> are not content that their lives should remain mere alternations be-
> tween bed and the factory. They demand time to look about them,
> time to see their homes by daylight, to see their children, time to
> think and read and cultivate their gardens — time, in short, to live.
> That is very strange, perhaps, but that is the request they have made
> and are making with increasing force and reason as years pass by.
>
> No one is to be pitied for having to work hard, for nature has
> contrived a special reward for the man who works hard. It gives
> him an extra relish, which enables him to gather in a brief space
> from simple pleasures a satisfaction in search of which the social
> idler wanders vainly through the twenty-four hours. But this reward,
> so precious in itself, is snatched away from the man who has won it,
> if the hours of his labour be too severe to leave any time for him to
> enjoy what he has won.

Three years later, when he was Home Secretary, Churchill was to
introduce a complicated Mines Bill of 123 clauses which legislated
for further important safety measures.

Churchill threw himself into the detailed day-to-day work of the
Board of Trade with his wonted enthusiasm. He was guided by Sir
Hubert Llewellyn-Smith, the Permanent Secretary, and by Arthur
Wilson Fox, head of the Commercial, Labour and Statistical depart-
ment, who, on the latter's death a few months later, was succeeded by
G. R. Askwith, an outstanding negotiator and administrator. Eddie
Marsh had moved with Churchill from the Colonial Office as his
private secretary.

One of the tasks of the Board of Trade was to assist in the conciliation and arbitration of industrial disputes. The Conciliation Act
passed in 1896 enabled the Board of Trade to appoint a conciliator
in trade disputes. In the first two years of the Liberal administration,
while Lloyd George was at the Board of Trade (1906–7) a total of
fifty-nine industrial conciliation cases were dealt with; but as many

cases came before the Board in the third year, 1908, as in the two previous years put together. This was work which Churchill relished. He was a firm believer in conciliation. 1908 was the worst year since 1892 for industrial disputes, and the new President was determined to play an effective part in preventing a breakdown of order. His handling of the shipbuilding dispute and the Lancashire cotton lockouts of 1908 illustrate his goodwill and good offices at this time.

At the beginning of the year the depression already described had forced shipbuilders on the Tyne to reduce wages. Five thousand shipwrights refused to agree to this and struck on January 21. In the following month 14,000 engineers went on strike owing to wage reductions. Lloyd George had unavailingly sought to conciliate the parties in February and March. The shipbuilding employers proclaimed a lock-out on May 2 which was extended to the Mersey and the Clyde. Churchill came back from his by-election campaign at Dundee for consultations in London with his advisors at the Board of Trade and the employers concerned, and three weeks later a settlement was reached through his personal intervention.

A reduction of 1s. 6d. a week in wages was to be coupled with the setting up of "permanent machinery" for future negotiations. The terms were finely drawn: they were accepted, but only just — by 24,745 votes to 22,110 on a ballot of the ship-workers.

The engineering dispute dragged on from February through the summer. In August the employers threatened that if it did not end there would be a national lock-out of the Amalgamated Engineers, Steam Engine Makers and Machine Workers. The union asked Churchill to intervene and a conference was held on September 9 at which it was agreed by the union that the wage reductions of six months before would be accepted and the employers promised that no further reductions would take place for six months. Again, the union members only just agreed to the terms, by 4,609 to 3,739 votes.

The cotton industry was also suffering from economic difficulties, and on July 24 the master cotton-spinners decided to reduce wages by 5 per cent. The cotton unions, at a conference with the employers on August 4, refused to recommend the acceptance of this reduction. Three weeks later notice was given that wages would be reduced from September 21, and that if the men did not accept this, they would be

locked out. The reduction was, however, opposed by the overwhelming majority of spinners and cardroom operatives, and the lock-out
started: 120,000 men were affected in the Bolton and Oldham areas of
Lancashire and thousands of weavers were also thrown out of work
for want of yarn. The lock-out lasted until November, when the
employers agreed to postpone the reduction of wages until March.

Nearly eight years as member for two Lancashire seats had made
Churchill thoroughly conversant with the workings of the cotton
industry and its problems, both from the point of view of the management and that of the unions. He naturally felt that his experience in
this field would be of assistance to the Board of Trade in its efforts to
effect a settlement, and even when he was on his honeymoon he
caused Board of Trade officials to send him detailed reports on the
progress of the negotiations. At the same time, he made proposals to
both sides of the cotton industry for a new "sliding scale" scheme that
would take into account the varying conditions of trade to supplement the existing conciliation machinery.

It was while he was on his honeymoon that Churchill also entered
into correspondence with Reginald McKenna, the First Lord of the
Admiralty, in order to persuade him to bring forward certain naval
construction plans for 1909 to the autumn of 1908. "The distress on
the Tyne and Clyde cannot fail to be exceptionally acute during the
whole of the coming winter and will produce a grave unrest among
the artisan classes greatly to the prejudice of all the most essential
interests of the Government." He explained that he had been
strongly impressed by the complaints which leading people in shipbuilding circles make of the uneven and indeed spasmodic manner
in which naval construction is regulated. Churchill feared that "if
events take their usual course, I suppose we shall have to face a winter
of starvation and stress on the Clyde and Tyne, with great numbers
of respectable Trade Unionists reduced to the gutter. . . . After
infinite misery has been caused and widespread discontent created,
next year upon a reviving trade, the Admiralty will have a very large
shipbuilding programme drawn up to an artificial level not to be
sustained by ordinary market demand, and have everybody working
under unsatisfactory conditions of overtime." Churchill therefore
suggested to McKenna that seven or eight of the next year's smaller

ships should be brought forward in construction. He had already consulted Lloyd George at the Exchequer on this plan and won his consent.

McKenna replied favourably — he pointed out that "in ordinary circumstances nothing of the kind that you suggested as the subject of discussion could be undertaken without having a supplementary estimate. It so happens however that this year owing to the engineers' strike our full estimated expenditure up to date has not been made, and a margin is therefore left me with which I can expedite my programme." He added, "not 7 or 8, as you suggest, but 21 ships will be in the course of construction in the very minimum of time."

Despite his successes in the first few months, Churchill became convinced that "there was a need for the creation of a more formal and permanent machinery" for industrial conciliation. He therefore proposed, in a memorandum dated September 1, a Standing Court of Arbitration. There were to be two representatives for labour, two for the employers and a Chairman appointed by the Board of Trade. These adjudicators would vary according to the nature of the dispute in question, and would be selected from three panels of qualified personnel nominated by the Board of Trade. Churchill's conciliation scheme did not require fresh legislation, and was thus put into practice straight away. During the year 1909 when the scheme was first in operation, courts of arbitration, formed at the request of the parties concerned, were used to settle a dispute of boot-and-shoe operatives at Northampton, of coal-miners at Dunkerton (near Bath), of iron-workers at Falkirk, of copper-smelters at Briton Ferry (South Wales), of carters at Londonderry, of axle hammermen at Newton in Lancashire and of Scottish iron-moulders.

The idea of intervention by the state in trade disputes had begun with Rosebery's handling of the coal strike in 1893 and had been reinforced by Lloyd George in his settling of the 1907 railway strike. Churchill, however, sought to make government action more systematic, and in particular to enable his department to intervene at an earlier stage of disputes than hitherto. He was thus able to play a more active and positive part in the conciliation of differences between capital and labour.

While at the Board of Trade Churchill showed great interest in the question of Daylight Saving, or the introduction of Summer Time. A bill, based on a suggestion of Mr William Willett of Brighton was introduced by Robert Pearce, Liberal MP for Leek, in the 1908 Parliamentary Session. The object was to ensure an extra period of daylight during summer evenings. The Bill provided that on each of the first four Sundays in April of each year the hour between 2 and 3 a.m. should consist of forty minutes, and on each of the first four Sundays of September should consist of eighty minutes. The Bill was read a second time on March 27 and referred to a Select committee of the House of Commons. They reported in favour of the measure on July 2, but the Government did not take it up, although Churchill used the Board to gather information on the question from employers and trade unions.

In the following year the Bill was introduced again, but in a different form. It now proposed that from the third Sunday in April to the third Sunday in September local time should be one hour in advance of Greenwich Mean Time. Churchill spoke in the debate on 5 March 1909. He said that it was a measure on which the executive was not going to dictate to the country. "It is one of those subjects on which a representative assembly ought to guide opinion and upon which opinion must be allowed to form gradually and slowly." The Government's position was described as one of "benevolent neutrality," but this did not prevent Churchill expressing his "strong support for the measure." He pointed out that it would have no apparent effect on people's lives. "An extra yawn some morning in April, an extra snooze some morning in September, otherwise the great mass of the human race will be quite unconscious that a change had occurred, except that the evenings appear to be unexpectedly and pleasantly longer." He believed its benefits greatly outweighed the disadvantages. He admitted certain difficulties existed over the despatch of continental mails and steamers, and that it may cause some inconvenience to farmers in harvest time. But he dealt scornfully with other objections like "rural labourers had no watches and therefore would not be able to know the time," "inconvenience might be caused to those who wish to gamble in stocks," "in restaurants, ladies like to dine by artificial light," and that "children will object to go to bed in consequence of the undue prevalence of light."

Churchill saw an extra hour of daylight as "a great boon for the wage-earning classes." He rejected the idea that employers would attempt to impose excessive overtime and destroy the effectiveness of the measure. "Overtime is not regulated by the sun but by the strength of working-class organisations." One hundred and fifty extra hours of light for the working classes each year would enable them "to visit parks and cultivate gardens to an extent which they are unable to do now." He stressed that the Bill was only an "experiment" and favoured it being referred once again to a Select Committee. Apparently in the previous year the Bill had not been treated seriously and the evidence submitted had not been full enough for the committee to reach a decision. The Bill was given a second reading by 130 to 94 and referred to the Select Committee.

Despite the support for the measure of many local Chambers of Commerce, of Borough Councils and Trade Unions, the Committee reported adversely on Willett's Bill. It felt that, as the *Annual Register* put it, "in view of the diversity of opinion and the probability that important interests might be inconvenienced" the proposed measure was inopportune. It was not until 1916 under conditions of war that the hours of daylight were extended in the summer time.

*

When the newly-married Churchills had returned from their honeymoon they squatted in Churchill's old house 12 Bolton Street. But at the end of February 1909 the lease expired and they looked for a house elsewhere. They found what they wanted at 33 Eccleston Square, and in March 1909 Churchill took an eighteen-year lease at £195 per annum.

The house in Eccleston Square was made ready more quickly than would be possible today. Churchill and his wife were anxious to move in earlier as their first child was expected in July. In their correspondence the expected child was referred to as the PK or Puppy Kitten — evidently to cover either eventuality as to the child's sex. They had varying *petits noms* for themselves of which the favourites in the early years were Pug and Kat. On the following pages are some examples of how they ended their letters with little drawings of these animals.

fondebest love to you a
the Pit . Your loving husband

a tranquil pug.

P.S. I have not spoken
to a single Cat
of any sort except my
witta !!!!

Clemmie

The Wow   The Woo

Your loving

Clemmie

loving husband

W.

with fondest love

W.

this is the
galloping pug — for European travel

A good deal of work needed to be done before Eccleston Square was ready to receive its new owners, and Churchill took a keen interest in the preparations that were being made for his new permanent home. "The marble basin has arrived," he reported to his wife who was staying at Blenheim. "Your window is up — a great improvement. All the bookcases are in position (I have ordered two more for the side window of the alcove). The dining-room gleams in creamy white. The Big room is papered. The bathroom well advanced." She gave directions as to the carpeting — in Churchill's room Nathan Laski's carpet, in her own the blue bedroom carpet from Bolton Street, a new carpet for the dining-room, as the old red stair-carpet was really too shabby for this purpose.

Churchill approved entirely. "You certainly have made a judicious selection of carpets and I entirely approve it," he wrote on April 28. "The bookshelves are being put in the cases & the colour is being most attractively polished." His wife longed to see the library and begged to be allowed to come up to London to help her husband put the books on the shelves.

Churchill was very much concerned that his wife should rest for the months before the baby was due to arrive. "I think," he wrote to her on May 4, "I was thoughtless to dwell upon the need of your resting so much before your mother but I could not help feeling anxious when I pictured you surrounded by all that stir and bustle. It is only in these critical months that you will find me a tease. . . . I think the arrangements you are making at Eccleston are excellent & I am only anxious that you should not wear yourself out in them."

On May 31 Jack's wife, Lady Gwendeline gave birth to her first child — John George. "It seems to have been a most smooth and successful affair," Churchill wrote to his wife. "Goonie dined out, walked home, slept soundly till 2. Then felt the premonitory sensations wh precede the act of destiny. And at 4 or 5 all was gloriously over — & another soul — escaping from its rest or unrest in the oceans of the spirit world crept timidly up on to a frail raft of consciousness & sense — there to float — for a while. She hardly had any pain and Philips was most skilful. My dear Bird — this happy event will be a great help to you & will encourage you. *I* rather shrink from it — because I dont like your having to bear pain & face this ordeal. But we are in the grip of circumstances, & out of pain joy will spring & from passing weakness new strength arise."

Mrs Churchill's baby arrived six weeks later on July 11.

She was christened Diana on August 9. Like her father the child had red hair. Her mother was a good deal run down after the birth of the child and so spent some weeks in Sussex with Lady Blanche Hozier, a separation which brings its usual crop of letters to chronicle and illuminate this account. The separation of lovers delights the heart of the biographer.

It is said that Mr and Mrs Stanley Baldwin only spent one night of their married life apart — hence no such correspondence as that which will continue to adorn this tale of a truly happy and lifelong marriage.

"The PK is very well," Churchill wrote to his wife on August 31, "but the nurse is rather inclined to glower at me as if I was a tiresome interloper. I missed seeing her (the PK) take her bath this morning. But tomorrow I propose to officiate!" He was delighted by the experience. After bathing her he wrote on September 2: "She is awfully strong & her little hands shut like a vice on one's fingers. She looks vy beautiful & is greatly improving in shape & size." And on the first anniversary of their marriage he wrote from Strasbourg: "Kiss especially the beautiful PK for me. I wonder what she will grow into, & whether she will be lucky or unlucky to have been dragged out of chaos. She ought to have some rare qualities both of mind & body. But these do not always mean happiness or peace. Still I think a bright star shines for her."

On that first anniversary he had written to his wife: "You have been so sweet and good to me that I cannot say how grateful I feel to you for your dear nature and matchless beauty." And the previous week he had written:

WSC to his wife
(*CSC Papers*)

EXTRACT

6 September 1909

Dearest Clemmie do try to gather your strength. Don't spend it as it comes. Let it accumulate. Remember my two rules — No walk of more than ½ a mile: no risk of catching cold. There will be so much to do in the autumn & if there is an Election — you will have to play a great part. All these last 8 months you have been weighed down with your tremendous effort. But when you are quite recovered I shall find you such a lot of work to do that you will call me a beast. My darling I do so want your life to be a full & sweet one, I want it to be worthy of all the beauties of your nature. I am so much centred in my politics, that I often feel I must be a dull companion, to anyone who is not in the trade too. It gives me so much joy to make you happy — & often wish I were more various in my topics. Still the best is to be true to oneself — unless you happen to have a vy tiresome self! Goodnight my sweet Clemmie, give my love to your Mamma and Nellinita — and keep yourself the fondest wishes of my heart — now & always.

The course of true love did not always run clear. No doubt their frequent separations contributed to occasional small friction.

WSC to his wife
(CSC Papers)

EXTRACT

10 November 1909   Board of Trade

Dearest it worries me vy much that you should seem to nurse such absolutely wild suspicions wh are so dishonouring to all the love & loyalty I bear you & will please god bear you while I breathe. They are unworthy of you & me. And they fill my mind with feelings of embarrassment to wh I have been a stranger since I was a schoolboy. I know that they originate in the fond love you have for me, and therefore they make me feel tenderly towards you & anxious always to deserve the most precious possession of my life. But at the same time they depress me & vex me — & without reason.

We do not live in a world of small intrigue, but of serious & important affairs. I could not conceive myself forming any other attachment than that to which I have fastened the happiness of my life here below. And it offends my best nature that you should — against your true instinct — indulge small emotions & wounding doubts. You ought to trust me for I do not love & will never love any woman in the world but you and my chief desire is to link myself

to you week by week by bonds which shall ever become more intimate & profound.

Beloved I kiss your memory — your sweetness & beauty have cast a
glory upon my life.

You will always find me your

loving & devoted husband

W

*

When he arrived at the Board of Trade Churchill is reported to
have observed that "there is nothing to do here: LG has taken all the
plums." Yet he soon found that the department could be fashioned
into an instrument for carrying out an experiment in social welfare
perhaps unprecedented in English history. In partnership with Lloyd
George he carried out a remarkable programme of radical reform to
help the exploited, the unemployed and the needy.

The three landmarks in Churchill's administration of the Board
of Trade, which covered less than two years, were legislation concerned with sweated labour, the creation of an intricate system of
labour exchanges, and most of the spadework for the Bill on Unemployment Insurance which Sydney Buxton introduced shortly after
he succeeded Churchill at the Board of Trade.

No neat definition can describe the sweated labour system. It essentially concerned the unskilled and unorganised section of the working
classes, that chiefly involved in the clothing trades like tailoring and
dressmaking, though it was also widespread in the docks. The introduction of machinery and the creation of large productive units in
the country's staple industries led to an abundant, even excessive
supply of unskilled and inefficient labour. This latter fact was crucial
to the whole system. As J. A. Hobson observed in his book *Problems
of Poverty*:

> ... the displacement of hired labour by new mechanical inventions
> kept in perpetual existence a large margin of unemployed or half
> employed who form the most hopeless and degraded section of the
> city poor. They furnish a body of reckless starving competitors for
> work, who keep down the standard of wages and life for the lower
> grades of regular workers affected by this competition.

The harsh struggle for employment in the docks in the 1880s had led to much public sympathy for the dockers. It was less easy to arouse sympathy for those trades which remained almost immune to public scrutiny. The competition of sempstresses, tailors, shirt-finishers and fine sewers, was conducted more quietly and privately and was less intense than the open labour market of the docks. The influx of Eastern European immigrants into London, Leeds and Manchester in the 1890s and 1900s made the problem worse. In London in particular, Whitechapel and St George's in the East End attracted many immigrants, particularly Jews, into the sweated labour trades. This uncontrolled entry of the unskilled and the poor accentuated the difficulties imposed by the lack of effective legislation to maintain minimum wages and standards in the multiplicity of private work-shops which sprang up in the East End of London.

For twenty years the sweated labour question had been a constant source of agitation by social critics such as Charles Booth and Hobson. Beatrice Potter, the future Mrs. Webb, gained experience of the tailoring and dressmaking trades of Whitechapel and campaigned for reform through the Fabian Society. Mrs Ramsay MacDonald, wife of the first Labour Prime Minister had founded the Women's Industrial Council. In Parliament, too, some attempt was made to face the problem. In 1888 Lord Dunraven got the House of Lords to set up a Committee to enquire into the sweating system, but it proved inconclusive and ineffective. The same could be said of the Factory and Workshops Acts of 1891. A mere extension of the Factory Acts to cover the domestic workship was no solution, as it would have been almost impossible to have penetrated into the dark recesses where much of this work went on.

A parliamentary committee which reported in 1908 alleged that in 1906 there had been over 1,000 breaches of the law and only three prosecutions. It was also clear that nearly a quarter of the medical officers of health did not even bother to submit reports on the sanitary condition of workshops to the Home Office, although the law obliged them to do so. In fact, after twenty years of sporadic and ineffective attempts to deal with sweated labour, there was a real need for a fresh and more vigorous approach to the problem.

So reformers sought a solution by advocating a general minimum

wage rate. Since the early 1890s, the State or local authorities had
been prepared to insist on every contractor signing a fair wages clause
guaranteeing the current wage paid by the corporation. The example
of Australia was often cited by reformers as a blue-print for the reform
of sweated labour. Trade Boards were set up there in 1896 and
minimum wage rates enforced. Sir Charles Dilke, MP for the Forest
of Dean, whose public position was greatly respected despite the
scandalous divorce case in which he had been involved, was much influenced by Deakin's Australian social legislation and introduced a
Wages Board Bill in every parliamentary session after 1900. The
Government finally decided to act and set up a committee of enquiry.
Yet when Dilke's Bill reached its second reading on 21 February 1908
Herbert Gladstone, the Home Secretary, remained unsympathetic.
He sought delay pending the final report from the Select Committee
on Home Work, while at the same time he rejected the principle of a
minimum legal wage being guaranteed for all workingmen by the
state.

Churchill showed more courage in the 1909 session of Parliament
with his Trade Boards Act. True, he was concerned at the outset to
overcome existing *laissez-faire* prejudices. He argued, when introducing his Bill on 28 April 1909: "It was formerly suggested that the
workings of the law of supply and demand would naturally regulate
and eliminate." Yet:

> . . . where in the great staple trades in the country you have a power-
> ful organisation on both sides, where you have responsible leaders
> able to bind their constituents to their decision, where that organisa-
> tion is conjoint with an automatic scale of wages or arrangements
> for avoiding deadlock by means of arbitration, there you have a
> healthy bargaining, which increases the competitive power of indus-
> try, enforces the progressive standard of life and productive scale
> and continually weaves capital and labour more closely together,
> but where you have what we call sweated trades, you have no or-
> ganisation, no parity of bargaining, the good employer is undercut
> by the worst. The worker whose whole livelihood depends on the
> industry, is undersold by the worker who only takes the trade up
> as a second string, his feebleness and ignorance generally renders
> the worker easy prey to the tyranny of masters and middlemen —

only a step higher up the ladder than the worker — and held in the
same relentless grip of forces — where those conditions prevail, you
have not a condition of progress, but a condition of a progressive
degeneration . . . there is no power of self-cure within the trade.
While the general advance of industrial life has been constant these
morbid patches have remained depressed.

Churchill's Bill was only to be applied to certain scheduled trades.
It set up Trade Boards which were to fix minimum rates for time-
work and also, if they thought fit, fix rates for piecework for the trades
under their jurisdiction. Any employer who paid less than the minimum rate could be fined up to £20 and £5 for each day after the
conviction, if the offence continued.

The Trade Boards consisted of an equal number of representatives
of employers and employed, "with an element of impartial and enlightened officialism so widely seen in Germany's social legislation."
Churchill made it clear that the Boards were not elective. The Board
of Trade itself was to "decide whether the minimum wage rate had
got sufficient backing in the trade to render enforcement of it by
prosecution a useful and effective process." The effectiveness of the
Bill depended on factory inspectors, special peripatetic inspectors
appointed under the Act by the Board of Trade, and on public
opinion.

Above all, Churchill warned, the Bill depended on "the powerful
band of employers, perhaps the majority, who from high motives and
self interest or a combination of the two, would form a vigilant and
instructive police, knowing every turn and twist of the trade, and who
will labour and must labour, to protect themselves from being undercut by the illegal competition of unscrupulous rivals."

"The Trade Boards Bill has been beautifully received and will be
passed without a division," Churchill wrote to his wife from the
Treasury Bench in the House during the debate on 28 April 1909.
"A. Balfour & Alfred Lyttelton were most friendly to it, & all opposition had faded away." Indeed, the only discordant note came from
Sir Frederick Banbury, an extreme protectionist, who believed that
the Bill was the thin end of the wedge, that it would eventually lead
to state intervention in the fixing of wages and conditions in all
industries.

The Bill covered 200,000 workers — of whom 140,000 were women and girls. In 1913 it was extended to five more trades and 170,000 additional workers. It was a measure beyond the dreams and expectations of the most ardent Fabians. Even though he was to be in the years immediately following less forward in promoting minimum wage proposals in general, Churchill's determined attack on sweated labour proved a notable first attempt to introduce the idea of a National Minimum into British labour legislation.

The schemes for compulsory unemployment insurance and for the allied Labour Exchanges were probably Churchill's greatest achievement at the Board of Trade. It ensured for him a place among the architects, if only of the foundations, of the modern welfare state.

Unemployment had been the recurrent handmaiden of nineteenth-century industrial society. While it was seen as a blot on the capitalist system, there were few who felt that anything could be done to solve the problem. Under the Poor Law the indigent and the unemployed obtained relief, but action could not be taken to prevent unemployment in the first place. Since Joseph Chamberlain had in 1886 urged local authorities to provide work in public parks, roads or forests, government attention to unemployment had been only sporadic and irresolute.

Churchill was to use his energy to move into a new field where no other politician had dared to enter.

As early as 4 January 1908 Churchill, while still Under-Secretary at the Colonial Office, had written to Henry Wilson-Fox, Manager of the British South Africa Company about unemployment insurance. In a terse letter from Cairo on his way home from East Africa, he compared the English and German systems of social security and concluded that "in one respect the German system has an enormous advantage. It catches everybody." Whereas in England "the meshes of our safety net are only adapted to subscribers and all those who are not found on any of those innumerable lists go smashing down on the pavement." He already saw "the need to underpin the whole existing social security apparatus with a foundation of comparatively low grade state safeguards."

The Webbs were at this time seeking support in the Government for their own projects for labour exchanges. Beatrice Webb sent a paper on the scheme to Churchill, who was greatly interested. Mrs Webb remarked in her diary of 11 March 1908: "Winston Churchill dined with us last night, we talked exclusively shop. He had swallowed whole Sidney's scheme for boy labour and unemployment, had even dished it up in an article in *The Nation* ["The Untrodden Field in Politics"] the week before. He is most anxious to be friendly and we are quite willing to be so."

In the letter to Asquith on March 14, already quoted about his post in the new Government, Churchill spoke of "dimly seeing across gulfs of ignorance . . . the outline of a policy which I call the Minimum Standard. It is national rather than departmental." He doubted then his ability or experience to carry the policy out. Yet he also stressed what had to be done. Among other constructive schemes like technical education for youth and the decasualization of labour, he believed "means must be found by which the state can within certain limits and for short periods augment the demand of the ordinary market for unskilled labour, so as to counter-balance the oscillations of world trade." He concluded that "underneath, though not in substitution for, the immense disjointed fabric of social safeguards and insurances which has grown up by itself in England, there must be spread — at a lower level — a sort of Germanised net work of State regulation and intervention."

To aid him in finding a way through the complexities which surrounded this problem Churchill enlisted the aid of two remarkable men, Sir Hubert Llewellyn-Smith and William Beveridge. Llewellyn-Smith had just become Permanent Secretary to the Board of Trade. Coming from a Quaker family he spent his early years doing social work at Toynbee Hall in London's East End, where he helped the dockers' leader Ben Tillett at the time of the 1889 dock strike. After joining the Board of Trade he distinguished himself as a negotiator. It was he who was mainly responsible under Churchill's direction for the scheme of unemployment insurance.

To deal with the equally tortuous problem of labour exchanges Churchill, on the advice of the Webbs, called in William Beveridge, a twenty-nine-year-old Oxford don who, like Llewellyn-Smith, had worked at Toynbee Hall. His articles in the *Morning Post* advocating the establishment of labour exchanges had lately brought him into prominence, and he had himself served on the Central Unemployed Committee for London. These two men worked together on their inter-related plans. Thirty-five years later, Churchill, as head of the wartime Coalition Government, was to recall Beveridge to the nation's service to prepare his massive study which formed the basis of the great new strides which, under the name of the Welfare State, were to be introduced largely, with the general approbation of all political parties, by the Labour Government of Clement Attlee in 1945–50.

Throughout 1908 Churchill made the general public aware of his "new departure." The 1908 parliamentary session had seen the establishment of old-age pensions of a non-contributory nature for those over seventy — a scheme initiated at the Treasury by Asquith and implemented by Lloyd George. Churchill at Dundee on October 10 explained its significance for the future. He said that it marked "the assertion into our social system of an entirely new principle in regard to poverty and that principle once asserted cannot possibly be confined within its existing limits." He believed that they had "opened a door which will not soon or easily be closed. The Members of both Houses of Parliament have been led to the verge of the cruel abyss of poverty and have in solemn session assembled to contemplate its depth and gloom."

> All alike have come to gaze — none have remained unmoved. There are some distinguished and eminent men, who have started back appalled by what they have seen, and whose only idea is to slam the door on the grim and painful prospect which has been revealed to their eyes. . . . But that is not the only spirit which has been awakened in our country — there are others, not less powerful, and a greater number, who will never allow that door to be closed, they have got their feet in it, they are resolved that it shall be kept open. Nay more, they are prepared to descend into the abyss, and grapple with its evils — as sometimes you see after an explosion at a coal mine a rescue party advancing undaunted into the smoke and steam.

Churchill described unemployment as the problem of the hour, and urged that it had become "a paramount necessity for us to make scientific provision against the fluctuations and setbacks which are inevitable in world commerce and in national industry." The 1908 depression had illustrated the frailty of England's prosperity which could be undermined by "the backwash of an American monetary disturbance or a crisis in the Near or Far East." These independent economic forces had "the effect of letting loose upon thousands of humble families and households all the horrors of a state of siege or a warlike blockade." Churchill concluded that "the social machinery at the basis of our industrial life" was "deficient, ill organised and incomplete." He listed three vicious conditions which made England peculiarly susceptible to any outside disturbance of international trade.

Firstly, he saw "the lack of any central organisation of industry, or any general and concerted control either of ordinary government work, or of any extraordinary relief works." He felt it should be possible for "some authority in some Government Office" to "exert a powerful influence over the general distribution of government contracts," after foretelling "the whole situation in advance." He adopted an almost Keynesian position, when he advocated the need to have "in permanent existence certain recognised industries of a useful, but uncompetitive character, like afforestation, managed by public departments and capable of being expanded or contracted according to the needs of the labour market, just as easily as you can pull out the stops or work the pedals of an organ." This would at least limit, if not eradicate, unemployment.

The second "vicious condition" he saw as the plight of the casual unskilled labourer, "whose whole life and the lives of his wife and children are embarked in a sort of blind, desperate, fatalistic gamble with circumstances beyond his comprehension or control." The third condition was that of boy labour — Churchill was very concerned at the youth of England being thrown on the labour market at a tender age — "running wild at fourteen."

Churchill appealed to the humanity and patriotism of the upper classes to help those in need. He also promised that large schemes were afoot, "properly prepared and scientifically conceived for dealing with the evils mentioned." Churchill's speech was well-received. Herbert Samuel wrote to him on the following day saying that he had been following the problem of unemployment very closely during the last ten years and that "your speech of last night was the first made by any leader which has seemed to me on the right lines."

On 11 December 1908 Churchill presented his memorandum on Insurance and Labour Exchanges to the Cabinet. He spoke of the responsibility of employers to their workmen and the need to give concrete expression and embodiment to it. He favoured low benefit scales, which would not be higher than the lowest earnings of workmen in the trade but which would support him without privation — "so as not to remove thrift, whether by saving or insurance." There was to be a system of compulsory contributory Unemployment Insurance to which both employer and employed were to contribute. "The unemployed benefit proposed will in the majority of cases enable the workman to tide over a temporary depression without selling up his home or losing his status. It will give him the necessary time to seek new employment if it is evident that the total stringency will be prolonged or perhaps permanent."

Mr James Wilson, Mr Harold Wilson's father, heard Churchill say after a meeting at Manchester, "Had I the powers of a dictator I would cause the word Insure to be inscribed on the lintel of every house in the land." Churchill had said on another occasion: "Insurance brought the miracle of averages to the rescue of the masses."

Labour Exchanges and Unemployment Insurance were to be inseparable. "All foreign experiments have shown that a fund for insurance against unemployment needs to be protected against unnecessary or fraudulent claims by the power of notifying situations to men in receipt of benefit as soon as they become vacant. The insurance scheme, on the other hand, will be the lever of the most valuable kind to bring the Exchanges into successful operation — for the employers, interested in reducing friction in the passage of workmen from job to job, and in not drawing fresh men into a trade while any man already insured in it is standing idle, will turn naturally to the use of a Labour Exchange." The plan for insurance had in fact almost reached completion by then. It was to cover a group of trades comprising 3,000,000 people in building and works of construction, engineering and shipbuilding, with the power of subsequent extension. Half the cost of the insurance scheme was to be met by a compulsory contribution of 2d. a week deducted by the employer from the workmen's wages — one-quarter (1d. a week) by the employer and one-quarter (1d. a week) by the Treasury. The benefits to be paid were 7s. 6d. a week for five weeks, 6s. a week for another five weeks,

5s. for another five weeks. Fuller details of the scheme may be found in the Companion Volume.

In a letter to Asquith on December 26, Churchill said that he would not press his "unemployment insurance plan until LG had found a way of dealing with infirmity or (which is possible) had found that there was no way." He felt that "the Insurance policy must be presented as a whole — for it would never do to exact contributions from masters and men in successive layers," and he proposed to go ahead with "the simple project of Labour Exchanges" alone in 1909. He believed this would also give more time to bargain and to discuss the insurance scheme with the trades and workmen specifically concerned. It was this prudent delay on Churchill's part which has robbed him in the public mind of a good deal of the credit for unemployment insurance. As he was to write to his wife on 22 April 1911: "Lloyd George has practically taken Unemployed Insurance to his own bosom and I am I think effectively elbowed out of this large field in which I gave so much thought and effort. Never mind! There are many good fish in the sea." When it was enacted as Part 2 of the National Insurance Act of 1911 it was merged with Lloyd George's schemes and it was Lloyd George who got most of the credit, as well as, admittedly, most of the abuse — "9d. for 4d." was tied by the Tories round the neck of Lloyd George rather than that of Churchill. Rough justice should have dictated 7d. for 3d. round Lloyd George's neck and 2d. for a penny round Churchill's. Perhaps the laurels should have been more appropriately shared. Perhaps so, too, should have been the criticism of their rabble-rousing partisan speeches. Lloyd George is remembered for his provocative Limehouse speech which Mrs Churchill attended on 30 July 1909. Churchill had acquired from his father a vitriolic tongue, and the reader will already have seen some pungent examples that fell from it. As he turns the pages, he will be regaled with still further specimens which, though they enraged his Tory opponents and drew censure from the King at the time, do not seem to have left posterity the reproach of a comparable Limehouse against him. Perhaps this was because he indulged his polemics so often and it would have been impossible to fix any precise location for the outpouring of his at times almost merciless oratory.

Churchill's relations with Lloyd George will be a persistent theme throughout these volumes. The formidable Welsh Radical who emerged almost from the caves of Wales to the centre of the British political scene and who was to make himself the master of the nation in what till then had been her most grievous hour long exercised a fascination for Churchill. It was a fascination which was reciprocated. A friendship was forged between them which had its ups and downs: but with many disagreements on public affairs it remained firm to the end. Everybody, even those who did not know him, called Churchill Winston. Very few called Lloyd George, David: Churchill was one of the few. They co-operated wholeheartedly in all the legislation of the pre-war Liberal Government. Yet there was certainly a rivalry between them. Either might have emerged as the great leader in the First World War: Gallipoli settled that role. Churchill was the younger man, and he was to have a more glorious role in an even more deadly struggle twenty years later. It must have given him some satisfaction that it fell to him to recommend his leader in the First World War to the Sovereign for an Earldom in 1945.

Churchill significantly concluded his letter to Asquith of 26 December 1908: "I feel we must look ahead and make bold concerted plans for the next two years. I look to the large measures of Finance and Unemployment wh are pending to justify our retention of office. I believe that there is an impressive social policy to be unfolded wh would pass ponderously through both Houses and leave an abiding mark on national history."

Three days later Churchill wrote from Blenheim to Asquith in a similar vein and sent a copy of the report from the trade union delegation led by Arthur Henderson which had just returned from Germany where they had been studying Insurance and Labour Exchanges.

WSC to H. H. Asquith

EXTRACT

29 December 1908   [Blenheim]
  Copy

. . . I have been revolving many things during these few days of tranquillity and I feel impelled to state to you the conviction that has for a long time past been forming in my mind. There is a tre-

mendous policy of social organisation. The need is urgent and the
moment ripe. . . . The minister who will apply to this country the
successful experiences of Germany in social organisation may or may
not be supported at the polls, but he will at least have left a memorial which time will not deface of his administration. . . .

He spoke of the two years which remained for the Government to
put its social programme into action, noting "the very class of legislation which is required is just the kind the House of Lords will not
dare to oppose." "The steps forward" that Churchill listed were:
Labour Exchanges and Unemployment Insurance, national infirmity
insurance, special expansive state industries — afforestation and roads
— modernized Poor Laws, railway amalgamation with State control
and guarantee; and a new education bill. He wanted to "thrust a big
slice of Bismarckianism over the whole underside of our industrial
system, and await the consequences whatever they may be with a good
conscience."

In January and February 1909 Churchill paved the way for his
schemes by a series of public speeches devoted to social reform. At
Birmingham on January 12 he claimed that "the main aspirations of
the British people are social rather than political. They see around
them on every side and almost every day spectacles of confusion and
misery which they cannot reconcile with any conception of humanity
or justice . . . they see on the one hand the mighty power of science
backed by wealth and power to introduce order, to provide safeguards, to prevent accidents, or at least to limit their consequences."
Yet "they wonder why so little has been done here. They demand
that more shall be done. . . ."

On February 5 at Newcastle Churchill spoke of "the great mission
of Liberalism" which was "now comprehensive and inclusive to bring
in the rearguard of society left behind struggling in the defiles behind
the position conquered by the main army . . . to bring the people into
government, to open all careers freely to the talent of every class, to
associate ever larger numbers with offices of authority." The path
was being prepared for the advances of 1909.

Churchill had to convince his Cabinet colleagues as well as Parliament and the country. He noted in a letter to his wife on April 27:
"My Unemployment Insurance plan encountered much opposition
from that old ruffian Burns & that little goose Runciman, & I could

not get any decision yesterday from the Cabinet. Asquith is however quite firm about it, & I do not doubt that in the end it will come safely through." He introduced his Labour Exchanges Bill in the House of Commons on 19 May 1909. It was designed to secure the more efficient organization of the labour market, to increase the mobility of labour and, in the words of the Royal Commission on the Poor Law, to mitigate "the misery of tramping after problematical work" and last, but not least, to institute machinery indispensable to the proper administration of a system of unemployment insurance. "Modern industry is national," said Churchill in the course of his speech of May 19. "The facilities of transport and communications knit the country together as no other country has ever been knitted before. Only labour has not profited by this improved organisation." To counter the fears of Labour members, Churchill stressed that the exchanges "were not to be the cause of sending working men gadding about the country from pillar to post." He also made it plain that his scheme was not a panacea for unemployment. He saw the main function of the plan "to reduce friction which has attended the working of the existing economic and industrial system."

The benefits under the Bill would be manifold. It would, first of all, provide information about the quantity and quality of the demand for labour in different trades and in different regions. The exchanges were to tell "workmen where not to go and where to go." They would diminish local and accidental unemployment and grapple with the evils of casual employment, which the Royal Commission had regarded "as the original fountain of so many of the greatest evils of our social life."

Churchill suggested the Bill would also dispose of "the need of wandering in search of work," and in consequence the vagrancy laws could be tightened up. He imaginatively hoped that "in association with school employment bureaux, which so many educational authorities are now starting in Scotland and to a lesser extent in England," the Labour Exchanges would have "the effect of enabling us to guide to some extent the new generation into trades" which were not "overworked or declining" and "to prevent the exploitation of boy labour."

The scheme was to be closely geared to a system of unemployment insurance. The introduction of Labour Exchanges enabled a clear distinction to be drawn between "the vagrant and loafer on the one hand, and 'bona fide' workmen on the other." An "elaborate and effective system of testing the willingness to work" would now exist. Churchill compared the much admired German system to his own, and maintained that his was on a "higher level and on a larger scale" than that "in any other country up to the present time."

Under the scheme, drawn up by a departmental committee at the Board of Trade under Beveridge, the whole country was to be divided into ten divisions, each with a Divisional Clearing House and presided over by a divisional chief, all co-ordinated with a national clearing house in London.

Distributed among these ten divisions would be between 30 and 40 first-class Labour Exchanges in towns of 100,000 upwards; about 45 second-class Labour Exchanges in towns of 50,000 and more, and about 150 minor offices and sub-offices. Third-class exchanges with waiting-rooms were to be established in the smaller centres. The control of this system was to be exercised by the Board of Trade. Advisory committees were to be set up consisting of equal numbers from both sides of industry with an "impartial officer" as chairman, "whose whole interest was to preserve the confidence of both parties and who was at the same time to be quite outside local jealousies and difficulties."

Churchill estimated that the scheme would cost less than £170,000 per annum, rising to not more than £200,000 when the period of building began. He was determined to bring this national system into "simultaneous operation all over the country, so far as practicable" on 1 January 1910. He envisaged the exchanges as being more than mere institutions for facilitating the smooth working of economic laws. "We hope that the Labour Exchanges will become industrial centres in each town. We hope they will become an office where the Trade Board will hold its meetings as a natural course, and that they will be open to Trade Unions, with whom we desire to co-operate in every way on the closest and frankest terms, while preserving our impartiality between capital and labour." The exchanges were in some cases to "afford facilities for washing, mending, and non-alcoholic refreshments to persons attending them." Travelling expenses were to be advanced on loan to workmen for whom situations had been procured, if the Management Committee thought fit.

Churchill conceded that the exchanges were to be voluntary for he argued that "to establish a system of compulsory exchanges eliminating casual labour, before making preparation for a reform of the Poor Law would be attended by administrative breakdowns and deadlock." The introduction of unemployment insurance was vital to the success of the exchanges; "being voluntary, there was a great danger that the higher ranks of labour — skilled workers, members of strong trade unions — would not think it necessary to use them, but would use the excellent approaches they had established for themselves." If that happened, Churchill saw that "the exchanges would only be used by the poorest and weakest in the labour market," and they would relapse into purely distress machinery from which the Government were trying to extricate and separate them. As he put it: "The exchanges and unemployment insurance were complementary. They were man and wife, mutually supported and sustained by each other."

The Labour members at the outset favoured his proposals. Arthur Henderson said that "it is one of the most far reaching statements, which has been delivered during the time I have been associated with Parliament." He dubbed the scheme "the Right to Work Bill in penny numbers." There was general support for both schemes from Conservative members too. The *Daily Telegraph* said "compulsory insurance is clearly a gigantic undertaking . . . it is well known that the Poor Law Commission found responsibility of recommending any particular scheme so heavy that they shirked undertaking it." David Shackleton, who was later to become labour adviser at the Home Office under Churchill, concluded that "we have heard for the first time schemes given forth to us which hold out some hope to us as labour men — that we are going to do something in this Parliament for the relief of the oppressed worker, who is unfortunately thrown on his own beam ends, without the slightest chance." In a later debate on 18 June 1909 Churchill maintained that "there is a consensus of agreement among all parties on the question of Labour Exchanges, which scarcely exists on any other similar question."

Despite the initial enthusiasm of Labour members in the Commons, the trade unions were sceptical, even hostile to the scheme.

Churchill dispelled many fears by clearly underlining that the exchanges would not, as was apparently sometimes the case in Germany, become a source of cheap surplus labour for industry or a potential instrument to break up official strikes. He held joint meetings with the T.U.C. and employers throughout 1909 to discuss his unemployment schemes. He envisaged the Board of Trade's role as essentially that of arbiter and conciliator between capital and labour. In this way he repudiated the idea that the Bill would enable an employer to use the Labour Exchange as a source of blackleg labour during an industrial dispute.

In the autumn of 1909 Churchill visited Germany on army manoeuvres at the invitation of the Kaiser, but also visited the Labour Bureaux at Strasbourg and Frankfurt on Main. "I have to go over to the Town Hall," he wrote to his wife from Strasbourg on September 14. "Mayor Adicker is to receive me & show me the Labour Exchange. There is no doubt I have got hold of a tremendous thing in these Exchanges. The honour of introducing them into England would be in itself a rich reward." He told his constituents at Dundee on December 28: "When I was in Germany in October I visited Labour Exchanges. I saw at each hundreds of workmen who were unemployed through the severe trade depression which the high German tariff had been unable to prevent, and which their reformed land system, their excellent state railways and wonderful methods of afforestation have only partially relieved."

Churchill clearly owed much to the German example in social policy and for his plan to deal with poverty and unemployment by insurance. He said about the German unemployed whom he had met — "Some of the poor fellows, at the lowest level of German life, had returned twenty times to Labour Exchanges in a vain search for work." But, he added, "there was not one of them among forty or fifty I questioned who had not in his pocket an insurance card stamped and in order, which entitled him to benefit in sickness, in invalidity, in infirmity, or old age." He said that the worker was ensured "an honourable maintenance proportionate in some degree to his skill and regularity as a worker." Churchill exclaimed — "My heart was filled with admiration of the patient genius which had added these social bulwarks to the many glories of the German race, and I was also filled with hope that we might soon in our own country, with our much greater national wealth, acting with Friendly Societies, establish broadly and forever a system of National Insurance which should embody and carry further all the experience which the Germans have slowly acquired and should comprise insurance against unemployment in addition."

The first exchanges were opened on 1 February 1910. On that day Churchill paid a visit to the seventeen exchanges which had opened in London. In an interview with the *Daily Telegraph* Churchill warned: "People must not expect too much from these exchanges. I have never claimed for them a higher position than they really can occupy, in fact. They are a piece of social mechanism, absolutely essential, I believe, to a well-ordered community. . . . I am confident, however, that fifteen or twenty years hence people would as soon do without telephone exchanges or electric trams as do without a National system of Labour bureaux." By the end of two months 214 state employment exchanges were functioning. When the National Insurance Act of 1911 came into force there were 414 exchanges. The exchanges were particularly successful, from the start, in assisting the movement of workers from one area to another. In 1910, 24,290 applicants were found jobs outside the areas of the exchanges in which they were registered. Loans for railway fares were frequently given by the exchanges.

The National Insurance Act did not become law until 11 December 1911. Churchill had left the Board of Trade for the Home Office in February 1910. It fell to Lloyd George to carry the Bill through the House of Commons. By the time it was enacted Churchill had become First Lord of the Admiralty and for the time being social legislation was behind him.

Contributions began on 15 July 1912: benefits six months later. The relative prosperity during 1913–14, when unemployment fell to under 2 per cent, helped the schemes to get started — 1,000,000 claims were made in 1913–14 and over 550,000 individuals received benefits. 2,250,000 were insured and contributions exceeded expenditure by £3,185,000.

On the outbreak of war, new functions were found for the exchanges in the mobilizing of the country on to a war footing. They were to become recruiting centres for the armed forces and for vital industries. Then, between the wars they were at the centre of the schemes inaugurated by successive Governments to deal with a situation in which the number of unemployed never dropped below one million and was for many years above two million. It was then that the real necessity for Labour Exchanges became apparent to all: and even though they could not make substantial inroads on unemployment they did ensure that this grim problem would be handled in an orderly fashion.

The climate of opinion had certainly helped Churchill to carry through his social legislation at the Board of Trade. The 1908 economic depression and the Tariff Reform threat had heightened the Government's awareness of the problem of unemployment. The rise of the Labour Party and the constructive help of the T.U.C. Parliamentary Committee had spurred him on. Yet no other figure in the Asquith government, except Lloyd George at the Treasury, did so much as Churchill in the social field. The other Liberal ministers involved in social policy pale into insignificance alongside his achievement. John Burns, Herbert Gladstone, and Sydney Buxton lacked the will or inclination to do what Churchill had done. He transformed the Board of Trade, particularly the invigorated Labour Department, into a power-house for social legislation.

The labour unrest of 1911–13, the Great War and the great depression have led the public to forget Churchill's constructive achievements in domestic politics. These may have smacked of paternalism; but they represent the first determined efforts of any politician to deal with issues which until then had been regarded as either insoluble or beyond the realms of government responsibility.

Perhaps Beatrice Webb in her diary for 30 November 1910 best expressed contemporary opinion on both Churchill and Lloyd George, when she wrote:

> The big thing that has happened in the last two years is that LG and Winston have practically taken the limelight *not* merely from their own colleagues, but from the Labour party. They stand out as the most advanced politicians. And if we get a Liberal majority and payment of members, we shall have any number of young Fabians rushing for Parliament, fully equipped for the fray — better than the

Labour men — and evolving themselves behind these two Radical leaders.

Events, however, did not take this turn; when Lloyd George pulled down Asquith the events that followed encompassed the destruction of the Liberal Party and inevitably paved the way for the rise to power of the Labour Party.

10

The Parliament Act

WHILE CHURCHILL was at the Board of Trade and later, when he went to the Home Office in February 1910, the clash between the two Houses of Parliament dominated British politics. The 1906 election had given the Liberals a majority of 82 over all other parties, and when the 54 Labour and 83 Irish nationalists voted with the Liberals — as they did in the main — they had a majority of 356 over the 157 Conservatives. The result was seen as a repudiation of the Conservative Party, which had ruled almost continuously for twenty years. During those twenty years the Liberal Party had become increasingly dominated by the Radicals, many of the Whig landlords having seceded in 1886 to the Tories because of their opposition to Irish Home Rule. Now the Liberal triumph had almost entirely removed the moderate urban Conservative MPs from Parliament. The Tory rump therefore for the most part represented the landed and agricultural interest.

The Tories did not readily accept the consequences of their dramatic and catastrophic defeat at the polls. Most imagined that things would go on in the same old way; but in private Balfour recognized that something tremendous had happened. To Lord Knollys, the King's private secretary, he wrote: "We are face to face, no doubt in a milder form, with the Socialist difficulties which loom so large on the Continent. Unless I am greatly mistaken, the election of 1906 inaugurates a new era." But in public, he took a different line: speaking at Nottingham he cheered his supporters with the assertion that "the great Unionist Party should still control, whether in power or opposition, the destinies of this great Empire." Balfour now felt it his duty to thwart the doctrinaire views of the new Liberal Government and his instrument was to be the House of Lords in which the Tories had an overwhelming majority.

For some years after the Reform Act of 1832 the Lords, under the guidance of the Duke of Wellington, had avoided serious conflict with the Liberal Governments of those days. To Bagehot, writing in his *The English Constitution* (1867), they had become a "pacific assembly" of "timid peers," aged lawyers, or as abroad, "clever *littérateurs.*" He saw the constitutional role of the House of Lords as a "revising and suspending" body which was able "to reject bills on which the House of Commons was not yet thoroughly in earnest . . . and upon which the nation had not yet become determined." From the 1860s onwards, however, the House of Lords tended increasingly to resist the measures of Liberal ministries. Only Lord Salisbury's moderation had prevented the House from throwing out Gladstone's Bill to disestablish the Irish Church in 1869. Salisbury, writing to Lord Carnarvon in 1872, expressed his belief that the Lords were obliged to give way "when the judgment of the nation had been challenged at the polls and decidedly expressed."

Only Disraeli's influence had ensured that Gladstone's Ballot Bill of 1872 and the abolition of religious tests at Oxford and Cambridge passed through the Lords. Indeed, Gladstone's Bill to abolish the system of purchase of Army commissions had failed and the reform had had to be made effective by letters patent. Again, only the Liberal Government's firmness in 1881 had prevented the mutilation of the Irish Land Bill and the amending of the Arrears Bill in 1882. In 1884, Gladstone had to accept dictation from the Lords to incorporate a redistribution of seats with his extension of the franchise to agricultural labourers. And in his final ministry the House of Lords threw out the second Home Rule Bill by 419 votes to 41. As can be seen from these figures, the Liberals were by this time heavily outnumbered in the Lords. As early as 1868 Lord Granville estimated an anti-Liberal majority of 60 to 70 in the House. Always in a minority of some sort, the movement of the Whig section over into the Liberal Unionist Party in the 1880s had weakened Liberal support further. The Dukes of Devonshire, Argyll and Bedford and the Marquess of Lansdowne joined the Tories: as Rosebery wrote to the

Queen in April 1894, Gladstone's zealous demand for Irish Home Rule had driven "the great mass of Liberal peers into the arms of the Conservative majority."

From the beginning of the 1906 Parliament, Balfour prompted Lord Lansdowne, the Conservative leader in the House of Lords, to use that majority to mutilate or destroy selected government measures. The Education Bill, which sought to revise the Act of 1902 and benefit the Nonconformists, was thrown out by 132 to 52. The Plural Voting Bill, which sought to correct an obvious electoral anomaly, failed on its second reading by 143 to 43. A Licensing Bill failed to gain the approval of their Lordships. The Lords, however, discriminated in the use of their veto. They accepted radical social welfare or labour legislation which would appease organized labour, such as the Trade Disputes Act which made trade unions (but not individual members) secure against legal liability. Old-age pensions, Labour Exchanges and sweated labour legislation later hardly caused a murmur in the Lords. But the Lords and the Conservative Party in the House of Commons were in combination to thwart any distinctly partisan legislation. Thus the Tories could claim that they were acting in the national interest and not merely defending the interests of their own, the propertied, class. This they had successfully done in 1893 by rejecting Gladstone's Home Rule Bill — at the next election the nation had endorsed their decision. Now, however, democratic ideas were gaining influence and the Government had a much larger majority. As Lloyd George strikingly said: "The House of Lords has long ceased to be the watchdog of the Constitution. It has become Mr Balfour's poodle. It barks for him. It fetches and carries for him. It bites anybody that he sets it on to." Campbell-Bannerman realized the seriousness of the situation. In the King's Speech for 1907 it was stated that "serious questions affecting the working of our Parliamentary system have arisen from unfortunate differences between the two houses. This important subject is now under consideration with a view to a solution of the difficulty."

*

Churchill had given his views on the House of Lords as early as February 1907, while he was still Under-Secretary of State at the Colonial Office. At Manchester Free Trade Hall on February 4 he spoke of the coming fight by the Liberal Government against "the fortress of negation and reaction." Churchill pointed to the "plain absurdities in the composition of our hereditary chamber where a man acquires legislative functions simply through his virtue in being born, where the great majority of the members never come near the place from year's end to year's end, where if they go mad or are convicted of a crime or become mentally incompetent to manage their estates or acquire an unwholesome acquaintance with intoxicating beverages, nevertheless they are still considered perfectly fit to exercise the highest legislative functions."

He pointed to the discretion with which the Lords accepted or rejected Liberal bills — which he described as "the spoke in the wheel and the dog in the manger." He put it down to "party tactics, pure and simple."' The only question which they asked themselves, he said, was: will this Bill serve the Conservative Party? In the House of Commons the Party might be in a humiliating minority, but Balfour had considerable power to thwart the Liberal Government. "Mr Balfour is no longer Prime Minister of this country. He sits in Opposition, in a lonely, solitary place on the left of the Speaker's chair. But he has power. He has the power to write a note — on a half sheet of notepaper — and to give it to a messenger and send it 200 yards down the corridor to the House of Lords. And by writing that note, he can mutilate or reject or pass into law any clause or any bill which the House of Commons may have spent weeks in discussing." The "half sheet of notepaper" was a reference to Balfour's compromise plan for Tariff Reform which he had enumerated at Sheffield in October 1903.

Churchill ridiculed George Wyndham's suggestion that the role of the House of Lords was that of an umpire. "It looks to me like the attitude of the footpad who waits for a dark night to stab his enemy rather than the act of an impartial chamber of review." He went on to attack the landed aristocracy which composed the House of Lords. He reviewed the two possible courses of action which had been advocated for the Government. The first was the idea of "filling up the cup" — that is, allowing the Lords to continue mutilating legislation until the situation was seen to be intolerable by the people, and then to have an election. He found this suggestion "foolish and unwise." "There are more ways of killing a cat than drowning it in cream, and I am certainly not in favour of a Liberal Government going on sending up bills to the House of Lords for them to throw out until the country gets exasperated — the policy of bowling lobs for the House of Lords to sky in the hope that the spectators will take pity on the bowler."

He found the second suggestion of an immediate dissolution very weak and humble. Churchill favoured going on soberly, patiently, firmly. "We have got to pass one or two good Radical Budgets first. We have got to formulate and develop our policy upon the land first — we have got to educate the country on the constitutional issue involved in the present position of the second chamber. The battle between Lords and Commons has to be fought out in Parliament first — then it will be fought out afterwards in the country. A great constitutional issue has been raised. . . ."

Churchill spoke of the "greatest and finest weapon" which the Lower House possessed — the power of the purse. "It is in our power to control the expenditure of every penny of the vast sums of money which are raised for the public service, to issue it where we will and to whom we will from the public Exchequer, to direct it to whatever objects we may select and under whatever conditions or provisions the House of Commons may choose to decree and affirm." He concluded: "we shall be simple-minded people if we were, at the first difficulty which confronts us, to throw up our commission and to come hurrying back to the country asking for a fresh mandate without ever having attempted to use those noble and formidable weapons which under the constitution of a free country have been so abundantly placed at our disposal."

While he was a backbencher, Churchill had spoken as if he were an Under-Secretary, now, as an Under-Secretary, as if a member of the Cabinet; and when he reached the Cabinet he was apt to speak as if he were Prime Minister. Today, Under-Secretaries, and even Cabinet Ministers, are expected to confine their oratory to the work of their own departments. Churchill never took this view, nor indeed did many of his gifted contemporaries. Lloyd George and F. E. Smith were wont to range freely over the whole field of politics — domestic and foreign.

On 2 May 1907 Churchill contributed an article to *The Nation* entitled: "A Smooth Way with the Peers." All he proposed was the inclusion of Privy Councillors in the Upper House to balance "the frivolous, lethargic, uninstructed or disreputable elements." He thought this would lead to a "harmonious balance between the parties" and that "a keener air of real responsibility, of more equal conflict, of fairer partisanship, would blow."

In June 1907 Campbell-Bannerman introduced a resolution in the Commons spelling out Liberal policy on the House of Lords: it stated that the Commons needed the power "to secure within the limits of a single parliament their prevailing decision." During the Commons debate on this resolution Churchill said the Lords had "placed themselves in a new position in the sense that never before had their old position been taken up so nakedly, so brazenly and so uncompromisingly."

Churchill believed that "to dispute the authority of an elected body fresh from its constituents is a deliberate incitement to the adoption of lawless and unconstitutional methods." And he ended this provocative speech: "In the main the lines of difference between the parties are increasingly becoming ties of cleavage between rich and poor . . . if we persevere we shall wrest from the hands of privilege and wealth the evil, ugly and sinister weapon of the Peers' veto, which they have used so ill, for so long."

F. E. Smith challenged Churchill the next day. "We do not ask for permanency from you, or consistency from Ministers, but we might have some degree of consistency as the fleeting weeks pass. For three weeks a man may hold the same view. Did the right honourable gentleman think at the time he contributed that article to *The Nation* that the best method of dealing with the House of Lords was to hold occasional sterile conferences with them? On the contrary, he had advanced his Privy Councillors scheme. Is that still the right honourable gentleman's view?" Churchill somewhat lamely suggested: "The honourable member will understand that I was only recommending one way which I deemed a smooth way of dealing with the House of Lords." Smith replied: "The right honourable gentleman in another place [Manchester] has observed that there are more ways of killing cats than by choking them with cream. I may be allowed to add that there are more ways of addling a political egg than by giving it to an Under-Secretary to sit on."

However, Churchill's aggressive policy towards the Lords was not shared by his colleagues. Campbell-Bannerman's talk of a suspensory veto was probably considered too drastic by Asquith. Campbell-Bannerman indeed appeared ready to deal with the powers, but not the composition, of the Upper Chamber. Yet, for all the radical talk, Campbell-Bannerman felt unable to act on his own resolution.

The rejection in 1908 of a Licensing Bill designed to curb alcoholism among the working classes and reduce the number of public houses by one-third particularly infuriated Churchill, who by this time had entered the Cabinet as President of the Board of Trade. Lucy Masterman has recorded in her diary a dinner in the House of Commons on 26 November 1908: "Churchill was perfectly furious at the rejection of the Licensing Bill by the Lords, stabbed at his bread, would hardly speak: murmured perorations about 'the heart of every Band of Hope in this country sinking within them.' He went on: 'We shall send them up a budget in June as shall terrify them, they have started the class war, they had better be careful.' He believed the Government would last 'two or three years, if they survive the budget. That'll be the teeth.' "

The dispute between Lords and Commons was brought to a head by the Budget — the "People's Budget" which Lloyd George introduced in 1909. This 1909 Budget may seem moderate by modern standards, but it was not regarded as such at the time. Lloyd George sought an extra £4 million for the Exchequer to pay for old-age pensions as well as for the First Lord's (McKenna) seven new Dreadnoughts — and he resolved to find it by increasing taxation on the better-off sections of the community, especially the property owners. The germ of the idea, which was to bear fruit much later, in Socialist policies, was that budgets should not merely pay for the expenses of the Government but should be regarded as a means of redistributing the nation's wealth. His proposals included a 25 per cent estate duty on property of £1 million and over, an increase in Income Tax from 1*s.* to 1*s.* 2*d.* in the pound, a 20 per cent tax on unearned increment on land values, and other land taxes.

Tory opposition to the tax on unearned increment was wittily epitomized by Eddie Marsh: "Earned increments are sweet, but those unearned are sweeter." Churchill and Lloyd George positively relished the prospect of a fight with the Lords. Churchill wrote to his wife on 28 April 1909, the eve of the Budget: "Tomorrow is the day of wrath! I feel this Budget will be kill or cure. Either we shall secure ample funds for great reforms next year or the Lords will force a dissolution in October."

It has been much disputed whether Lloyd George put land taxes in his budget as a deliberate provocation of the House of Lords which, since the reign of Charles II, had lost the right to amend a money bill but could throw it out altogether. During the middle 1930s, the author visited him at Churt and Lloyd George volunteered that he had done it with this purpose, regarding it as essential to clip the power of the Lords. He said: "Asquith was a much stronger Prime Minister than most people imagined. If he said he'd back you up he would see you through. He told me he would support the land taxes. When it came to the final discussion in Cabinet, Asquith asked me to explain the position to them. When I had done so, he observed: 'The Chancellor has given us a very cogent account of his proposals. I think they are of such importance that every member of the Cabinet should say how he feels about them.' Asquith went round the table, and everyone spoke against them, including your father." With a twinkle in his eye Lloyd George added, "I always thought your father had a soft spot for dukes — Blenheim and all that. Asquith then said, 'We have had a very full and frank expression of opinion from every member of the Cabinet and it seems to me that the weight of the argument rests with the Chancellor.' "

Margot Asquith relates in her autobiography how, on the day after the Finance Bill had received its third reading in November 1909, Lloyd George gave a dinner to those of his colleagues who had assisted him in piloting the Bill through the Commons (it took 70 parliamentary days and 554 divisions). The division records of those who attended were printed, a little invidiously perhaps, on the menu cards. Of those present, only the Chief Whip, J. A. Pease, and the Solicitor-General, Samuel Evans, bettered the record of the Chancellor. Churchill, strangely enough, was bottom in attendance in the division lobby, despite an accusation by the Conservatives on August

17 that he had been "wearing his pyjamas" in the Chamber, under some other clothing, in order to sleep more easily between divisions. (In fact, never in his life did he wear pyjamas.) He had taken a prominent part in the debates: his poor showing in the division lists may be accounted for by the fact that, as President of the Budget League, an organization designed to tell the people the advantages of the budget, he was carrying on the fight up and down the country.

In a speech on May 22 in Manchester Free Trade Hall, he showed his peculiar historical insight, his premonition of changing times:

> The wonderful century that followed the battle of Waterloo and the downfall of Napoleonic domination, which secured to this small island so long and so resplendent a reign, has come to an end. We have arrived at a new time. We must realise it. And with that new time strange methods, huge forces, larger combinations — a titanic world — has sprung up around us. The foundations of our power are changing. To stand still would be to fall — to fall would be to perish. We will go forward into a way of life more earnestly viewed, more scientifically organised, more consciously national than any we have known. Thus alone shall we be able to sustain and renew through the generations to come the fame and power of the British race.

On July 18, addressing the Scottish Liberal Association in Edinburgh, he drew a clear distinction between land as a source of profitable investment on the one hand, and industry and commerce on the other:

> Fancy comparing these healthy processes with the enrichment which comes to the landlord who happens to own a plot of land on the outskirts or at the centre of our great cities, who watches the busy population round him making the city larger, richer, more convenient, more famous every day and all the while sits still and does nothing. The roads are made, the streets are made, the railway services are improved, electric light turns night into day, electric trains glide to and fro, water is brought from reservoirs a hundred miles off in the mountains, and all the while the landlord sits still.
>
> Every one of these improvements is effected by the labour and at the cost of other people — yet his [the landlord's] land value is enhanced. When the land is finally sold, it is sold by the yard or inch

at ten times, twenty times or even fifty times its agricultural value on which alone hitherto it has been rated for public service.

Churchill constantly and powerfully advocated the need for social reform in his speeches. He spoke of the dangers of class conflict. On September 4 at Leicester, for example:

> If we [carry] on in the old happy go lucky way, the richer classes ever growing in wealth and in number, the very poor remaining plunged or plunging ever deeper into helplessness, hopeless misery, then I think there is nothing before us but savage strife between class and class, and its increasing disorganisation with the increasing waste of human strength and human virtue.

Lloyd George too beat the same drum, especially in his famous Limehouse speech on July 30 specfically attacking the dukes. "A fully-equipped duke" he said, "costs as much to keep up as two Dreadnoughts, and dukes are just as great a terror and they last longer." He ridiculed the nobleman — "he has one man to fix his collar and adjust his tie in the morning, a couple of men to carry a boiled egg to him at breakfast, a fourth man to open the door for him in and out of his carriage, and a sixth and seventh to drive him."

As well as the dukes and the Tories, the King himself was bitterly offended. He complained to Crewe, through Knollys, that such a speech, "full of false statements of Socialism in its most insidious form and of virulent abuse against one particular class" could "only have the effect of stirring up 'class' against 'class,' and of stirring up the worst passions of its audience. It is hardly necessary, perhaps, to allude to its gross vulgarity."

Yet Churchill, even more than Lloyd George, was an object of abuse. For his attack on the peers he was regarded as a traitor to his class. Cartoons of the day mischievously pointed out the incongruity of the young Liberal radical castigating the landed classes and then retiring to Blenheim for a weekend in the country. His having left the Conservative Party heightened the hostility and rancour felt towards him by members of his own class. Lloyd George's radicalism was understandable because of his Welsh Non-conformist background; but Churchill's was not. Nevertheless he had his inner doubts. He wrote to his wife on 30 August 1909: "Today I have been working at my speech for Leicester again, and am gradually getting some material together but of doubtful merit. I cannot make up my mind whether to be provocative or conciliatory and am halting between the two. But on the whole I think it will be the former!"

On September 4 at Leicester he spoke of "the small fry of the Tory party splashing actively about in their proper puddles" and of Balfour — "who aims to lead — who has been meaning to lead for six years if he only could find out where on earth to lead to." He talked of the Lords being brought into the political struggle to reinforce the Tory Party in the Commons — "They have been forced to fall back on their dukes. These unfortunate individuals, who ought to lead quiet, delicate, sheltered lives, far from the madding crowd's ignoble strife, have been dragged into the football scrimmage, and they have got rather roughly mauled in the process. . . . Do not let us be too hard on them. It is poor sport — almost like teasing goldfish. . . . These ornamental creatures blunder on every hook they seek, and there is no sport whatever in trying to catch them. It would be barbarous to leave them gasping on the bank of public ridicule upon which they have landed themselves. Let us put them back gently, tenderly into their fountains — and if a few bright gold scales have been rubbed off in what the Prime Minister calls the variegated handling they have received, they will soon get over it."

Later in this speech he said: "If the struggle comes, it will be between a representative assembly and a miserable minority of titled persons who represent nobody, who are responsible to nobody and who only scurry up to London to vote in their party interests, their class interests and in their own interests."

Churchill's Leicester speech led to the "extraordinary thing" of the King's secretary, Lord Knollys, writing to *The Times* about it. Churchill wrote to his wife on 12 September 1909, during his visit to Germany: "He and the King must really have gone mad. The Royal Prerogative is always exercised on the advice of ministers, and ministers and not the Crown are responsible — and criticism of all debatable acts of policy should be directed to ministers — not to the Crown. This looks to me like a rather remarkable Royal intervention and shows the bitterness which is felt in those circles. I shall take no notice of it. It will defeat itself."

A report of a recent speech by Lord Rosebery on the Budget was forwarded to Churchill. He commented: "All reports seem to confirm my view of Rosebery's speech — tedious, undistinguished, inconclusive. He really reminds me of a rich selfish old woman grumbling about her nephew's extravagance." To Lord St Davids he commented: *"Il a manqué une belle occasion de se taire."*

As the autumn passed by it was evident from Conservative reaction to the Budget campaign that the Lords would probably reject the Budget. Churchill wrote to his wife on 3 November 1909: "We had an exciting Cabinet this morning on the question of what we should do if the Lords reject — as is now assumed. I took a very clear line, but was almost alone at first, but gradually they all came round to my view, and that in the face of Lloyd George's and the Lord Chancellor's dissent. I am in quite friendly relations with LG but more formal and independent than before." According to Wilfrid Blunt, Churchill told him in September 1909 that "the Budget was very popular and that the Government will win on it if it comes to a General Election, but it will not come to that. The Lords will not fight. Some day there will be a great Constitutional fight, which he thinks the Commons will win, though at present the Lords would have all the physical force in their hands — army territorials and boy scouts."

On 14 November 1909, a week before the debate on the Budget began in the Lords, Churchill spoke in Bristol. He accused the Lords of being "a proud Tory faction," who thought "they were the only persons fit to serve the Crown. They regard the government as their perquisite and political authority as merely an adjunct to their wealth and titles. They cannot bear to see a government representative of and resting on the middle and working classes, a government supported by nonconformists and trade unions, which cares nothing and less than nothing for fashionable influences before which they have always bowed. All the House of Lords can do — if they go mad — is to put a stone on the track and throw the train of state off the line and that is what we are told they are going to do."

The struggle over the Budget was as much a political as a constitutional one. The main resistance of the Tory Party, despite Balfour's leadership, came from tariff reformers frustrated after having lost power, and the landed aristocracy, fearful of the effects of the land

taxes on their wealth. Churchill's cousin Ivor Guest, who had left
the Tories at the same time as Churchill on the issue of Free Trade,
was none the less concerned:

WSC to his wife

EXTRACT

4 May 1909

. . . Ivor Guest has just been to me in a great state. His father transferred his estates over to him 2 years ago, in order to avoid death
duties. The law allows this — if more than one year before the
death. Now we make five years necessary to prevent this rather
shabby kind of evasion: Ivor has only just realised that he will have
to pay after all! Result — fury.

Perhaps he will even resign his seat.

This is a great worry to me. It would ruin his career — & cost me
a friend & ally. . . .

The period during which money and estates could be made over to
heirs and thus avoid death duties was extended in 1909 to end five
years before death instead of twelve months. A few weeks later
Churchill was writing from Lord Wimborne's place in Dorset:

WSC to his wife

EXTRACT

1 August 1909   Canford Manor

. . . There is no one here but family. Poor old Wimborne moons
about wearily — on the brink. Cornelia is a tower of strength. There
are lots of grandchildren, sons & daughters. But there is a feeling
of sunset about the place — & I meditate upon the vacuity & imper-
manence of human things. . . .

But Wimborne survived till 1914 and the estates were saved.

Inside the Conservative Party the tariff reformers appeared to be
in the ascendancy after 1906. They believed that protectionism could
be the vehicle for moderate social reform, even if it involved dearer
food prices. To men like Austen Chamberlain and F. E. Smith the

activities of the Liberal Government were undermining the validity of this argument. The week before the Budget was voted on in the House of Lords, Milner said in Glasgow: "It is our duty to try to prevent it and damn the consequences." Despite the reasoned pleas of the Unionist Free Traders, Lord Balfour of Burleigh and Lord James of Hereford, Lansdowne led his Tory peers into the lobby to throw out the proposition that "the Bill be now read a second time" by 350 to 75. Asquith, after moving a resolution in the Commons on 2 December 1909 "that the action of the House of Lords in refusing to pass into law the financial provision made by the House for the service of the year is a breach of the Constitution and a usurpation of the rights of the Commons," prorogued Parliament on December 3 and the General Election campaign began.

*

The Liberals approached the electorate with high confidence. They believed that their election cry of "Peers *v.* People" would ensure that they retained their large majority. Consequently they placed the issue of the House of Lords and the Budget at the forefront of their election campaign. Asquith opened it at the Albert Hall on December 10 with what was taken by many to be a forthright declaration of war against the House of Lords:

> I tell you quite plainly and I tell my fellow countrymen outside that neither I nor any other Liberal minister supported by a majority in the House of Commons is going to submit again to the rebuffs and humiliation of the last four years. We shall not assume office and we shall not hold office unless we can secure the safeguards which experience shows us to be necessary for the legislative utility and the honour of the party of progress.

This was taken by some to imply that the King had guaranteed to create peers if the Liberals should win and the House of Lords remain obdurate. On December 15, the King's secretary, Lord Knollys, told Asquith's secretary, Vaughan Nash, that "the King had come to the conclusion that he would not be justified in creating new peers (say 300) until after a second General Election. . . . The King regards the policy of the government as tantamount to the destruction of the House of Lords."

In view of the nearness of the election the King was wise to make this stipulation in so grave a matter. It is not known whether Asquith revealed the true position to all of his colleagues, but most of them, without mentioning "guarantees," spoke as if such a sanction would be available in such a situation. J. A. Spender and Cyril Asquith wrote in their Life of Asquith: "Asquith, therefore, entered upon the election of January 1910 with the knowledge that not one but in all probability two elections would be necessary before King Edward could be persuaded to exercise his prerogative, if, as was practically certain, the House of Lords resisted the Liberal scheme for limiting its powers."

Outwardly it looks as if Asquith had not told Churchill of the King's decision. On a number of occasions, Churchill argued that if the Liberals received a mandate from the people, "the veto of the House of Lords will be restricted, so that the will of the people's representatives can be carried into effect within the lifetime of a single Parliament" (Dundee, January 4). He assumed that Asquith had received the King's assent that peers would if necessary be created to push through a Bill which would end the Lords' veto. "If the Lords win they will have asserted their right, not merely to reject the legislation of the House of Commons, but to control the finances of the country, and if they lose we will smash to pieces their veto."

For the election campaign Churchill published a pamphlet of 150 pages entitled *The People's Rights*. The positive issues advocated in the pamphlet were "defence of Free Trade, the carrying of the Budget with the land and social reforms dependent upon it, and the settlement for ever of the evil, ugly veto of the Peers, which they have used so ill so long."

Churchill certainly did not restrain himself in his attacks on the Lords. On December 8 at Liverpool he taunted: "If these distinguished pro-consular administrators were to get wearied of the burden of state, there are 400 or 500 backwoods peers meditating upon their estates on the great questions of government or studying *Ruff's Guide* [*to the Turf*] and other Blue books or evolving problems of

Empire at Epsom. Every one of them, a heaven-born or God-granted legislator, knows what the people want by instinct and every one of them with a stake in the heart of the country." At Leven on January 9 Churchill turned his fire on Lansdowne. "His career represents privilege and favour from the beginning to end; consistent and unbroken spoon-feeding from start to finish — that is the royal road to favour and employment. He is the representative of a played out, obsolete, anachronistic Assembly, a survival of a feudal arrangement utterly passed out of its original meaning — a force long since passed away, which only now requires a smashing blow from the electors to finish it for ever." At Inverness on January 13 he said of the Lords: "Just as they clutched greedily at the last sour, unpalatable dregs of the bottle before it was torn away from them at the last election, so now when they see a possible chance of obtaining power and place, they kick over the whole table in an ugly wish to jam their noses in the trough."

Some 250 meetings were addressed by peers who usually took part in politics. Curzon went to Oldham on 16 December 1909 to defend the hereditary principle. He quoted the French historian Ernest Renan who had said that all civilization had been the work of aristocracies, and Maine who said that a democracy in England would have prevented the Reformation and other great political and economic reforms.

Balfour at Hanley on January 4 played on anti-German prejudices. He favoured a big navy and saw "Socialism *v.* Tariff Reform" as the real issue. Lansdowne accused the Liberal Party of stirring up class hatred.

As the campaign wore on the emphasis in Churchill's speeches changed noticeably from the Lords to Free Trade. The old issue of Free Trade *v.* Protection was once more fought out. Perhaps the seductive tariff propaganda cry of "Tariff Reform means work for all" was gaining converts among wage-earners. At Dundee on January 15 he argued: "The lie of protection has been inverted to give the propertied classes means of warding off the insistent claims for social and remedial legislation for the masses of the population. . . . Every advocate of reaction and monopoly would know that by blatant newspapers, by public house organisation and influence, by the pressure of the privileged class on their dependents and upon those who were

affected by them, by flagrant misrepresentations, by thrusting hum-
bugging statistics, and false misleading theories before the electorate,
it was possible to go on in the old evil ways, trample on reform, and
cast all progress under foot" if Free Trade was overturned.

At the election in January 1910 Churchill retained his seat at
Dundee. The Labour candidate, Alexander Wilkie, the other member for the two-member constituency, who had stood on the same
platform, was 382 votes behind Churchill's majority over the Tory
of 6,195. Churchill had had a majority of 2,209 at the by-election in
1908.

Churchill (L)	10,747
Wilkie (Lab)	10,365
Seymour-Lloyd (C)	4,552
Glass (L.U.)	4,339
Scrymgeour (Prohibitionist)	1,512

In the country as a whole the Unionists had a net gain of 116 seats,
which gave them 273 in the House of Commons. The Liberals with
275 seats had a clear majority of only two over the Tories. The
verdict of the electorate was, as the *Annual Register* said, "obscure
and indecisive." The great Liberal majority of 1906 had vanished.

When one thinks of what had happened only four years before,
the result must be regarded as almost a defeat for the Liberals. Their
survival from now on depended on the Irish vote, which had to be
appeased with the promise of Home Rule. "The general sky is
black," wrote the usually exuberant Morley to Churchill on February
15. Some Liberals like "Lou Lou" Harcourt in a letter to Asquith
were inclined to blame the loss of seats on "Lloyd George's speeches
and Winston's earlier ones." Margot Asquith was more outspoken:

Mrs H. H. Asquith to WSC

EXTRACT

10 February 1910   10 Downing Street

Private — Burn

. . . Believe me cheap scores, hen-roost phrases & all oratorical want
of dignity is out of date. You have only to say to yrself "Margot
Asquith is a little boring & over-earnest but she is right. Loyalty,

reserve & *character* pay more than all the squibs & crackers. I have got a beautiful young wife, an affectionate heart & a love of amusement. I will make the Court, the Colonies, the West and the East ends of London change their whole view of me. I won't see a Press man & I wont have my name coupled with anyone's & I shall thrive on being liked instead of loving abusive notice & rotten notoriety."

I have never said anything of you that I was not prepared to say *to* you & I hope you will never feel that I am not *absolutely* trustworthy & true. I have a great feeling for Clemmy she is *so* rare not to be vain of her marvellous beauty.

Yrs
M.A.

Mrs H. H. Asquith to WSC

12 February 1910   10 Downing Street

... It is I confess a real deep grief to me — & I am *no funk* — to see how want of moderation & self control has smashed our splendid majority — a little imagination & knowledge of the wiser sort of

voter — a stronger navy, less violence in the Budget, a little dignity
& silence this horrible crisis wd *never* have come. We've lost the confidence of a large body of wise opinion & the question is, can we go
slowly bravely & *above all* silently forward to win it again? I don't
mind owning to you & Clemmy I am a very *very* sad woman watching Henry with his loyal kind splendid nature drowning slowly.

Yours in perfect sincerity
MARGOT ASQUITH

Asquith, it should be remarked, had not complained. Writing to
Churchill on February 1, he offered his warmest thanks and best
congratulations on his work during the election. "Your speeches from
first to last have reached high-water mark, and will live in history."

The substantial Liberal losses narrowed the Prime Minister's room
for manoeuvre. He now depended for his secure continuance in
power on the 41 Labour members and 71 Irish Nationalists. Initially,
some alarm was felt that neither of these two parties would support
the Government wholeheartedly. Keir Hardie made a threatening
speech at the Labour Party conference at Newport on February 10,
and some Irish members had expressed hostility to the budget measure which introduced a £1,200,000 increase in the spirit duty and
would have a deleterious effect on the Irish whiskey trade.

Yet neither of the two parties would be likely to ally with the
Tories as long as their interests were taken care of by the Government. The Irish nationalists and their leader Redmond were now
in a strong position to force the Government to bring forward a third
Home Rule Bill. The abolition of the veto of the House of Lords
was necessary to its success, and the Nationalists and the Labour
Members would certainly be ready to support a resolute government
reform of the Lords. Keir Hardie even argued that the recent election
had ensured that "the ministers were returned not to reconstitute but
to destroy the House of Lords."

How much Churchill's mind was exercised by the question of the
House of Lords is shown not so much by his fulminations on the
platform as by the serious private study he gave to the matter. He
wrote a long speculative memorandum to Asquith on the House of
Lords, dated 14 February 1910, thrashing out the problem. It is preserved in the Asquith Papers. He said that the Government were not
committed to the Campbell-Bannerman plan which advocated a joint

assembly comprising the House of Commons and a number of elected
peers. Churchill went on: "The time has come for the total abolition
of the House of Lords." If the Lords were to remain the Tory Party
would find ways of controlling it, whatever reforms might be introduced. He recognized that it could not be abolished before the next
General Election and he weighed the problem of what, if anything,
should be put in its place. He favoured a second chamber subordinate
to the Commons: "it must be based upon the roots of the whole body
of the parliamentary electors"; it must be less in numbers than a
quarter of the House of Commons, elected from very large constituencies; it should have no power to "touch bills certified by the
Speaker of the House of Commons to be Money Bills and consequently no power to make or unmake Governments." He added a
few suggestions of a "consequential nature," such as representatives
from the Dominions and eligibility of peers to stand for Parliament.
Four days later Churchill set out some tactical considerations which
had occurred to him:

WSC to H. H. Asquith

18 February [1910]   Board of Trade
Copy

Prime Minister,
   We are becoming involved in a perfectly unreal dispute with our
own supporters. The Irish, the Labour party & I daresay half our
own men say "Veto before Budget," because they think (or pretend
to think) that withholding the Budget means putting pressure on the
Lords to pass the Veto. Surely a triumph of absurdity! It is the
refusal of the necessary votes in supply that alone could embarrass a
new Government — & about these there is no dispute & no danger.
On the other hand we say "Budget before Veto" because we feel that
our duty as Ministers obliges us to safeguard the national finances.
   But the situation has changed.
   When "Veto first" meant "Veto *Bill* first" there would have been
real injury to the Finances owing to the delay involved. Now that
"Veto first" means nothing more than "Veto *Resolutions* first" & only
a week or ten days is in question — no injury to public interests can
occur.

One has only to realise how artificial the point in debate has become, to feel reassured about the outcome.

Your own statements are perfectly compatible with either course. If the Budget is to be "the first act" that means the first completed controversial business of the new Parliament. Nothing prevents "the first *step*" being taken to lay the Veto policy before Parliament at any time or in any form you may consider convenient.

I write this note — because I hope our full freedom to take the best path — agreeably to our public declarations, & the national interest — will not be restricted by the false points of dispute around wh our discussions have revolved.

W S C

There was considerable dismay among members of the Liberal Party when Asquith informed the House of Commons on February 21 that he "had no guarantees from the King" on the creation of peers. "In my judgment it is the duty of responsible politicians in this country, as long as possible and as far as possible, to keep the name of the sovereign and the prerogatives of the crown outside the domain of party politics. If the occasion should arise, I should not hesitate to render such advice to the Crown as in the circumstances the exigencies of the situation appear to warrant in the public interest. But to ask, in advance, for a blank authority, for an indefinite exercise of the Royal Prerogative, in regard to a measure which has never been submitted to, or approved by, the House of Commons, is a request which, in my judgment, no constitutional statesman can properly make, and it is a concession which the Sovereign cannot be expected to grant." In fact, he had taken soundings to procure such a promise, and had been rebuffed, as is shown by the memorandum to Nash on page 318.

Asquith's admission that there was no guarantee renewed the hesitations and divisions within the Government and in the Liberal Party generally. Asquith informed the King on February 25 that "certain ministers were of the opinion that the wisest and most dignified course for ministers was at once to tender their resignation to Your Majesty." Churchill certainly did not approve of such tactics. Balfour might have formed a government which, brought down by a coalition of the Liberal, Labour and Irish Parties, might then have triumphed in a general election. Balfour might unexpectedly have done as well as Campbell-Bannerman had done in 1906, in circumstances not entirely dissimilar. Churchill believed that it was the Government's duty to fight on. After some hesitation Asquith determined to see the issue through. In a speech at Oxford on March 18 he declared that the House of Lords must be rebuilt on a democratic basis.

Resolutions were put down on the order paper of the House of Commons to deal with reform of the Upper House. The Government's measures were three-fold. First, the Lords should not be allowed either to amend or to reject a money bill, and the definition of a Money Bill was to rest with the Speaker, acting in accordance with certain specified rules. A Money Bill was defined as "the imposition, repeal, remission, alteration or regulation of taxation." Tacking of non-financial proposals on to Money Bills was consequently prohibited; since 1862 Chancellors had combined all money bills into one budget to overcome the piecemeal rejection previously practised by the Lords. Indeed, the definition of a Money Bill was so clearly given, that Speaker Lowther was to inform the 1911 Parliament that according to its provisions he would have had to invalidate much of Lloyd George's controversial People's Budget. Secondly, the Lords were given the power of delay of two years and one month for other legislation. A Bill was to become law without the assent of the peers after three successive sessions, if in the third session it had not been passed by the House of Lords without amendments, other than those agreed to by both Houses, within twenty-eight days of being received by the Upper House. The delaying powers given to the Lords replaced their absolute veto with a suspensory one. The third measure reduced the maximum duration of Parliament from seven years to five.

At Manchester on 17 March 1910 Churchill ridiculed Lord Rosebery's proposals to leave the Lords with the substance of their veto powers. Churchill went so far as to assert that it was now a matter of "The Crown and the Commons acting together against the encroachments of the Lords." The King, who was at Biarritz, was displeased, and Sir Frederick Ponsonby, his assistant private secretary, wrote to Lord Althorp, the Lord Chamberlain: "The King thinks that as I am writing to you privately I might mention the following matter. The somewhat nebulous allusions to the Crown in Winston Churchill's speech seem to have received various interpretations from various quarters, and it has been most distasteful for the King to find speeches, letters to the Press, and leading articles discussing the point and attributing various opinions to His Majesty. The King thinks that you might privately tell the PM that he hopes that as far as possible Cabinet Ministers will refrain from mentioning His Majesty's name in their speeches or referring to him in their discussions."

For all the anger and hostility of the Tory Party and the Lords, it had to be admitted that the three measures which comprised the Parliament Bill were moderate. Churchill, speaking on March 31 in the Commons in the debate on them, stressed that, "under these resolutions, the Lords would, in the first two years, be the effective power of delay even in regard to those measures forming a specific subject of appeal to the electorate and in the second two years the power possessed by the Lords would be the tremendous power of correction and discrimination."

In view of the marked moderation of the resolutions, Asquith was in no mood to back down. He wrote to the King in Biarritz in early April: "Ministers came to the conclusion that [in the event of a Lords rejection of the resolutions] it would be their duty at once to tender advice to the Crown as to the necessary steps — whether by the exercise of the prerogative or by a "referendum *ad hoc*," or otherwise — to be taken to ensure that the policy, approved by the House of Commons by large majorities, shall be given statutory effect in this Parliament. If they found that they were not in a position to accomplish that object, they would then either resign office or advise a dissolution of Parliament, but in no case would they feel able to advise a dissolution, except under such conditions as would secure that in the new Parliament the judgment of the people as expressed at the election, would be carried into law."

The Budget passed through the Commons on April 27 by 324 to 231. The Lords assented to it in a few hours, without even a division. Apparently they were prepared to accept the verdict of the 1910 election on the People's Budget. Asquith now felt sure, thanks to the patience of Lord Knollys, that the King would be prepared to use his prerogative and create new peers if the Lords refused to accept the

Parliament Bill. However, on May 6 Edward VII suddenly died. Asquith saw that the new King "with all his fine and engaging qualities" was without political experience, and he felt that "we were nearing the verge of a crisis without example in our constitutional history."

As Sir Harold Nicolson wrote: "King George V was faced, immediately on his succession, with an unprecedented constitutional problem of which he had little previous knowledge and in which he was accorded no consistent guidance." Sir Arthur Bigge, the new King's private secretary, and Knollys gave conflicting advice. The King was "unaccustomed to ambiguous phraseology" and "totally unable to interpret Mr Asquith's enigmas."

The only precedents for the creation of peers were those of Queen Anne in 1712 who created twelve to avert opposition to the Peace of Utrecht, and of William IV who reluctantly agreed to Lord Grey's demand for 80 new peers if that were necessary to secure the passage of the Reform Bill: in the event, no additional peers were needed. On May 18 Asquith had an audience with George V at Buckingham Palace. The King wrote in his diary: "I gave an audience to the Prime Minister. We had a long talk. He said he would endeavour to come to some understanding with the Opposition to prevent a general election." Asquith's statement gave the new King a respite of six months. This was used without success to seek an agreed settlement with the Tory opposition.

Churchill's attitude during that summer is difficult to fathom. He was apparently coming to the conclusion that some compromise settlement to the Lords issue was possible. Despite his personal friendship with F. E. Smith, too many difficulties and antipathies existed between Churchill and the Conservatives for him to seek agreement with them. Yet he was ready to explore with Lloyd George the possibility of a "political truce" during which they would form a coalition, though perhaps with little hope of success.

Lloyd George had advocated a national coalition in a memorandum to Asquith on August 17 in which he asserted that a national government would enable the two Parties to shed their extremist wings and reach common agreement on the constitutional question, on a federal solution for Ireland, a general social welfare programme, and even compulsory military training. Akers-Douglas, the Tory whip, told Balfour that the Party would not agree to such a proposal. The Tory leader was forced to refuse, adding: "I cannot become another Peel in my party." Lloyd George grieved that his proposal was turned down. In his *War Memoirs* he described this rejection as "the supreme instance" of the damage done when party politics "stand seriously in the way of higher national interests. In the year 1910 we were beset by an accumulation of grave issues — rapidly becoming graver. . . . It was becoming evident to discerning eyes that the party and parliamentary system was unequal to coping with them." The grandiose dream of a national government, no doubt under the leadership of Lloyd George, vanished.

If Lucy Masterman's diary is to be believed, Churchill lost interest in the scheme when he found that Lloyd George had decided not to include him in his Cabinet. Mrs Masterman writes that "he flew into a rage and there was rather a comic scene" when "he worked himself up into an astonishing state of indignation, pouring forth rhetorical denunciation of the whole affair." One minute he was denouncing their Lordships, and now, according to Mrs Masterman, "he was more and more passionate in favour of coalition, praising government by aristocracy and revealing the aboriginal and unchangeable Tory in him." In weighing such recollections it must be remembered that apart from the fallibility of human testimony Churchill was a great talker. He would in private often develop and air scores of opinions which never matured into conviction or action. Asquith wrote of him to Venetia Stanley, "Winston thinks with his mouth."

In his interview with the King, Asquith had agreed to a Constitutional Conference. It met for the first time on June 17. The Government was represented by Asquith, Lloyd George, Crewe and Augustine Birrell, and the Unionist Party by Balfour, Lansdowne, Austen Chamberlain and Lord Cawdor. Churchill was not a member. The main questions discussed by the two parties were the relations of the two Houses in regard to finance, and the provision of some machinery to deal with persistent disagreement between the two Houses, whether by limitation of veto, joint sitting, referendum or otherwise. They also considered changing the composition of the Upper House so that it would act and be regarded as acting fairly between the great parties in the State. After a number of abortive meetings it became clear that there was no common ground between the two Parties.

On 11 November 1910, what J. L. Garvin, editor of *The Observer,* described as "the Truce of God" was called off. The unreal Party harmony of the previous three months was replaced by bitter inter-Party strife. Irish Home Rule clouded the sky to prevent any workable compromise. The friction of the last four years could not so easily be overcome.

In default of any agreement between the two Parties, Asquith had to go ahead with his Lords plan, which was now approved by his Cabinet. Asquith received secret guarantees from the reluctant monarch on November 16 to create enough peers to pass the Parliament Bill if the Liberals won a second election.

In the following year Lord Derby wrote a memorandum which gives perhaps the clearest account of the King's side of the story:

Memorandum by Lord Derby
(Derby Papers)

20 August 1911

At Bolton Abbey today HM was good enough to tell me all that led up to his giving his guarantees with reference to the Veto Bill. Asquith went down to York Cottage last November and told the King he wanted an immediate dissolution, that he had arranged all dates, etc, and that he wanted to make the announcement at once so that it should all be over by Xmas. The King asked him why he wanted it, that Parliament was still very young and the Govt had got a good majority. Asquith, who was in a very bullying mood, said that it was to pass the Veto Bill and as his side was ready and ours wasn't he wanted it at once, that it was no good sending the Veto resolution up to the House of Lords as they would only refuse it, and much time would be lost.

The King absolutely refused to give the dissolution until the resolution had been first submitted to the H. of L. This was before dinner. After dinner Asquith returned to the attack but the King still refused. The next morning Asquith, seeing the King meant what he said — gave way. The King said: "Remember I only give you the dissolution, I give you no guarantee as to the creation of peers."

"No," said Asquith, "I quite understand that. I would not dream of asking you for that."

The King afterwards went to London and here saw Asquith and Crewe. When they asked him for guarantees he complained that this was putting a pistol to his head and asked Asquith what he (A) would do if he refused. The answer was "I should immediately resign and at the next election should make the cry 'The King and the Peers against the people'." He then appealed to Crewe, who said that he supported Asquith and that the whole Cabinet was united on the subject. He further urged that they were asking the King to do nothing unconstitutional. He begged to be allowed to see Arthur Balfour and Lansdowne but this was peremptorily refused. They bullied him for an hour and a half and he then told them that he would give guarantees if they got a majority and asked to be allowed to make this public.

He said: "I have been forced into this and I should like the country to know it." They declined and said that this was a confidential pledge and must be kept so. In fact they bullied him and in his own language "behaved disgracefully to me."

Certain things he told me incidentally are of interest. "They sent a cabinet memo to my father but I have no idea, nor would they tell me, what his answer was. . . ."

"I had no idea of how my father would have dealt with the request, he never mentioned the subject to me at all. . . ." "I was given to understand that Balfour would have refused to form a Government — I know now that was not true."

"Morley's words with reference to the creation of peers — which he read — on the final draft were written and submitted to me for my approval. I insisted they should be."

"People must have been mad who thought I should only create enough peers to give a bare majority. I should have been forced to create 450, and as I told Asquith, I should never have held up my head again."

"There was only one name I told him whatever happened I should refuse to accept — and that was de Forest."

*

Much of the weight of piloting the Parliament Bill through the Commons fell upon Churchill. He was often in charge of Govern-

ment business — particularly after dinner — and Asquith had devolved on him the task of writing the nightly letter to the King on
that day's proceedings in the Commons.

WSC to his wife

EXTRACT

22 April 1911   Home Office

. . . On Thursday night the PM was vy bad: & I squirmed with embarrassment. He could hardly speak: & many people noticed his condition. He continues most friendly & benevolent, & entrusts me with
everything after dinner. Up till that [time] he is at his best — but
thereafter! It is an awful pity, & only the persistent freemasonry of
the House of Commons prevents a scandal. I like the old boy and
admire both his intellect & his character. But what risks to run. We
only got him away the other night just before Balfour began the
negotiations wh I conducted but wh otherwise wd have fallen to
him — with disastrous consequences. The next day he was serene,
efficient, undisturbed. . . .

Parliament had been dissolved on 28 November 1910 and the
country had to endure its second election in under twelve months.
Churchill once more took up the radical cause against the Lords. In
his manifesto to the electors of Dundee he claimed that "the whole
machinery of representative government had been brought to a standstill," and that "the Tory Party regard themselves as the ruling caste,
exercising by right a Divine superior authority over the whole
nation." Speaking in Dundee on November 14, he said: "All that
friendly discussion, prolonged in earnestness and candour for so
many months, could do, has been done and has been done in vain,"
for "at the end of every legislative avenue loomed the portals of Lansdowne House." He told a meeting at Highbury Athenaeum on
November 22: "I have not come here tonight to attack individual
peers. There is no hatred of peers, as peers, among the British people.
It is their functions and powers which are deservedly the objects of
popular displeasure." He demanded "a fair and equal constitution,"
which could only be possible, when "the harsh and cruel veto" of the
Upper House had been "shattered into fragments so that they were

dust upon the ground." Three days later, on November 17, at a meeting of the Manchester Liberal Federation in the Free Trade Hall he
was markedly more aggressive. He dismissed the reforming attempts
of the Lords as "a mockery and a sham" and as "an attempt to confuse the issue and grab more power for the particular class which
these noblemen represent." At Lambeth on November 28 he accused
the Tories of "seeking to build up a new House of Lords on a narrow
franchise, removed from popular influence." It would be a "House
of swells, who were removed from the ordinary methods of control."
At Colchester on the following evening, Churchill ridiculed the peers
for now talking of widening their social composition. He said "he
was not satisfied that the old devil would be carried out and the
House swept clear. A whole troop of much more powerful and vindictive fiends might occupy the comfortably prepared apartment.
I have heard of people repenting on their death beds but I have never
heard of a person saying on his death bed 'I repent' and then making
a declaration far worse than the worst things that he's ever done in his
whole life."

At Sheffield on November 30, his thirty-sixth birthday, Churchill
was enthusiastically on the offensive. He radiated optimism at the
thought of future victory. He claimed that the Lords were on the
run. "Only a year before the patriotic, fearless and impartial back-
woodsmen had been summoned from their sylvan retreats at the
imperious call of the Tory whips to stand between the nation and a
Socialist scheme that would ruin our trade and go far to destroy the
fabric of English society."

Now, Churchill said, "frantic appeals for quarter and mercy rend
the air, the white flag hangs over the Tory club, over many a noble
residence and public house. All the colours, tents, baggage, and
ammunition are scattered along the line of flight. England has never
witnessed such a spectacle since the days of Naseby and Marston Moor
and at the head of the rout, in the very forefront of retreat, gleams the
white banner of their leader, a leader whom we heard say in this very
building 7 years ago, 'I am a leader who means to lead' — Balfour is
now like Charley's aunt, still running."

It was not only Tories who were shocked by Churchill's method of
invective. As we have seen, Margot Asquith after the previous elec-

tion had gone so far as to urge silence upon him. He did not allow this to discourage him: he did not weary, as he was apt to say, from well-doing. Though there may have been some rivalry between him and Lloyd George, Churchill was not trying to out-do him on the platform. He was merely repeating the technique which Lord Randolph had found so effective in turning out Mr Gladstone. That had made Lord Randolph the darling of the Tory masses. Understandably, the Tories did not like it when they were forced to take the same medicine from Lord Randolph's son. And many of them were not as tough as Mr Gladstone.

At Parkstone on December 12, where he spoke for his cousin Freddie Guest, who was the Liberal candidate for East Dorset, Churchill looked beyond the victory over the Lords. Perhaps a coalition government would be possible. "After all, deep and wide as our party differences are, strong as are the contrasts of feeling and conviction, of temperament and interest, which mark and diversify our political life, the overwhelming majority of the British people stand true and clear for peace abroad, for law and order at home, for a reconciliation of races within the United Kingdom, fot the unity and consolidation of the Empire, for a supreme and unchallengeable Navy, for a better, a fairer, juster and more scientific organisation of the social life of the people, a due correction of the abuses of wealth and monopoly, religious equality and industrial progress." Churchill hoped common ground could be found between the parties on "the great schemes of National Insurance, the reform of the Poor Law, the development of our national resources, in the training of our youth, in relieving the Imperial Parliament from congestion by a well-considered plan of devolution: in prison reform, and even in a reform of the electoral laws and redistribution." He regarded the unity in political life, as exhibited at the coronation of George V, as "manifest of a deep and fundamental unity which underlies the clamorous conflicts of British national life." He sought a return to such "a season of rejoicing amity, concord and good feeling." On 17 December 1910 Churchill wrote to his wife — "Well we are through. I am resolved that nothing shall turn me from the veto *sans phases, sans trêve, sans merci*. The slightest wavering would be absolutely fatal."

The result of the December General Election showed almost

negligible changes in terms of seats. The Liberals lost three seats and the Unionists two, Labour and the Irish Nationalists gained two each and the Liberal net majority fell from two to one. Nothing had been proved; but the Government, armed with its guarantees, decided to go ahead. Churchill now returned the compliment which Asquith had paid him after the first 1910 election:

WSC to H. H. Asquith
(Asquith Papers)

EXTRACT

3 January 1911

My dear Prime Minister,

I have been pondering ever since the election was decided over the general position of our affairs, and as my view has not changed at all with reflection, I write it to you for what it is worth. But first let me tell you what everyone feels — that your leadership was the main and conspicuous feature of the whole fight. It is not always that a leader's personal force can be felt amid all that turmoil. You seemed to be far more effectively master of the situation and in the argument than at the Jan election, and your speeches stood out in massive preeminence whether in relation to colleagues or opponents. Balfour made heroic exertions considering his health; but you fairly beat him all along the line, and I noticed that Liberal audiences responded to your name with increasing enthusiasm as the days wore on. The result was decidedly a victory, and decidedly your victory. The course now seems to me to be quite plain, smooth and safe. We cannot parley with the Tories on any question until we can meet them on fair and equal terms. We cannot resume discussions where we argue and they decide, where we propose and they pronounce. The veto must be restricted as an indispensable preliminary to any co-operation between parties on the reform of the Lords, on Ireland, or on any other subject.

We ought to go straight ahead with the Parliament Bill and carry it to the Lords at the earliest date compatible with full discussion. We are I conceive perfectly free to accept any amendments not affecting the principle which appear useful in themselves or likely to conciliate opposition. It would be disrespectful to the House of C to suggest we were not. . . . I would myself like to add to these a provision enabling Peers to stand for the H of C on renunciation of their privileges and its counterpoise, ministers to be allowed to speak in both Houses.

We should state at the proper time that after the veto has been restricted we shall be quite ready to discuss the future composition of the Lords with the Conservative leaders in the true spirit of the conference: and that we do not attempt to prejudge what arrangements for adjusting differences wd be appropriate in regard to an assembly wh was not one-sided in its character.

We ought as early as possible to make it clear that we are not a bit afraid of creating 500 peers if necessary: that we believe ourselves beyond doubt possessed of the power, and will not shrink from using it. Such a creation would be in fact for the interest of the Liberal party and a disaster for the Conservatives. It wd be possible to make a list of men whose local and civic reputations stood so high with both parties in cities and councils that the attempts to ridicule their character or to compare them unfavourably with the present nobility wd fall flat. We should at a stroke gain a great addition of influence in the country. The wealth and importance of British society could easily maintain 1000 notables much more easily than 300 a century ago. The enlarged Peerage wd serve as an admirable body if 200 or 400 could be chosen. As we should have a majority on the panel, we should obtain a majority in the Chamber; and our representatives wd be far more capable and determined politicians than the Tory nobles. We shd at any rate for some years be able through the agreement between the Liberal majorities in both Houses to dispense with any other inconveniences (to us) and the two years delay and the 3 sessions procedure. All these considerations are obvious to the Tories. Without the provocation we shd not be justified in taking such an extreme step. But let us make our Tory friends realise at the outset that we regard such a creation coolly and in a matter of fact mood, that we shall make no bones about it, if the need arises, and that we have no doubt who wd suffer from the event.

I do not believe we shall get the chance. The Parliament Bill ought to receive the Royal assent before the Coronation. Two months for the discussion in both Houses will be ample for such a short and simple measure. One thing we must not put up with is any dilatory vapourings in the Lords about constitutions in general. If the Bill does not make proper progress we should chink [?] the coronets in their scabbards. Until the veto is out of the way there can be no peace between parties and no demonstration of national unity. The quicker and more firmly this business is put through, the better for all.

After the veto has been restricted I hope we may be able to pursue one *politique d'apaisement.* The circumstances of the year and the questions which have to be settled are favourable to such a policy. I trust that some of the disappointment of defeat may be mitigated by a Liberal grant of Honours (following the precedent of the last Coronation) to prominent members of the Opposition: Privy Councillorships to Bonar Law and FE; Order of Merit for Joe [Chamberlain]; a proportion of Tory peers and baronets — something for the Tory press — if you could find a little place for Neil [Primrose, Rosebery's younger son] it would please Rosebery in spite of himself.

Then on policy — we shd offer to confer with the Conservatives not only on the reform of the Lords, but on Ireland. On the Poor Law, on boy labour, and Insurance there is already common ground. I should like you to come to an understanding with Balfour about the Navy, if necessary letting him and Cawdor have full access to all Admiralty information. We should not hesitate to make a good arrangement with Portugal and France.

The sharp edge may be taken off the license duties, where they are really cutting too deep. Death duties ought not to fall on landed estates more than once in 25 years. We ought to pursue a national and not a sectional policy. You will have the power to do all this because of the unshakeable confidence wh the Liberal masses will give to the leader who restricts the veto of the Lords by strong and fearless action. You will be strong enough to pursue a sober and earnest policy without the stimulus of undue partisanship — and it is my hope that after triumphing in the storms of faction, Liberalism may enjoy that measure of national approval wh is due to those who have not merely been successful but right upon many of the great questions of the day. All this may lead us further still.

These are my feelings at the present juncture wh I put before you in all sincerity, trusting that you will share many of them and that you will not resent the expression of any. . . .

*

On May 28 of this year a son was born to the Churchills. Prior to his birth they called the prospective baby "Chum Bolly." No one remembers why. Mrs Churchill plainly expected a boy, for in a letter from Penrhos written on April 18 she wrote: "I am counting the days till May 15th when the Chum Bolly is due. I hope he will not have inherited the Pug's unpunctual habits!" She was right about the sex but miscalculated as to the timing, for unlike his father who had been born seven weeks prematurely, he was a fortnight late, thereby disappointing his mother's hopes right from the start of better punctuality than his father.

About a month before Churchill was engaged in a slight fracas in the House of Commons with Lord Winterton, the Member for Horsham. In a letter already quoted he wrote to his wife:

WSC to his wife

EXTRACT

22 April 1911   Home Office
                                        [*Probably from Blenheim*]

My Beloved,

You will see from the enclosed *Hansard* what a little pig Winterton made of himself. I ought not to have called out his name in my position — but the House was thoroughly good tempered & I did not expect him to take such a nasty line. I have done with him. He showed real malignity — wh I never forget. No evil consequence has arisen — & no one attached any importance to the incident except myself.

Our party to the Gaiety was vy amusing. "Peggy" is so good. I must take you to see it. There are some poisonous allusions; but the piece is belief & sermons. George Grossmith asked me to come & see him & I went behind to see a stage full of pretty cats in all their warpaint! There is a good song "What has become of the girls I used to know" "Many said 'No' but some said yes" etc. Vy amusing — you wd laugh! . . .

There is a vy nice & remarkable party here. All clever patriotic young Empire Builders out of work. Practically the whole of Milner's "Kindergarten." These young men whom he gathered from the Universities to govern S.A. after the war. They all regard me as the devil incarnate, & are only just beginning to realise that I am not so bad as they have always thought.

You might have been amused. I played golf better this afternoon — & slept 10 hours last night. We shall be up all night Monday & I am going to put the screw on the Parliament Bill as it has never been put before in the next few days. We must get on. No peace till after the shock.

Lansdowne is seriously ill, & Wernher dying.

Wire me when you return & bring your P K & C B with you my sweet darling Clem pussie bird —

Your loving & devoted husband
W

Mrs Churchill replied loyally saying that she thought Winterton's conduct had been "detestable."

The next letter from Churchill was five days after the boy's birth. Churchill was in camp with the Oxfordshire Hussars. The boy's name had not yet been decided upon.

WSC to his wife

EXTRACT

2 June 1911   Blenheim Camp

My sweet and beloved Clemmie,

The weather is gorgeous and the whole Park is gala glories. I have been out drilling all the morning & my poor face is already a sufferer from the sun. The air however is deliciously cool. We have 3 regiments here, two just outside the ornamental gardens, & the 3rd over by Bladon.

I have 104 men in the squadron & a vy nice new young officer — Valentine Fleming's younger brother — "the lesser flamingo." F.E. is here and everything promises to be vy pleasant. Many congratulations are offered me upon the son. With that lack of jealousy wh ennobles my nature, I lay them all at your feet.

My precious pussy cat, I do trust & hope that you are being good, & not sitting up or fussing yourself. Just get well & strong & enjoy the richness wh this new event will I know have brought into your life. The chumbolly must do his duty and help you with your milk, you are to tell him so from me. At his age greediness & even swinishness at table are virtues.

We are all going to bathe in the lake this evening. The water is said to be quite warm. No cats allowed! How I wish you were here, it wd be such fun for you — there are lots of young men to [talk] with & sounds of music, & beautiful trees & all sorts of things, including in a corner your ever loving & devoted Pug.

Always my darling your own loving Winston.

The Tories threaten to move a vote of censure on me after Whitsuntide. I hope they will. They are really too idiotic. . . .

Two thousand kisses my sweet birdling

Your own for ever

This goes to you by the King's messenger who is taking the box.

Mrs Churchill replied the next day saying that though Blenheim sounded fun and she missed the "fun and glitter" she was "very happy" in London "contemplating the beautiful Chumbolly who grows more darling & handsome every hour, & puts on weight with every meal; so that soon he will be a little round ball of fat.

"Just now I was kissing him, when catching sight of my nose he suddenly fastened upon it & began to suck it, no doubt thinking it was another part of my person!"

WSC to his wife
(CSC Papers)

EXTRACT

5 June 1911   Blenheim

Secret
Lock up or destroy

My dearest,

Both your letters have now arrived. You should address them Q.O.O.H. [Queen's Own Oxfordshire Hussars]. Blenheim Camp, not Palace, (wh latter produces delay).

I am so glad you are both progressing well. Ten ounces since last Tuesday is indeed good. I hope he is helping you as well as himself! . . . Yesterday afternoon I went for a long drive and walk with the King [of Portugal]. He is really a vy charming boy — Full of gravity & conviction, & yet in spite of his sorry plight — a boy brimful of life & spirits. He has a great air, natural and compulsive. He is extremely clever and accomplished. We made great friends. In harmony with my duty & British interests, I will do my best to help him. He wants to come & dine at [33] Eccleston [Square] to meet a few men. I am suggesting Friday 16th. You could receive him on a sofa in the library & then go up again to bed — if you felt well enough. He told me much about his views of Portugal & his hopes of returning soon by a *coup d'état*. I had to be extremely guarded so as not to raise false hopes, or encourage adventures in wh I shd not share the risks. I talked to him about the Church — such a strong ally, but demanding such a heavy price, & entailing so many powerful foes in a modern state. You will see the difficulty for yourself. It is his main prop. Yet priestly rule & ascendancy will always I trust encounter staunch resistance from free & enlightened men. He said nothing cd be achieved without religion. He began our talk by saying — Mr Ch! I am not a leader of the democracy. I am a King and it is as a King I must manage my affairs.

I must say I do not see why we should be in a hurry to recognise this provisional Republic. Their leaders still condone & glorify the murder of King Carlos, & the State Museum exhibits the ghastly trophies of that event. The elections have been carried by force & terrorism. But on the other hand — the Catholic Church has ruined every country in wh it has been supreme, & worked the downfall of every dynasty that ruled in its name. How then to reconcile Past & Present — and to do this without sapping those stubborn forces upon wh the counter-revolution must rely. These are deeper problems than the inquiring mind of this intelligent, good Master & devout young exile has yet reached.

King Manuel of Portugal had been forced to flee his country when his fleet fired on Lisbon in October 1910 in support of a republican revolution. From Lisbon he travelled to Gibraltar, whence King George V had him brought to England in the Royal Yacht *Victoria and Albert*. Manuel was never to recover his throne; he died in England in 1932 at the age of forty-three.

We all marched past this morning — walk, trot & gallop. Jack & I took our squadrons at the real pace and excited the spontaneous plaudits of the crowd. The Berkshires who followed cd not keep up & grumbled. After the march past I made the general form the whole Brigade into Brigade Mass and gallop 1200 strong the whole length of the park in one solid square of men & horses. It went awfully well. He was delighted. No news about the night march yet.

Yes Balfour has written to A. [Asquith] protesting agst FE being made a PC [Privy Councillor] & to FE to tell him so.

There is a lot of soft sawder about his great position & prospects and about Hayes Fisher's long services (as a wretched Whips room hack & county council wirepuller) & his misfortunes (due entirely to AJB); but the main purpose is pretty plain. They want to keep him (FE) back.

The result is important either way. If FE does not get it, he will not forgive Balfour. If he does, Balfour will not forgive him. But what an insight into the fatuous & arrogant mind of the Hotel Cecil, wh even at its last gasp, would rather inflict any amount of injury upon the Tory party than share power with any able man of provincial origin. So may it long continue.

And now my sweet little darling with my fondest love I sign myself your devoted friend & husband

W

Churchill was later to give an account of the transaction of how FE became a Privy Councillor in his *Great Contemporaries:*

His son tells us of his becoming a Privy Councillor at the Coronation in 1910. I think I had something to do with that. I knew Mr Asquith thought highly of him, and liked his mind with refined professional appreciation. I urged his inclusion as a Privy Councillor in the non-party honours list. The author tells us of the curious reaction which this proposal when made by the Prime Minister produced upon Mr Balfour, then leader of the Opposition. I do not think it was jealousy or fear of subsequent complications. Mr Balfour had his long-built-up ideas about how patronage and promotion should be distributed among members of the party over which he and his uncle had reigned for a generation. At any rate he opposed it, and in order to carry the proposal it was found necessary to confer another Privy Councillor-ship upon Mr Bonar Law. This probably turned the scale in favour of Mr Bonar Law's leadership, and may traceably have altered the course of history.

Churchill continued to keep Mrs Churchill informed:

WSC to his wife
(*CSC Papers*)

7 June 1911   Blenheim

My dearest,

I am going to come home tomorrow & will reach you before dinner. I am longing to see you & the Ch B. again. He really seems a wonder to put on weight. I will have dinner with you in your room my darling & tell you all my news & give you lots of kisses on your dear cheeks & dearest lips.

We have been out all day sham fighting, & as usual opinions differ about the result. The party has gone and the Palace is solitary except for Goonie.

With much love
Always your devoted husband
W

Three weeks before the coronation on June 22 of George V, Mrs Churchill had written to her husband that she was to see the Coronation from the King's box — a special favour granted because she was a nursing mother. The King had made the gesture even before the Chum Bolly was born:

Lord Knollys to WSC

29 April 1911   Buckingham Palace

My dear Churchill,

I spoke to the King today about his giving Mrs Churchill a ticket for his Box in Westminster Abbey on the occasion of the Coronation. He said he should have much pleasure in giving her one, and you may like to know that he was very nice about it.

Yours sincerely
KNOLLYS

I explained to him what you meant when you alluded in your letter to the "crisis."

WSC to his wife

(CSC Papers)

25 June 1911   Hartsbourne Manor
                                      Bushey Heath
                                      Herts

My darling Clemmie,

It rained all the morning so I stayed in bed & ruminated amid my boxes. At luncheon [J.M.] Barrie arrived — but I am vy sorry to say that he went off again unexpectedly this afternoon without my ever having a talk with him. I am vexed at this because I am sure I like him — and always something crops up to prevent my getting to know him.

Curzon cd not come — ill. But Mamma is here and Muriel [Wilson] comes to dinner. Maxine [Elliot, his hostess] is so nice. She has a new bullfinch — arrived only last night & already it sits on her shoulder and eats seeds out of her mouth. See how much these innocent little birds know! I went for a long walk in the rain with Alex Thynne — and talked all the time. I like him. He is just one of these young Tories who wd have followed my father or me with perfect satisfaction. But now — without leaders or ideas or plan — they drift off into all sorts of foolish backwaters of thought.

Maxine sends you her best love. She & I spent a long time last night singing your praises. Did the Cat's ear burn!

The general turn-out on Friday made a great impression. Everyone admired the cat, the carriage, the horses and the tiger — separately, but in combination they fairly lifted the sultana. It really was great fun, & I am sure you will long look back to our drive & will like to tell the P.K. & the Chumbolly all about it [the Coronation] — so it will become a tradition in the family & they will hand it on to others whom we shall not see. Dear me, I have thought of you with tender love to-day. May all blessings be yours & all good fortune.

I did not tell you that I wrote at gt length to Grey about Portugal & made out a vy strong case for non-recognition of those sanguinary swine.

He has agreed to take the first step I advocated — i.e. to write to the other Powers in such a way as to give them a strong lead to say that they think the time is premature.

I am sending this up by a special messenger who will find your address in London & will send it off to-night so that I hope it will reach you early tomorrow morning.

With fondest love
Your own ever loving
Husband W.

Do ask Grey to be godfather — I am sure it is a vy good idea, & will give him great pleasure. I am always hearing nice things he has said about me. He likes and wistfully admires our little circle. What do you think?

Mrs Churchill replied from Seaford where she had taken her two children to lodgings. She agreed to Sir Edward Grey: he accepted. She also raised the question of a "Fairy Godmother" for the Chum Bolly. The "Fairy Godmother" was Lady Ridley, a daughter of 1st Baron Wimborne and wife of the second Viscount Ridley. The other godfather was F. E. Smith. On October 26 the Chum Bolly was christened Randolph Frederick Edward in the crypt of the House of Commons.

*

The new Parliament had been opened on February 6 and the Parliament Bill read a first time on February 22. Asquith opened the debate and Churchill, winding up, particularly attacked the Tory proposal to hold a referendum to decide contentious issues. He maintained that this would "exchange the stable foundation from which this House has long been able to administer the affairs of Empire" for "a nice tossing sea of frenzied electioneering." Churchill spoke of "parliament and its representative institutions being swept away by the worst forms of Jacobinism, Caesarism and anarchy." He accepted that the Parliament Bill would still leave the Lords with considerable power and authority, and that although "it does not give us an equal constitution, it is at any rate a tolerable and workable constitution for all classes of His Majesty's loyal subjects."

The Bill went through the Commons by 351 to 227, and a week later for a second time by 368 to 242, despite continued Tory hostility. Throughout the spring the House of Commons battled their way remorselessly through the Parliament Bill discussing and defeating over 900 amendments.

On May 15 the Parliament Bill received its third reading in the Lower House, Churchill making a notable contribution to the debate. He was becoming more and more aware that, despite the hysteria and hostility of the Lords, the Bill would not reduce their actual powers as considerably as many thought. He therefore sought to damp down the opposition of the House of Lords. "The powers retained by the House of Lords will not merely be effectual, but, as I think has been borne in upon us every day we have discussed this matter, they will be very formidable and even menacing." It was true that under this measure they would not have an absolute veto, but they would "retain living and effective power, all the more effective because it would be maintained within these reasonable limits, to mould and shape the laws of the country according to the views and interests of the Tory Party at present." Churchill said he was "aghast at our own moderation": his radical speeches now seemed to have lost all relevance. "We regard this measure as territory conquered by the masses from the classes — a province won by the people in two elections which have been fought upon it. . . . We shall no longer face each other as master and servant. We shall meet each other on a true and proper basis of responsible partners in the trust and inheritance of our country and Empire." The Bill was despatched to the Lords who did not reject it but sought to amend it instead.

Mrs Churchill's life, while still with the children at Seaford, was enlivened by receiving frequent bulletins from Churchill on the passage through Parliament of the Bill. On June 28 he wrote: "The Veto fight is deepening. Look at today's *Westminster* cartoon. The Cabinet this morning accepted the LG–Winston view of tactics — the wisest and boldest. There will be no weakness: and I think the situation is good." And again on July 5: "Meanwhile the Lords go on tearing the Veto Bill to shreds. I shall be glad when the crisis comes."

WSC to his wife

EXTRACT

14 July 1911   Home Office

. . . Things are clearly tending to a pretty sharp crisis. What are you
to do with men whose obstinacy & pride have blinded them to their
interests and to every counsel of reason. It would not be surprising
if we actually have to create 500. We shall not boggle about it when
it comes to the pinch. . . .

WSC to his wife

EXTRACT

2 August 1911   Home Office

. . . The Lords crisis is comical & complicated. The "diehards" are
about 100 (with the whole party at their back). Lansdowne has 324
abstainers: of whom 50 to 60 will follow Cromer & St Aldwyn into
the Government Lobby. We have 75 wh with stray bishops & Court
officials may be 85. *But* at least 20 perhaps more of Lansdowne's abstainers say that if any Unionists follow Cromer and vote with the
Government, they will hold themselves freed from their pledge to
Lansdowne and vote against the Government. Thus a creation wd
be necessary, or at least it is a damned near thing! And if one single
peer is made Lansdowne & his gang will all vote against the Govt.
What a whirlpool! . . .

WSC to his wife

EXTRACT

6 August 1911   Blenheim

. . . It is quite likely that the Tories will be so angry & excited after
dinner that they will not let me be heard. But still I must have something ready on the "wretched-man I do not wish-by-any-words-of-
mine-to-add-to-the-anguish-which-you-no-doubt-feel" tack. All the indications now are that the Bill will be carried by about 80 Liberals,
4 Bishops 4 King's friends (Knollys, Bigge [since June: Lord Stam-
fordham] etc) & 25 to 40 Independent Unionists against 70 to 80
diehards. If anything goes wrong we make 350 Peers at once. Sunny

is going to speak on both the Vote of Censure & the Lords' Amendts. He is in the best of tempers & spirits. . . .

Churchill said in the Commons that the passage of the Parliament Bill would "mark a new era in our politics — an era not of strife but of settlement." After all "there was a greater degree of agreement between the parties in the House of Commons on many large aspects of public policy than existed before in living memory." Apparently, now "all the outworn controversies of the Victorian period had been honourably settled and cleared out of the way." Churchill made his last contribution to the Lords' struggle on August 7. Once again he stressed the moderation of the Liberal measure. "I know the day will come when we shall be reproached by some of those to whom we look in the country for the singular moderation with which at this memorable opportunity we have used our power, and for the fact that at this opportunity we have still left the Conservative Party possessed of notable advantages which are denied and perhaps will for ever be denied to those who sit on this side of the House. . . ."

Events since January 1911 had witnessed a significant lurch towards extremism in the Conservative Party. The activities of F. E. Smith and Austen Chamberlain in aligning themselves with Lord Halsbury and his diehards indicated that the Lords issue was being increasingly used to undermine Balfour's leadership of the party. Asquith's delay in informing the Tories of the guarantee which he had been given by the King, and the extremists' belief that the whole tactic was simply a bluff, helped to lead the "Ditchers" (those who would die in the last ditch) on the road of no return, when Morley made it plain in the Lords that the Government meant business. The Parliament Bill passed through the Lords in the sweltering heat of late July, thanks to Curzon and Lansdowne, by 131 votes to 114. The conflict in its final stages had torn the Conservative Party apart. Balfour decided to resign rather than curb his Right Wing. Despite Churchill's hope that settlement of the Lords' issue would lead to harmony and peace in English politics, one problem led to another. Asquith had relied on the support of the Irish Nationalists. Now that they had helped to diminish the powers of the Upper House, they demanded their reward. Irish Home Rule now became the decisive and bitter issue.

II

Home Office

CHURCHILL HAD UNDERTAKEN a considerable speaking tour before
the first 1910 election. This, coupled with his speeches during the
election, had won him wide popular acclaim and had particularly
commended him to his colleagues. It was clear that he deserved promotion: in what form he did not know. On January 20 Lord Morley,
with whom he was obviously becoming increasingly intimate, wrote
to him:

Lord Morley to WSC

EXTRACT

20 January 1910   Flowermead
                                                Wimbledon Park

. . . Your position has now risen to the first order. Those are the
moments that most demand circumspection.
    I had a long talk — two in fact — with R.B.H. [Haldane]. . . .
The first Lord could not be changed — they think — without being
slighted. But if you cared for H.O., no doubt it would be at
your disposal. R.B.H. himself thought the L.G.B. [Local Government Board] the place with finest opening. I ought to say that he
had seen the PM, but how far he represented any views of the PM,
I don't know. I gathered that the PM had not yet at all considered
the line of future transmutations. . . .

Churchill had already, when he went to the Board of Trade,
averred his dislike of the Local Government Board. Although still
interested in socal legislation he aimed higher than "Mrs Webb's soup

kitchen." Asquith, though full of good will, did not at this time envisage a large-scale reconstruction. He was not in the mood of the "good butcher" which he was later to quote Gladstone as saying was a prerequisite of a good Prime Minister. Indeed, to a man of Churchill's ardent optimism and ambition Asquith's proposal must have seemed bleak.

The Prime Minister wrote from Cannes, where he was seeking the pale wintry sunshine of the Côte d'Azur while the final results of the General Election came in. It is true that he had held East Fife with a satisfactory majority of 2,059 in January 1910 but in view of the close outcome of the election in which every seat was to count Asquith's absence at this time exemplified his Roman sense of detachment. The votes had been cast: he could not influence the count: he might as well attend to his health before a rigorous session.

H. H. Asquith to WSC

1 February 1910   Chateau de Thorenc
                                                              Cannes

Secret

My dear Winston,

I must first offer you my warmest thanks & best congratulations on your work during this election. Your speeches from first to last have reached high-water mark, and will live in history.

There must be a certain amount of Cabinet reconstruction.

It has occurred to me that, in view of the character & composition of our re-arranged forces, you might see your way to take what is bound to be one of our most delicate & difficult posts — the Irish Office.

Twice in my experience, it has been held, under not more arduous conditions, by men (on each side) of the weightiest calibre — Balfour & Morley.

I don't press it on you, for I know well how keen you are on your great projects at the Board of Trade. And I should quite understand & appreciate a negative answer.

But it seems to me to offer, in existing circumstances, an avenue of great possibilities.

Yours always
H. H. ASQUITH

I am here till the end of the week.

Churchill must have been disappointed by this offer, particularly by the sting in the tail that he might remain at the Board of Trade. The salary and the status of that office had been raised to the level of a Secretaryship of State, but Churchill suggested that he himself should not get the increased salary. A change of office was therefore desirable on private grounds apart from any public considerations. Such money as he had saved from his lecture tours and his Life of Lord Randolph had long been expended; he had virtually no private income; he had a wife and a child; Members of Parliament were still not paid and his salary was £2,500 a year — half of what he had been led to expect. In these circumstances his answer to the Prime Minister was forthright, guileful and masterly. As so often, he took great care over it. He made two drafts with his own hand before he sent off the following holograph letter:

WSC to H. H. Asquith

5 February 1910   Board of Trade
Secret
Copy

My dear Prime Minister,

Your letter only reached me last night.

I am sensible of the compliment you pay to my personal qualities in suggesting that I should go to Ireland at this juncture, & I realise the peculiar importance to the Government of the successful conduct of that post. I am the more grateful to you for not pressing me to undertake it. The office does not attract me now. There are many circumstances connected with it which repel me. Except for the express purpose of preparing & passing a Home Rule Bill I do not wish to become responsible for Irish administration. And before that situation can be reached, we must — it seems to me — fight another victorious battle in the constituencies.

Three years or four years ago I would have gone; but now I am sure that it would be more in the interests of the Government that Birrell should stand to his post. The Nationalists respect him & trust him. He has all the threads in his hands. He has been through the unpleasant process of being disillusioned.

I do not know what other reconstruction you contemplate, but for myself I should like to go either to the Admiralty (assuming that place to become vacant) or to the Home Office. It is fitting, if you will allow me to say so — that Ministers should occupy positions in the Government which correspond to some extent with their influence in the country. No Minister holding an office of the second class can play a large part without producing awkward and doubtful relations with some of his colleagues in more important positions; & this in spite of much personal good will. It is convenient and it is fair that a true balance should be established. At a time so critical & with struggles so grave impending, there should be a generous appreciation of the real forces which contribute to the strength of the party & of your government.

One word more. Two years have passed since you offered me the Board of Trade as a Secretaryship of State. It has not been possible — for reasons wh I have loyally recognised — to make that offer good; but the fact that it was made will I am sure weigh with you at the present time — sufficiently at any rate to justify me in writing openly.

Let me finally thank you for the kindness of your letter. It gives me the greatest pleasure to know that you are satisfied with my work.

Believe me, Yours vy sincerely
WINSTON S. CHURCHILL

Asquith decided that he should go to the Home Office. Churchill was thirty-five. Only one Home Secretary had been younger — Sir Robert Peel at thirty-three.

The Home Secretary was and is the Principal Secretary of State — the "First" Secretary as he was widely called when Mr R. A. Butler held that office. Its origins go back more than two centuries. In congratulating him on his promotion George Nathaniel Curzon wrote to Churchill of "so fine and high an office." Secretaries of State of various kinds go back a long way; at one period there was only one, at another, three. Eventually, in 1782, George III divided the functions between a Secretary of State for the Home Department and a Secretary of State for Foreign Affairs: Lord Shelburne was appointed for the Home Department; Charles James Fox for Foreign Affairs. Other Secretaryships of State have been created since, but the Home Office has always retained the titular primacy.

Churchill succeeded Herbert Gladstone, eldest son of the Grand Old Man. Gladstone was made a peer and went out to become the first Governor-General of the newly created Union of South Africa.

Other changes in this small ministerial reshuffle involved Sydney Buxton, who took Churchill's place at the Board of Trade, and who was succeeded as Postmaster-General by Herbert Samuel; and J. A. Pease, who became Chancellor of the Duchy of Lancaster and who was succeeded as Government Chief Whip by the Master of Elibank.

The ramifications of the duties pertaining to the Home Secretary were no less than those which Churchill had left behind him at the Board of Trade. They included: the maintenance of law and order; the efficiency of the police service; the control and administration of prisons and borstal institutions; the treatment of offenders, including juvenile offenders; the efficiency of the probation service; the organization of magistrate's courts; legislation on criminal justice. He advised the Crown on the prerogative of mercy where a sentence of death had been passed. He was concerned with the supervision of the fire service; the care of children by local authorities and voluntary societies; the regulation of the employment of children and young persons; the control of immigrants and aliens and the naturalization of aliens; the law relating to parliamentary and local government elections. In addition, many miscellaneous subjects were dealt with, including the mines, explosives, dangerous drugs, poisons, intoxicating liquor, shops, public safety, entertainments, by-laws on good rule and government and other subjects, cremations and burials, betting and gambling; addresses and petitions to the King, ceremonials and formal business connected with honours.

Among these important duties, the principal matters in which Churchill was involved and with which he had to deal were: Strikes: Advice on Prerogative of Mercy: Prison Reform: The Mylius Affair: Women's Suffrage: Accidents in Mines: Sidney Street: Shops Act and Early Closing: Aliens Bill: House of Commons Letter to the King.

Since few of these topics are inter-related it has been thought best to deal with them seriatim.

*

As we have seen in Chapter 9, the prosperity of the country had taken a downward turn in 1908. By the time Churchill went to the Home Office there had been some recovery, but unemployment was to remain around 4 per cent. Today this figure would seem very high: anything above 2 per cent has by implication been stigmatized as "unacceptable." Although the foundations of the welfare state had been laid in 1908 little benefits had so far come to the people. Nonetheless, there had been until 1910 comparatively little industrial unrest, even in the two years following the 1908 depression. By 1910 things were on the mend. Yet Churchill was to find when he went to the Home Office that he had to face a series of strikes far more serious than the country had known before.

There were three principal strikes during his two years at the Home Office — The Newport strike of transport workers; the Rhondda Valley strike of coal-miners; and the national railway strike of 1911. Each of these strikes was on a larger scale than the previous one and passions tended to mount. At the Board of Trade, which had functions now handled by the Ministry of Labour, it would have been Churchill's task to have sought conciliation: that now fell to his successor, Sydney Buxton. Churchill's task was now the unpopular one of maintaining law and order.

The strike at Newport docks arose over a loading dispute between the Empire Transport Company and Holder Brothers, shippers, on the one hand and the dockworkers union. The employers attempted to use labourers supplied by the Shipping Federation; these were prevented from working by the dockers and forced to leave town. Although the dispute only involved two or three hundred men the stoppage brought the docks to a standstill and there were soon reports of looting.

Churchill first heard of the trouble from his Permanent Under-Secretary when he was staying with his aunt, Lady Wimborne, at Canford in Dorset.

Sir Edward Troup to WSC
(Home Office Papers)

TELEGRAM

19 May 1910 Home Office

Three representatives of Empire Transport Company called this morning to represent that, in connection with strike of stevedores loading vessel, serious disturbances have occurred, that police have failed to give adequate protection and that their free workmen have been assaulted and intimidated. They ask Home Secretary to intervene. I have told them local police are entirely responsible, and if numbers insufficient should obtain assistance from other forces.

I have also communicated with Board of Trade who had not heard of dispute but Mitchell is now communicating with firm and they will watch the case and give help if possible. Meantime may I telegraph to local police to remind them of their responsibility to maintain order and prevent outrage or intimidation?

TROUP

The looting gave rise to apprehension among the local authorities. Churchill's experience at the Board of Trade had made him sensitive to a situation of this kind.

WSC to Sir Edward Troup
(Home Office Papers)

TELEGRAM

19 May 1910 Canford

You are authorised to telegraph as you propose but if any public announcement is made it should be stated that I have asked the Board of Trade to intervene and that Mitchell had already proceeded to Newport. The Empire Transport Company should be made to realize that employing large droves of men from London to break the strike is a very strong order. Do not on any account give them or the public the impression that we approve their action.

CHURCHILL

The situation deteriorated and soon there were requests for extra police to be sent down from London:

Mayor of Newport to Home Office

TELEGRAM

21 May 1910   Town Hall
                                                    Newport
                                              Monmouthshire

Serious riots anticipated here in consequence of dock strikes. At
meeting of borough magistrates here this morning it was unanimously resolved that the War Office be requested to hold in readiness
two hundred infantrymen and one hundred mounted men to assist
the local police and five hundred imported police. Duplicate of this
telegram sent Secretary of State for War.

MAYOR

Chief Constable Newport to Home Office

TELEGRAM

21 May 1910   Newport

My telegram yesterday informing you of our additional police requirements to protect life and property is unanswered. Imported
labour arrives tomorrow. It is essential we should have 250 Metropolitan Police to reach here by two o'clock Sunday afternoon. We
have wired the Commissioner requesting these men to be sent. Please
wire if we can rely upon your co-operation.

SINCLAIR

Sir Edward Troup to WSC

TELEGRAM

? 21 May 1910   Home Office

Chief Constable of Newport in telegram which missed yours asks for
250 Metropolitan Police tomorrow. [Sir Edward] Henry is replying
that he will send men if conditions mentioned in your telegram are
accepted and he is getting his men ready.

TROUP

The extra police asked for were sent. There was some unexplained delay in their departure, but meanwhile the situation was still deteriorating. The Chief Constable of Newport telegraphed to the Commissioner of Police that imported labour from London was arriving and that he must have reinforcements at the latest by 2 p.m. on the Sunday. In the absence of the Metropolitan Police reinforcements more police were sent from Bristol, Merthyr, Glamorgan County and Monmouthshire County, in all 180 men.

At this stage the strike did not seem any more serious than others in the past and on Friday Churchill left for a short holiday at Lucerne. He was only to be gone a week, but he instructed Troup to keep him fully informed by cipher.

WSC to Sir Edward Troup
(*Home Office Papers*)

TELEGRAM

21 May 1910   Folkestone

Action approved. If they want more they must have more. My address for telegrams all tomorrow is Hotel du Palais Lucerne.

CHURCHILL

Sir Edward Troup to Chief Constable Newport

TELEGRAM

21 May 1910   [Home Office]

Your telegram of yesterday fully answered in Home Secretary's telegram to Mayor sent this morning. If all local resources are exhausted Home Secretary will sanction despatch of Metropolitan Police on terms mentioned in his telegram.

TROUP

Mayor of Newport to Sir Edward Troup

TELEGRAM

21 May 1910   [Town Hall
                                                       Newport]

I am in receipt of your wire, and Head Constable now shown me your telegram just received. All local resources exhausted and am promised tomorrow sixty men from Bristol and forty from Merthyr, and am hoping to get forty from Glamorgan County and like number from Monmouthshire County: but these latter eighty are doubtful as demonstration is to be made in Cardiff tomorrow and Cardiff City can render no assistance. Imported labour arrives in two sections tomorrow, one by rail, the other by water. In these circumstances shall require 250 Metropolitan foot and 50 mounted policemen. Am providing accommodation for these. Please wire that I can rely upon their being sent in terms of your telegram.

MAYOR OF NEWPORT

[*Note from Troup*]: I arranged with Sir E. Henry to send the 300.

C.E.T.

Sir Edward Troup to Mayor of Newport

TELEGRAM

21 May 1910

Your telegram received. Commissioner of Police has been authorised to supply the force for which you ask.

TROUP

Sir Edward Troup to Sir Edward Ward
[*Permanent Under-Secretary of State for War*]

21 May 1910   [Home Office]
Copy

Dear Ward,

I understand that the Newport Magistrates have telegraphed to the War Office asking you to hold troops in readiness.

The state of things at Newport is serious, and Mr Churchill, before he left, had considered the possibility of their applying for troops. He is most anxious to avoid their being used, and is doing all he can by offering to supply Metropolitan Police and otherwise to avoid the necessity; but of course if the Mayor or Magistrates requisition them, they must be ready to go. Mr Churchill asked me specially to impress on the War Office that *mounted troops* should be sent. They are far more effective than infantry in dealing with a riot, and the risk of their employment leading to loss of life is much less.

Yours sincerely
EDWARD TROUP

Mayor of Newport to Sir Edward Troup

TELEGRAM

22 May 1910   [Newport]

Further to telegrams of today, Newport labour dispute just been
settled in conference with Mayor and representatives of masters and
men, and with assistance of Board of Trade. Police and military
assistance not now required. Have communicated direct with Scotland Yard and officer commanding troops at Chester to this effect.

WSC to Sir Edward Troup
(*Home Office Papers*)

TELEGRAM

22 May 1910   Lucerne

Am very glad˙ to hear of settlement. Please send official to Board
of Trade expressing satisfaction also appreciation of Mr Mitchell's
excellent work. Telegraph to Houlder Brothers as follows: Begins:
I desire to thank you personally for the assistance you have rendered
in the friendly settlement of a dangerous dispute and for the consideration with which you have treated me throughout. I trust your
difficulties will not recur. Churchill. Ends. Also send civil letters to
Mayor of Newport and Head Constable. Telegrams tomorrow will
find me till 5 o'clock at Grand Hotel, Goeschenen, Switzerland. Shall
not reach Venice till Wednesday. Wire full details. Foregoing complimentary messages are not to be sent if you see any serious reason
not known to me against them in any case.

CHURCHILL

Because of the strike at Newport troops had been alerted at
Chester, but the early settlement brought about by the Mayor of
Newport and a representative of the Board of Trade made their
despatch unnecessary. It was equally found unnecessary to send the
detachment of the Metropolitan Police.

The second strike began in the coal mines at Rhondda in early
November of the same year. It arose out of a dispute concerning
wage differentials in the working of hard and soft seams. On this
occasion many men were involved, estimates varying between 25,000

and 30,000, and many different pits were affected. Again there was looting and the local authorities appealed to the War Office for troops. On hearing of this, Churchill consulted the Secretary of War, Haldane, and they agreed instead to send police, but to hold some troops in reserve near by. Churchill's whole conduct in the matter has since been grotesquely distorted, and it has become a part of socialist demonology that Churchill sent troops who fired upon the miners of Tonypandy. Socialist propagandists have sought to make martyrs of the miners of Tonypandy comparable to those of Tolpuddle in 1834. Tonypandy in reality is only distinguished from the other Welsh villages involved because of the high degree of looting in which the miners indulged; but a lie once started can seldom be overtaken. Fortunately, a contemporary account of the truth survives in words written before the lie had ever been born:

WSC to The King

[? 10 November 1910]
Copy [? Draft]

Reports to-day from the whole of the Rhondda Valley are satisfactory. Absolute order has been maintained around all the threatened collieries. A few trifling incidents of window-breaking have occurred in two of the villages. The 1,400 Police at the disposal of the Chief Constable will, it is expected, be able not merely to prevent attacks upon the collieries but to control the whole district and to deal promptly with any sign of a disorderly gathering large or small. No need for the employment of the military is likely to occur. They will be kept as far as possible out of touch with the population, while sufficiently near to the scene to be available if necessary.

With regard to the action taken by the Home Office on Tuesday, the following facts should be known:

The 400 Cavalry and Infantry which were sent for by the Chief Constable on Monday night were not started by the Secretary of State for War or by the Home Secretary, but were sent, pending superior instructions, by the General Officer Commanding of the Southern Command. Up to 10 o'clock on Tuesday morning the Home Office had no knowledge of this movement or of the necessity for it. At

11 o'clock Mr Churchill, after consulting with Mr Haldane and communicating by telephone with the Chief Constable of Glamorgan at
Tonypandy, definitely decided to employ Police instead of Military
to deal with disorder, and, while moving troops near to the scene of
disturbance, to keep them in the background until it was certain that
Police methods had proved insufficient. From this policy there has
been no change whatever. 300 Metropolitan Police, of whom 100
were mounted, were ordered to start for Pontypridd as fast as trains
could be got to convey them. This force of picked constables experienced in the handling of crowds was for every purpose better suited
to the needs of the situation than an equivalent body of military.
Infantry soldiers can if attacked or stoned only reply by fire from
long-range rifles which often kills foolish sightseers unconnected with
the riot, or innocent people at some distance from it. The Chief Constable of Glamorgan concurred in the substitution of the Metropolitan Police for the Infantry, who were halted at Swindon, and the
Cavalry were told to proceed no further than Cardiff and to await
further instructions there. General Macready [Commander of the
2nd Infantry Brigade] was specially selected to take charge of any
military forces which might be required to support the police. He
proceeded at once to Cardiff where it was intended the Cavalry
should remain pending further developments. As, however, the
special trains conveying the Metropolitan Police were not expected
to reach the scene of the disorder until about 9 pm on Tuesday night,
both General Macready and the Chief Constable were authorised
to move the troops forward if they considered it necessary. The train
conveying the Metropolitan Police was delayed for about an hour in
reaching its destination. All the attacks of the rioters upon the
Glamorgan Colliery were, however, successfully repulsed by the Chief
Constable with the County Police at his disposal, and when the
Metropolitan Police arrived the rioters had already been beaten from
the collieries without the aid of any reinforcement either of London
Police or Military. The insensate action of the rioters in wrecking
shops in the town of Tonypandy, against which they had not the
slightest cause for animosity, when they had been foiled in their
attacks upon the colliery, was not foreseen by anyone on the spot,
and would not have been prevented by the presence of soldiers at
the colliery itself. There is no reason to believe that the first contingent of the Metropolitan Police with the local police forces already
gathered was not and is not sufficient to deal with the situation in the

district without additional help. With the view however of increasing the strength of the police force in the district to a point which will obviate all risk of having to use the military, two further contingents, aggregating 500 additional police, have been sent from London. The whole district is now in the effective control of the police, and there appears to be no reason at present why the policy of keeping the military out of direct contact with the rioters should be departed from.

King George V to WSC

TELEGRAM

10 November 1910   Sandringham

Many thanks for your full report with regard to Riots in Wales. Glad you are satisfied with the latest news and I trust that matters will soon settle down. Trust that it is not true that all the horses have been lost in one of the mines.

GEORGE R.I.

A study of the contemporary Press confirms the facts set out in Churchill's letter to the King. The fact that Churchill did not use troops against the miners is underlined by the fact that Lord Northcliffe's *Times,* "ever strong upon the stronger side" as Hazlitt had earlier said of it, attacked him for not having used troops.

Under the heading THE BREAKDOWN OF TRADE UNIONISM a lengthy *Times* leader of 9 November 1910 said in part:

The Chief Constable of Glamorgan very properly took a most serious view of the disturbances on Monday, and lost no time in making arrangements for dealing effectually with any renewal. He felt already on Monday night that the police could not cope with the situation alone, and applied to the local military authorities for troops. Yesterday, it appears, both cavalry and infantry were despatched by train for South Wales, but were stopped at Swindon in consequence of a consultation between the Home Secretary and Mr Haldane. It was thought preferable to send more police instead and to hold back the troops. Accordingly 70 mounted men and 200 ordinary constables belonging to the Metropolitan Police were sent down from London, while the infantry already on the road were detained at

Swindon and the cavalry proceeded to Cardiff, but no further. The Home Secretary took upon himself a grave responsibility in interfering with the arrangements demanded by the Chief Constable and acceded to the military authorities; and late last night he so far reconsidered his decision as to send on a squadron of cavalry to Pontypridd at the junction of the two disturbed valleys. The Chief Constable knows the local conditions and the character of the men with whom he has to deal; he has the fullest information and can command the best advice; and he is responsible for order in the district. If he asked for troops it was no doubt because he was convinced that they were needed. If he thought that additional police would suffice, he would have asked for them, for no police officer cares to bring soldiers on the scene if he can help it. No doubt the motive for countermanding the arrangement was the fear that the presence of the military would exasperate the strikers. But it would be difficult to increase the excitement they have already shown, and the sight of the London police is just as likely to have that effect as the presence of soldiers, while the latter would be more efficient if dire necessity arose and more likely to overawe the rioters.

The renewed rioting late last night seems to have been of a most determined character, and if loss of life occurs, which we fear is more than possible, the responsibility will lie with the Home Secretary. The conciliatory message which he sent yesterday to the miners is well meant, of course, but it shows a very inadequate grasp of the situation, and the somewhat maudlin tone in which it is couched is more likely to excite ridicule than respect.

Mr Churchill hardly seems to understand that an acute crisis has arisen, which needs decisive handling. The rosewater of conciliation is all very well in its place, but its place is not in face of a wild mob drunk with the desire of destruction. Men's lives are in danger, not to mention the poor horses; and the Home Secretary offers an interview between Mr Askwith and some representatives of the men. We have the utmost respect for Mr Askwith and his capacity for dealing with labour disputes; his services will be most valuable at the right time. But the heart of the whole trouble, as he at least knows, if the Home Secretary does not, is that the men will not listen to their leaders. Their whole conduct is in flat violation, not only of the agreement which their representatives signed last April, but of the advice and entreaties of the executive committee of their union, and also of the votes recently given by their comrades.

The *Manchester Guardian* the next day rebuked *The Times* and said in an editorial:

> Mr Churchill was violently attacked in yesterday's *Times* for a decision which in all probability saved many lives. It needed some courage after the Chief Constable had asked for troops to stop the troops which were on their way and to send policemen instead. But, as usual, the brave course was also the wise one. The attacks of the powerhouse were beaten off by the local police before the reinforcements came up. Defeated at the mine, the rioters then began to pillage the shops in the village street, and it was while they were at this sorry work that the first batch of London police arrived. One can imagine what would have happened if the soldiers instead of the policemen had come on the rioters while they were pillaging. Bayonets would have been used instead of truncheons; the clumsier methods of the soldiers would have exasperated the crowds, and instead of a score of cases for the hospital there might have been as many for the mortuary. And morning would have brought not shame and repentance but deep anger over someone's death and sullen resentment at being treated not like citizens who had lost their heads but like enemies of the State. It is true that the disorders of the night at one time seemed so serious that Mr Churchill decided to allow the troops to move up into the district so as to be in readiness for anything that might happen. But he never wavered in his determination not to employ the troops unless the disorders passed beyond the control of the police, who were being constantly reinforced throughout the whole of the day. As far as can be seen his policy promises to be completely successful, and in the meantime negotiations are in progress which will, we hope, see the authority of the men's leaders re-established over the anarchy of the last few days. A rougher handling of the situation would not only have been less efficacious for the matter in hand — the restoration of order — but it would have led almost certainly to an extension of the area of stoppage and to excesses on both sides of which no one could have foreseen the end. The right use of the police is one of the things that we understand better than they do in France; and Mr Churchill's policy promises better than that of M. Briand.

In the light of the facts so clearly shown in the public prints of the time, it is all the more remarkable that the Tonypandy label should have hung around Churchill's neck all his life. The lie was still being energetically spread 5 years ago and received what should have been its quietus in a brilliant article by Sir Alan Herbert in the *Spectator* of 28 June 1963. Yet the rumour persists and has even been improved upon. Shortly before this volume went to press the author was informed that in January 1967 an Oxford undergraduate, discussing Churchill's career with his tutor, asserted with some confidence that "Churchill had ordered tanks to be used against the Welsh miners at Tonypandy." His tutor commented that this showed remarkable far-sightedness on Churchill's part, as the tank had not yet been invented.

In June 1911 another wave of strikes began in the docks. Starting in Southampton they quickly spread to other ports, the largest taking place at Salford and lasting from mid-June until July 10. It was· clear, however, from the general industrial unrest which accompanied these strikes and from the sympathy and active support which the dockers were receiving from other unions, particularly the transport workers, that industrial action in Britain had reached a new and somewhat alarming phase. G. R. Askwith, who had worked closely with Churchill when at the Board of Trade and who was Chairman of the Fair Wages Advisory Committee, had already drawn up a considered analysis of the situation and warned of the exceptional difficulties that now lay ahead.

Churchill seems to have accepted Askwith's warnings, for he expressed his own views in an undated minute probably written towards the end of July:

> Those conversant of labour matters in *practice* anticipate grave upheaval. Serious crises have been in recent years, and very often lately, surmounted only by a narrow margin of safety, and now specially a new force has arisen in trades unionism, whereby the power of the old leaders has proved quite ineffective, and the sympathetic strike on a wide scale is prominent. Shipping, coal, railways, dockers etc etc are all uniting and breaking out at once. The general strike "policy" is a' factor which must be dealt with.
>
> While control can probably be maintained, even in a dozen or more simultaneous Tony Pandys or Manchesters [*he meant the contiguous Salford*], control would be more difficult if the railways went, and inadequate control must mean great uncertainty, destruction of

property, and probably loss of life. Such protection or repression must be coupled with civil action on the lines of prevention and peace.

Quite soon the dangers which both Askwith and Churchill had foreseen became apparent. From the beginning of August onwards partial strikes of railwaymen, ostensibly in support of the dock workers in various parts of the country, began to break out. The railwaymen had a grievance of their own in that the railway companies were still refusing to recognize the unions as negotiating bodies. The combination of dock and railway strikes, together with subsequent dismissals by the railway companies, resulted in threats of grave shortages of food in London, Liverpool and Manchester, accompanied by considerable unrest and some rioting.

All this took place in the sweltering heat of the hottest summer on record. On August 9, the day the London meat and fruit markets came to a standstill and, incidentally, while the House of Lords was coming to the end of its historic debate on the Parliament Bill, the temperature in London was never below 90° in the shade between 11.30 a.m. and 6.30 p.m. and went as high as 100° at Greenwich. What had started in the London Docks as a dispute ostensibly concerned with wages and demarcation was now degenerating into a wave of nation-wide sympathy strikes among transport workers, particularly railwaymen. This was the first serious manifestation of a general strike which was eventually avoided in this instance and which the nation did not have to face until 1926.

Both at the Board of Trade and at the Home Office Churchill had hitherto taken an active part in forwarding the machinery of conciliation in industrial disputes. He took the initiative in the appointment of David Shackleton, a Labour MP, as industrial adviser to the Home Office in the autumn of 1910, and, in the summer of 1911, gave G. R. Askwith help and encouragement in the establishment of the Industrial Council. More and more now, as reports of food shortages, unrest and rioting came in from all parts of the country, was he concerned with the maintenance of law and order and, as part of this, with the maintenance of essential supplies. When he accounted to Parliament for his actions on August 22 he made a speech in which

there occurs a passage which, read in the cold light of historical
analysis more than fifty years later, seems high flown and even
absurdly exaggerated. There is little doubt though that at the time it
reflected the considered views and attitudes of the overwhelming
majority of responsible opinion:

> I have a right to ask the House to look at the emergency with which
> we were faced, and which alone would justify the strong and unusual
> measures which we thought it necessary to take. Let the House
> realise it. In that great quadrilateral of industrialism, from Liver-
> pool and Manchester on the West to Hull and Grimsby on the East,
> from Newcastle down to Birmingham to Coventry in the south — in
> that great quadrilateral which, I suppose, must contain anything be-
> tween 15 to 20 millions of persons, intelligent, hard-working people,
> who have raised our industry to the forefront of the world's affairs
> — it is practically certain that a continuance of the railway strike
> would have produced a swift and certain degeneration of all the
> means, of all the structure, social and economic, on which the life
> of the people depends. If it had not been interrupted it would have
> hurled the whole of that great community into an abyss of horror
> which no man can dare to contemplate. Let me remind the House
> that at this time, before the railway strike began, we had had a pro-
> longed interruption of the entry of food supplies from Liverpool and
> Manchester; the ports on the other side were closed by the railway
> dispute, and the lines from north to south were being cut off. I am
> sure the House will see that no blockade by a foreign enemy could
> have been anything like so effective in producing terrible pressure on
> these vast populations as the effective closing of those great ports,
> coupled with the paralysis of the railway service. Meanwhile, the
> populations of the south, the east, and the west, of this island would
> have remained comparatively unaffected by what was going on —
> not suffering themselves, and yet almost helpless to come to the aid
> of their fellow countrymen.
>
> The honourable member (Mr Ramsay MacDonald) spoke of medi-
> aeval methods. This is a new peril. I do not know whether in the
> history of the world a similar catastrophe can be shown to have
> menaced an equally great community. I remember a gentleman who
> had returned from the East telling me of the breaking of the great
> Nimrod Dam of the Euphrates in the fifteenth century. It had been
> built in times of antiquity, but had been neglected by the ignorant

conquerors of the country. In the fifteenth century it broke, and there were no means of repairing it. Above the Dam there was a great canal running 300 or 400 miles, and along the banks of that canal four or five million persons lived in a fertile province. Immediately the Dam broke the water flowed out of the canal, and, though history gives no details, it is certain that the enormous population who lived by that artificial means, except for a few thousands who lived on pools by the canal or found their way across the desert, were absolutely wiped from the book of human life. These are the considerations which it is no exaggeration to say have to be borne in mind at this present juncture.

A typical incident occurred in Liverpool on August 14, and it is well described in a telegram from the Head Constable of Liverpool to the Home Office:

[The rioting] took place in an area where disorder is a chronic feature, ready to break out when any abnormal excitement is in force. The object of the riot was purely and simply attack on the police, whom they tempted into sidestreets in which barricades of sanitary dustbins and wire entanglements were placed. The riot began about eight, and the troops were called out with natural reluctance on the part of the police officer in charge at 11.40. The mob pursued the same tactics, stoned troops and police from the windows and house tops, but troops and police worked admirably together, and reduced the neighbourhood to peace about 2.30 and the former returned to quarters. Twenty prisoners were taken from the streets and houses. The troops fired a few shots (officers' revolver shots I think) at the house tops, whence the stones came. Six privates of the Yorkshire regiment and two constables received minor injuries. Both military and police behaved admirably, and the experience of working with the former has been valuable to the officers of the police, who will call the latter out more readily in future. A great deal of damage to houses and shops, especially public houses and provision shops, but food does not seem to have been the object, as the bread was thrown about the street. Troops engaged were Yorkshire regiment — 200 of all ranks.

The Lord Mayor of Liverpool and the Mayor of Birkenhead sent a joint telegram to Churchill asking him to send a warship to the

Mersey with instructions that if needs be blue-jackets would work the ferries and HMS *Antrim* was in fact sent. Lord Derby wrote to Churchill from Harrogate that he had had an earnest telephone message from the Lord Mayor of Liverpool complaining that people in London did not realize that this was no ordinary strike riot but that "a revolution was in progress." Derby went on: "the City is in a state of siege — the hospitals have but two days supply — and in forty-eight hours all poor people will be face to face with starvation and God alone knows what happens when that moment arrives." And the King telegraphed to Churchill:

The King to WSC

TELEGRAM

16 August 1911

Accounts from Liverpool show that the situation there more like revolution than a strike. Trust that Govt while inducing strike leaders and masters to come to terms will take steps to ensure protection of life & property.

Local feeling runs so high that you cannot expect reason to prevail yet and a settlement must be forced on both sides. Can you not induce labour leaders to assist or would they be afraid to be on the side of law and order?

Strongly deprecate half-hearted employment of troops: they should not be called on except as a last resource but if called on they should be given a free hand & the mob should be made to fear them.

GEORGE R.I.

It was, of course, the employment of troops that aroused the bitterest political passions. Until August 15 Churchill's attitude to the use of troops remained the same as it had been in the previous year in the case of the South Wales riots. He encouraged Chief Constables to enroll Special Constables, and he made it clear that he wished the local authorities to make the fullest use of the police before calling in troops. Nevertheless, together with Haldane, he made a point of ensuring that troops in sufficient numbers were available and at all the most likely points of disturbance, ready to be called in if need be by the authorities. Until the middle of August the directive given to police and military was the same as that given by General Macready in the Salford strike earlier in June: that it was for the police to take such action as might be necessary, and the military were not to act until called upon by the police, and only when the Officer in Command of the military was satisfied that all the resources of the Police were exhausted.

... "[These instructions] in no way over-ride or modify the instructions laid down in the King's Regulations and the Manual of Military Law for the use of the Military in the aid of the Civil Power." [i.e. that the Military may not act unless help is specifically requested by the Civil Power.]

As late as August 17 Churchill sent a letter to all Chief Constables directing them to make the maximum use of the police. But on the following day the threat of a general railway strike grew more serious and it was in order to protect the railways from possible sabotage and those railwaymen who continued to work, particularly those on signal boxes, from possible injury that new orders were issued to "all Mayors and Chief Constables in the Disturbed Areas." As Churchill telegraphed to the Mayor of Birkenhead on August 19: "Officers commanding the various Military areas to use their own discretion as to whether troops are or are not to be sent to any particular point. The Army Regulation which requires a requisition for troops from a civil authority is suspended."

This action was taken after the railwaymen's leaders had given notice of a national railway strike. On August 18 the Prime Minister had offered the railwaymen a Royal Commission, but this was turned down on the grounds that it would be too slow to report. When they refused it, Asquith is reported to have said, "Then your blood be on your own head." That evening every member of the railway service received the following telegram: "Your liberty is at stake, all railwaymen must strike at once."

Churchill telegraphed to the King on August 18 "that the railway strike will now be fought out." He himself had no standing in the negotiations which were conducted by the Board of Trade. He was concerned solely with protecting the railways, maintaining supplies and keeping order.

In a communiqué issued on August 19 Churchill declared: "The

Government are taking and will take all necessary steps to make sure that supplies of food, fuel and other essentials, shall not be interrupted on the railways or at the Ports . . . any serious breakdown . . . would lead to the starvation of great numbers of the poorer people . . . the Government believe that the arrangements which have been made to safeguard the working of the railways and to maintain order would prove effective. If not other measures of an even larger scope will have to be taken promptly . . ." Throughout that day the Home Office was being inundated with requests for help such as the following from the Mayor of Birkenhead: "6 p.m. 50 infantry have been withdrawn from the town. There have been several collisions between strikers and police. I do not think that I have sufficient forces at my disposal. If you cannot send me more military or naval support, I cannot answer for the safety of life or property." And five hours later at 11.30 p.m: "I have no reply to my telegram of this afternoon. Please send more troops at once. It is urgent. I cannot see my way to preserving life and property unless I can have more assistance." The Mayor of Birkenhead did not know, but by the time he despatched this telegram the railway strike was off.

It was the Chancellor of the Exchequer, Lloyd George, who played the leading part in persuading the railway unions to abandon the strike. This was due in the main to the employers' agreeing to recognize the unions as negotiators. It may also have been due, as was widely supposed at the time, to the frank revelations by Lloyd George, that the country was being threatened by Germany as a consequence of the crisis resulting from the Agadir incident and that the Germans would not hesitate to use the paralysis into which the country was falling in order to attack Britain. Or it may be, as Churchill claimed, that the strike collapsed "because it was obvious and certain that any Government must, with the whole force of the State, exert itself to prevent such a catastrophe, and because it was certain that in taking such action they would be supported by the good sense and resolution of the whole mass of the people." More probably it was a combination of all three factors. The railway strike was over and, wonderful to relate, there was very little bloodshed. The troops fired, when they did fire, with great caution and deliberation, usually over the heads of the crowds. Ironically, it was two days after the settlement of the strike that the only fatality from the use of troops occurred. This was at Llanelly, where four people were killed after a train had been held up by rioters, the engine driver had been knocked senseless and looting had begun. This calculated violence by the strikers exceeded anything which had occurred hitherto. The King telegraphed to Churchill on August 20:

The King to WSC
(Royal Archives)

TELEGRAM

20 August 1911
Copy

Your telegram informing me that the Railway Strike has been declared at an end has given me the greatest satisfaction. I take this opportunity of thanking you for the very full accounts you have given me during this anxious time. Glad the troops are to be sent back to their districts at once: this will reassure the public. Much regret unfortunate incident at Llanelly. Feel convinced that prompt measures taken by you prevented loss of life in different parts of the country. Trust in very short time normal state of affairs will be resumed.

GEORGE R.I.

For all the criticism that came Churchill's way from the Labour members of Parliament for his attitude to the use of troops during this strike, there is little doubt that the King's telegram represented public opinion at the time. But Labour was not to forget Churchill's part in this strike — even though they were soon to muddle it with Tonypandy, doubtless because Tonypandy comes easier to the English tongue than Llanelly.

*

Churchill, as already stated, was the second youngest man ever to hold the office of Home Secretary; almost certainly he was the only Home Secretary ever to have been in prison. He was, of course, a prisoner of war and his jailors the humane Boers, but the loss of freedom had irked him greatly, and he felt he had some affinity with the life of the prisoner. He has described how, apart from his school-days, his days as a captive were the unhappiest of his life. Home Secretaries of modern times usually aspire to be "reforming" Home Secretaries, but Churchill had a personal motive stronger than most. He sought to help prisoners in every way, short of escaping.

Asquith told Churchill in a letter dated 2 October 1911 that when he was at the Home Office in 1895, though he had not the time to accomplish much, he was able to leave behind him Sir John Ruggles-Brise, an outstanding Chairman of the Prison Commissioners. This remarkable man who was to remain in this post until he reached the retirement age in 1921 was behind many of the penal reforms initiated by the Liberal administrations between 1906 and 1914. Under Churchill's predecessor, Herbert Gladstone, Probation and Borstal Institutions were introduced to deal with young offenders, and Preventive Detention was introduced to deal with the recidivists, or habitual criminals. But the overwhelming problem which Gladstone had been unable to tackle and which still confronted Churchill on his arrival at the Home Office was that too many people were being sent to prison. Of the 184,000 who were imprisoned in 1908–9, more than half were committed in default of payment of a fine, and a third for drunkenness. Clearly here were areas where reform was necessary and urgent.

Churchill's strong sense of the shame that a prison sentence could bring, combined with a desire to nullify the propaganda value that suffragettes enjoyed from exposing the prison conditions to which they were condemned, led to his first pronouncement of intentions in the House of Commons in March 1910: "I feel, as did my predecessor, that prison rules which are suitable to criminals jailed for dishonesty or cruelty or other crimes implying moral turpitude, should not be applied inflexibly to those whose general character is good and whose offences, however reprehensible, do not involve personal dishonour." He promised that the so-called political prisoners should be treated separately in that they should not be forced to wear prison clothing, should not be searched or forced to take the regulation bath, should be allowed food from outside, to take regular exercise and to talk while so doing. This amelioration of conditions for prisoners of this kind — which still prevails to this day — was generally welcomed and

Churchill personally enjoyed a good deal of praise from the press and the public for this action. This caused Gladstone to complain in two private letters to Churchill that the latter had merely taken up schemes which Gladstone had drawn up but had not had an opportunity to carry into practice, and that Churchill should have acknowledged his debt to his predecessor (Gladstone had not seen the reference to his predecessor quoted above). Churchill replied with spirit: "I think it might interest you to read the series of Minutes which led up to the decision. They will show you that my action was independent, and will perhaps enable you to see how it was I failed to ascribe proper importance to your point of view."

For the next three months Churchill busied himself in studying the problems of the prison services. He took pains to work out the costs where extra funds were involved, and he was willing to listen to outside evidence from such eminent men as W. T. Stead and Wilfrid Scawen Blunt, both of whom had been imprisoned in their time, and John Galsworthy whose play *Justice* had recently been performed. "I have always admired his pluck and his capacity," Galsworthy wrote to Churchill's aunt, Mrs John Leslie. "I now perceive him to have a heart and to be very warm."

The result of Churchill's studies was presented to the House of Commons on July 20, when on the Prisons Vote he announced far-reaching reforms. While some had to wait four years before they became the subject of legislation, the spirit of these reforms was carried into effect straight away. They were of lasting significance and remain outstanding, even when compared with the other great measures of the period.

First and most revolutionary was the proposal to alter the regulations for the payment of fines:

> There are almost an unlimited number of cases of men whose character is well known, who have committed an offence for which they are properly punished by a fine, who could pay if time were allowed them, but who, in default of having the money with them in their pockets, are hurried off to gaol. Let the House see what an injurious operation that is. The State loses its fine, the man goes to prison, perhaps for the first time. A shocking event. He goes through all the formalities for a four or five day sentence that would apply if he

were sentenced to a long term of penal servitude. He is photographed, taken off in a Black Maria, and his fingerprints are taken. All these painful processes are gone through just as in the case of a long sentence. Further, more than half the people committed to prison in default of paying fines are committed for the offence of drunkenness; and in the case of drunkenness the enforcement of a fine is a far better punishment than a committal to prison; for his release is very often celebrated by a prisoner but a fine effectively enforced means a period of temperance.

This proposal to allow "time to pay" had been in the air for some time. The Surrey magistrates had been doing something of the kind since 1909, but there were doubts among the Prison Commissioners and the Home Office staff, particularly Troup, whether it was advisable to introduce this·on a national scale because of the lessening of the deterrent effect. Churchill pushed this measure into the open and it was accepted as a principle of national policy. In ten years the result was dramatic. Whereas 95,686 were imprisoned for non-payment of fines in 1908–9, the number in 1918–19 was 5,264. Whereas 62,822 were sent to prison in 1908–9 for drunkenness, the number in 1918–19 was 1,670. And despite the Royal example, the consumption of alcohol had not decreased markedly during the war.

The second important proposal was an extension of the Children Act of 1908 to cover offenders between sixteen and twenty-one. The main clauses were that: (*a*) no young person between sixteen and twenty-one should be sent to prison unless he is incorrigible or has committed a serious offence; (*b*) that if it is necessary to send him to prison, the sentence must be for more than a month; (*c*) that he is not to receive a sentence that is merely punitive but positively of a curative and educative character; (*d*) that the full Borstal sentence should be relaxed in the case of youthful offenders; and that (*e*) some form of disciplinary correction (drill) should take place outside prison in the case of those youthful offenders guilty of petty crimes (gambling, rowdyism and swearing).

In support of this measure, Churchill said: "The House will, I think, sympathise and will support me in any steps that may be necessary to prevent these undesirable commitments [to gaol]. The evil only falls on the sons of the working classes. The sons of other classes commit many of the same offences. In their boisterous and exuberant spirits in their days at Oxford and Cambridge they commit offences for which scores of the sons of the working classes are committed to prison, without any injury being inflicted on them . . . [because they could afford to pay the fine]. At least 5,000 lads committed for these offences every year would be saved from the knowledge of gaol if only some such method of correction as I have indicated could be devised with proper regard for the nourishment of the boy. It would inflict a punishment on him which would not injure him, but, on the other hand, might actually benefit him." These reforms only produced results gradually, but the progress was steady. In 1910 there were 12,376 boys and 1,189 girls under twenty-one in prison. In 1919 there were only 3,474 and 762 respectively. Churchill went on to confirm that the relaxation for political prisoners announced in March should become part of the new Prison Rules.

He also made an important amendment in the Rules relating to solitary confinement. This was now to be reduced to one month, except in the case of recidivists or others who actually desired solitary confinement. Churchill proposed that lectures and concerts should be given in every prison: this provoked considerable opposition from Earl Winterton, one of his sharpest critics, on the grounds that Churchill was making prison life too comfortable. When Winterton came to write his own memoirs in 1955, however, he described Churchill as a "good Home Secretary — he humanised and improved the penal system."

Last, but almost as important as his proposals for giving "time to pay," were Churchill's recommendations for the supervision of released convicts by the establishment of a central after-care association, composed of official members and representatives of the Prisoners' Aid Societies. He also proposed that police supervision after release should be suspended and that the ticket-of-leave or licence system be abolished. This was probably as energetic an attempt to deal with the after-care of prisoners as has been made by any Home Secretary before or since.

The first reactions were generally favourable. Galsworthy in a letter to *The Times* on 23 July 1910 wrote: "These changes are one and all inspired by imagination, without which reform is deadly, and by common sense without which it is dangerous." But Sir Edward

Clayton, a former Inspector of Prisons and Secretary to the Prison Commission, expressed the more conservative and popular view when he wrote in the January 1911 issue of *Nineteenth Century and After*: "I believe that these changes are in the right direction, and all that requires to be guarded against is, that we do not ignore the poorer classes outside the prison walls while we do so much for the worst classes of our population."

When Churchill returned from his holiday, he began a series of visits to prisons with his Under-Secretary C. F. G. Masterman, and in the case of Dartmoor, with Lloyd George. It was on the occasion of this visit to Dartmoor that Churchill and Lloyd George met "the Dartmoor Shepherd," one David Davies. This man was described by Churchill in a minute as one who "enjoyed a melancholy celebrity for the prodigious sentences he had endured, for his good behaviour and docility in prison, and for his unusual gift of calling individual sheep by name." His record was, as Churchill said, "certainly not less terrible for the punishment than for his crimes." Since his first conviction in 1870 he had been sentenced ten times, including seven years' penal servitude for burglary in 1871, ten years' for stealing a watch and chain in 1877, fifteen years' for burglary in 1887 and five years' for stealing £1 6s. 6d. in 1902. Never in committing these offences, all of which were of a trivial character, did he offer violence. He was, in fact, a most docile person who, during his frequent stays on Dartmoor, tended the flock of sheep there with loving care. It was his last conviction, however, which aroused the wrath of the Chancellor of the Exchequer and the compassion of the Home Secretary. This was in 1909, when Davies was sixty-eight; he was found guilty of robbing an offertory box of two shillings, and was sentenced to three years' penal servitude and ten years' preventive detention. During the election campaign in November 1910 Lloyd George contrasted the Lords, descended from "plunderers of the poor," with the Dartmoor Shepherd who, he said — incorrectly — had been sentenced to thirteen years' penal servitude for stealing two shillings. Churchill remitted the sentence of ten years' preventive detention and the Shepherd was released at the end of the year. Moreover, Davies was found a job at Wrexham at the beginning of January, but he disappeared from it the next day. Great were the derision and the sarcasm with which the episode of the Shepherd was discussed in the press and in the House.

Davies was eventually found in April, when he was arrested for house-breaking. He was sentenced later to nine months' imprisonment. Though Churchill was subjected to a good deal of ridicule on account of this case, it did serve to highlight some of the deficiencies of the prison system in general and of the new preventive detention rules in particular.

His visit to Pentonville was similarly productive of Parliamentary questioning. Seeing a number of young offenders in the prison he enquired into their cases, and finding that seven of them were serving sentences for trivial offences he commuted their sentences. "I must confess," he said in the course of an adjournment debate in the House on 21 February 1911, "I was very glad of the opportunity of recommending the use of the prerogative in these cases, because I wanted to draw the attention of the country by means of cases, perfectly legitimate in themselves, to the evil by which 7,000 or 8,000 lads of the poorer classes are sent to gaol every year for offences which, if the noble Lord [Earl Winterton, who had raised the matter] had committed them at College, he would not have been subjected to the slightest degree of inconvenience."

Churchill never missed an opportunity of pressing forward with his schemes for penal reform. He quickly grasped that proper classification of prisoners was the "essence of penology," though Eddie Marsh had to report to Churchill on 23 August 1910 that Ruggles-Brise "burst into Homeric laughter when he read that it would be easy for the Prison Commissioners to classify into 20 groups." On 26 September 1910 Churchill drew up a lengthy memorandum for Asquith outlining a Bill, "a scientific & benevolent measure, dealing with prisons & the punishment of offenders . . . well suited to the Coronation Year." His main objective was to do away as far as possible with short sentences — a laudable objective which successive Home Secretaries for more than fifty years were to find elusive. He proposed four lines of advance towards this objective — the greater use of probation for young offenders; the abolition of imprisonment for debt; an extension of the "time to pay" principle; and "suspended sentences" for those sentenced for certain trivial offences to a month or less. Asquith was sympathetic — though he had doubts about abolishing imprisonment for debt. But in the wake of Lloyd George's budget and the Parliament Bill there was little time left for other measures, and Churchill was never able to present his ideas to Parliament in the shape of a Bill. Thus he never got any penal reform on the statute book: but those reforms which he was able to carry out without parliamentary sanction were to shine for years and to serve as milestones and signposts to future reformers.

*

Among the minor problems with which the Liberal Government was afflicted the most vexatious was the question of women's suffrage. The suffragists or suffragettes, as the women agitators were called, did not concern themselves much with the Tories who were then a small minority in opposition. The attitude of Liberal ministers varied; some like Asquith consistently opposed them from first to last, others like Grey, Birrell and Burns were sympathetic. Churchill's attitude was somewhat ambivalent. He had first encountered these formidable women, whose leaders were Mrs Emmeline Pankhurst and her two daughters Christabel and Sylvia Pankhurst, when he was speaking at a pre-election meeting at North-West Manchester in 1905. He was then Under-Secretary of State for the Colonies and was supported on the platform by the Foreign Secretary, Sir Edward Grey. While they were addressing the meeting they were frequently interrupted by Christabel Pankhurst and her friend Annie Kenney. Police and stewards escorted these ladies from the hall. They were brought before the magistrates and fined, but refused to pay and were imprisoned for a week. When Churchill heard this he offered to pay their fines totalling fifteen shillings, but the suffragettes preferred the martyrdom of prison, which indeed became one of their main techniques in the ensuing period of militant agitation.

At the General Election of 1906 his meetings were much disturbed by suffragettes and some disorder occurred. The reader will remember the account in Chapter 4, pages 119–120. In spite of the support of Lady Dorothy Howard, he was again badgered by suffragettes who caused disorder at several meetings at his by-election at North-West Manchester in 1908, and at the second by-election at Dundee. The ringleader there was a Miss Maloney. At the end of 1909, just before the first of the 1910 elections, he was attacked by Miss Theresa Garnett with a dog-whip at Bristol railway station. Shortly after he had been assaulted by this woman he received a deputation of suffragettes to whom he said: "I am bound to say I think your cause has marched backwards." By now it was clear that there was a concentrated attack being carefully organized against individual leaders.

Miss Christabel Pankhurst to Miss Cullen
(British Museum)

17 July 1909

Dear Miss Cullen,

   Mr Winston Churchill is to address a meeting at Norwich on Monday 26 July. I wonder if you would go there a few days beforehand to rouse the people and get a great crowd at his meetings. . . . No doubt you can get hospitality while in Norwich and the Union would gladly pay out of pocket expenses. I am writing to the I.L.P. to say we shall send someone about the middle of next week, and whoever goes will be prepared to address their Sunday meeting.

Yours sincerely
CHRISTABEL PANKHURST

   Six days later Miss Pankhurst wrote again to Miss Cullen saying: "We send you another helper in the person of Miss Jarvis. She is ready for arrest." Many of them courted prison, some went on hunger strikes and had to be forcibly fed. All this became distasteful to many people whatever their views on votes for women.

   In the spring of 1910 a non-party Conciliation Committee was set up to get agreement to promote some legislation on female suffrage. Lord Lytton was its President and H. N. Brailsford acted as secretary. They were particularly concerned to receive the support of Churchill. Brailsford wrote to him on April 13 asking him to lend his name to the Conciliation Committee's activities:

H. N. Brailsford to WSC

13 April [1910]   32 Well Walk
Private   Hampstead

Dear Mr Churchill,

   You were good enough to say, when I talked to you about the new non-party suffrage committee, that you would give it a general support, provided you approved the documents which it proposed to publish.

I enclose (1) a letter which will be sent to all members of Parliament — not for publication. (2) a declaration which they will be asked to sign. It *may* be published, though it may be expedient not to do so. (3) a private memorandum (which you need not trouble to read) intended for Liberals only, which of course is not for publication and commits no one but myself.

What I venture to ask of you is that you should allow us to quote you in the covering letter (No 1) as one of the "Rt Hon X.Y.Z." who "welcome the formation of the committee and would favour a solution on non-party lines." The formula is vague & not I think at all compromising to you. It does not commit you either to the municipal basis, or to procedure by private Bill. But it would greatly help us if you would give us your blessing even in these very general terms. We are asking Sir Edward Grey, Lloyd George, Arthur Balfour, Alfred Lyttelton and Bonar Law to lend us their names in the same way. We are hopeful of getting Sir E. Grey & Alfred Lyttelton — nearly sure in fact. I don't know yet what success those of our friends who are approaching the others have had. Mr Balfour in private goes quite as far as this, and he is considering whether he ought to let us use his name.

Please note that the letter (No 1) will go to MP's but not to the press.

Sincerely yours
H. N. BRAILSFORD

Churchill agreed in principle to do so, with a proviso:

WSC to H. N. Brailsford

19 April 1910   Home Office
Copy

Dear Mr Brailsford,

Owing to great pressure of business I have not been able to study your papers, which I see you sent me on the 13th April, until this morning. Pray accept my expression of regret for the delay. I should be willing to allow myself to be quoted in the manner you suggest as "welcoming the formation of a Committee and favouring its solution on non-party lines," provided that the others whom you mention, or most of them, are willing to come forward too. Perhaps you will write to me on this, and let me know what progress you have made.

I do not wish to be committed at the present juncture to any special form or basis in or upon which the franchise is to be granted to women. I have not sufficiently studied the bearings of the municipal franchise which you now favour. I am, however, anxious to see women relieved in principle from a disability which is injurious to them whilst it is based on grounds of sex.

Yours sincerely
WINSTON S. CHURCHILL

A provisional draft of a Conciliation Bill giving the vote to women possessed of a household qualification was included with Brailsford's letter. Churchill had agreed to support the Committee if his colleagues did but he made no mention of the Conciliation Bill as such. In the next few weeks Churchill began to have doubts about the Bill which was proposed by the Committee. A Bill, called the Parliamentary Franchise (Women) Bill, was to be introduced into the Commons on July 11 by David Shackleton and had been drawn up by the Conciliation Committee. Churchill told Lord Lytton in a private interview at the Home Office on June 6 that he did not think that "any effective legislation on female suffrage could be introduced during the 'present' session of Parliament;" he also expressed doubts as to the form the bill would take when it was eventually introduced. Churchill asked Lytton to leave with him a copy of the Bill so that he could consider it. Churchill then sent the Bill to the Whips and other leaders of the Liberal Party for their views. Within a few hours of the interview Lytton wrote Churchill a long letter expressing his disappointment at the latter's attitude to the problem. Churchill replied about three days later stating that the Government would not be able to find the time to introduce a suffrage bill in the present Parliament, and further that he now learned that the Bill itself was "open to many objections on the grounds of being partial and undemocratic." On July 12 Churchill spoke on the Bill in the House and opposed it, arguing that as women had not made the most of their opportunities in municipal government, there was no reason to think that they would do better in the parliamentary field. He saw that there were two grievances, the refusal of the vote for women political workers and, more serious, the slur of inferiority on the sex in general. He had hoped that the Committee would have considered the removal of these grievances by "fancy" franchises or by adult suffrage at twenty-five: they had not.

Many working women might gain the vote but be immediately disfranchised by their receipt of poor relief. Many rich men could give qualifications of property to their wives and daughters and so multiply plural voting. Prostitutes would lose the vote by marriage and regain it on divorce. The Bill could not be commended democratically.

When Churchill spoke and voted against the Bill, which was carried by 299 to 189, it cannot have been any surprise to Lytton; however Lytton had not passed on the result of his interview to Brailsford, who was furious and accused Churchill of treachery.

H. N. Brailsford to WSC

12 July 1910   32 Well Walk

Sir,

I beg to inform you that in discussing your conduct in today's debate, I shall be obliged to describe it as treacherous. You knew when you "welcomed the formation" of the Conciliation Committee the nature of the Bill which it was drafting.

I shall further state that you said what was false when you gave the House to understand that you are in favour of adult suffrage. You told me that you are strongly opposed to the duplicated vote of married women.

If you consider yourself insulted, I am at your service, and will study your convenience in making arrangements for a meeting.

I am, Sir, Faithfully yours
H. N. BRAILSFORD

WSC to H. N. Brailsford

[12 July 1910]   Home Office
Copy

Sir,

I was never consulted in any way as to the nature of the Bill. I never saw the Bill until after it was made public. As soon as I had examined it & had the opportunity of consulting others I wrote to

Lord Lytton that it was "one-sided" and "undemocratic." He has no doubt kept my letter. You are right in saying that I welcomed the formation of a Committee on non-party lines. You know perfectly well that you had no authority to use my name in connexion with the Bill — which I now learn you have done freely — but only in connexion with the formation of a Committee.

With regard to the question of adult suffrage — you ought not to repeat for public purposes private conversation or such fragments of it as you can remember, or think you can remember. This is rather a well-known rule: but if your strong feelings lead you to break it, I can only say that I discussed with you quite freely at your request the objections & difficulties which attach to every solution of the woman's franchise question. Among other things I pointed out that adult suffrage would be largely a duplication of the existing franchise. That is quite true: & that is one reason why I should prefer the first solution I indicated to the House yesterday — if it were possible. If it is not possible, I am at the proper time & circumstances willing as I told my constituents in Dundee at the last election to vote for adult suffrage.

Your accusation of "treachery" is not well-grounded. Under what obligations had you or your friends ever placed me? For the last five years you have disturbed or tried to disturb almost every meeting I have addressed. During the last four elections that I have fought your organisations have opposed me with their utmost strength: & if I have been returned on three occasions it has been in spite of every effort on the part of the militant suffragists to prevent me.

You personally have received from me nothing but courtesy, & the sympathy which I felt — and feel — for you in your earnestness & distress. You had no right or reason to suppose that I was not an entirely free agent to give my vote & counsel in Parliament, agreeably with my public pledges, & according to my judgement.

Yours faithfully
WINSTON S. CHURCHILL

Churchill's next important encounter with the suffragette movement was during the aftermath of 18 November 1910, which has gone down in suffragette annals as "Black Friday." On that day Asquith was proposing the dissolution of Parliament prior to the second 1910 election. This meant that all hope (not that there was much anyway) of the Conciliation Bill getting any farther in the

House was finished; the Conciliation Committee which had got the Bill through its second reading would have to start all over again in the new Parliament. The Women's Social Parliamentary Union was holding a meeting in the nearby Caxton Hall and resolved to hold a demonstration in Parliament Square. The police were there and fighting broke out and lasted for six hours. Hitherto the police had made arrests as soon as they reasonably could; this time it developed into a free-for-all. Stories of women being punched, kicked, pinched and grabbed by the breasts seem well authenticated; one old lady protested that she had been violated. Whatever actually did happen, it is clear that the police, following the policy of delaying arrests, had then behaved with unusual violence. Even so, by the end of the day, over two hundred arrests had been made.

Both the suffragettes and one of the leading authorities on women's suffrage seemed convinced that the Government had begun on a new, more aggressive policy against the militants. There is no evidence whatever for this statement. Indeed, Churchill's letter to Sir Edward Henry, head of the Metropolitan Police, indicates that there had been some serious breakdown between the Home Secretary's instructions and the instructions that the police were actually given. "It was my desire to avoid this [the scenes that had occurred] even at some risk, to arrest large numbers and then subsequently to prosecute only where serious grounds were shown and I am sorry that, no doubt through a misunderstanding, another course has been adopted. In future I must ask for a strict adherence to the policy outlined herein."

Hostile critics, however, did not take this view at all; the release of all prisoners taken on "Black Friday" was regarded as a device for preventing their grievances being publicly aired in court. Churchill was again to appear in an unfavourable light on 22 November 1910 in the so-called "Battle of Downing Street." After a scuffle outside Number 10, Asquith was hustled into a taxi and Birrell's knee was badly hurt. Churchill appeared on the scene, and, shouting to a group of policemen who were scuffling with Mrs Cobden-Sanderson, he said: "Take that woman away; she is obviously one of the ringleaders." This remark was overheard by Hugh Franklin who was a relation by marriage of Herbert Samuel. Franklin was a militant suffragist and one of those arrested on "Black Friday." On 26

November 1910 Churchill, after addressing a meeting at Bradford which had been interrupted throughout by Hugh Franklin and his friends, boarded the evening train for London. On his way to the dining-car Franklin attacked him with a whip shouting, "Take that you dirty cur." Franklin, described as a "Cambridge Undergraduate," was charged with assault and sentenced to six weeks' imprisonment. Churchill was blamed for the behaviour of the police on "Black Friday" and on 9 December 1910 by Franklin, in an article in *Votes for Women* in which he stated: "When Mr Churchill, as the chief policeman, orders his thousands of trained servants to become a set of real hooligans, no one is left to act as protectors of law and order."

Churchill considered taking legal action against the author and sought the advice of the Solicitor-General:

Sir John Simon to WSC

TELEGRAM

14 December 1910

My dear Churchill,

    I return the *Votes for Women* cutting which Marsh sent me. It is of course scurrilous to a degree, & I am sure will be generally resented by decent people. But I would strongly urge you *not* to take proceedings on it. The cases are very rare in which a Minister ought to defend himself by himself taking action in the Courts for injurious statements, and it seems to me that for the Home Secretary personally to pursue a creature who has already been sentenced for an assault on him would be most unwise. The violence & hysteria of these people prevent what they say having any importance. . . .

On 2 December 1910, while speaking at Dundee, Churchill gave one of the fullest explanations of his position on the question of female suffrage:

So far as he himself was concerned he was still of opinion that the sex disqualification was not a true or a logical disqualification, and he was therefore in favour of the principle of women being enfranchised. But he declined utterly to pledge himself to any particular

Bill at the present time. He would not vote for any Bill which he considered would have the effect of unfairly altering the balance between parties by giving an undoubted preponderance to the property vote; and he would not vote for any Bill unless he was convinced that it had behind it the genuine majority of the electors. That was his position, and it was very desirable that they should not build any undue hopes on any words he might say. He had no desire to extend to them any encouragement which might afterwards afford ground for their reproaches. Whatever he had admitted in friendly discussion on this subject, he had always found it was only the excuse for renewed abuse and insult, and every step taken in friendship towards their bodies had only met grosser insults and more outrageous action. He was confident that while these tactics were employed the opinion of this country would be rendered less favourable and not more favourable to the cause which they keenly had at heart.

By the spring of 1911, the accusations and counter-accusations provoked by "Black Friday" had died down; attention was now concentrated on the second Conciliation Bill. After the Liberal victory in December 1910, a new Conciliation Committee had been formed and a new Bill drafted which incorporated none of the features which Churchill had found so objectionable in the first Bill. The second Conciliation Bill was presented to the House on 5 May 1911 by Sir George Kemp, a Liberal industrialist. Though the Bill passed by a large majority (167), no front-benchers spoke and the passage of the Bill was delayed by its being referred to a committee of the whole House. The suffragettes were further reassured by a letter from Asquith to Lord Lytton which asserted that the Government were "unanimous in their determination to give effect, not only in letter, but in spirit" to the women's demands.

The large majority that the Conciliation Bill won, and Asquith's undertaking that, despite his personal hostility to women's suffrage, if the Commons agreed on a measure it would be made law, led to a widespread decline in militancy in the summer and autumn of 1911. In addition, the House of Lords crisis and the wave of strikes in July and August made it tactically unwise to start large-scale agitations; Mrs Pankhurst left in the summer for an extensive tour of America.

The Liberal Government had mixed feelings about the question of an extension of the franchise. Only 60 per cent of the adult male population had the vote in 1911, and many Liberals felt that a franchise based solely on the male propertied voter gave an unfair advantage to the Conservative Party. Asquith announced on 7 November 1911 that he would propose a Reform Bill to the 1912 session which would extend the franchise, simplify registration procedure and abolish plural voting. He added that it would be left to the House of Commons to decide whether women should be granted their suffrage under this Bill.

The militant suffragettes attacked the proposal. They believed that the Government were seeking to adulterate the women's vote, and the WSPU now resorted to stone throwing and later, arson. Churchill now became increasingly concerned at the course of events:

WSC to Master of Elibank

18 December 1911   Admiralty

My dear Alick,

We are getting into vy gt peril over Female Suffrage.

Be quite sure of this: — the Franchise Bill will not get through without a dissolution if it contains a clause adding 8,000,000 women to the electorate. Nor ought it to get through.

How can the PM honourably use the Parlt Act to force it upon the King, when he has himself declared it to be a "disastrous mistake." In the second year of passage of this and the Home Rule Bill the Tories will demand a dissolution. Votes for women is so unpopular that by-elections will be unfavourable. The King will be entitled obviously to say to his Prime Minister, "You cannot conscientiously advise me to assent to this vast change. The Constituencies have never been consulted. No responsible Govt is behind it. You do not believe in it yourself." The King will dismiss the Ministry & Parliament will be dissolved on the old Plural voting register. We shall be in confusion ourselves. With us will go down the Irish cause.

The situation wh is developing is vy like the Trade split in the Tory party in 1903. I do not understand LG at all. My one hope was the referendum wh alone gave a reasonable & honourable outlet. He knew my view. And yet he has gone out of his way to rule it out at the vy beginning. He is exactly like Joe in 1903: It is with

most profound regret that I watch these developments. I have been
through it before. Do not I beseech you my friend moderate the
danger.

What a ridiculous tragedy it will be if this strong Government &
party which has made its mark in history were to go down on Petti-
coat politics! And the last chance of Ireland — our loyal friends —
squandered too! It is damnable.

No doubt you have made some deep calculations as to voting in
H. of C. Please let me know what they are. But I do not think there
is any safety there. If LG & Grey go on working themselves up, they
will have to go, if female suffrage is knocked out. And the PM's
position will become impossible if it is put in.

The only safe & honest course is to have a referendum — first to
the women to know if they want it: & then to the men to know if
they will give it. I am quite willing to abide by the result.

What I cannot stand is making this prodigious change in the teeth
of public opinion, & out of pure weakness.

Alexander the Great (your forerunner) said that the peoples of
Asia were slaves because they were not able to pronounce the word
"No." Let you & me avoid their pusillanimity & their fate.

Your sincere friend

w

He wrote to Sir Edward Grey in a similar vein:

WSC to Sir E. Grey

20 December 1911   Admiralty
Copy

My dear Grey,

I am getting increasingly anxious about the woman's suffrage situation. If you and George are going to make a strong campaign in
favour of adding 6,000,000 voters to the franchise, it will become increasingly difficult for those who do not think such a change at this
juncture likely to be good for the country, not to participate actively
in some counter movement. I do not think the Prime Minister's position is tenable except on the basis that the question is regarded as an
unimportant one. But it cannot remain unimportant and as it approaches the domain of decisive action, it will not improbably dominate other issues. How can he possibly use the provisions of the
Parliament Act to force through a measure which he has stated pub-

licly he would regard as a disastrous political mistake? This strong Government on whose continuance so much depends may easily come in two and be utterly discredited by proceedings on the present course. With every wish to respect other people's feelings I could not remain silent on such a topic indefinitely. I see with great apprehension you and George working yourselves up into enthusiastic champions of the cause. I know how sincere natures gather force and conviction from motion and activity. After a point you may well persuade yourselves that woman's suffrage is not merely the most important but the *only* question in politics. If so you will find it very difficult to regard me as anything but an opponent. It is because I am so deeply disturbed at the prospect I see ahead that I write to urge that an effort should be made to see whether we cannot come together on a referendum — men or women or both — I do not care. Your own honesty and candour will I am sure lead you to admit that the opinion of the country has never yet been tested on this subject.

Yours very sincerely
WINSTON S. CHURCHILL

These are the three questions on the answer to which the issue will be decided:

1. Do the women really want it?
2. Would it be for the good of the country to give it now?
3. Have the electors ever expressed any conscious opinion?

W S C

Finally, on December 21, he wrote to the Prime Minister:

WSC to H. H. Asquith

21 December 1911
Private & Personal

My dear Prime Minister,

I apprehend great danger to the Govt over women's suffrage. There are 3 main questions wh must be answered satisfactorily.

1. Is there a real desire on the part of great numbers of women to assume political responsibilities? 2. Wd this addition to the Electorate be for the good of the country now? 3. Has the country ever been effectively consulted?

Your own position appears to me to be likely to become extraor-

dinarily difficult from the moment that a female suffrage amendment
is included in the Govt Bill; for you will then be accused of using
the machinery of the Parliament Act to force upon the Sovereign
& upon the constituencies a vast change for wh no organised Govt or
party will become responsible, on wh the Electors have never pronounced, & wh you yrself have characterized as a "disastrous political
mistake." Further, if yr colleagues are going to take the field & work
themselves up into a keen enthusiasm for Female Suffrage, then members of the Govt who do not agree with them will be forced to
express themselves in a contrary sense. You yrself may even be drawn
into the fray. This anomalous condition may possibly be tolerated
so long as the question is academic or of small importance; but if it
became imminent & important & real, the Govt wd be utterly discredited. It is certain that as the issue became more real passion will
rise in regard to it & make it a subject of overwhelming importance.
What a ridiculous tragedy it wd be if this strong Govt from wh so
much is hoped were to come to grief in this ignominious way, &
perish like Sisera at a woman's hand.

What about the King: will he not be pressed to use the prerogative
of dissolution in 1913 in the same way as he was pressed to use the
prerogative of creating peers in 1911? I cannot help thinking that in
all the circs wh I foresee he might be justified. He wd certainly not
be disinclined. If we had to fight an election, in confusion ourselves,
with Home Rule on our shoulders & with the Plural Voter still active,
we shd be beaten decisively; & with us wd fall the Irish cause, with
all the hopes wh are centred upon it. I am quite sure that the adding
of 8,000,000 women to the register will never be achieved without
some form of appeal to the nation. Nor ought it to be. I have written since their speeches both to Grey & to Lloyd George pointing out
these dangers & explaining that I cd not indefinitely remain silent;
& last night by arrangement we all three dined together to discuss the
difficulty. We had a vy valuable talk, & both were vy much inclined
to adopt a suggestion wh I put forward, & wh LG developed, that is,
that if the women's clause were carried, the adult suffrage register
shd be forthwith constructed, & as soon as this was complete the
whole mass of the women to be enfranchised shd, either by referendum or initiative, decide whether they wd take up their responsibilities or not. In order to get them (Grey & LG) to adopt this position,
I shd have to go with them on the democratic amendment, so that
we cd all work together; & I am bound to say that any objections

to the change wd be greatly diminished if 3 or 4,000,000 women, representing as they wd every household in the country, had specifically asked for it. Also, it wd probably get smashed wh again wd be a solution. The conciliables refrained from coming to any fixed agreement, but we parted with a feeling that unity on these lines was not impossible.

If the Tories were to say, why don't you have a referendum on Home Rule as well as abt the women, our answer (debating) is clear. We have no objection at all to applying the same principle to Ireland & having a referendum on the Irish question to the Irish people.

I hope whatever happens nothing will be said to close up this loophole of escape, wh is the only one I can see. . . .

Churchill now returned to his suggestion of a referendum on women's suffrage, which he had first mentioned in the December 1910 election campaign. He even wrote to Lord Curzon, president of the Anti-Suffrage League, on 7 January 1912 to try to get him to back a *non-party* referendum. Curzon, in reply, was not particularly enthusiastic.

The Franchise Bill was not passed in 1911, and in March 1912 the second Conciliation Bill which had been passed in the House of Commons by 167 votes in 1911 was now defeated by 14 votes on its third reading. Paradoxically Churchill now supported it. The decrease in support for the suffragette cause must be attributed to the increasingly violent action of its supporters during the preceding months.

Most of the militant suffragettes were keenly patriotic and devoted themselves to war work unsparingly. In 1915 Asquith promised that the women would receive the vote at the end of the war. This was one political promise which was kept in its entirety. Liberal fears were justified, for even with no property qualification there soon developed a built-in Conservative majority among women voters. Indeed, Emmeline and Christabel Pankhurst joined the Tory Party in 1918. Christabel also became a religious fanatic prophesying the imminent second coming of the Lord. Sylvia played a part in founding the Communist Party in Great Britain; but her work did not find favour in Lenin's eyes.

*

A relatively minor incident, which has always been associated with Churchill's name, usually to his detriment, took place at this time. Just before the end of 1910 a gang of burglars was detected late at night trying to tunnel their way into a jeweller's shop in Houndsditch from the house next door. Of six policemen who sought to apprehend them three were killed and two were wounded, a police casualty rate not to be approached again until 1966. The murderers, identified as a gang of Letts, were tracked down to 100 Sidney Street in the East End of London. Here they fortified themselves and fired upon the police, who by this time were armed. The Home Secretary was called to the telephone by the Home Office to give authority for a detachment of Scots Guards from the Tower of London to be called in. After consulting with his advisers he gave this authority, although the soldiers had already been summoned in anticipation of it. The reason troops were called in was that the police were only armed with revolvers, which did not have the same range and power as the rifles of the soldiers or of the Mauser weapons with which the Letts were armed. It was even thought prudent to call in the Horse Artillery from their barracks in St John's Wood, but in the event they were not required.

Churchill at once went to the Home Office where no more seemed to be known. Characteristically he drove immediately to the neighbourhood of Sidney Street and watched the siege at close quarters. He did not intervene in the conduct of the siege. "I made it my business, however," he recorded in a passage of a letter to the coroner which was not subsequently made public, "after seeing what was going on in front to go round the back of the premises and satisfy myself that there was no chance of the criminals effecting their escape through the intricate area of walls and small houses at the back of No 100 Sidney Street." When he returned from this expedition he found that the house had caught fire and the fire brigade had arrived.

It was at this stage that Churchill intervened. In evidence at the inquest on January 18 Churchill said: "A junior officer of the fire brigade came up to me where I was standing and said that the fire brigade had arrived, and that he understood he was not to put out the fire at present. Is this right? Or words to that effect. I said: 'Quite right; I accept full responsibility.' I have to make it clear that these words referred to the specific question asked me and that I confirmed and supported the police in their action. From what I saw it would have meant loss of life and limb to any fire brigade officer who had gone within effective range of the building. . . . It would be quite untrue to say that I took the direction out of the hands of the executive officers. I had not in any way interfered with the arrangements made by the police. I was only there to support them in any unusual difficulty as a covering authority." The fire was allowed to continue: when it had burnt itself out the police entered and found two bodies, one of whom had been shot and the other asphyxiated. The leader of this Lett gang of murderers, burglars and anarchists, "Peter the Painter," was not found and was never heard of again.

In a letter about the House of Lords which already has been quoted in the previous chapter, there occurs this paragraph:

WSC to H. H. Asquith
(*Asquith Papers*)

EXTRACT

3 January 1911

. . . I was interrupted in copying out this letter by the Stepney affair from wh I have just returned. It was a striking scene in a London street — firing from every window, bullets chipping the brickwork, police and Scots Guards armed with loaded weapons artillery brought up etc.

I thought it better to let the House burn down rather than spend good British lives in rescuing those ferocious rascals. I think I shall have to stiffen the administration and the Aliens Act a little, and more effective measures must be taken by the police to supervise the dangerous classes of aliens in our midst. . . .

Churchill's presence at the siege was much criticized both in the Press and in Parliament and by the public. Post cards were sold in large numbers showing Churchill at the scene of the "battle," a typical caption being "The Battle of Stepney — Mr Winston Churchill surrounded by detectives and armed police." The incident was recorded by the early newsreel cinema camera and the bill boards announcing the showing of the film proclaimed "Mr Churchill in the danger zone." Eddie Marsh, who had accompanied Churchill, enjoyed what he called the unique experience of seeing himself on the movies and sustaining public obloquy. "I make the most gratifying appearance as almost the central figure of 'Mr Churchill directing the operations' at the Palace [Theatre], which is nightly received with unanimous boos and shouts of 'shoot him' from the gallery — why are the London music-hall audiences so bigotedly and uniformly Tory?"

Churchill himself in later life felt that perhaps he should not have yielded to his "curiosity" by going to Sidney Street. In the House of Commons Arthur Balfour summed the matter up: "He was, I understand, in military phrase, in what is known as the zone of fire — he and a photographer were both risking valuable lives. I understand what the photographer was doing, but what was the right honourable gentleman doing?"

One immediate result of the Sidney Street incident was a demand for stricter regulations against the entry of aliens. It will be remembered that Churchill himself had strenuously opposed the aliens regulations which the Tory Government had introduced in 1904–5; and it was largely because of opposition such as his that the Aliens Act of 1905 proved to be ineffective and difficult to operate. The King was one of the first to bring up the question. "He hopes," wrote his private secretary, Sir Arthur Bigge, on 5 January 1911 "that these outrages by foreigners will lead you to consider whether the Aliens Act could not be amended so as to prevent London from being infested with men and women whose presence would not be tolerated in any other country." Churchill hastened to reassure the King. In a letter dated January 6 he said he had it in mind to ask Parliament "to give the police power to arrest any alien who has no visible lawful means of earning a living." He also thought that aliens should be forbidden to possess fire-arms without a special licence and that a breach of this rule should render them liable to a fine, imprisonment or deportation. Churchill argued against any wholesale tightening of laws against the entry of aliens though he hoped the courts would use their power to expel aliens more freely.

This was not a subject which gave any pleasure to the radical majority in the House. Josiah Wedgwood, soon to be one of his

staunchest supporters, begged Churchill not to be rushed into exceptional laws against anarchists: "It is fatally easy to justify them but
they lower the whole character of a nation. You know as well as I do
that human life does not matter a rap in comparison with the death of
ideas and the betrayal of English traditions. Rebelling against civilisation and society will go on anyhow and this is only a new form of
the disease of '48; so let us have English rule not Bourbon." Nevertheless, Churchill on January 19 circulated to his Cabinet colleagues
a draft bill which contained the following principal provisions:

1. An alien convicted of an offence was to be considered liable to
expulsion.
2. Penalties for harbouring illegal immigrants to be increased.
3. Aliens to require special permission to carry fire-arms.

He wrote in the accompanying memorandum to the Cabinet: "Two
naughty principles are involved . . . a deliberate differentiation between the alien, and especially the unassimilated alien, and a British
subject, and . . . that an alien may, in certain circumstances, be
deported before he has committed an offence."

The bill was introduced into the House under the Ten Minute
Rule on April 18 but no time was found to proceed with it. Churchill
persuaded the Commons to give a second reading to a Private Members' Bill dealing with aliens a little more harshly in the hope that in
Committee an amalgam of his bill and the Private Members' Bill
might emerge. But nothing came of it: no parliamentary time was
made available and the aliens regulations were not in fact revised
until 1915.

*

One of the most distasteful and testing tasks that was until recently
the duty of the Home Secretary was that of advising the Sovereign on
the prerogative of mercy in capital cases. It was always Churchill's
habit to have on his desk the name of anyone who had been sentenced
to be hanged and the date of his execution. In his two years at the
Home Office forty-three such cases came before him. He recommended
twenty-one for clemency: in twenty-two cases the law took its ap-

pointed course. Churchill always gave very close personal attention to his duty in this matter, and he formed a rule of examining the whole case himself. If there was doubt in his mind he sought to clarify it by writing a memorandum in which he thrashed it out with himself and then submitted it for the opinion of his advisers at the Home Office. Only then did he come to a conclusion; and even this conclusion was left to the last minute to provide for any new consideration or evidence that might arise. His handling of such matters is exemplified by the following case, in which all the relevant details are supplied, though the name, following an unbroken tradition, is withheld.

This case is of particular interest since the evidence on which the accused was convicted was wholly circumstantial. Between the conviction and the appeal certain information came into the hands of the Home Office. Some of the witnesses asked to identify the accused had been improperly given a glimpse of him by the local police through a half-open door before the identification parade.

Till then the appeal concerned matters of law only. But when these and other doubts about the evidence were brought to Churchill's attention, he authorized the following announcement:

> The Home Secretary, in view of applications he has received questioning the justice of the conviction and of certain evidence brought to his notice which may possibly be regarded as material, has, in the exercise of the power conferred on him by Section 19 of the Criminal Appeal Act of 1907, referred the whole case to the Court so as to enable the Court to deal with it as if there were an appeal on grounds involving questions of fact.

The new evidence was accordingly placed not only before the Appellate Court but also before the appellant's counsel. In spite of this, the Court rejected the appeal. The Lord Chief Justice, Lord Alverstone, wrote to Churchill:

> We disposed of [this man's] case today and in reality there is an overwhelming case against him. There is only one matter that I need point out to you. It is suggested in some of the petitions to you that neither of the pistols were sold to him. As a matter of fact there is no doubt that he did purchase one of the pistols in 1907 and that it would

have been proved but for the fact that there was a technical objection because the gun-maker could not swear that the entry made was an entry of his own transaction but might have been an entry of a fact communicated to him by an assistant. This prevented the fact being proved but you can easily ascertain what the true facts are.

Churchill's next act was to put ten questions to his advisers, Sir Edward Troup and Mr Ernley Blackwell, an Assistant Under-Secretary, as follows:

1. The second pistol: was it ever sent back as requested to the gunsmith? Have they received it?

2. About how many people left the train [at the station]?

3. How many people were travelling in the first two carriages of the train?

4. How was it that the bag was not found at the foot of the [mine's] airshaft till June? Is the bottom of an airshaft frequently visited?

5. When was [the accused brother's] statement made? Is it a deposition on oath or merely a letter?

6. Was there in fact a carriage at the rear of the train with "reserved" on one of the compartments? Who was it reserved for?

7. Mr Blackwell enquires by pencil comment "Where is the brown coat." Prisoner in his evidence states: "I have it here." (In court.) Is this so?

8. What is the time taken between [the two stations] (by train)?

9. LCJ suggests in appeal: bag thrown out of window — it appears to me very improbable — what are your views?

10. There is a story that about a fortnight before the murder passengers travelling in the same train heard shots fired and a bullet came through the window of one of the carriages?

When he had received such answers as it was possible to supply he dictated the following memorandum which he sent to Troup:

The evidence against the prisoner may be considered in three sections. First, the evidence of [the four witnesses] fixing the position of the prisoner in the train. Secondly, the account given by the prisoner of his movements from the time he left [the station] at 11.10 till he returned to his [home station] by the 1.40. Thirdly, subsidiary contributory evidence bearing on pistols, bloodstains and his financial position.

It is upon the first and second sections that the full weight of the conviction must rest. Unless we can be satisfied that these two sets of circumstances are alone sufficient to justify the verdict, the extreme penalty ought not to be enforced. If we are so satisfied, the subsidiary evidence may be considered on its merits as additional proof.

I have considered in the first instance the prisoner's own account of his movements particularly between 11.10 and 1.40. His account of his illness is not necessarily absurd. Why should it be? He suffered from piles — he would know the symptoms. They are not impossible symptoms. On the other hand he could easily invent them. But the kind of things he says he did in view of this malady carry no belief. He cannot remember whether it was a hedge, a railing, a gate or a fence through which or over which he got into the field. He returned to [the station] so hurriedly that he was hot, although it was [a cold time of the year]. He had eased himself in the field by lying down. Yet on arrival at [the station] instead of lying down or resting in the Waiting room, he wandered off into the town. He says that he returned to [this station] rather than to [another nearer one] because there was a refreshment room at [the first]. He does not tell us that he went into the refreshment room.

His errand to the Colliery is of the most shadowy description. Even more unsubstantial is his reason for visiting the "drift" between [the two stations]. The fact that he had paid similar visits to [the manager] exactly a fortnight previously, i.e. on pay day, cuts both ways and deeper against than for him.

His action on arriving at [the] station appears unreasonable. He had been carried on already beyond his intended destination. He proposed to travel back to [his home] by the 1.40. He had only therefore $2\frac{1}{2}$ hours to walk $5\frac{1}{8}$ miles, to find [the manager] at the Colliery and to transact his business with him. He could have got a train back by waiting 10 minutes. To explain his action he has to fall back upon his desire to visit the "drift" between the [two stations]. Nothing could be less convincing than his statement on this point. His account of his movements and motives, whether in examination or cross-examination, cannot be believed. It is not reasonable. It is quite uncorroborated. If nothing else were known about the prisoner but his own account of his movements between 11.10 and 1.40, the gravest suspicions would be aroused.

The crux of the case is however his position in the train and in relation to [the murdered man]. Three witnesses saw him and [the murdered man] together. [One] saw them together as if in company. He knew them both. [Another] knew the prisoner well. [And the third] knew [the murdered man] well. The evidence of these three directly counters the prisoner's statement that he never was in company with [the murdered man] and that he took his seat in the rear of the train. [One of the witnesses'] evidence appears to be perfectly trustworthy, in spite of the improprieties connected with the identification at [the] gaol. Nothing shakes the combined evidence. It stands by itself, if [the murdered man's wife's] sensational recognition is entirely excluded [after leaving the box, where she had failed to recognise the prisoner, she saw him from another angle and recognised him instantly]. It is completed by the prisoner's own statement that he travelled in a carriage with four or five or six passengers, not one of whom he can recall, although his attention was drawn to the importance of the point within three or four days of the murder — not one of whom has come to corroborate him, widely as this case has been made public. If [the three witnesses'] evidence is believed, the prisoner must be disbelieved and the conclusion is of the utmost consequence.

Now here we have two perfectly separate sets of highly incriminating circumstances. Either, if the prisoner be disbelieved, goes far to establish his guilt; taken together they complete the case against him. There is no reason to doubt the evidence of [two of the witnesses]. Only the most extraordinary series of accidents could possibly have led to an error. How incredible is it that the man who was the victim of such an extraordinary series of accidents should be the same man who, by quite another series of occurrences, should be able to give such an untrustworthy account of his actions after leaving [the] Station. Just as the evidence of [the two witnesses] fits together like a bracelet, so do the two sets of circumstances, namely, those which fix the prisoner's position in the train and those by which he accounts for his movements after leaving [the station]. I have been unable, though I have searched for it, to find any ground for differing on all these points from the conclusions to which Judge, Jury, Court of Appeal and the Home Office experts have, from such different points of view, successively and independently arrived.

The third section of the evidence consists of various separate circumstances, most of which tend, though in very different degrees, to strengthen and confirm the case against the prisoner, not one of which discloses any fact out of harmony with his guilt. First, the bloodstains. Accepting fully that the medical evidence concerning their age is unsatisfactory and not to be relied on, the fact that they are there on the glove and in the trousers pocket remains for what it is worth. Second, the pistols. One pistol, the .250, was certainly in the possession of the prisoner before the crime. As to the [other] pistol, all that can be said is that the prisoner received it under an assumed name, and at a different address. It may well be that both sets of bullets, small and big, were fired by the one pistol; but that theory, or any conclusions drawn from it, do not affect the evidence of his possession of the pistols, so long as we do not attach undue importance to that possession. Third, the prisoner's financial position. No one can doubt that he was pressed for money. The statement of [the prisoner's brother] again taken for what it is worth, which is not much, throws some light upon the mood in which the prisoner would face such difficulties.

The fact that he was carried on beyond [one station to the next one] by mistake on this fateful day, when so many other strange circumstances affected him; the conflict of his story with the evidence of [one of the witnesses] and the method by which the bag could have been carried through a slit in the coat on the right-hand side, all fit in just where they would naturally fit in in the chain of evidence.

The following questions may be asked: Can the prisoner be believed when he says he travelled at the rear end of the train, in a compartment containing five or six other persons? Can his account of his actions between 11.10 and 1.40 at or near [the station] be believed? Can his statement that he was not in financial straits be believed? The answer to each and all of these questions is clearly, No. And that answer leads directly to the conclusion of his guilt.

It should further be remembered that all these questions of fact have been pronounced upon and decided by a Jury under the guidance of one of the most humane and able Judges on the Bench, and by three Judges sitting as a Court of Appeal. The whole question of facts as well as of law was submitted to the Court of Appeal. All additional information which could tell in the prisoner's favour was placed before the Court of Appeal. All information that could tell against him was withheld. The careful and trained investigations of Mr Blackwell and Sir Edward Troup have led them to endorse the verdict of the Jury and the Judgement of the Court of Appeal. My own conclusions are the same.

Home Office

The verdict must be upheld. The execution of the sentence follows on this necessarily. The murder was one of the most cold-blooded, deliberately planned and brutally executed crimes for sordid ends that can be cited. The law must take its course.

W S C

Churchill was shortly due to go on holiday abroad. The Foreign Secretary, Sir Edward Grey, was to be in charge of the Home Office in his absence. Accordingly, Churchill forwarded the papers to Grey who replied:

Sir E. Grey to WSC

Dear Churchill,

I return these papers. Unless there were a rule never to confirm a sentence on circumstantial evidence I do not see how you could do otherwise than acquiesce in the decision of the jury, the Judge and the Court of Appeal.

I shall treat the case as settled unless something is brought before me which has not been before the authorities including yourself who have dealt with the case.

The impression made upon me by the prisoner's account of his own doings is unfavourable, otherwise I should have felt reluctance to accept the conclusion to which the circumstantial evidence points.

Yours sincerely
E. GREY

No grounds for a reprieve were found, and the convicted murderer was duly executed. Two weeks later Grey wrote:

Sir Edward Grey to WSC

EXTRACT

Balmoral Castle

Dear Churchill,

Since the execution of [the convicted murderer] the work from the H.O. sent to me has been infinitesimal. One warrant to open letters from an absconded criminal and one flogging of 12 lashes to an incorrigible tramp who misbehaved in prison & when being removed to a punishment cell bashed one warder in the face with a pair of loose handcuffs, hit a second, and pulled a third to the ground by the testicles.

Nothing new turned up about either of the capital cases, except one or two obviously bogus stories in the case of [the convicted murderer]; but the constant stream of letters pointing out the weak points of the evidence & ignoring the strong points was very uncomfortable. I think this part of your job is beastly & on the night before the men were hung I kept meditating upon the sort of night they were having, till I felt as if I ought not to let them hang unless I went to be hung too.

I heard a good deal about the case in his home county, all going to prove that he was guilty, but I didn't repeat any of this to the H.O. so that they should not be influenced adversely to him by anything outside the evidence, & in consequence be reluctant to give him the benefit of any new fact. . . .

And Churchill replied:

> *WSC to Sir Edward Grey*
>
> *Honor* off Mytelene
>
> My dear Grey,
> I am very much obliged to you for taking my work & for your kind letter. I know you must have felt keenly the painful duties wh I put upon you. There was however no doubt as to the course to pursue. The only capital decision with wh I have been dissatisfied during my tenure was about a man I reprieved just before I started on grounds wh I do not feel wholly convinced were adequate. He has since committed suicide! To most men — including all the best — a life sentence is worse than a death sentence . . .

All his life Churchill supported capital punishment. Yet when it fell to him to take the decision in a particular case he found it most painful. Conscious of his direct responsibility he would brood long over each case.

*

Towards the end of 1910 Churchill was afforded an opportunity of cementing his relationship with the new King by performing signal services in what was largely a personal matter. For many years a strange story had been going around that King George V had contracted a secret marriage in Malta in 1890 while he was serving with the Mediterranean Fleet. The marriage was supposed to have been contracted with a daughter of the Commander-in-Chief, Admiral Sir Michael Culme-Seymour. This legend was revived when the King succeeded to the Throne in 1910 and it was propagated by one Edward F. Mylius in November in a Republican and anarchist broadsheet the *Liberator,* published in Paris. Mylius asserted that the King's marriage in 1893 to Princess, later Queen, Mary, was "sham, shameful and bigamous and an offence against the Church." Churchill at once initiated steps to prosecute Mylius. Having obtained the opinion of the Law Officers that the *Liberator* contained a criminal libel on the King, Churchill proposed to Asquith at the end of November that an information for criminal libel on the King should be laid, thus "enabling the falsity of the libel to be demonstrated" and making possible a conviction. Such action, Churchill wrote to Asquith on November 26, "should be taken and The King's good name cleared from such cruel and widely circulated aspersions."

It was now for Churchill to make all the preparations. With infinite care he co-ordinated the opinions and actions of the Law Officers of the Crown whom he summoned to a conference, of the Director of Public Prosecutions, and of the Commissioner of Police. He presided over the intricate detail connected with the accumulation of evidence, with the seizure of the libellous newspaper and eventually with the arrest, charge and detention of Mylius, pending trial. Throughout these proceedings during December Churchill kept the King informed of what was being done. The King's personal advisers were divided as to whether or not proceedings should be taken against Mylius. Sir Frederick Ponsonby, who had served as Assistant Private Secretary to Queen Victoria and to King Edward VII, was against such a step. Sir Arthur Bigge, on the other hand, who had been Private Secretary to the King for many years before he came to the Throne, was in favour. Churchill urged the King to take this opportunity "to strike at the libel and sweep the falsehood out of existence once and for all" — "the opportunity has now presented itself and may not come again of dealing with it in a tangible form and in a person not quite of the lowest class." He quite frankly put all the contingencies of the case before the King "especially those of which your Majesty is the sole judge":

WSC to The King
(*Royal Archives*)

EXTRACT

22 Dec 1910

Dictated

. . . it has become clear that Mylius would be able, if he chose, to claim that the article in the *Liberator* should be read as a whole, not only that part which affects Your Majesty, but that which asperses the late King and the Prince Consort, the reading of this article in Court would of course give it a universal publicity, and it is possible that the prisoner might also put some offensive questions. All this would be irrelevant to the point to be decided, and would not affect, except perhaps to aggravate it, the sentence of the Court; but Mr Churchill feels that he must be precisely assured that Your Majesty has read the article in its entirety, and is indifferent to the possibility of a certain amount of scandalous and offensive imputations upon others besides Your Majesty obtaining incidentally public expression. Mr Churchill does not himself regard this possibility as any valid argument against action. No doubt a man like Mylius, with his back against the wall, will spatter any dirt he can in the course of his defence. . . .

On Christmas Eve Churchill, who was at Blenheim, telegraphed Bigge asking for an urgent reply: "The legal tackle is now perfect and I can move at any time." Bigge replied: "The King wishes you to proceed as previously settled," and he later added, "His Majesty, after due consideration and admitting that the reading of the article in full would be unfortunate, sees no reason why the proceedings should be stopped." The King, said Bigge, "appreciates your carefulness to provide for every eventuality in this delicate question."

The greatest care was taken over the arrest of Mylius to ensure that there were no possible grounds for saying that all formalities had not been fully complied with. Once Mylius was arrested, Churchill made it his business to ensure that every facility should be given for Mylius's defence. For example, Churchill learned that Mr Newman, who had been Dr Crippen's solicitor, was likely to be engaged for Mylius. "As this gentleman's professional reputation is now under a cloud," Churchill wrote to the King, "[Mr Churchill] is in doubt whether he should allow this." The Judge gave Mylius fourteen days' extension of his time, not because it was insufficient but because it was thought better not to deprive the authorities of a chance of saying that they had given ample opportunity to the defendant for filing a plea of justification.

Mylius received letters in prison from the publisher of the *Liberator*, William James, of a kind which would normally not have been forwarded to a prisoner. Churchill gave instructions that Mylius should be allowed to receive them. "HM," wrote Bigge to Churchill on 18 January 1911, "is glad that Mylius was allowed to have these letters agreeing as HM does with you that Mylius should have no excuse for complaining that he had not been given every possible facility for preparing his defence."

As the day of the trial came nearer Churchill once again gave earnest consideration as to whether or not the King should appear as a witness and what should be done if a subpoena were issued. Churchill was against the King appearing, although the King had expressed himself willing to do so if necessary. And if Bigge or the King were to be presented with a subpoena, they were merely to accept it and say nothing. No subpoena, however, was issued and on the eve of the trial, on 31 January 1911, Churchill assured the King that "everything is in order, that the strength of the case from all points of view inspires Your Majesty's servants with complete confidence, and that they have every hope and expectation that by tomorrow night the cruel and malicious falsehood which has so long offended Your Majesty will have been effectually disposed of for ever."

The case took place in the King's Bench Division before the Lord Chief Justice and a special jury on February 1. It was proved in evidence that the wife and two daughters of Sir Michael Culme-Seymour did not come out to Malta until 1893; that his younger daughter died unmarried two years later without ever having spoken to the King; that his other daughter, now married, had not met the King between 1879, when she was eight years old, and 1898; and finally and transcendentally that the King had not been in Malta between 1888 and 1901. Mylius, who was not represented by counsel, claimed that as he was being tried for criminal libel, the King ought to have been in Court as a witness. When this objection was overruled, he refused to proceed with his case and was convicted and sentenced to twelve months' imprisonment.

Churchill had throughout been in charge of the affair. He had taken the responsibility upon himself, consulting only, it appears, the Prime Minister, the Attorney-General and the Solicitor-General among his colleagues. This caused Lord Morley to protest:

Lord Morley to WSC

1 February 1911   Privy Council Office
                                                        Whitehall

My dear Winston,

   I have written to the PM, that I should wish to raise at the Cabinet the proceedings about the libel on the King. It seems to me to be a profound mistake — and in any case, as it affects the Sovereign personally, the Cabinet ought to have been consulted.

Yrs

M

Churchill as always treated the King with ceremony, and after the trial was over he wrote:

WSC to The King
(Royal Archives)

1 February 1911   10 Downing Street

Sir,

   I cannot add anything to the full reports wh appear in all the newspapers of the trial today of the defendant Mylius, or to the account wh Sir Arthur Bigge will doubtless give Your Majesty. But I should like to offer my respectful and sincere congratulations to Your Majesty upon the entirely successful & satisfactory character of the whole proceedings in Court. I am confident that their reception throughout the Kingdom & the Empire will indicate the wisdom & propriety of taking action; & that Your Majesty's subjects will admire the robust and manly courage with which Your Majesty has not shrunk from an ordeal wh could not but be painful and anxious, and has sought regardless of personal feelings to defend Your Majesty's personal honour. In the result the truth has been established on unchallengeable foundations, justice has been done upon a miscreant, & Your Majesty's royal dignity has been in no respect compromised or flouted.

I have the honour to remain Your Majesty's faithful servant & subject

WINSTON S. CHURCHILL

Curiously, no reply from the King survives, but on February 3 the Chief Whip, the Master of Elibank, wrote to Churchill: "I was at Buckingham Palace today. I can see there is real gratitude for your exceeding care and sympathy in their recent troubles."

*

Among the responsibilities that devolved on the Home Secretary was that of the coal mines. It so happened that during Churchill's first year at the Home Office mining accidents caused the greatest toll of deaths since statistics were first kept. Two disasters in particular roused the conscience and the sympathy of the nation: that at Whitehaven in May 1910 when 132 lives were lost, and that at the Pretoria Pit near Bolton on 21 December 1910 when 320 miners were killed. The extent of public sympathy may be gauged from the fact that nearly £250,000 was raised in public subscriptions for the dependents.

1910 was also the year in which a Royal Commission, first set up in 1906, reported on the mines. The Home Office had announced for some time that new legislation concerned with safety in the mines was overdue, but apart from introducing a small Bill concerned with the provision of rescue apparatus Churchill felt that he would have to wait until the Royal Commission had reported before introducing fresh legislation. This he did in the form of the Coal Mines Bill, a comprehensive measure containing 123 clauses which was given a second reading on 17 March 1911. It dealt with such measures as the promise of exits for easier escape; tests for gas and for pit props; a regulation that no one should henceforth work under an unsupported roof; stricter regulations for safety such as search of miners for matches; fixed standards of ventilation and the building of pit-head baths and their compulsory use by the miners at a fee of one penny a week. Further provisions related to the employment of children and women in the mines, and a large number of amendments in Committee, chiefly at the instance of the Government, strengthened the Bill when it received its third reading in December: particular provision was made to lessen cruelty to pit ponies.

From the beginning Churchill was greatly concerned that the inspectorate of the mines should be strengthened. Churchill wrote a personal letter to Lloyd George on 3 March 1911 — "This is not a matter for departmental correspondence but between ourselves" — in which he made detailed proposals by which Lloyd George could raise £80,000 a year to spend on experiment and inspection. "I hope you will realise how much [the miners' leaders] expect we shall rise to the challenge of this frightful death roll, and come to the rescue of this great community of labouring men." Lloyd George accepted Churchill's proposal.

*

While the Coal Mines Bill was another outstanding achievement to be credited to Churchill, his Shops Bill was virtually a failure. The problem of shop-opening hours was a long-standing one and associated with a history of sustained agitation. Churchill attempted an ambitious solution and presented a Bill to Parliament on 4 July 1910 which contained six principal provisions:

1. Maximum hours of work should be 60 a week, as against 80 or so in many businesses.
2. Intervals should be especially set aside for the meals of shop assistants.
3. The amount of overtime should be regulated.
4. One early closing day a week.
5. Sunday closing, except for Jewish shops which should stay open until 2 p.m. and shops which sold food, drink, and newspapers.

6. The existing regulations on sanitation and ventilation to be strengthened.

While these sensible proposals commended themselves to a wide range of public opinion from the King downwards they were entirely opposed by those who had anything to do with shopkeeping. Those who employed labour pointed out that the Bill penalized them at the expense of self-employed shopkeepers. The Sunday laws were objected to by the Jews because the 2 p.m. closing meant that the total of their shop-opening hours was less than that of the Gentiles: while the non-Jews complained that the opening of Jewish shops on Sundays represented unfair competition.

Three years later the Whitechapel and Spitalfields costermongers presented Churchill with a charming table ornament which took the form of a costermonger's barrow in appreciation of what he had done for them under the Act — virtually the only successful part of it.

Churchill presented an amended version of the Bill on 6 March 1911, the earlier Bill having been crowded out by the dissolution at the end of 1910. But the attempts to reconcile the various provisions proved abortive. Churchill displeased the Jews by specifying that Jewish shops should only serve Jewish customers and he displeased the Archbishop of Canterbury and the Lord's Day Observance Society by suggesting that Sunday opening might be considered in large towns. The Bill was decimated in Committee and when it finally received its third reading all that it contained was the provision of intervals for assistants' meals and one early closing day a week subject to the arbitration of Home Office officials. Churchill complained at its third reading that one could judge the character of the proposals now embodied in the Bill "from the long succession of pages from which the Grand Committee went inch by inch, which are now waste paper." It was not until after the war, in the Shops Act of 1920, that it was possible to tackle the issues in the way that Churchill had wanted.

*

Apart from the routine administration of his office and the reforms which he instituted a great weight of parliamentary business fell upon Churchill — much of it extraneous to his own department, such as the passage through the Commons of the National Insurance Bill and the introduction of a Trade Union Bill. A very large share of the passage of the Parliament Bill to reduce the power of the House of Lords became his responsibility. Asquith, in addition to being Prime Minister, was leader of the House; but Churchill on a number of occasions was asked to deputize for him, winding up some of the important debates. In addition, Asquith devolved upon Churchill the task of writing the nightly letter on the work of the House to the Sovereign. This process of devolution has now run its full course and what was once an important as well as a ceremonious duty which had been relished by Gladstone, Disraeli and Lord Randolph is now discharged by a junior whip. This "chore" at the end of a hard day's work was not as laborious as might have been thought, since it could be written while on the Treasury bench or, when pressed, dictated immediately afterwards from notes. Churchill doubtless relished the task all the more because he was not Leader of the House of Commons, and it was therefore a tribute both to his sense of the House of Commons and to his literary style that the job came his way. He had superabundant energy and could always find time for anything; he was never work-shy.

Altogether, over a period of two years, he wrote 138 letters. They will all be found in the Companion Volumes: here a few specimens must suffice.

WSC to The King
(Royal Archives)

22 February 1910   House of Commons

Mr Churchill with his humble duty to Your Majesty has the honour to report that the situation in the House of Commons, though not clear or satisfactory, has become distinctly less critical than last night.

The debate upon the Address to Your Majesty in reply to the gracious speech was resumed by Mr Barnes, the Leader — or it would be more accurate to say — the spokesman of the Labour Party. This gentleman voiced strong opinions upon the various topics of the hour with a considerable flavour of Scotch good sense; and the tenor and purport of his remarks was evidently to strengthen the position of the Government and under guise of vehement counsel to support sober action.

Mr F. E. Smith who as Your Majesty knows is a vy good speaker upon the Conservative side followed him with a smart general attack upon the Government which Mr Churchill is informed — for he had to leave for a Cabinet Council — was a successful Parliamentary performance. The Debate hereafter became Hibernian in its character. Mr O'Brien expressed his detestation of the Budget and of Mr Redmond's policy and person with eloquence, and Mr Moore from Belfast — a strong Conservative — delivered a long and sarcastic diatribe against the Irish Nationalist Party, the Government and the supposed relations of the two. Mr Churchill had been deputed by the Cabinet to make a further statement in the Debate. He therefore followed Mr Moore and while adhering to the policy declared yesterday by the Prime Minster, endeavoured to make it clear to the House that the Government had no intention of delaying the issue which must soon arise when the proposals for dealing with the House of Lords and the relations between the two Houses are laid before Parliament.

The House listened with a very apparent sense of anxiety and oppression to the speech and every word was attended to with severe concentration. Upon the whole, however Mr Churchill feels that an easier and friendlier feeling towards the Government was created among its own supporters, and Your Majesty will be glad to hear that Mr Walter Long who followed commented favourably upon the "improvement" in Mr Churchill's "manners" towards the Opposition which appeared to have resulted from his transference to the Home Office.

No developments of any real interest are expected tonight, and Mr Churchill feels that it is improbable that any will take place during the next fortnight.

The fiscal amendment of the Opposition is to be the first business tomorrow.

[WINSTON S. CHURCHILL]

Churchill did not always confine himself to a bare account of the debate. Sometimes he felt it his duty to acquaint the King with a full account of the state of Parliamentary business.

WSC to The King

EXTRACT

25 February 1910   Home Office
Copy

Reviewing the events of the week Mr Churchill feels that the position of the Government has become one of the utmost weakness. There can be no doubt that their supporters in the House and still more in the country are thoroughly disheartened and deeply angered by two grave disillusionments: first that Your Majesty's Ministers are remaining in office without any real prospect of carrying their Legislation upon the Lord's Veto; and secondly that the simple question (to them) of the limitation of the Veto according to Sir Henry Campbell-Bannerman's plan should have been clouded by the intention to deal with the constitution of the Second House. It is impossible that the wide and almost universal feeling which now exists should not make its effect upon the policy which it will be open to Ministers to pursue.

Monday will be a climacteric in the existence of this short-lived Parliament. Mr Churchill does not mean to suggest to Your Majesty that the Government will be defeated. He thinks that even if Mr Redmond votes against them with their discontented followers as he has formally announced his intention to do, it is improbable that the Opposition will wish to turn out Ministers upon a question like taking the time of the House — a matter that is to say which would be absolutely vital to them (the Opposition) should Your Majesty recur to them for the conduct of public affairs. But unless the Prime Minister is able to make a statement which will reassure his supporters as to the simple issue of a limitation of the Veto being adhered to, and as to the resolution of the Government upon that point, the general situation must degenerate rapidly.

If however such a statement could be made a very sensible and marked improvement would be produced, and the necessary financial business, including the great estimates of nearly 41 millions for the Navy might be expeditiously transacted.

Mr Churchill has ventured to place the absolute facts of the situation in the House of Commons, as he sees them, before Your Majesty.

[WINSTON S. CHURCHILL]

Sometimes he presumed to draw upon his reading of history for the King's enlightenment.

WSC to the King
EXTRACT

28 February 1910   House of Commons
Copy

. . . Lord Hugh Cecil who was listened to with much consideration
on his return to the House followed with a speech of historic flavour.
He reminded the House of the various precedents which exist for the
extraordinary use of the Royal Prerogative in the creation of Peers
— to show that they were very bad precedents and applied to very
evil circumstances and occasions. Mr Churchill has always felt that
the destruction of the Whig majority in 1711, and the squandering
of the fruits of all the Duke of Marlborough's victories by the Treaty
of Utrecht, through the creation of 12 new peers, is a singularly unsatisfactory example from the history of the past. Lord Hugh Cecil
quoted at length the fierce terms in which the Hanoverian House of
Commons impeached the responsible author of these transactions. . . .

And again:

WSC to the King
(*Royal Archives*)
EXTRACT

14 March 1910   Home Office

. . . It is unsatisfactory from many points of view that so large an
element of instability should enter into the political situation and
that Your Majesty's Ministers should live from day to day under
the shadow of the axe. He has however passed the Sunday in the
fascinating task of reading the volume of the letters of the late
Queen and the correspondence relating to the Ministries of Lord
John Russell and Lord Palmerston with their precarious majorities
and their swiftly changing constructions; and he finds it comforting
to reflect that all came out right in the end, that the Queen's Government was faithfully carried on in spite of the utmost party confusion and many personal rivalries which now happily do not exist. . . .

He took the opportunity in these letters to praise the good work of
his colleagues, and seems to have singled out for favourable mention
those members of the Opposition like F. E. Smith and Lord Hugh
Cecil who were his personal friends. In March 1910 he wrote:

WSC to The King
(*Royal Archives*)

EXTRACT

30 March 1910   Home Office

. . . Today the debate has been excellently well maintained. First
an amusing and indeed a masterly speech by Mr F. E. Smith, who
has now become one of the principal figures upon the Opposition
benches; then a rejoinder very apt in point and argument by Mr
Simon, also a young King's Counsel of distinguished ability; thirdly
Lord Hugh Cecil who was vehement and surprising in manner and
matter. . . .

When the King died it fell to Churchill to write the letter of con-
dolence to the new King from the House of Commons. The final
letter was written in Marsh's hand but the first draft was in Churchill's:

King Edward had never thanked Churchill for these letters as Queen Victoria had thanked Lord Randolph when he was the leader of the House of Commons; but Churchill had no reason to suppose that his animated and sometimes chatty reports were received with anything except pleasure. Consequently, when King George succeeded his father, Churchill continued to write in the same vein.

Sometimes Churchill used his nightly letter to awaken the interest of the new King in some measure for which his own department was responsible, such as the Aliens Bill.

WSC to The King
(Royal Archives)

EXTRACT

19 April 1911   Home Office

... Your Majesty was pleased earlier in the year to take some interest in this question, and Mr Churchill has endeavoured to profit by the expression of Your Majesty's wishes wh then reached him. He ventures to send (in another box) a copy of the Bill. Sir Edward Henry thinks it will be vy useful. Some of the supporters of the Government are not however vy pleased about it, and the Minister must walk warily lest the flock rebuke him. . . .

Sometimes he had lively scenes to report, somewhat in the fashion of a schoolmaster reporting the recalcitrant boys in his form to the headmaster:

WSC to The King
(Royal Archives)

24 July 1911

Mr Secretary Churchill with his humble duty to Your Majesty: The Prime Minister was this afternoon subjected to prolonged organised insult & interruption from a section of the Conservative party, among whom Lord Hugh Cecil & Mr Goulding were the most prominent. For more than 25 minutes he attempted to deliver his speech, but in spite of the Speaker's appeals the Conservatives continued their rowdy and unreasonable disorder. He therefore confined himself to stating the course wh the Government would adopt without further argument or explanation.

It was therefore a great triumph of restraint on the part of the majority of the House, including as it does the Labour & Irish parties that they listened patiently and politely to a long & controversial speech from Mr Balfour, who acknowledged their courtesy & expressed regret for the behaviour of his friends.

Sir Edward Grey then rose and in a few impressive sentences told the Opposition that the Prime Minister would be the only spokesman of the Government and its supporters, & that if they would not listen to argument from him, "no one on these benches will take his place." Action would however follow on the lines wh the Prime Minister had marked out.

Mr F. E. Smith who had been himself vy disorderly attempted to continue the debate; but of course the House would not listen to him & the Speaker after some further clamour had arisen, held that a condition of grave disorder had been reached, & adjourned the House under the Special rules.

The feeling on the Government side is one of sober resolve. The violence of The Opposition was limited to a section only of their party. The irritation of the Conservatives is no doubt natural: but their claim to govern the country whether in office or opposition and to resort to disorder because they cannot have their way will not in any circumstances be acquiesced in by the majority of the House of Commons.

Mr Churchill should add that Mr Balfour pointedly asked the Prime Minister *when* he had received the "guarantees," & the Prime Minister refused to answer. This will however probably be pressed.

All of wh is humbly submitted by Your Majesty's faithful & devoted servant.

WINSTON S. CHURCHILL

WSC to The King
(Royal Archives)

26 July 1911   Home Office

Mr Secretary Churchill with his humble duty to Your Majesty: There was some recrudescence of disorderly conduct at Question time yesterday owing partly to the irritation of the supporters of the Government at the events of Monday & mainly to the provocative atti-

tude of Lord Hugh Cecil and his friends. A large section of the Conservative party deeply & sincerely regrets the shameful scene wh was
then created. The ugliest feature was the absence of any real passion
or spontaneous feeling. It was a squalid frigid organised attempt to
insult the Prime Minister & to prevent debate. The ringleaders are
however making themselves a distinct force as against Mr Balfour &
there is no doubt that a great many Unionists in the country who are
dissatisfied with his leadership will take the opportunity of supporting the rebels. It is noticeable that Mr Goulding & others acting with
him did not rise from their seats to welcome their leaders with the
rest of the party, & no doubt had he appealed to them to desist from
disorder they would have vy likely refused him. The spectacle of
Lord Hugh Cecil, Mr F. E. Smith & Mr Worthington-Evans now all
concentrated below the gangway revives something of the old force
of the Fourth Party in the eighties: & this should be carefully watched
if it develops as it may lead to considerable changes within the
Unionist party itself.

The rest of the sitting was occupied in the peaceful discussion of
the revenue Bill when the methods of Valuation were debated.

Submitted by Your Majesty's faithful servant.

WINSTON S. CHURCHILL

Churchill sometimes allowed some moralizing to creep into his
letters: he was to discover that this was not as pleasing to the King as
he had hoped:

WSC to The King

EXTRACT

10 February 1911
Copy

. . . As for tramps and wastrels there ought to be proper Labour
Colonies where they could be sent for considerable periods and made
to realise their duty to the State. Such institutions are now being
considered at the Home Office. It must not however be forgotten
that there are idlers and wastrels at both ends of the social scale. . . .

The King was evidently so distressed by this letter that he caused
Knollys to write a remonstrance, not to Churchill but to the Prime
Minister's Private Secretary:

Lord Knollys to Vaughan Nash
(Asquith Papers)

11 February 1911   Buckingham Palace

My dear Nash,

The King thinks that Mr Churchill's views, as contained in the enclosed, are very socialistic. What he advocates is nothing more than workshops which have been tried in France & have turned out a complete failure. In 1849 Louis Blanc introduced them in Paris and we all know what was the result: they were in reality the fore-runner of the street fighting in June of that year when so many thousands lost their lives.

HM considers it quite superfluous for Churchill in a letter of the description he was writing to him, to bring in about "idlers and wastrels at both ends of the social ladder."

Yours sincerely
KNOLLYS

Asquith evidently passed on Knollys' letter to Churchill, who was much taken aback, mortified, indeed affronted at this rebuke after all the trouble he had been taking: he did not hesitate to make his feelings plain:

WSC to The King

13 February 1911
Copy

Mr Secretary Churchill with his humble duty to YM. He has received with deep regret the expression of YM Displeasure wh has reached him through the PM upon a phrase wh occurred in his Parly letter of Friday last. Mr Churchill has never been offered any guidance as to the form wh such letters shd take and he consequently pursued the course he had been accustomed to follow when His late Majesty was on the Throne, namely with deep respect to write freely and frankly upon the events issues and feelings of the debates in the H. of C. His late M. on several occasions conveyed to the Home Secy His approval of the form and style of these letters, wh were frequently of a discursive character and frequently contained expressions of personal opinion upon the subjects under discussion. Mr Ch now gathers that YM desires that he shd confine himself to a narrative of the debates. He is of course most anxious to meet YM wishes in every respect: and in this case the result will be a lightening of his labours wh at this season are severe. He ventures however to point out that very excellent summaries of the debates, far better than any that he could write in the time and space available appear in all the news-papers, and that the use of the Parly letter has greatly diminished from this modern cause. YM is also apprised before the letter is despatched by telegram of the actual course of business. If the letter is merely to repeat at slightly greater length than the telegrams a summary of the debate wh has at the same time been published verbatim in the newspapers, its usefulness in informing YM of facts and issues in the H. of C. will not be great. Mr Ch will also feel a serious difficulty in writing these letters in the future after what has occurred, for fear that in a moment of inadvertence or fatigue some phrase or expression may escape him wh will produce an unfavour-able impression on YM. He therefore wd earnestly desire that YM wd give commands that the duty shd be transferred to some other Minister who wd be able to write with the feelings of confidence in YM gracious and indulgent favour, wh Mr Ch deeply regrets to have lost.

With regard to the particular phrase wh has caused YM's dis-pleasure, wh Mr Ch understands is "It should be remembered that there are idlers at both ends of the social scale" Mr Ch cannot un-derstand why this shd be thought to be Socialistic in its character. The Govt contemplate measures to deal with vagrancy and the pun-ishment and reform of tramps and incorrigible loafers by means of labour colonies on the continental system, and the HO is already studying the subject with a view to drafting a bill. It is a national difficulty wh stands in the way of such measures that the reproach may be uttered that even-handed justice wd require that all persons shd render some service to the State whether rich or poor. To say this is not to attack the wealthy classes, most of whom as Mr Ch knows well have done their duty in many ways: but only to point to those particular persons whose idle and frivolous conduct and lack of public spirit brings a reproach to the meritorious class to wh they belong. Mr Ch therefore adheres most respectfully to the truth and sincerity of the opinion wh he expressed in endeavouring in a few sentences to give YM a correct impression of the issue in the H. of C. on Friday last.

All of which is submitted with great respect by YM faithful servant.

W S C

Knollys replied:

Lord Knollys to WSC

14 February 1911   Buckingham Palace

My dear Churchill,

The King desires me to acknowledge the receipt of your letter of yesterday — he regrets that your feelings should have been hurt by anything which the Prime Minister may have said to you in consequence of HM having taken exception to two passages in your House of Commons Letter of the 10th Instant.

In one of those passages you appeared to advocate the, what is called, "Right of Work" scheme, although in the division on the debate the Government voted against it.

You then implied that a comparison could be fairly drawn between "Tramps and Wastrels" whom you would relegate to "Labour Colonies," and "idlers and wastrels" at the other end of the social scale.

I cannot conceal from you that the King would have preferred it, had you seen your way to suppress this remark, to which moveover an obvious answer might be offered that the cost of support in one case falls on the State and does not do so in the other.

These personal views were of course your own, but they were contained in a communication from a Cabinet Minister to the King.

HM feels that in certain contingencies, difficulties and embarrassments would inevitably arise were individual Ministers to express in official, though private letters, written daily during some months of the year to the Sovereign, their own views on important questions, which opinions might not be in agreement with those of their colleagues.

The King directs me to add that your letters are always instructive and interesting and he would be sorry if he were to receive no further ones from you in the future. At the same time he would not wish you to continue them if you feel disinclined to do so.

I ought to mention that I know King Edward took the same view of your "House of Commons letters" as the present King does, but he also did not always appear pleased with certain occasional passages in them.

With reference to your statement that you "have never been offered any guidance in the form" of your letters, I hope you will forgive my saying that you have never asked for any, or else it would of course have been most cheerfully given. It would give me great pleasure to show you some "House of Commons letters" from Lord Palmerston, Lord Beaconsfield and Mr Gladstone, which are bound up and are in my room, if you would care to see them.

Yrs sincerely
KNOLLYS

He also wrote to Nash:

Lord Knollys to Vaughan Nash
(Asquith Papers)

15 February 1911   Buckingham Palace

My dear Nash,

I think Mr Asquith may like to see W. Churchill's letter to the King with reference to the PM lecture to him.

I don't think the tone of the letter is quite a proper one nor has he taken the matter in the right way.

So far (7.30 pm) he has not answered me, but if he does I will send you on his letter. Of course the matter will end here unless he says he does not want to write any further "House of Commons letters" to the King, & then we must think of someone else.

Yrs sincerely
KNOLLYS

Churchill explained:

WSC to Lord Knollys

EXTRACT

16 February 1911   The Home Secretary
Copy

. . . I own to you that I was surprised and grieved to receive through the PM a formal notification of the King's displeasure. I have greatly valued the privilege and honour of conducting the Parly correspondence with HM. I have always endeavoured to place HM in possession of the best infn of the H. of C. situation at my command. In writing these daily letters and trying to make them interesting and readable, it is always possible that some sentiment or opinion may occur wh has not received the severe and deliberate scrutiny and reconsideration wh should attach to a State Paper. In these circs a Minister would wish that the most favourable construction wd be placed upon his words and sincerity, or that if the case were to require it some friendly suggestion or guidance might be conveyed to him from some person like yourself near to the King. The slightest indication of HM wishes and feelings wd always be studied by me with the most prompt and earnest attention. But I felt and feel that the serious and exceptional step of a formal significn to the Home Sec through the PM of the King's displeasure was utterly undeserved on this occasion, and bore no proportion to any error unconsciously committed. It was this that led me to express the pain I felt, and to ask to be relieved of a duty wh I felt might expose me to further possibilities of forfeiting HM favour.

In view of your letter and of the fuller information which you give me upon HM views and wishes, I will be glad to continue to keep the King informed of what passes in the H. of C. . . .

[WINSTON S. CHURCHILL]

Knollys replied:

Lord Knollys to WSC

17 February 1911   Buckingham Palace

My dear Churchill,

I have shown your letter of yesterday to the King, and he desires me to thank you for continuing your "House of Commons letters" which are always very interesting.

He also wrote to Nash:

Lord Knollys to Vaughan Nash
(Asquith Papers)

17 February 1911   Buckingham Palace

My dear Nash,

I enclose you Churchill's reply. He means it to be conciliatory I imagine, but he is rather like "A Bull in a China Shop."

I have merely thanked him for his letter & told him that the King is glad to hear he is going on with his "House of Commons letters."

I could have added, but I did not, that he is quite wrong in what he intimates would have been the right way of finding fault with him. At least I imagine so as surely the PM is the proper medium for conveying a reproof from the King to a member of the Cabinet.

Queen Victoria used always to send remonstrances to Lord Palmerston through Lord John Russell.

Yrs sincerely
KNOLLYS

Thus ended this altercation which Churchill conducted with proper deference but with proper spirit. He seems to have been undeterred from continuing in his bad old ways by the Royal reproof which, he felt, had been unjustly administered to him.

12

Home Rule

CHURCHILL HAD BEEN born and bred a Unionist, not merely a Tory Democrat. When Mr Gladstone had embraced Home Rule for Ireland in 1886 Lord Randolph Churchill, who was an ardent supporter of the union between England and Ireland, had been determined to play the "Orange card." "Pray God it may turn out the ace of trumps," he wrote to his friend Lord Justice Fitzgibbon. It did. The idea of putting the overwhelmingly Protestant population of the six counties of Ulster under a Catholic-dominated Parliament in Dublin was as repugnant to many Englishmen as it was to the men of Ulster. The "Orange card," revived memories of the Battle of the Boyne in 1690 when Dutch William had overpowered the forces of James II, who had already fled from England dropping the Great Seal in the Thames on his way. It inevitably rallied to the Union all those who placed their faith in the Protestant Succession that had been assured by William of Orange and his co-sovereign Mary who, though a daughter of James II, was staunchly attached to the reformed faith.

"Ulster will fight and Ulster will be right," Lord Randolph had proclaimed. With this simple master-stroke, which he had been the first to discern, he broke the power of Gladstone and the Liberal-Radical hegemony, attracted to his side the greatest Whig lords and more than any other man made Lord Salisbury Prime Minister and ushered in twenty years of almost unbroken Tory rule. His reward in the first stop-gap ministry of caretakers had been the India Office and a seat in the Cabinet at the age of thirty-six: and a few months later, after the great electoral victory later in 1886, the Chancellorship of the Exchequer and the Leadership of the House of Commons.

The succession to the leadership of the Tory Party and to 10 Downing Street was his for the waiting. But wait he would not: within six months he picked a quarrel with his colleagues on some trifling matter in the estimates and resigned. Of course he thought he would pull down Salisbury and the Government and have the immediate succession. He very nearly succeeded; it took twelve days to find a successor at the Treasury. His coup had failed: he was never to hold office again.

Churchill was eleven years old at the time of these stirring events. He grew up in a family which partly grieved at Lord Randolph's folly and partly resented Lord Salisbury's refusing to invite Lord Randolph back after all he had done to make the Tory victory possible. Churchill, while still a twenty-two-year-old subaltern in India, had acquired a fine contempt for the Tory Party; but he remained unwavering in his support of the cause on which Lord Randolph had mounted to fame and glory. Hence his letter to his mother quoted in the previous volume about Home Rule being the only impediment to his entering Parliament and joining the Liberal Party.

As we have seen in Volume I (page 332) in his first speech three months later at Bath he had said:

> And the great Liberal party which in 1882 was vigorous, united, supreme, is shrunk to a few discordant factions of discredited faddists, without numbers, without policy, without concord, without cohesion, around whose necks is bound the millstone of Home Rule.

Indeed, in a letter to Bourke Cockran dated 27 April 1896 (an extract of which is quoted in Volume I, page 271, and the full text of which is given in its Companion Volume, page 670–1) he had written in a prematurely mature mood of cynical realism:

> Nor will the civilised world compel us as you suggest to a prompt settlement. How could they with Justice? Does Russia give up Poland? Does Germany surrender Alsace and Lorraine? Does Austria give up Hungary? Does Turkey release Armenia? — or Spain grant autonomy to Cuba? One more instance, should the United States accede to the demand for Confederate independence? And one more argument. You may approve of Home Rule on principle. But I defy

you to produce a workable measure of it. He will be a bold man who
will rush in where Mr Gladstone failed.

Even after he had crossed the Floor in 1904 he wrote to the President of the North-West Manchester Liberal Association: "I remain
of the opinion the creation of a separate Parliament for Ireland
would be dangerous and impracticable." And in his speech of acceptance as candidate for North-West Manchester on 17 July 1904 he
maintained, albeit in a moderated form, his reservations about Home
Rule. He said:

> On the Policy of administrative Home Rule — as my father said in
> 1890 — I do not look forward to the day when there shall be created
> a separate Parliament to be a rival of, and perhaps an enemy of the
> central government here at home.

At this time the Liberals were in opposition and though an election might come at any time there were few votes to be gained by the
advocacy of Home Rule. Declarations for Home Rule were few and
half-hearted. Asquith was to say at Sheffield in April 1905: "There is
no question, say what you like, of a Home Rule Bill being introduced
into the next session." In October 1904 Churchill had already
shuffled into line with this Laodicean attitude when he said at Carnarvon Boroughs on October 19 when speaking for Lloyd George,
that there should be "an extension of local self-government" as it was
demanded "both by cramped nationalities who wanted to mind their
own business in their own way and also in the interests of Parliament
itself." And in his Election Address for the 1906 General Election he
went no further than to write:

> I shall support no Irish legislation which I regard as likely to injure
> the effective integrity of the United Kingdom, or to lead, however
> indirectly, to separation. I am persuaded that considerable adminis-
> trative reforms are required in the government of Ireland, and I
> would gladly see the Irish people accorded the power to manage their
> own expenditure, their own education and their own public works
> according to Irish ideas.

So little had he moved from his earlier position that he found it
possible in the course of the campaign on January 12 to give credit to

the Conservative Government for its administration of Irish affairs particularly in land settlement. He went on: "I do not think that we should be frightened from dealing with the question because we have the harsh and senseless reiteration of the cry of Home Rule. I do not think we ought to be prevented from endeavouring to carry out the administrative reforms which are admitted by the common sense of representatives of all parties to be urgently demanded in Ireland at the present time."

The result of the 1906 election left 83 Irish Nationalist Members in the House of Commons with no bargaining power at all. Campbell-Bannerman, although not yet pledged to Home Rule, was sympathetic to the cause and certain minor measures were introduced in the first years of the Liberal administration to alleviate Irish grievances. The Labourers (Ireland) Act gave $3\frac{1}{4}$ per cent loans for housing and made possible the erection of 30,000 labourers' cottages. An Irish University Act provided Dublin a Catholic seat of learning, without any Protestant influence. The Administrative Council in Ireland Bill, however, was rejected by the Irish Members as inadequate.

On 30 March 1908 John Redmond, the leader of the Irish party, introduced a Home Rule resolution in the House of Commons. The Chancellor of the Exchequer, Asquith, deputizing for Campbell-Bannerman who was to resign within a few days, said he could not vote for the resolution as it stood because it did not explicitly recognize Imperial supremacy, nor could he if it required the present Parliament to undertake Home Rule legislation. An amendment asserting the supremacy of the Imperial Parliament which Redmond accepted, though describing it as meaningless, was carried by 313 to 157. Churchill, of course, voted with the Government.

Redmond commenting on the result of the resolution said:

> The vote of the House of Commons declaring by a majority of 2 to 1 in favour of granting a full measure of Home Rule to Ireland as the only effective remedy for the present ills of our country and the declaration of Mr Churchill mark a distinct advance in the progress of the Home Rule cause.

In April Asquith became Prime Minister; Churchill was appointed President of the Board of Trade and went into the Cabinet at the age of thirty-three. Churchill's rise to Cabinet rank was thus quicker though less dramatic than that of Lord Randolph: he beat his father by three years, and his career was to prove incomparably more durable. His life-span was to be very nearly double that of his father. So far his observations on Ireland had been those of a subaltern, a backbencher and an Under-Secretary. Asquith as Prime Minister allowed his colleagues a wider latitude of expression than a modern Prime Minister would tolerate; but henceforward when Churchill spoke he had to remember the doctrine of the collective responsibility of the Cabinet and make sure that he carried with him the approval of his colleagues, and above all, that of the Prime Minister. This was one of the reasons why he so often circulated his opinions in writing to the Cabinet or for Asquith's individual eye. He was not only seeking to mould opinion but in default of any contrary argument to obtain a tacit licence to air his own policies in public.

Asquith's succession to 10 Downing Street brought a change of attitude in the Irish nationalists toward the Government. Whereas Campbell-Bannerman, without any precise commitment to Home Rule, had seemed to be moving in that direction, Asquith was, in the main, either obstinate or apathetic. The fact that he was Prime Minister seemed a definite set-back to the aspirations of the Irish Party.

Churchill was keen to use every available means in his fight to be returned at the by-election in North-West Manchester which followed on his appointment as President of the Board of Trade. In spite of a rather bleak letter from Redmond he sought in a manly fashion to persuade the Irish leader to rally the Irish vote in Manchester. Like the Democratic Party in the United States at the same period, the Liberal Party always sought to gain the votes of under-privileged minorities such as the Jews and the Irish.

John Redmond to WSC

EXTRACT

[? April 1908]

Dear W Churchill,

I was speaking to Mr Whitley (the local leader of the United Irish league in Manchester) today about the Irish electors in your division.

I told him that, under the existing circumstances which you fully understand, I did not believe they would vote for you.

No doubt if you made a very strong and explicit Home Rule declaration and if he strongly advised them to do so, a portion of the
Irish vote might be got to go for you — but only a portion and you
probably would lose quite as many votes because of your declaration.

Further I think he would, in any case, have great difficulty in asking the Irish vote to support the Government just at this moment. . . .

WSC to John Redmond

7 April 1908   Colonial Office
Copy
Private

Dear Mr Redmond,

I am very much obliged to you for your letter and I fully appreciate the friendly spirit in which it is written.

Your countrymen will make a mistake if they fail to support me
now. Their alternative is to vote for an ultra-Unionist who has spent
some part of the autumn in denouncing the Government for not
applying the Crimes Act to Ireland, and who hopes to secure the
Protestant vote by denouncing the University Bill.

My vote for your resolution will undoubtedly expose me to considerable attack, as it will rightly be interpreted as being another
step forward on my part towards a full recognition of Irish claims
to self-Government.

I shall not however regret it, whatever be the treatment to which
I may be subjected: and your friends may rest assured that any action
they may take — however injurious and as I think miscalculated —
will not prevent me from doing my best as opportunity may offer to
serve the interests and sustain the hopes of Irishmen and from promoting that effective recognition of their national claims to the
management of purely Irish affairs which I believe to be right in
itself, and entirely compatible with the interests of the British people.

Believe me that the courtesy and consideration of your letter will
always be a pleasant recollection to

Yours very truly
w s c

Redmond was an upright man. He had realized that Irish opposition in Manchester was focussed much more on Asquith than it was
on Churchill: so he did not encourage Churchill to get into trouble

with his own party by making promises which could not do him any good. He preferred to gain his confidence and goodwill, doubtless in the hope of winning his support for Irish legislation at a more propitious time. If this was his assessment he calculated shrewdly. With increased responsibilities Churchill became more progressive on many issues. The more he studied the Irish problem the more convinced he became that something must be done about Ireland. Churchill always liked to take the lead in any matter in which he was concerned. Thus it was that when the further life of the Government depended upon embracing Home Rule, Churchill became one of the foremost champions of that cause. It often happens that when necessity drives men's minds it quickens them towards the justice of a cause which they have hitherto neglected. Such is politics, the cynic may exclaim, but such too is life itself.

Accordingly in the middle of the campaign Redmond advised the Irish electors of North-West Manchester not to support Churchill at the by-election, i.e. to abstain: he did not advise them to support Joynson-Hicks or the Socialist candidate, Dan Irving.

WSC to H. H. Asquith
(Asquith Papers)

18 April 1908
In the train

My dear Prime Minister,
    The Irish are not at present, according to my information, in a state to receive with any thankfulness the suggestion that "the half-way house" is still open if they themselves will take a real responsibility for it. They are *grateful* at having lost it. They dare not now admit the error or ask for it again. I have no doubt that before the end of this Parliament a conjunction favourable to a Council Bill will stand. But it would be as you apprehended useless to try anything now. I shall not therefore use the discretionary freedom you gave me yesterday on that point.
    The local Irish leaders are going to ask me three questions tomorrow at a public meeting. I enclose them with the answers I propose to give. They have taken me a good deal of time to concoct and I should have been glad to have had an opportunity of discussing

them with you, but that is impossible. I have adopted Lloyd George's phrase, [with] which I understand you agree, about a "free hand next time." I have chosen a slightly different formula about Catholic schools, and have carefully put this forward "in my opinion." But I really don't see how the contrary can be contended.

A telegram to the Midland Hotel would reach me tomorrow morning in case you think it necessary. But I hope you will agree with the answers as drafted.

T P [O'Connor] thinks that the full and active support of the Irish party will be secured on these lines in the present contest. It may be however that all the central body will do is to leave the decision to the local people. In this case some of the Catholic voters may go wrong. In no case will there be any hostile action taken by the politicians.

It is no joke fighting such a contest as this.

Yours ever

W S C

Questions and Answers

1. Is Mr Churchill in favour of Home Rule, meaning an Irish Parliament for the management of purely Irish affairs, with an executive responsible thereto, in accordance with the resolution recently adopted by the House of Commons?

Yes. In common with the rest of His Majesty's Government I voted in favour of Mr Redmond's motion which was couched in almost the same words as your question with the addition of the words — "subject to the supremacy of the Imperial Parliament," which, let me remind you, was accepted by Mr Redmond.

2. Is Mr Churchill of opinion that Home Rule ought to form a leading issue in the programme to be put before the electors at the next General Election by the Liberal Party, and will he, as a member of the Cabinet, use his best endeavours to have this done?

At the last election I precluded myself as did others of my colleagues from attempting what is called "the larger policy" in respect of Ireland during the present Parliament. By that I am bound so far as this Parliament is concerned.

I have for some time resolved not to be fettered in that way in any subsequent Parliament. I am encouraged by the striking success of a bold and generous policy in South Africa to approach Irish difficulties in a similar spirit — and when this Parliament has reached its close, I am strongly of opinion that the Liberal party should claim authority to deal with the problem of Irish self government as indicated in Mr Redmond's resolve.

3. Would you indicate what steps you have in mind to give effect to the statement in your election address with regard to the treatment of Catholic schools?

With the concurrence of the Prime Minister and others of my colleagues I have stated that provision must of course be made for the case of the Catholics whose religious faith diverges so widely from that of the great majority of the people of these islands that a special type of school is rendered necessary.

In my opinion it is of high importance that in any settlement of this vexed question which may be arrived at, and of which there are now good hopes, no school or class of school should be placed in a position which would be detrimental to the educational and purely secular interests of the children attending them.

For some reason the answers to questions 1 and 2 are missing from the Asquith Papers; only the third, to which Asquith seems to have suggested an amendment, is there in its unamended form. We may suppose from Churchill's next letter, in reply to a note from Asquith which does not survive, that Asquith returned the two answers to which he had agreed and only kept the original third one to which he had proposed an amendment. The last sentence of Churchill's draft of the third answer had read:

In my opinion it is of high importance that these schools, if occupying a position necessarily different from that of the National and Protestant system of education, should not be placed in a position which would be detrimental.

WSC to H. H. Asquith
(*Asquith Papers*)

19 April 1908

My dear Asquith,

I was very much relieved to get your note. A deputation consisting of Devlin and Kettle MP arrived late last night with the enclosed questions from Redmond. To them I tacked the answers agreed upon. They pressed hard for more precise language, especially the addition to the second answer of the words "in accordance with the principles of Mr Redmond's resolution." But I said you had approved the particular form of the answer and I would not alter a word. "If they do not like it, they must smash the crockery." They are rather superior fellows and we got through our business in a very friendly way. The local Irishmen are red hot to vote for me — but I do not yet know what will be decided. I think I shall get 3 quarters at the most — 4/5ths at the lowest.

I altered the answer on Education as you will notice, in order to avoid the appearance of a special preference to Catholics by the use of general terms.

The Easter holidays have delayed our canvass and the returns to date while not at all unsatisfactory are still quite inconclusive.

Yours ever

W S C

Four-fifths is of course larger than three-quarters; Churchill was no better at fractions than Lord Randolph had been at decimals. Asquith seems to have wished to obfuscate the answer about the Catholic schools to avoid giving offence to the Non-conformists. From what we know of Asquith it would have been characteristic of him to have wished the issue to be blurred.

On reflection, and with polling day only four days ahead, Churchill decided to make a radical advance on the Irish question. Speaking in his constituency he said:

My opinion on the Irish question has ripened during the last 2 years when I have lived in the inner or nearly in the inner councils of Liberalism. I have become convinced that a national settlement of the Irish difficulty on broad and generous lines is indispensable to any harmonious conception of Liberalism — the object lesson is

South Africa. . . . At the next election I am strongly of the opinion
that the Liberal party should claim full authority and a free hand
to deal with the problem of Irish self-government without being
restricted to measures of administrative devolution of the character
of the Irish Councils Bill.

This speech caused the Irish Party to claim that the Liberals had
altered their position on Home Rule, and to put a gloss on Churchill's words. Churchill immediately telegraphed to Asquith saying
that he proposed to repeat the words he had used in his speech. He
wrote to Asquith on the same day, sending him a verbatim report of
his speech and saying that the Liberal Party were not "bound by Irish
gloss" which was being put on his speech, "but only by precise and
carefully considered words." He concluded his letter by saying:
"Jews, Irish, Unionist Free Traders and the Protestant League are all
now safely penned in the same cage together. Please God they do not
fight before Friday morning." He was nearly always an optimist. He
continued to report to Asquith at every turn of events: "At two meetings I was asked 'whether I accepted Mr Redmond's interpretation'
of my speech. I parried." Asquith told Churchill by telegram that
Joynson-Hicks had telegraphed him and asked him direct whether
he accepted the Irish interpretation of Churchill's speech. He did
not reply to Joynson-Hicks but told Churchill that it was not within
his or anyone else's power to give pledges at this time "as to what
issues will be before the country at the General Election." Churchill
replied on April 23, the day before polling, that he would that evening "say specifically that I am bound by my own word and no others."
   Churchill lost the by-election, as has been described in Chapter 8.
Probably Redmond was right, that the Irish vote could not be shifted.
In fact, however, the Irish vote probably played only a minor part in
determining the issue. In Chapter 8 it was argued that Free Trade
being now firmly established and under no threat from the Tories,
many of the Unionist Free Traders who had voted for Churchill at
the General Election returned to their natural allegiance; more especially since Home Rule was daily becoming a more urgent issue.
   Churchill's defeat by 429 votes caused great joy among the Unionists. In *Carson* by H. Montgomery Hyde there is printed an extract
from a letter which Carson wrote to his Egeria, Lady Londonderry,

Churchill's cousin by marriage: ".... I have been trying to picture your feelings at Winston's defeat. I am bound to say I felt almost a savage satisfaction and I think the effect on the Government must be serious. I think W. Churchill really degrades public life more than anyone of any position in politics, and I doubt if he will ever mature into the kind of serious and reliable politician the majority of people have confidence in. ...." This gloating was to be short-lived. The Government's fortunes were unaffected and Churchill himself, as we have seen, was to be comfortably returned by Dundee within a few weeks.

Irish affairs simmered on without any striking event till the rejection of Lloyd George's Budget in the spring of 1909. It was then that the Liberal Government decided to break the power of the Lords. They embarked on this undertaking overwhelmingly for domestic purposes: but to the Irish the main objective of curbing the veto of the Upper House was to stop them throwing out Home Rule as they had done in 1893. The Lords had felt safe in doing this and would have felt safe in doing it again, since the cause of Union with Ireland still enjoyed popular support in the Kingdom's main island. The bulk of the Liberal Party had probably supported Asquith in his apathetic attitude, which consisted of favouring Home Rule without entering into any precise commitments as to how or when it should be brought about. To the more perspicacious of the Lords Ireland loomed visibly on the horizon. Their motives in clinging to the veto were not entirely selfish. Lloyd George's land tax cannot have struck as much terror as some of them affected to believe. Indeed, they eventually let the budget through, *including the land taxes,* before the veto was abolished, and there were not above twenty whose considerable estates in Ireland might be threatened by Home Rule. Too little justice has been given to the Lords and to the Unionist Party generally for an attachment to the Union as strong as that which animated the American Republican Party in 1860 when it decided to oppose by force the secession of the Southern States, which it regarded as rebellion. Ever since the time of James II Ireland had been regarded as the back door for an attack by France upon England: the Union seemed to many essential to the defence of Britain.

Confronted by the high, reckless attitude of the Lords in throwing out a Money Bill, Asquith decided to ask the King for a dissolution.

The tide had been running strongly against the Liberals ever since 1906; it was the natural reaction to their overwhelming victory in that year. Already the Tories had gained twenty-eight seats between the General Election of 1906 and 1910. The cry of "the peers versus the people" did not make as big an appeal as the Liberals had hoped. This was partly because it was found necessary to make further concessions about Ireland. Asquith went no farther than he deemed absolutely necessary and spoke in characteristically ambiguous terms. Opening the campaign in the Albert Hall on 10 December 1909 he said that the new Liberal Government would safeguard the supremacy and authority of the Imperial Parliament while setting up in Ireland a system of full self-government in regard to purely Irish affairs. He said "in the new House of Commons the hands of a Liberal Government and of a Liberal majority will, in this matter, be entirely free."

Though the Liberals tried to put a brave face on it, the election was a defeat. They came back with a majority of two over the Unionists; so they had to rely on the support of the Irish Nationalists who had 82 seats and the Labour Party with 41. Even before the full results of the election were known, Churchill realized that the Government would have to come to terms with the Irish Nationalists and that Home Rule in some form was inevitable. He was prepared to play a leading part.

Wilfrid Blunt wrote on February 10:

Lunched, as arranged, with Winston and Clementine. He had just been at the Cabinet in Downing Street, and arrived late, looking rather grave; but he soon cheered up, and began talking about the situation . . . There is to be a "general post," but nobody knows who is to get what. He would like the Home Office. He would not take Ireland, unless it were to grant Home Rule. I questioned him as to his understanding of the Home Rule to be given, and he said it would be complete Parliamentary Government for all Irish affairs in Dublin, including finance, police, and everything, but not the power of levying Custom duties against England, or altering the land settlement, and, of course, none of levying troops or of treating with foreign Powers. He would have the Irish members still sit at Westminster, but in diminished numbers.

And three days later, the day before the final results, Blunt wrote in his diary:

> February 13 — John Redmond called on me, and we had a long hour's talk about the situation in England and also in Ireland. I began by giving him my view of the deadlock; the impossibility Asquith was in of getting the King to coerce the Lords, and that I did not think Asquith or Grey or Haldane were really in earnest about Home Rule, though Churchill and Lloyd George were. He said he quite agreed with this view. He believed in Asquith to the extent that he would trust him if he made a promise in so many words, but he had not quite done so about Ireland. What he had promised was full self-government, subject to the control of the Imperial Parliament. Churchill, he believed, was quite sincere. He had a very high opinion of him. Churchill had told him once that it was the ambition of his life to bring in a Home Rule Bill as Chief Secretary.

The Irish were not slow to see their opportunity and to stake out a claim. Redmond speaking at Liverpool on March 20 said: "With us this question of the veto is the supreme issue. With us it means Home Rule for Ireland."

The Budget was passed in the Commons in April with the support of the Irish Nationalists. Some thought that they would have been in a better bargaining position over Home Rule if they had, with the help of the Tories, thrown it out. Blunt wrote in his diary on June 20:

> Unless the Irish get rid of Asquith, Grey and Haldane, they will never gain what they want. They certainly had bad luck with the King's death on May 6 but it was a mistake their allowing the Budget to pass.

In a letter of June 6, T. P. O'Connor wrote to Redmond: "WC said — and over and over again — before I said anything on the point — that he would not accept any settlement, by whomsoever made which did not permit the Liberal party to pass into law — with or without the consent of the House of Lords — Home Rule, Welsh Disestablishment and other measures which he mentioned as typical Liberal measures."

Churchill was seeking at this time to saturate himself in the background of the Irish situation. He sought the aid of Redmond, who put him on to Stephen Gwynn, the Nationalist MP for Galway and also a journalist and author, and who sent Churchill half a dozen books on Ireland.

*

Attempts to reach a settlement about the Lords, some behind the scenes and some at a Constitutional conference, ended abortively. These, and the pressures brought upon the new King, have been described in a previous chapter. Amidst vacillations and uncertainty the Government drove forward with a fresh appeal to the electorate. Parliament was dissolved on November 28 and the General Election was held between December 2 and 20. Ten days earlier Churchill in a speech at Islington had spoken with sympathy of the Irish Members at Westminster:

> For over 30 years these men — these same men, some of them, mind you, whose parliamentary gifts, are such as they could not, except for being in the Irish party, have failed to rise to the highest eminence in the public service — for 30 years these same men have laboured with that hope deferred that maketh the heart sick and they have laboured without taint of personal motive — without thought of personal gain — for one cause, the cause which every Englishman who loves the freedom and honour of his country, whatever his opinion for or against Home Rule — must treat with consideration and respect.
>   . . . The hour is coming for the reconciliation of the English and Irish people . . . The sky is already brightening and there is promise of the dawn for which Mr Gladstone waited so long — but which he did not live to see.

He saw Ireland free in all that properly concerns itself, loyal to the Crown and with reviving prosperity ready to take her place with the colonies.

> A settlement will gain the heartfelt sympathy of that great English-speaking Republic across the water and lead to the discomfiture of every European rival of the greatness of our country.

With the reconciliation which he had presided over in South Africa still fresh in his memory, he believed the Irish, as "those brave Boers had done" once their grievances were overcome, would "take their place — in a true and indissoluble Union of Empire." Once the Irish question had been solved there would be a "calmer, richer, fuller national life open to the people of both islands."

On 24 February 1911 Churchill circulated a paper to the Cabinet on his views on "Devolution." The scheme had originally been devised in 1903 by Sir Antony MacDonnell, the Permanent Under-Secretary in Dublin, and Lord Randolph's friend, Lord Dunraven, who was sympathetic to the idea of Home Rule. Finance and local legislation were to be transferred to a parliament in Dublin. There were to be two parliaments in London: an Imperial executive with power over foreign policy, colonial administration and naval and military affairs; and an English executive dealing with internal affairs, like its counterpart in Dublin.

Churchill in his memorandum said:

> It seems to be absolutely impossible that an English Parliament, and still more an English Executive, could exist side by side with an Imperial Parliament and an Imperial Executive, whether based on separate or identical election. Imperial affairs could not in practice be separated from English party politics, which consist principally of domestic questions. The persons who are prominent in British party politics will be so mainly because of their following in England on internal questions; and it is not conceivable that such persons, having acquired mastery in the decisive field of home politics, would be willing, or would be able, to surrender the control of foreign, colonial, military, and naval affairs to another class of Ministers or politicians. The external sphere touches the internal at almost every point. The fortunes of the country abroad and at home are interdependent and indissoluble. Persons are trusted by the nation to manage the external affairs of the country because of the confidence and support accorded to their political action on great social, economic, and political issues at home; and the principles which are affirmed by the nation in domestic politics have always governed, and will always govern, the character and conduct of external affairs. No separation of the issues is possible in practice, and none is desirable. The strong positions of a British Foreign Minister,

Chancellor of the Exchequer, or Minister of Defence are based upon the support of vast organised party followings which come together for all purposes, but primarily for domestic purposes, and would be incompetent for action in either sphere alone.

He listed three contingencies under which he considered the break-up of power to be unworkable. First: a Liberal majority in both the Imperial Parliament and the English Parliament, in which case the Prime Minister of the Imperial Parliament would also be the Prime Minister of the English Parliament. Second: a Conservative majority in the Imperial Parliament and a Liberal majority in the English Parliament: "This would produce an immediate and violent collision between two bodies of almost equal strength . . ." each trying to over-throw the other. And third and most unlikely: a Liberal majority in the Imperial Parliament and a Conservative majority in the English Parliament. This would produce a Liberal leader of the Opposition in the English Parliament more powerful than the Prime Minister. The situation "could not be reconciled with any conception of reason or good government."

On March 1 Churchill circulated another paper in which he put forward a basis for discussion on devolution. He said that the Impe-rial Parliament must remain unaltered and intact. He suggested that there should be ten regional authorities set up in the United King-dom, including Ireland, embracing all local government, County Councils, education, housing, Poor Law, agriculture, police, fisheries, roads, etc. The Imperial Parliament would retain all powers not specifically devolved. Thus Ireland would gain a measure of self-government and the whole kingdom would be divided into a more de-tailed and up-to-date idea of the Anglo-Saxon system of the heptarchy to which he frequently recurred as a desirable goal in later life.

*

Nine months were to elapse between the second 1910 election and the placing on the Statute Book of the Parliament Act in August 1911. Already, during the election campaign, the Tory leaders had

foreseen and foretold what this would mean for the Union. Balfour
said in an election speech on November 23:

> Let everybody realise that the House of Lords is to be destroyed, not
> in the least because the electors of the United Kingdom who value
> the British Constitution want it to be destroyed, but because that
> section of the electors who do not value the British Constitution
> want to get Home Rule.

Austen Chamberlain said at Oldham on 8 December 1910:

> What are the Government going to do, if they have a majority — a
> sufficient majority? They are going to abolish the veto of the House
> of Lords, they are going to establish Home Rule in Ireland.

On August 7–8, when the Commons were discussing the Lords
amendments which had been moved by Lansdowne, it fell to Churchill to answer for the Government: Asquith was absent with laryn-
gitis. Late on August 7 he told the House that the Government intended to bring forward a Home Rule measure in the course of the
Parliament. The Tories immediately challenged the announcement.
So this was what the Parliament Bill really meant, they claimed: it
had nothing to do with the reform of the House of Lords — it was
just a dodge to get Home Rule through Parliament without consulting the people. The next day Lord Hugh Cecil and Carson made
bitter speeches in support of their motion to defer consideration of
the Lords Amendments for three months. It was no use sending the
Bill to the House of Lords, argued Cecil, as it had ceased to be a free
assembly. He attacked Asquith and the Government:

> I conceive that the Government and the Prime Minister have been
> guilty of high treason. That is my point. Undoubtedly it is high
> treason to overthrow the liberties of either House of Parliament.

He demanded a referendum:

> I suggest that the disagreement between the two Houses should be
> referred by special Act of Parliament to the electorate to decide . . .
> I am not suggesting a dissolution of Parliament. The thing should
> be referred to the people in this form: "Will you have the Parlia-

ment Bill with Lord Lansdowne's Amendment or without Lord
Lansdowne's Amendment?" . . . But I do not suppose the Government will accept it. They know they would be beaten. They know
that except for the purpose of party rhetoric the will of the people
has not been conclusively obtained, and anyone opposite who has a
fair judgment will agree in his secret heart that the will of the people
on this particular issue of Lord Lansdowne's Amendment is on our
side and against you.

And he turned on those peers who were willing to support the Bill
against their own convictions:

I cannot conceive how any self-respecting person can give a vote
against his convictions under the pressure of a Government of which
he disapproves in the case of a Bill which he thinks is ruinous to the
country. We have called the Peers who are to be created "puppet
peers," but there is something worse than being a puppet: it is to
be a puppet's deputy.

Passions ran high. Carson challenged Churchill's announcement
about Home Rule. When the King was asked to give the guarantee
to pass the Parliament Bill, did he know that a Home Rule Bill
would be introduced in the same session? Carson believed the King
had been "trapped," the House of Lords had been blackmailed. In
his reply, Churchill claimed that everyone knew perfectly well that
Home Rule was part of the Government's programme. Had not a
Tory amendment to exclude Home Rule from the scope of the Parliament Bill been debated and defeated in April? As to the King's
position "it is right and proper to say that His Majesty was fully acquainted in November with the true facts of the political situation
and with all the matters in dispute between the various parties in the
State, among which Home Rule was unquestionably one of the more
important."

This passage in Churchill's speech drew a mild complaint from the
King. This time, though, it was of a much less personal nature than
that of Churchill's nightly Parliamentary letter to the King described
in Chapter 10. The message was not sent through Asquith's secretary,
Vaughan Nash: the matter was dealt with more directly, and was not
so calculated to offend Churchill.

Lord Knollys to WSC

EXTRACT

9 August 1911   Sandringham

. . . people will imply from these words that the Home Rule question formed part of the conversation which took place between the King and the PM and Lord Crewe. This however would be an entirely erroneous impression, as no reference to Home Rule was made either by HM to the PM and Lord Crewe, or by them to the King. But your words will lead people to suppose that his consent to the creation of Peers under hypothetical circumstances was given, not only for the purpose of enabling the Parliament Bill to be passed, but likewise for the Home Rule Bill.

In a great political crisis like that which is now going on, the King stands in a very helpless and peculiar position, as he is unable to defend himself; and the point in question is he thinks so important a one for him, that he would be glad if you would take steps to explain that nothing relating to Home Rule passed at the audience on 16th of November. . . .

On October 4 Churchill spoke at Dundee on the subject of Home Rule.

Next year we propose to introduce the Home Rule Bill and we propose to carry it forward with all our strength. It is 18 years since this subject has been debated in Parliament, and many things have happened in the interval.

Ireland is almost timeless, much more timeless than our own island. Ireland is much more prosperous than she was. Local government institutions are established and at work. The land of Ireland is redeemed or in the process of redemption by British credit — a solid social foundation of small landowning farmers has been created. . . .

All the self-governing colonies are favourable to Home Rule — we are now in the full tide of a successful experiment in regard to self-government. South Africa and Canada are the fruits of the Imperialism of peace and freedom. . . .

It is our duty to exhaust every effort which sympathy and earnestness can inspire to understand the reasonable difficulties of Ulster

and to allay unfounded alarm — and provide sure and effective safeguards for civil and religious equality and freedom.

On 8 November 1911 Balfour yielded to the persistent nagging
"Balfour must go" campaign. He had had enough. The BMG campaign had been in the main directed against his vacillating attitude
on Tariff Reform, which had not satisfied either wing of his party;
but staunch Unionists felt also that he was not wholeheartedly with
them over Ireland. His successor, Bonar Law, a man of markedly inferior parts, and in large measure a pliant tool of Sir Max Aitken,
his fellow Canadian, who had been knighted in the Coronation
Honours, was numbered among the diehards on Ireland. Bonar Law
and Churchill were temperamentally antagonistic; they were always
to remain so.

*

With the Parliament Bill out of the way in August 1911 Home
Rule once again became one of the chief issues in political debate.
On 8 February 1912 Churchill was due to speak in the Ulster Hall
in Belfast. The announcement of this meeting caused much excitement and the fact that he was to speak in the Ulster Hall where
Lord Randolph had proclaimed "Ulster will fight and Ulster will be
right" was thought particularly provocative. A cool exchange of
letters between Churchill and his kinsman, Lord Londonderry, took
place:

WSC to Lord Londonderry

EXTRACT

17 January 1912   33 Eccleston Square
Copy

. . . If you & your friends choose at the outset of this great Controversy to resort to riot, & to endeavour to prevent peaceable discussion, I shd be quite content in the interests of the Home Rule cause
to leave the object lesson to the judgement of Great Britain & of the
self governing Colonies. No cruder assertion could be made of a
claim to ascendancy than an open declaration by the Ulster Conservatives that they will not allow their fellow-countrymen from whom
they differ the right of public meeting.

No more naked admission of argumentative embarrassment cd be afforded than that a British Minister cannot in the interests of Unionism be allowed to speak to those in Belfast who wish to hear him on the subject of Home Rule.

If the position wh you & your friends have adopted is that you will endeavour by force to deny the right of public meeting, & will prevent discussion if you can, then the responsibility for the consequences must rest with you; & it may be a very direct & personal responsibility. If however it is not against the right of public meeting that you wish to demonstrate, but only against the right of meeting in a particular hall, while I venture to think the country will consider such an objection not very reasonable, it shall if practically possible be met. We do not seek quarrels about trifles. We seek to debate matters serious to us and serious to you, wh will shortly become the subject of prolonged national & parliamentary examination. . . .

As often happened the first draft was in Churchill's hand and, as below, the final letter in Marsh's:

WSC to Lord Londonderry

25 January 1912   Admiralty
Copy

My Lord,

  The very grave and direct personal responsibility which will fall upon you if serious rioting occurs in Belfast on the occasion of my visit, makes me sure that you will not lightly seek to widen the grounds of quarrel. For my part I only care about one essential thing. It is my duty to keep my promise to the Ulster Liberal Association, and to assert our

My Lord,
    The very grave and direct personal responsibility which will fall upon you if serious rioting occurs in Belfast on the occasion of my

visit, makes me sure that you will not lightly seek to widen the grounds of quarrel. For my part I only care about one essential thing. It is my duty to keep my promise to the Ulster Liberal Association, and to assert our right of free speech and public meeting. If, as I now gather from the newspapers, the main objections of yourself and your friends are directed against our holding our meeting in the Ulster Hall, then, although such claims are neither just nor reasonable, I will ask the Ulster Liberal Association to accede to your wish. There will thus be no necessity for your friends to endure the hardships of a vigil, or sustain the anxieties of a siege. Neither will it be necessary for you to break the law in an attempt to deprive us forcibly of the use of property to which we are lawfully entitled. It is not a point of any importance to me where I speak in Belfast. On the contrary, I desire to choose whatever hall or place is least likely to cause ill-feelings to the Orange Party.

It has, however, become of importance to the public liberties that the meeting should take place in Belfast on the 8th of February; & I intend to hold it there, in lawful exercise of the elementary rights of citizenship.

Yours faithfully
[WINSTON S. CHURCHILL]

Churchill released this letter to the press the same evening he sent it to Londonderry, who first read it in the papers the following morning.

Lord Londonderry to WSC

26 January 1912   Mountstewart
                                                  Newtownards
                                                  Co Down

Sir: —

I have read in the Press your letter directed to me, but of which I have not yet received any copy.

In the interest of the peace and order of the great city of Belfast I note with satisfaction that you have abandoned the idea of holding a meeting in the Ulster Hall in that city.

I only regret that before you had announced your intention of holding such a meeting you did not consider how inevitable it was that such an intention could only intensify the feelings of bitter resentment and hostility to Home Rule which existed amongst the loyal citizens of our City.

By selecting the Ulster Hall with its historic traditions and the memories connected with your late father's visit in 1886, and the advice he then gave to the people of Ulster, I have no doubt you intended directly to challenge the genuineness of the oft-expressed determination of those who have made up their minds never under any circumstances to allow themselves to be degraded from their present position under the Imperial Parliament; and so far as you could by a choice of the locality to falsely represent that those who are unalterably opposed to you were adherents of the policy you come to advocate.

Against such an attempt which was only the culmination of many acts of insult and arrogance towards the loyalists of Ulster, the Ulster Unionist Council felt bound in the most emphatic manner to protest with a full knowledge that peace and order could not be preserved if a meeting under such circumstances took place.

So far as the Council is concerned its main objection in the interests of law and order are removed, if you determine to hold your meeting outside the districts which passionately resent your action, and if you do so it certainly would be no party to and would strongly deprecate any attempt to interfere with your meeting.

At the same time having regard to the intense state of feeling that has been created by your proposed action, the Ulster Unionist Council cannot accept any responsibility with reference to your visit to Belfast and they do not desire to give any assurances that they might be unable to fulfil. With reference to the place where you propose to hold your meeting it is not for the Ulster Unionist Council to make any suggestion. As a Member of the Government you have access to all the information in the possession of the Executive Authorities in Belfast, who, no doubt, thoroughly understand the situation and have already given you full particulars.

I only desire to add that as regards your references to the necessity of upholding "the elementary rights of citizenship," (by which no doubt you mean the right of free speech) which appear almost cynical having regard to the action of your Government in repressing it in the House of Commons, I believe the citizens of Belfast and of the Province of Ulster are as jealous supporters of that principle as any of the inhabitants of the United Kingdom, and I repudiate the sug-

gestion that their opposition to your provocative action was prompted
by any desire to interfere with that precious heritage.

Yours faithfully
LONDONDERRY

WSC to Lord Londonderry

27 January 1912   Admiralty
Copy

My Lord,
   You are wrong to think that the Ulster Hall was "selected" by me
as a "challenge" to you or your friends. Beyond consenting, in fulfilment of an old promise, to make a speech for the Ulster Liberal
Association before the meeting of Parliament, I had nothing to do
with the local arrangements. I am told, and you no doubt are aware
of it, that the Ulster Hall was only "selected" by the Liberal party in
Belfast, after other alternatives had fallen through, because it happened to be free on the date in question. You know quite well that
it is a Hall by Act of Parliament open to all parties, and that many
Home Rule meetings of importance — one of them as lately as last
month — have been freely held there. It is therefore the Ulster
Unionist Council who seek to fasten a quarrel, and search for
grounds of offence where none are intended.
   For my part I can truly say that I had no other idea or intention
than to discuss in public, according to the long established custom
of British politics, matters which are serious to us, and which we
freely recognise are serious to you. The rightful interests of the
Protestants of Ireland must be the deep concern of every British
Government. They will be respected by all who faithfully strive to
reconcile Ireland to the British Empire, and to see an end to hatreds
which disturb the foundations of the Estate.
   As to public order, I have invited no assurance from you. I rely
upon the law of the land and upon the sense of justice of the citizens
of Belfast. Unless a riot is covertly or openly organised and strangers
are brought in for that purpose, I am confident that nothing will
happen unworthy of the prosperity and honour of the city.
   One word more. Your letter forces me to refer to a personal matter. Your Lordship has a claim, to which I bow, to remind me of the
memory of Lord Randolph Churchill. You were his friend through
evil as well as good days. The Unionist party, who within a few

months of the very speech which is now on their lips pursued him
with harsh ingratitude, have no such right.

Yours faithfully
WINSTON S. CHURCHILL

As a result of these protests the meeting was transferred from the
Ulster Hall which lay in the strongly Protestant area to a large
marquee at the Celtic Road football ground in the Catholic working-
class district. Members of the government were also worried about
what might happen in Belfast.

Master of Elibank to WSC

EXTRACT

Stafford Hotel
St James's Place

31 January 1912

. . . The Police report that great quantities of bolts & rivets have
been abstracted from the yards, and many revolvers have been taken
out of pawn. My own feeling is that there will be no serious riot,
but that isolated disturbance may take place is probable.

In any case I implore you not to bring Mrs Churchill with you:
her presence might be a source of great embarrassment, and moreover you cannot satisfy yourself that she does not run considerable
risk.

Forgive me for writing thus freely — but I know you well enough
to do so.

And Mrs Churchill must also forgive me for interfering with a
very natural impulse and in accordance with what all would expect
of her. . . .

Extraordinary precautions had to be taken to protect Churchill
and his wife who had insisted on accompanying him. The *Manchester Guardian* reported that the railway line from Larne, where
the Churchills landed in Ireland, to Belfast was patrolled by police
to prevent sabotage. A hostile crowd of nearly 10,000 greeted them
outside the Grand Central Hotel in Belfast, where they were staying.
On February 9 *The Times,* describing the drive from the hotel to the
Celtic Road, reported, "As each car made its way through, men thrust
their heads in and uttered fearful menaces and imprecations. It

seemed to me," wrote the *Times* reporter, "that Mr Churchill was taking a greater risk than ever he expected. . . . Yet he never flinched and took hostility visualised as well as vocalised calmly and no harm befell him." The *Manchester Guardian* said that the back wheels of the Churchills' car were lifted eighteen inches off the ground by the angry crowd before the police beat them off. Four battalions of infantry guarded the route.

When Churchill's party reached the Falls neighbourhood — the Roman Catholic district of Belfast, there was "a transition from scowls to smiles." *The Times* reported Churchill as having commented. "It was splendid. The wicked dug the pit and they tumbled into it themselves." It was a wet afternoon and Churchill addressed the crowd of 5,000 Irish Nationalists, and a handful of Unionist hecklers. He told them that the main safeguard for the Protestants of Ulster and Ireland would be the Irish Parliament, "which will be so constituted, both in its House of Commons and in its Senate, as to be fully and fairly representative of the Irish nation — of Protestants as well as Catholics, of urban interests as well as of agricultural interests, of minorities even more than majorities." And then he went on to set out six further safeguards which would provide the "additional rampart" for the protection of the Protestants.

First, the Crown will be able to refuse assent to an unjust Bill.

Secondly, the Imperial Parliament will be able to repeal such a Bill or enact another law.

Thirdly, the Home Rule Bill will contain provisions safeguarding religious freedom and fair play for both Protestants and Roman Catholics.

Fourthly, if any law passed in Ireland transgressed the limit laid down by the Home Rule Act, then the Privy Council would be able to declare it void.

Fifthly, the Home Rule system will be worked in the face of Great Britain as well as Ireland. The Imperial Parliament is overwhelmingly Protestant, and would certainly resent any attempt to act in a spirit of religious intolerance or unfairness.

Sixthly, the power of the Imperial Parliament to interfere is unquestioned in law, and equally unquestioned in fact, for all military forces will be under the Imperial control. . . .

He continued:

> We look forward to a time which has long been retarded and which
> we believe is now, when this island — instead of being a disruptive
> force in the British Empire — shall be transformed into a new centre
> of Union, when the harsh and lamentable cry of reproach which so
> long jarred upon the concert of Empire will die away, when the
> accursed machinery, by which the hatred manufactured and pre-
> served will be broken for ever.

And remembering his experience in South Africa, he continued:

> We have made friends with our enemies — can we not make friends
> with our comrades too? . . .

He said that the division of Ireland damaged the unity of the Empire. He recalled how Ireland had suffered in the past and talked of
hope for the future:

> Only think if we had their aid instead of their enmity, their help
> instead of their opposition, how much smoother our path would be,
> how much quicker our progress, how much brighter our fortunes.

Two months later on April 9 Carson took the chair at a Unionist
meeting at the showgrounds of the Royal Agricultural Society outside
Belfast. Bonar Law, Londonderry and Walter Long addressed a
crowd of 100,000 people. Bonar Law said:

> The Government have erected by their Parliament Act a boom
> against you to shut you off from the help of the British people. You
> will burst that boom. That help will come and when the crisis is
> over men will say to you in words not unlike those used by Pitt —
> You have saved yourselves by your exertions and you will save the
> Empire by your example.

Carson repudiated conciliation. "Even if both parties in Great
Britain were committed to Home Rule, Ulster would still resist."
    On April 11 the Home Rule Bill was introduced; on April 16 it
was given its first reading and on April 30 its second reading. On
this occasion Churchill addressed the House; having expressed annoyance at the fact that the resurrection of such an old issue should

still cause division between the two parties he said that he spoke "from a point of view of one of many of its younger Members to whom the controversies of the 1880s and 1890s never made their appeal and one of those many Members of the House whose active political life lies wholly or almost wholly in the new century."

> I look at the Irish issue with a "modern eye" happily emancipated from the prejudices and passions of a bygone generation. . . . The Home Rule movement in its whole course and character has been a modifying and moderating movement designed to secure the recognition of Irish claims within the circuit of Empire. . . .
>
> At one sweep of the wand, they [the Ulstermen] could sweep the Irish question out of life and into history and free the British realm of the canker which poisoned its heart for generations. If they refuse, if they take to the boats, all we say is they shall not obstruct the work of salvage and we shall go forward at any rate to the end.

He then accused Bonar Law of "almost treasonable activity": "These speeches he and Sir Edward Carson have been making at large gatherings in the country, have not been warnings to the Government, but incitements to the Orangemen. As the detestable incidents which have lately taken place in Belfast prove they have been only too well interpreted by those to whom they were addressed. . . . Had British statesmen and leaders of great parties in the past allowed their thoughts so lightly to turn to projects of bloodshed within the bosom of the country, we should have shared the follies of Poland."

Bonar Law replied to Churchill's rebuke at a Unionist rally at Blenheim on July 27 accusing the Government of being "a revolutionary committee which has seized upon despotic power by fraud. In our opposition to them we shall not be guided by considerations or bound by the restraints which would influence us in an ordinary constitutional struggle. . . . They may, perhaps they will, carry their Home Rule Bill through the House of Commons but what then? I said the other day in the House of Commons and I repeat here that there are things stronger than Parliamentary majorities. . . . I can imagine no length of resistance to which Ulster can go in which I should not be prepared to support them, and in which, in my belief, they would not be supported by the overwhelming majority of the British people."

In August Churchill wrote to Redmond seeking to find an honourable and peaceful solution to the problem.

WSC to John Redmond

EXTRACT

31 August 1912

. . . The opposition of three or four counties is the only obstacle which now stands in the way of Home Rule. You and your friends ought to be thinking of some way round this. No doubt you are, with your usual political foresight.

The Unionist Party have now staked their whole power to fight Home Rule on this foundation. Remove it, and the path in my judgement is absolutely clear. I do not believe there is any real feeling against Home Rule in the Tory Party apart from the Ulster question, but they hate the Government, are bitterly desirous of turning it out, and see in the resistance of Ulster an extraparliamentary force, which they will not hesitate to use to the full.

I have been pondering a great deal over this matter, and my general view is just what I told you earlier this year — namely that something should be done to afford the characteristically Protestant and Orange counties the option of a moratorium of several years before acceding to an Irish Parliament. I think the time approaches when such an offer should be made — and it would come much better from the Irish leaders than from the Government. No doubt that the winter session will be critical. Much is to be apprehended from a combination of the rancour of a party in the ascendant and the fanaticism of these stubborn and determined Orangemen. These opinions are personal so far as I am concerned — they have not been arrived at from consultation, they are for your private eye alone. . . .

In an open letter to Sir George Ritchie, Chairman of the Dundee Liberal Association, on September 8 Churchill wrote: "The vital thing is to set up before the General Election the Irish Parliament in Dublin. Once set up it can never be cast down. As Pym said, 'None have gone about to break up Parliaments, but that Parliaments have broken them up.' " He thought that anything short of that might easily be brushed away by a Tory administration with a sub-

servient House of Lords. The act of setting up an Irish Parliament
would lead to peace and conciliation.

> The economic pressure which the rest of Ireland could gradually
> bring to bear upon Belfast, and the feeling of confidence which
> would be created if the Irish Parliament was a dignified and success-
> ful body, would, I believe, overcome misgivings of the Orangemen,
> or at any rate, of a majority in the Orange counties, in the course of
> a few years. . . .
> I would also, if I had my way, at an early stage in the proceedings
> take power to delay the operation of the Act in regard to certain
> counties where it was clear that the majority were opposed to it. In
> this way no excuse or opportunity would be given for any act of
> violence or organised resistance to the law, and the Orange party
> would be broken up and could be dealt with in detail. . . .

*

When Parliament reassembled in the autumn, Unionist threats of
rebellion and civil war in Ulster, particularly on the part of Bonar
Law, had reached such proportions that the Cabinet did not feel
that it would be possible to make any progress with the Home Rule
Bill without the sort of parliamentary sanctions against the Tories
that had proved necessary to the discharge of public business against
the Irish Nationalists in the previous century. Then it had been necessary to introduce the closure or *clôture* as it was known in the
French Assembly, for the Irish had made all legislation impossible
in order to draw attention to their grievances. Now the same tactics
were to be employed against the Unionists, who claimed to be the
upholders of parliamentary government and the Constitution. Accordingly on October 10 Asquith announced that the closure accompanied by the "guillotine" would be introduced. This meant that a
timetable for the Bill would be announced and that discussion would
cease at a set hour each day so that whatever the merits of the argument the Government's business might be accomplished at the hour
and on the day which had been predetermined and for which parliamentary sanction had already been obtained. This announcement
was received with indignation from the Unionists. Bonar Law tabled

an amendment which stated that while admittedly the Constitution was in suspence, the House declined to restrict discussion, denounced the resolution as the climax of an ignoble conspiracy and stated that the time allocated was totally inadequate. He warned that Ulster might explode at any moment; if Home Rule were forced upon it, Heaven help Great Britain; if there were bloodshed the guilt would be on the Ministry. Churchill retorted that those who "talk of revolution ought to be prepared for the guillotine."

While this matter continued to agitate the Parliament Churchill was touring the country as First Lord of the Admiralty talking about sea-power; but at the same time he was also pressing the cause of Home Rule upon the electorate. He talked a good deal about devolution and developed his somewhat utopian plan for the revival of the heptarchy. This was not one of his bellicose periods: he stressed that there should be no violence and urged courses of moderation upon his hearers. Though he played a leading part in pressing for Home Rule his heart was now fully engaged with the Navy. The safety of the country preoccupied every waking moment and he saw an Irish settlement as vital for the safety of England.

Despite the strong powers which the Government had taken to ensure the passage of their business through the Commons the ingenuity and enterprise of the Tory backbencher Sir Frederick Banbury led to a snap vote over the financial provisions of the Home Rule Bill on November 11. In the afternoon, with only two Cabinet Ministers in the Chamber and Liberal attendance slack, the Government was defeated by 21 votes. The Unionist attendance was good and seemed to denote a pre-concerted plan. The Unionists were delighted; in their exuberance they shouted the traditional chant, "Resign, resign." Asquith then moved the adjournment which was carried without a division. As each Minister left the Chamber the Opposition called out irrelevantly "Good-bye, good-bye; take your pension: good-bye": irrelevantly, for even if they had resigned, there were no pensions to be had — not even, as there is today, £4,000 a year for the Prime Minister.

Two days later Asquith moved that Banbury's amendment be rescinded. The motion was successfully carried, and great uproar resulted. As Churchill left the Chamber he mockingly waved his handkerchief at the Opposition. A Unionist Member, Ronald McNeill, an Ulsterman, lost his sense of parliamentary decorum and threw the Speaker's Copy of Standing Orders which lay upon the table. It hit Churchill and drew blood. His friend Jack Seely escorted him from the House. Many years later McNeill served as Financial Secretary when Churchill was Chancellor of the Exchequer in Stanley Baldwin's Government. Churchill had then to reprove McNeill for bringing his lunch to the Treasury in a cardboard box. After the Second World War the book was sent to Churchill and it reposes today in the author's library at Stour. What might have been an ugly scene was aborted by Will Crooks, Labour Member for Woolwich, who started singing "Auld lang Syne." The following day in the House McNeill made a full apology which the First Lord accepted. The Speaker suggested that McNeill's conduct should be overlooked, but he urged that his action should not be regarded in the future as a parliamentary precedent for the throwing of books.

*

By August of 1913 the Home Rule Bill was nearing the end of its passage through Parliament. It had passed twice through the Commons and had been rejected twice by the Lords. The Parliament Act ensured that the Lords could not prevent it becoming law after the third reading in the Commons; thus it would become effective by the middle of 1914. The Ulster situation was still deteriorating. Carson's threat to set up a provisional government was beginning to take on a more concrete shape and the Government realized that it was more than mere bluff. Nearly half a million Ulster men and women had signed, under the exhortation of Carson and other Unionist orators, the "Solemn Covenant" which pledged them to use "all means" to defeat Home Rule and, if a Home Rule Parliament were forced on them, to refuse to recognize its authority. Volunteers were drilling in Ulster and an armed clash seemed imminent.

Bonar Law, as in March 1912, again sought to involve the Crown in the Irish issue by urging the King to dissolve Parliament. It is clear that the Tory leaders thought that they would be more successful in putting pressure on the King than they would be in attempting a compromise with the Government.

Asquith refused to accept this unconstitutional move and maintained that the King had no right to dismiss an elected Government with a majority in the House of Commons. The King now tried to interest the Tory leaders in compromise talks and invited Bonar Law and Lansdowne to Balmoral. On the Liberal side there were signs that a negotiated settlement might be acceptable. Loreburn, the former Liberal Lord Chancellor wrote to *The Times* suggesting a conference or direct communication between the Party leaders in order to prevent possible bloodshed.

Asquith disclosed to the King that he was sceptical as to whether Carson or Redmond would support Loreburn's proposals. He was alarmed that the King had taken Bonar Law's suggestion of dissolution seriously and authorized Churchill to warn the King against any further unconstitutional overtures by the Unionists:

H. H. Asquith to WSC

12 September 1913　　　　　　　　　　　　　Hopeman Lodge
　　　　　　　　　　　　　　　　　　　　　　　　Hopeman
Secret　　　　　　　　　　　　　　　　　　　　Morayshire

My dear Winston,

I understand that it is your turn to go to Balmoral next week: so I send a word of friendly warning.

You will find the Royal mind obsessed, and the Royal tongue exceptionally fluid and voluble.

I have just sent there a Memn, in which I have endeavoured, with all plainness and faithfulness, to make clear what are, *and what are not* the functions of a Constitutional Sovereign in regard to legislation.

The important thing is to emphasise the dangers of rejection, when the ship is just reaching port. An ungovernable Ireland is a much more serious prospect than rioting in 4 counties — serious (and, if possible, to be avoided) as the latter is.

As to a round table, I am all for it, provided the confabulations are to proceed upon some definite basis, and not to be mere talking at large.

　　　　　　　　　　　　　　　　　　　　　　　Yours always
　　　　　　　　　　　　　　　　　　　　　　　H H A

Churchill was further authorized to discuss the possibility of informal talks with Bonar Law who was also going to be at Balmoral. Bonar Law reported to Carson on these talks and said that he had told Churchill that the situation was desperate for both Parties but worse for the Liberals; he had said that "we would stick at nothing when it came to the point," that as soon as the Bill was passed Carson would take control of Ulster and allow no other authority in that area. Churchill spoke, according to Bonar Law, in a "half-hearted way" of stopping sea and rail communications, but Bonar Law said that that would interfere with the whole of Ireland as well as England and Scotland. Bonar Law said that if the Home Rule Bill were passed and the whole of the Unionist Party supported Ulster, the Unionist members may be turned out of the Commons and in this case "undoubtedly we should regard it as civil war." "Does he [Churchill] suppose the Army would obey orders to exercise force in Ulster?" Having stated his position clearly to Churchill Bonar Law felt sure that Asquith would suggest a private meeting with Landsdowne or himself. On September 17 Stamfordham recorded in his diary that Churchill's talk with Bonar Law had been a "long and pleasant one." He wrote that Churchill was hopeful of a solution. "History teaches us that in such cases British common sense generally triumphs." Lord Stamfordham's account continues:

Lord Stamfordham's Diary
(Royal Archives)
EXTRACT

17 September 1913

. . . Up till now he had not been in favour of a conference & thought the right time for it had not arrived & that things must get worse. But he has changed his opinion & now believes that if the Opposition will come into Conference with reassurable proposals, the Govt which has always been ready to consider any suggestions, would gladly treat with them. He has always admitted that Ulster has a case. If Ireland has the right to claim separate government from England, Ulster cannot be refused similar exemption from Government by an Irish Parliament. But he strongly resents that Ulster should talk of "Civil War" & do everything in her power to stir up

rebellion before even the H.R. bill is [debated] let alone before the
Irish Parliament is set up, from which rule they look for persecution
& tyrannical injustice. Naturally the Opposition wish to turn out
the Government.

But it is not "playing the game" to try & do this by trying to raise
a threat of civil war.

Personally he would take a very strong line if the Navy or Army
hesitated to put down any opposition to the responsible executive
— Ireland has been earnestly waiting for the fulfilment of her dream
for the past 30 years. Is it likely that she can now stand by & see the
cup almost at her lips, dashed to the ground. If by chance the Bill
is killed we shall be faced with similar difficulties in S & W Ireland.
If only Sir E. Carson does not go too far arrangements will be arrived at. The Irish party will consider any scheme for securing
their objects peacefully. . . .

Asquith replied favourably to Churchill's report on his talks with
Bonar Law. "I always thought (and said) that, in the end, we should
probably have to make some sort of bargain about Ulster as the price
of Home Rule," he wrote to Churchill on September 19. He listed
three points which now would bear careful consideration.

1. The recent developments of Carsonism have much stiffened the
backs of some moderate men against any seeming concession to bluff
and blackmail.

2. Secrecy in these matters is nowadays impossible. What is going
on always leaks out — generally in the shape of perverted and misleading gossip.

3. Consultations from which both Redmond and Carson were excluded — I do not mean corporally, but in the sense of not being
taken into counsel — would (apart from other difficulties) be only
of provisional value.

He discredited Bonar Law's threats of organised disorder as "almost
puerile in their crudity." A repetition of the row in the previous
November only on a larger scale "would be repellent to the best elements in their party, and be taken in the country as an admission
that the game was up. There is no folly, however, of which the present Tory leadership is incapable."

Lansdowne, concurring with Bonar Law's position, commented on the Balmoral talks in a letter to him dated September 20: "The fact that Winston Churchill should have been authorised to speak to you is interesting and may be significant — but it may have been only an attempt to draw your fire." On September 23 Balfour wrote to Bonar Law agreeing that a dissolution would be the best thing for the Unionist Party before the Home Rule Bill could be passed. However, he explained the King's fears of the Crown being compromised by such action, which would not only affect the monarchy at home but also "in the great Dominions, where the Home Rule policy has always found favour."

Meanwhile F. E. Smith had the idea of excluding Ulster from any arrangement for Irish Home Rule. He had put this idea forward in conversation with the King at the end of September and again in his speech at West Branwich on his return to England from a tour of inspection of Ulster Volunteers which he had made with Carson at the beginning of October. F. E. Smith's ideas did not commend themselves to his more diehard colleagues, and he wrote to Churchill:

F. E. Smith to WSC

5 October 1913   4 Elm Court
                                                       Temple

Dear W,

I think you will agree that I have played up well. I hope you will do the same now.

Couldn't you ask — what does Sir Ed Carson mean by exclusion? Does he mean that he and his friends will abandon a factious opposition in that part of Ireland when they are in so small a minority? Does he mean that he and his friends will remember that they are Irishmen and apply their ability and influence to make the experiment a success in the South?

But you can do the thing much better than I can suggest. Only do play up. I have run no small risks and incurred considerable censure.

Yours ever

F E

Carson is most reasonable. I think he wd be glad to meet you.

Churchill's friendship with F. E. Smith was very close at this time; they worked tirelessly behind the scenes to produce an accommodation over Irish and other matters that might hamper national unity. Both were alive to the German danger and the need of Britain to face it. They saw each other so often that they probably did not correspond very much. In any case, the above is one of the few letters that survives between them.

On October 8 Asquith wrote to Bonar Law in the light of the Balmoral talks. He said that anything "in the nature of a 'conference' . . . between the leaders of the parties under existing conditions, is out of the question," but he did agree to the idea of "an informal conversation, of a strictly confidential character" between himself and the Tory leader. On the same day Churchill made a conciliatory speech at Dundee. He said that the claim of Ulster for special consideration could not be ignored and that far-reaching alterations to the Bill were possible — but only by agreement and goodwill. The following day he spoke at Lochee where he said that the Government would stay the full course and go to the country in 1915 with an Irish settlement in complete form on the Statute Book.

Difficulties over a settlement came, however, from both sides. T. P. O'Connor, the Irish Nationalist MP for the Scotland Division of Liverpool, wrote to Churchill on October 7 expressing the disquiet of the Irish Party at the trend of events. "The Nationalists were irreconcilably hostile to any break up of the country. . . . They would positively prefer a postponement of Home Rule for some years rather than consent to such a mutilation of the country." O'Connor was also opposed to a conference as he thought that the Tories would "lay down impossible terms." Carson and Lansdowne on the other hand realized that the desertion of Unionist forces in South and West Ireland would follow an Irish settlement. Lansdowne wrote to Carson on October 11: "If the overture which has been made by Asquith to Bonar Law leads to further discussion, we shall have an extremely difficult hand of cards to play." He was also pessimistic about a settlement.

On October 18 Churchill spoke at Manchester; his speech was mainly devoted to a renewal of the proposal for a Naval Holiday. But as usual at this time he also spoke of Ireland. He continued to tread the uneasy path between the two antagonistic forces. He laid great stress on the fact that a settlement could only be compatible with the principle of an Irish Parliament and an executive responsible to it and not destructive of the unity of Ireland.

Another friendship across the floor of the House of Commons which Churchill nourished in these bitter years was with Austen Chamberlain, the son of the famous Joe who had wrecked the Liberal Party over Home Rule and the Tory Party over Tariff Reform. When the elder Chamberlain had separated himself from Balfour in 1903 to preach the gospel of Tariff Reform, Austen had been promoted from Postmaster-General to Chancellor of the Exchequer. This was a Balfourian sop to Joe to dissuade him from kicking over the traces altogether. Austen had a good mind and a handsome appearance. He affected his father's monocle, but not his orchid. Austen's friendship with Churchill was to be lifelong. Though he filled many of the highest offices, like his father he never reached the summit, as did his half-brother Neville, a man of more meagre parts and understanding. Of Austen, Churchill was to write in *Great Contemporaries,* "he always played the game, and he always lost."

In late November 1913 Austen Chamberlain discussed the Irish problem with Churchill on board the Admiralty yacht, *Enchantress.* Afterwards Chamberlain prepared a long and detailed memorandum for Bonar Law on the "very frank but also very discursive" talks they had had. It illustrates how far Churchill was prepared to go at this time in order to reach a settlement. Churchill suggested that the Government would be prepared to exclude Ulster, at least for a limited period until she had "voted herself in," thus antagonizing Redmond upon whose support the Government had relied so much in the past. They discussed in detail all the points on which both sides might give concessions. In his memorandum on their conversation Chamberlain gave a graphic account of what passed between them.

In answer to W's opening remark I said that I had assumed that Asquith's Ladybank speech meant that he was prepared upon conditions to exclude Ulster. He replied: "We have never excluded that possibility — never." Of course Redmond hated it, but they were not absolutely bound to R. and he was not indispensable to them.

They would not allow Ulster to veto Home Rule, but they had never excluded the possibility of separate treatment for Ulster. This was repeated more than once in the course of our talk. He added that he and Lloyd George had proposed to the Cabinet Committee on the Bill to exclude Ulster from the first. Loreburn had been particularly opposed to this. "I asked them," said W. "But how far are you prepared to go? Are you ready to plant guns in the streets of Belfast and shoot people down?" Loreburn would only say pompously: "I shall be prepared to do my duty."

W. said that there were three ways of dealing with Ulster:

(1) Home Rule within Home Rule, e.g. grant to her the nomination of all executive officers within the province.

(2) Exclusion for a fixed term — say so long that two general elections must have intervened — and then exclusion if Parliament had not otherwise decided in the interval.

(3) Exclusion till Ulster voted herself in — the Bill to provide that a vote should be taken in 5 or 10 years.

I replied that I thought it quite useless to enter on conversations at all unless the Govt was prepared at least to take the third course, i.e. exclusion till Ulster voted for inclusion.

He pressed a little for (2) saying that some concession on this point might make it much easier to meet Carson's wishes on the boundary question. "There was a fringe of Covenanters in Counties whose exclusion Carson could not ask for. They would be a great difficulty to Carson." Concession by us on (2) might enable them to solve this difficulty on terms more favorable to Carson. I did not ask what the Counties were, merely saying that I thought Ulster would regard the suggestion as a trap. She would say: We are to disarm now that we may more easily be gobbled up afterwards.

W. repeated more than once that exclusion was possible as part of a compromise or settlement by common assent — even, as I understand, if the assent was merely passive. And he said more than once that tho' he was prepared to put down disorder ruthlessly, he did not consider that they "had the right" to coerce men in the position of Ulstermen into submission to Home Rule.

I spoke of my speech at Bromsgrove on Thursday last. "Very important," said W. "Oh very important — yours and Lansdowne's. We had them before us at the Cabinet." I said I had better say at once that it was made — not indeed without some knowledge of my colleagues views but without any consultation with them.

It was done wholly on my own responsibility and committed no one except myself. I had received strong remonstrances on the subject — (here I rather exaggerated their number and importance) — and delay was not making for peace. If the House once meets the opportunity for peace will be gone. You will break the H. of C. in the process. That is bad, but worse remains behind. You will break the army, and then how is government to be carried on by anyone at home or abroad? That is why I spoke. He elaborated this argument dwelling on the dangers of strikes and so forth, and on the effect on India, South Africa, etc.

I said that my idea was that the bare exclusion of Ulster was the worst and most humiliating solution for them and it did not satisfy us. The Bill without Ulster was only one degree worse than the Bill with Ulster. So we must change the issue. They would say we always wanted HR all round. "That is true," he interrupted "we only adopted this course because in face of your opposition it was the most we could hope to carry!" "Very well," I rejoined, "you would say that, and I should say that this was the old Liberal Unionist policy."

W. attached great importance to my statement that though the scheme must be equally applicable and equally applied Ireland might be dealt with first. I said I put that in to meet Asquith's condition.

He suggested that it would be well to find out exactly what delegation of powers we had in mind and whether my "federalism" was or was not at all equivalent to what they had in mind. I replied that I had not thought it my business to make a plan but why did not A. resume his conversations with Bonar Law. He would then find out whether B.L. was prepared to consider such a solution, and how far he could carry agreement. He said that A. could not make any advances at present. He did not think the time had come. Leaders might be prepared but parties were not. Public opinion had got to have a shock. Both sides had to make speeches full of party claptrap and no surrender, and then insert a few sentences at the end for the wise and discerning on the other side to see and ponder. "A little red blood had got to flow" and then public opinion would wake up, and then — ! "And you must remember that we think that time is on our side. We shall give no provocation. The Ulstermen will have no excuse, and we think that public opinion will not support them if they wantonly attack."

I said that this was very dangerous. It was a gamble on bloodshed. They might win, or we might win, but either way there was a national disaster. I did not suggest that A. should make public advances but why should he not at once resume his conversations with B.L.

"Oh," said W., "he means to do that. He will do that. But they could not scrap their Bill before they knew that there was agreement as to a substitute." "Well," I replied, "you ask me for a scheme. I have not got one. But suppose A. were to go to B.L. and offer as part of a federal settlement by consent:

(1) To reserve all powers not specifically delegated.

(2) To reserve customs and excise.

(3) To reserve the Post Office.

(4) To reserve the judiciary, or at least all appointments to the High Court.

(5) To give Ulster its own Parliament.

I believe that B.L. who doubtless would be in consultation with his colleagues could not refuse such an offer and I do not think that A. would find it very difficult to draw up eight or ten propositions as to the powers remaining to be delegated."

We discussed 1 and 4 a little. W. did not raise any objection. To 2 and 3 A. had already agreed. 5 followed from our whole conversation.

W. again spoke of the feeling of parties that we must wait etc. and then said (and this he repeated more than once) "that we ought to be prepared to turn the corner" by the exclusion of Ulster, and afterwards we could see what more could be done, whilst I again pressed the danger of delay if anything was to be done at all.

And so we travelled more than once over the same ground, but this includes all that is important in regard to Ireland.

Incidentally he told me that A. was "supreme" in the Cabinet but very self-contained, reserved and slow to speak. "He holds the casting vote and he thinks it unfair to use it until all have spoken."

Also A. had told him that "B.L. was a much better man to do business with than Balfour." I see I have omitted to say that in the course of our conversation I said to him that, though I would try to find a more conciliatory way of expressing myself if our talk were more formal, he would understand that my root objection to H.R.

was to the idea of "Ireland a Nation." That was separation and must
issue in separation. He replied that that was to deny the Irish a sentiment of any satisfaction in the enjoyment of its Parliament. "You are
like the R.C. Church which admits the necessity of the marriage bed
but holds that you must find no pleasure in the enjoyment of it.
But," he went on, "there can be no nation as long as they accept a
subsidy and we can always bring them to book by withholding
supplies."

Chamberlain summed up the meeting by saying: "The impression
left on my mind by the whole conversation is that W. genuinely
wants a settlement and that so do Lloyd George, Grey and Asquith,
but that as to the means they have no clear idea. And that the hot
and cold fits succeed each other pretty quickly; that A. means to 'wait
and see' and will not give his 'casting vote' till the last moment."

However, speaking in Leeds before the National Liberal Federation on November 27, Asquith adopted a more resolute position on
Home Rule. He claimed that the Bill was a well-conceived and carefully considered measure with adequate safeguards against religious
or political persecution. He said that he would not be intimidated by
violent threats, but was ready to listen to reasoned demands for compromise. He stressed the unity of opinion in the Cabinet and concluded by saying that the Government would not betray the trust
which the majority of the Irish people committed to their charge.
Chamberlain was not pleased by Asquith's speech and wrote to
Churchill:

Austen Chamberlain to WSC

29 November 1913   9 Egerton Place

Secret

My dear Winston,
   "And what do you think of it all?" as Rosebery once said to a
meeting. You told me that Asquith would say nothing at Leeds. I
thought that dangerous, but he has done infinitely worse.
   When he spoke at Ladybank we thought his offer was made in good
faith & that he meant business. Selborne, Lansdowne & I, in the
order named, all advanced to meet him, thereupon he withdraws.

He may say what he likes, but he *has* slammed the door in our faces. It is difficult now to think that the Ladybank offer was made in good faith & impossible to believe that he means business. He has blown conciliation to the winds.

Could I have foreseen the terms of his speech (which I have only just been able to read in full) I would have talked navy shop with you — or the fashions or feminism or anything *except* the Irish question!

Well! He has chosen, but I would not have his responsibility on my hands. He would scarcely have spoken differently if he had deliberately set himself to provoke strife. I presume that he knew what he was doing.

Yrs sincerely
AUSTEN CHAMBERLAIN

PS We all three (i.e. my wife, Joe & myself) have the pleasantest memories of our trip & of your kindness.

Asquith and Bonar Law had met privately on three occasions to discuss the possibility of a solution to the Ulster problem, but these meetings came to nothing. The forces on both sides remained irreconcilable. Redmond had told Asquith on November 17 that the Nationalists would go no farther than autonomy for Ulster under the final supremacy of a Dublin Parliament. It is clear that neither Carson nor Bonar Law would accept anything less than at least the temporary exclusion of Ulster from the provisions of the Home Rule Bill. At the beginning of 1914 all compromise talks on Ireland had failed.

Meanwhile the intransigence of Ulster dominated men's minds. Sir Horace Plunkett, a moderate Unionist who had once sat for a Dublin seat and who later accepted Home Rule, wrote to *The Times* on 10 February 1914:

> If the Home Rule Bill passes through Parliament, without substantial modifications, there will break out in Ireland either civil war or unpremeditated and uncontrolled sectarian outrages.

The same day *The Times,* now dominated by Northcliffe, wrote in a leader on Carson's Volunteer Movement:

It is not the single act of a handful of obscure plotters and of no single class. It is the rising of a whole organised community, permeated, from peer to labourer and artisan, by an unshakeable determination to maintain the full rights of British citizenship bequeathed to them by their father.

It was in this atmosphere that Asquith introduced a compromise plan into the House of Commons on March 9 without the support of the Unionist Opposition. An Amending Bill was passed to modify the Home Rule Bill. This enabled each of the Ulster counties to decide by a plebiscite in favour of exclusion for six years from the enactment of the Home Rule Bill. At the end of that period the counties were to be incorporated with the rest of Ireland. The settlement would have given the Tories two general elections in which to reverse Home Rule. If they won neither of them they would not be able to change the nature of the Irish Settlement. Carson denounced Asquith's proposal, calling it "sentence of death with a stay of execution for six years."

13

The Curragh

IT SEEMED NOW as if all hope of a peaceful settlement had been destroyed. The actions and language of Ulster Unionists and Tory politicians could not be dismissed as mere bluff. Early in 1914 Bonar Law seriously contemplated using the remaining power of the Lords to reject the passage of the annual Bill which was necessary to permit the maintenance of a standing army in time of peace. The rejection of the "Army Annual," as it was known, and which had always been a formality, would have destroyed the Government's power to act in a national emergency. The loss of the supreme arbitrament of force on which in the final analysis all civilized Government must depend would have led to widespread bloodshed and anarchy. The police would have been impotent to deal with the situation which seemed imminent in Ulster.

A Government report for Ireland in January 1914 indicated that there was likelihood of disorder in Belfast, Antrim, Cavan, Donegal, Down, Tyrone and Londonderry. The Tyrone report from the District Inspector dated January 8 stated that the Ulster Volunteers intended to disarm all police without bloodshed and to seize all arms at military barracks in Ulster; wax impressions of the keys of military stores and magazines were reported to be in the possession of the Volunteers. The report added that "while there is to be no premature outbreak of hostilities, if any attempt is made to seize the arms of the Volunteers, the Volunteers are to resist with arms." Asquith reported this information fully to the King on March 13:

H. H. Asquith to the King
(Royal Archives)

EXTRACT

13 March 1914   10 Downing Street

. . . The Cabinet met yesterday. Some considerable time was given
to a discussion of the military situation in Ulster, suggested by the
latest series of police reports, which indicates the possibility of attempts on the part of the "volunteers" to seize, by coups de main,
police and military barracks, and depots of arms and ammunition.
A small committee of the Cabinet consisting of Lord Crewe, Birrell,
Churchill, Col Seely and Sir John Simon was appointed to look into
the matter in all its aspects, and report to the Cabinet. . . .

In the light of these reports plans were naturally drawn up to cope
with what seemed likely to be a dangerous emergency. There were
not many troops in Ulster and if the situation deteriorated it would
be necessary to reinforce them with units from the garrison at the
Curragh outside Dublin. Churchill was due to speak at Bradford on
March 14, and it was felt in Government circles that he should utter
a strong warning to Ulster. Lord Riddell wrote in his Diary:

Lloyd George told Churchill — "This is your opportunity. Providence has arranged it for you. You can make a speech that will ring
down the corridors of history. I could not do it. You are the only
member of the Cabinet who could make such a speech. You are
known to have been in favour of conciliation for Ulster. Now you
can say that having secured a compromise Ulstermen will have to
accept it or take the consequences."

The firm and measured tones in which Churchill spoke at Bradford
had been approved in advance by Asquith. So too had the grave and,
as some thought, provocative words with which he concluded. He
started by emphasizing his own and the Government's record of conciliation, he agreed that there was a strong case for special treatment
for Ulster, that the Government's Bill was constructed so that far-
reaching amendment was possible, but that this must come about only
by agreement. The Government refused to be influenced by threats.
He attacked Carson, who, he said, was engaged in "a treasonable

conspiracy." Asquith had asked "If Home Rule were to fail now, how would you govern the rest of Ireland?" Captain Craig, later Sir James Craig and then Viscount Craigavon, first Prime Minister of Northern Ireland, had replied: "We have done it before." Churchill commented on this: "There you get a true insight into the Tory mind — coercion for four-fifths of Ireland is a healthful, exhilarating and salutary exercise — but lay a finger on the Tory one fifth — sacrilege, tyranny, murder!"

He concluded by saying:

> As long as it affects the working man in England or nationalist peasants in Ireland there is no measure of military force which the Tory party will not readily employ. They denounce all violence except their own. They uphold all law except the law they choose to break. They are to select from the Statute Book the laws they will obey and the laws they will resist. . . . The veto of violence has replaced the veto of privilege. But if it should happen that the Constitution of the maintenance of order stand in the path of some Tory project, stand in the path of the realisation of some appetite or ambition which they have conceived, then they vie with the wildest anarchists in the language which they use against the Constitution, against law, order and all the means of maintaining order. And that is the political doctrine they salute the 20th century with.
>
> We are not going to have the realm of Great Britain sink to the condition of the Republic of Mexico . . . If all the loose, wanton and reckless chatter we have been forced to listen to these months is in the end to disclose a sinister revolutionary purpose, then I can only say to you "Let us go forward and put these grave matters to the proof."

The next day *The Times* commented: "His speech was rather that of a minister, who having carried the claims of his own Department against the formidable menace of the Radical rank and file (Naval Estimates) seemed to think it necessary to show that on an occasion he could shout defiance with the rest." *The Times* was wide of the mark. It is true that Lloyd George had encouraged him to make the speech but the words were very much his own, and certainly represented a mood shared by all the strongest elements in the Cabinet. Of course, the speech did not commend itself to the pacifist faction.

THE CURRAGH

N

Miles
0 10 20 30 40 50

===== Boundary of Six Counties

In his memoirs Sir Almeric Fitzroy described a luncheon party at 10 Downing Street shortly after the speech:

> The Prime Minister instanced the enthusiasm with which the speech was received, and the cheers with which Winston was greeted in the House of Commons, as a proof that it corresponded to the feelings of the party. Lord Morley reminded him that a great Prime Minister [*Walpole at the commencement of the Seven Years War*], who once lived in that house, on being told of the popular delirium with which the declaration of war had been welcomed, replied, "They are ringing their bells now, but in no long time they will be wringing their hands."

Riddell telephoned his congratulations and said: "It was absolutely necessary that there should be some plain speaking." Redmond regarded the speech as "superb" — "proof of what is our last word is also the last word of the Government." Lord Fisher wrote to Churchill on March 17: "I should say it's probably the best speech you ever made."

The crisis was now coming to a head. Asquith told the King on March 18 that the committee investigating the military situation in Ireland, of which Churchill was a member, had reported to the Cabinet that the depots of arms and ammunition at Armagh, Omagh, Enniskillen and Carrickfergus were in danger of being "rushed" and that the War Office had instructed the General Officer Commanding Forces in Ireland, Sir Arthur Paget, to have these places adequately guarded. Seely, Secretary of State for War, said that there were 23,000 regular troops stationed in Ireland but only 9,000 of these were in Ulster. Asquith's report to the King continued:

> The First Lord of the Admiralty stated the forthcoming practice of the 3rd Battle Squadron would take place at Lamlash on the Scottish coast, seventy miles from Belfast. He said the Admiral commanding in Irish waters had already taken precautions for the protection of coastguard stations. A cruiser will be stationed at or near Carrickfergus, and two or three destroyers sent to the South of Ireland.

Paget, in reply to the War Office instructions to reinforce the four garrisons in Ulster, said that "in the present state of the country" he was of the opinion "that such move of troops would create intense excitement in Ulster and possibly precipitate a crisis." He felt justified therefore in not moving the troops but he was keeping "a sufficient number in readiness to move at short notice should the situation develop into a more dangerous state."

The Government intended to act against Ulster by reinforcing its weak garrisons in the North. Most of the Army officers were Tories and many of them had connections of blood and property with Ulster; indeed, for the most part Irish regiments and Irish officers were involved. As a result of representations made by Paget and by Brigadier-General Gough, Commanding the 3rd Cavalry Brigade, the War Office became doubtful of the fidelity of the officers, particularly in the Cavalry Brigade. Thus occurred what was known at the time as the Curragh Mutiny, but what historians now agree should be more properly called the Curragh Incident. For though there was wide-spread disaffection on the part of the officers at the Curragh and gross dereliction of duty by the Director of Military Operations at the War Office, Henry Wilson, who betrayed the Government secrets to Bonar Law, no actual refusal to obey orders took place. The Incident arose in the main through the weakness of Seely and the disloyalty of Wilson. The situation was aggravated by the stupidity of General Paget and the strange perversity of Brigadier-General Gough. It was largely due to the tact and firmness of Major-General Sir Charles Fergusson, Commanding the 5th Division, of which Gough's cavalry brigade was a part, that the effects of widespread disaffection were not more serious than they were. But for him it might have been a mutiny.

By March 18 Paget had become alarmed at the turn of events and went to London for talks at the War Office. The meetings between Paget, the Cabinet sub-committee on Ulster, the army chiefs Ewart, Macready and French, and Asquith were held on March 18 and 19. No official record was kept of the series of meetings; McKenna, now Home Secretary, claimed in the House on April 8 that this was because "the oral instructions did not differ from the written ones of March 14." Churchill, however, wrote a long, undated memorandum in which he records what took place at the meetings and what took place in the days following them:

Memorandum by WSC

Admiralty

It is necessary that a clear understanding should be reached on the following points:

(1) Sir Arthur Paget received no orders or instructions for any movement of troops, beyond precautionary moves for guarding depots of ammunition and artillery at Dundalk. These movements were assented to in principle by Cabinet, and their details were approved at a conference, presided over by the Prime Minister, between members of the Cabinet, principal members of Army Council, and Sir Arthur Paget. No one believed that these precautionary moves were provocative or would lead to bloodshed. But it was necessary to take the possibility into consideration. As C in C in Ireland, and as a military officer carrying out those approved operations, Sir Arthur Paget had full discretionary power if new and totally different circumstances arose; if the depots were attacked or the columns marching to reinforce them were opposed, to make such dispositions of the force under his command as the emergency might require; and he was told that if necessary as the result of such events, large reinforcements would be sent to him from England. Six contingencies, separate or in combination, had to be borne in mind:

1st Armed opposition to the small bodies of troops moving to reinforce the depots.

2nd Attacks on those depots themselves, or on artillery at Dundalk.

3rd The blowing up or destruction of the railway lines.

4th The outbreak of a serious conflict in Belfast between the Protestant and Catholic elements following upon the proclamation of a Provisional Government, or arising from the general excitement.

5th Widespread sporadic disorders in the south and west of Ireland requiring use of large numbers of troops to protect scattered Protestants from reprisals made on them by the Catholic population.

(6th was added) viz — as organised on Paget's suggestion: Warlike movement of the Ulster Volunteers under their responsible leaders, created the impression in their minds that active operations of an aggressive and offensive character, and on an extensive scale, were to be undertaken at once against Ulster; and they transmitted this impression in a still cruder form to their Brigades and Regiments.

All these contingencies were present in Sir Arthur Paget's mind;

he was bound to be prepared for them; but none of them belong to the precautionary movements alone authorised by the Government, or were a probable or legitimate consequence of them.

When Sir Arthur Paget discussed the precautionary moves their contingent possibility of disaffection among the officers had to be considered. The Secretary of State gave him orally for his guidance in dealing with individual cases of officers refusing to act, should they occur, the following two principles:

First, that officers ordered to act in support of the Civil Power should not be permitted to resign their commissions, but must, if they refused to obey orders, be dismissed from the army.

Secondly, indulgence might be shown, as asked, to officers who were domiciled in or had special connection with Ulster.

There was no intention on the part of the Government or of the Secretary of State, or of any other member of the Government, or of the Army Council, that these two rules given for Sir Arthur Paget's guidance in case of grave emergencies arising, should be put as a test or a trial to the whole body of officers in the Irish command; nor did Sir Arthur Paget intend to do so; nor did he do so. When Sir Arthur Paget returned to Ireland, the grave anxiety which he felt that the precautionary moves would be misinterpreted or would be the signal for a violent counterstroke on the part of the Orange army, made him feel that he must know what officers and units he could rely upon if the worst came to the worst.

Upon his own initiative he summoned a conference of general officers and told them, not only of the precautionary moves, but of his anxieties at what might follow from them. These [views?] formed from Sir Arthur Paget's statement created the impression in their minds that active operations of an offensive and aggressive character, and on an extensive scale, were to be undertaken at once against Ulster; and they transmitted their impression in a still cruder form to their brigades and regiments. For this there was no warrant in any instructions which had been given by the Secretary of State or by the Government or any member of it to Sir Arthur Paget; nor was it intended by Sir Arthur Paget in anything which he said to his generals.

It has been repeatedly stated that Sir Arthur Paget said that the provocation would come from Ulster, and on this has been founded the charge that steps had been taken to arrange for or foment such provocative action on their part. This imputation is an astonishing perversion of the truth. The members of the Government who attended the conferences at which Sir Arthur Paget was present in London, were deeply impressed by that officer's strong sense of humanity and forbearance.

He repeatedly assured us that in no circumstances which could arise would he allow his troops to fire upon the Orangemen until the troops had themselves been fired at for some time and suffered effective loss from that fire. He impressed this point upon the Generals who met him in conference on Friday morning in order to make it clear to them that no aggressive action was contemplated by the orders on which he was acting and in order to make it clear to them the gulf which existed between the purely precautionary moves which he had been authorised to make, and the grave but improbable consequences which might follow from them. Indeed, on the Saturday when he visited the Cavalry Brigade at the Curragh in order to reassure the officers who had been thrown into such natural consternation and distress by the question put to them, Sir Arthur Paget went so far as to say that, not only would he never give the order for the troops to fire until they had first been attacked and had suffered loss, but that he intended himself to walk out in front and be shot down by the Orangemen before any firing in reply would be ordered of the troops. It is an extraordinary instance of the perversions of the truth which malice and rumour can effect, that these statements should have been twisted into a foundation for the vilest of calumnies.

To sum up:

1. While Sir Arthur Paget had discretionary power to take any action which a great and sudden emergency might require, he had received no directions from any quarter to take any action outside the precautionary moves for guarding the depots; and no orders were ever issued by him (except stand-by orders) for any purpose or plan outside these moves.

2. Sir Arthur Paget was never directed to subject the officers under his command to the test of whether they would declare themselves ready to take the offensive in military operations against Ulster, or be dismissed the service; nor did he intend at any time to force that alternative upon them.

3. So far from lending himself to any scheme intended to provoke wantonly a collision with the Ulster volunteers, Sir Arthur Paget

WSC with officials of the Board of Trade;
Edward Marsh at the door

Drafting a bill at the Board of Trade. Mr Churchill: "Oh I understand
all these figures, right enough. What we've got to do, gentlemen, is to
put some — er — *humanizing ginger* into 'em."

Max Beerbohm, 1909

MOVING TO 33 ECCLESTON SQUARE, 1909

Mrs. Churchill with a friend

WSC AND
MRS CHURCHILL
VISIT THE FIRST
LABOUR EXCHANGE,
WHITECHAPEL, 1910

LADY RANDOLPH CHURCHILL

WSC, Home Secretary, and Reginald McKenna, First Lord
of the Admiralty, on their way to the Cabinet, 1909

WSC AND THE KAISER AT THE GERMAN ARMY
MANOEUVRES, 1909

WSC AND DAVID LLOYD GEORGE

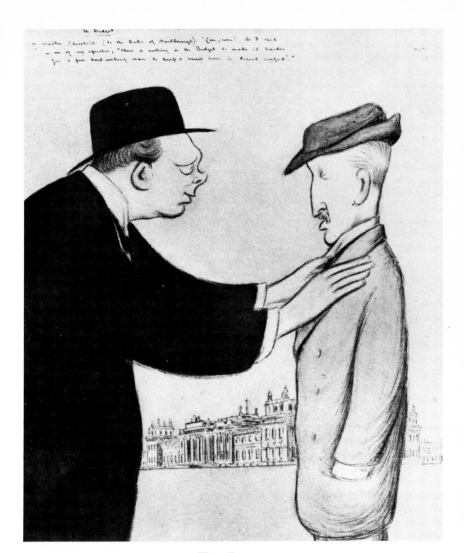

THE BUDGET

Winston Churchill (to the Duke of Marlborough) : "Come, come! As I said in one of my speeches, 'there is nothing in the Budget to make it harder for a poor hard-working man to keep a decent home in comfort.'"

Max Beerbohm, 1910

John Redmond

Sir Edward Carson

F. E. SMITH

ANDREW BONAR LAW,
1911

MRS CHURCHILL WITH
HER DAUGHTER DIANA,
1910

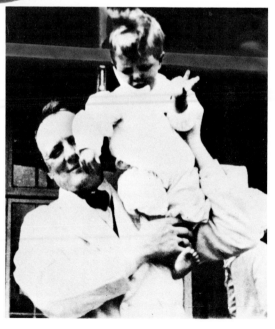

WSC WITH THE AUTHOR
AT THE SEASIDE,
1912

DESIGN FOR AN ADMIRALTY CHRISTMAS CARD

Bernard Partridge, *Punch*, 11 December 1912

WSC WITH
JACK SEELY

LORD NORTHCLIFFE
AND WSC AT HENDON

WSC INSPECTS HMS *Mercury*, 1912

WSC AND MRS CHURCHILL LAND FROM
HMS *Enchantress*, CHANNEL ISLANDS, 1913

WSC WITH PRINCE LOUIS OF BATTENBURG

NEPTUNE'S ALLY

Bernard Partridge, *Punch*, 25 May 1914

CAPTAIN
GILBERT WILDMAN-
LUSHINGTON, R.M.

WSC AFTER FLYING OVER THE FLEET, 1914

resolved to observe every conceivable precaution which courage and humanity could suggest, to avoid a collision and to prevent blood-shed; and on this he was acting in the fullest harmony with what he knew were the wishes and hopes of the Government.

The course which events took in the next few days have been well described by many writers including Sir James Fergusson in his *The Curragh Incident*. He was the son of Major-General Sir Charles Fergusson, the commander of the 5th Division. The first event, from which all other mistakes, follies, absurdities and mis-judgements were to follow, stemmed from the resignation of the Com-mander of the 3rd Cavalry Brigade, Brigadier-General Gough. It is not possible here to give a detailed account of how Gough and fifty-seven officers out of seventy resigned their commissions: how Gough then came to London and was persuaded by unauthorised assurances from Seely to withdraw his resignation and persuade his brother officers to do likewise: how Gough persuaded Seely to put these assur-ances in writing: how a Cabinet, at which Seely was not present as he was explaining the affair to the King, approved the assurances: how Gough further persuaded Seely to add more assurances in writing to those of the Cabinet: how Gough set up a trust for his daughter and handed the document to the trust for safekeeping so that he could not hand it back to the Government: how all this news was leaked by Henry Wilson to Bonar Law: how embarrassing this proved to Asquith: and how this proved fatal to Seely's retention of the War Office.

Churchill was but little involved in these transactions. It is his action in ordering the 3rd Battle Squadron to Lamlash that we must examine. Churchill had promised Paget the use of naval vessels in certain circumstances to carry troops by sea to Dundalk and Carrick-fergus if the Northern Railway Company of Ireland refused to do so. The presence of the Battle Squadron at Lamlash would have facili-tated this operation. On March 19 Churchill signalled the following orders from the Admiralty:

WSC to the Vice Admiral Commanding 3rd Battle Squadron

TELEGRAM

19 March 1914   Admiralty
Secret

Proceed at once at ordinary speed to Lamlash, sending *Britannia* to
Gibraltar. After clearing Ushant hand over command temporarily to
Rear Admiral and proceed in your Flagship — to Plymouth, from
where you are to proceed to London and report yourself at the
Admiralty. Your Flagship should at once rejoin Squadron at Lamlash to which place you will proceed overland from London. Acknowledge and report dates of arrival.

[w s c]

WSC to HMS New Zealand

TELEGRAM

19 March 1914   Admiralty
Secret

Secret. Issue at once the following orders to Captain Johnson of
Attentive. (begins) Proceed with *Attentive* and *Pathfinder* to Kingstown at such speed as to arrive by noon tomorrow. A staff officer will
be sent from Dublin to communicate with you on arrival. You are to
embark one Company Bedfordshire Regiment, one half in each ship
and proceed to Belfast Lough so as to arrive off Carrickfergus at
daybreak on Saturday 21st instant. The troops are to be landed at
once. You should then take *Attentive* to Bangor, County Down,
land yourself in plain clothes and proceed to Holywood Barracks
and interview General Sir Nevil Macready as to co-operate with
military in certain eventualities. You should comply with requests
made so far as practicable without landing men. Captain of *Pathfinder* is to personally arrange with senior military officer in Carrick-
fergus for guarding the ammunition and other government stores
there. This place is to be defended against attack by every means,
and if co-operation of Navy is necessary, by guns and searchlights
from the ship. You may if necessary exchange stations of the two
ships provided one is kept at anchor off Bangor and one off Carrick-

fergus. Day leave may be given to reliable men during daylight hours, (ends). Acknowledge and report time of leaving.

[w s c]

WSC to HMS Gibraltar

TELEGRAM

19 March 1914   Admiralty
Secret

Gibraltar and *Royal Arthur* are to proceed at once to Kingstown Ireland to embark tomorrow 550 Infantry equally divided and proceed to Dundalk where ships should anchor not before daybreak on Saturday and at once disembark the troops. Report time of probable arrival at Kingstown.

[w s c]

On March 21 Churchill approved the order to embark four to eight field-guns on board the *King Edward VII*, flagship of the Admiral in command of the 3rd Battle Squadron at Devonport. The telegram of approval was timed 2.30 p.m.: at 6.40 the order was cancelled. The *King Edward VII* was then ordered to sea to "meet the squadron in the Channel for commencement of tactical exercises." Eight destroyers of the squadron, which had sailed for Lamlash that morning, were now ordered to "return to Southampton at once." Fergusson suggests that Asquith was kept in ignorance of these movements. He told the House of Commons on March 24, "In view of the prevalent excitement in this country, and the fact that the precautionary measures in Ireland had been peacefully carried out, I suggested to Churchill that the movement of the ships should be delayed."

The King, however, complained that he was not kept fully informed; he wrote to the Prime Minister on March 21:

... I must further ask that I am kept fully informed of any proposed employment of the Navy in connection with Ulster, especially as I see in the press that some excitement has been caused already in Ireland by the movements of some ships and I have heard nothing from the First Lord of the Admiralty. . . .

On March 25, during the second reading of the Consolidated Fund Bill, Lord Charles Beresford asked Churchill to explain the movements of the 3rd Battle Squadron. Churchill replied: "It was decided a fortnight ago by the Cabinet that a naval force comprising a Battle Squadron with attendant vessels should be stationed at Lamlash, so they would be in proximity to the coasts of Ireland in case of serious disorders arising": this, together with the Prime Minister's own record of the Cabinet meeting of March 18, disproves Fergusson's assertion that Asquith was ignorant of the matter. So well did Asquith cover his own responsibility that he even deceived his own daughter. In *Winston Churchill As I Knew Him* she wrote:

> . . . Winston ordered the Third Battle Squadron of eight battleships to concentrate at Lamlash in the Isle of Arran, stationed a cruiser near Carrickfergus, and sent two or three destroyers to the South of Ireland. My father knew nothing of these orders, given to the fleet on March 19th, until the morning of the 21st, when he promptly countermanded them. But the Admiralty had already announced them in a statement and the fat was in the fire.

Churchill's reply to Lord Charles Beresford was evidently disbelieved and Asquith's denial of responsibility seems to have established itself in history.

Churchill stated that the reason for the countermanding of the Battle Squadron's orders was "because the precautionary movements of the military in Ireland had been effected without opposition from the army of 100,000 which has been raised to resist the authority of Crown and Parliament." This statement infuriated the Opposition. Leo Amery interjected: "Will the right honourable gentleman state whether he expected and hoped that purely precautionary movements to look after stores would lead to fighting and bloodshed?" Churchill angrily repudiated what he called a "hellish insinuation." The Speaker asked him to withdraw such violent language, and with great reluctance he did so.

The debate continued on an acrimonious level. The Opposition had plainly cast Churchill as the villain of the piece. He was in no mood to truckle to their jibes: indeed, he courted them. He attacked Balfour and Bonar Law, "who emulates the former's dialectical force without his dialectical subtlety, to show that it is always right for soldiers to shoot down a Radical or Labour man." This produced a stormy scene in the House and there were cries of "Resign," "Traitor" and "Withdraw." Churchill was not overawed; he concluded:

> ...I earnestly suggest that when we have got to a point when rebellion, organised, avowed, applauded, and stimulated is set on foot against the ordinary workings of our legislature — when attempts to deal with that rebellious movement if it should be necessary, are to be countered — sometimes by exciting speeches, sometimes by newspaper articles, and sometimes by social influence — when attempts are made to paralyse the Executive in dealing with rebellion by fomenting stimulating suggestions of mutiny in the Army and Fleet, when that has been actually reached in our sober, humdrum, prosaic British politics, it is about time for serious, responsible people in all parts of the House, and all parties, to see if they cannot do something to make the situation a little better.

Ever since his speech at Bradford Churchill, with the assent, indeed the encouragement of the Prime Minister had assumed growing responsibilities for Irish affairs. Doubtless it was felt that his earlier record of seeking conciliation and his known friendship with Austen Chamberlain and F. E. Smith fitted him to resist the unlawful and even treasonable activities of Carson in Ulster. Though at this period Churchill was often the Government's spokesman, no documentary evidence can be found to justify the extraordinary personal malevolence of which he was made the victim. He never feared taking responsibility nor was he wont to lay the blame on others when events wore an ugly aspect. His metal was the very reverse of Asquith's. He knew that he had great aptitudes for leadership and he always grasped any opportunity to exercise it. If there was a battle he always aspired to be in the front line, even if not in actual command. It was not until he was sixty-five years old and qualified to draw the old age pension that the leadership of the country was entrusted to him. Meanwhile, all his attempts at leadership, whether they succeeded or failed, were fitting him for that supreme service to the State for which he had long decided he had been born into the world.

The abuse that was now levelled at him was equal to any that he was to receive in his career. He was accused of plotting a pogrom. *The Times* on March 23 said that Seely, French and Churchill had "mismanaged the whole affair . . . These three men are responsible for an episode without parallel in the history of the Army." In a speech in the House on March 30 Churchill referred to a letter Lord Roberts had published in the Press inciting all officers in the forces to hold themselves justified in "taking or supporting any measure" to prevent Home Rule being put into effect. At a Unionist rally in Hyde Park on April 4 Lord Charles Beresford referred to Churchill as a "Lilliput Napoleon — a man with an unbalanced mind, an egomaniac — whose one absorbing thought was personal vindictiveness towards Ulster." At the same rally Carson called him "Lord Randolph's renegade son who wanted to be handed down to posterity as the Belfast butcher who threatened to shoot down those who took his father's advice." Lord Robert Cecil spoke of Churchill's "dark and tortuous mind." Leo Amery, who took an active part in attacking Churchill at this time, wrote later in his *My Political Life*: "Churchill was indeed in our eyes the villain of the piece, the author of the 'Plot' or 'Pogrom' — with Asquith and Seely as his weak accomplices." Lord Beaverbrook, in his *Men and Power*, said that Bonar Law "always accepted the 'Pogrom' theory of the Ulster crisis, blaming Churchill as the real leader."

These contemporary opinions greatly damaged Churchill's reputation and lingered in the minds of his opponents for many years. Sir Henry Wilson wrote to Bonar Law when Churchill was invited to join Lloyd George's War Coalition in 1916: "A man who can plot the Ulster Pogrom, plan Antwerp, and carry out the Dardanelles fiasco is worth watching." Churchill wrote to his wife:

WSC to his wife

EXTRACT

23 April 1914

. . . The "Ulster Pogrom" is in full swing as you will read in the papers. We have now published everything and I am confident these wild charges will become gradually discredited. Bonar Law has exceeded himself in rudeness to the Prime Minister and feelings are on all sides bitter to a degree unknown hitherto.

Seely goes about like a disembodied spirit, trying to return from the wastes of the infinite to the cosy world of man. He is terribly hard hit and losing poise. The world is pitiless to grief and failure.

The Federal and conciliation movements are going forward well and there is a tremendous undercurrent on both sides towards a settlement. . . .

On the night of April 24/25 Carson's Ulster Volunteers in a brilliantly conceived and executed operation landed military equipment estimated by the *Annual Register* at 35,000 rifles and 3,000,000 rounds of ammunition. These figures cannot be regarded as exact, estimates differ; but it was gun-running on a large scale, and it gave substance alike to the threats of Ulstermen and to apprehension about them.

WSC to his wife

EXTRACT

27 April 1914   In the train

. . . tomorrow I am to reply to Austen Chamberlain's voice of censure on the "Pogrom." The situation has from a parliamentary point of view been altered much in our favour by the gun-running escapade of the Ulstermen. They have put themselves entirely in the wrong, and justified to the full the modest precautions which were taken. My line will be a very stiff one. . . .

After Chamberlain had reiterated the Opposition's charges of Government incompetence over the Curragh incident and the whole of the Ulster question, Churchill opened the case for the Government by referring to Chamberlain's motion as "uncommonly like a vote of censure by the criminal classes on the police." The gun-running of three days before had hardened public opinion against Ulster and made possible this audaciously robust opening; but with public opinion veering towards the Government Churchill found it possible once more to hold out hopes for conciliation. In effect he asked Carson to say: "Give me the amendments to the Home Rule Bill which I ask for, to safeguard the dignity and the interests of Protestant Ulster, and I in return will use all my influence and good will to make Ireland an integral unit in a federal system." Robert Harcourt, a Liberal MP and brother of "Lou Lou" Harcourt, the Colonial Secretary, wrote to Churchill expressing general Liberal unease at his conciliatory proposals:

Robert Harcourt to WSC

EXTRACT

28 April 1914

My dear Churchill,

I hope you will not resent it as an impertinence if I write to you with the utmost frankness.

It is absolutely vital that you should realize the extent of the fury — for no milder term will fit the facts — which has been aroused in the Irish party and among large numbers of our Liberal colleagues by the offer to Carson with which you concluded your speech. I do not deal with merits of the proposal — I am concerned with the fact of its reception. Devlin is beside himself with rage and is openly telling everyone that you have betrayed the Irish cause. Radicals, and among them the most active and talented debaters in the party, are comparing your action with Seely's surrender to Gough.

A number of Liberals went to Illingworth tonight and he is going to speak to the Prime Minister before the Cabinet tomorrow. They are afraid of an open row on the floor of the House which may shatter the whole basis of the Coalition. . . .

Though I myself have had some part in the Federal movement I felt so strongly that this was not the moment to parley with the enemy that I absolutely ignored the question in my speech. I give you my opinion for what it is worth and it is this — that unless the Prime Minister states unmistakably that your offer was not the decision of the Cabinet there is a definite danger of an open rupture. . . .

The Times's response to Churchill's conciliatory words was bleak; the next day it wrote: "Mr Churchill learned on Saturday that there were men in Ulster who could plan a coup rather more successfully than himself, and discovery perhaps chilled his ardour."

WSC to his wife

29 April 1914

. . . I have just come back from the Pogrom debate. You must read all about it. We smashed the "plot" altogether, but as you will see I yesterday at the end of my speech greatly daring and on my own account threw a sentence across the floor of the House of Commons to Carson which has revolutionised the situation, and we are all back again in full conciliation. This is the biggest risk I have taken. . . .

On April 30 Asquith replying to a question on the First Lord's speech said that Churchill had made his conciliatory suggestion on his own responsibility; but he was entirely in sympathy with it. There was little response from the Tories. Balfour contented himself with saying that it was "an outburst of demagogic rhetoric." Churchill, writing that day to his wife said: "You will see by the papers, that the daring and perilous stroke I made has transformed the political situation. It was an inspiration . . . !"

All through the summer the contending factions remained at arm's length. On July 18 the King summoned a conference of all parties involved at Buckingham Palace. Asquith and Lloyd George represented the Liberals: Bonar Law and Lansdowne the Tories: Redmond and Dillon the Nationalists: and Carson and Craig the Ulstermen. The conference met between July 21 and 25. On the second day Churchill wrote to Grey, anxious that the Irish quarrel should not lead to civil war:

WSC to Sir Edward Grey

EXTRACT

22 July 1914

. . . Failing an Irish agreement there ought to be a British decision. Carson and Redmond, whatever their wishes, may be unable to agree upon Tyrone — they may think it worth a war, and from their point of view it may be worth a war. But that is hardly the position of the 40 millions who dwell in Great Britain; and their interests must when all is said and done be our chief and final care. . . . I do not want good tactical positions for war. I want peace by splitting the outstanding differences, if possible with Irish acquiescence, but if necessary over the head of both Irish parties.

While this conference was sitting Churchill wrote to his wife on July 22: "On leaving the Palace Redmond and Dillon were followed by a cheering crowd, and as they passed the barracks, the soldiers of the Irish Guards ran out waving and cheering in a very remarkable demonstration. This will make Europe take unfavourable views of the British situation — which serious though it is — they will greatly exaggerate! . . ." This letter was written two days before the Austrian ultimatum to Serbia. It is clear that despite the Irish distraction Churchill's mind had all this summer been strictly concentrated on the German menace.

The Buckingham Palace conference ended without agreement on July 25. Churchill had written to his wife on the previous evening:

WSC to his wife

EXTRACT

24 July 1914   Admiralty

. . . We are to go ahead with the Amending Bill, abolishing the time limit and letting any Ulster county vote itself out if it chooses. The Irish acquiesced in this reluctantly. We must judge further events in Ulster when they occur. No one seems much alarmed. . . .

As the world plunged towards war Ireland still dominated the scene. Churchill was later to describe the transition from this domestic crisis to the imminent glare of world war in *The World Crisis.*

And so, turning this way and that in search of an exit from the deadlock, the Cabinet toiled around the muddy byways of Fermanagh and Tyrone. One had hoped that the events of April at the Curragh and in Belfast would have shocked British public opinion, and formed a unity sufficient to impose a settlement on the Irish factions. Apparently they had been insufficient. Apparently the conflict would be carried one stage further by both sides with incalculable consequences before there would be a recoil. . . .

The discussion had reached its inconclusive end, and the Cabinet was about to separate, when the quiet grave tones of Sir Edward Grey's voice were heard reading a document which had just been brought to him from the Foreign Office. It was the Austrian note to Serbia. He had been reading or speaking for several minutes before I could disengage my mind from the tedious and bewildering debate which had just closed. We were all very tired, but gradually as the phrases and sentences followed one another impressions of a wholly different character began to form in my mind. This note was clearly an ultimatum; but it was an ultimatum such as had never been penned in modern times. As the reading proceeded it seemed absolutely impossible that any State in the world could accept it, or that any acceptance, however abject, would satisfy the aggressor. The parishes of Fermanagh and Tyrone faded back into the mists and squalls of Ireland, and a strange light began immediately, but by perceptible graduations, to fall and grow upon the map of Europe. . . .

Eight years after the outbreak of war, it fell to Churchill as Colonial Secretary to introduce the Irish Free State Bill into the House of Commons. On this occasion he said:

Of course, all this trouble in regard to boundaries surrounds the boundaries of Fermanagh and Tyrone. I remember on the eve of the Great War we were gathered together at a Cabinet Meeting in Downing Street, and for a long time, an hour or an hour and a half, after the failure of the Buckingham Palace Conference, we discussed the boundaries of Fermanagh and Tyrone. Both of the great political parties were at each other's throats. The air was full of talk of civil war. Every effort was made to settle the matter and bring them together. The differences had been narrowed down, not merely to the counties of Fermanagh and Tyrone, but to parishes and groups inside the areas of Fermanagh and Tyrone, and yet, even when the differences had been so narrowed down, the problem appeared to be as insuperable as ever, and neither side would agree to reach any conclusion. Then came the Great War. . . . Every institution, almost, in the world was strained. Great Empires have been overthrown. The whole map of Europe has been changed. The position of countries has been violently altered. The mode and thought of men, the whole outlook on affairs, the grouping of parties, all have encountered violent and tremendous changes in the deluge of the world, but as the deluge subsides and the waters fall we see the dreary steeples of Fermanagh and Tyrone emerging once again. The integrity of their quarrel is one of the few institutions that have been unaltered in the cataclysm which has swept the world. That says a lot for the persistence with which Irishmen on the one side or the other are able to pursue their controversies. It says a good deal for the power which Ireland has, both Nationalist and Orange, to lay her hands upon the vital strings of British life and politics and to hold, dominate and convulse, year after year, generation after generation, the politics of this powerful country. . . .

With the threat of war Bonar Law and Carson proposed that the second reading of the Amending Bill be postponed and the differences between parties should for the moment be buried. Redmond acquiesced. In a moving speech on the eve of war he said that "our Nationalist Catholics in the South would be only too glad to join arms with the armed Protestant Ulstermen in the North" to defend the coasts of Ireland. But the next day he wrote to Churchill:

John Redmond to WSC

4 August 1914   House of Commons
Private

My dear Mr Churchill,
    I want to write you a purely informal letter & make an urgent appeal to you.
    In making my speech yesterday I was quite aware that I was taking very great risks. My people are sincerely anxious to make friends with this country but, naturally enough, they are still full of suspicion & if the Home Rule Bill be postponed they will consider themselves sold & I will be simply unable to hold them. In that event deplorable things will be said & done in Ireland & the Home Rule cause may be lost for our time.
    My suggestion is that the Royal Assent should be given to the Bill, that a pledge should be given that an Amending Bill would be introduced in the winter & that pending the disposal of the Amending Bill no step whatever would be taken to put the original Bill into operation.

I am convinced if this course be adopted that we will be able to agree with Carson on the terms of the Amending Bill. If it be not adopted, if we separate for 2 or 3 months with the Home Rule Bill still unpassed bitterness will grow & settlement become more difficult. Besides, it is not fair play, to subject us to all the risks & chances that may arise in the next 2 or 3 months.

The enactment of the Bill is, after all, in the circumstances, only the settlement of the principle & surety that we are entitled to. Furthermore in the *present* temper of the Unionist Party after my speech you can afford to take the course I suggest.

The Prime Minister knows my views & I think agrees with them. Now I urgently appeal to you to help me. Will you?

Very truly yrs
J. REDMOND

The British Isles went united into the war. Asquith announced on September 15 that the Home Rule Bill was to be put on the Statute Book, but that its operation was to be suspended for the duration of the war.

An unreflecting reader of the story of the Home Rule crisis which convulsed British politics in the four years prior to the First World War might conclude that the line which Churchill pursued was ambivalent if not erratic. To some extent this can be explained by the fact to which he sometimes referred in later life that in embracing Home Rule under the pressure of events he was proving disloyal to the policies of Lord Randolph who always remained his political hero. The more his conduct and speeches are scrutinized the more harmony will be detected between the two apparently contradictory principles of the policy he pursued. It seemed strange that he was the Minister who was prepared to go the furthest in taking action against Ulster while simultaneously being the one who was most forward in seeking an agreed settlement with the Tories. To Churchill's mind, which in this period was perhaps in its most brilliant and flexible prime, there was no contradiction in driving these two seemingly unmatched horses in tandem. All his life he believed that you could only be just and magnanimous and pursue a policy of appeasement from a situation of strength. Four decades later, at the time of the Korean War, speaking in the House of Commons, he said:

Appeasement in itself may be good or bad according to the circumstances. Appeasement from weakness and fear is alike futile and
fatal. Appeasement from strength is magnanimous and noble, and
might be the surest and perhaps the only path to world peace.

Moreover, though he was more ready than most if necessary to use
force against Ulster, he was of all the Liberal Ministers the one who
was the most ready to contemplate an at least temporary exclusion of
Ulster from the provisions of the Home Rule Bill. To the public eye
and even to his colleagues he must have seemed the least serviceable
contact with the Tories, for they regarded him as a turncoat and were
even more bitter against him than they were against Lloyd George.
That is probably why Asquith did not ask him to be one of the
Government's representatives at the abortive Buckingham Palace
Conference. But apart from his intimate friendship with F. E. Smith
and his growing accord with Austen Chamberlain, he had a waxing
and reciprocal affinity with those Tories who believed that war with
Germany was coming and that an Irish settlement was essential for
that reason if no other. Many past bitternesses were at least temporarily assuaged in the minds of those Tory leaders who believed in a
strong Navy by their knowledge of Churchill's work at the Admiralty.
Though this unperceived link between himself and the opposition
failed at this time to procure an Irish settlement, the contacts established proved serviceable to national unity when war came, and were
to be of further service when Churchill and Smith (by then Viscount
Birkenhead) were to be among the British negotiators of the Irish
Treaty of 1922.

14

First Lord

DURING HIS EARLY years in the Liberal Party Churchill had supported the foreign policy which was broadly acceptable to the Radical wing of the party. Though he would have been a Liberal Imperialist if he had belonged to the party at the time of the Boer War, so far as the continent of Europe was concerned he was virtually an isolationist. Nurtured on the slogans of Lord Randolph Churchill, he believed in Peace, Retrenchment and Reform. He believed that with an unchallengeable navy Britain could take as much or as little part in any great war as she chose. A small army was enough for home defence and for Imperial garrisons. According to this view, if Britain's interests should ultimately involve her in a European war, a great army could be brought into being, trained and armed, while the Royal Navy maintained her sea communications throughout the world and kept the island inviolate. All this had been instinctive in his criticisms of Mr Brodrick's Army. He clung to this view until at least 1908. On 17 August 1908, on the morning of which his engagement to Miss Clementine Hozier was announced, he spoke at Swansea. Lloyd George at the time was in Germany, and Churchill doubtless wished to speak words that would quicken the growing feeling of goodwill which existed at that time between Britain and Germany. He said:

> I have been astonished and grieved to read much of the wild language which has been used lately by people who ought to know better — by Lord Cromer in the House of Lords and by Mr Blatch-

ford in the *Clarion* about our relations with Germany. I think it is greatly to be deprecated that persons should try to spread the belief in this country that war between Great Britain and Germany is inevitable. It is all nonsense. In the first place, the alarmists have no ground whatever for their panic or fear. This country is an island, and no Government which is in power in this country in the near future, or likely to be in power, will depart in any degree from the naval policy which shall secure us effectively from outside invasion. All parties are pledged to those reasonable measures of naval defence which secure our peaceful development in this island, which free us from the curses of continental militarism, and which can never be a menace to any other great power in the world. I say, in the second place, there is no collision of primary interests — big, important interests — between Great Britain and Germany in any quarter of the globe. Why, they are among our very best customers, and, if anything were to happen to them, I don't know what we should do in this country for a market. While there is no danger of a collision of material interests, there is no result which could be expected from any struggle between the two countries except a destruction of a most appalling and idiotic character. People said it would be well worth their fighting for the sake of our trade. Gentlemen, it is never worth while fighting for the sake of trade. In a month of fighting you would destroy more wealth than the successful trade of five years would produce if every one worked 12 hours a day. We are told there are colonies which could be seized by Germany. Why, nothing will alter the destiny of great communities like Canada, Australia, South Africa, and India. They are pruning their own path and their own destiny, and that destiny will not be altered in the future as a result of any struggle between European powers. What remains as a prize to be fought for by two great countries? Nothing but tropical plantations and small coaling places scattered here and there about the world. Look at it from any point of view you like, and I say you will come to this conclusion in regard to the relations between England and Germany, that there is no real cause of difference between them, and although there may be snapping and snarling in the newspapers and in the London clubs, these two great peoples have nothing to fight about, have no prize to fight for, and have no place to fight in. What does all this snapping and snarling amount to, after all? How many people do you suppose there are in Germany who really want to make a murdering attack on this country? I do not suppose in the whole of that great population of 50 or 60 millions of inhabitants there are 10,000 persons who would seriously contemplate such a hellish and wicked crime; and how many do you think there are in this country? I do not believe there are even that number to be found in our country if you exclude the inmates of Bedlam and writers in the *National Review*. But we are told that though they may be few — these mischief-makers, snappers and snarlers — they are very influential. I am not sure there are not more influential people on the side of peace for which His Majesty the King has worked nobly, and I think it is clear now that there are laurels to be gained by European Sovereigns working for peace which are much more glorious and which bring them the applause of a far wider circle and enable them to write a much finer page in the history of their own times than was ever gained by barbarous and purposeless battles. But even if the 15,000 persons whom we will say in Germany and this country desire to make war on one another. (A voice, "Not one would fight.") I agree. They are not the people to fight, but soldiers and sailors; those others like to stay at home and read about it. Even if those persons were as influential as one would think from the noise they make and the chatter they keep up, what about the rest of us? What about the 100 millions of people who dwell in these islands and Germany? Are we all such sheep? Is democracy in the 20th century so powerless to effect its will? Are we all become such puppets and marionettes to be wire-pulled against our interests into such hideous convulsions? I have a high and prevailing faith in the essential goodness of great people. I believe that working classes all over the world are recognising they have common interests and not divergent interests. I believe that what is called the international solidarity of labour has an immense boon to confer upon all the peoples of the world. I was reading the other day of a story in the war between Germany and France in 1870. The Germans were occupying part of the French territory, and a visitor saw the German soldiers, who were of the hostile garrison, when not on duty, working in the fields by the side of French peasants helping them to get in their crops. One of the German soldiers was asked, "Why do you do that to your enemy?" Said the German, "War is all very well for the swells, but poor people have to help one another." I have come here this afternoon to ask you to join with me in saying that far and wide throughout the masses of the British dominions there is no feeling of ill-will towards Germany.

I say we honour that strong, patient industrious German people, who
have been for so many centuries a prey to European intrigue and a
drudge amongst the nations of the Continent. Now in the fulness of
time, after many tribulations, they have by their virtues and valour
won themselves a foremost place in the front of civilization. I say we
do not envy them their good fortune; we do not envy them their
power and their prosperity. We are not jealous of them. We rejoice
in everything that brings them good; we wish them well from the
bottom of our heart, and we believe most firmly the victories they
will win in science and learning against barbarism, against waste, the
victories they will gain will be victories in which we shall share, and
which, while benefitting them, will also benefit us.

Churchill had always been aware of the importance of the navy
for Britain. His early parliamentary speeches, in which he attacked
Brodrick's army scheme, showed his clear appreciation of the importance of naval supremacy. Then he had said:

I do not defend unpreparedness; but with a supreme Navy all unpreparedness can be redeemed: without it, no preparations, however
careful, can avail.

In 1908 Churchill's naval views appeared to change. He joined
with Lloyd George in seeking to cut down the McKenna Naval Estimates. A prolonged Cabinet crisis in January and February had
already resulted in the proposed increase in the Estimates for 1908–9
being halved, while Lord Tweedmouth was First Lord. Tweedmouth
was succeeded by McKenna in April 1908. McKenna at once agreed
with the Sea Lords to lay down four and if necessary six Dreadnoughts in 1909. Sir John Fisher, the First Sea Lord, called this proposed increase "perhaps the greatest triumph ever known." Churchill
and Lloyd George thereupon embarked upon a concentrated campaign to stop at four Dreadnoughts. When, on 8 December 1908,
McKenna recommended to the Cabinet a new programme of six
Dreadnoughts, Churchill and Lloyd George began a strong opposition. Their intention was to devote money to social reform rather
than naval armaments, believing that Britain's preponderance at sea
was answered. Though Churchill differed with McKenna as to the
precise necessities of the navy he never wavered from the principle of

British naval supremacy. When the Cabinet subcommittee on the Army Estimates met in 1908 he urged the need to maintain naval supremacy. He considered a strong Royal Navy to be the best guarantee of European peace and British security. The following letters show the troubled progress of the controversy over the 1908 Naval Estimates.

David Lloyd George to WSC

21 December 1908   Treasury Chambers

My dear Winston,
    I cannot go away without expressing to you my deep obligation for the assistance you rendered me in smashing McKenna's fatuous estimates & my warm admiration for the splendid way in which you tore them up.
    I am a Celt & you will forgive me for telling you that the whole time you were raking McK's squadron I had a vivid idea in my mind that your father looked on with pride at the skilful & plucky way in which his brilliant son was achieving victory in a cause for which he had sacrificed his career & his life.
    Wishing Mrs Winston Churchill & yourself a merry Xmas & a very happy New Year.

I remain Ever yours sincerely
D. LLOYD GEORGE

Starting Friday for the South of France. Should anything occur to you on which you would like to communicate with me write me Prince de Galles Hotel, Cannes.

David Lloyd George to WSC

[Postcard]   House of Commons

Dear Winston,
    Can you come to my room soon? I have gone farther into the figures. They are much more serious than even your ingenious computations would suggest.

D. L L G.

David Lloyd George to WSC

EXTRACT

Hotel Prince de Galles
Riviera Palace
3 January 1908 [1909]   Cannes

My dear Winston,

The Admiralty mean to get their 6 Dreadnoughts. Murray sent me a message through Clark that the Admiralty have had very serious news from their Naval attaché in Germany *since our last Cabinet Committee* & that McK is now convinced we may have to lay down *8* Dreadnoughts next year!!!

I feared all along this would happen. Fisher is a very clever person & when he found his programme was in danger he wired to Davidson for something more panicky — & of course he got it.

Can we not secure *reliable* information on this through the Foreign Office — or even through the German Embassy as to what the Germans are really doing.

Frankly I believe the Admirals are procuring false information to frighten us. McK feels his personal position & prestige is at stake. He has postponed his visit to the South of France in order to organise the intelligence for the next fight. The [*Admiralty Yacht*] *Enchantress* is waiting outside Monte Carlo for him!

Could you not get Grey to write to the Embassy or see Metternich? I do not believe the Germans are at all anxious to hurry up their building programme, quite the reverse. Their financial difficulties are already great. Why should they increase them?

During January and February 1909 the Cabinet discussion revolved around the question — four or six Dreadnoughts? Lloyd George and Churchill, in wishing to limit the construction to four, argued that, if German construction did proceed more rapidly than at present, a further two could be sanctioned by Parliament before the next Estimates. The demand for six came from McKenna, Grey, Runciman and Haldane; while Lloyd George and Churchill were supported by Morley, Loreburn, Burns and Harcourt. Behind the scenes, Fisher was campaigning for eight, and popularizing the cry: "We want eight, we won't wait."

Churchill's determination to stop at four was sharply criticized. Lord Knollys wrote to Lord Esher on 10 February 1909: "What are Winston's reasons for acting as he does in this matter? Of course it cannot be from conviction or principle. The very idea of his having either is enough to make anyone laugh."

Asquith took the side of those who wanted six Dreadnoughts. On February 20 he wrote to his wife that "Winston and Ll.G. by their combined machinations have got the bulk of the Liberal press in the same camp . . . [they] go about darkly hinting at resignation (which is bluff) . . . but there are moments when I am disposed summarily to cashier them both." On February 24 Asquith proposed in Cabinet a compromise which satisfied both sides: four Dreadnoughts were to be laid down in 1909–10, and a further four no later than 1 April 1910 if they could be shown to be necessary by comparison with the German programme. This compromise gave rise to the sarcastic comment against the little navy supporters that they had asked for four, had fought against six, and had got eight. But only four were laid down in 1909. Yet in November 1908, after he had studied Germany's financial position, Churchill wrote a memorandum from the

Board of Trade in which he stated the belief "that there are practically no checks upon German naval expansion except those imposed by the increasing difficulties of getting money."

In *The World Crisis* Churchill reflected on this prolonged dispute that "there can be no doubt whatever that, so far as facts and figures were concerned, we were strictly right. The gloomy Admiralty anticipations were in no respect fulfilled in the year 1912. The British margin was found to be ample in that year. There were no secret German Dreadnoughts, nor had Admiral von Tirpitz made any untrue statement in respect of major construction." But he also considered in retrospect:

> . . . although the Chancellor of the Exchequer and I were right in the narrow sense, we were absolutely wrong in relation to the deep tides of destiny. The greatest credit is due to the First Lord of the Admiralty, Mr McKenna, for the resolute and courageous manner in which he fought his case and withstood his Party on this occasion. Little did I think, as this dispute proceeded, that when the next Cabinet crisis about the Navy arose our roles would be reversed; and little did he think that the ships for which he contended so stoutly would eventually, when they arrived, be welcomed with open arms by me.

Churchill's battle to keep down the Naval Estimates continued until February 1911. The following two letters show his desire to keep the Estimates for 1911–12 as low as possible, using Colonial construction to help achieve this, and casting a critical eye over the high cost of maintaining "foreign" fleets in the Mediterranean, Atlantic and Pacific:

WSC to Lord Crewe
(Lloyd George Papers)

14 February 1911
Copy
Secret

My dear Crewe,

I suggest to you that the Estimates Committee might be asked to consider the following conclusions in order to produce some result from our impotent discussions.

1. That Haldane's estimates have increased by £750,000 during the last three years, and that this must be regarded as an increase in the permanent cost of the Army.

2. That an arrangement should be made with N.Z. and if possible with Australia which will secure us one or both of the Colonial ships in the North Sea in the period 1914–16; and that we should therefore sanction 4 new ships this year and (if both the Colonials are secured) 4 next year.

3. That we do not recommend any artificial inflation of this year's Estimates to those of next year.

4. That we report that McKenna has reduced the protected cruiser programme by two, with consequent savings.

5. That a Cabinet Committee assisted where necessary by experts should overhaul the whole question of British fleets abroad.

6. That we invite the favourable attention of the Cabinet to the recommendations of the Committee on Public Expenditure 1903 in regard' to an Estimates Committee of Members of the House of Commons.

As to Runciman [President, Board of Education], we have not heard him; but I really do not see where the money is to come from, however good his case. The PM seems to think that Lloyd George will have to come up. Thursday afternoon is the only time I have free this week. I hope we shall be able to agree upon that at any rate!

Yours sincerely
W S C

WSC to David Lloyd George
(Lloyd George Papers)

14 February 1911   Home Office
Secret

My dear David,

The Cabinet Committee did nothing this morning. Crewe was unable to be present except for a very few minutes. I brought the *Daily Mail* article to the notice of the Committee. McKenna declared the Admiralty had nothing to do with it. It is not accurate in all respects. There never has been any talk of six. And our discussion has mainly turned on the Colonial ships. I send you a memorandum which I circulated to the Cabinet Committee only, in the hopes of coming to an arrangement with McKenna which would be helpful and which would enable us all to come in. He did, however, nothing but raise difficulties and resist. The Committee will, I think, report in favour of four ships contingent upon an arrangement being made to retain one or both of the Colonial Dreadnoughts during the period 1914–1915. If two ships could be built, namely four this year and four next year, instead of two fives, you would get a reduction of nearly a million-and-a-half each year from that cause alone. Mc-Kenna announced this morning that as the result of pressure he would build two fewer unarmoured cruisers, effecting a saving next year of £450,000, and the year after of about £300,000. The Cabinet Committee were dead against increasing the expenditure this year artificially, and the Estimates are being provisionally printed on the basis of an increase of £3,800,000. McKenna also told us this morning that the cost of the foreign fleets of this country, the Mediterranean, Atlantic, Pacific, &c, was £5,000,000 a year. I believe myself that there is a great field for reduction here, as, after all, the sea is all one, and naval supremacy must be settled at the central point.

Runciman has not yet been before us, and I doubt very much whether there is much use in our seeing him in your absence.

Owing to the Prime Minister having promised our fellows two days' debates on Army and Navy Estimates together, it is now said that the Naval Estimates must go to press in the course of the next two or three days. We shall discuss this further at the Cabinet tomorrow, and if necessary we shall have to ask you to come up for a meeting of the Estimates Committee on Thursday afternoon, and probably there will have to be a special Cabinet on Friday.

I send you also a note which I dictated this morning, which I have shown nobody, on the inconvenient method by which we are always committed nearly a year ahead to ships which are not wanted until long after we have been bound, and which cost nothing in the year in which they have been sanctioned and millions of money in the years which follow.

I think on the whole Crewe is inclined to recommend that something may be done about the Colonial vessels. There are no other prospects of relief as far as I can see.

Unless you have come up on Thursday, I will meet you at Walton Heath at 11 o'clock on Friday.

                                                   Yours always

Churchill's search for naval economy was based upon his reluctance to see public money squandered, and was sustained by his belief that Germany constituted no threat to Britain. This belief was shared by many Liberals before 1911, and to them suspicion of German intentions seemed ill-informed and short-sighted. But in 1911 this faith in Germany's good intentions was rudely shaken, and Churchill was among the first to see the need to change his views, and to seek policies consistent with the danger.

For Churchill's mind the decisive event came in July 1911. This was the provocative action of Germany in sending a gunboat, *Panther*, to the Moroccan port of Agadir, to which the French had claims, as a demonstration of their dissatisfaction and as a protest against the way in which Britain, France and Spain had earlier in the month disregarded German claims in the African continent.

This was a musical comedy of gunboat diplomacy. Sometimes the currently held derisory views on gunboat diplomacy are wide of the mark. "Showing the flag" had often pacified whole areas of primitive natives without a shot being fired. It was often a most beneficent instrument of law and order, no more menacing than the policeman on his beat, save for the reserve power which lay behind both. But to use a gunboat as a counter in the disputes of great powers was plainly silly. That is doubtless why that action was ascribed, perhaps unfairly, to the Kaiser himself. He was probably not as silly as some of his advisers. But this was more than silly; for though it could achieve nothing of value to Germany, it alerted the Chancelleries of Europe, perhaps more than was warranted, certainly more than was intended, to the growing ambition of Germany.

In those days statesmen did not make inflammatory speeches to hysterical mobs. The conduct of diplomacy among the great powers was in the hands of trained and skilful diplomats who all spoke the same language, French. Even the nuances of diplomatic jargon were so nicely expressed in that precise language that there was little room for misunderstanding. There was no United Nations where clownish statesmen could beat the table with their shoes. All was courteous and urbane. The sending of the *Panther* to Agadir could not have procured a square centimetre of Africa for the Germans. What it did was to make everyone sit up and focus their attention on the expanding sea power of Germany. Her armies had already threatened her continental neighbours; her growing navy could only be a menace to Britain. Though the event caused little public stir it caused a change of values in the governing minds of every great power in the world.

Mrs Churchill was abroad at the time:

WSC to his wife
(CSC Papers)

EXTRACT

3 July 1911

. . . The German action in Morocco has caused a flutter. The French want us to send a "bat" [*bateau*] to Agadir. This would be a serious step on which we should not engage without being ready to go to all lengths if necessary. There is to be a special Cabinet tomorrow on this question. . . .

WSC to his wife
(CSC Papers)

EXTRACT

5 July 1911   Home Office

. . . We decided to use pretty plain language to Germany and to tell her that if she thinks Morocco can be divided up without John Bull, she is jolly well mistaken. . . .

Churchill was at the Home Office during the Agadir crisis. On a sheet of Home Office paper he recorded his thoughts. He did not, as was his custom, circulate this to the Cabinet, but he doubtless spoke in these terms to his closest colleagues, who at this time were Asquith, Grey and Lloyd George.

Memorandum by WSC

[Undated]   Home Office

It is true G. has some (minor) claims about Morocco wh if amicably stated we should be glad to see adjusted either there or elsewhere — subject to Britain being safeguarded — wh ought not to be difficult.

Her action at Agadir has put her in the wrong & forced us to consider her claims in the light of her policy & methods.

We are bound to give diplomatic support to F. in any discussion about Morocco: but are entitled to tell France if necessary & to make public fact that this is only diplomatic if we think she is unreasonable.

If no settlement is reached between F. & G. & deadlock results we must secure Brit interests independently. This again ought not to be impossible.

If Germany makes war on France in the course of the discussion or deadlock (unless F. has meanwhile after full warning from us taken unjustifiable ground) we shd join with France.

Germany should be told this now.

[w s c]

It is doubtful if at this time any other member of the Cabinet, except Grey, would have gone so far as Churchill was prepared to go in the hypothetical circumstances which he had predicted: but from now on Churchill at least considered that Britain's self-interest involved obligations to France and regarded her as our natural ally if war should come. All the Cabinet, however, took note of the menace and Lloyd George, who since his Boer War days had been regarded as a pacifist and was to show himself one again until the very eve of the war, felt moved to utter a warning. It so happened that he was the first Cabinet Minister who was due to make a public speech after Agadir. Probably prompted by Churchill, and after consultation with the Foreign Secretary, the Chancellor took the opportunity of a speech he was to make at the Mansion House on July 21 to interpolate these words.

I believe it is essential in the highest interests not merely of this country, but of the world, that Britain should at all hazards maintain her place and her prestige amongst the Great Powers of the world. Her potent influence has many a time been in the past, and may yet be in the future, invaluable to the cause of human liberty. It has more than once in the past redeemed continental nations, who are sometimes too apt to forget that service, from overwhelming disaster and even from national extinction. I would make great sacrifices to preserve peace. I conceive that nothing would justify a disturbance of international goodwill except questions of the gravest national moment. But if a situation were to be forced upon us in which peace could only be preserved by the surrender of the great and beneficent position Britain has won by centuries of heroism and achievement, by allowing Britain to be treated where her interests were vitally affected as if she were of no account in the Cabinet of nations, then I say emphatically that peace at that price would be a humiliation intolerable for a great country like ours to endure.

Neither the *Panther* nor Agadir was mentioned, and his words passed almost uncomprehended over the heads of his City audience, but they were heard where they were meant to be heard. Churchill himself was much perturbed. He tells us in *The World Crisis* how the diplomatic situation developed:

Four days later, at about 5.30 in the afternoon, the Chancellor of the Exchequer and I were walking by the fountains of Buckingham Palace. Hot-foot on our track came a messenger. Will the Chancellor of the Exchequer go at once to Sir Edward Grey? Mr Lloyd George stopped abruptly and turning to me said, "That's my speech. The Germans may demand my resignation as they did Delcassé's." [In 1905 Delcassé, the Foreign Minister, was forced to resign during the Moroccan crisis after German pressure.] I said, "That will make you the most popular man in England" (he was not actually the most popular at that time). We returned as fast as we could and found Sir Edward Grey in his room at the House of Commons. His first words were: "I have just received a communication from the German Ambassador so stiff that the Fleet might be attacked at any moment. I have sent for McKenna to warn him!" He then told us briefly of the conversation he had just had with Count Metternich. The Ambassador had said that after the speech of the Chancellor of the Exchequer no explanation could be made by Germany. In acrid terms he had stated that if France should repel the hand offered by the Emperor's Government, the dignity of Germany would compel her to secure by all means full respect by France for German treaty rights. He had then read a long complaint about Mr Lloyd George's speech, "which to say the least could have been interpreted as a warning to Germany's address and which as a matter of fact had been interpreted by the presses of Great Britain and France as a warning bordering on menace."

Sir Edward Grey had thought it right to reply that the tone of the communication which had just been read to him rendered it inconsistent with the dignity of His Majesty's Government to give explanations with regard to the speech of the Chancellor of the Exchequer. The First Lord arrived while we were talking, and a few minutes later hurried off to send the warning orders.

They sound so very cautious and correct, these deadly words. Soft, quiet voices purring, courteous, grave, exactly-measured phrases in large peaceful rooms. But with less warning cannons had opened fire and nations had been struck down by this same Germany. So now the Admiralty wireless whispers through the ether to the tall masts of ships, and captains pace their decks absorbed in thought. It is nothing. It is less than nothing. It is too foolish, too fantastic to be thought of in the twentieth century. Or is it fire and murder leaping out of the darkness at our throats, torpedoes ripping the bellies of half-awakened ships, a sunrise on a vanished naval supremacy, and an island well-guarded hitherto, at last defenceless? No, it is nothing. No one would do such things. Civilization has climbed above such perils. The interdependence of nations in trade and traffic, the sense of public law, the Hague Convention, Liberal principles, the Labour Party, high finance, Christian charity, common sense have rendered such nightmares impossible. Are you quite sure? It would be a pity to be wrong. Such a mistake could only be made once — once for all.

A few days later at a garden party at 10 Downing Street Churchill happened to meet Sir Edward Henry, the Chief Commissioner of Police. To his surprise he learned from him that as Home Secretary he was technically responsible for the safety of all the reserves of naval cordite some of which were stored in magazines in London, one of them hard by the Serpentine. Churchill at once returned to the Home Office and telephoned to the Admiralty. The Admiral in charge refused to accept any responsibility and declined to send a detachment of marines to guard these hitherto neglected but vital magazines. Accordingly, Churchill rang up Haldane at the War Office and persuaded him to send a company of infantry to each magazine. This was the first of many actions which in a long life was to gain for Churchill the reputation in pussyfoot circles of being an alarmist. He always maintained that it was better to be alarmed before a catastrophe rather than after.

There was to be a secret meeting of the Committee of Imperial Defence on August 23. To instil in this important body an alertness such as he felt himself, he circulated a lengthy memorandum ten days in advance. It can be read in full in *The World Crisis.* Here a résumé must suffice.

In the memorandum Churchill assumed that an Alliance existed between Britain, France and Russia, and that they had been attacked by Germany and Austria. He considered that the decisive military operations would be between France and Germany.

> The German army is at least equal in quality to the French, and mobilizes 2,200,000 against 1,700,000. The French must therefore seek for a situation of more equality. This can be found either before the full strength of the Germans has been brought to bear or after the German army has become extended. The first might be reached before the ninth and thirteenth days; the latter about the fortieth.

He stressed that the German attack would break through the line of the Meuse on the twentieth day and that the French would then fall back on Paris and the south. "All plans based upon the opposite assumption ask too much of fortune." He showed how the impetus of the German advance would be weakened as it progressed.

> By the greater losses incidental to the offensive (especially if they have tested unsuccessfully the French fortress lines);
> By the greater employment of soldiers necessitated by acting on exterior lines;
> By having to guard their communications through Belgium and France (especially from the sea flank);
> By having to invest Paris (requiring at least 500,000 men against 100,000) and to besiege or mask other places, especially along the sea-board;
> By the arrival of the British army;

> By the growing pressure of Russia from the thirtieth day;
> And generally by the bad strategic situation to which their right-handed advance will commit them as it becomes pronounced.

The result of this would mean that by the fortieth day Germany "should be extended at full strain both internally and on her war fronts" and that this strain would become daily "more severe and ultimately overwhelming" unless they could win a victory. It was then that "opportunities for the decisive trial of strength may occur."

> Such a policy demands heavy and hard sacrifices from France, who must, with great constancy, expose herself to invasion, to having her provinces occupied by the enemy, and to the investment of Paris, and whose armies may be committed to retrograde or defensive operations. Whether her rulers could contemplate or her soldiers endure this trial may depend upon the military support which Great Britain can give; and this must be known beforehand, so that we may know, before we decide, what they would be prepared to do.

Churchill then outlined the measures Britain should take, including 107,000 men to be sent to France on the outbreak of war and 100,000 troops of the British Army in India who should be moved at once out of India, enabling them to reach Marseilles by the fortieth day.

> This fine army, almost entirely composed of professional soldiers, could be assembled around (say) Tours by the fortieth day, in rear of the French left (instead of being frittered into action piecemeal), and would then become a very important factor in events. The Russian army would also by then be engaged in full force on the eastern frontiers of Germany and Austria, and the power of the three allies should then be sufficient either to hold the Germans in a position of growing difficulty, or if desirable, to assume the offensive in concert.

Churchill next examined the needs of home defence, and suggested that a volunteer system would be adequate for six months, but that then a half million men should be raised compulsorily for home defence and the already trained volunteers be sent to France.

The steady augmentation of British military strength during the progress of the war would, however, put us in a position by the end of the twelfth month to secure or re-establish British interests outside Europe, even if, through the defeat or desertion of allies, we were forced to continue the war alone. No lesser steps would seem adequate to the scale of events.

This was one of the most prescient strategic documents that Churchill ever wrote. Its forecast of the military timetable of the German invasion of Belgium and France proved right almost to the day. When the Germans were pouring through Belgium and France in 1914 Churchill circulated this memorandum once more to the Cabinet in order to encourage his colleagues "with the hope that if the unfavourable prediction about the twentieth day had been borne out, so also would be the favourable prediction about the fortieth day." It is noteworthy as the work of a Home Secretary. It shows an acceptance of the doctrine of Cabinet responsibility in its positive aspect. Today even its negative aspect seems to be in decline. Ministers increasingly confine themselves to their own departments and give little aid to their colleagues.

This memorandum did not make much impact upon the Committee of Imperial Defence. Balfour was a member of the CID and must have read it. But there is no known reaction from him. When, however, he re-read it in the early days of war he wrote to Eddie Marsh, on 8 September 1914, "it is a triumph of prophecy!"

Mrs Churchill was still abroad:

WSC to his wife
(CSC Papers)

EXTRACT

2 August 1911   Home Office

. . . Today the news about the big thing is that the bully is climbing down & it looks as if all would come out smooth and triumphant. . . .

WSC to his wife
(CSC Papers)

EXTRACT

6 August 1911   Blenheim Palace

. . . There is no doubt the Germans are going to settle with the French on a friendly basis. They sent their *Panther* to Agadir & we sent our little Panther to the Mansion House: with the best results. . . .

WSC to his wife
(CSC Papers)

EXTRACT

24 September 1911   Balmoral Castle

. . . L.G. . . . electrified their Majesties by observing that he thought it would be a great pity if war did not come now. They are of course repeating this statement somewhat freely. I shall practise caution. . . .

Churchill's mind was now busy revolving many ideas to prevent war and to maintain Britain's integrity if war should come. Henceforward his correspondence dwelt increasingly on the war danger.

WSC to Sir Edward Grey

30 August 1911   [Home Office]
[Copy]

Perhaps the time is coming when decisive action will be necessary. Please consider the following policy for use if and when the Morocco negotiations fail.

Propose to France and Russia a triple alliance to safeguard *(inter alia)* the independence of Belgium, Holland and Denmark.

Tell Belgium that, if her neutrality is violated, we are prepared to come to her aid and to make an alliance with France and Russia to guarantee her independence. Tell her that we will take whatever military steps will be most effective for that purpose. But the Belgian Army must take the field in concert with the British and French

Armies, and Belgium must immediately garrison properly Liège and Namur. Otherwise we cannot be responsible for her fate.

Offer the same guarantee both to Holland and to Denmark contingent upon their making the utmost exertions.

We should, if necessary, aid Belgium to defend Antwerp and to feed that fortress and any army based on it. We should be prepared at the proper moment to put extreme pressure on the Dutch to keep the Scheldt open for *all* purposes. If the Dutch close the Scheldt, we should retaliate by a blockade of the Rhine.

It is very important to us to be able to blockade the Rhine, and it gets more important as the war goes on. On the other hand, if the Germans do not use the "Maestricht Appendix" in the first days of the war, they will not want it at all.

Let me add that I am not at all convinced about the wisdom of a close blockade, and I did not like the Admiralty statement. If the French send cruisers to Mogador and Saffi, I am of opinion that we should (for our part) move our main fleet to the north of Scotland into its war station. Our interests are European, and not Moroccan. The significance of the movement would be just as great as if we sent our two ships with the French.

Please let me know when you will be in London; and will you kindly send this letter on to the Prime Minister.

WSC to David Lloyd George
(*Lloyd George Papers*)

EXTRACT

31 August 1911   Home Office

. . . I have had a talk with [Henry] Wilson today. He entirely agrees that great strategic advantages wd be immediately derived from our being able to move into a friendly Belgium, and from our being able to threaten the German flank in conjunction with the Belgian army. He also concurs fully in the policy of my letter to Grey. He tells me however that Sir W. Nicholson [CIGS] is much more doubtful abt the utility of the Belgian army. Will you tell me what you think abt my letter? I hope we shall be in pretty close accord. I think there is no doubt yr view is sound — that we shd get hold of the Belgians; and I think yr phrase "pivoting on Antwerp" is much more correct than "based on Antwerp," wh I had rather loosely employed.

Meanwhile, according to the newspapers, the Belgians are taking steps to hold the Liège–Namur line, either of their own accord or at French prompting. This is excellent. We are bound by treaty to protect Belgian neutrality. Its violation wd be an undoubted *casus belli,* independently of other "griefs." The Belgians must however be made to defend themselves. How do we know what their secret relations with Germany are? All their interests are with the French; but it is possible that British neglect & German activities may have led to some subterranean understanding — for instance, that the Germans shd not go above the Namur–Liège line, & that the Belgians, in consideration of this, should forbid either British or French troops to come to their aid. This wd deprive us at once of the Belgian army and of the strategic position on the German flank, as well as of a *casus belli* wh everyone here wd understand. Wilson said in conversation that Anglo-Belgian cooperation, promptly applied to the German flank, might mean the subtraction of as much as 10 to 12 divisions from the decisive battle front. But I have grave misgivings lest we may be too late, and that the Belgians are got at already.

I hope also that you will think well of the idea of meeting any fresh German move at Agadir, not by sending ships in concert with the French, but by moving the fleet to its Scottish station, where it wd be at once the most effective & least provocative support to France, & a real security to this country. It is not for Morocco, nor indeed for Belgium, that I wd take part in this terrible business. One cause alone cd justify our participation — to prevent France from being trampled down & looted by the Prussian junkers — a disaster ruinous to the world, & swiftly fatal to our country.

Yours ever
w

WSC to H. H. Asquith

EXTRACT

13 September 1911   Home Office
Copy

. . . Are you sure that the ships we have at Cromarty are strong enough to defeat the whole German High Sea fleet? If not they shd be reinforced without delay. Are 2 divisions of the Home Fleet enough? This appears to be a vital matter.

I cannot measure the forces, but the principle is clear that the fleet concentrated in the North Sea shd be strong enough without further aid to fight a decisive battle with the German Navy.

And something must be allowed for losses through torpedo surprise.

Are you sure that the Admiralty realise the serious situation of Europe? I am told they are nearly all on leave at the present time. After his revelations the other day I cannot feel implicit confidence in [Sir Arthur] Wilson. No man of real power cd have answered so foolishly.

The Admiralty have ample strength at their disposal. They have only to be ready and to employ it wisely. But one lapse, as stupid as that revealed at our meeting, and it will be the defence of England rather than that of France which will engage us.

Excuse plainness. Clemmie and I are much looking forward to our visit to you on the 27th.

Yrs vy sincerely

W S C

WSC to Reginald McKenna

EXTRACT

13 September 1911   Home Office
Confidential

My dear McKenna,

The maintenance of the food supply in time of war and the prices resulting from its insecurity, touch public order very closely. I had a long talk with Sir Frederic Bolton [Chairman of Lloyds] the other day, and he spontaneously and most earnestly confirmed the impression which I had begun to form in my mind, that on the outbreak of war the British Government should guarantee to pay full indemnity for all British or neutral ships sunk or captured by the enemy in the course of bringing necessaries of life and manufacture to this country. I believe this not to be a substitute for but a necessary counterpart of a supreme and effective naval defence. If the naval defence is perfect the additional cost of paying indemnity would be nominal, but its advantage in preventing artificial enhancement of insurance rates will be none the less real. Even if only one ship in a hundred were sunk or captured the rise in insurance would be enormous and the consequent effect upon food prices, and thereafter on public order, very serious.

On the other hand, in this case the full cost of insurance to the Government would only be one per cent. It seems to me that the sound and dignified policy, equally agreeable to the Naval prestige and practical interests of this country, would be for us to say, on a declaration of war, that Great Britain is prepared to maintain the complete security of the seas for all vessels trading with the United Kingdom who conform to certain conditions, and that if and in so far as we fail to make this good by naval force we will pay full compensation for all loss resulting. The result would seem to be that we should continue to get our food and raw material at world prices, although no doubt the prevalence of war would tend to some unavoidable enhancement of these. I asked Sir Frederic Bolton to write me out a statement of his views and of his plan, and I send it to you herewith together with some other papers on the subject, hoping that you will let me know the opinion you have formed, for you have no doubt had many other opportunities for studying the subject.

You asked me the other day at the CID about the maintenance of order in this country in the time of war. I am sure that it depends almost exclusively upon the poorer people being able to purchase a certain minimum amount of the staple foods, especially bread, at prices which they can afford; and the Government will be forced to secure them this ration at all costs, paying themselves the difference in some form or another between the normal and war prices. The method indicated by Sir Frederic Bolton seems to me to be much the best way of effecting this purpose.

WSC to David Lloyd George

(Lloyd George Papers)

14 September 1911   Home Office
Secret & Personal

My dear David,

Seely tells me that having to make some official enquiries at the Admiralty today he found that practically everybody of importance & authority is away on his holidays, except Wilson himself who goes tomorrow. The War Office cannot understand this at such a time, & Sir William Nicholson expressed his surprise to Admiral Wilson last night that he shd find it possible to leave the office so denuded. He was told in reply that everything was ready, & that all that was necessary was to press the button, which could as well be done by a clerk as by anyone else. I can only say I hope this may be so.

Sir Arthur Nicolson [Permanent Under-Secretary, Foreign Office, later Lord Carnock] saw Cambon this morning, who repeated what we already know about the French reply to the German amendments, and also said that he still believed in his own mind that Germany wd give way, & that everything wd be settled. Cambon said he had no reasons for this view, except that it was his own feeling & that of M. de Selves. Certainly there is not much confirmation of it in the papers we have seen.

While waiting to see Nicholson at the W.O., I had a talk with Kitchener. He was much more respectful about French chances & military qualities, & he told me that Huguet, the French military attaché, had told him that the winter was the best time for Germany because at that season Russia cd not move. According to the W.O. there is no truth in this. The bad months for Russia are the spring & summer, when there is a great deal of rain & slush in Poland. The good months are from September to the end of February.

The City is bad this afternoon, but there is no other news. I am going to spend Sunday with Grey on my way North to Freddie Guest. Write to keep them progged up through any method that is open to you.

Keep this letter to yourself.

Yours ever
WINSTON S. CHURCHILL

David Lloyd George to WSC

EXTRACT

15 September 1911   Balmoral Castle

. . . I had a long talk with Balfour. He is very much worried — as you are — about the Navy. He is by no means happy about the Admiralty. He has no confidence in Wilson's capacity for direction and leadership. He thinks the Admirals too cocksure.

If there is war he will support us.

Benckendorff [Russian Ambassador] is here. He told the King that if Germany attacked France Russia would certainly throw herself into the conflict. Of that he had no doubt.

Have you heard from the War Office that owing to the drought there is no water in that part of Belgium which the Germans must march through? That *may* have something to do with the delay.

Knollys does not believe in war. Benckendorff also says the Germans played the same with them over Persia as they are engaged in playing over Morocco with France. They made vital alterations in the draft, then pleaded they were merely verbal. Eventually they gave in when they realised that Russia meant to be firm. Who can tell? I am not sure they know themselves. I think the chances are still against war. . . .

Though many of his colleagues on the CID and in the Cabinet may have disregarded Churchill's clamant appeals to thought and action and the pacifists may have thought him an alarmist, his memoranda and letters deeply impressed the Prime Minister. In *Great Contemporaries* Churchill was later to write of Asquith:

He was always very kind to me and thought well of my mental processes; was obviously moved to agreement by many of the State papers which I wrote. A carefully-marshalled argument, cleanly printed, read by him at leisure, often won his approval and thereafter commanded his decisive support. His orderly, disciplined mind delighted in reason and design. It was always worth while spending many hours to state a case in the most concise and effective manner for the eye of the Prime Minister. In fact I believe I owed the repeated advancement to great offices which he accorded me, more to my secret writings on Government business than to any impressions produced by conversation or by speeches on the platform or in Parliament. One felt that the case was submitted to a high tribunal, and that repetition, verbiage, rhetoric, false argument, would be impassively but inexorably put aside.

Asquith does not seem to have resented the fact that his Home Secretary was concerning himself so vigorously in military and in naval matters. On the contrary, Churchill's activities convinced him that he must replace McKenna at the Admiralty.

Late in September Churchill was invited to stay with the Prime Minister in Scotland. In those days Churchill still occasionally played golf, after a fashion — more for the companionship of Asquith and Lloyd George than for any serious addiction to the pastime. He has recorded how coming home from the links the Prime Minister asked him "quite abruptly" whether he would like to go to the Admiralty. Churchill replied: "Indeed I would."

A fuller account of Churchill's visit to Archerfield, Asquith's Scottish home, given in Haldane's *Autobiography*, suggests that there was more argument about the appointment between Haldane and Churchill than the latter has recorded:

> I drove over to Archerfield as soon as I had got to Cloan. As I entered the approach I saw Winston Churchill standing at the door. I divined that he had heard of possible changes and had come down at once to see the Prime Minister.
>
> It was as I thought. Churchill was importunate about going himself to the Admiralty from the Home Office, where he was. He had told Asquith that the First Lord must be in the Commons. As I was by now in the Lords this looked like a difficulty. But I said the situation was too critical to permit of any such difficulty standing in the way. I had no desire to be First Lord, but if a real Naval War Staff were to be created and the Admiralty were to be convinced of its necessity, that must be done by someone equipped with the knowledge and experience that were essential for fashioning a highly complicated organisation. Now where was he to be found?
>
> Obviously Churchill had been pressing Asquith hard. I returned to Cloan and came back the next day. Churchill was still there, and the Prime Minister shut me up in a room with him. I took the initiative. I told him that his imaginative power and vitality were greater than mine, and that physically he was better suited to be a War Minister. But at this critical moment it was not merely a question of such qualities. The Navy and the public had to be convinced, and they would be most easily convinced of the necessity of scientific preparation for naval war by someone who already had carried out similar preparations with the only Service in which they had been made or even thought of. I was satisfied that in all probability I could accomplish what was wanted within twelve months, and if he would look after the Army till the end of that time I would return to it and he could then take over the Admiralty.

There was nothing in the idea which the Prime Minister had that the [Lord] Chancellorship would soon be vacant and that I might fill the post. The Great Seal might go anywhere so far as I was concerned at this moment. It was a question of executing a great plan if the emergency arose. And I said that, to be frank, I did not think that Churchill's own type of mind was best for planning out the solution that was necessary for the problem which at the moment was confronting us.

However, Churchill would not be moved, and Asquith yielded to him.

Haldane was disappointed by Asquith's decision, but he took it well. He did everything in his power to help the new First Lord to set up the Naval War Staff.

*

It was in a stern mood but with a buoyant heart that Churchill embarked upon his new duties. Largely under the tuition of Henry Wilson, Director of Military Operations and later Chief of the Imperial General Staff, alertness to the German menace had quickened in him. He already had a belief in the probability that Germany meant to make war: his years at the Admiralty were to turn that belief into a conviction.

It is not possible to find a shorter or more pithy account of his first day at the Admiralty than in his own words in *The World Crisis*.

Mr McKenna and I changed guard with strict punctilio. In the morning he came over to the Home Office and I introduced him to the officials there. In the afternoon I went over to the Admiralty; he presented his Board and principal officers and departmental heads to me, and then took his leave. I knew he felt greatly his change of office, but no one would have divined it from his manner. As soon as he had gone, I convened a formal meeting of the Board, at which the Secretary read the new Letters Patent constituting me its head, and I thereupon in the words of the Order-in-Council became "responsible to Crown and Parliament for all the business of the Admiralty." I was to endeavour to discharge this responsibility for the four most memorable years of my life.

Churchill's arrival at the Admiralty got a mixed reception. It must be remembered that party feeling was at its height and that no individual was so abhorrent to the Tories as the new First Lord. *The Times,* in an editorial of 27 October 1911, gave him a guarded welcome:

> His countrymen will wish him well in the discharge of the great and vital duties he has undertaken, and few will be so ungenerous as to anticipate that he will fail to rise to the full height of his responsibilities. . . . some of Churchill's antecedents may perhaps inspire misgiving, but this must not be allowed to deprive him of fair play, or to forestall a dispassionate appreciation of his actions on their merits.

The *Spectator* contrived to be most disagreeable: it believed that "his office duties were only themes for newspaper advertisement and pegs on which to hang his turgid speeches." *The Economist,* on the other hand, though friendly, was wide of the mark as to the reasons for Churchill's appointment and as to the light in which he regarded his new task. They believed he had "the energy, the resource, and the capacity that should enable him to increase the efficiency of the whole administration, put spirit and confidence into the service, effecting large entrenchments, and avoiding such fiascoes as airships which cannot fly, and battleships which cannot either get into harbour or fire their own broadsides."

Not only was opinion divided between different people and different papers but some people themselves had divided opinions and emotions about Churchill. Thus:

Duke of Connaught to Princess Louise
(Royal Archives)

EXTRACT

8 November 1911   Government House
                                   Ottawa

. . . Personally I think Winston Churchill will do just as well at the Admiralty as McKenna & I don't think you will find him agree to a dangerous reduction of the Navy. I know him well & have done so for more than 17 yrs. I *loathe* his speeches, but he is young & impulsive still & "all found" he is not a bad fellow & I know he is favourably much devoted to Georgy [King George V]. . . .

An important reason for the change of First Lord arose after a dispute in the Committee of Imperial Defence on 23 August 1911. The War Office had been anxious to obtain assurances from the Admiralty that six British divisions could be transported immediately to France if the need arose in order to join the left flank of the French Army. The Admiralty, represented at this Committee by Sir Arthur Wilson, refused to give this assurance. Immediately after the meeting Haldane had told Asquith that he could not remain responsible for the War Office unless his general staff could receive full support in their planning from the Admiralty. There could be no doubt that Churchill would not prove as reluctant as McKenna to authorize plans to be made for the swift transportation of an Expeditionary Force to France. Fisher had only ceased to be First Sea Lord the year before. His influence at the Admiralty was still strong. His pre-war correspondence shows that he thought it wrong to send a British Army to fight beside the French on the Continent.

But the main reason why McKenna was replaced by Churchill as First Lord was that the former was unwilling or unable, because of Admiralty resistance, to create a Naval War Staff, for which the Prime Minister had been pressing. The main obstacle to this necessary innovation was the First Sea Lord, Sir Arthur Wilson, who, after a distinguished life at sea had now, for over two years, been at the head of his profession. He was sixty-nine years old, and had won the VC fighting on land against the Dervishes.

Churchill, in *The World Crisis,* later wrote an agreeable account of Wilson:

He was, without any exception, the most selfless man I have ever met or even read of. He wanted nothing, and he feared nothing — absolutely nothing. Whether he was commanding the British Fleet or repairing an old motor car, he was equally keen, equally interested, equally content. To step from a great office into absolute retirement, to return from retirement to the pinnacle of naval power, were transitions which produced no change in the beat of that constant heart.

Everything was duty. It was not merely that nothing else mattered. There was nothing else. One did one's duty as well as one possibly could, be it great or small, and naturally one deserved no reward. This had been the spirit in which he had lived his long life afloat, and which by his example he had spread far and wide through the ranks of the Navy.

It made him seem very unsympathetic on many occasions, both to officers and men. Orders were orders, whether they terminated an officer's professional career or led him on to fame, whether they involved the most pleasant or the most disagreeable work; and he would snap his teeth, and smile his wintry smile to all complaints and to sentiment and emotion in every form. Never once did I see his composure disturbed. He never opened up, never unbent. Never once, until a very dark day for me, did I learn that my work had met with favour in his eyes. . . .

The system of counter-mining in use for forty years in the Navy, and the masthead semaphore which continued till displaced by wireless telegraphy, were both products of his ingenuity. He was an experienced and masterly commander of a Fleet at sea. In addition to this, he expressed himself with great clearness and thoroughness on paper, many of his documents being extended arguments of exact detail and widely comprehensive scope. He impressed me from the first as a man of the highest quality and stature, but, as I thought, dwelling too much in the past of naval science, not sufficiently receptive of new ideas when conditions were changing so rapidly, and, of course, tenacious and unyielding in the last degree.

The First Lord had no better luck than his predecessor in persuading the First Sea Lord in the matter of the Naval War Staff. He merely produced a "powerfully reasoned and unqualified refusal." Thus it was that the First Lord had no alternative but to ask for his resignation. The Commander-in-Chief of the Home Fleet, Sir Francis Bridgeman, was appointed in Wilson's place. He seemed to be willing to co-operate in the new venture. Balfour's secretary, J. S. Sandars wrote a letter to his Chief which shed some light upon these transactions and which suggests that the First Lord was not going to find it as easy to get his way as he had perhaps hoped.

J. S. Sandars to A. J. Balfour
(Balfour Papers)

EXTRACT

14 December 1911   4 Carlton Gardens
Confidential   Pall Mall

My dear Chief,

I think you were interested in the appointment of a new Board of Admiralty which Winston brought into existence immediately on taking office. Various reasons were assigned for this unexpected action. And, if you will recollect, some of us thought that the most plausible reason was that the Government desired to have the services of McKenna at the Home Office, where Winston had been an undoubted failure, for the purpose of the forthcoming Welsh Disestablishment Bill. I understand the real reason was quite different.

Bridgeman, the new First Sea Lord came to see me on Sunday afternoon, and we had a very long talk. He told me that the Government has been profoundly dissatisfied with McKenna's want of information concerning the capacity of the Navy to undertake the tasks suggested for it at recent meetings of the Defence Committee. . . .

Bridgeman related to me that McKenna was highly indignant at his removal from the Admiralty, and that he had gone into the Home Office in the most irritated condition of mind, and full of resentment against the man who had taken his place. So much for that. I asked Bridgeman how he came to leave command of the Home Fleet. He said that Winston had sent for him, never mentioning what he wanted him for, and to his great surprise he was pressed to accept the post of First Sea Lord, although he had been Commander-in-Chief of the Home Fleet less than a year. He did his best to decline, but Winston was insistent. Winston told him that he was satisfied he should never be able to work with Wilson, and that he had satisfied himself that he could work with him (Bridgeman). In the result much against the grain Bridgeman had to consent. . . . Winston's first official act was to put into Bridgeman's hand the letter which he, Winston, had addressed to Wilson requesting him to relinquish his post, for Winston had declined to see Wilson. Bridgeman told me that the letter was a fine example of what a letter ought not to be under such circumstances, especially having regard to the

high standing and conspicuous services of the outgoing First Sea
Lord. He told me that it was a plain notice to quit, coupled with a
solatium that he might have a peerage if he liked. The letter was
sent, and of course under these circumstances, Wilson, without any
grace whatever, promptly declined the honour. . . .

In November 1911 Churchill consulted General Sir Douglas Haig,
who had just returned from India, where he had served as Chief of
Staff to the Commander-in-Chief, and who was about to take up his
command as GOC Aldershot Command. Haig, like Churchill, had
served as a cavalry officer at Omdurman and in South Africa. There
is no record of any friendship having developed between them at that
time but Duff Cooper in his *Haig* quotes a letter from Haig, then a
Major, written from Omdurman to Sir Evelyn Wood, the Adjutant-
General, in which he says he is sending the letter by "young Churchill, who is going North by steamer today." So it is probable that
they met.

Haig supplied Churchill with "a masterly paper" on Staff organization, which was in itself "a formidable commentary on existing naval
methods." A part of the Admiralty resistance to the creation of a
Naval War Staff arose from the fear that it would lead to the growth
of an élite body of officers withdrawn from the practical day-to-day
work of the Navy and dwelling, brooding and planning in some irra-
tional hothouse of their own. It was felt that they would be intellectual landlubbers who would inevitably find themselves in conflict
with the commanders at sea. In a memorandum dated 6 January
1912 Churchill set out the case for a Naval War Staff and, in particular, sought to allay these misapprehensions. Its opening para-
graphs speak for themselves:

> In establishing a War Staff for the Navy it is necessary to observe
> the broad differences of character and circumstances which dis-
> tinguish naval from military problems. War on land varies in every
> country according to numberless local conditions, and each new
> theatre, like each separate battle-field, requires a special study. A
> whole series of intricate arrangements must be thought out and got
> ready for each particular case; and these are expanded and refined
> continuously by every increase in the size of armies, and by every

step towards the perfection of military science. The means by which superior forces can be brought to decisive points in good condition and at the right time are no whit less vital, and involve far more elaborate processes than the strategic choice of those points, or the actual conduct of the fighting. The sea, on the other hand, is all one, and, though ever changing, always the same. Every ship is self-contained and self-propelled. The problems of transport and supply, the infinite peculiarities of topography which are the increasing study of the general staffs of Europe, do not affect the naval service except in an occasional and limited degree. The main part of the British Fleet in sufficient strength to seek a general battle is always ready to proceed to sea without any mobilization of reserves as soon as steam is raised. Ships or fleets of ships are capable of free and continuous movement for many days and nights together, and travel at least as far in an hour as an army can march in a day.

Every vessel is in instant communication with its fleet and with the Admiralty, and all can be directed from the ports where they are stationed on any sea points chosen for massing, by a short and simple order. Unit efficiency, that is to say, the individual fighting power of each vessel and each man, is in the sea service for considerable periods entirely independent of all external arrangements, and unit efficiency at sea, far more even than on land, is the prime and final factor, without which the combinations of strategy and tactics are only the preliminaries of defeat, but with which even faulty dispositions can be swiftly and decisively retrieved. For these and other similar reasons a Naval War Staff does not require to be designed on the same scale or in the same form as the General Staff of the Army.

Naval war is at once more simple and more intense than war on land. The executive action and control of fleet and squadron Commanders is direct and personal in a far stronger degree than that of Generals in the field, especially under modern conditions. The art of handling a great fleet on important occasions with deft and sure judgment is the supreme gift of the Admiral, and practical seamanship must never be displaced from its position as the first qualification of every sailor. The formation of a War Staff does not mean the setting up of new standards of professional merit or the opening of a road of advancement to a different class of officers. It is to be the means of preparing and training those officers who arrive, or are likely to arrive, by the excellence of their sea service at stations of high responsibility, for dealing with the more extended problems which await them there. It is to be the means of sifting, developing, and applying the results of actual experience in history and present practice, and of preserving them as a general stock of reasoned opinion available as an aid and as a guide for all who are called upon to determine, in peace or war, the naval policy of the country. It is to be a brain far more comprehensive than that of any single man, however gifted, and tireless and unceasing in its action, applied continuously to the scientific and speculative study of naval strategy and preparation. It is to be an instrument capable of formulating any decision which has been taken, or may be taken, by the Executive in terms of precise and exhaustive detail.

The First Lord realized the complexity of his task, and writing afterwards in *The World Crisis* expatiated on it:

. . . Thus when I went to the Admiralty I found that there was no moment in the career and training of a naval officer, when he was obliged to read a single book about naval war, or pass even the most rudimentary examination in naval history. The Royal Navy had made no important contribution to naval literature. The standard work on Sea Power was written by an American Admiral (Admiral Mahan). The best accounts of British sea fighting and naval strategy were compiled by an English civilian (Sir Julian Corbett). "The Silent Service" was not mute because it was absorbed in thought and study, but because it was weighted down by its daily routine and by its ever-complicating and diversifying technique. We had competent administrators, brilliant experts of every description, unequalled navigators, good disciplinarians, fine sea-officers, brave and devoted hearts: but at the outset of the conflict we had more captains of ships than captains of war. In this will be found the explanation of many untoward events. At least fifteen years of consistent policy were required to give the Royal Navy that widely extended outlook upon war problems and of war situations without which seamanship, gunnery, instrumentalisms of every kind, devotion of the highest order, could not achieve their due reward. Fifteen years! And we were only to have thirty months!

It was not surprising that the Naval War Staff was still a primitive

weapon when war came in August 1914 and that it failed to be per-
fected in the harsh stress of war.

*

Sir John Fisher, who had ceased to be First Sea Lord in 1910, had
known Churchill since 1907 when they had met in Biarritz and
Fisher had greatly enthused him on a variety of naval topics. Their
friendship had waxed rapidly and Fisher soon started the series of
extraordinary letters with which he often bombarded him. The first
that survives dates from the earliest time of their friendship; in it
Fisher discussed the sugar strikes and riots which were taking place in
St. Lucia at this time:

Sir John Fisher to WSC

27 April 1907   Admiralty

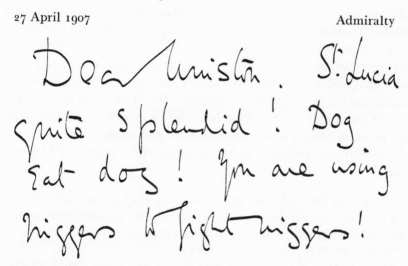

Dear Winston,

St Lucia quite splendid! Dog eat dog! You are using niggers to
fight niggers! For God's sake don't send British Bluejackets inland
amongst sugar canes on this job or we shall have to set up a War
Office inside the Admiralty & goodness knows *one* War Office is

enough! I enclose a very secret paper. *Don't let anyone see it.* The best thing ever written in the English language bar the Bible & Robertson's Sermons & letters from a Competition Wallah. Kindly return the print with your improvements in the margin — study it closely.

Ever yours

J. A. FISHER

Remember wh I told you "History is a record of exploded ideas"

At that time Churchill was still Under-Secretary at the Colonial Office. Doubtless he was pleased that this great man should impart such secrets to him so casually. Later he was to learn that Fisher did this on a widespread scale and did not scruple to leak information to the Press, and in particular to J. L. Garvin, the editor of Mr William Waldorf Astor's *Observer,* whenever he thought it could help his cause against the enemy, his colleagues, or his Chief.

Fisher had become involved in a deadly controversy with Lord Charles Beresford, who managed to intersperse high command in the Navy with voluble and ferocious outbursts in the House of Commons. The controversy in its essence was purely personal, but it embraced every imaginable topic of naval tactics, strategy and armaments, and it split the Navy from top to bottom. But Fisher prevailed. The wounds given and taken did not heal and produced a most unhealthy state of mind among naval officers ashore and afloat.

Churchill later recalled his first meeting with Fisher in *The World Crisis*:

He was then First Sea Lord and in the height of his reign. We talked all day long and far into the nights. He told me wonderful stories of the Navy and of his plans — all about Dreadnoughts, all about submarines, all about the new education scheme for every branch of the Navy, all about big guns, and splendid Admirals and foolish miserable ones, and Nelson and the Bible, and finally the island of Borkum. I remembered it all. I reflected on it often. I even remembered the island of Borkum when my teacher had ceased to think so much of it. At any rate, when I returned to my duties at the Colonial Office I could have passed an examination on the policy of the then Board of Admiralty.

Fisher and Churchill met quite often, and in between the correspondence prospered:

WSC to Sir John Fisher
(Lennoxlove Papers)

EXTRACT

19 January 1908
Secret

My dear Fisher,

I return you herewith the papers you sent me, having read them with great interest. The historical argument is most reassuring and makes very good reading besides.

I am very glad to see the unhesitating acceptance and even assertion by the Admiralty of what I have always considered the fundamental proposition of home defence, *viz* that the land force need only be sufficient to compel the enemy to employ more than 150,000 men. This premise I have always regarded as establishing (a) a real function for the Volunteers, Militia and Yeomanry and (b) removing the contention that we require a large *regular* army for home defence.

I understand of course that your Memorandum is selective and not comprehensive in its treatment of the subject. I think, however, you should face more squarely the one unique operation which falls in the third or intermediate category of half-raid half-invasion attack. Would it or would it not be worth while to sacrifice 60,000 men for the pleasure of burning London to the ground? Would it or would it not be possible to accomplish this, if it were thought worth while? This is to my mind the only doubtful point and all other descents in the United Kingdom remote from the capital would be purely irrelevant operations from a military point of view and would only confer upon the British Government an immense accession of resisting power through the resulting infuriation of the whole people.

I do not suggest that the destruction of London would be decisive; but it would be a staggering blow at the commencement of a long war. I would hang the people who did it. . . .

When Fisher resigned as First Sea Lord he received a peerage. The correspondence continued:

Lord Fisher to WSC

2 March 1910   Kilverstone Hall
Private

My dear Winston,

Now that I am absolutely free of the Admiralty I suppose I may venture to ask to be welcomed once more into your arms unless in the meanwhile you've got to hate me! My only official attachment now is the Defence Committee (on which as I told you *long ago* you ought to be & I've said it again lately behind your back!) but on the Defence Committee I only survey the Admiralty from an Olympian height and its right perspective! How is the beloved Marsh. Is he still with you? I hope so. What an awful hash you have made of your stunning majority of 124? I am no politician but if from the first you had walked straight for the Lords your progress would have been irresistible! Now it's all vacillation! I hope I am not kicking your shins! But I do detest cowardice whatever party it is! The Budget was nothing as everyone had got to see that through!

I hope I may send my best love to Mrs Winston.

Ever yours
FISHER

I'm told the Government is sure to be kicked out in June — if so it will be the Government's own doing! What would Dizzy have said with a majority of 124?

WSC to Lord Fisher
(Lennoxlove Papers)

3 March 1910   Home Office
Private

My dear Fisher,

I am truly *delighted* to get your letter. I stretched out several feeble paws of amity — but in vain. I like you vy much indeed — & I am only sorry that the drift of events did not enable us to work together. Your elevation to the Peerage was a source of real pleasure to me; & was a partial recognition of the great service you have rendered to British Naval supremacy.

I have deeply regretted since that I did not press for the Admiralty in 1908. I think it would have been easily possible for me to obtain it. I believe it would have been better for us all.

But my best wishes will always go with *you,* & I do hope we shall be able to meet & have a good talk before long.

Yours vy sinly
WINSTON S. CHURCHILL

We shall pull through all right.

Lord Fisher to WSC

7 March 1910   Kilverstone Hall
Private

My dear Winston,

You've sent me a very nice letter!

> "To my faults a little blind"
> "To my virtues more than kind"

I belong to no party and am no politician! Only a patriot! I said to Rosebery

> "Sworn to no party — of no sect am I"
> "I can't be silent — and I will not lie!"

So what I now say to you is purely disinterested: Say to T. P. O'Connor who I always think so sensible "It's the only chance that ever will offer for Ireland" and it's the only chance that ever will offer for England to get unity so let the 124 be solid for 2 years definite — you can't do with less! If the Government go out in the next 18 months they won't come in again for 20 years! *That's sure!* If the 124 are solid for 2 years or more then you stay in for 20 years! I'm no prophet only an outsider but before the Election I said the majority would be 120 and wrote it to a friend. I was only 4 out! Kindly burn this letter.

You'll all be d——d idiots if you lose this splendid opportunity!

Ever yours
F

So far, in naval matters, Fisher had been his mentor. Thus the very first thing the new First Lord did on reaching his new office was to seek counsel from his friend:

WSC to Lord Fisher
(*Lennoxlove Papers*)

25 October 1911   Home Office

My dear Lord Fisher,

I want to see you vy much. When am I to have that pleasure? You have but to indicate your convenience & I will await you at the Admiralty.

Yours vy sincerely
WINSTON S. CHURCHILL

There is no doubt from what Churchill later wrote that even at this moment he toyed with the idea of bringing Fisher back. He was later to speculate in *The World Crisis*: "I wonder whether I was right or wrong." Looked at from a greater distance the reader may incline to the view that it would have been better to take Fisher in then rather than three years later. When Churchill became First Lord, Fisher was seventy-one years old; when he invited him back he was seventy-four. People can grow old quickly at that age and the Fisher of 1914 was not the Fisher of 1911. Moreover, Churchill and Fisher would have had three years of working together in peacetime to cement their alliance. Instead, it was to be shattered at the end of nine months on the sharp and agonizing rocks of war.

Of the advice which Fisher urged upon the First Lord nothing was more pressing than the need for the appointment of a suitable Naval Secretary. He thrust a number of names upon him but concluded by saying "but you have heaps of time to choose and it *must* be a personal choice." It was not for nothing that Fisher had written in the log-book of the *Vernon*, "Favouritism is the secret of efficiency." Among the naval officers who asked to see the new First Lord in his early days at the Admiralty was David Beatty, at the age of forty, the youngest Rear-Admiral in the Navy, who for two years had been on half-pay and who was under something of a cloud because he had declined what was considered a suitable appointment in the Atlantic Fleet. Good looking and addicted to fox-hunting, Beatty was a brilliant figure in London society and some felt that his attachments were more on land than at sea. Ten years earlier he had married Miss Ethel Marshall Field, the beautiful, wilful and dominating heiress of the Marshall Field department store in Chicago.

Churchill had never met him, save before Omdurman when Beatty tossed Churchill a bottle of champagne from his gunboat on the Nile. Churchill took to him at once. He found that he thought of war problems "in their unity by land, sea and air" and was struck with "the shrewd and profound sagacity of his comments expressed in language singularly free from technical jargon." Thus Beatty, who was to command the Battle Cruisers at Jutland, and in 1917 the Grand Fleet, moved into the room beside the First Lord's as head of his Naval Secretariat and was in hour to hour touch with him throughout the working day.

The First Lord announced his new Board on November 28, a month after taking office.

First Sea Lord: Admiral Sir Francis Bridgeman (formerly C-in-C Home Fleet)

Second Sea Lord: Vice-Admiral Prince Louis of Battenberg (formerly commanding 3rd and 4th Divisions)

Third Sea Lord: Rear-Admiral Charles Briggs (no change)

Fourth Sea Lord: Captain William Pakenham (formerly commanding HMS *Collingwood*)

Civil Lord: George Lambert MP (no change)

Parliamentary and Financial Secretary: T. J. Macnamara MP (no change)

Permanent Secretary: Sir W. Graham Greene (no change)

Apart from Sir Francis Bridgeman's promotion to replace Sir Arthur Wilson, the most significant change was the latter's replacement as Second Sea Lord by Prince Louis of Battenberg. The Battenbergs came from a minor princely house but Prince Louis had married Princess Victoria of Hesse, who was a granddaughter of Queen Victoria. This led to a friendship between the families of Battenberg and Saxe-Coburg-Gotha. Prince Louis had already settled in England as a boy because of his mother's friendship with Queen Victoria's daughter, Princess Alice, the mother of Prince Louis' future wife. Prince Louis' mother was a Russian countess, Julia Theresa von Hauke, who on her marriage had been created Countess of Battenberg. Prince Louis had early been intended for the Royal Navy and went to the *Britannia* in 1868, rising, through various appointments to the rank of vice-admiral and commanding the third and fourth divisions of the newly created Home Fleet.

Churchill's appointment of Prince Louis as Second Sea Lord was warmly welcomed, not only in Royal circles. Lord Selborne, a Tory who had been First Lord from 1900 to 1905, and had been High Commissioner in South Africa at the time of the Transvaal Constitution, had not always seen eye to eye with Churchill in South Africa but although a political opponent, he warmly endorsed the appointment.

Lord Selborne to WSC

29 November 1911   Brooks's
Private   St James Street

My dear Churchill,

Accept my very sincere congratulations on your appointment of Prince Louis.

He is the ablest officer the Navy possesses and, if his name had been Smith, he would 'ere now have filled various high offices to the great advantage of the country, from which he has been excluded owing to what I must characterise as a stupid timidity.

He has in fact nearly had his naval career maimed because he is a Prince & because of his foreign relationships. I have stated what I think of his ability — I can only add that a better Englishman does not exist or one whom I would more freely trust in any post in any emergency. I think I know one of the special tasks you have in hand. I bequeathed that task as an urgent legacy to Fisher nearly seven years ago and gave him all the material for its fulfilment. To my surprise & disgust on my return from South Africa I found he had done nothing; I say "surprise" because I thought it would have been a job after his own heart, but obviously I was wrong.

Prince Louis is just the man to help you.

Yrs sincerely
SELBORNE

Though, like King Edward VII, Prince Louis spoke with a heavy German accent, he had become entirely anglicized and his supreme interest in life was the welfare of the Royal Navy. Churchill recorded in *The World Crisis* that: "It was recounted of him that on one occasion, when he visited Kiel with King Edward, a German Admiral in high command had reproached him with serving in the British Fleet, whereat Prince Louis, stiffening, had replied, 'Sir, when I joined the Royal Navy in the year 1868, the German Empire did not exist.' "

*

The years 1912 and 1913 were to witness a scandal which smirched the fair reputation of the Liberal Government. The long and complicated tale of the Marconi scandal has been admirably told by Frances Donaldson in her book of that name. There is no need to re-tell it here except in so far as Churchill was affected.

The matter arose in the following way. In March 1912 a contract was signed between the Postmaster-General and the Marconi Company to set up a chain of wireless stations throughout the Empire. Suspicion was first aroused by a gamble that took place in the shares of the Marconi Company. In August 1910 the shares had stood at £2. 8s. 9d., by March 1912 they were quoted at £6. 15s. 0d. and by April at £9. In April there were issued new shares in the American Company which were entirely separate from the British Company. There followed a series of newspaper attacks, many of them of a libellous character; the attack was initiated by Cecil Chesterton, the brother of the more celebrated G. K. Chesterton, in a paper called the *Eye Witness*. The main line of attack was levelled at the Attorney-General, Sir Rufus Isaacs, the Chancellor of the Exchequer, Mr Lloyd George, and Mr Herbert Samuel, the Postmaster-General. Most of the attack was pure innuendo, but questions in Parliament led to the appointment of a Select Committee of Enquiry by the House of Commons.

While the Enquiry was sitting the libel was given new life by *Le Matin*. This Paris newspaper suggested that Samuel had entered into an arrangement with Rufus Isaacs, and his brother, Godfrey Isaacs, Managing Director of the Marconi Company, whereby they bought shares and made a profit when the contract was signed. On this Samuel and Rufus Isaacs issued a writ for libel against *Le Matin*. The two leading Tory lawyers F. E. Smith and Carson were retained by the aggrieved Liberal Ministers and this prudent move which was much resented by some Tories to a large extent disarmed the Opposition's criticism of the Ministers. *Le Matin* had apologized for the libel as soon as a writ was issued, did not defend the case and paid the costs.

When the matter was first raised in the House, both Lloyd George and Isaacs had denied that they had shares in the Company. In the course of the case against *Le Matin,* it was thought judicious to reveal that they had had shares in the American Company. Whether, if Isaacs and Lloyd George had disclosed four months earlier to the House of Commons the true position, they would have got off scot free, it will be doubted; but the fact that they were so disingenuous as to wait four months before revealing the whole truth of the matter must be held very damaging to them in their conduct as public men. However, the two Ministers were vindicated because the Liberal Party had an automatic majority on the Select Committee. If Asquith had wavered in his support of the two Ministers, they would surely have been ruined. As it was those who attacked them and alleged corruption really saved the Ministers. The Ministers ought not to have speculated in the shares and they ought not to have been disingenuous to the House of Commons. But nothing they had done was corrupt.

Churchill did all he could to help Lloyd George and it was probably that at this time their lifelong friendship was cemented. In *Old Men Forget* the late Lord Norwich quoted Churchill as saying many years afterwards that if the affair had been properly handled by the Tories they might have brought down the Government, but "Some of them were too stupid and, frankly, some of them were too nice."

The services which Churchill rendered to Lloyd George were threefold. Firstly, he was largely responsible for persuading Northcliffe not to play the matter up unduly, secondly, he persuaded F. E. Smith and Carson to appear in the libel action against *Le Matin* and thirdly, when Asquith was going to reply in the Debate on the report of the Select Committee, he paced frequently between the rooms in the House of Commons of the Prime Minister and the Chancellor and persuaded the former to use no words which would provoke Lloyd George's resignation. Perhaps, however, an even greater service was the evidence he gave when he was summond from the Admiralty to give evidence before the Select Committee.

He had been summoned because the Editor of the *Financial News* had repeated a vague rumour that another Minister was involved and when pressed had named Churchill as that Minister. Churchill vehemently and passionately attacked the Select Committee for summoning him at a moment's notice upon "a most insulting charge . . . that, having had dealings in Marconi shares, I sat silent while friends and colleagues came forward and voluntarily disclosed their exact position — that I sat silent while they were subjected to gross ill-usage and covered with every species of calumny and insult, that all the time I sulked in the background, keeping my guilty knowledge to myself and desiring to conceal it from your Committee." Churchill went on:

> And am I to understand that every person, Minister or Member of Parliament, whose name is mentioned by current rumour and brought forward by a witness who says he does not believe it, is to be summoned before you to give a categorical denial to charges which, as I have pointed out, have become grossly insulting by reason of the fact that the Minister in question, it is suggested, has concealed up to this moment what his position was? . . . I am grieved beyond words that a Committee of my fellow-members in the House of Commons should have thought it right to lend their sanction to the putting of such a question. Having said so much, I will proceed to answer your question. I have never at any time, in any circumstances, directly or indirectly, had any investments or any interests of any kind — however vaguely it may be described — in Marconi telegraphic shares, or any other shares of that description, in this or any other country in the inhabited globe.

Lloyd George survived the scandal to become Prime Minister. Sir Rufus Isaacs was an equally durable character. In his youth he had been hammered on the Stock Exchange and made bankrupt, though it should be recorded that he later repaid his debts in full. Now within a few months of the Marconi affair he was appointed Lord Chief Justice.

As Attorney-General Isaacs had a right to the Lord Chief Justice-ship and if Asquith had not appointed him it would have been tantamount to admitting a stain on his honour. He continued to rise and shine in the political world, serving as Ambassador to the United States during the war and as Viceroy of India afterwards. In fact, neither Isaacs nor Lloyd George made any money out of their financial speculations. They merely lost a little.

Churchill took the opportunity of a speech at the National Liberal Club on 1 July 1913 to vindicate his colleagues. He did so with a good deal of righteous indignation: so much so that one cannot but feel that he had been embarrassed by their activities. In *The Times* of July 2 he is reported in part as saying:

> . . . If there had been the faintest touch of dishonour or breach of public duty in the conduct of my right honourable friends, no services, however great, no prospects of future service, however vital, however hopeful, would have enabled us to march with them. But when we know on the evidence, on the mature conclusion even of their most bitter opponents, that no stain of any kind rests upon their integrity or upon their character, what kind of curs should we be if we allowed them to be trampled down by a campaign of calumny and slander unequalled in recent annals? (Loud cheers). And those who thought that this event and the cruel suffering it has entailed upon them would make any difference to their career of usefulness in public life and in the Liberal Party, little knew the constant, discriminating, and fearless loyalty of democracy to its leaders. They reckoned without the National Liberal Club; they reckoned without our noble chairman; and they reckoned without the Prime Minister of this country. (Cheers) They reckoned without that broad yet searching justice which great peoples, and this people above all others, mete out to men who have served them well.
>
> I said just now that my right honourable friends had suffered for our sake. The Attorney-General has few enemies in politics. He has as few as any man who takes an active and prominent part in public affairs can make, and in the great profession of which he is the chief, and the chiefest ornament, a life-long test has produced him nothing but friends.
>
> My right honourable friend the Chancellor of the Exchequer is more bitterly hated in certain powerful classes — certain great organized confederated groupings of public opinion — he is more bitterly hated and more relentlessly pursued than even Mr Gladstone was in the great days of 1886. I do not know how one can measure the degree

of hatred with which he has been pursued in certain quarters. I do not believe my right honourable friend the Attorney-General would ever have been attacked in the way he has been but that they wanted to strike at Mr Lloyd George. (Cheers) I do not know how you can measure the degree of hatred, but let me give you two most striking instances which afford some method of measuring it. We have Lord Robert Cecil rising in his place in the House of Commons and saying that there are things which he could not put in his report because he has no evidence, because he cannot prove them, but which he is, nevertheless, prepared to impart privately to any member of Parliament who asks him. A more disgraceful statement never issued from the lips of a member of a Select Committee of the House of Commons. (Loud cheers) And if anything could make it more odious and contemptible it is that it should be uttered by one who has been fraudulently posing as a fair-minded, impartial man, and lending a smooth pretence of gentlemanly culture to the dirty work he had set himself to do. (Loud cheers)

At a later stage it came out that the Master of Elibank, the Liberal Chief Whip, had not only had some shares for himself but also for the Liberal Party. He was away in Bogota, in South America, at the time on some business of Lord Cowdray. Later, audiences would shout "Bogota, Bogota" whenever his name was mentioned on the public platform. However, he was vindicated with the rest. Churchill's warm-hearted harangue did not deter Rudyard Kipling from writing his celebrated attack on Sir Rufus Isaacs when a little later he was appointed Lord Chief Justice. His poem "Gehazi" may be found in his collected works and the author has printed it in his *Lord Derby "King of Lancashire"*. The Marconi ministers in the poem, however, were duly grateful.

Master of Elibank to David Lloyd George
(Lloyd George Papers)

EXTRACT

20 August 1913   Bogota
                                                       Colombia

. . . *it was just like him.* I have always regarded him as a really true friend who will always stand by one in foul or in fair weather — and that speech for its warmth of feeling for his injured friends and its scathing attack on their traducers will show to many what we already knew that in time of trouble Winston is the first to spring to the side of his friends. . . .

15

Britain's Naval Defence

THE DOMINANT question in 1912, for the nation as a whole, as well as for the Admiralty, was that of German intentions. Many people were content to regard the Agadir crisis as an unfortunate incident that was best forgotten, and to look forward to many years of increasingly friendly and constructive co-operation with Germany. Churchill, more perhaps than any other public figure and certainly more than any other Minister, sensed the growing German danger, and sought, both in his departmental activity and his speeches to alert the public and to prepare the Navy for the dangers which confronted it. Churchill had twice watched German Army manoeuvres as a guest of the Kaiser; he had pondered long and deeply over German intentions. Through Sir Ernest Cassel the First Lord had received, when by the courtesy of the Kaiser, the details of the German Navy Law which was to be introduced in May 1912. The proposals themselves were not at this stage particularly alarming. It must be assumed that the Kaiser's motive in letting Churchill see them was to procure a situation of goodwill and confidence for the more serious steps that he and his naval experts had in mind for later in the year.

This seemingly amiable gesture did not put Churchill off his guard. Cassel had been born in Germany, but had made his fortune in England. He had been a friend of Lord Randolph's, as well as of King Edward VII when the latter was still Prince of Wales. Churchill inherited his father's friendship and Cassel had himself proved a good and sagacious friend to him. Churchill in fact entrusted the money he had made from his writings and his lecture tour to Cassel, and it had been well cared for. After the war, when the Crown successfully prosecuted Lord Alfred Douglas for criminal libel that Douglas had perpetrated on him, Churchill revealed in his evidence that Cassel had given him £500 as a wedding present.

Cassel's loyalty to the land of his adoption was never in doubt, and in these uncertain years of mounting anxiety before the war he provided a useful liaison not only with the Kaiser but also with many of the most powerful men in Germany. Shortly after he had communicated the news of the new German Navy Law to the First Lord he wrote proposing that Churchill should have exploratory talks with the Kaiser. Cassel's letter does not survive, but its import may be divined from Churchill's answer.

WSC to Sir Ernest Cassel

7 January 1912   Admiralty
[Copy]
Private

My dear Cassel,
    It will not be wise for me at this juncture to have any parley with your august friend. If the King were to visit Germany & I went with him, both hypothetical conditions, I shd be honoured by being permitted to discuss the great matters wh hang in the balance. But the occasion wd have to arise naturally & I shd have to be empowered by Grey & the Prime Minister. Even then all that cd be said on our part wd be that till Germany dropped the Naval challenge her policy wd be continually viewed here with deepening suspicion & apprehension; but that any slackening on her part wd produce an immediate détente with much good will from all England. Failing that I see little in prospect but politeness & preparation. [*Sentence deleted*: What is mere imperialism to them is life & death to us.]
    I deeply deplore the situation for as you know I have never had any but friendly feelings towards that great nation & her illustrious Sovereign & I regard the antagonism wh has developed as insensate. Anything in my power to terminate it, I wd glady do. But the only way I see open is one which I fear Germany will be reluctant to take.
    Will you then as you think best disengage me with the greatest

respect from the suggestion, using so far as your judgment inclines you, what is written here. Always my dear Cassel your vy sincere friend,

WINSTON S. CHURCHILL

I will try & come to see you one day this week.

Meanwhile Churchill had caused an analysis to be made of the exact implications of the proposed German Navy Law. He was then in a position to broach the whole matter with the Foreign Secretary.

WSC to Sir Edward Grey

EXTRACT

31 January 1912   [Admiralty]

Observations

It seems certain that the new Navy Law will be presented to the *Reichstag* & that it will be agreed to, even the Socialists not resisting. The naval increases are serious & will require new & vigorous measures on our part. The spirit may be good, but the facts are grim. I had been thinking that if the old German programme had been adhered to we shd have built 4,3,4,3,4,3 against their 6 years programme of 2,2,2,2,2,2. If their new programme stands, as I fear it must, & they build 3,2,3,2,3,2, we cannot build less than 5,4,5,4,5,4. This maintains 60% superiority over Germany only in Dreadnoughts & Dreadnt Cruisers. It will also be 2 keels to 1 on their additional 3 ships.

The matter of a 4th squadron in full commission is also a serious and formidable provision. At present, owing to the fact that in the 6 winter months the 1st & 2nd squadrons of the [German] High Sea Fleet are congested with recruits, there is great relief to us from the strain to wh we are put by German naval powers. The addn of the 3rd squadron will make that strain continual throughout the year. The maintenance in full comm of 25 battleships wh after the next 4 or 5 years will all be Dreadnts exposes us to constant danger only to be warded off by vigilance approximating to war conditions. A further assurance against attack is at present found in the fact that several of the German Dreadnts are vy often the wrong side of the Kiel

Canal wh they can't pass through & must therefore make a long detour.

The deepening of the Canal by 1915 will extinguish this safety signal. The fact that the defenders are always liable to be attacked when not at their ordinary . . . [?] strength by an enemy at his selected moment & consequent maximum strength means that our margins wd have to be vy large. Agst 25 battleships we cd not keep less than 40 available within 24 hrs. This will involve addnal expense.

The German increase in personnel must also be met. I had intended to ask Parlt for 2,000 more this yr and 2,000 next. I expect to have to double these quotas. On the whole the addn to our estimates consequent upon German increases will not be less than 3 million a year.

This is certainly not dropping the naval challenge.

I agree with you that caution is necessary. In order to meet the new German squadron we are contemplating bringing home the Meditn battleships. This means relying on France in the Meditn & certainly no exchange of system wd be possible, even if desired by you.

The only chance I see is roughly this. They will announce their new programme, & we will make an immediate & effective reply. Then if they care to slow down the *"tempo"* so that their Fleet Law is accomplished in 12 and not in 6 years, friendly relations wd ensue, & we, though I shd be reluctant to bargain about it, cd slow down too. All they wd have to do wd be to make their quotas biennial instead of annual. Nothing wd be deranged in their plan. 12 years of tranquillity wd be assured in naval policy. The attempt ought to be made.

Yrs vy sincly

w s c

On 7 February 1912 Churchill left London for Belfast, where he was to speak in support of the Home Rule Bill. While waiting for the train to leave London he read in the late edition of the evening papers the Kaiser's speech on opening the Reichstag, in which he announced increases in both the Army and Navy. Knowing of the as yet unpublished Navy Law, and reading the Kaiser's words, Churchill "sustained a strong impression . . . of the approaching danger." He determined to speak frankly; and on February 9, at Glasgow, made what was perhaps his most important public speech as First Lord.

The purposes of British naval power are essentially defensive. We have no thoughts, and we have never had any thoughts of aggression, and we attribute no such thoughts to other great Powers. There is, however, this difference between the British naval power and the naval power of the great and friendly Empire — and I trust it may long remain the great and friendly Empire — of Germany. The British Navy is to us a necessity and, from some points of view, the German Navy is to them more in the nature of a luxury. Our naval power involves British existence. It is existence to us; it is expansion to them. We cannot menace the peace of a single Continental hamlet, no matter how great and supreme our Navy may become. But, on the other hand, the whole fortunes of our race and Empire, the whole treasure accumulated during so many centuries of sacrifice and achievement, would perish and be swept utterly away if our naval supremacy were to be impaired. It is the British Navy which makes Great Britain a great power. But Germany was a great power, respected and honoured all over the world, before she had a single ship. . . .

If to-day our position is eminently satisfactory we owe much to the foresight and resolution of Mr McKenna. . . . Whatever is needed for the safety of the country will be asked for by the Government, and granted by the representatives of the nation with universal assent. There is no need for anxiety in regard to our shipbuilding capacity. There is no chance whatever of our being overtaken in naval strength unless we want to be. . . . But what of the men? We have to-day 135,000 men in the active service ratings of the Navy. The great bulk of them are long-service men who have begun as boys and have been trained as a life-long profession to the naval service. We have no difficulty in recruiting for the Navy . . . and there is no doubt whatever of our ability to make any increases which may be necessary, and which I think will be necessary, in the personnel of the Navy. We have great reserves of seamen in this country. There are measures which may be taken to make a greater use of our reserves than has hitherto been found possible, and I have given directions for that part of the subject to be carefully studied by the naval experts upon whom I rely. Our reserves, both from the Royal Navy and from the Mercantile Marine, are a great resource, and this island has never been, and never will be, lacking in trained and hardy mariners bred from their boyhood up to the service of the sea.

Whatever may happen abroad there will be no whining here, no signals of distress will be hoisted, no cries for help or succour will go up. We will face the future as our ancestors would have faced it, without disquiet, without arrogance, but in stolid and inflexible determination. We should be the first Power to welcome any retardation or slackening of naval rivalry. We should meet any such slackening not by words but by deeds. . . . If there are to be increases upon the Continent of Europe, we shall have no difficulty in meeting them to the satisfaction of the country. As naval competition becomes more acute, we shall have not only to increase the number of ships we build, but the ratio which our naval strength will have to bear to other great naval Powers, so that our margin of superiority will become larger and not smaller as the strain grows greater. Thus we shall make it clear that other naval Powers, instead of overtaking us by additional efforts, will only be more outdistanced in consequence of the measures which we ourselves shall take.

Churchill's Glasgow speech caused an immediate and prolonged outcry. The Germans resented the remark that for them the Fleet was "in the nature of a luxury." As Churchill himself wrote in *The World Crisis,* "The *Luxus Flotte* became an expression passed angrily from lip to lip in Germany." Liberals in England disliked what they considered the speech's threatening tone; yet when Lord Haldane returned from his Berlin Mission to discuss closer Anglo-German relations he told the Cabinet that "so far from being a hindrance to him in his negotiations, the Glasgow speech had been the greatest possible help."

On February 14 Churchill circulated a translation of the proposed new German Navy Law to his Cabinet colleagues, together with a covering note in which he pointed out "the extraordinary increase in the striking force, of ships of all classes," resulting in the creation of a Fleet of five battle squadrons which would be "extremely formidable," particularly as the battle squadrons would each be attended by a battle-cruiser squadron and by flotillas of destroyers and submarines, four-fifths of which would be maintained in full permanent commission. On the next day Churchill circulated the following Memorandum to the Sea Lords:

Memorandum by WSC

15 February 1912   [Admiralty]
[Copy]
Secret

1. The naval situation disclosed by the new German Navy Law renders the formation of an additional Battle Squadron in Home waters necessary. We cannot afford to keep fully commissioned battleships abroad during these years of tension. The first ten days and especially the first five days of war wd require the maximum immediate development of naval power in the North Sea and the Channel. Once our mobilisation has been effected and even before any naval decision has been obtained it shd be possible, if desired, to detach a Battle Squadron for the Mediterranean. But the greatly increased striking force wh Germany is organising, and against wh we must *always* maintain sufficient margins, makes it necessary that all fully commissioned battleships, whether eventually destined for the Mediterranean or not, shd be retained in the main theatre of operations until our mobilisation is complete, or the enemy's fleet beaten.

2. Proposals shd be made for carrying out this policy. As it is not now possible to reduce the total number of ships in full commission, but on the contrary some increase is necessary, there is no longer any financial saving to be looked for. The alternative of basing one of the battle squadrons on Gibraltar and [Castletown] shd not be excluded from consideration. The Atlantic fleet wd thus be recalled, and the Mediterranean battle squadron moved into the Atlantic station. It wd not then be necessary to strengthen the Mediterranean cruiser squadron.

The number of vessels for wh we shall have to provide accommodation may make it necessary to use Gibraltar to the full. The diplomatic aspect wd be better also.

Both places shd therefore be examined by the staff in their strategic and administrative aspects. The question is urgent.

W S C

In early March Churchill circulated to the Cabinet, and sent to the King, a memorandum in which he stated bluntly the full implications of the German Navy Law, which "practically amounted to putting about four-fifths of the German Navy permanently on a war footing."

On March 9 Churchill wrote to Fisher to tell him that he intended to "announce publicly the policy of the two keels to one on all increases above the existing German Navy Law." On March 18 Churchill introduced his first Naval Estimates in the House of Commons. These were largely what his predecessor McKenna had envisaged. At the same time he laid down the new principle for the future: "Sixty per cent in Dreadnoughts over Germany as long as she adhered to her present declared programme, and two keels to one for every additional ship laid down by her." This did not immediately involve expenditure beyond that proposed by McKenna, namely, £44 million. Naval expenditure had been rising for some years, as the following figures show:

1907–8	31,251,156
1908–9	32,181,309
1909–10	35,734,015
1910–11	40,419,336
1911–12	44,392,500

"Unlike McKenna's speeches on the estimates," Professor Marder wrote in *From The Dreadnought to Scapa Flow,* Volume I, "which were apologetic and sometimes confused, Churchill was almost brutally clear and frank." Colonel Charles à Court Repington wrote privately to Churchill:

Colonel Charles à C. Repington to WSC

EXTRACT

21 March 1912   Maryon Hall
                                                     Hampstead
My dear Churchill,

The opinion of an amateur looker-on regarding our naval affairs may not be of much interest, but I should like to offer you my warmest congratulations upon your masculine handling of our naval policy, and to tell you how completely I am in accord with the policy which you have announced. I suppose that there must be a little yapping from Berlin for a week or so, but if your speech is read in its complete text I cannot help hoping that the Germans will see the point of it all.

From my point of view you have converted me from an attitude of suspicious mistrust of the Admiralty into one of complete confidence and I think that this is so because for the first time policy seems to be based on war considerations and not on any other. Of course it is all promise at present and not performance and I hope that you may some day explain our theory of battleship distribution at home in time of peace, and of commerce protection in war, but, assuming that I am what Palmerston used to call a fair foolometer — I suppose that most people in the street will share my views and that you will have the great merit of having stabilised a national policy which will prove enduring.

The point of your great speech on March 18 which appeals to me most is that in which you guarantee to meet at one average moment the naval force of an enemy at his selected moment. There is a whole world of difference between this and the past. . . .

Lord Esher was also impressed.

Lord Esher to WSC

26 March 1912   The Roman Camp
Private   Callander N.B.

My dear Winston,

I have been meaning for ages to write you a line of affectionate congratulation.

In my time — extending now over 30 years of public life — no such speeches have been made as yours — so straight and so daringly truthful.

Ever yours
ESHER

Esher was a strange and enigmatic creature. He was an intimate in Court circles and was on familiar terms with politicians of both parties. Some may think him an embryo of those busybodies like Tom Jones and Philip Kerr (later Lord Lothian) who, as members of the "Cliveden Set" did our country so much harm between the two wars, barging about in every field with high-minded irresponsibility. Esher was a tremendous gossip, but he did more good than harm. He was often a catalyst in the shaping of policy. As a founder member of the Committee of Imperial Defence he did most valuable work. His massive memoirs and diaries are a real contribution to history. The documents of his mission to Paris 1914–18 are at the British Museum, and remain under seal until 1981. Moving freely in the background, he shunned public office. The only offices he ever adorned were:

Private Secretary to Lord Hartington	1878–1885
Liberal MP for Penryn and Falmouth	1880–1885
Secretary of the Office of Works	1895–1902
Lieutenant Governor of Windsor Castle	1901–1928
Governor of Windsor Castle	1928–1930

and his son, in his Preface to the Esher diaries, adopted the unusual course of printing a list of all the jobs he was offered and yet refused. Since he will often recur in this story, it may be of interest to list the appointments which it was claimed he declined.

1886	Editorship of the *Daily News*
1891	Editorship of the *News Review*
1898	To write the Life of Disraeli
1899	Under-Secretaryship for Colonies
1900	{ Under-Secretaryship for War { Governorship of Cape Colony
1903	Secretaryship of State for War
1905	GCB
1908	Viceroyalty of India
Date Uncertain	Earldom

The Times considered Churchill's Estimates speech "one of the best expositions, perhaps, indeed, the best exposition of naval policy which has been made since Lord George Hamilton's famous statement in 1889." The Kaiser described Churchill's speech as "arro-

gant"; Bethmann Hollweg, the German Chancellor, wrote that Churchill "seems to be a firebrand past praying for." But Churchill's
instinct was a sound one, for within two months the Kaiser had
removed the conciliatory German Ambassador Metternich from London, a clear sign that he was not in earnest about an Anglo-German
rapprochement, and on May 21 the German Navy Bill was passed
into law by the Reichstag.

Churchill was not content to watch the mounting growth of armaments. He still hoped that it might be possible to persuade the
Germans to call a halt, if only temporarily, to their accelerated programme of naval construction. But when in April he proposed a
"Naval Holiday" the Kaiser replied that such an arrangement could
only be made between allies. In an attempt to break the deadlock
and reduce German suspicions, Churchill wrote a letter to Sir Ernest
Cassel intended for the Kaiser's eye. It was conciliatory and frank,
but led to no positive change in the German refusal to come to some
agreement.

WSC to Sir Ernest Cassel

EXTRACT

14 April 1912   Admiralty
[Copy]

My dear Cassel,

I am deeply impressed by the Emperor's great consideration . . .
and I take this opportunity of saying again that we have been
throughout equally innocent of any offensive design. I suppose it is
difficult for either country to realise how formidable it appears to the
eyes of the other. Certainly it must be almost impossible for Germany with her splendid armies and warlike population capable of
holding their native soil against all comers, and situated inland with
road & railway communications on every side, to appreciate the sentiments with which an island state like Britain views the steady &
remorseless development of a rival naval power of the vy highest
efficiency. The more we admire the wonderful work that has been
done in the swift creation of German naval strength, the stronger,
the deeper & the more preoccupying those sentiments become.

Patience, however, and good temper accomplish much: & as the

years pass many difficulties & dangers seem to settle themselves peacefully. Meanwhile there is an anxious defile to be traversed, and what
will help more perhaps than anything else to make the journey safe
for us all is the sincere desire for goodwill & confidence of wh Ballin's
letter & its enclosure are a powerful testimony. . . .

Herr Ballin, director of the Hamburg-America Line, in his letter
had told Cassel that it was Churchill's "frankness and honesty" in
proposing a Naval Holiday which had "flustered the whole world,
and especially the leading parties in Germany, and has caused a
torrent of indignation in the Press."

On 4 May 1912 Churchill was one of the speakers at the annual
Royal Academy banquet. The other guests included the Prime
Minister, who spoke on art. Churchill, whose interest in painting
had not yet been aroused, took the opportunity to describe what he
called the sole aim of naval policy: "the development of the maximum war power at a given moment, and at a particular point. Everything in the naval world is directed to the manifestation at a
particular place during the compass of a few minutes of a shattering,
blasting, overbearing force." Churchill also ventured a prophecy:
"I believe that if any two great civilized and highly scientific nations
go to war with one another, they will become heartily sick of it before
they come to the end of it."

On May 9 and 10 the King inspected the Fleet at Weymouth. The
Prime Minister was also present. Two major advances were demonstrated during the inspection: aeroplanes detected submarines beneath the surface, and explosive bombs were dropped from aeroplanes. The King, Prince Albert and A. J. Balfour all travelled in a
submerged submarine, and according to the *Annual Register* "the
satisfactory state of the first British line of defence . . . was impressed
on the public."

The *Pall Mall Gazette* gave an account of Churchill taking Lord
Morley and A. J. Balfour down into one of the turrets of the *Orion*
to show them how the guns of a super-Dreadnought worked. Despite
the "cramped and oily quarters, with a mass of machinery penning
them in on either side" the visitors were impressed. The *Gazette*
commented that "Mr Churchill, quite a naval enthusiast, seems to

instil into his guests some of his own keen appreciation of Naval men and material."

On May 15 Churchill was the chief guest of the Shipwrights' Company at Fishmongers Hall. He spoke on the horrors of war and then went on: "It is much more likely, I say it with sincere conviction, that war will never come in our time and perhaps will have passed from the world, at any rate for the period which our most adventurous imagination enables us to foresee."

Churchill determined to press forward with his policy of preparedness. He was supported in his endeavours by A. J. Balfour, who, though regarding an Anglo-German war as a virtual impossibility, as did many Liberals, saw the dominant need to maintain British naval supremacy. Balfour had been a member of the Committee of Imperial Defence from its inception: when Prime Minister he had strongly approved the Committee's formation. He remained on the Committee when he became Leader of the Opposition.

A. J. Balfour to WSC

22 March 1912   4 Carlton Gardens
Dictated
Private & Confidential

My dear Winston,
I return you the documents you were so very kind as to send me. I have read them with the deepest misgiving.

A war entered upon for no other object than to restore the Germanic Empire of Charlemagne in a modern form appears to me at once so wicked and so stupid as to be almost incredible! And yet it is almost impossible to make sense of modern German policy without crediting it with this intention. I am told that many good observers in France regard a war in May as inevitable. Personally, I am more disposed to think that, if war comes, it will come when the disparity between our Naval Forces is less than it is at present. But imagine it being possible to talk about war as inevitable when there is no quarrel, and nothing to fight over! We live in strange times!

Yours sincerely
ARTHUR JAMES BALFOUR

*

Early in 1911 F. E. Smith had introduced Churchill to a remarkable young Canadian millionaire, William Maxwell Aitken, who had arrived in England the year before, at the age of thirty-one. He had made a large fortune by organizing a series of mergers and had decided to settle in England in order to take up Joseph Chamberlain's policy of Tariff Reform as a means of binding the Empire more closely together. He knew little about English politics when he arrived, but within a year had found out so much that he was able by his machinations, when Arthur Balfour resigned the leadership of the Tory Party, to procure the leadership of the Party in the Commons for his friend and fellow Canadian, Andrew Bonar Law. The two preeminent contenders for the succession were Walter Long and Austen Chamberlain. Aitken, by pushing now one, now the other, managed to produce a stalemate so that both men to avoid splitting the Party stood down in favour of Law. It was a fantastic achievement. This gifted and, to many people, sinister character, will frequently reappear in the remaining volumes of this story.

Aitken was naturally excited by the proposal which Churchill encouraged at this time, that Canada should make some contribution to Imperial defence, and offered to do what was in his power to help should Churchill visit Canada, as was then being suggested:

Sir Max Aitken to WSC

[Undated]

Private

Dear Mr Churchill,

About Canada. If you go you will have a great reception and if properly looked after it might easily be a turning point. Chamberlain intended to go to Canada but illness interfered. Had he gone it's my belief the Country would have been aroused and Imperial Preference forced on England. You would have regarded that as disastrous, and I am only illustrating the possibilities in Canada, which is like America, and can be swayed by the right person. I was Secy to the Nova Scotia Committee which was making the Chamberlain arrangements.

I don't think any other person can arrange your reception as efficiently as I can. Please forgive the conceit. I know you won't do anything for Imperial Preference but you are aiming for the same end and your plan may be as efficient. I don't think so, but that makes no difference.

There is an objection to me you must know about. I created all the big trusts in Canada. None of them are bad trusts but the Western farmers attack me very often and sometimes very offensively. I don't care. But you might not like an intimate connection. I can best illustrate the position when I tell you that my relation to Canada was in a small way the same as Morgan's relation to America. I'm done now and in fact for eighteen months past I have steadily pulled out. But the trusts remain, and will and can remain with or without tariffs. In fact there are more efficient trusts in England than in Canada or America. If you don't think so I'll prove it to you. Transportation not tariff is the corner stone of the Trust.

If you don't mind the objection I would take care to relieve you from the incubus if it developed. And if you are to be my guest it won't so appear. Probably it doesn't make any difference at all, and I exaggerate it.

Another matter for your consideration is the Canadian political situation. To efficiently organise your reception I would have to use both liberals and conservatives. I couldn't get them together if Canada is then in the midst of an election. And you couldn't avoid political chairmen etc. I think this requires consideration.

On behalf of Mrs [Lady] Aitken as well as myself I urge you to go with us on such date as you may fix via New York — because I have all the transportation I require by that route. If you would rather go West alone we will start you on your way, meet you on return.

Please don't tell anybody I admitted I organized any trusts, please forgive me for this very long letter.

Yours faithfully
W. M. Aitken

If you would rather go West alone we will start you on your way & meet you on return.

Please don't tell anybody I admitted I organized any trusts, & please forgive me for this very long letter

Yours faithfully
wm.aitken

WSC to Sir Max Aitken

5 May 1912   Blenheim

My dear Aitkin [*sic*],

It is with vy great reluctance that I have come to the conclusion that our Canadian project must stand over till next year. I am vy much indebted to you for the kindness with wh you have offered to smooth my path. I shall look forward to availing myself of your powerful aid in the not distant future.

I hope you will come & dine on Tuesday night to meet Louis Botha. I hope LG may be there too.

Yours sincerely
WINSTON S. CHURCHILL

Other Conservatives were less content with Churchill's conduct of naval affairs. Walter Long, who had failed to become Leader of the Conservative Party in 1911, wrote to Bonar Law:

Walter H. Long to Andrew Bonar Law

EXTRACT

27 May 1912   Schinznach les Bains
Confidential   Switzerland

. . . I was very glad to observe the caution and brevity with which you referred to W. Churchill and his naval policy: apparently he is doing right, but I don't trust, or believe in, him, I profoundly distrust Fisher who is behind him (this accounts for Garvin's support) and in my opinion we ought to watch his action very closely, especially in the Mediterranean, and with a hostile, rather than a friendly eye. I know the best men *in* the Navy regard W.C. and all his works with profound suspicion and have misgivings: they look to us to see through W.C's trickery and be ready to detect and fall upon his misdeeds. . . .

Churchill persevered. The new German Navy Law of May 1912 confirmed the German intention to challenge Britain's naval supremacy. On July 2 Churchill, in a Cabinet memorandum, stressed that the Law would result in an "extraordinary increase in the striking force of ships of all classes, immediately available throughout the year." Many Liberals felt that if Britain would relax the pace of naval building the Germans would do likewise. But the seventy-six-year-old Earl Brassey, who had been Civil Lord of the Admiralty in Gladstone's second administration, and was the founder of the *Naval Annual,* stressed in a letter to Churchill the rightness of his policy, and encouraged him to continue on the lines laid down in his Glasgow speech.

Lord Brassey to WSC

8 July 1912   Spithead
                                                 Sunbeam R.Y.S.

Dear Mr Churchill,

Having lately spent a week at Kiel and seen much of the chief people I briefly report.

I have come away convinced that building ships to the full limit of our requirements gives no offence. The cry of the pessimists, the discussions and the comparisons are not pleasant to Germany: they fully accept the ships.

I am assured that they have reached the limit of possible expenditure on the Navy. If the Glasgow speech policy is steadily and quietly pursued, the party in Germany opposed to costly rivalry will gain.

I should add that Admiral Holtzendorff, commander in chief of the High Sea fleet, is against further increase of dimensions.

The same lesson is impressed at Spithead when we take into view the danger to the large ships from the torpedo and mine in the dark hours.

Yours sincerely
BRASSEY

Churchill had arranged a review of the Fleet at Spithead which took place on July 9. It was designed to show off British naval supremacy and to prepare Parliament for the forthcoming Supplementary Naval Estimates. There were 223 ships present from the First, Second and Third Home Fleets; including forty-four battleships, five battle cruisers and twenty-five armoured cruisers. The Prime Minister and the First Lord attended in the Admiralty Yacht *Enchantress* and

members of the Lords and the Commons in the Union Castle liner
Armadale Castle.

Churchill's enthusiasm for naval affairs was remarkable. He was
more than "quite" a naval enthusiast, as the *Pall Mall Gazette* had
described him. He made frequent journeys on the Admiralty yacht
Enchantress, visited all the naval stations off the British Isles, toured
shipyards, and mastered most aspects of naval administration. He
took an interest in the problems of the lower deck. A visit to a submarine in June 1912 prompted the *Daily Express* to write: "He had
a yarn with nearly all the lower deck men of the ship's company,
asking why, wherefore, and how everything was done. All the sailors
'go the bundle' on him, because he makes no fuss and takes them by
surprise. He is here, there, and everywhere."

Lloyd George felt that the Navy had become "an obsession" with
Churchill and told Riddell that he had rebuked Churchill for this:
"You have become a water creature. You think we all live in the sea,
and all your thoughts are devoted to sea life, fishes and other aquatic
creatures. You forget that most of us live on land."

A week after Lloyd George had delivered this lecture, Churchill
received a letter from one of his father's friends which must have
given him pleasure.

Sir Frederick Milner to WSC

11 July 1912   91 Lancaster Gate

Dear Winston Churchill,

I was looking through some old letters, & came upon one from you
written at the time you brought out your Father's life. In it you say
you look upon me as one of the best of your Father's friends, & that
though you feared I could not approve of the step you had taken,
you hoped to retain my respect, & would value any expression of my
opinion. . . .

For some time after you joined the Radicals, I confess I could follow you with no sympathy. The violence & bitterness of your language, and your extreme views against your own class filled me with
sorrow and dismay. I could not help contrasting your conduct with
Randolph's after he gave up office, and it was almost impossible to

believe that you could so suddenly and completely have changed all your opinions, which you had so vigorously advocated but a short time before.

From the first, I always recognised your great abilities; and I remember well imploring Arthur Balfour to try & conciliate you, as I consider you the greatest asset in our Party, but it seemed to me you were prostituting these abilities on the sordid altar of Party.

Gradually however your speeches became less bitter & more statesmanlike. At the Home Office I thought you did really useful work. . . . Since your appointment to the Admiralty you have done admirable work, and have gained my respect and esteem. You have the opportunity of your life now. The future welfare of your country lies in your hands, and I believe you will rise to the position. I am now able to watch your career with sympathy and deep interest. You have a difficult job, and many diverse interests to satisfy, but you have abilities second to none, & I only hope your health may stand the strain, for it will be a severe one. . . .

On July 11, at the 118th meeting of the Committee of Imperial Defence, Churchill made an important statement on naval policy. The Canadian Prime Minister, R. L. Borden, was present, as well as Asquith, Lloyd George, Haldane, Morley, McKenna, Grey, Harcourt, Crewe, Seely, Fisher, Sir John French and General Henry Wilson. Churchill outlined the history of German naval development, explained the problems which faced the Admiralty, and answered questions about naval policy. He opened with a broad survey of the naval situation:

Committee of Imperial Defence
118th meeting

11 July 1912

. . . The whole character of the German fleet shows that it is designed for aggressive and offensive action of the largest possible character in the North Sea or the North Atlantic — action, according to the memorandum accompanying their first Bill, against the strongest naval Power at some moment when that Power will not be able, owing to some duty which it may have to discharge to its Colonies or to some other part of the Empire, to keep all its forces concentrated to meet the blow. The structure of the German battleships shows clearly that they are intended for attack and for fleet action. They are not a cruiser fleet designed to protect Colonies and commerce all over the world. They have been preparing for years, and are continuing to prepare, on an ever larger scale a fleet which, from its structure and character, can be proved by naval experts to have the central and supreme object of drawing out a line of battle for a great trial of strength in the North Sea or in the ocean. I will not go into technical details, but the position of the guns, the armament, the way the torpedo tubes are placed — all these things enable naval experts to say that this idea of sudden and aggressive action on the greatest scale against a great modern naval Power, is undoubtedly the guiding principle of German naval policy. When you go to the smaller types of vessels, the same principle can be traced. In their torpedo boat destroyers, which they call torpedo boats, speed has been the principle essentially that they have gone upon, and that they have developed. We on our part have developed gun power and strength to a greater extent, because our destroyers would play the more defensive rôle of protecting our battle fleet against the attack of the enemy's destroyers. Their torpedo boats are undoubtedly designed with a view to developing an attack upon the great ships of the navy that they may be opposed to, whereas ours have in view the object of destroying the torpedo craft of the enemy which would be trying to make an attack. That again is a very significant fact. Now we come to the submarine. If there ever was a vessel in the world whose services to the defensive will be great, and which is a characteristic weapon for the defence, it is the submarine. But the German development of that vessel, from all the information of defence into one of offence, that is to say, they are building not the smaller classes which will be useful for the defence of their somewhat limited coastline, but the large classes which would be capable of sudden operation at a great distance from their base across the sea. So I think I am justified in saying that the German fleet, whatever may be said about it, exists for the purpose of fighting a great battle in the North Sea, both with battleships and with all ancillary vessels, against some other great naval Power which is not referred to by them.

We are sometimes told that the Germans only think of fighting a battle which will leave the greater naval Power seriously weakened after the battle is over; they will have been destroyed themselves and the greater naval Power will be weakened. I do not think anyone who respects the German nation and knows to how high a degree they carry their study of the military art on sea and on land will be much impressed by that. Anything more foolish than to spend all these millions year after year and to make all these efforts and sacrifices and exertions for no other purpose than certainly to come off second best on the day of trial cannot well be imagined; and I think it is useless and foolish to shut one's eyes to the fact that whatever may be the intention of the German Government, and whatever may be the intention of the German people, which is quite a different thing, the spirit and purpose of the inception and of the prolonged development of the German navy is such as to lead only to one conclusion, and that is that it is intended for a great trial of strength with the navy of the greatest naval Power.

I was going to say, but of course that is a matter for the Foreign Office, that we have no quarrel with Germany. There are questions on small points of foreign policy, but there is no quarrel at all, and everybody has done their best to avoid anything which increases antagonism and so forth. But the fact remains, and it cannot be doubted, that if the British navy were out of the way, either beaten in battle or in some other way had disappeared as a factor, a far wider prospect and a far more brilliant prospect would be opened to German action in any quarter of the world, if, of course, it has any such ambition.

I do not pretend to make any suggestion that the Germans would deliver any surprise or sudden attack upon us. It is not for us to assume that another great nation will fall markedly below the standard of civilisation which we ourselves should be bound by; but we at the Admiralty have got to see, not that they will not do it, but that they cannot do it. That is the view we take of the duties which are placed upon us, and I should like to tell the Committee that that involves a very great strain indeed. The advantages of the initiative are self-evident. I have spoken in public about the contrast between the average moment of one Power and the selected moment of another. That makes a great difference; it may make as much as 20 to 25 per cent difference in the number of ships that can be brought immediately into the line. There is this great distinction which should be drawn between naval war and land war. On the continent of Europe you have great armies living side by side across a purely political frontier, but there is a cushion, a pad, which is a

great buffer between them and the actual development of great operations of war, that is, mobilisation. The whole male population has
to be withdrawn from its ordinary employment, the whole life of the
country has to be suspended, and a vast operation of mobilisation
has to be begun, the very first signs of which would be immediately
apparent to the other country before anything of a decisive or critical
character could take place. No such security stands in the way of a
sea operation. The ships which were assembled the other day at Spithead, or which are now assembled at Kiel and at Wilhelmshaven, can
begin fighting as soon as they bring the ammunition up from
below to the gun, and absolutely no preliminary steps need be
taken which would be noticeable by any foreign Power, however
great the vigilance might be. That being so, I say that there is a
great deal of truth in the statement which was made last night in the
House of Commons by Mr Bonar Law, when he said that this great
concentrated fleet, ever growing in efficiency and strength, within
twelve or fourteen hours' steam of our shores, was almost a loaded
cannon continually pointed at us. Of course they may say that our
fleet is similarly pointed at them, but nothing that we can do on the
sea can menace the freedom or security of Germany, nothing that
we can do on the sea can make any difference to that which makes
life worth living for them. For us the matter is very different. Any
serious misfortune which happened to us at sea would produce immediately the ruin of the greatness of this country, and the disruption
of the many parts of the Empire now united to us.

*

During 1912 politicians and the Press discussed in detail the problems of the Mediterranean. Should Britain seek there to hold the
naval balance against Austria and Italy, as she held it against Germany in the North Sea? An Admiralty War Staff memorandum of
June 1912 recognized that Italy and Austria, although technically
allies, were building *against* each other, and that as the French could
be assumed to be with Britain, the balance of naval power could
favour Britain even without British Dreadnoughts.

On 18 March 1912 Churchill told the House of Commons that the
4th Battle Squadron based on Gibraltar could act eastwards or west-
wards as required. He was criticized by Lord Esher who, in a letter

to the King on May 30 called Churchill's statement "dust in the eyes of the public." According to Esher, the 4th Battle Squadron would be required in the North Sea at the outset of war, and could play no part in the Mediterranean. Esher advised the King that the choice lay between "such increases of Naval Power as will ensure sea command in the Mediterranean, or the substitution of a conscript for a voluntary Army, or the abandonment of Egypt and Malta and a complete reversal of the traditional policy of Great Britain in regard to her trade routes and military highways to the East."

Churchill was not unaware of Lord Esher's views. In January 1912 Asquith had sent him a "highly confidential" memorandum written by Esher which, in Asquith's view "has much good sense in it." The memorandum stressed the need for Britain to maintain and increase her naval power in the Mediterranean. Churchill's answer had been forthright:

> It shd not be supposed that mastery on the seas depends on the simultaneous occupation of every sea. On the contrary it depends upon ability to defeat the strongest battlefleet or combination wh. can be brought to bear. This ability cannot be maintained by a policy of dispersion. The sea is all one, and war is all one. The supreme strategic principle of concentration of superior force in the decisive theatre, and the supreme tactical principle described by Napoleon as *"frapper la masse"* must govern all naval dispositions. All the rest will come *"par surcroit."* Dispersion of strength, frittering of money, empty parades of foolish little ships "displaying the flag" in unfrequented seas, are the certain features of a policy leading through extravagance to defeat.
>
> Some doubt seems to be thrown on these "fundamentals" by Esher's examples and the tone in wh they are referred to. So far as the Cte of ID is concerned, it appears to me that if Admiralty contemplate an important change like the concentration in Home Waters, they wd of course consult the Prime Minister. It would then rest with him whether the CID shd be involved. Personally, I shd be glad of its support.
>
> However the ultimate responsibility of the First Lord must not be impaired. He cannot be expected to be responsible for faulty dispositions, or what he thinks are such!
>
> W S C

Haldane supported Churchill, and had written to him confidently on January 24 that "whenever we have a case it will decide our way and we should in consequence have the PM at our backs. You and I must always be responsible for policy, and if we secure the head of the Govt we shall be in a still stronger position."

*

Many people have considered that Fisher, though he never commanded a fleet in war, was the greatest sailor since Nelson. He was certainly one of the most exciting letter writers of all time. His letters, carefully collected and brilliantly edited by Professor Marder, are an enormous contribution to the political as well as to the naval history of those days. In his introduction to Volume I of *Fear God and Dread Nought,* Marder quotes Lord Acton: "History is better written from letters than from histories." Acton added, "No public character has ever stood the revelation of private utterances and correspondence. Be prepared to find that the best gives way under closer scrutiny." Fisher's letters were more indiscreet than Churchill's, but they have not destroyed his character any more than Churchill's will be found to have destroyed his. None the less, Fisher's letters do betray indiscretion and vanity of great rarity.

Churchill had continued to correspond with Fisher over the years. Churchill was anxious to use Fisher to preside over an enquiry into the use of oil-burning boilers for naval ships. In April he wrote to Fisher, who was in Naples, and sent the letter out by King's messenger. Churchill used some arguments in favour of the Dreadnought design which Fisher found acceptable. In Fisher's reply of April 22 he set out seven points on design in new ships and expressed his pleasure that Churchill "appreciated Jellicoe." He also thanked Churchill for writing:

> Also, I ought to thank you for your words as to myself, that "the adoption on a great scale of the Big Gun in such good time" is one of the "finest acts of foresight and wisdom by which your naval administration has been distinguished."

But interlarded with all this occurred the following passage:

I regret that in regard to what you say and what you have done in the appointments of Sir Hedworth Meux, Sir Berkeley Milne, and Sir Reginald Custance, I fear this must be my last communication with you in any matter at all. I am sorry for it, but I consider you have betrayed the Navy in these three appointments, and what the pressure could have been to induce you to betray your trust is beyond my comprehension. You are aware that Sir Berkeley Milne is unfitted to be the Senior Admiral afloat, as you have now made him. You are aware that Sir E. Poe should have been Commander-in-Chief at Portsmouth, failing your promise to Admiral Egerton, and you must have been as cognizant as I am of Custance's views and animus.

Churchill was a proud man so he must have wanted Fisher's services very badly to put up with such an insult. Perhaps he did not take Fisher's insults at their face value. He continued to seek Fisher's advice. One can hardly believe that he would have persevered had he known that Fisher was writing to Esher, as was revealed by Marder in *Fear God and Dread Nought,* a few days later on April 29:

Winston, alas! (as I have had to tell him) feared for his wife the social ostracism of the Court and succumbed to the appointments of the two Court favourites recently made — a wicked wrong in both cases! Winston has sacrificed the Country to the Court, and gone back on his brave deeds of December 5th last! so I've done with him!

In fact, Fisher's letter to Churchill did not contain the further insult about his wife; but it seems to have come naturally to Fisher to suggest to Esher that it did. A week later we find him boasting to his son, Cecil, on May 6:

Well! as regards Winston Churchill, *"amantium irae amoris integratio est."* No doubt, I sent him an awful letter, and he really has replied very nicely that no matter what I like to say to him, he is going to stick to me and support all my schemes and always maintain that I am a genius and the greatest naval administrator, etc, etc, etc.

He added:

I've had a very nice telegram from Winston. However, there is no getting over the fact that he truckled to Court influence when

McKenna, under greater pressure, did not! and I have rubbed this into WC and he don't like it! McKenna was splendid! I will not go in the Admiralty Yacht. WC is coming out for 7 or 8 weeks, I believe. Still, for the good of the Navy I am reluctantly feeling compelled to continue my advice to him as to new Dreadnought and other vital fighting business.

Meanwhile Churchill, unruffled, wrote to Fisher:

WSC to Lord Fisher
(*Lennoxlove Papers*)

15 May 1912   Admiralty

My dear Fisher,

The Prime Minister & I are coming to Naples on the 24th for a few days en route for Malta & Gibraltar in the *Enchantress*. I shall look forward to having a good talk with you & I therefore defer replying to your last letter, wh I was so glad to get. If the consequences of recent appointments were to be what you apprehend I shd feel your censures were not undeserved. But they will not be. The highest positions in the Admiralty & in the Fleet will not be governed by seniority; & the future of the Navy rests in the hands of men in whom your confidence is as strong as mine.

No change of Government will take place in the near future: & no change of Government would carry with it any change of policy in this respect.

For the rest let us wait till we can talk freely. Writing is wearisome & unsatisfactory.

Yours vy sincerely
WINSTON S. CHURCHILL

Fisher was writing to Esher on the same day:

. . . You are now responsible! I've condoned Winston's damnable lapse! but I've "rubbed it in" while doing so that it is quite incomprehensible to me how he could be a Hero last December and a Poltroon in April! and that ever since Cromwell it has always been "the People's Navy" and "the Court Army"! and no Admiralty ever yet in history were sent on board the Flagship of the Second-in-

Command while the Sovereign flew his standard in the ship of the Commander-in-Chief! It's quite wrong and unprecedented! but I fear Bridgeman and Battenberg are powerless against Winston! Winston told Jellicoe that I was the one he entirely and fully leaned on! and yet you see he sold me! (He told Jellicoe this only last week in confidence!) Jellicoe has an unbounded admiration of Winston! He says he's wonderful! . . .

I have declined to go with WC in the Admiralty Yacht. He is coming out here. Don't mention to him or anyone else, please, that I was asked. . . .

Churchill further sent two telegrams encouraging Fisher to come on board the Admiralty Yacht. After Fisher had received Churchill's letter of May 15 he wrote to Gerard Fiennes, assistant editor of the *Pall Mall Gazette:*

I've just had a letter [of May 15th] that the Prime Minister and WC are coming direct here from England to spend "a few days" with me and to talk of things that can't be written about!

Evidently wishing it to be known, he concluded his letter:

They arrive here in the Admiralty Yacht on May 23, but this is all private. However, if you see the arrival of the *Enchantress* at Naples in the newspaper, with the Prime Minister and WC, then it's public property, and also that I am here! I have not told anyone but you. I thought it would interest you and might be useful as a piece of news, if you can get it by other means from Naples when they arrive. . . .

Marder in a footnote points out that he "promptly told his son, Esher, [Arnold] White [the author], [Lionel] Yexley [Editor of the *Fleet*], [J.A.] Spender, and possibly others!"

On May 22 the First Lord, the Second Sea Lord, Prince Louis of Battenberg, the Prime Minister and his daughter Violet Asquith boarded the *Enchantress*. They sailed the same day and arrived in the bay of Naples on May 24. Despite what had gone before all went splendidly. Miss Asquith, now Lady Asquith, recorded in her diary:

Friday 24th May 1912. We reached Naples this morning and anchored in the harbour under grey skies, Vesuvius hidden in the clouds, no sun or colour anywhere. In many ways it looked rather like a Scotch shipping town — (I hope all this is not an omen?) Some of us went on shore in a pinnace — straight to the Museum where we saw the most wonderful treasures (ecstatic enumeration follows) . . . Back to the Yacht for luncheon — and *there was Lord Fisher!* in the flesh (but not yet in the bag). I examined him minutely and tried to diagnose his mood and his potential placability. His eyes, as always, were like smouldering charcoals — lighting up at his own jokes. He was very friendly to Father and Prince Louis but glowered a bit, I thought, at Winston. To me he retailed a stock of anecdotes, puns, chestnuts and riddles which might have come out of crackers. (I expect that all "great men" of action talk like this — at least to women?) After luncheon he dragged us off *à contre cœur* on a long expedition to a most hideous modern Pompeian villa belonging to some friends of his called —— Poor Father bled — aching to get back to the Museum. Winston endured for oil's sake, but behaved as though he were barely conscious. I played up for all I was worth and perjured myself in praise of the most monstrous objects. . . . As the day wore on I noticed signs of mellowing in Lord F. which I feel will turn to melting before long. I whispered at tea to Winston: "He's melting." His mind was far away. He gazed at me blankly and said in a hard, loud voice: "What's melting?" Distracted I replied: "The butter," which brought me an "old-fashioned look" from our hostess, who eyed the bread and butter anxiously. When we got back to the *Enchantress* Lord F. and W. were locked together in naval conclave. . . . I'm sure they can't resist each other for long at close range.

The next day she wrote: "Danced on deck with Lord Fisher for a very long time before breakfast."

Fisher made the most of the visit. He wrote to Lady Fisher from Lucerne on May 28:

WC said the King was always talking about me to him, and had acknowledged how much I had done, but that I was absolutely wedded to certain ideas he couldn't approve of. WC turned round to him and said that everything now that was said at home and abroad of the "present overwhelming supremacy and efficiency of

the British Navy" was solely and only and entirely due to me! and
that "there would shortly be 16 ships with $13\frac{1}{2}$-inch guns, when not a
single German ship had anything but a 12-inch gun, which, compared to the British $13\frac{1}{2}$-inch gun, was only a pea-shooter!" and he
said the King shut up then. I also heard indirectly from Esher that
Winston Churchill always sticks up for me to all the Court people
besides the King! About the only grateful politician I have ever met!
(except Lord Spencer). Selborne, Cawdor, Balfour, and all the rest
have never said one word in my defence! I speak of men as I find
them, and no such black ingratitude has ever been shown me in this
world as the Tory Party have shown me! It is all in black and white,
and they will all be exposed in due course! I don't wonder at the
Country becoming socialistic! . . .

And to Gerard Fiennes he wrote:

> I was nearly kidnapped and carried off in the Admiralty Yacht! They
> were very sweet about it! My old cabin as First Sea Lord all arranged
> for me! I had a good time and came out on top! The Prime Minis-
> ter is "dead on" for my coming back, and he has put things so forcibly
> to me that, with great reluctance to re-enter the battle field, I prob-
> ably shall do so! But not a word of this, except perhaps in the very
> deepest confidence to dear Garvin. I had great talks with the Prime
> Minister upon every sort of subject ("China to Peru!"). No doubt
> I am "all there" with him! (This sounds rather egotistical, I fear!)
> Don't breathe a word.

Churchill had also enlisted Fisher's help in influencing Asquith.
"The Prime Minister is coming to Naples: he will come and see you,"
Churchill had written to Fisher on January 10. "Talk to him about
the Mediterranean and about shifting the bases." In May Churchill
explained to Haldane that Admiralty war plans for the previous five
years "have provided for the evacuation of the Mediterranean as the
first step in a war with Germany."

WSC to Lord Haldane
(Haldane Papers)

6 May 1912   In the train
Secret

My dear Haldane,

The Malta Conference can settle nothing. I hope they will however have the advantage of concentrating the PM's attention upon
important questions in a way that wd be impossible in the rush of
business over here. The actual point has been settled long ago by the
brute force of facts. We cannot possibly hold the Mediterranean or
guarantee any of our interests there until we have obtained a decision
in the North Sea.

The War-plans for the last 5 years have provided for the evacuation
of the Meditern as the first step consequent on a war with Germany
& all we are doing is to make peace dispositions wh approximate
to war necessities. It wd be vy foolish to lose England in safeguarding Egypt.

Of course if the Cabinet & the House of Commons likes to build
another fleet of Dreadnoughts for the Meditern the attitude of the
Adm'l will be that of a cat to a nice fresh dish of cream. But I do
not look upon this as practical politics. It wd cost you 3 or 4 millions
a year extra to make head against Austria & Italy in the Meditern &
still keep a 60% preponderance in the North Sea. All the above is
true, independent of anything France may do. If she is our friend,
we shall not suffer. If she is not, we shall suffer. But if we win the
big battle in the decisive theatre, we can put everything else straight
afterwards. If we lose it, there will not be any afterwards. London
is the key of Egypt — don't lose that.

Considering you propose to send the whole Br Army abroad, you
ought to help me to keep the whole Br Navy at home.

Whatever the French do, my counsel is the same, & is the first of
all the laws of war — overpowering strength at the decisive point.
I cd meet you & Grey on Thursday night after dinner, but shall not
be back during the rest of this week.

Yours very sincerely
WINSTON S. CHURCHILL

The Mediterranean question was discussed in detail at the end of
May and early in June, when Churchill, Asquith and Kitchener, then

Agent-General in Egypt, met at Malta. Churchill and Asquith arrived in the *Enchantress,* and Kitchener was summoned from Egypt. Although a final decision was left to the Committee of Imperial Defence, Churchill reached a provisional agreement with Kitchener which was in harmony with Churchill's view.

Note of Draft Arrangement concerted with Lord Kitchener

The new arrangements for the naval forces in the Mediterranean in time of peace will be: —

(*a.*) 2 battle cruisers — preferably 3.

(*b.*) A cruiser squadron of 4 armoured criusers; 2 to be "Devonshires," the other 2 to be of the same class as soon as circumstances permit.

(*c.*) The present smaller vessels on the station (less *Yarmouth*).

(*d.*) The present torpedo craft and submarines stationed at Malta.

The Mediterranean (Fourth) Battle Squadron will be based on Gibraltar, the *Yarmouth* being the attached cruiser. The Squadron will be raised to an ultimate total of 8 ships, as follows: —

The 2 "Lord Nelsons" to join the 4 "Duncans" about January or February 1913

The *Dreadnought* and *Albermarle* towards the end of 1913, as crews become available.

This Squadron will cruise in the Mediterranean as much as possible, but will be available for service elsewhere if seriously required in peace, or in case of war.

The Malta Dockyard to be maintained on its existing scale.

The Submarine Flotilla and, if necessity should arise, the Destroyer Flotilla, at Malta to be increased so as to provide an adequate system of local defence.

A Flotilla of Submarines capable of overseas action, with a battleship of the *Royal Sovereign* class, manned by a suitable nucleus crew, as a parent ship, to be based on Alexandria. The land defences of the port, erected by the Egyptian Government, to be sufficient to ensure their safety, the Admiralty agreeing to provide the necessary guns and mountings.

While returning to England in the *Enchantress,* Churchill prepared a long memorandum on the Naval situation in the Mediter-

ranean, in which he argued his case before the CID in a masterly
fashion.

NAVAL SITUATION IN THE MEDITERRANEAN

5 June 1912

Secret

The new German Navy Law provides for keeping 25 battleships in
full permanent commission. There will also be 4 battleships of the
Reserve, which will have full crews on board, and may consequently
be used at very short notice. Against this we cannot keep less than
33 battleships in full commission, and all of these must be either in
home waters or constantly and easily available. We are straining our
margins even by basing one squadron of 8 on Gibraltar. While that
squadron is abroad we shall only have an equality with the Germans
in numbers of fully commissioned ships. We have, in addition, 8
battleships with full nucleus crews (5th battle squadron), and these
compare in readiness with the 4 German reserve battleships above
mentioned. It will be nearly 2 years before we have the men to man
the 6th battle squadron with full nucleus crews. It will be seen, therefore, that we have no great superiority in the numbers of vessels ready
at short notice, even when the arrangements which we are making are
complete. We have of course, substantial superiority in quality, particularly in the older ships, but we are all agreed that the proportion of 33 to 25 fully commissioned ships is the very least in numbers
that will provide for the safety of Great Britain.

2. We cannot afford to keep 6 battleships in the Mediterranean
in full commission. It is not so much the ships, but the men that are
wanted. It is a waste of our limited resources to use full complements
to man inferior ships. . . .

3. We have hitherto always been able to keep a fleet in the Mediterranean equal to that of our rivals for the time being, whoever
they were. Formerly, it was France, now they may be said to be Italy
and Austria, separately or together. Unless we can face Italy and
Austria in the Mediterranean, it would be a faulty strategic disposition to keep a battle squadron there. Neither Austria nor Italy have
any Dreadnoughts actually commissioned at present; but in a few
months the first Italian Dreadnought will be ready, and thereafter

both Powers will continue to be reinforced at short intervals by very powerful modern units, until by January 1915 Austria and Italy together will dispose of no less than 10 Dreadnought vessels. Against this, or half this force, the 4 "Duncans" and the 2 "Swiftsures," hitherto stationed at Malta, could offer no effective resistance. They would only be a cheap and certain spoil. We should be simply leaving a weak division of old ships to be overwhelmed in a subsidiary theatre, while the crews might have manned much better ships in the decisive theatre. The Malta squadron can do great good at home, and no good where it is.

4. It would be both wrong and futile to leave the present battle squadron at Malta *to keep up appearances*. It would be a bluff which would deceive nobody. The influence and authority of the Mediterranean Fleet is going to cease, not because of the withdrawal of the Malta battleships, but because of the completion of the Austrian and Italian Dreadnoughts. It will cease certainly and soon whether the Malta battleships are withdrawn or not, only in the latter case we shall have more to lose in a subsidiary theatre and less to win with in the decisive theatre. . . .

5. If it were decided to maintain a purely British local superiority in the Mediterranean as well as adequate margins in the North Sea, it would be necessary to build and man an entirely new and additional squadron of modern battleships for that purpose. This would be a very extravagant policy, and is not necessary to the fundamental safety of the British Empire or to our ultimate victory and supremacy at sea. It would commit us to a two-Power standard against Italy and Austria in the Mediterranean, plus a 60 per cent. preponderance always ready against Germany in home waters. This could not be justified by our primary needs. But anyhow this alternative, extravagant though it would be, is not open to us. There is no time, even if Parliament voted the money, to build a special squadron of Dreadnoughts for the Mediterranean. We could not get them ready soon enough; and if they were ready we could not provide trained officers and seamen for them. We have therefore got to face the fact that the naval control of the Mediterranean is swiftly passing from our hands whatever we do, while we remain single-handed.

6. . . . It must be plainly recognised that we must adopt the *rôle* in this minor theatre appropriate to the weaker naval Power, and while in the North Sea we rely on the gun as our first weapon, we must in the Mediterranean fall back mainly on the torpedo. The

Admiralty would propose to leave a sufficient force of armoured and protected cruisers based on Malta to discharge all the diplomatic functions which our responsibilities entail. For the defence of Malta it will be necessary to build and organise a strong flotilla of submarines and to reinforce the destroyer flotilla already there. If Malta and the Malta Channel obtain the reputation of being a nest of submarines and torpedo craft, and is effectually so defended, it would not be worth the while of Austria or Italy to risk either battleships or transports in an attempt to capture it by a regular attack. Unless they were prepared to pay an altogether disproportionate price for the island, the only two dangers to be apprehended would be surprise or starvation. . . .

7–10. . . .

11. The contingencies which we must bear in mind may be classed in their order of probability, as follows: —

(i.) *Great Britain* v. *Germany.* — In this case the Mediterranean would not be involved.

(ii.) *Great Britain and France* v. *Germany and Austria.* — In this case the position in the Mediterranean would be secure. [Because of French Mediterranean preponderance.]

(iii.) *Great Britain and France* v. *the Triple Alliance;* or

England, France, and Russia v. *the Triple Alliance.* — The arrangements proposed above would in this case be adequate for the Mediterranean.

(iv.) *Great Britain alone* v. *Germany and Austria.* — It is probable that by good management we could maintain ourselves simultaneously in both theatres once our mobilisation was complete; but a great many risks would have to be run in the subsidiary theatre until a decision was obtained in the North Sea.

(v.) *Great Britain alone* v. *the Triple Alliance.* — The situation would then be grave, and we should certainly suffer heavy losses in the Mediterranean; but there would be very good hopes, so far as the next three or four years are concerned, that we should be able to prevent the hostile fleets in the Mediterranean and the North Sea from joining, and to attack them separately in superior strength.

Churchill reinforced his arguments in a further memorandum on the Naval Situation circulated to the Cabinet on 26 June 1912. He urged his colleagues to read it in conjunction with his memorandum

of June 5, and asked for a swift decision. He put his arguments succinctly.

> To hold the Mediterranean single-handed will cost from 15 to 20
> millions capital expenditure, plus *personnel* and upkeep, and can-
> not be fully achieved till 1916.
>
> There are therefore four courses: —
>
>   *a.* To reduce our margins in the North Sea, which my naval
> advisers state will imperil the country.
>   *b.* To abandon the Mediterranean, which would be very in-
> jurious.
>   *c.* To build a new fleet for the Mediterranean, which will cost
> 15 to 20 millions and cannot be ready before 1916; and,
>   *d.* To make an arrangement with France and leave enough ships
> in the Mediterranean to give her undoubted superiority, as
> proposed in my memorandum of 16th inst.

McKenna took up the cause of those who wanted to divide British
naval power between the North Sea and Mediterranean, and circulated a memorandum to the Cabinet sharply critical of Churchill's
arguments. To this Churchill replied in a further memorandum, in
which he stated bluntly that in the opinion of his advisers the balance
of forces in the Mediterranean under McKenna's scheme "would be
such as to expose a British fleet, equal to nearly a third of our total
battleship strength and manned by 12,000 of our best officers and
seamen, to certain destruction."

Churchill ended his reply to McKenna with the brief, laconic sentence: "The arguments here adduced have the full concurrence of
the First and Second Sea Lords, and all figures and statements of fact
have been verified by the War Staff."

Churchill's persistence was largely successful. On July 4, at the
117th meeting of the Committee of Imperial Defence, it was agreed
after much discussion, in which the First Lord took an ample share,
that "there must always be provided a reasonable margin of superior
strength ready and available in Home waters. This is the first re-
quirement. Subject to this we ought to maintain, available for Mediterranean purposes and based on a Mediterranean port, a battle fleet
equal to a one-power Mediterranean standard, excluding France."

The Committee of Imperial Defence had not decided as Churchill wanted as far as the Mediterranean was concerned. But although ships were to be maintained at Malta, the dominant needs of the North Sea would be upheld. Churchill was therefore able to pursue his policy with greater ease. When Lord Roberts wrote to him on July 10 urging the need to strengthen Britain's position in the Mediterranean, Churchill replied confidently:

WSC to Lord Roberts

12 July 1912   [Admiralty]
Copy

My dear Lord Roberts,
    There are several important points in your letter with which I am not quite sure that I find myself fully in agreement. The massing of our fleet in home waters does not arise out of the military weakness of these islands solely, but from their dependence on ocean communication, a dependence wh no military strength could cure. Secondly, the need of being always ready without a mobilisation to meet a hostile attack requires larger margins in peace of ships of the first line than wd perhaps be necessary a fortnight after war had broken out. It does not follow from our present dispositions that considerable forces cd not be detached for service in the Mediterranean or beyond it, once our mobilisation is complete. Surprise, the only chance of the weaker naval power, is our bugbear, & to guard against it, not merely for a few weeks, but year after year indefinitely, is our burden.
    It wd be possible under actual and prospective Admiralty arrangements, if it were necessary, to provide a substantial naval force for service in the Eastern Mediterranean; but we shd have to make civil arrangements in this country wh wd amount to a practical mobilisation.
    I admit that to maintain a naval war singlehanded with the Triple Alliance, & a great land war for the protection of Egypt against Turkey simultaneously is beyond our powers. The circumstances are formidable but also unlikely. It seems probable however that a decisive naval victory wd open up a series of situations wh wd lead to the capitulation of any force landed in Egypt in the interim.

Even Lord Esher seemed willing to make a gesture of amity and reconciliation, despite his previous hostility to Churchill's plans. While still hoping to convert Churchill to a more pro-Mediterranean view, he wrote nevertheless in a conciliatory manner:

Lord Esher to WSC

[undated]   The Roman Camp

My dear Winston,

You have probably heard from Jackie [Fisher] and others that I am strongly and irreconcilably opposed to "abandoning" the Mediterranean, but I don't want you to think that I am opposed to *You*. Because of your youth, zeal, assiduity and great powers of mind, you are the only member of the government for this vital post which you occupy. Your speeches, as I said to you, are the best and frankest, upon naval and kindred matters, since Dizzy's.

First, as you know, I have liked you since, as a child, you sat on my knee; and have admired your brilliance ever since you became a man.

So much for the personal aspect of this affair.

I see your strategical aims and entirely sympathize with your wish to be overwhelmingly strong at this crucial moment and at this crucial point in War.

There are, however, other considerations. When I wrote to you about your great speech, you will remember that I took exception to that portion of it which related to the Mediterranean Fleet.

For years I have been associated, very intimately, with a Society now very numerous and powerful, whose *raison d'être* was to press for "Two keels to one ——"

The whole object of this scale of shipbuilding was (a) to fight with a margin of 60% in our favour, at a moment's notice (b) to keep our prestige unimpaired, in *Peace,* in the Mediterranean.

Holding so strongly these views, and adhering to these engagements, you can realise what a shock it has been to me to find the country on the verge of abandoning the principle which underlies them.

Good, however, is certain to come out of this controversy. You will find the nation *anxious to give you the ships and men* you require

for the double purpose — perhaps all the more anxious as you have
not pressed for either. Please do not reply. I *may* come up for the
CID.

Always your friend
ESHER

Show this to your wife.

While at the Admiralty, Churchill sought to guide foreign policy
in the direction of closer Anglo-French relations. In his view the
existing situation was unsatisfactory. There was no alliance with
France, but instead, as he wrote to Asquith and Grey on 23 August
1912, "we have the obligations of an alliance without its advantages
and above all without its precise definitions." Already, on July 17,
Churchill had taken an initiative towards closer Anglo-French naval
co-operation when he informed the French Naval Attaché, the Comte
de Saint-Seine, of Britain's Mediterranean decisions, and added that
"I thought that France would be wise to aim at a standard of strength
in the Mediterranean equal to that of Austria and Italy combined."
But Churchill, while anxious for conversation and general understanding with France, was opposed to any agreement which would
result in "tying us up too tightly with France and depriving us of
that liberty of choice on which our power to stop a war might well
depend." When in August the Cabinet agreed to authorize naval
conversations between Britain and France, Churchill, in a memorandum for Asquith and Grey, warned against too great a commitment
to France.

> The point I am anxious to safeguard is our freedom of choice if the
> occasion arises, and consequent power to influence French policy be-
> forehand. That freedom will be sensibly impaired if the French can
> say that they have denuded their Atlantic seaboard, and concentrated
> in the Mediterranean on the faith of naval arrangements made with
> us. This will not be true. If we did not exist, the French could not
> make better dispositions than at present. They are not strong enough
> to face Germany alone, still less to maintain themselves in two
> theatres. They therefore rightly concentrate their Navy in the Medi-
> terranean where it can be safe and superior and can assure their
> African communications. Neither is it true that we are relying on

France to maintain our position in the Mediterranean. . . . If France did not exist, we should make no other disposition of our forces.

Circumstances might arise which in my judgement would make it desirable and right for us to come to the aid of France with all our force by land and sea. But we ask nothing in return. If we were attacked by Germany, we should not make it a charge of bad faith against the French that they left us to fight it out alone; and nothing in naval and military arrangements ought to have the effect of exposing us to such a charge if, when the time comes, we decide to stand out.

This is my view, and I am sure I am in line with you on the principle. I am not at all particular how it is to be given effect to, and I make no point about what document it is set forth in. But how tremendous would be the weapon which France would possess to compel our intervention, if she could say, "On the advice of and by arrangement with your naval authorities we have left our Northern coasts defenceless. We cannot possibly come back in time." Indeed (I added somewhat inconsequently), it would probably be decisive whatever is written down now. Everyone must feel who knows the facts that we have the obligations of an alliance without its advantages, and above all without its precise definitions.

W S C

The Anglo-French naval discussions took place, and led to an agreement signed on 10 February 1913 which laid the foundations of naval co-operation not only in the Mediterranean but also in the Straits of Dover, the western Channel and the Far East. The phrasing of the agreements was such that Churchill's anxieties were allayed. The British and French Navies were to co-operate so that *should* Britain decide to enter a war in which France was involved, the maximum efficiency could be ensured. But there was no alliance. Churchill was to agree in January 1914 with Prince Louis' proposal to reject a French suggestion for putting into use joint Anglo-French signal books. Nevertheless, co-operation was close. The signal books had been drawn up by the two Admiralties. And in the same month Churchill was to agree to an Anglo-French exchange of intelligence about the Austrian and Italian Fleets.

As we have seen, immediately after Agadir Churchill had mooted the idea of an Anglo-Russian-French defensive alliance. This proposal found few "takers," and subsequent reflection and, doubtless, discussions with the Foreign Secretary led him to the more cautious attitude outlined above. But when the German power was about to be unleashed upon France, proximity to the danger led him to urge his colleagues that we had some obligations of honour as well as of self-interest to prevent the High Sea Fleet coming down the Channel.

Meanwhile the implications of the new German Navy Law had sunk into the minds of his colleagues and still more into the minds of the Conservative Opposition. Possibly because public opinion was at that time unprepared for an increase in the Estimates, he had been content in March to go along gently with the McKenna Estimates, which were themselves an increase of nearly £4 million over the previous year. But he now realized that the time for action had come. It was necessary to introduce Supplementary Estimates. Compared with the trouble he was to experience in getting the 1913–14 and 1914–15 Estimates through the Cabinet, there was so little opposition to these July Supplementaries that retrospectively their importance seems to have diminished in his mind. Though they passed quite easily through the Cabinet and the House, yet they were of considerable significance, amounting as they did to an extra £5 million.

On July 12 Churchill explained the various essential increases in the Estimates in a letter to Lloyd George. He pointed out that the previous year's Estimates had been kept artificially low as the Admiralty "did not want our Estimates to go up before the German Navy law was settled." The coal strike of autumn 1911 had also led to underspending, and greater expenditure would be needed than had been anticipated. The adoption of heavier guns by Germany, Japan and the United States "has forced us to advance also." The increases in dockyard wages raised the needed sum still higher. The total sum was likely, in Churchill's estimate, to reach £50 million, an increase of £5 million over the original Estimate. Churchill suggested that Lloyd George should meet the difference "by imposing new direct taxation."

Churchill took the opportunity of pointing out that the Cabinet decision to build ships for the Mediterranean fleet, to which he had been opposed, would amount to over £8 million over the next four

years and that it would "place an undue strain on the taxpayer to
raise the money by annual Finance."

At a Cabinet meeting on July 16 Lloyd George passed a note
across to Churchill, on which Churchill pencilled a neat reply:

Cabinet Notes
(Lloyd George Papers)

Bankruptcy

Stares me in

the face

Youre only chance is to get
£5,000,000 next year
and put the blame on me.
Then you will be its clover
again for the rest of the Parliament.
WSC

16 July 1912   10 Downing Street

L L. G: Bankruptcy stares me in the face

w s c: Your only chance is to get £5,000,000 next year — and put
the blame on me. Then you will be in clover again for the
rest of the Parliament

                                                        W S C

Churchill introduced his 1912 Supplementary Estimates in the
House of Commons on July 22. These Estimates, having been approved by the Cabinet, passed through the House of Commons with
the minimum of debate. After explaining the scope of the new German Navy Law he warned the House that "the strain we shall have
to bear will be long and slow." As the First Lord's strong measures
increasingly gripped the public imagination, leader writers and public men sought for all earlier and earlier precedents for comparison.
The Times had compared a speech of his with that of Lord George
Hamilton; Esher with Disraeli; and now the *Western Daily Mercury*
with Lord St Vincent who had been First Lord in Nelson's day.
"Within the scope of a few months he has gained a mastery of his
mighty subject as no predecessor has ever shown since the dim days
of Lord St Vincent. . . . His eyes are fixed upon Germany as he speaks.
He tells Germany so, neither in arrogant nor aggressive terms, but
with firm courtesy which befits one strong nation talking to another
strong nation." The *Daily Sketch* described Churchill as "a much
more versatile person than Pitt ever was, and with all he has done he
is still on the right side of thirty-eight."

                               *

The First Lord's next proposals, the Estimates of 1913–14, were
to meet with far more Treasury and Cabinet opposition. In the end,
after much argument, the First Lord obtained authority for Estimates
of £49 million. This meant in effect that the Supplementary Estimate which had gone through so easily — doubtless on the basis that
it was "once and for all" — had now become built in to the general
continuing structure of naval expenditure. Whereas the Supplemen-

taries were in part due to the Cabinet's decision to strengthen the Fleet in the Mediterranean, and partly due to rising costs, the new Estimates provided for formidable additions of capital ships — three battleships and one battle cruiser — in addition to what was building. He also required £470,000 a year for an increase in the pay of naval ratings, which in some cases amounted to 3*d.* a day.

Churchill set out his argument for his Estimates in two letters to Lloyd George. In the first he pointed out, on October 29, that he could not be held responsible for the general increase in the price of materials "which is particularly marked in all forms of warship building." Shipbuilding material was up more than 5 per cent — and gun machinery between 10 per cent and 12 per cent. This would add some £500,000 to the four new battleships. The cost of torpedo boats was £125,000 greater than in the previous Estimates, mainly on account of the need for increasing their speed by 3 or 4 knots to equal the speed of the German torpedo boats. In a draft letter of November 3 the First Lord proposed to take up what threatened to be a more serious point of dispute:

WSC to David Lloyd George

3 November 1912   The Wharf
                                                   Sutton Courtenay
                                                         Berks

Private & Personal
Not sent

My dear David,
   My naval advisers take a serious view of the decision of the Cabinet about the Pay of the Men: and I may at any time be confronted by the resignation of the Sea Lords in a body. This would of course make my position quite untenable: for I fully share their view that the scheme we had passed with so much care was an extremely moderate one. As I cannot yet believe that you wish to bring about a smash, & as I am determined to be guiltless shd that be the result, I am preparing new proposals to meet you & your friends as far as possible. It is not possible that these proposals shd be confined to the crude or arbitrary limit of £300,000 p.a. I have obtained from

the Prime Minister the assurance that the decision of Friday's cabinet does not preclude me from making a further proposal. In putting such a proposal forward I must make it clear (1.) that it is without prejudice to the existing Admiralty Scheme, wh we regard as the only satisfactory treatment of the subject: & (2) that my putting it forward must be conditional upon my obtaining the support of my naval advisers wh I have not yet got.

If you wd like to discuss this with me before it is brought before the Cabinet I am at your service, & I shd be glad to hear from you when I shd come. I shall be ready any time after Thursday.

From what you said the other morning about my "having looked out for opportunities to squander money," it has occurred to me that you may perhaps prefer that final decision on the Pay question shd be deferred until the Estimates can be surveyed as a whole.

In that event I could tell the House that the Pay scheme wd not be completely settled until the beginning of December. This wd cause murmuring but wd not be impracticable. In the meantime the main question could be determined.

All my present indications show that the rise in prices will affect the whole range of the estimates as provisionally forecast by me.

If we are to separate, it had much better be on the great issue of Retrenchment v. National Defence, than on a small matter of £170,000 a year for Sailors Pay. These large political issues ought not to affect personal friendships nor will they so far as I am concerned whatever the consequences. Little petty squabbles about matters wh do not affect gt issues are far more trying.

Yours ever

W

But this letter was never sent.

During his period at the Admiralty, Churchill continued the policies, so vigorously initiated by Fisher as First Sea Lord, of improving the pay and conditions of naval ratings. This was no doubt due to his years of social reform both at the Board of Trade and the Home Office as well as to his association with Fisher. Pay was the first and most pressing. It had remained almost unchanged for sixty years at a disgracefully low level. Having reached a compromise with Lloyd George at the Treasury the pay of older Able Seamen was raised by 3d. a day to 1s. 11d. and that of Petty Officers by 6d. a day to 3s. 2d.

It was not as much as Churchill had hoped for but it was well received in the Fleet.

Churchill also reformed naval discipline. He set up a committee under Admiral Brock to review naval justice. This committee received a great deal of evidence, both written and verbal, and produced a report which was in the main accepted by the Board of Admiralty. The recommendations, which included changes in the administering of summary punishments (those awarded by the Commanding Officer) and improvements in the internal administration of ships, were quickly introduced. Naval Detention Quarters instead of civil prisons were set up for naval offenders. Again these reforms were welcomed by the Lower Deck and complaints which were freely expressed in the sailors' magazine *The Fleet* were greatly reduced.

A few elderly Warrant Officers were commissioned after many years' service, more as a reward for long service than a serious step in rank. They never held commands at sea. Churchill introduced a scheme by which young Warrant and Petty Officers could be given educational training ashore and then sent to sea as officers. This scheme was an immediate success and continues today in an improved and expanded form. It was much appreciated by the Lower Deck who realized their talents and merits could be revealed and used to advantage. Churchill also advanced another reform which had been dear to Fisher's heart. In 1913 the fees at Osborne and Dartmouth were reduced by nearly 50 per cent for a quarter of the new entrants each year: it was not until 1947 that the system of free education for all naval cadets was introduced. These naval reforms were even noticed by Churchill's critics. In 1916 the *Navy League Annual,* which was hostile to him at a time when Churchill had been driven with discredit from the Admiralty, was to write:

> But the important element of British sea power is not the ships, essential as they are, but the officers and men. Whatever mistakes in naval policy Mr Churchill may or may not have committed, the nation owes him a debt of gratitude for the persistence with which during his period of office at the Admiralty he demanded from Parliament repeated increases of the personnel while at the same time making more adequate provision in respect of pay and laying on a surer foundation the system of promotion from the Lower Deck to commissioned rank.

Churchill was anxious to find items on which economies could be made. There was clearly no means of reducing the building programme, but opportunity for economy soon presented itself elsewhere.

WSC to Lord Stamfordham
(Royal Archives)

5 November 1912   Admiralty

My dear Stamfordham,

My attention has been drawn to some very large estimates wh have been presented for the refit of the *Victoria & Albert* [the Royal yacht], & I have also been looking into the expenditure of the last five years on this vessel. I am sure the King would be surprised to see the enormous charges wh are made for quite small things. I know His Majesty wd disapprove anything in the nature of wasteful or extravagant expenditure apart from what is properly required for the maintenance of the yacht in the highest condition. I am asking Sir Francis Hopwood & the Director of Dockyards to go down to Portsmouth this week & go through the new estimate for £13,000 with the Commodore; & after I am more fully informed His Majesty wd probably wish me to lay the result of the investigation before him.

Yours very sincerely
WINSTON S. CHURCHILL

Note by Stamfordham: —

5 November 1912

Am sure HM wd deprecate unnecessary expendre or extravagance & that he will be glad to know result of Sir F.H's investigations.

s

Further note: —

Read by the King 6.11.12.

This approach was successful.

Sir Francis Hopwood to WSC

16 December 1912   The Reform Club

First Lord,

I had a talk with the King about the Royal Yacht and took him through items and estimates. He was very much impressed with the extravagance of many of the demands. Once in two years for most of them is his opinion.

He will also personally examine proposals, when general renewals become necessary, for materials and so forth which will be much less expensive and more seaworthy than those used now.

He is going to send for the Commodore and will tell him that next year he must consider and report how little is required and not how much. For this year we have cut the Estimate in half and when we take into consideration that a lot of items will be bi-annual and not annual it is better than that.

F H

Note:
Good. WSC 16 December 1912.

*

Before the end of 1912 Churchill had warned the Treasury that they must expect much higher Naval Estimates in 1913–14. As always, he mustered his figures with extreme clarity and put forward his arguments with care and precision. Writing privately to Lloyd George he drew his attention to the seriousness of the proposed Austrian construction of three extra Dreadnoughts.

WSC to David Lloyd George
(Lloyd George Papers)

18 November 1912   Admiralty
Private

My dear David,

Look at this. Do you realise what it means if it is true?

It is no use being vexed with me and reproaching me. I can no more control these facts than you can.

Should the Austrians build 3 extra Dreadnoughts *beyond anything yet foreseen* or provided against, we shall have to take further measures. What measures I cannot now say: but an *equal* provision in some form or another will be necessary.

However, it may all prove to be rumour. But I don't think so; my information has for some time pointed in this direction.

Yours ever

W S C

To his Sea Lords Churchill outlined what would be needed for the 1913 Estimates in a memorandum of 8 December. He asked the Sea Lords for specific proposals and insisted that "it is my desire that the new programme should be stated in the most moderate terms possible so far as number of units are concerned, and that there should be an unshakeable foundation for every item put forward." To Lloyd George Churchill sent a warning note on December 9: "prices may harden against us still more." And he continued:

I should be very glad to go with you or with the Cabinet Committee into the causes which have led and are leading to the general increase in naval expense. The increase is out of all proportion to the programme of new construction. The new programme for the year 1913–14 contains nothing abnormal: 5 capital ships which have already been announced to Parliament, against 3 German; the usual annual programme of 20 destroyers against the German 12; 1,000,000*l.* for submarines against the 1,000,000*l.* they are spending; 4 or 5 small cruisers, according to the standard; and the usual proportion of yard craft and miscellaneous auxiliaries. All these subjects proceed on lines which are very clearly marked out, and are well known to you and to the public. The increased number of men proposed for the year (5,000) is no more than my predecessor has proposed, and has already been brought to your notice and to the notice of Parliament. . . .

While I regard it as my duty to aid you in any way in my power in regard to the methods by which the necessary naval services are financed, and to fall in with your general policy so long as the interests of the country do not suffer, I must again state my opinion that the proper and courageous course is to take Parliament fully into your confidence and to meet the expense either by new taxation or by a substantial diminution during these years of strain of the Sinking Fund.

Any other course will expose you in 1914–15 to difficulties greater than those which now confront you without your having the strength which you now possess to carry your policy for the urgent reasons which justify the expenditure.

I am prepared to take the whole responsibility of the present and prospective naval expenditure upon myself. Everything that is not uncontrollable and automatic can be fully justified in detail to Parliament and the public, in consequence of naval developments elsewhere; and I am sure the Government have only to put their case plainly and boldly to the House of Commons to receive from one source or another, without any serious difficulty, the sums which are necessary for the safety of the State.

Lloyd George was certainly not the only critic of Churchill's policies. In his diary Lord Riddell recounts, for 5 December 1912:

He is too concentrated on his particular office. He has not got the art of playing in conjunction with others. He does not understand the method which made the Welsh footballers so successful — the fine art to which they brought passing the ball from one player to another. When we refuse him anything, he talks of resigning. I think he was very near going back to the Tories some little time ago, but he would have made a mistake. He would have been like a woman who had run away from her husband and then gone back after a long interval.

The First Lord and the Admiralty had already decided to build a new, fast squadron of battleships, which would outclass everything of their weight at sea in fire-power, speed and armour. This decision involved the use of oil instead of coal and not only for this fast battle squadron of the *Queen Elizabeth* type but also for other ships as well. Coal was to be had in abundance; oil had to be brought from great distances overseas and ample stores must be kept at home if communications should be ruptured through some alien commerce raider. In *The World Crisis* Churchill explained the cardinal importance of the decision:

The three programmes of 1912, 1913 and 1914 comprised the greatest additions in power and cost ever made to the Royal Navy. With the lamentable exception of the battleships of 1913 — and these were afterwards corrected — they did not contain a coal-burning ship. Submarines, destroyers, light cruisers, fast battleships — all were based irrevocably on oil. The fateful plunge was taken when it was decided to create the Fast Division. Then, for the first time, the supreme ships of the Navy, on which our life depended, were fed by oil and could only be fed by oil. The decision to drive the smaller craft by oil followed naturally upon this. The camel once swallowed, the gnats went down easily enough.

Already in June, as mentioned earlier, he had invited Lord Fisher to preside over the Royal Commission on Oil Supply:

WSC to Lord Fisher

11 June 1912   [Admiralty]
[Copy]

My dear Fisher,
We are too good friends (I hope) and the matters with which we are concerned are too serious (I'm sure) for anything but plain language.
    This liquid fuel problem has got to be solved, and the natural, inherent, unavoidable difficulties are such that they require the drive and enthusiasm of a big man. I want you for this viz to crack the nut. No one else can do it so well. Perhaps no one else can do it at all. I will put you in a position where you can crack the nut, if indeed it is crackable. But this means that you will have to give your life and strength, and I don't know what I have to give in exchange or in return. You have got to find the oil: to show how it can be stored cheaply: how it can be purchased regularly and cheaply in peace; and with absolute certainty in war. Then by all means develop its application in the best possible way to existing and prospective ships. But on the other hand, your Royal Commission will be advisory and not executive. It will assemble facts and state conclusions. It cannot touch *policy* or action. That would not be fair to those on whom I must now rely. Nor would you wish it. Its report must be secret from the public, and its work separate from the Admiralty. I cannot have Moore's position eclipsed by a kind of Committee of

Public Safety on Designs. The field of practical policy must be reserved for the immediately responsible officers. Research however authoritative lies outside. All this I know you will concur on.

Then as to *personnel*. I do not care a d—n whom you choose to assist you, so long as (1) the representative character of the Committee is maintained, and (2) the old controversies are not needlessly revived. Let us then go into names specifically.

Further, "Step by Step" is a valuable precept. When you have solved the riddle, you will find a very hushed attentive audience. But the riddle will not be solved unless you are willing — for the glory of God — to expend yourself upon its toils.

I recognize it is little enough I can offer you. But your gifts, your force, your hopes, belong to the Navy, with or without return; and as your most sincere admirer, and as the head of the Naval Service, I claim them now, knowing well you will not grudge them. You need a plough to draw. Your propellers are racing in air.

Yrs ever in warm regards
w.

The Royal Commission was not to report until July 1913; but the First Lord must have known that he was likely to get a satisfactory answer, for all planning for the five *Queen Elizabeths* was well in hand before the end of 1912.

Churchill sought wherever possible to reduce expenditure. He was particularly anxious that the governments of the Empire should contribute to the general development of naval power. He sent a copy of the following letter to Lloyd George: it was a plea to Asquith and Lord Crewe, the Secretary of State for India, that the Indian Government should increase its contribution to Imperial Naval Defence.

WSC to H. H. Asquith

EXTRACT

13 December 1912

My dear Prime Minister,

You are asked from time to time questions in regard to the contribution which India pays towards the Imperial Naval Defence and the special services rendered her by the Admiralty.

I hope that in replying nothing will be said which will appear to definitely close the question of an increased contribution.

The case is indeed a very strong one from many points of view. . . .

After detailing some of the ways in which the Indian Government could help, the First Lord continued:

The action of all the great dominions in greatly increasing their naval contributions or in making important new contributions constitutes a new fact of much significance. They have all revised and extended their contributions since the date when the Indian contribution was last fixed by Lord Rosebery's Arbitration.

You will realise that I am only asking that these questions may be fairly considered between Departments and by the Cabinet before they are prejudiced by answers in the House. . . .

*

In the chapter "The Romance of Design" in the first volume of *The World Crisis,* Churchill reviewed what he considered to be the major advances in naval construction before the war. When he became First Lord twelve ships were building on the slips with their main armament the 13.5-inch gun. This fired a shell of 1,400 pounds, compared with the 850-pound shell of the 12-inch gun. It was to Fisher that this major advance was due. The new First Lord "immediately sought to go one size better," and asked Fisher's advice, which was at once forthcoming: a 15-inch gun should be developed without delay. "No one who has not experienced it," wrote Churchill, "has any idea of the passion and eloquence of this old lion when thoroughly roused on a technical question. . . . He was steadfast and even violent. So I hardened my heart and took the plunge. The whole outfit of guns was ordered forthwith."

Churchill's next concern was speed. "Smashing up the tail of an enemy's Fleet . . . is not comparable to smashing up his head"; a division of fast ships would be able to "curl round the head of the enemy's line" and fire upon the leading warships, "throwing his whole formation into confusion."

From this idea Churchill developed the Fast Division, drawing upon the expert knowledge of Sir Philip Watts and Sir Henry Oram and obtaining from the Naval War College full details of the speeds which would be needed to outmanoeuvre the German Fleet as it would be in 1914 and 1915. It was more than ever apparent from the statistics which were then prepared that the power to drive these ships at the necessary 25 knots could only be obtained by the use of oil fuel. To secure this he again approached Fisher, as well as entering into negotiations with the Anglo-Persian Oil Company, and carrying through the House of Commons in 1913 the Anglo-Persian Oil Convention which ensured for the Royal Navy an adequate oil supply of its own free from the risks of foreign control or private speculation. Britain's 51 per cent, in interest alone, apart from capital appreciation, certainly paid the cost of all battleships thereafter built.

The 15-inch gun, the Fast Division and oil were the three major advances which the First Lord initiated and over whose development he presided. But he also inherited one legacy from Lord Fisher, the Dreadnought, which had become in the public mind the principal advance in naval technology and guarantee of British Naval superiority. This was an exaggeration, as the existence of these "all big-gun battleships" at once made the smaller British as well as German warships less effective.

The Dreadnought gave the Royal Navy an important advantage over the German Fleet, but it also weakened the overall superiority which rested upon the total number of ships of all sizes and armaments. It made the German battleships obsolete; it did the same thing for all the existing British battleships, and we could never gain so great a preponderance with the Dreadnoughts as we had with the old battleships. On the other hand, foreign navies were toying with the idea of the "all big-gun battleships": if they had to come, it was well that Britain led the way. The Dreadnoughts were Fisher's creation. He had fought for them within both naval and political circles. While First Sea Lord he had accelerated naval construction and secured the building of 22 battleships of over 16,000 tons between 1906 and 1912, as well as 12 light cruisers, 65 destroyers, 62 submarines and many other smaller vessels. Churchill commented on this in *The World Crisis:*

This tremendous new Navy, for it was nothing less, was a providential aid to the Admiralty when more than two years later the real German submarine attack began. Its creation on such a scale is one of the greatest services which the nation has owed to the genius and energy of Lord Fisher.

*

Churchill's questing activity in these years before the war is well described by him in *The World Crisis:*

While the discussions of the invasion Committee were at their height during the spring and summer of 1913, I prepared a series of papers in support of the Admiralty view, but also designed to explore and illuminate the situations that might arise. They show the hopes and fears we felt before the event, what we thought the enemy might do against us, and the dangers we hoped to avoid ourselves. They show the kind of mental picture I was able to summon up in imagination of the tremendous period which was so soon to rush upon us. My intention also was to stimulate thought in the Admiralty War Staff, and to expose weak points in our arrangements. For this purpose I entered into an active discussion and correspondence with several of the ablest Admirals (notably Admiral Beatty, Admiral Lewis Bayly, and Sir Reginald Custance), seeking to have the whole matter argued out to the utmost limit possible. I caused war games to be played at the War College in which, aided by one or the other of my naval advisers, I took one side, usually the German, and forced certain situations.

Doubtless the Sea Lords sometimes had good grounds for thinking they were being treated in an arbitrary fashion; but for the most part the First Lord sought to make his opinions prevail by persuasion and argument. This, too, could cause resentment. Admirals and Generals are seldom trained to expound or defend propositions in lucid or compulsive prose. This inability often caused ill-feeling and obstruction. Sir William Robertson, later Chief of the Imperial General Staff, was wont to resist all new arguments or facts with the uncompromising: "Well, I've 'eard different." Among the First Lord's more imaginative papers designed to destroy the prevailing complacency was one which dealt with the hypothetical landing by Ger-

man troops on the East Coast just at the time when a British expeditionary force would be moving over to join the left flank of the
French Army.

Memorandum by WSC

[16 April 1913]
Confidential   Admiralty

THE TIME TABLE OF A NIGHTMARE

Saturday, April 1. — Germany, convinced that the Powers of the
Triple Entente are bent on war, determines to start with the advantages of the initiative and surprise.

During the early part of the year there had been considerable tension between France and Germany over a dispute about an African
boundary. The anxiety which existed had been relieved in response
to the mediation of the British Government about the middle of
March, when Germany suddenly made several important concessions
to meet the French view.

Another cause of apprehension had been the special manœuvres
which the Germans had proposed to hold in Alsace in the last week
in March, as this would have entailed corresponding increase in the
French forces on the frontier. These were cancelled as soon as the
negotiations were brought to a happy conclusion, and a test mobilisation of a Division on a full war scale was substituted at Stettin.
The Emperor proceeded to Stettin himself on the 30th March to review and inspect the garrison instead of attending the Alsace manœuvres as had been contemplated. A general *détente* was apparent
in consequence of these events.

The London newspapers of the 29th March observed "that the
change of the manœuvres from Alsace to Danzig removed the last
outstanding cause for European apprehension, and that this event,
taken in conjunction with the reasonable and conciliatory attitude
adopted so spontaneously by Germany in the recent negotiations,
was a bright and effective rejoinder to French Arrogance and British
suspicion."

April 1, 4 *pm.* — Failure of telegraphic communication with Germany reported to the Admiralty by the G.P.O. (The Admiralty did
not attribute any special significance to this, even when it was con-

firmed two hours later from Paris. A strike of German telegraphists had been threatened for some time in Germany.)

April 1, 8.30 *pm.* — Telegram received at the War Office from the French War Office that a rumour is current in Brussels that Liège has been occupied by German soldiers in motor-cars. Rumour discredited in official quarters, but adding that telegraphic communication with Germany has completely failed. It is thought that the strike of German telegraphists is the cause both of the telegraphic breakdown and of the rumour.

No special action taken.

April 1, *Midnight.* — Cipher message received at Foreign Office from the French Government, stating that the German Order to mobilise had been given at 9 *am* that day, that Liège had been occupied by the Germans without fighting; that Germans in motor-cars and with cavalry were penetrating and overrunning Belgium; and that the French Order for mobilisation had just been given.

Sunday, April 2, 12.30 *am.* — Clerk completes the decipher and communicates at once with Admiralty, War Office, and the Foreign Secretary.

Meanwhile private confirmation has been received at the Admiralty and the War Office, and telegrams reporting the invasion of Belgian territory have been received in the offices of the Sunday newspapers and forwarded at once both to the War Office and the Admiralty.

(Actually the first overt act of war took place about 6 *pm.*)

April 2, 1 *am.* — Resident Clerk at the Admiralty summons by telephone the Director of Operations Divisions, who was on duty in London, and arouses the First Sea Lord.

(Either the First Sea Lord or the Second Sea Lord is *always* in London night and day.)

April 2, 1.30 *am.* — "Warning Telegram" despatched.

Necessary Admiralty staff summoned by telephone and messengers.

April 2, 3 *am.* — First Sea Lord in telephonic communication with First Lord, who was at Portsmouth.

Orders issued for completing the Second Fleet, and "Take up War Stations" telegram despatched.

It is assumed that both First Sea Lord and First Lord acted to the above extent without consulting higher authority.

(It must be realised that no one in England had any right to assume that Great Britain would necessarily be involved in a Franco-

German quarrel. No decision had yet been taken by the Cabinet. There was no reason to expect any German attack on this country until after such a decision.)

April 2, 3 am. — All Second Fleet ships began completing at the Naval Ports.

April 2, 3 am. — Commander-in-Chief, Home Fleets, receives "Warning" and "Take up War Stations" messages by wireless.

The disposition of the Fleet was as follows: The Second Fleet was completing in the Home Ports. The First Fleet, except the 3rd Battle Squadron in the Mediterranean, and all the cruisers were (where they are now, 16 April 1913) with Sir George Callaghan off Lands End and the South Coast of Ireland engaged in tactical exercises. They were, on the average, only half full up with coal. As soon as the warning telegram was received the Commander-in-Chief signalled to assemble the First Fleet. While assembling, the telegram "Take up War Stations" was received, and by 4.45 *am* Sunday, the 2nd April, all ships were proceeding northward to their stations through the Irish Channel. The Battleships at 15 knots, Cruisers 18 knots, Flotillas 20 knots. The Commander-in-Chief also sent an urgent message to the Admiralty by wireless for coal and oil to be sent immediately to Oban and Rosyth, there being none in the North Sea north of Harwich.

April 2, 5 am. — Authority received from the Prime Minister for general mobilisation of the Fleet and Army. Orders issued accordingly.

The telephone worked well.

April 2, Sunday, 9 am. — Cabinet meets to consider specific demand of the French Government for the support of six Divisions.

April 2, Noon. — Telegram despatched promising they will be sent.

April 2, Noon. — Up to this moment the Cabinet believed that the question of whether Great Britain would be involved in the war or not rested with them.

April 2, 1 pm. — News received from Harwich that German battleships and cruisers are bombarding the forts.

April 2, 3.30 pm. — News received in London that the Harwich forts have been silenced.

Three German light cruisers entered and anchored in the harbour. The forts were occupied by men from the battleships and cruisers outside. These men were not part of the ships' companies, but had been brought for this purpose. Weather calm, clear, smooth. (The tide being low at 2.30, only light cruisers could get into the harbour; the battleships bombarded the forts at 8,000 yards range.)

April 2, 3 pm. — The British Fleet was in latitude 52° 12' north, longitude 5° 42' west, and 17 miles east of the Tuskar; cruisers 30 miles ahead, flotillas 50 miles ahead — all steaming northwards. From this position to the entrance to the Skaggerak it is exactly the same distance (855 miles) whether they go through the Pentland Firth or through the Straits of Dover; but the distance to Harwich is only 505 miles, which at 15 knots they could do in 33 hours, arriving off Harwich at midnight on the 3rd–4th; and in this position they would be no further from the Skaggerak, and consequently from their chance of intercepting the enemy's battle fleet, than if they had gone North about. It was therefore decided, on the news from Harwich, to bring the fleet thither by the shortest route.

The Admiralty therefore wirelessed the Commander-in-Chief to turn south with all his ships, and to proceed at once to Harwich, ready if necessary to follow the German Fleet across the North Sea, and to endeavour to bring it to action. It was owing to this latter possibility and the shortness of coal in his ships that the Commander-in-Chief did not increase his speed above the 15 knots he was going before. The whole fleet turned at 3 *pm.*

Admiralty simultaneously ordered mine-sweeper to sweep and keep swept the passage through the Downs, and informed Commander-in-Chief that they had done so.

[Both movements of the Fleet, although contradictory, were natural on the information available in each case. The first, to the north, was merely precautionary; the second, southward, was the necessary answer to an actual attack.]

April 2, 3.30 pm. — Reports from Harwich that German transports are entering the harbour and disembarking troops at the various jetties, but mainly at the Parkeston Quay.

The German ships were not attacked on arrival off Harwich by destroyers because the southernmost patrol craft had gone to Yarmouth, their station, on the order to take up war stations, and the Nore Defence Flotilla were guarding the mouth of the Thames from the ships reported to be off the estuary, and their station did not include Harwich. During the night of the 2nd–3rd, however, they made several attacks and succeeded in sinking some of the German warships.

The order for German troops to assemble was issued at 9 *am* on the 1st April. The embarkation was completed at 3 *pm,* and the vessels put to sea with lights lit at 6 *pm* on the same day, and lay under escort 20 miles off the English coast until the German warships had silenced the batteries at Harwich (four 6-in guns), and their landing parties had obtained virtual possession of the town. It is possible that 4,000 or 5,000 men had been put on board some days previously for some manœuvres which had been ordered. The transports did not land men on the beach, but steamed into the harbour and anchored, the smaller ones going alongside the jetties.

April 2, 5 pm, the place being in German possession, four other German vessels averaging 7,000 tons, filled with artillery and ammunition, steamed into the port and their unloading commenced. By 6 *pm* the whole of the infantry had landed and was taking up an extended line around the town on both sides of the port.

The German escorting force consisted of the first three squadrons of the High Sea Fleet, which had been exercising off Heligoland during the previous week, and of four armoured cruisers and eight light cruisers. This force remained in observation off Harwich, covering the landing operations, until 6 *pm* 3rd, when the German Fleet sailed, steering across the North Sea, leaving three light cruisers in Harwich to protect transports.

April 2, 5 pm. — Two German battle cruisers and forty destroyers with three depôt ships occupied Scapa Flow and closed the Pentland Firth 2nd April. Their whereabouts was reported to the Admiralty, who ordered the Admiral of Patrols to endeavour to clear the Firth.

During the afternoon of Sunday, the 2nd April, the presence of German submarines and minelayers, supported by cruisers and armoured ships and a destroyer flotilla, are variously reported to the Admiralty as being off the Estuary of the Thames and towards the Straits of Dover.

The submarines from Queensferry and Dundee went to sea and tried ineffectually to get in touch with the German ships.

Monday, April 3, 3 am. — The German battle cruisers, destroyers, and depôt ships withdrew from Scapa, and proceeded to establish a destroyer base at Balta Sound in the Shetlands. There the German flotillas were joined by four transports and eight supply ships and colliers from the Baltic, and established themselves strongly.

April 3, 6 pm. — The British Fleet steamed up the Channel, and at 6 *pm,* the 3rd April, the flotilla was in sight of the German Fleet off Harwich. The latter, which was under weigh, proceeded at once at a high speed for the Elbe and Jade Rivers, and owing to a freshening easterly wind with an increasing sea were easily able to keep ahead of the British flotilla. The British cruisers and Battle Fleet were off Harwich by 9 *pm* and midnight respectively, and continued the pursuit, but without success, the German Fleet having too good a start. The British Fleet then withdrew to their war stations, and to coal and oil at Rosyth, except two cruiser squadrons which had been ordered to remain off Harwich, to blockade it, on their arriving there at 9 *pm*.

.   .   .

Meanwhile, on the night of the 2nd April, while the mobilisation at Chatham was in full activity, five German airships appeared over the dockyard and basins at intervals between the hours of 11 *pm* and 5 *am,* and dropped from 15 to 20 tons of explosives. A state of the utmost confusion and disorder was created by this attack, to which no effective reply could be made. The Power House escaped injury, but both caissons of the North Lock at the eastern entrance were so damaged that the water in the Eastern basin fell to sea level, causing much damage. The *Canopus, Flory,* and *Ocean* were sunk, and the *Jupiter* was seriously damaged. Several of the largest workshops were completely wrecked, the process of mobilising was absolutely arrested, and a panic ensued among the townspeople and the dockyard labourers. One of the airships was brought down by a lucky shot from an improvised high-angle howitzer, but the others went off uninjured. It was twelve hours before the process of mobilising could be resumed, and that only in a very partial and crippled fashion.

The repairing plant was, to a large extent, wrecked and wholly thrown into confusion. The 3rd April was consumed in restoring order in the Port and in improvising some kind of gun mountings capable of firing at a high angle. The Dockyard workmen evinced the greatest reluctance to go into the yard, and many of them, with the inhabitants of the surrounding district, fled to some distance from the Admiralty property. The General Officer commanding ordered all lights to be extinguished in the Dockyard at night in anticipation of a renewed attack, and, though this did not take place, the whole of Chatham and its resources, with the single exception of the flotillas and the Second Fleet ships lying at Sheerness, were seriously crippled for a week.

Several attempts were made by the Nore defence flotilla to attack the Germans outside Harwich with some success. Only a portion of the floating defence could be sent on account of the reports of German ships off Dover, &c.

Sunday, April 2, 5 pm. — Harwich was in complete possession of the enemy, the greater part of whose infantry had already landed, and who were developing a strong line of outposts on the landward side along an arc of about 3 miles radius, and preparing to push forward advance guards along both the Ipswich and Colchester roads.

A considerable quantity of rolling stock had been seized.

The German General in Harwich telegraphed by wireless to the Commander-in-Chief of the High Sea Fleet and to the Commander-in-Chief at Hamburg that he had effective possession of the town and port.

From the moment when they believed that their intentions were exposed, viz, 8 *pm* on the night of the 1st April, orders were issued by the German Government to seize all shipping in the German ports which had not already been requisitioned for the Expeditionary Force of 20,000 which was then embarking. A further force of 30,000 men, consisting of the remaining 12 battalions of the Xth Corps (7,000), 5,000 marines, and 18,000 men from the mobilised division at Stettin, who had begun entraining at 9 *am* on the 1st April, was ordered to embark as rapidly as possible, and as soon as the capture of Harwich was reported these ships were ordered to leave individually for that port as fast as they could be filled up with men.

(After October next the whole number could be found from the IXth and Xth Corps alone.)

From noon till 7 *pm* the 2nd April, seventeen more vessels of various sizes, averaging 3,000 tons, and including four with artillery and ammunition (no horses), were despatched from the German North Sea ports to Harwich; and from daylight on the 3rd to 4 o'clock in the afternoon ran safely into port at Harwich under the protection of the captured batteries and the escorting cruiser squadron. These ships travelled singly at great risk, and were therefore able to go faster (about 14 knots) than a body of transports together. Owing to the considerable steam traffic between Harwich and Flushing and Esbjerg, the Germans had no difficulty in getting pilots for their transports, their own people having studied the route for years. The despatch of transports from the German ports ceased at 7 *pm* on the

2nd April on news being received that the British fleet, preceded by flotillas, was passing Land's End on the way up Channel.

Monday, April 3. — The last vessel to cross the sea made Harwich at 4 *pm*.

If the Germans had been bolder, they could have sent at least seven other vessels which were loaded.

At 6 *pm*, 3rd, as described, the German fighting ships left Harwich for the Elbe and Jade Rivers, leaving three light cruisers, twenty-four destroyers, and three submarines (all of which had accompanied the transports, the submarines following them) to protect the landing. During the night of the 3rd April, the disembarkation of the rest of the German transports was effected with the exception of the artillery, which was not accomplished till twenty-four hours later, and then not fully. In the interval, from the seizure of Harwich at 2 *pm* on the 2nd April to 4 *pm* on the 3rd April, 45,000 infantry and 60 guns had entered Harwich harbour together with seven ships containing ammunition and supplies. The Germans carried with them ten days' supplies and emergency rations. The town and port of Harwich contained sufficient stores and victuals for another fortnight.

April 3, 10 pm. — At 10 *pm* the 3rd April the British blockade of Harwich was complete. Blockading forces: two armoured cruiser squadrons and the Thames Flotillas, thirty boats, supported by five Second and Third Fleet battleships and armoured cruisers from Sheerness and Chatham (the rest unavailable).

April 3, 10 pm. — Bombardment of Harwich by the British armoured cruisers begins. Replied to by the forts and the three German light cruisers in the harbour.

It was necessary at all hazards to harass the disembarkation of the invaders, and the British cruisers were ordered to continue the bombardment, changing stations frequently to minimise risks. By midnight the Harwich guns were silenced and part of the town in flames. Five vessels in the harbour, some partially filled with troops, were sunk, and others damaged.

April 3, 10 pm. — From darkness onwards continued attacks by the German destroyers in Harwich to drive off the British cruisers and protect the disembarkation. Both sides having a vital object to contend for, the losses were very heavy. The German torpedo attack did not stop till their flotilla was practically destroyed, but before this could be known, *i.e.*, at midnight, the British had lost 7 ships, sunk or holed by torpedoes, including 5 of the best armoured cruisers — more than half the force engaged.

. . .

Tuesday, April 4, 1 *am.* — The German expeditionary army, leaving 3,000 men in the forts and improvised entrenchments to hold Harwich pending the disembarkation of their artillery, marched 5 miles inland to be out of range of the naval bombardment. The vessels containing stores, ammunition, and guns, which had not been unloaded before the bombardment commenced, were run on the tide as high up the river as their draught permitted. It must be recognised that only a proportion of their cargo could be landed.

Desultory skirmishes with the local territorials marked the German advance during the 4th, and firing continued along their outpost lines throughout the night. During this day and the night which followed, the different units and parts of units of the German Army which had effected the landing were reorganised into three divisions of infantry and cyclists, and camped facing west on the line Bromley–Manningtree.

Wednesday, April 5. — All British fleets and squadrons, less casualties and the Harwich blockading force, were in their war stations, the First Fleet anxious for coal and oil.

Mobilisation of the Third Fleet complete, except Nore Division.

German Army enters Colchester under strong advance guards, bringing their supplies along the railway. Skirmishing with the local Territorials reinforced by three partially formed regular battalions not included in the Expeditionary Force.

Thursday, April 6. — The transportation of the British force to France continues, and now includes portions of five divisions already despatched in transports; 60,000 more being railed southward for embarkation.

The German army marches from Colchester, where they have found ample supplies, on Chelmsford.

April 6, 4 *pm.* — Passage of the Blackwater. 6,000 regulars and 65,000 territorials driven from their entrenched positions, and defeated with a loss of 8,000 killed and wounded, and all their stores, camps, and artillery.

The British army, which had been very hurriedly gathered to delay the advance, consisted almost entirely of untrained men and wholly of unorganised units, 6,000 prisoners and 70 guns were taken on the field. German loss 1,800.

April 6, Midnight. — German advance guard (cyclists) enters Chelmsford, capturing 4,000 fugitives who had taken refuge in the town.

On this day the transportation of the British army to the Continent reaches its maximum, and in spite of the disorders elsewhere the whole was proceeding smoothly. Portions of all six divisions are now in transit. Flexibility of the railway system has permitted the transport of the troops to the south to be effected practically without hindrance, in spite of the invasion of the Eastern Counties.

Friday, April 7. — The German army halt at Chelmsford to rest and to organise the captured artillery.

Transportation to France continues. Three-fifths of the army have now left.

April 7, Afternoon. — Serious rioting in London to prevent the departure of troops. Enormous crowds, converging on Westminster, were repeatedly charged by the mounted police, and finally fired on by the two battalions of Guards which had been assigned to the duty of protecting His Majesty's person. From this time on, the movement of the troops to the south was increasingly hindered by the population, who endeavoured everywhere to prevent the departure of troop trains by invading the lines, tearing up the rails, or laying themselves in front of the engines. Continued collisions between the military and the people at all points of entrainment and detrainment reported.

Saturday, April 8. — German army marches south from Chelmsford to the line Harlow–Ongar–Billericay.

In spite of the delays on the railroads through ignorant popular manifestations, the transportation of the army continues, though many units and portions of units are delayed.

Sunday, April 9, 3.40 pm. — House of Commons: Leader of the Opposition asks the Government what steps they propose to take to protect London, and particularly whether some part of the expeditionary army should not be employed for that purpose. Ministers reply that the word of England has been passed that six divisions shall be on the French flank by the 13th day; and it would be impossible to arrest the movement now without betraying an ally at the supreme and decisive moment; that in any case portions of all the divisions and most of the brigades have already gone; and that it would be impossible to organize regular field units from the remainder in less than a week. Also stated that to keep the remainder would thoroughly disorganise and dislocate the whole army already transported. The Government were relying on the advice of the military authorities, and were resolutely determined not to be deflected from the course they had marked out by popular clamour. Various Territorial divisions were assembling to cover London, and an improvised brigade made up from the reservists of the Household Brigade would be sent to the front as soon as the tranquillity of the capital permitted.

April 9, 3.45 *pm.* — Adjournment of the House moved by the Leader of the Opposition. Practically all the members on both sides, excepting the Government Bench, stood up to support it.

April 9, 11 *pm.*—Government defeated by 617 votes to 22. Ministry resigns. New Ministry formed. Sole object and policy: "To save London."

German advance guards reach Waltham Abbey, Romford, and Woolwich. Continuous street fighting commences at all points of contact.

Monday, April 10, 3 *am.* — All transportation of troops to the Continent stopped.

Orders issued for those already landed to return. French authorities refuse railway transport for the return journey.

The position when the transportation was arrested was that 110,000 regular soldiers had crossed the Channel, and 50,000 were still in the United Kingdom. All the infantry had gone and the forces left behind although considerable, bore no relation to the units of an army, and comprised parts of five divisions and eleven brigades.

Orders given to concentrate all regular troops on London.

German army continues its advance in three divisions, fighting their way through the suburbs of London, being resisted by the civil population, and large numbers of Territorials without organisation of any kind, and reinforced piecemeal from hour to hour by the regular units brought back from the south.

Fifteen thousand naval reservists from the Home Ports, and the whole of the complements of the Third Fleet ships mobilised at Portsmouth, brought to the capital, and thrown into the fight as they arrive.

Large Yeomanry and Territorial Forces following the invaders from rear.

During this day the German advance only amounted to 3 or 4 miles along their main front.

April 10, 8 *pm.* — German advance definitely arrested on the line Tottenham–Dagenham–Woolwich.

Tuesday, April 11. — Germans completely invested in the triangle Tottenham, Woolwich, Romford.

British forces reorganising on all fronts.

Wednesday, April 12. — General attack by British on German positions; continuous street fighting; enemy gradually worn down. (No regular infantry from the expeditionary force could be present, even if their orders for recall were effective, before the 17th or 18th.)

Thursday, April 13. — Four large German transports carrying between them 12,000 men, coming from the Baltic and profiting by rough and misty weather, evade the British patrolling cruisers, and land at Blyth covered by 2 cruisers.

Friday, April 14. — German raiding column from Blyth enters Newcastle, the North having been completely denuded of troops by the supreme need of London.

Raiding force makes preparations for defending the town, where supplies are ample.

British attacks upon the German army near London continue, and the enemy's lines are continually restricted.

April 14, 4 *pm.* — Great battle on the line of the Meuse begins. British troops on the left (mainly infantry) heavily engaged.

April 14, *Midnight.* — German destroyers from the Shetlands attack the British Battle Fleet in its war station, 80 miles north-east of Peterhead, sinking one and holing five of the best ships. The injured vessels were beached to avoid sinking, there being no repairing plant of any kind available on the East Coast.

(This is intended to illustrate the vexatious consequences of the enemy holding a base in the Shetlands, at a time when our fleet is compelled to be in the North Sea.)

Saturday, April 15. — Total defeat of the French and the Franco-British left on the line of the Meuse. The British army was too weak to maintain its position, and none of the divisions were complete with their proper proportion of the various arms. Above all it was deficient in artillery and cavalry, the transportation of which had been abruptly stopped. In the circumstances, the resistance which they offered cannot be considered discreditable, and the immense losses they sustained in the battle and during the retreat are a proof of the severity of the fighting.

The attack on the German army near London is continued from all sides with unceasing vigour, and the enemy's position becomes continually more restricted.

April 16, 17, 18 *and* 19. — French armies and remnants of the British force in full retreat from the line of the Meuse.

Enemy near London still holding out.

Newcastle raiders fortifying themselves practically unmolested.

No serious operations against the enemy in the Shetlands possible pending the settlement of the London business.

All British warships were riveted on the vital task of preventing further disembarkations.

April 19, *Midnight.* — German Commander-in-Chief near London offers to capitulate on terms of being conveyed out of the country. He states his ability to hold out for several weeks more, and declares that rather than surrender at discretion he will shoot the 10,000 prisoners who are in his hands, and destroy all the plant in Woolwich Arsenal.

Terms accepted. It was indispensable to concentrate on the Newcastle raiders with the minimum of delay, and to clear the Shetlands.

Wednesday, April 20. — The second phase of the war begins.

The memorandum brought varying reactions from the naval personnel to whom it was circulated. Admiral Lewis Bayly, commanding the 3rd Battle Squadron, thought that the Germans were unlikely to try and seize a large town. Churchill replied: "I cannot myself believe that the streets of a town constitute any real obstacle to a landing from the quays. A street is after all only a road along which men can march; and where do you get so many roads as you do in the streets of a town? The more streets there are the more easy it is to advance through a town. No system of barricades can be improvised in a few hours which good troops cannot easily turn or pierce. Columns move forward quite easily along parallel roads; and if the civil population attempt to resist them, they are of course dealt with according to the rigours of war."

In 1940 Churchill was to take a more robust view of the potentiality of the civil population resisting in the towns.

The only serious objections came from Admiral Sir Henry Jackson, the newly appointed Chief of the War Staff. He argued that normally the German High Sea Fleet would be in the Baltic and that if it were not, it would excite apprehensions which would alert our own naval precautions. In the second place, Jackson did not believe that British troop movements to France would continue once the German invasion had started. Thirdly, he regarded the military possibilities envisaged by the First Lord as "sensational" and "satirical." Finally, he disliked the "alarmist" style with which the document had been presented.

In the First Lord's reply he took up Sir Henry Jackson's points:

> In time of peace the fact of the German fleet being in the North Sea does not excite apprehension, nor in ordinary circumstances alter the regular exercises of the British fleet. These are prescribed for some time in advance, and their dates are no doubt very often known abroad.
>
> . . . If so unwise a policy were followed as to send away or promise to send away the whole regular army in the circumstances assumed in my memo., no censure or punishment would be too serious for the public officers and personages concerned. That is exactly the moral which I seek to draw. . . .
>
> What follows after the maximum invading force which can be got ashore has landed does not really concern the Admiralty; and the sensational sketch of the operations and events which followed was only intended to be illustrative of certain general propositions. It was intentionally cast in a satirical vein. But after all a *reductio ad absurdam* is not an unknown argumentative method. . . .
>
> I am sorry you do not like the style of the paper called "A Time Table of a Nightmare." It was written with the intention of raising certain very serious issues, and which I think will be apparent the more the facts and arguments are studied with attention. The title was chosen with the object of justly and accurately describing the character of the paper and of disarming and discounting the very criticisms which you make. Leaving, however, the question of style, on which opinions may easily differ, and which in any case is not of serious importance, and coming to the question of fact, I do not gather from your minute that there is much dispute. . . .

16

Palace and Admiralty

AT THE BOARD OF TRADE and the Home Office Churchill, while relying very much upon his official advisers, had already developed his natural instinct for command. Under his patent as First Lord he was "responsible to Crown and Parliament for all the business of the Admiralty." None the less, this seemingly wide power was shackled by provisions which made action difficult without consent of the Board of Admiralty. Some of the members, accustomed to the more easygoing ways of McKenna, grew restive under their new civilian chief. They did not scruple to let their views become known to the Opposition though not, it must be admitted, in the peculiarly peccant and aggravated form which had distinguished Sir John Fisher and was to become notorious in the case of Sir Henry Wilson at the War Office.

Admiral Sir Francis Bridgeman, who had become First Sea Lord when Sir Arthur Wilson resigned because of his resistance to the setting up of a Naval War Staff, had collaborated usefully with the First Lord in this matter; but there was an underlying *malaise*.

J. S. Sandars to A. J. Balfour
(Balfour Papers)

EXTRACT

10 October 1912   14 Egerton Gardens

My dear Chief,
    You may like a little gossip — it is about Winston & his colleagues at the Admiralty.

Bridgeman came to sit with me the other day. He is always very frank about his office, as he knows you are the only person to whom I pass on his views.

Winston, although promising not to offend again, has nevertheless outraged official decorum by the language of his official minutes. It appears he has been sending through his office and round the office the most peremptory orders to the Sea Lords. Bridgeman and Prince Louis met & agreed that respect & authority could not be maintained if Winston were allowed to issue papers couched in these terms. Bridgeman therefore met Winston on the latter's return to the Admiralty and plainly told him that he must mend his manners or his Board would have to take action. Bridgeman pointed out that as Winston could not give a single order outside the Admiralty building without the consent of the Board & that he was only *primus inter pares* the terms in which he had been addressing his colleagues was most improper. Winston at first contested this position; whereupon Bridgeman replied that in that event the Sea Lords would address themselves to Asquith & ultimately to the King. Winston then capitulated abjectly, broke into tears and talked in such a melancholy manner about himself that Bridgeman thinks he must be ill. I assured Bridgeman that I had never known the time when sympathy was not asked for Winston on grounds of health.

He has behaved better since; but the other day at the Board he exhibited great irritability and bad temper.

I asked Bridgeman how Winston was getting on in matters of Naval policy. Bridgeman replied that they had hoped that after the mess Winston made over the Mediterranean arrangement he would be more careful & less impulsive. However, he has recently had another fiasco. It appears that Borden [the Canadian Prime Minister] requested the Board of Admiralty to furnish him with some information about our ships, armament etc. in the North Sea. Winston told his colleagues that he would write the paper himself & then show it to them. He did: so the Sea Lords begged & implored him not to send the paper. They pointed out that it dealt with policy and that it was most dictatorial in its tone to the Canadian Govt & that it did not answer Borden's requirements.

However, Winston would send it. Borden promptly returned it, saying that the paper did not give the information for which he asked. Winston then prepared another paper on different lines and sent it to the Board, observing that they might criticize it, but that they should not alter it. The Board were equally opposed to this new paper, and took it upon themselves to rewrite the whole thing on their own lines. Winston was furious and told them he would take the papers to Asquith & if, as he expected, Asquith approved of his (Winston's) paper, he should send it. When the papers reached Asquith, Winston's paper was wholly disallowed: the Sea Lords' was adopted and that has gone to Canada. Winston is now denouncing Borden in the strongest language! . . .

On 28 November 1912 Churchill suggested to Bridgeman that he retire, hinting at Bridgeman's ill-health as a cause for alarm:

WSC to Sir Francis Bridgeman

28 November 1912   [Admiralty]

My dear Sir Francis,

I am very glad to hear from various sources that you have now somewhat recovered from the chill which so unkindly spoiled your holiday, and I trust you will continue to make good progress in spite of the drop in the temperature.

I have been meaning for some time to write to you about your health, which causes me concern both as a colleague and a friend. During the year that we have worked together I have seen how heavily the strain of your great office has told upon you, and I know that only your high sense of duty and your consideration for me have enabled you successfully to overcome your strong inclination to retire. That strain will not, I fear, diminish in the future; and if, by any misadventure, we were to be involved in war, I feel that the burden might be more than you could sustain.

If therefore you should feel disposed at this juncture to retire, I could not, whatever my personal regrets, oppose your wish, and I believe that such a step would be a relief to you.

It would be a cause of very great pleasure to me if I could feel that our association in so much important business had in no way been a cause of regret or dissatisfaction to you.

Believe me, Yours very sincerely
WINSTON S. CHURCHILL

Bridgeman replied cautiously, even cordially, and described Churchill's letter as "kindly-meant." He announced that he would be coming to London "as soon as the doctor will allow me." Churchill was in no mood to delay matters, however:

WSC to the King
(Royal Archives)

29 November 1912   Admiralty
Dictated

Mr Churchill with his humble duty to Your Majesty: he expressed in audience with Your Majesty the other day his increasing anxiety about the state of Sir Francis Bridgeman's health. He can no longer feel satisfied that this officer would be capable of bearing the immense responsibility and strain which would be cast upon him if by any misfortune we were involved in a great naval war. This conclusion once having been reached makes action imperative. Mr Churchill has therefore suggested to Sir Francis Bridgeman in terms of high consideration the propriety of his retirement at an early date. He will on this retirement becoming effective submit to Your Majesty a proposal for promoting Sir Francis Bridgeman to be an Admiral of the Fleet additional to the regular list. This distinction is well merited by Sir Francis by the great command he has held and the high esteem which he enjoys throughout the Navy.

Mr Churchill would then propose with the concurrence of the Prime Minister to submit to Your Majesty the name of Prince Louis of Battenberg to fill the office of First Sea Lord, and that of Sir John Jellicoe to succeed him as Second Sea Lord.

Before making these submissions Mr Churchill would be deeply grateful if he could receive from Your Majesty an intimation that Your Majesty's pleasure would be in accord with arrangements which Mr Churchill is convinced are required in the interests of the Navy and of the State.

WINSTON S. CHURCHILL

Lord Stamfordham replied on December 2 making it clear that the King "is very glad to approve your recommendation of Prince Louis of Battenberg to be First Sea Lord." At the same time the King opposed Churchill's suggestion that Bridgeman should be promoted to Admiral of the Fleet. Churchill wrote at once to Bridgeman on December 2 informing him that he had consulted with Asquith, and that his decision "must necessarily be final." But Bridgeman had no intention of accepting his demission, and before receiving Churchill's letter had himself written:

Sir Francis Bridgeman to WSC

3 December 1912   Copgrove Hall
                                                            Near Leeds

My dear Mr Churchill,

You will be anxiously expecting my reply to your very kind and sympathetic letter suggesting that if my health was not good enough to allow me to continue the duties of my office, I should apply to resign.

I have carefully thought the matter over, and as it seemed to be more a question for the doctors to give an opinion on, I have consulted them. Dr. Wexley-Smith, whom I usually consult, is of opinion that having now diagnosed thoroughly the malady, feels himself able to put me quite right, there being nothing organically wrong, but that I have been run down.

The change to this place has done me a lot of good, and I am returning to London on Monday next. I don't think I need go abroad. I shall remain in London for a week or ten days, and then come back for Christmas and return for good to the Admiralty at the new year. This plan is what I originally arranged for earlier in the year with the Second Sea Lord.

I wish I had taken your advice six or seven months ago and gone abroad. I should probably have avoided all this trouble.

Believe me, Yours very sincerely
F. B. BRIDGEMAN

On receiving Churchill's letter of December 2 Bridgeman seemed resigned to his fate. "I now understand that you expect me to resign," he wrote, "and I am happy to be able to meet your wishes." Bridgeman's letter was dated December 4; ten days later the *Morning Post* carried an account of confidential Admiralty business:

Morning Post

14 December 1912

MR CHURCHILL AND SIR FRANCIS BRIDGEMAN

We are enabled to publish some particulars regarding the resignation of Admiral Sir Francis Bridgeman, the correctness of which is vouched for on the very best authority. Some time ago the late First Sea Lord took the initiative in urging his colleagues on the Board of Admiralty to tender their resignations on the subject Pay and Manning in the Navy. This resolution was conveyed to the Prime Minister by Mr Winston Churchill, and it is not unreasonable to suppose that the result was the recent statement by the First Lord providing a general increase of pay. It will be remembered that in the House of Commons on Wednesday last, Sir C. Kinloch-Cooke [Unionist MP for Devonport] asked the First Lord whether it was a fact that the Sea Lords had threatened more than once to resign during the last month. In answer to this Mr. Churchill said: "There is absolutely no truth in the suggestion." This statement is in obvious conflict with the facts which we put before our readers; but no doubt the explanation is that the wording of Sir C. Kinloch-Cooke's question left some opening for the First Lord's answer. When he acquiesced in Mr Churchill's suggestion that he should retire, Sir Francis Bridgeman was offered the honour of Admiral of the Fleet, which, however, he refused.

Churchill wrote at once to Sir Francis:

WSC to Sir Francis Bridgeman

14 December 1912   [Admiralty]

My dear Sir Francis,

The enclosed extract from the *Morning Post* raises several serious issues on which it is necessary that I should know exactly where you stand. For such a gross breach of official confidence, I am certain you cannot be directly responsible. But it seems to me probable that the question of your resignation will now be the subject of acrimonious debate in Parliament, and I must be free, if necessary, to deal fully and plainly with the facts. I have done my best to guard and sustain your professional reputation and personal dignity, and if I am to continue to do so with success it is essential that I should have your concurrence in making certain statements.

First. That no difference existed between us on the question of manning, and that you were satisfied with the provision (5,000) proposed for next year's increase. On this point I hold, of course, your assent on the official papers; but it will be better if I can state it with your permission.

Secondly. That you concurred in and accepted the scale of improved pay now published. On this point I hold your signed acceptance of the proposals, subject of course to your desire to get more if the money could be found. It will again be very advantageous if I can make this statement with your concurrence. If the matter is disputed, I should be forced to state that during your whole tenure as Second Sea Lord you made no proposals for increasing the pay, and that no proposals for increasing the pay either of officers or of men emanated from you during your tenure as First Sea Lord. Those proposals were initiated solely by me, though I acknowledge the loyal support which I received from you and from the other Sea Lords in my negotiations with the Treasury. No difference of view existed between us on the subject. You were willing to resign if necessary to strengthen my hands during the discussion, but no resignation was tendered by you or any other members of the Board, and you and all the other Sea Lords concurred in the conclusion finally reached.

I hope that it may not be necessary to argue out all these details in public. I shall not in the least shrink from doing so.

Thirdly. I desire to state that I have your authority that no other cause of difference or disagreement in policy or view existed between us which had led, or was about to lead, to your resignation.

Your agreement in the above plain statements of fact will, I believe, enable me to close the incident without further unpleasantness. But unless I have your authority to make such a statement on behalf of us both it may be necessary — though I should regret it from every point of view — for me to publish to Parliament my letter to you of the 28th November, together with your replies of the 29th and the 3rd December; my second letter to you of the 2nd December and your reply dated the 4th.

It may also be necessary for me, if the point of your ill-health is disputed, to state that you wrote on the 25th November to Prince Louis as follows: —

"I have been very depressed lately about my health: two attacks of bronchitis within a few months, and coming on top of appendicitis, seems to have weakened my constitution, and I sometimes feel inclined to give up my post. However, I am now up and about the house, and it will, I hope, pass off. The fact is, I really ought to go somewhere warmer than England to spend the winter — an impossibility so long as one remains at the Admiralty." It may also be necessary for me to refer to your letter to my Naval Secretary of November 26th, in which you say that you had actually taken up your pen to write out your resignation overnight, but that feeling better in the morning you had changed your mind.

It would be very painful to me to go into these details, or to have to prove to the House of Commons, inch by inch, the facts which led me to the conclusion that your physical strength and energy were no longer equal to the duties of your office. But if I am challenged by persons who the public may think (though some of them are no friends of yours) are acting on your behalf, I shall be forced to vindicate the action which I took, at this dangerous period in international affairs, in asking you to relinquish your post.

Let me, then, recapitulate the three statements which I desire to make upon our joint authority: —

1. That no difference existed between us on the question of manning, and that you were satisfied with the provision proposed for next year's increase.

2. That you concurred in, and accepted, the improved scale of pay as now published.

3. That no cause of difference or disagreement in policy or view existed between us which had led, or was about to lead, to your resignation.

As it is important that I should receive your answer before Monday, the messenger is instructed to await your convenience.

Yours very sincerely
WINSTON S. CHURCHILL

Bridgeman telegraphed in reply ". . . agree to all you say. I don't know where *Morning Post* article came from, but it's untrue." But when Churchill sought a statement from Bridgeman confirming that they had been in agreement on matters of general policy, Bridgeman insisted that Churchill made it plain "that on other matters we have differed to the extent that I suggested resignation." To this Churchill replied:

WSC to Sir Francis Bridgeman

18 December 1912   [Admiralty]

Dear Sir Francis Bridgeman,

I cannot accept the statement contained in your telegram just received by me. You have never on any occasion tendered your resignation to me. No resignation by you was threatened or impending at the time of your retirement. My letter to you of the 28th November imparted to you the fact that I did not "consider your health and strength sufficient to bear the strain of a war." In spite of this, however, you still proposed in your reply to continue in office. This alone proves that there was, in the words of my question, "no difference in general policy between us which had led, or was about to lead, to your resignation," and it is unworthy of you not to accept an opportunity of dissociating yourself from statements which are unfounded, and known to be unfounded by those with whom you worked.

I shall certainly not place any reliance upon your authority in any statement I may have to make, or quote you in any way as agreeing with me.

Yours very truly
WINSTON S. CHURCHILL

On December 20, during the debate on the Christmas adjournment, Churchill was attacked in the House of Commons over Bridgeman's retirement. Bonar Law said that Bridgeman had been "brutally ill-used." Although Churchill replied at length, quoting correspondence, and stressing that Bridgeman's retirement was due to ill-health, Conservative critics were not entirely convinced:

Lord Charles Beresford to Andrew Bonar Law
(Bonar Law Papers)

20 December 1912   1 Great Cumberland Place

My dear Bonar Law,
Your speech today quite cheered me up. It was really quite excellent and put the grave part of Sir Francis Bridgeman's resignation clearly before the public. Churchill was not clever. He let out that a colleague of his on the Board had received a private letter from Sir Francis which was shown to Churchill and used as a lever to oust Sir Francis. The letter was sent to Battenberg, who appears to think that it was not a bad thing to use it, in order to step into Sir Francis' shoes. There is a great deal more to be found out over this disgrace-

ful affair. Certainly things went far more in the direction of getting
at the truth than we thought last night.

I wish you a happy Xmas.

Yours very sincerely

CHARLES BERESFORD

But the "truth" as Beresford saw it was mostly from a tainted
source. On December 21 Churchill asked the King to warn Bridgeman "of the deplorable folly of persisting further on disclosures damaging only to himself." Lord Stamfordham replied on the same day
that the King "would prefer to give no advice and to leave the matter
in your hands to be dealt with as you deem best."

Bridgeman, unaware that the King had given Churchill a free
hand, wrote pugnaciously on December 21:

Sir Francis Bridgeman to WSC

21 December 1912   Grosvenor Hotel

Dear Mr Churchill,

I observe that in the reports of yesterday's debate in the House of
Commons, in the course of your speech you thought proper to quote
passages from private letters written by me to Prince Louis of Battenberg and to Admiral Beatty.

I beg to remind you that in my letter to you, replying to your
letter of the 15th December last, in which you stated that *"it may also
be necessary"* for you to quote from my letters to Prince Louis and
Admiral Beatty, I made it a condition of granting my permission to
do as you proposed, *"that if, as you seem to intimate, you should
publish my private letters to yourself and to officers serving at the
Board of Admiralty, I must ask you to be good enough to include this
letter with the other correspondence."* I think you will agree with me
that I had some right to expect that you would comply with my
request, I see, however, that you have quoted the letters in question
without fulfilling the condition expressly stated by me. I feel, therefore, that I have now no choice but to urge that you will forthwith
publish the whole correspondence which has taken place between us,
with regard to my resignation.

I desire also to reserve my right of sending this letter, together
with your reply, to the press.

I am returning to Copgrove to-day, where all letters should be addressed.

Believe me, Yours truly
F. B. BRIDGEMAN

Churchill replied at once:

WSC to Sir Francis Bridgeman

21 December 1912

Dear Sir Francis Bridgeman,

I see no reason to object to a further publication of the correspondence between us, so far as I am concerned, and if you desire it I will make arrangements to send it to the press in time for Monday. The correspondence must, however, be sufficiently full to convey from the series of letters and telegrams a true impression to the public. I should propose, therefore, to begin with my letter of the 6th December and your answer to it of the 8th December, in which you first refer to the alleged occasion of your having threatened resignation. From this letter there should, however, be omitted the recommendations of particular officers which you made to me, as there is no need to bring them in. This letter concludes with your good wishes to the new Board and to myself, and it is essential that it should be included. I should propose to publish my letter of the 9th December, omitting irrelevant references to individuals. It will be necessary that my letter of the 14th December should be published, in which I ask you certain specific questions, and your telegram in answer, in which "you absolutely agree to all I say." Then in its proper place will come your letter written from the Grosvenor Hotel later in the same day, when under what influence I cannot determine you go back on your spontaneous first thoughts and allow yourself to become the tool of party attack. My letter of the 16th December must be published, as it deals with the alleged incident of your threatening resignation, and shows the proper proportions of the affair. In this connection I may remind you that it is the Naval Secretary, and not the First Sea Lord, who by long-established custom advises the First Lord on naval appointments, and that even if it were true that you threatened to resign, which I was certainly not aware of, it would have been a most unreasonable and improper oc-

casion. Had your resignation been tendered on such a subject I
should have been bound to accept it forthwith. I should propose
further to publish your letter of the 17th December and your telegram of the 18th December, together with my answer of the same
date. The correspondence could conclude, if you desire it, with yours
of to-day's date and this answer to it.

You have no claim, and have never had any claim, to prevent my
making use, if necessary for a public purpose, of information as to
your state of health, and your view of your state of health, which had
reached me through official channels. Admiral Beatty, as Naval
Secretary, was bound in duty to acquaint me with what you had
written, just as he would have done if any flag officer in high command afloat communicated to him that his health was so bad that he
was on the verge 'of resignation. Your letter to Prince Louis was in
no sense a privileged document, and it would have been improper
in any officer serving on the Board of Admiralty to withhold such
information from the responsible Minister. It was your duty, indeed,
which I am at last reluctantly compelled to remind you of, to have
written to me yourself of your misgivings as to your ability to discharge your office. I thought it would be more considerate to you to
establish, as I was bound to do for the satisfaction of Parliament,
your ill-health from your own words rather than to prove the fact
by going into details. I could, of course, have pointed out instead
that you have only been able to attend three out of six meetings of
the Committee of Imperial Defence, and that on one of those three
occasions you were forced to leave from sudden faintness. But it was
hateful for me to dwell on such things in public.

If you desire that a further publication shall be made I shall not
resist your wish. But I warn you most earnestly that it would be
deeply injurious to your reputation. That is the last service which I
can render you.

Yours very truly
WINSTON S. CHURCHILL

Bridgeman, meanwhile, had seen the King. It was clear that he
would have to accept Churchill's ruling. The influence which he had
with certain Conservatives did not extend to the Court.

Sir Francis Bridgeman to WSC
(Royal Archives)

23 December 1912   Copgrove Hall
Copy
Most Secret

Dear Mr Churchill,

Yr letter of Sat 21st reached me at 5 pm after my interview with His Majesty.

The threatening character of this letter is such that I should have desired to reply with emphasis. However after a conversation with a High Personage I had already been led to the conclusion that the publication of our correspondence wd not conduce to the interests of the Service.

I accordingly withdraw my claim that the complete & unedited correspondence which has passed between us shd be published.

I have to add that HM who adopted a wholly impartial attitude at my audience, desires that his influence in the matter should not be the subject of conversation.

I shall do my utmost to fulfil HM's wishes tho' you will readily appreciate the circumstances which impel me to communicate this fact to yourself.

y.v.t.
F. B. BRIDGEMAN

However, Bridgeman did not seem to bear Churchill any malice. Soon after his resignation he wrote a letter to Stamfordham in which he loyally defended the First Lord.

Sir Francis Bridgeman to Lord Stamfordham
(Royal Archives)

28 December 1912   Copgrove Hall

My dear Stamfordham,

Thank you for returning the letters so promptly, it certainly was a smart performance, only possible under such an organisation as appears to prevail at the Palace!

I do hope the whole business is now at an end, but I hear rumours of a deep-laid agitation against Churchill; I am using every bit of influence I possess to arrest it and have asked Balcarres to do the same. I am afraid Beresford is difficult to hold & I unfortunately can do nothing with him. My difficulty of course lies in the fact that if I am too emphatic it cd be thought I had something to hide, wh of course is not the case. Also that it is of primary importance that HM's influence shd be concealed.

To you I am indebted for a great deal, & I don't know how to thank you.

My wife joins me in wishing you & yours a happy new year.

Believe me, Yours very truly

F. B. BRIDGEMAN

Admiral Bridgeman's departure still left other leak-holes unplugged at the Admiralty. Sir Francis Hopwood, whom Churchill had guilelessly brought with him from the Home Office, always seems to have thought it his duty to keep the Sovereign informed of any departmental gossip which came his way. He had accompanied the Duke of Connaught to the Delhi Durbar in 1903 and clearly had aspirations to be a courtier as well as an administrator. Although he was an Additional Civil Lord his sympathies lay more with the Admirals than with his civilian master.

Sir Francis Hopwood to Lord Stamfordham
(Royal Archives)

9 November 1913   13 Hornton Street
Private.

My dear Stamfordham,

There is a fierce quarrel raging between Churchill and his Naval Lords. C. very foolishly travels round the coast holding reviews and inspections & so forth without reference to Naval opinion and regulation. He is also much addicted to sending for junior officers & discussing with them the proceedings of their superiors; this naturally enrages the latter & is very mischievous to the former. It is on the score of breaches of discipline that the present trouble has been founded. The facts as described to me are as follows: Churchill interviewed a Lieutenant of the *Vernon* & encouraged him to put forward some scheme or other about torpedo working. The Captain of the *Vernon* refused to forward it to the Commander-in-Chief at the Nore *en route* to the Admiralty whereupon the Lieutenant said

"Then I shall send it direct to Mr Churchill who invited (or ordered) me to do so..." Then the row began. The Captain of the *Vernon* wrote in strong terms of complaint to the Commander-in-Chief who wrote on in equally strong terms to Jellicoe criticising the First Lord's method. Now somehow Churchill had heard that this correspondence had begun. Perhaps the Lieutenant at the *Vernon* had written him to say he had got into trouble. But anyhow Churchill sent his Private Secretary to Jellicoe to say that if any despatch came from the C-in-C at the Nore on the subject he (Churchill) desired to see it immediately. It did come & Jellicoe finding it couched in strong terms determined, in order to keep the peace, to send it back for some amendment. Jellicoe accordingly returned the despatch with a private letter of his own enclosed. When a few hours later C. found the despatch had been sent back he went dancing mad & on his own sent a telegram to the General Post Office asking that the letter should be found & returned at once to *him*. He also telegraphed to the C-in-C Nore to return the letter to him at the Admiralty unopened. He got it back from the GPO, & so came into possession of the correspondence & also Jellicoe's private letter with comments! To get out of the difficulty of the latter he professes not to have read it! Jellicoe has of course intimated that he will resign. Churchill has now announced that he will get rid of both the C-in-C Nore & the Captain of the *Vernon*. On that issue Moore & Pakenham both want to go. Prince Louis felt that way at first but Jellicoe tells me that Churchill has talked the First Sea Lord over. Churchill is reported to have told the 4 Naval Lords that if any one of them desired to criticise his methods he should expect them to resign as they could not work together.

C. has not mentioned the subject to me, all this comes from the Admirals. Of course it is very private but The King may be interested in the facts as unless differences are composed there may be a resignation & some publicity at any moment. It is deplorable.

Ever yrs
FRANCIS S. HOPWOOD

Sir Francis Hopwood to Lord Stamfordham
(Royal Archives)

10 November 1913

My dear Stamfordham,

There are evidences of saner mind. I think there will be a climb down if a way can be found. Perhaps it would be well to keep my letter back until tomorrow as one does not want to worry HM if the crisis is going to pass. If it blows over he can read what has happened with an equable mind.

The real difficulty will be to find a way of sufficiently scolding the C-in-C to satisfy Churchill without really affecting that officer unduly!

Ever yrs
Fs. S. H.

No record survives of Churchill's side of the story. It certainly seems that in his desire to get first-hand information he unduly ruptured the chain of command: but Hopwood's account may have been exaggerated.

The First Lord always encouraged his associates by precept no less than by example to express themselves cogently on paper. This led him to deal somewhat unkindly with Rear-Admiral Arthur Limpus, who since April 1912 had been serving as Naval Adviser to the Turkish Navy.

Admiral Limpus to WSC

Wednesday   Constantinople
3 December 1913

Dear Mr Churchill,

It may fairly be said that something tangible has been done, and a success scored which should retain a predominant British interest here in naval affairs for many — probably 30 years.

Hard negotiating has been going on from the latter parts of September until today. Often we are at it from 9.30 a.m. till 6.30 p.m. with a very brief lunch interval; but today the Directors have gone back to England with the matter settled. Twice the negotiations so nearly failed that I wrote for your help. But at the last moment the difficulty was surmounted and the letters were not sent.

If it interests you, you shall have the whole yarn when I return; just now there is no need to trouble you with more than the first two pages of the first letter. They follow this page: —

29 October 1913   Constantinople

Dear Mr Churchill,

As regards influence in naval matters in Turkey we are now, in my opinion, face to face with the German Government. If I am correct, then it is not to be expected that the Armstrong Group can successfully compete, unless the British Government will accord to them its support. The situation is as follows: —

The Turks have built the *Rechadieh*. They need a dock for her. Their arsenals in the Golden Horn are crumbling — have nearly crumbled to decay. They need capable management, workmen, and money. Then they could be used both for the navy and commercially. But in the future their main arsenal must be outside the Golden Horn. I have persuaded the Armstrong Group to take this business up. They have formulated in writing certain terms upon which they will do so. The Turk Govt has accepted these terms, in principle, in writing, and invited directors with full powers to come here & discuss & settle details. Sir Vincent Caillard (Vickers) and Sir Charles Ottley (Armstrong) arrived on Wedn 22nd Oct. The Min of War Djavid Bey, and I have discussed the matter with them. [*Note by WSC on a typed copy of this letter:* this seems to be the end of the old letter]

Djavid Bey left for Berlin Oct 29th and the Government gave us Haladjian Effendi (an ex Minister of Public Works) in his place. The agreement was re-drafted 13 times! But now it is settled.

It may well be considered not only as the day of the renaissance of the Turkish Navy, though it may very well be that, but more important still, as a really vital nucleus for the building up of a large industry in Turkey.

The final scene was interesting to me because I was called upon to address all the Ministers in Council on the general bearing of the agreement. However, thank goodness it is *done*. Here it is in outline: —

3 parties to the agreement, Government, the public debt, and the Group (Armstrong Vickers). They form a Compagnie Cointeressée. Object, naval & commercial construction & repair works. Duration, 30 years. Govt gives . . . [?] Existing docks & arsenals, and, aided by the public debt, guarantees the interest & sinking fund on the £1,300,000 capital and agrees to have all its work done by the Societé Imperiale Ottomane des Docks &c, and, what the Societé cannot do is

to be done in England. The Group finds the capital, finds the management & direction & certain English workpeople, and engages to put the existing plant in to order, install a floating dock near Ismidt with the necessary nucleus of workshops on shore & a model village. Engages to be in a position to execute certain classes of work in certain definite times, & to so train the Turkish personnel that at the end of the term it shall be handed back to the Governmt as a going Turkish concern.

That is a rough outline of the agreement.

Of course the unforeseen is always to be reckoned with, but barring the unforeseen a really useful work has been born. Its nationality is very distinctly British, and if I do not mistake, undesirable aliens are shut out for 30 years. If that is so, then quite apart from the other odds and ends of work that have been done, we have justified our mission both to the Turks & to those who sent us.

It is bad to shout too soon, but the appearance of the infant is so healthy that the temptation to cheer a little is strong.

Sincerely yours
ARTHUR H. LIMPUS

The First Lord, while disposed to compliment Limpus on what he claimed to achieving did not like the style in which this naval "yarn" had been concocted.

WSC to Admiral Limpus

10 December 1913   [Admiralty]

Copy

I have received your letter of the 3rd instant, and I am glad to hear from you and from other quarters of the agreement which has been reached between the Turkish Government and Messrs Vickers. I recognize that you have played a useful and effective part in the negotiations, and I congratulate you upon the result.

I find it necessary to criticise the general style and presentment of your letters. A flag officer writing to a member of the Board of Admiralty on service matters ought to observe a proper seriousness and formality. The letters should be well written or typed on good paper; the sentences should be complete and follow the regular English form. Mere jottings of passing impressions hurriedly put together without sequence, and very often with marked confusion, are calculated to give an impression the reverse of that which is desirable. You do not do yourself justice in these matters. No one can be so busy as not to be able to cast a letter to a superior in a proper form. You should make up your mind beforehand exactly what you mean to say, and study to say it in the clearest and shortest way, if necessary re-drafting your letter. In your latest communication three letters appear to be mixed up without beginning or end. Knowing the good work which you did in South Africa and your zeal in your Turkish mission, I am able to dispel from my mind the impression which the chaotic character of your correspondence would otherwise convey.

*

King George V always took a very great interest in the Royal Navy. It was not for nothing that he had seen fifteen years' service, and was known as the Sailor King. Churchill, as we have seen, always kept him fully informed with possibly decisive results in the matter of the Estimates. Like his First Lord, the King took a keen interest in small details. This led to a controversy between the King and the First Lord that was conducted with spirit and deep knowledge of British history and naval traditions on both sides. In such a matter the King naturally prevailed.

In November 1911, shortly after becoming First Lord, Churchill submitted the names *Africa, Liberty, Assiduous* and *Oliver Cromwell* for the new battleships being laid down. The King would only accept *Africa.* When the King proposed *Delhi, Wellington* and *Marlborough* in March 1912, the First Lord accepted *Marlborough,* persuaded the King to change *Wellington* to *Iron Duke,* and opposed *Delhi.* To this Lord Stamfordham replied:

Lord Stamfordham to WSC

EXTRACT

7 March 1912   Buckingham Palace

My Dear Churchill,

The King quite agrees with you that *Iron Duke* will be a more suitable name than *Duke of Wellington* and he gladly approves of the former for one of the new Dreadnoughts.

But the King is sorry that he does not like giving up the *Delhi*. Indeed he holds strongly to it as an appropriate name for one of the others: and as the chief point in his choice was the fact that it would mark the year in which the change of capital in India was made, to bestow it upon a ship to be laid down later on would have little significance — nor does he care about so naming a *Cruiser* . . .

The First Lord at once agreed to the name *Delhi* for one of the new battleships.

In October 1912 the First Lord submitted four further names for the capital ships of 1912–13, *King Richard the First, King Henry the Fifth, Queen Elizabeth* and *Oliver Cromwell*. Churchill informed the King that he had consulted with the Prime Minister about the name *Oliver Cromwell* "and finds him in full accord with the view that the almost unequalled services which the Lord Protector rendered to the British Navy should find recognition in Your Majesty's Fleet." But the King was not influenced by the combined arguments of his Prime Minister and First Lord.

Lord Stamfordham to WSC
(Royal Archives)

29 October 1912   Buckingham Palace

My dear Churchill,

The King wishes me to return the enclosed submission as he feels sure there must be some mistake in the name of *Oliver Cromwell* being suggested for one of the new Battleships. For that name was proposed for one of the ships of last year's programme; His Majesty was unable to agree to it and on his return from India personally explained to you the reasons for his objection.

The King's opinion on the subject has in no way changed and in these circumstances he naturally regrets at having again to ask that some other name be submitted.

Believe me, Yours very truly
STAMFORDHAM

The First Lord was determined to persevere in his choice. He replied at once to Stamfordham with a variety of arguments, stressing that he had the support not only of Asquith but also of other colleagues, whom he did not name. He tried also to allay royal fears about naming a battleship after a regicide.

WSC to Lord Stamfordham
(Royal Archives)

EXTRACT

1 November 1912   Admiralty

. . . Oliver Cromwell was one of the founders of the Navy, & scarcely any man did so much for it. I am quite sure that nothing in history will justify the view that the adoption of such a name would constitute any reflection, however vague, upon His Majesty's Royal House. On the contrary, the great movement in politics & in religion of which Cromwell was the instrument, was intimately connected with all those forces which, through a long succession of Princes, have brought His Majesty to the Throne of a Constitutional & a Protestant country. The bitterness of the rebellions and tyrannies of the past has long ceased to stir men's minds; but the achievements of the country & of its greatest men endure. His Majesty is the heir of all the glories of the nation, & there is no chapter of English history from which he should feel himself divided.

I am satisfied that the name would be extremely well received; & that it would mark in a way that little else could the permanent ascendency in this country of monarchical over republican ideas. . . .

These arguments were not successful. Lord Stamfordham replied on November 4, reminding him of the strong Irish opposition in 1895 to a statue of Cromwell which it had been proposed to erect out of public funds. The Government had been defeated by a majority of 137 on this issue. Stamfordham quoted six speakers from the parliamentary debate, including A. J. Balfour, "who had disputed the point that Cromwell was the founder of the Naval Power of England" and had stressed that "as to Parliamentary Government he absolutely succeeded in uprooting the whole system."

The First Lord took up the challenge. He consulted Lord Morley, who provided a comprehensive answer to Stamfordham's points, replete with relevant quotations from Macaulay and Mahan. This enabled the First Lord to draft a full reply to Stamfordham on November 6, making copious use of Morley's case and quotations. This concluded with a strong argument: "To come down from historic heights, may I remind you that the monument to Oliver Cromwell was *provided* by Lord Rosebery, of whom I would venture to say two things: (1) that in his historic sentiment and conviction he is representative of many many Englishmen and Scotchmen in both political camps; (2) that even when he does not fully share their sentiment he has an extraordinarily acute flair for it.

"It would surely be a strange paradox to refuse Cromwell's name to a battleship when his commanding effigy stands conspicuous in the very spot where of all others in the realm historic reverence and honour for great rulers of every line are most naturally and irresistibly awakened in English hearts."

But the First Lord does not appear to have sent this letter. On the day on which it was drafted Prince Louis informed him that "all my experience at the Admiralty & close intercourse with three sovereigns leads me to this; from all times the Sovereign's decisions as to names for H.M. Ships has been accepted as final by all First Lords." Prince Louis concluded his letter with the warning that he was inclined to think "the service as a whole would go against you in this choice." The First Lord redrafted his letter in a much modified form:

WSC to Lord Stamfordham
(Royal Archives)

16 November 1912   Admiralty

My dear Stamfordham,

In the face of the accredited historians like Gardiner, Firth, and others, it is really impossible to deny Oliver Cromwell's share in the strength and greatness of the Navy. There is besides the marked and indisputable fact that he brought the name and power of England into a recognised prominence over the Continent of Europe which has not many times been equalled and has never been surpassed. It certainly seems right that we should give to a battleship a name that never failed to make the enemies of England tremble.

It has been my duty to place before the King in this and my last letter to you the good and serious reasons which have led me to submit this name. If they do not weigh with His Majesty I shall not on such a subject press my advice further. Meanwhile, I enclose you two quotations, for which I am indebted to the erudition of Lord Morley.

Yours sincerely
WINSTON S. CHURCHILL

Stamfordham replied briefly on November 20 that "nothing which had been said or written during the controversy had induced the King to alter his opinion," and asking the First Lord to submit some other name. This Churchill did on the same day: "I bow to the King's wish about the battleship's name and will submit the name *Valiant* as a substitute." This was accepted.

In August 1913 the First Lord informed Sir Frederick Ponsonby, the King's Assistant Private Secretary, that "I am strongly of the opinion that the Navy ought not to be without a *Pitt* and an *Ark Royal*." In his letter he stressed the historical association of these vessels, and enclosed their past history.

Ponsonby's reply was not encouraging:

Sir Frederick Ponsonby to WSC
(Royal Archives)

5 August 1913   HM Yacht *Victoria & Albert*
                                 Cowes

My dear Churchill,

Many thanks for your letter which I have submitted to The King.

His Majesty was well aware that both *Pitt* and *Ark Royal* were old names with historical traditions but sees nothing in the records of former vessels to render a revival of these names so essential.

The King agrees with you in thinking that it is well when possible to keep alive the old names but considers that certain exceptions should be made. French names should now be avoided in case they

might wound the susceptibilities of the French people. Monosylla-
bles are as a rule a mistake when applied to Battleships although they
may well be used with smaller vessels.

The King knows how carefully all these questions are considered
at the Admiralty and how well the old records are kept. His Majesty
thinks you will, therefore, have no difficulty in selecting two other
old names in the place of these two which he dislikes.

Yours sincerely
F. E. G. PONSONBY

The First Lord again replied at length, arguing in favor of the
names he had chosen, and of his own responsibility in the matter.

WSC to Sir Frederick Ponsonby
(Royal Archives)

8 August 1913   Admiralty

My dear Ponsonby,

I am very sorry to learn from you that the King does not like the
names *Pitt* and *Ark Royal* for two of the battleships of this year's
programme. I am convinced that they are from many points of view
the best choice that could be made. The name "Pitt" recalls the two
famous statesmen under whom the most martial exploits of our race
have been achieved. It was suggested to me as a specially appropriate
name for a British battleship by the Prime Minister. The *Ark Royal*
which, as is shown in the accompanying memorandum, was the flagship at the defeat of the Armada, revives the glories of the Elizabethan period as the *Warspite* did in the programme of 1912–13. For
both these names, were precedent indispensable, precedent exists. It
is not desirable to confine the naming of battleships solely to vessels
associated with the Nelsonic epoch though they assuredly should play
a principal part.

With regard to the *Pitt* in particular, I cannot feel that the reasons
to which you refer in your letter ought to weigh either with the
Admiralty or with the King against doing honour to one of the greatest names in the history of this or any other European country. It
would of course be possible if the King desired it to call the vessel
the *William Pitt*; but there are great advantages in brevity, and I do
not recommend this alternative.

I would venture to observe that in this field, as in others where opinions so easily differ, a definite responsibility for advice attaches to the Minister who for the time being is entrusted by His Majesty with the duty of presiding over the Admiralty Board. If public criticism through the Press or in Parliament is directed upon the naming of battleships, whether from the point of view of the exclusion or inclusion of certain names, it is essential that it should be borne solely by the First Lord of the Admiralty and that no one should have the right to suppose that His Majesty's personal act is in any way involved.

It has been a cause of regret to me that on several occasions in the past the names which it was my duty to submit to the King have not been favoured by His Majesty and that this subject has led to an extensive correspondence. I have therefore been led to examine the past history of this branch of naval administration. I find that the custom of bringing the names of battleships to the Sovereign's notice did not exist during the reign of Queen Victoria, except in cases where it was proposed to name a ship after the Sovereign or a member of the Royal Family, and was only introduced in the last reign in connection with the proposal to institute a "King Edward the Seventh" class of battleships. In these circumstances it occurs to me that the King might prefer not to be troubled at all in the matter, and that I should revert to the practice invariably followed up to a quite recent date.

Perhaps you will kindly let me know whether the King would like me to renew my submission in its amended form or to proceed in accordance with the older usage.

> Yours sincerely
> WINSTON S. CHURCHILL

Lord Stamfordham, who had been on leave, returned, and wrote a decisive reply:

> *Lord Stamfordham to WSC*
> *(Royal Archives)*

20 August 1913   Balmoral Castle

Having returned from leave I am desired by the King to write to you regarding the names of *Pitt* and *Ark Royal* suggested for two of the new Battleships, about which you and Ponsonby have been in correspondence.

In your letter of the 8th August you refer to "ministerial responsibility." It would undoubtedly be the duty of the First Lord to point out any objections to giving effect to the wishes of the Sovereign if they involved questions of organisation, efficiency, or expenditure: but in the present instance no such questions arise.

Battleships have to be named so as to distinguish them: but for all practical purposes they might equally well be numbered and lettered, like submarines.

The actual names are a matter of fancy, sentiment, and suitability, though, as you say, this is a field where opinions easily differ.

The King assumes that in submitting the names for his approval you expected to have His Majesty's views upon your selection: and His Majesty cannot help thinking that the Officers and Men of the Royal Navy would like to feel that the Ships were named with the approval of the Sovereign, all the more so as the King was himself for many years in the Service.

You mention that you find the custom of bringing the names of Battleships to the Sovereign's notice practically did not exist during the reign of Queen Victoria. But, speaking with 20 years experience of Her Majesty's methods of business, I cannot imagine one of her Ministers submitting a question for approval except on the understanding that due regard, if not actual effect, would be given to any expression of Her Majesty's pleasure.

The King's objections to the above two names have already been stated in the previous letters. But His Majesty noticed from the records you sent that the two vessels called *Pitt* were used as Coal Depots: two previous ships of that name being respectively a captured French Privateer, and a vessel bought from the East India Company and changed from *Pitt* to *Doris*.

Moreover, up till now there has been no case of a ship in the Royal Navy bearing the name of any of our great Statesmen.

The King quite recognises the interest and trouble which you have taken in this matter, and indeed in everything connected with the great Service over which you preside. But at the same time his Majesty yields to no one in his concern for all that affects the daily life of the Sailor, with which the name of the Ship, wherein he lives, and wherein he may have to fight, must always be closely associated.

Under these circumstances the King hopes that you will see your way to carry out his wishes and submit two other names, which, together with the three already agreed upon, would meet with His Majesty's approval.

Would it not avoid difficulties if in the future you were to ask to see the King and talk over such matters with his Majesty before sending in the formal submission? As you know, the King is only too glad to receive you at any time.

STAMFORDHAM

17

Naval Estimates Crisis

IN EARLY 1914 the First Lord had to address himself to the serious business of preparing the Naval Estimates for 1914–15. These, as it turned out, were to be of crucial importance in maintaining British supremacy at sea. His previous Estimates had been largely inherited from his predecessor though he had added to them considerably by supplementary Estimates. He had now been in charge of the Admiralty for more than two years and these were the first Estimates which were entirely his. He had had the time to study naval strategy and naval requirements down to the smallest detail. He rightly suspected from the outset that he would encounter stern opposition from numerous colleagues in the Cabinet. He had made himself master of all the arguments and there was no matter great or small which he had not got at his fingertips. He was to require all his knowledge, his powers of persuasion and his determination, if need be to resign, in order to carry the Cabinet with him. The successful process, by which he marshalled his arguments and gained acceptance for what he judged to be imperative, shows his powers of statesmanship at their highest and constitutes an achievement which will long be thought to have been an imperishable service alike to the Royal Navy and to the nation.

While the First Lord was preparing his Naval Estimates the first hint of future criticism occurred in a letter which Margot Asquith wrote to Lloyd George from 10 Downing Street on 17 November 1913: "Don't let Winston have too much money — it will hurt our party in every way — Labour & even Liberals. If one can't be a little economical when all foreign countries are peaceful I don't know *when* we can."

Churchill circulated his memorandum on the proposed estimates to the Cabinet on 5 December 1913. He sought an increase of £2,985,500 over the previous year's Original and Supplemental Estimates, bringing the total to £50,694,800. This increase was made up to a large extent from the rise in the cost of naval construction which resulted from a general rise in prices of about 15 per cent. As Churchill explained in his memorandum "during the year 1912 . . . the boom in the shipbuilding trade caused an advance in the price of materials of about 15%." This involved an automatic and uncontrollable addition to the cost of those battleships already under construction of about £320,500 each, and put an additional burden of about £1,200,000 on the new construction. The First Lord had sought economies; four capital ships were to be laid down instead of the five of the previous year and twelve destroyers instead of twenty. But there were other aspects of construction in which he sought increases.

He wished to provide greater reserves of oil and sought an extra £475,000 for this. Sir John Jellicoe, the second Sea Lord, had impressed on him the need for a six months' reserve supply. Churchill also sought a further 5,000 men, and the continued extension of the 6-inch armament to all battleships, a policy which had been decided on before he had gone to the Admiralty. Fisher was bitterly opposed to the calibre of these guns which he thought excessive for fighting off torpedo-boats. A further technical advance from the 18-inch torpedo to the 20-inch would involve an extra cost of £217 for each torpedo and £500 for each torpedo tube.

In his memorandum the First Lord went into specific details for every aspect of both increased and decreased expenditure. He summed up the main causes of the increases in this memorandum:

First: From the decisions of policy to increase the programmes of new construction and the number of ships maintained in full commission in consequence of the new German Navy Law, and the decision to increase the numbers and pay of the personnel.

Secondly: From the increase in the size, speed, armament, equipment, and cost of warships of all kinds necessary to keep pace with the similar vessels building all over the world.

Thirdly: From the introduction and development of new services, principally Oil Fuel, Air Service, and Wireless Telegraphy.

Fourthly: From the general increase in prices and wages, and particularly in the cost of coal, oil, steel, and all materials used in connection with shipbuilding.

It was clear from this Memorandum that Churchill realized the need to economize wherever possible. As well as reducing the number of new capital ships and destroyers he decided to save £180,000 by not holding the Grand Manoeuvres but by substituting for them a general mobilization of the Third Fleet: "The test is one of the most important that can be made, and it is surprising we should have continued for so many years without ever once making it." As events turned out this proved both far-sighted and fortunate in the extreme.

During the first Cabinet meeting to discuss the Naval Estimates the First Lord, in a note which he passed to Lloyd George, expressed some of the deeper anxieties which he felt as a result of the German Navy Law and outlined a broader policy than that contained in the detailed estimates themselves: "In order to guard against any sudden expansion of German construction, not hitherto expected, it seems imperative that we should forthwith increase the plant necessary to turn out guns and turrets for Dreadnought vessels to a capacity of at least 12 vessels a year." Churchill hoped to maintain "an adequate balance of naval strength against Germany for the ensuing three years" and "to secure a substantial preponderance" by 1920.

One private comment on this Cabinet meeting has survived:

H. H. Asquith to Miss Venetia Stanley
(Montagu Papers)

EXTRACT

8 December 1913   10 Downing Street
Midnight

. . . We had a Cabinet which lasted nearly 3 hours, 2¾ of which was occupied by Winston. Tomorrow, I make (I hope) my last speech for a long time, on Land! I trust you are praying for me. . . .

Other members of the Cabinet disliked the estimates and sought to cut them back substantially. The Postmaster-General, Herbert Samuel, proposed that only two capital ships should be built, that the number of men should be reduced, and that fewer submarines and light cruisers should be built. Churchill answered Samuel's criticism in a memorandum of 13 December 1913. He pointed out that the construction of four battleships "only just maintains the 60% standard." He circulated to the Cabinet a series of papers on the comparative strength of the British and German Fleets, the increase of personnel, and the cost of submarine and light cruiser construction. From these papers it was clear that were Herbert Samuel's proposals to be accepted Germany would swiftly gain the advantage. Other ministers took up Samuel's call for economy, but Churchill was not without supporters in the Cabinet and received a warning from the Secretary of State for War:

Jack Seely to WSC

12 December 1913   Blatchington House
Seaford
Sussex

My dear Winston,

Simon was in most truculent mood yesterday about your estimates. He kept on muttering to me that it was scandalous and so on. I disagreed with him and asked him what practical criticism he had to make. He said "what we want is a clear statement shewing what Germany was spending four years ago and what she is spending this year, and the same figures for ourselves; you will then see that our advance in expenditure is out of all proportion to theirs." Now, you can fight your corner better than anyone, so I hesitate to make a suggestion to you but if, as I believe to be the case, Simon is entirely wrong, and that comparing like with like including loans and other charges in the German figures as in our own, our increase is proportionately less, it seems to me it would be well worth your while to make the point clear next Monday.

Yours ever
JACK

Lord Riddell's Diary contains a full account of the growing crisis:

December 13th, 1913 — The Navy estimates and the Ulster question are causing serious differences in the Cabinet. There is, no doubt, strong opposition to Winston on both. I saw McKenna to-day. He has been working up the case for reducing the estimates, and is strong against concessions to Ulster. Evidently much worried. The story published to-day about the Ulster settlement dinner is incorrect. LG was not there. The diners were Winston, Lord Morley, F. E. Smith and Austen Chamberlain. Masterman says the outlook is black. Devlin tells him that the Irish Party will not consent to anything in the nature of exclusion for Ulster, and that the Irish leaders could not, if they would, carry such a proposal with their followers. Ministers (LG, Masterman, McKenna, etc) are talking of civil war as a possibility.

. . . Masterman says that Samuel, Hobhouse, Pease and Runciman have formed a combination against Winston on the estimates. McKenna was very bitter regarding the Ulster dinner.

LG whom I saw later, said, "I shall be no party to driving Winston out of the Cabinet. I do not agree with some of my colleagues."

R: He was very loyal to you over the Marconi business.

LG: Yes, I know, and shall never forget it. Of course I have been too easy during the past two years regarding the Naval estimates. When he went to the Admiralty I made a bargain with him about expenditure. He has not kept it. He has been extravagant. Now the feeling against him is very strong. I think, however, he will amend his figures to meet the views of the party. . . .

18th. — Things are in a critical state. There are grave disputes in the cabinet regarding the Naval estimates. Winston is being bitterly attacked in the Liberal papers. Samuel, Simon and Runciman are doing their utmost to force him out of the Cabinet. Masterman says he thinks he is sure to resign, but whether he will resign over the estimates or Ulster remains to be seen.

LG says the position is acute. Evidently he sees that the party are strong against Winston and is considering his position. He told me today that Samuel, Simon, Runciman and Co are doing their utmost "to down Winston." Also that the Prime Minister has received strong protests from some of his most influential supporters in the country. He said that Seely made a sort of "bleating speech" in Winston's defence, but received no support.

I said, "Will Winston resign?"

"Not now," replied LG, "but I think he will later on. If he is wise, he will try to fall in with the views of the Cabinet, and if I were you I should advise him to do so. His Guildhall speech was a piece of madness. [*Churchill had spoken at Guildhall on November 13 of larger estimates, submarine development and aerial superiority.*] The public will not stand provocative speeches of that sort. They are quite unnecessary. Winston has been a loyal friend to me, but there comes a time when one cannot allow oneself to be influenced by personal considerations of that sort."

Masterman says he thinks Winston may resign and the result may be serious for the Government. He also remarked that LG did a fatal thing for Winston when he persuaded the PM to send him to the Admiralty, and that since he has been there he has lost all touch with Liberalism and has become a man of one idea. He added, "It is a curious history. During McKenna's time at the Admiralty Winston and LG strongly objected to the Naval estimates and LG threatened to resign. A stormy interview took place between the PM, LG and McKenna, at which McKenna was much upset. The dispute was ended by McKenna undertaking to reduce the estimates."

Later I called on the McKennas. Saw Mrs K. McK. She says that McK. felt he could not join in the attack on Winston and that Winston is certain to resign, but will probably go out on Ulster and not on the estimates, which will be a better thing for the party. Seely called on McKenna last night. S. said he had not seen Winston, but McKenna thought he came to ascertain how the land lay. Mrs McK. also told me that the PM is furious about Winston's speech at the Guildhall — that he did not know what W. was going to say, and was astonished. 19th; Called to see LG at Downing Street. Found him in his bedroom, dressing. He told me he had not been very well and that the doctor said he had been working too hard.

Churchill acted on Seeley's advice when the Cabinet met on 16 December 1913. He had circulated a series of papers in which he substantiated the need for an increase in Naval expenditure. But it was at this meeting that Lloyd George joined the malcontents. The notes which passed between them at the Cabinet have survived:

Cabinet Notes
(Lloyd George Papers)

WSC to David Lloyd George

16 December 1913   10 Downing Street

I consider that you are going back on your word: in trying to drive
me out after we had settled, & you promised to support the Estimates.

David Lloyd George to WSC

I agreed to the figure for this year & I have stood by it *& carried it*
much to the disappointment of my economical friends. But I told
you distinctly I would press for a reduction of a new programme with
a view to 1915 & I think quite respectfully you are unnecessarily stubborn. It is only a question of a 6 months' postponement of laying
down. That cannot endanger our safety.

D. L L. G.

WSC to David Lloyd George

No. You said you would *support the Estimates.*

The Estimates included the new programme.

On the day after this Cabinet meeting Sir Francis Hopwood reported to Lord Stamfordham on the growing crisis:

Sir Francis Hopwood to Lord Stamfordham
(Royal Archives)

17 December 1913   Admiralty

Confidential

My Dear Stamfordham,

Following hard on the description of forthcoming finance I sent
(the figures were agreed with the Chancellor of the Exchequer) another difficulty has cropped up. The Cabinet has become thoroughly
scared by the Radicals who are for a smaller navy, and is putting
pressure upon Churchill to reduce the *programme.* This he cannot
do for the simple reason that he was fool enough to tell the world

what his programme was going to be for about half a dozen years ahead. To this he is bound hand and foot. It is said that practically all the Cabinet is for a reduction in programme. What they mean by it I cannot imagine for the numbers are deeply committed. Not only did they not dissent when Churchill made his speech about building 4.5.4.4.4.4 battleships in each year but they made themselves a party to the despatch laid on the table of the Canadian Parliament in which the coming programme is set forth. To cut the programme hardly reduces the Estimates at all for next year. Building 2 battleships instead of 4 reduces the estimates in the second year, *viz* 1915–16. In the first year very little is spent upon them. The only way of largely reducing estimates is to knock off construction on ships already building which is of course absurd.

They are odd people indeed! Is it possible they are riding for a fall or do they merely want to shed Winston?

Yrs ever

FRANCIS S. HOPWOOD

The First Lord informed the Prime Minister on December 18 of the importance of adhering to the Estimates. Were the number of capital ships for 1914–15 to be reduced below four, Churchill wrote, "there is no chance whatever of my being able to go on . . . Germany every month is more drawn to naval understanding. The Dreadnought era will eventually pass away. A weakening, a reversal, an upset now, will ruin everything. My loyalty to you, my conviction of your superior judgement and superior record on naval matters prompt me to go to all possible lengths to prevent disagreement in the Cabinet."

Churchill also sought to enlist the support of the Foreign Secretary:

WSC to Sir Edward Grey

EXTRACT

25 December 1913   [Admiralty]
[Copy]

. . . So far as my personal position is concerned I do not seek help about the 4 battleships: for I see my duty quite plainly and am willing to pay any forfeit the fates may exact while on that path. But I hope in these weeks you will turn over in yr mind the effect which the abandonment of programmes, definitely matched against the series in the German Navy Law, would have upon the position of England in Europe. My statements on the subject were not made without consultation & agreement; and such as they were they were spoken in the name of Britain. We have offered the Germans to reduce or drop our quota if they will do the same. They have refused: and now it is suggested — seriously — that we should do for nothing what only last October we said we would not do except they did the same. The country will be made ridiculous before the whole world. *I can* clear my reputation by immediate resignation. But what happens to an individual minister is of very small importance compared to the public interest. . . .

I am sure that to desert the programmes which have been set up (and never before criticised except for their moderation) while Germany goes on her path unmoved & unwavering would be to mar very seriously the high prestige and authority which the country has acquired abroad during the eight years of your work at the Foreign Office.

Believe me it is not for my own personal interest that I write. I am inflexible — thank God — on some things. It was good of you to intervene to postpone the decision when we last met. But unless a very serious disaster to national policy is to happen you will have to rouse yourself and exert the influence which you at the Foreign Office alone command.

If there be any point on which you have doubts — I mean as to the necessity of particular services or standards, or as to the thriftiness & prudence of Admiralty administration, let me have the opportunity of giving you the fullest information. . . .

The controversy over the Estimates was not confined to the Cabinet. His aunt Cornelia wrote to him:

Lady Wimborne to WSC

18 December 1913   Templeton House
                                                      Priory Lane
                                                      Roehampton
Dearest Winston,
    I am going to write very frankly, and I know you won't take it amiss, because I love you and care so much for your career. I have an

instinct you are going wrong. Even the ablest of men may wreck their political life witness your dear Father by an error of judgement and I who saw him eating out his heart in years of disappointment feel I can't keep silence. You are breaking with the traditions of Liberalism in your Naval expenditure; you are in danger of becoming purely a "Navy man" and losing sight of the far greater job of a great leader of the Liberal party. Peace, retrenchment and reform must ever be its policy and you are being carried away by the attraction of perfecting your machine for war and expenditure.

What will it lead to as regards yourself — the Tories are already counting on your return to them which is absolutely unthinkable, and would indeed break one's heart. But to lead the Liberal party you must respect its traditions, and I believe nothing is doing the present Govt so much harm as this naval expenditure. They will either have to drop you or suffer defeat.

I am sure this is the situation, and it is because I feel it is so critical as regards your own future that I beseech you to pause. If you are looking to some different combination of parties it is a delusion. Tories will always be Tories, a Tory democracy is a myth. Liberalism has the promise of the future, and will always attract all the talent and ideals of men.

I won't say any more and I don't want any answer if you will only read mark and digest the reflections of one who has lived through a good bit of political life and cares for you a good deal.

Yrs affecy

C. WIMBORNE

Shortly before Christmas Lloyd George circulated a paper to the Cabinet in which he insisted upon the need to cut down on naval construction and to abandon the 60 per cent margin.

WSC to Prince Louis of Battenberg

26 December 1913   Admiralty

My dear Prince Louis,

The paper which the Chancellor of the Exchequer has circulated to the Cabinet must be regarded as a most serious challenge to the whole of our policy. I shall be glad if you and your Naval colleagues will devote your close attention not only to it but to the restatement of the case for the programmes and standards the Admiralty are pursuing.

I could not in any circumstances remain responsible if the declared programme of 4 ships were cut down. But my responsibility is greater than anyone else's and I hold my naval colleagues perfectly free to review the situation without regard to the action which I should take in the circumstances which may now be apprehended.

I am preparing a more general statement on the Naval position as a whole, and we can compare our separate productions later.

Yrs vy sincerely
W S C

Churchill prepared a long reply to Lloyd George's memorandum, together with appendices and diagrams. "Upon the whole," he wrote to his Private Secretary, Masterton-Smith, "I think this is the best case I have ever had anything to do with."

Churchill had earlier been able to limit his demand to four capital ships on account of the Canadian Government's willingness to pay for three Canadian Dreadnoughts. In July 1912, when Churchill had urged Canada at the Committee of Imperial Defence "to take part in the defence of the British Empire" the Canadian Prime Minister, R. L. Borden, had been most enthusiastic, had invited the First Lord to visit Canada with Asquith and Sir Max Aitken had offered to help organize the visit. In March 1913 Borden had agreed to Churchill's suggestion that the three Canadian Dreadnoughts should form part of a Dominion Squadron. With this knowledge Churchill had been able to cut back on British Dreadnoughts. But in November 1913 Borden warned Churchill that his Navy Bill might fail to pass the Senate, and on 3 January 1914 Borden telegraphed that he could not guarantee their construction. Borden was proved right: the Bill passed the Commons but was defeated by the Senate in May. Churchill had therefore, at the very moment when the Chancellor was demanding reductions in the Estimates, to propose a further increase of £2½ million to make up for the loss of the Canadian ships.

On 1 January 1914 Lloyd George had made public his opposition to increased naval expenditure. In an interview published in the *Daily Chronicle* he declared that had the present armament figures remained at the 1887 level a saving of 4*s.* in the pound on local rates would have been effected. He pointed out that Lord Randolph Churchill had considered even the 1887 expenditure "bloated and extravagant." According to the Chancellor of the Exchequer the Estimates could now be reduced, both because Anglo-German relations seemed more cordial than in past years and because in his view the continental countries were concentrating more on land than naval armaments, thus precluding a German challenge to British naval power. Lloyd George gave this interview on the basis of the Estimates and in ignorance that more was to be asked for because of the backsliding of the Canadians.·

The First Lord was hunting the wild boar with his friend the Duke of Westminster in France when Lloyd George's interview was published. He wrote to Masterton-Smith at the Admiralty: "The Chancellor of the Exchequer's interview in the *Daily Chronicle* is a fine illustration of his methods, and I should imagine that it would deeply vex the Prime Minister." This was indeed so:

H. H. Asquith to Miss Venetia Stanley
(Montagu Papers)

EXTRACT

Tuesday   10 Downing Street
6 January 1914

. . . I have had quite a stream of visitors this morning, mostly of the official type: Illingworth, Edward Grey, the Arch Colonel [Seely], and the Infant Samuel. They all mutter severe things about Ll. George and the needless folly of his "interview" which has set all Europe (not to mention the poor Liberal Party here at home) by the ears. I find that Winston does not return from his Paris fleshpots till Friday: meanwhile he preserves a dignified and moody silence. . . .

Sir Francis Hopwood continued to inform Lord Stamfordham of the course of the crisis:

Sir Francis Hopwood to Lord Stamfordham
(Royal Archives)

EXTRACT

5 January 1914   Hawkshead House

My dear Stamfordham,

Our affairs are very critical and Winston is returning in haste. The Cabinet being mad on general subjects now naturally descends to the particular — the Navy. . . . The Fact is the Cabinet is sick of Churchill's perpetually undermining & exploiting its policy and are picking a quarrel with him. As a colleague he is a great trial to them. But their battleground is very ill-chosen as in consequence of their indolence he has probably got chapter & verse for every item of the Naval Programme. For example; he has told the House of Commons how many ships he proposed to build each year & no member of the Cabinet objected. . . .

If Winston goes in consequence of a quarrel on general subjects he will have all the [advantage] of the fight chosen by his Colleagues on Naval Programmes. He will knock them about dreadfully in the country & this will have an effect on their general stability.

Then again a sad part of the quarrel is the effect it may have on Borden's Government. How is the Canadian Prime Minister to go on when he has staked his existence on giving us 3 battleships *in the name of emergency* when we say we can safely reduce the number of ships *without those three!* It ought to break him. Only one point remains and that is what should be the conduct of the Naval Lords in the crisis? If it comes to Winston's resignation he will press them fiercely to go with him. In my opinion they should not do so. The quarrel is political not administrative as it stands. I am sure that the true policy is for the Naval Lords to say that they will "wait & see" what a new First Lord proposes in the way of a programme & then consider whether they can agree on it. Then if they don't think it good enough they should resign. You will observe the important effect of this. The Sea Lords ought not to waste themselves on Winston but on his successor. The results then would be more marked. I do not think that this Government could stand the double shock.

Prince Louis ought to be impressed with the importance of seeing what a successor to Winston would propose before he decided on a course. I have impressed this opinion on all four of the Naval Lords but they may be driven out of it.

The whole affair may blow over but it looks very ugly. Winston
writes that he has his "back against the wall."

Sn yrs
FRANCIS S. HOPWOOD

Sir Francis Hopwood to Lord Stamfordham
(Royal Archives)

11 January 1914   13 Hornton Street

My dear Stamfordham,

I have been at home for a couple of days and have not seen Winston but on his arrival & after seeing the PM he wrote me "The situation is serious and may prove fatal to the Government unless it
should turn out that the Ch of Ex is only trying it on" . . . "I don't
want any of my Admiralty colleagues to get unnecessarily involved in
what may easily become a disastrous conflict."

This contradicts Hopwood's malicious prognosis in his previous
letter: "he will press them fiercely to go with him." Hopwood went
on:

I think myself that the Ch of Ex was only trying it on but in his
irresponsible way he may have created a position of so much aggrava-
tion that he cannot smooth it out again. In this connection it should
be borne in mind that Lloyd George did not originate the row — he
agreed to the estimates — it was McKenna, Samuel, Runciman &
Harcourt — all anti-Churchill men — then others followed. Now the
malcontents having got Lloyd George to commit himself to their
side in an interview to a newspaper may very easily refuse to let him
escape from the halter into which he has put his neck! Anyhow
things are not getting easier for HMG. "Patience" is the watchword!

Ever yrs
FRANCIS S. HOPWOOD

Lord Riddell recorded in his Diary on 9 January:

Mrs McKenna told me that Asquith dined with them last night. He
is very worried, and says he needs a rest cure. He does not mind
Winston resigning so much, but Grey is furious over LG's interview
in the *Daily Chronicle* and refuses to be placated.

10th. McKenna confirmed the above. He says that Grey may now side with Winston and that matters are serious.

The Cabinet met on January 12. The First Lord explained why it would now be necessary to add a further £2½ million on the Estimates. Asquith's comment on the meeting is not helpful:

H. H. Asquith to Miss Venetia Stanley
(*Montagu Papers*)

Monday   10 Downing Street
12 January 1914

. . . I have had another long dose of Winston today and am rather late.

The First Lord now assembled the principal memoranda which had passed and sent them to the King. In his covering letter he stressed the importance of his proposals:

WSC to The King
(*Royal Archives*)

EXTRACT

13 January 1914   Admiralty

. . . Mr Churchill is forced to regard the maintenance of the declared programme of 4 ships this year as a vital matter affecting the recovery strength of the Fleet. The advice wh he has received from his naval colleagues and the continuous study wh he has made of the whole naval situation during the last two years, leave him in no doubt as to what his duty wd be if the Cabinet decided to reduce the provision from 4 to 2 ships.

If this fundamental question were settled satisfactorily, Mr Churchill believes that the other difficult questions wd not be found incapable of solutions agreeable to the general interests of the Government & the special requirements of the Navy. . . .

The King's reply was encouraging, the more so since he wrote himself:

The King to WSC

18 January 1914   York Cottage
                                                        Sandringham

Confidential.

York Cottage,
Sandringham,
Norfolk.

Jan: 18ᵗʰ 1914

My dear Churchill

I was very glad
to receive your letter
of the 13ᵗʰ inst: & its

My dear Churchill,

I was very glad to receive your letter of the 13th inst & its most
interesting enclosures, but as Stamfordham explained to you, I wished
to read these carefully before sending you my reply. This I have
done & in my opinion your answer to the Treasury memorandum
especially the able manner in which you sum up the general situation
(page 16) establishes without a doubt the fact, that if the Government
are to carry out the Naval policy which they have already sanctioned,
this year's programme of 4 Battleships must be adhered to. I recognise the difficulties with which you are confronted, but it is you as
the head of the Navy, with the assistance of your expert advisers,
who are responsible to the Country that the Navy is maintained in
such a condition as to be able to carry out whatever the policy of
the Country may necessitate. Since you have been at the Admiralty

you have by your zeal & ability done great work for the Navy & I sympathize with you in your present position. I hope the question may be satisfactorily settled & that a solution may be found to the financial problem.

I have kept the papers you sent me.

Believe me, my dear Churchill, very sincerely yours
GEORGE R.I.

Asquith persuaded Lloyd George and Churchill to hold a "conference" in order to settle the points of dispute before the next Cabinet meeting. But at their meeting Lloyd George sought a pledge from Churchill that future Estimates would be less than the proposed 1914–15 ones. In a letter of January 19 Churchill made it clear that "no predecessor of mine has ever been asked or has ever attempted to forecast the Estimates of any but the coming year and I cannot undertake to do so now."

Asquith postponed a Cabinet meeting on January 23 in the hope of effecting a reconciliation between Churchill and Lloyd George, but during the ensuing days no compromise was reached:

WSC to David Lloyd George

26 January 1914   Admiralty

Draft

My dear David,

In Cabinet tomorrow it will be my duty to state that while I will do my best to work to the figures mentioned in my letter, I cannot be bound to them in any extraordinary or improper sense. While I am responsible, what is necessary will have to be provided. The estimates of 1914–15 have been prepared with the strictest economy. For all expenditure incurred or proposed there is full warrant & good reason. There is no act of Admiralty administration for which I am responsible wh cannot be vindicated to the House of Commons. I cannot buy a year of office by a bargain under duress about the estimates of 1915–16. No forecasts beyond the year have ever been made by my predecessors; & I have no power — even if I were willing — to bind the Board of Admiralty of 1915 to any exact decision.

I recognise your friendship, but I ask no favours & I shall enter into no irregular obligations.

I am now approaching the end of my resources, & can only await the decision of my colleagues & of the Prime Minister.

Yours sincerely
WINSTON S. CHURCHILL

David Lloyd George to WSC
(Lloyd George Papers)

27 January 1914   Treasury Chambers

My dear Winston,

I have striven hard for a friendly and honourable settlement without the slightest regard for the effect upon my personal position, but your letter has driven me to despair, and I must now decline further negotiations, leaving the issue to be decided by the Prime Minister and the Cabinet.

Your letter warns me — in time — that you can no more be held bound by your latest figures than you were by your original figure of £49,966,000. This intimation completely alters the situation. I now thoroughly appreciate your idea of a bargain: it is an argument which binds the Treasury not even to attempt any further economies in the interest of the taxpayer, whilst it does not in the least impose any obligation on the Admiralty not to incur fresh liabilities. Such understandings are surely not worth all the time and anxiety you and I have devoted to arriving at them.

In one vital respect the task of the Cabinet is simplified by your letter, for it demonstrates that you and your critics are in complete agreement as to the real value of your last proposals. The only certainty about them is that the Exchequer would this year have to find 56 millions — supplementaries included — for the Navy, whilst the reductions promised for 15/16 do not bind either the Board of Admiralty or the First Lord. Therein you and your critics agree. I have been repeatedly told that I was being made a fool of; I declined to believe it. Your candour now forces me to acknowledge the justice of the taunt. You proposed before Christmas to take 50 millions. As a compromise on that you proposed Friday last to take four millions more this year on condition of coming down 1½ millions next year. Not a sumptuous offer at best. Now you qualify that!

I have laboured these last few days — not to favour you or to save myself — but to rescue Liberalism from the greatest tragedy which has yet befallen it. I have a deep and abiding attachment for Liberal causes, and for the old Party, and the prospect of wrecking them afflicts me with deep distress. That is why I have been prepared to risk the confidence of my friends and to face the gibes and sneers from friend and foe alike with which I foresaw the publication of the figures would be greeted. I know too well that every paper would gloat over my humiliation. That I did not mind if the ship and its precious cargo could be saved. You decreed otherwise, and the responsibility is yours and yours alone.

Ever sincerely
DAVID LLOYD GEORGE

Lloyd George continued to canvass support for his determination to hold out against Churchill's Estimates. On January 23 he had informed C. P. Scott, the editor of the *Manchester Guardian,* of the details of Churchill's proposals, and Scott had replied "of course Churchill can play the mischief with this or any other plan but it won't be so easy and you can bring him to book. I feel it in my bones that the fight has got to be now or never." Charles Hobhouse, the Chancellor of the Duchy of Lancaster, wrote in similar vein to Lloyd George:

Charles Hobhouse to David Lloyd George
(Lloyd George Papers)

26 January 1914   67 Cromwell Road

My dear George,

I served under you so long that I think I ought just to let you know that I find myself still unconvinced by Churchill's figures. If I get a chance at Cabinet tomorrow I wish to express my dissent from and my distrust of them. My fear is that between them — him, the Labour party and the Tories — we shall come to hopeless grief.

Yrs sincerely
C. HOBHOUSE

Lloyd George appears to have been entrusted by Asquith with the task of mediating between the First Lord and his critics. He even seems to have sought acceptance from his colleagues for Churchill's proposed £54 million Estimates, if the First Lord would make pledges concerning the 1915–16 Estimates. But Churchill did not wish to commit himself to future limitations, nor did the critics of his Estimates relish a compromise on Lloyd George's lines. The Attorney-General wrote to Lloyd George:

Sir John Simon to David Lloyd George
(Lloyd George Papers)

26 January 1914   57 Kensington Court

Dear Lloyd George,
    After our talk this afternoon & before the Cabinet tomorrow, I think it well to write to make plain that I cannot hold myself bound to join you in acquiescing in Winston's figure of £54 millions. Our recent close association began because (as I understood) you sympathised with the criticism directed against so large a figure as £50 millions: the upshot of the crusade for economy is, so far, an increase of £4 millions: a conclusion at once tragical and laughable. No doubt the laugh is with Winston & those who agree with him; I only hope the tragedy is not for the whole Liberal cause.

Yours very try
JOHN SIMON

David Lloyd George to H. H. Asquith
(Asquith Papers)

27 January 1914

My dear Prime Minister,
    I have laboured in vain to effect an arrangement between Churchill & the critics of his Estimates which would save you and the Cabinet the necessity for entering upon an unpleasant & maybe a disastrous controversy.
    I have utterly failed . . . The economists have always contended that Winston's latest figures were not real & that he meant to take his £54,000,000 this year without honouring his promise of reduction for 1915–16. Winston's letter to me confirms this suspicion. . . .

The Cabinet met on January 29. Asquith reported on its deliberations to the King:

H. H. Asquith to The King
(*Royal Archives*)

29 January 1914   10 Downing Street

The main topic of discussion at the Cabinet meeting was the Navy
Estimates. Some points which were left outstanding in December
were settled without difficulty. It was agreed that the Supplementary
Estimate for the current year should be raised to $2\frac{1}{2}$ millions, and in
view of the pledges given by Ministers in the past, that the Estimates
for 1914–15 should provide for the Construction of 4 (not 2) Capital
ships. The total expenditure for 1913–14 will thus be £48,800,000;
and Churchill's revised figures show for 1914–15 a total of £52,-
800,000, and for 1915–16 £49,500,000.

Strong protests were made by the Chancellor of the Exchequer,
Lord Beauchamp, Sir J. Simon, Herbert Samuel and others, against
this scale of expenditure, the criticism being directed not so much to
the programme of new construction, as to the growing cost of maintenance, which has risen no less than 25 per cent in 3 years. It was
agreed that large economies might be, & ought to be, made under this
law.

The Chancellor of the Exchequer pressed especially for a definite
pledge of substantial reduction in 1915–16. He pointed out that according to his present forecast the Revenue in 1914–15 would show
an increase of about $3\frac{1}{2}$ millions, while the Expenditure (putting the
Navy at 52,800,000) would grow by over 12 millions, leaving an ad-
verse balance of about 9 millions which must be met by new taxation.
He had no hope of being able to commend such taxation to the
House of Commons, unless he could assure them that in the following year (1915–16) the bulk of the proceeds could be devoted to Education & the relief of local rates.

After a prolonged discussion, in which all the principal items in
the Estimates were exhaustively reviewed, the Prime Minister, after
warning his colleagues of the disastrous consequences of a split on
such an issue, suggested that the First Lord should examine again the
chief [items] of the charge for maintenance; and the final consideration of the [Estimates] was postponed until next Tuesday.

Asquith's appeal to the Cabinet seemed to encourage those who opposed the Estimates. The following protest was in the handwriting of Sir John Simon:

> *Lord Beauchamp and others to H. H. Asquith*
> (*Asquith Papers*)
>
> EXTRACT

29 January 1914

Dear Prime Minister,

Every member of the Cabinet must have been deeply impressed by the appeal which you made yesterday for the cultivation of a spirit of mutual accommodation in discussing the Navy Estimates . . . but the question remains whether the figure now put forward by the First Lord, and the plan now tentatively suggested by the Chancellor of the Exchequer for dealing with them, are calculated to make more certain the happy issue of the legislative programme to which you and we stand committed. . . .

We think it best to put before you in writing a summary of the general considerations (apart from any detailed criticism of this figure or that) which seem to us to justify our deep concern & uneasiness.

1. The effect of so enormous an increase in our Naval expenditure upon the German programme & policy is a matter of surmise; but such excuses as may be suggested cannot obscure the main fact — that the total is unprecedented; the increase is unexampled at a time of international calm; and the impression powerfully created that we are leading the way in yet more rapid outlay.

2. If the announcement of our figure were to be followed by further accelerations by Germany, the whole scheme for retrenchment in 1915–16 falls to the ground.

3. These proposals expose us to Parliamentary attack far more serious than the sporadic efforts of a few Liberal "economists." The Labour Party will surely be driven to go to any lengths in dissociating itself from such increases; defection by a substantial group on our own benches is likely; Ulstermen who profess that our defeat is the only protection against "civil war" will hardly resist the temptation offered.

4. The carrying through of Home Rule may vitally depend on the avoidance of disaster at bye-elections in the meantime. How are our prospects in this regard affected by such proposals?

5. Heavy taxation this year will be represented as the breakdown of Free Trade. . . .

If the difficulties which press upon us appear to you to be of weight, we ask that you should present them with all your authority to those who are disposed to favour a course of high expenditure and new taxation. From first to last our single desire is to promote absolute unity under your leadership, with a view of giving Home Rule the best possible chance under your guidance.

Yours most truly
BEAUCHAMP
C. HOBHOUSE
R. McKENNA
WALTER RUNCIMAN
JOHN SIMON

Sir John Simon to H. H. Asquith
(Asquith Papers)

[January 1914]

1. Dissolution now, if we were beaten, means that Parliament Act is utterly destroyed; House of Lords reconstructed on Tory Lines which only a revolution can alter; Home Rule and Welsh Disestablishment lost.

2. The probability of losing Gen Election is great, *not* because Country is against Home Rule or in favour of Admiralty Extravaganza, but because our *keenest* supporters will think we have given up causes to which we are pledged.

3. The loss of WC, though regrettable, is *not* by any means a splitting of party — indeed large admiralty estimates may be capable of being carried *only* because WC has gone.

4. The party wd feel itself strengthened in its Radical element & among the Economists; the feeling that the Cabinet *fights for economy* but pursues Home Rule unflinchingly is just what is wanted.

5. A majority of the Cabinet certainly takes this view.

Asquith himself seems to have hoped that the First Lord would be able to make concessions; but the latter had already done his utmost to keep the Estimates as low as possible.

H. H. Asquith to WSC

1 February 1914
Alderley Park
Chelford
Cheshire

Confidential

Confidential

1 Feb 1914

My dear Winston

Very largely in

deference to my appeal;

My dear Winston,

Very largely in deference to my appeal, the critical pack (who know well that they have behind them a large body of party opinion) have slackened their pursuit.

I think that you on your side, should (without "Confiteors" or "Peccavis" or the white sheet) show a corresponding disposition, and throw a baby or two out of the sledge.

Ever yours

HHA

WSC to H. H. Asquith

2 February 1914   [Admiralty]

Private
Copy

My dear P Minister,

For the last 4 or 5 months I have been striving by every means in my power to reduce the cost of the maintenance votes. They have been searched and scrubbed by Macnamara & his Finance Committee as they have never been before. I am circulating today papers on the 3 points — fuel, practice, ammunition, & minor repairs — wh were specifically raised at the Cabinet. These will I believe be found conclusive. If other points are mentioned they will be loyally and simply examined. But there is no part of my admin of this office wh has not throughout been conducted with severe economy; & this can be proved by reference not only to facts but to my minutes & directions at every stage. I see absolutely no hope of further reductions in the cost of maintenance & upkeep. The number of ships in commission is not I am sure susceptible of appreciable reduction — but each vessel & squadron can be discussed in detail at the Cabinet. The prognosis of 1915–16 is bad. The volume of ship building shows practically no diminution (under existing contracts & the reduced new programme 1914–15) & there is the inevitable rise due to numbers, & automatic charges. Knowing all I do abt the position I am certain that to produce in these circs 1915–16 Estimates at "under 50 m." wd be a prodigy; & no man in this country wd be able to do better. I can only promise to do my best. Everything possible has been done already for 1914–15.

Air has been reduced to £400,000, the [tear in text] programme (subject to Bd agreement) £1,750,000. 36 oil-burning destroyers have been laid up as the result of Cabinet discussions. These follow & accompany a long series of Deptal contractions, postponements, & excisions.

I do not love this naval expenditure & am grieved to be found in the position of taskmaster. But I am myself the slave of facts & forces wh are uncontrollable unless naval efficiency is frankly abandoned. The result of all this pressure & controversy leaves me anxious chiefly lest the necessary services have been cut too low. . . .

The sledge is bare of babies, & though the pack may crunch the driver's bones, the winter will not be ended.

Yours always

w

The Cabinet met again on February 11 to discuss the Naval Estimates. Churchill received support two days before from a source which through the centuries had always shown its support of the Royal Navy:

Sir Thomas Vansittart Bowater to WSC

9 February 1914   The Mansion House
                                                            London

Dear Mr Churchill,

I am desired to send you a copy of a resolution unanimously carried at a meeting of the City of London held today at Guildhall, under my presidency, on the subject of the Navy, *viz:* —

"That this Meeting of the Citizens of London begs to assure the Prime Minister and His Majesty's Government of the support of the Commercial Community in any measures — financial or other — that may be necessary to ensure the continued supremacy of the Navy and the adequate protection of the Trade routes of the Empire."

I venture to hope that the Government may welcome this assurance by the Citizens of the Capital of all political parties.

Believe me, Dear Mr Churchill, Yours very truly

T. VANSITTART BOWATER

Lord Mayor

In many memoranda and at a large number of Cabinets the First Lord had explained the need for both his original figures and for the new additions to cover the Canadian Dreadnought failure. Unlike the Chancellor of the Exchequer he had eschewed public debate. He had enlisted the support of the King, the Prime Minister and the Foreign Secretary. On the day before the Cabinet met he was confident that he would prevail.

Many years ago the author was told by his father an anecdote which has some bearing on the solution of this crisis. In 1962 the late Lady Megan Lloyd George confirmed it in detail.

There were many Cabinets about the Estimates, but the matter was not resolved and Asquith said Lloyd George and WSC must decide between themselves one way or the other. The point had been reached where both were determined to resign rather than yield. Lloyd George said to WSC, "Come to breakfast tomorrow at No 11 and we shall settle the matter." WSC arrived next morning fully expecting that he would have to resign. Lloyd George greeted him and said, "Oddly enough, my wife spoke to me last night about this Dreadnought business. She said, 'You know, my dear, I never interfere in politics; but they say you are having an argument with that nice Mr Churchill about building Dreadnoughts. Of course I don't understand these things, but I should have thought it would be better to have too many rather than too few.' So I have decided to let you build them. Let's go in to breakfast."

It is possible that Lloyd George involved his wife in the story to sweeten and cover his own retreat. It was doubtless with this breakfast episode in mind that Churchill wrote to his mother:

WSC to Lady Randolph
EXTRACT

10 February 1914   Admiralty

Dearest Mama,
   I think the naval estimates are now past the danger point & if so the situation will be satisfactory. But it has been a long and wearing business wh has caused me at times vy gt perplexity. . . .

Asquith described the Cabinet discussion in his letter to the King of February 11:

H. H. Asquith to The King
(Asquith Papers)

11 February 1914   10 Downing Street

The total of the Navy Estimates for 1914–15 was fixed at £51,580,000 and Churchill was willing that the Government should announce that the total for the following year should shew substantial reductions: he thinks he can practically guarantee a saving of £2,000,000.

A prolonged discussion took place on the question of accelerating the first 2 battleships in the 1914–15 programme, in consequence of Borden's admitted inability to make any progress with the Canadian contribution this year. Mr. McKenna & others were strongly opposed to this course, upon which in view of previous declarations Mr Churchill strongly insisted. In the end an agreement was come to that the acceleration should take place, but that Parliament should be clearly informed that in the event of Borden's continued default, the British Government was under no obligation to supply the 3 missing Canadian ships, and that our standard of construction is to be maintained at 60%.

Asquith's letter to the King does not make plain that in addition to the £51,580,000, £2,500,000 was agreed to in order to make good the Canadian disappointment.

The Naval Estimates for 1914–15 were issued on March 12 and introduced by the First Lord in the House of Commons on March 17. His speech lasted for 2½ hours and was described by the *Daily Telegraph* as "the longest and perhaps also the most weighty and eloquent speech to which the House of Commons have listened during the present generation."

During his speech the First Lord said:

The burden of responsibility laid upon the British Navy is heavy, and its weight increases year by year. All the world is building ships of the greatest power, training officers and men, creating arsenals, and laying broad and deep the foundations of future permanent naval development and expansion. In every country powerful interests and huge industries are growing up, which will render any check or cessation in the growth of navies increasingly difficult as time goes by. Besides the Great Powers, there are many small States who are buying or building great ships of war, and whose vessels may, by purchase, by some diplomatic combination or by duress, be brought into the line against us. None of these Powers need, like us, navies to defend their actual independence or safety. They build them so as to play a part in the world's affairs. It is sport to them. It is life and death to us. . . . It is not suggested that the whole world will turn

GERMAN DREADNOUGHT STRENGTH, 1914

BATTLESHIPS BUILT

Consecutive No	Ship	Launched	Displacement (tons)	Speed (designed) (knots)	Armour belt (max) (in)	Armament (excluding guns below 12 prs)	Weight of broadside, primary guns (lb)
1	Nassau	1908	18,600	19	11.81	12 — 11 in, 12 — 5.9 in, 16 — 3.4 in	5,376
2	Westfalen	1908					
3	Rheinland	1908					
4	Posen	1908					
5	Ostfriesland	1909	22,440	20.5	11.81	12 — 12 in, 14 — 5.9 in, 14 — 3.4 in	7,232
6	Helgoland	1909					
7	Thuringen	1909					
8	Oldenburg	1910					
9	Kaiser	1911	24,310	21	13.78	10 — 12 in, 14 — 5.9 in, 12 — 3.4 in, 4 — 13 prs	9,040
10	Friedrich der Grosse	1911					
11	Kaiserin	1911					
12	Prinzregent Luitpold	1912					
13	König Albert	1912	25,390	22 ?	?	10 — 12 in, 14 — 5.9 in, 12 — 3.4 in, 4 — 13 prs	9,040
14	Grosser Kurfürst	1913					
15	König	1913					
16	Markgraf	1913					

BUILDING

No.	Name	Year					
17	*Kronprinz*	1914	25,390	22	?	10 — 12 in, 14 — 5.9 in, 12 — 3.4 in, 4 — 13 prs	9,040
18	*Ersatz Wörth*	—					
19	*T*	—	} 28,050	22	?	8 — 15 in, 16 — 5.9 in	15,360 ?
20	*Ersatz Kaiser Friedrich III*	—	?				

BATTLE CRUISERS

No.	Name	Year					
1	*Blücher*	1908	15,550	25	6	12 — 8.2 in, 8 — 5.9 in, 16 — 3.4 in	2,204
2	*Von der Tann*	1909	18,700	25	6	8 — 11 in, 10 — 5.9 in, 16 — 3.4 in	5,376
3	*Moltke*	1910	} 22,640	27	11	{ 10 — 11 in, 12 — 5.9 in, 12 — 3.4 in	6,720
4	*Goeben*	1911		27	11		6,720
5	*Seydlitz*	1912	24,640	27	11	10 — 11 in, 12 — 5.9 in, 12 — 3.4 in	6,720
6	*Derfflinger*	1913	28,000	27	7	8 — 12 in, 12 — 5.9 in, 12 — 3.4 in	7,232

BUILDING

No.	Name	Year					
7	*Lützow*	1913 Bdg	} 28,000	27	7	{ 8 — 12 in, 12 — 5.9 in, 12 — 3.4 in	7,232
8	*Ersatz Hertha*						

BRITISH DREADNOUGHT STRENGTH, 1914

BATTLESHIPS BUILT

Consecutive No	Ship	Launched	Displacement (tons)	Speed (designed) (knots)	Armour belt (max) (in)	Armament (excluding guns below 12 prs)	Weight of broadside, primary guns (lb)
1	Lord Nelson	1906	16,500	18.5	12	4 — 12 in, 10 — 9.2 in, 24 — 12 prs	5,300
2	Agamemnon	1906					
3	Dreadnought	1906	17,900	20.9	11	10 — 12 in, 24 — 12 prs	6,800
4	Superb	1907					
5	Temeraire	1907	18,600	20.75	10	10 — 12 in, 16 — 4 in	6,800
6	Bellerophon	1907					
7	St Vincent	1908					
8	Vanguard	1909	19,250	21	10	10 — 12 in, 20 — 4 in	6,800
9	Collingwood	1908					
10	Neptune	1909	19,900	21	10	10 — 12 in, 16 — 4 in	8,500
11	Colossus	1910	20,000	21	11	10 — 12 in, 16 — 4 in	8,500
12	Hercules	1910					
13	Orion	1910					
14	Thunderer	1911	22,500	21	12	10 — 13.5 in, 16 — 4 in	12,500
15	Monarch	1911					
16	Conqueror	1911					
17	King George V	1911					
18	Centurion	1911	23,000	21	12	10 — 13.5 in, 16 — 4 in	14,000
19	Ajax	1912					
20	Audacious	1912					
21	Iron Duke	1912	25,000	21	12	10 — 13.5 in, 12 — 6 in, 2 — 3 in	14,000
22	Marlborough	1912					

BUILDING

No.	Ship	Year	Tonnage			Armament	
23	*Benbow*	1913	25,000	21	12	10 — 13.5 in, 12 — 6 in, 2 — 3 in	14,000
24	*Emperor of India*	1913					
25	*Queen Elizabeth*	1913					
26	*Warspite*	1913					
27	*Valiant*	—	27,500	25	13	8 — 15 in, 16 — 6 in, 2 — 3 in	15,360
28	*Barham*	—					
29	*Malaya*	—					
30	*Resolution*	—	25,750	21	13	8 — 15 in, 16 — 6 in, 4 — 3 in	13,360
31	*Ramillies*	—					
32	*Revenge*	—					
33	*Royal Sovereign*	—					
34	*Royal Oak*	—					

SHIPS BUILDING IN GREAT BRITAIN FOR FOREIGN POWERS AND REQUISITIONED FOR THE ROYAL NAVY

No.	Ship		Tonnage			Armament	
35	*Agincourt*	—	27,500	22	9	14 — 12 in, 12 — 6 in, 8 — 3 in, 2 — 3 in A.A.C.	12,900
36	*Erin*	—	23,000	21	12	10 — 13.5 in, 16 — 6 in, 2 — 3 in A.A.C.	14,800
37	*Canada*	—	28,000	23	9	10 — 14 in, 12 — 6 in, 2 — 3 in A.A.C.	16,560

1	*Invincible*	1907	17,250	26	7	8 — 12 in, 16 — 4 in	6,800
2	*Inflexible*	1907					6,800
3	*Indomitable*	1907					
4	*Indefatigable*	1909	18,750	25	7	8 — 12 in, 16 — 4 in	6,800
5	*Lion*	1910	26,350	28	9	8 — 13.5 in, 16 — 4 in	10,000
6	*Australia*	1911	18,800	25	7	8 — 12 in, 16 — 4 in	6,800
7	*New Zealand*	1911					
8	*Princess Royal*	1911	26,350	28	9	8 — 13.5 in, 16 — 4 in	11,200
9	*Queen Mary*	1912	27,000	28	9	8 — 13.5 in, 16 — 4 in	11,200

BUILDING

10	*Tiger*	1913	28,000	28	9	8 — 13.5 in, 12 — 6 in	11,200

upon us, or that our preparations should contemplate such a monstrous contingency. By a sober and modest conduct, by a skilful diplomacy, we can in part disarm and in part divide the elements of potential danger. But two things have to be considered: First, that our diplomacy depends in great part for its effectiveness upon our naval position, and that our naval strength is the one great balancing force which we can contribute to our own safety and to the peace of the world. Secondly, we are not a young people with a blank record and a scant inheritance. We have won for ourselves, in times when other powerful nations were paralysed by barbarism or internal war, an exceptional share of the wealth and traffic of the world.

We have got all we want in territory, but our claim to be left in undisputed enjoyment of vast and splendid possessions, largely acquired by war and largely maintained by force, is one which often seems less reasonable to others than to us. Further, we have intervened regularly, as it was our duty to do, and as we could not help doing, in the affairs of Europe and of the world, and great advantage to European peace has resulted, even in this last year, from our interference. We have responsibilities in many quarters to-day. We are far from being detached from the problems of Europe. We have passed through a year of continuous anxiety, and, although His Majesty's Government believe the foundations of peace among the Great Powers have been strengthened, yet the causes which might lead to a general war have not been removed and often reminds us of their presence. There has not been the slightest abatement of naval and military preparation. On the contrary, we are witnessing this year increases of expenditure by Continental Powers in armaments beyond all previous experience. The world is armed as it was never armed before. Every suggestion for arrest or limitation has so far been ineffectual. From time to time awkward things happen, and situations occur which make it necessary that the naval force at our immediate disposal, now in this quarter, now in that, should be rapidly counted up. On such occasions the responsibilities which rest on the Admiralty come home with brutal reality to those who are responsible, and unless our naval strength were solidly, amply, and unswervingly maintained, the Government could not feel that they were doing their duty to the country.

Three months later, when Churchill and Lloyd George were at a Cabinet meeting, they exchanged notes on the Estimates crisis:

Cabinet Notes
(*Lloyd George Papers*)

1 July 1914   10 Downing Street

LLOYD GEORGE: Philip Snowden in his weekly letter today says that
had there been any other Chancellor of the Exchequer your Naval
Bill would have been cut by millions.

WSC: There would also have been another First Lord of the Admiralty! And who can say — if such gaps were opened — that
there would not have been another Government — which does not
necessarily mean lower estimates.

The reader may care to study the tables on pages 664–8 which
show the capital ship position of Britain and Germany at the outbreak of war. They are reproduced from Appendix B of *The World
Crisis,* Volume I.

18

Eve of War

ONE OF THE First Lord's most enterprising and successful roles was
as founder of the Royal Naval Air Service. In *The World Crisis* he
gave a brief résumé of what he set out to achieve in the air as far as
the defence of Britain was concerned:

> The War Office claimed on behalf of the Royal Flying Corps com-
> plete and sole responsibility for the aerial defence of Great Britain.
> But owing to the difficulties of getting money, they were unable to
> make any provision for this responsibility, every aeroplane they had
> being earmarked for the Expeditionary Force. Seeing this and find-
> ing myself able to procure funds by various shifts and devices, I be-
> gan in 1912 and 1913 to form under the Royal Naval Air Service
> flights of aeroplanes as well as of seaplanes for the aerial protection
> of our naval harbours, oil tanks and vulnerable points, and also for
> a general strengthening of our exiguous and inadequate aviation. In
> consequence I had in my own hand on the eve of the war fifty effi-
> cient naval machines, or about one-third of the number in possession
> of the Army. The War Office viewed this development with dis-
> favour, and claimed that they alone should be charged with the
> responsibility for home defence. When asked how they proposed to
> discharge this duty, they admitted sorrowfully that they had not got
> the machines and could not get the money. They adhered however
> to the principle.

Churchill's first interest in aviation had been excited before he
went to the Admiralty. In 1909, when he was still President of the
Board of Trade, he had been appointed a member of the Committee

of Imperial Defence, and intervened in one of its earliest discussions
on aviation:

Report of the Sub-Committee on Aerial Navigation
(Asquith Papers)

25 February 1909   Committee of Imperial Defence

Mr C. S. Rolls had purchased a "Wright" aeroplane, and hoped "that
the Government would give him facilities for experimenting with it
on Government ground." He also offered his services to the Govt "in
the event of their wishing to benefit by the experience that he
gained."
    [Esher & Haldane agreed to this.]
    "Mr Churchill thought that there was a danger of these proposals
being considered too amateurish. The problem of the use of aeroplanes was a most important one, and we should place ourselves in
communication with Mr [Orville] Wright, and avail ourselves of his
knowledge."

When he arrived at the Admiralty he was immediately encouraged
by his friend Fisher to pursue this matter, which they had doubtless
often discussed:

Lord Fisher to WSC
EXTRACT

10 November 1911

... *Aviation* supersedes small cruisers & Intelligence vessels. You told
me you would push *aviation* — you are right — but don't take away
our splendid young Naval Officers who have been suckled on Gunnery
and sea fighting to do what civilians can do better. The civilian airman can always carry an expert for observing. . . .

The First Lord's early plans met obstruction from the Treasury,
particularly when he had to come out in the open and ask for an Air
Department at the Admiralty. Up to then he had relied, as he has
told us, on "various shifts and devices." In all, he was rebuffed three
times before he could get Treasury sanction for this modest but far-

sighted proposal. After the third rebuff he wrote to the Permanent Under-Secretary at the Treasury:

WSC to Sir Robert Chalmers

24 August 1912

Copy

My dear Chalmers,

I am much surprised to get a third refusal from the Treasury on the subject of the Air Department at the Admiralty.

I had rather hoped from our talk the other day that your objections were removed. I could not be responsible for the conduct of the Admiralty business unless this most vital subject of naval aeronautics received the attention and study it requires.

The organisation proposed is absolutely necessary and is already in being. It is most modest in scale and I should certainly not agree to its being broken up. I am very much distressed by these repeated refusals of the Treasury, which are injurious to the public service.

[wsc]

Even when Treasury sanction had been obtained all did not at first go well. Captain Murray Sueter, who was appointed Director of the Air Department, had obtained the rank of Commodore when the war began. He later commanded the Royal Naval Air Service in Southern Italy, rose to the rank of Rear-Admiral and from 1921 to 1945 was Conservative MP for Hertford.

WSC to Prince Louis of Battenberg

EXTRACT

7 December 1912

... After what happened yesterday, it is clear that the Air Department and Naval Aviation generally require to be continuously gripped and studied under one hand in order that a thorough and well considered policy may be maintained. Captain Sueter requires supervision, and the connection between the Army and Navy work must be close and harmonious. We must have a thoroughly good policy which can be advocated from every point of view.

The duties of the First Sea Lord are very heavy and I am inclined to think that the "Air" should be definitely and absolutely assigned to the Second Sea Lord. Sir John Jellicoe is the very man to shake the whole thing together, and, unless you differ, I should propose to assign this duty to him. . . .

Throughout his political life Churchill, while pursuing the broadest themes and dealing with the greatest topics, never hesitated to master as much small technical detail as was possible in the course of a working day. Sometimes people were apt to resent his interference in such minutiæ of business, but he never allowed his eye for detail to blind him to the main task he had in mind. And certainly Government departments are more apt to be kept on their toes when they feel they are liable to the investigation of an eye from the top instead of everything being conducted sluggishly through the usual channels. In the particular case of the formation of the Royal Naval Air Service the First Lord's attention to detail scarcely needs vindication, since the whole project was his own conception, and without him it would never have taken flight.

WSC's Minutes

EXTRACTS

21 December 1913

All the seaplanes of the 1914–15 programme, and as many others as can conveniently be adjusted, should have sufficient uniformity in their design to enable a standard wireless to be quickly and easily fitted or removed as a complete unit.

2. The above principle should be applied so far as possible to engines which should be interchangeable and capable of being removed or fitted in a few minutes.

3. More care and attention should be paid to the seating accommodations. At present, caprice of the makers appears largely to govern this. Proper consideration for the comfort of the pilot and observer, combined with an attempt to arrive at good principles in this field, would conduce to greater efficiency.

10 February 1914

The objectives of land aeroplanes can never be so definite or important as the objectives of seaplanes, which, when they carry torpedoes, may prove capable of playing a decisive part in operations against capital ships. The facilities of reconnaissance at sea, where hostile vessels can be sighted at enormous distances while the seaplane remains out of possible range, offer a far wider prospect even in the domain of information to seaplanes than to land aeroplanes, which would be continually brought under rifle and artillery fire from concealed positions on the ground, among trees, behind hedges, &c. Yet in spite of these tendencies the army is seeking to spend nearly 1,000,000£ this year on the aeroplane service, as against 400,000£ provided for this section (or should one not rather say, "pinion") of the Naval Flying Wing.

11 February 1914

I think the word "canteen" would excite misgivings in strict Scottish bosoms. "Institute" is a much better word. I should like the building to offer accommodation not only to naval ratings, but to officers. There should be two parts and two entrances. Bathrooms with hot and cold water are indispensable. There is no reason why a canteen should not be established, but this must be an incident and not an object. There should be at least two good rooms on the officers' side and one or two smaller ones. A squash court would be better than the second lawn tennis court. The whole should be described as "The Naval Flying Service Club and Institute." You want a garage for motor-car or motor-bicycles. There should be a nice verandah in front. I wonder whether a bowling-alley would not be better than a second billiard table.

3 March 1914

A small inter-Departmental Committee should be formed to draw up a detailed scheme before any appeal is made to the public. Two officers from each of the Naval and Military Wings, and a War Officer should form the committee, and a military officer of the General Staff with flying experience should preside.

2. The object in the first instance should be to establish certain well-marked flying routes along which at known intervals good landing-places will be available. It ought to be possible, by removing hedges and filling up ditches, cutting down trees in the fences, &c, to secure a succession of good landing places at comparatively small cost.

3. The Ordnance Survey should undertake the preparation of a regular flying map in consultation with the above Committee. This map, which must of course be made in sections, should study the country along these routes from a flying point of view. The routes themselves should be studied in the same way as motor car routes are studied, and descriptions and directions prepared.

4. An official letter should be addressed to the War Office asking for their assent and co-operation.

5 March 1914

Referring to my note about the provision of landing places, the Committee should also consider how such landing places should be made visible to airmen from aloft. To this end metal signs, coloured and numbered, should be planted in the same way as motor-car guides are now fixed on all our roads. Flags or other conspicuous aviation landmarks should be erected along the main aerial routes, like lighthouses at sea, so as to enable navigation to proceed with sureness. It ought to be possible for an airman flying along an aerial route to pick up a succession of points which would enable him to verify his position exactly in relation to each of which well-known landing places exist.

1 May 1914

The conclusion I have reached is as follows: The uniform of the Naval Air Service to be — Naval uniform with an eagle instead of an anchor on buttons, cap badges, epaulettes, and sword belt clasps, and an eagle over the curl on the sleeve.

Squadron Commanders to be given the acting rank for all purposes of Lieutenant Commanders. This will only affect six officers.

All the other ranks correspond normally.

18 May 1914

It is important that a war squadron of ten fighting aeroplanes should be created at Eastchurch as quickly as possible, in order to assign a definite military value to the personnel assembled, and so provide to some extent for the aerial defence of the Chatham Dockyard, the Chattenden magazines, and the oil-fuel tanks. So vital are these points that in the near future we must contemplate a large increase in the numbers of this squadron.

In the first instance the squadron should consist of two flights of four machines each, with one in reserve. The design of these aeroplanes should be reconsidered in the light of the latest experience. They should all be identical in pattern, should all come from one maker, and should have all their parts interchangeable. The engines should be capable of being exchanged in not more than half an hour, and two spare engines should be ordered with each flight. These machines should be kept quite separate from the practice and school machines, and eight of the ten should always be ready to fly.

4 June 1914

The engine controls of the new Maurice Farman are a good example of what to avoid in this class of work. They are awkward, flimsy, inconveniently shaped, and ill-secured to the fuselage. The switch is also cheap and common in the last degree. No one would put such fittings into a motor-car costing 1,000£. It is the falsest economy, both in money and in weight, to have these appliances of the gimcrack order. Five or six pounds in weight laid out in making good, solidly-attached controls, would be wise economy. When you open or close the throttle you ought to have a sensation like winding a watch, and there should be no question of any bending movement of the lever from side to side, but only a direct slide fore and aft. All these small fittings require thought and study to reach the best disposition, and a responsible proportion both of money and weight should be expended upon them, since they are vital to the safety of the machine.

7 June 1914

The wooden shed at Kingsnorth would be a fine quarry for the suffragettes, and it appears to me that it should be watched. The existing watchman informs me that he watches all night long, and on Saturdays from 12 noon till 7 o'clock next morning. This means that he probably walks round once or twice and goes to sleep for the rest of the time. The matter should have your attention, and a regular watch established pending the time when the men enter.

The First Lord frequently visited Chatham and Sheerness in the Admiralty yacht *Enchantress*. On these expeditions he was able to inspect Eastchurch aerodrome and discuss progress with the naval air pioneers. As First Lord he was an ex-officio member of the Aviation sub-committee of the CID and he took a prominent part in its work. A stream of memoranda and minutes flowed from his office, all devoted to the aim of encouraging flying in the Navy, both by improving the conditions of the officers and men concerned and by concentrating technical talent on aviation problems.

In a minute to the Second Sea Lord in December 1911 about the proposed new flying corps, he wrote:

2. Terms and conditions must be devised to make aviation for war purposes the most honourable, as it is the most dangerous profession a young Englishman can adopt.

3. No regard to military or naval seniority should prevent the real young & capable men who have already done so much for the new arm, from being placed effectively at the head of the corps of airmen. There is no doubt as to the danger. The number of flights for every death in aviation was 500 in 1910, and 1,500 in 1911. In 1912, it had risen to 5,000.

Brassey's Naval Annual, never an uncritical judge of Churchill's policies, said in 1914: "The First Lord showed particular interest in all matters relating to the Naval Air Service and made many flights in aeroplanes and seaplanes. No occupant of this high office of state has made corresponding effort to acquire a practical knowledge of the work of the Navy."

Fisher had always been in favour of airships and after leaving the

Admiralty in 1910 he continued to press this view. The Admiralty and the First Lord — particularly the First Sea Lord — were sceptical of the airship. This was largely due to an unfortunate accident in an early experimental one. The report of the Court of Enquiry, presided over by Admiral Sturdee, had been most unfavourable. No blame was attributed to the officers and men of the airship. The disaster was found to have been due to insufficient strength in the keel.

This caused the project to be abandoned but the interest in airships was later revived. Jellicoe was much impressed by a flight in a Zeppelin; a continental tour by Mr O'Gorman, the Superintendent of the Royal Aircraft Factory at Farnborough, and Captain Sueter and eulogistic reports from our attachés in Germany brought much information about progress abroad. On 25 April 1912 at the 116th meeting of the CID Churchill raised the airship question again and it was agreed to ask the technical committee to review the matter. Considerable controversy followed. The CID considered the question at four separate meetings. They listened to attacks on airships by Admiral Wilson, and support for airships by Churchill, Seely and others. At the 122nd Meeting of the CID on 6 February 1913 it was agreed that the navy should take over the development of airships and that an airship section should be formed with the help of the army experts. In July, the First Lord ordered two rigid and six non-rigid airships to reinforce the few small craft taken over from the army. But it was too late, and the navy started the war with no airship capable of operating with the fleet in the reconnaissance role.

The airship controversy was accompanied by a long dispute between Sir Arthur Wilson, who although no longer First Sea Lord was a Member of the CID, and the First Lord and his advisers. In January 1913 Wilson sent Churchill a memorandum attacking airships which used arguments which were hotly disputed by the experts and many of which today appear nonsense. Extracts from this paper show the fallacy of Wilson's arguments — "Airships when out of sight of land very soon lose their reckoning; in the North Sea it is doubtful if a more extended view would often be obtained from an airship than a cruiser, as the atmosphere is rarely sufficiently clear and the use of a telescope from an airship would be more difficult."

An interesting aspect of the controversy was Wilson's suggestion that a Dido-class cruiser should be converted to carry aeroplanes. The mainmast was to be removed and the after funnel hinged so as to allow a length of flight deck on which the aircraft would land. Derricks were to be fitted to transfer the aircraft from aft to the forecastle for taking off. This is the first practical proposal for an aircraft carrier which is in the Admiralty archives and it was welcomed by the First Lord. But nothing was done beyond the provision of seaplane carriers which had to stop both to hoist their seaplanes and to recover them. The *Courageous* in 1917 was the first ship to be used for the takeoff and landing of aeroplanes: thus four years were lost. It is difficult now to appreciate the reasons for this delay.

In any event the opponents of airships were wrong, at least in the short term. They would have been valuable in the war and particularly at Jutland for naval reconnaissance. In the long term they were doomed for military purposes by their slow speed and great size which made them extremely vulnerable to anti-aircraft and fighter attack.

Naval Aviation made rapid progress between 1911 and 1914, particularly with seaplanes. The alliance with Shorts, who set up a factory near Eastchurch, flourished and produced some excellent machines. Sopwith's help was also enlisted and he designed some good aeroplanes and seaplanes. Avros also built successful aircraft for the Navy. As the official historian says:

> The Naval Wing paid more attention than was paid by the Military Wing to the use of the aeroplane as a fighting machine. . . .
> The Military Wing, small as it was, knew that it would be entrusted with the immense task of scouting for the expeditionary force, and that its business would be rather to avoid than to seek battle in the air. The Naval Wing, being entrusted first of all with the defence of the coast, aimed at something more than observing the movements of an attacking enemy. Thus in bomb-dropping and machine-gunnery the Naval Wing was more advanced.

Naval experiments covered every aspect of sea and air warfare. Trials were carried out in early 1912 to discover whether submarines could be detected and attacked from the air. The officer concerned, a submariner turned aviator called Williamson, also put up a design for a ship to carry aircraft which would land on wires stretched across the deck. The use of W/T in aircraft received much attention. Bomb-dropping was practised and a few machine-guns and cannon were fitted in aircraft.

In 1913, the first torpedo was dropped from a British aircraft. The protection of ships and dockyards was seen as a naval responsibility and many experiments were made in the attack on airships from aircraft, using bombs, grenades and machine-guns. Night flying was also practised for the first time.

The *Hermes* was converted to carry seaplanes, and in the North Sea manœuvres of 1913, seaplanes from the *Hermes* aided one side and seaplanes from shore stations the other, with considerable success. At the outbreak of the war, the Royal Naval Air Service was flourishing. There were 39 aeroplanes, 52 seaplanes, a few small airships and about 120 pilots. The machines were good, the pilots well-trained and morale unequalled.

The First Lord's enthusiasm for this new weapon was not confined to planning, organization and procurement. He determined to be airborne himself. At that time it was rare for a civilian to fly at all, and for a civilian to handle the controls himself was even rarer. Thirty-two was considered the top age at which a man could take up flying. Churchill was thirty-eight when he made the first of the many and sometimes dangerous flights which he was to make both now and during the war. He never flew solo, or obtained a flying certificate, but he was to notch up many hours of flying time to his credit. Group Captain Ivon Courtney, who was one of Churchill's flying instructors in 1913, later recorded for the author the following reminiscence:

Before our first flight together he said to me: "We are in the Stephenson age of flying. Now our machines are frail. One day they will be robust, and of value to our country." He had already done quite a lot of flying. "I want some more instruction," he said. We had no headphones in those days. Once airborne we would shout at one another, and hope the wind carried something approximating to what we said across to the other fellow. One didn't normally use instruments; they were all in a box but we "old" fliers scorned them, we liked to fly on "ear" as it were. But WSC was fascinated by the instruments, and used to keep his head in the box. He took the instruments seriously, and he was right to do so. He saw that one day the box of instruments would be more important than the pilot's ear.

WSC and I would go up perhaps ten times in one day. He was far more keen than most learners to "go up again." He couldn't bear to make mistakes. He always wanted to correct them at once. I remember the time when, on landing, he bent an undercarriage. I imagined he would want to stop flying that day. But the shock did not deter him one bit. It made him more eager. So up we went again.

As an instructor one was *over*-careful with WSC. We were all scared stiff of having a smashed First Lord on our hands. Even I was frightened once, when we had an airspeed indicator on board. It was an experimental one, they were quite new, and most pilots preferred to judge speed by looking over the side. But WSC, fascinated by instruments as I said, gazed intently at the airspeed indicator, and neglected all else. The result — he was so buried in the box he nearly forgot to cut off the engine as we came over the hedge, and very nearly overshot the field. WSC was always bucketed about from one instructor to another. We didn't want to take on too much responsibility for him. The result was *good* because it gave him experience of many types of pilot; but it was *bad* because no pilot stayed with him long enough to let him go up solo. [Eugene] Gerrard [Captain RN, later Air Commodore] once said to me: "WSC has had as much as 25 hours in the air. But no one will risk letting him solo. If anything happened to WSC the career of the man who had allowed him a solo flight would be finished." WSC's capacity for concentration was truly amazing. Before most flights, the normal pupil is nervous and talks of nothing but trivialities. I remember calling for WSC one morning. He asked me to stay for breakfast. Jellicoe was there. Jellicoe and WSC spent the whole breakfast time pouring over official papers, and discussing intricate questions of naval tactics. Then WSC turned abruptly to me: "Well, Courtney, let us fly."

Those that were sceptical of heavier-than-air machines always deprecated WSC's interest in them. They said he was playing with a silly toy, and that it had no future. Then the war came, and these same sceptics saw the importance of the aeroplane. They began to clamour for greater activity in the very sphere in which they had shown such hostility. [Richard] Davies [Lieutenant RN, later Admiral, VC] said to me one day: "They have pissed on Churchill's plant for three years — now they expect blooms in a month."

An early warning of the dangers involved came from his cousin Marlborough:

Duke of Marlborough to WSC

EXTRACT

12 March 1913   15 Great College Street

My dear Winston,
    I do not suppose that I shall get the chance of writing you many more letters if you continue your journeys in the Air. Really I consider that you owe it to your wife family and friends to desist from a practice or pastime — whichever you call it — which is fraught with so much danger to life. It is really wrong of you. . . .

A little later Churchill started flying with Captain Gilbert Wildman-Lushington of the Royal Marines. He greatly enjoyed the company of Lushington and his young friends, and they made much of him. Later in the year, when a pilot had shot some wild duck for him from a plane and the officers were treating it as a great lark, he surprised them by making a short speech on aerial war in the future, including the arming of planes with weapons — until then they had been regarded as suited only for reconnaissance.
    On 29 November 1913 he had a particularly agreeable and interesting day in the air with Lushington. A good account is preserved in a letter which Lushington wrote the next morning to his fiancée, Miss Airlie Hynes:

Captain G. W-Lushington to Miss Airlie Hynes
(Airlie Madden Papers)

EXTRACT

30 November 1913   RA Flying School

Darling loved one,
    Yesterday turned out to be quite a strenuous day for us, the First Lord and his coterie arrived about noon. We had 17 ma-

chines out & besides that there were three private machines, the
Dunne, Mr Ogilvy's & Professor Huntingdon's, the air seemed absolutely thick and congested. I started Winston off on his instruction about 12.15 & he got so bitten with it, I could hardly get him
out of the machine, in fact except for about ¾ hour for lunch we
were in the machine till about 3.30. He showed great promise, &
is coming down again for further instruction & practice. I think I
did myself quite a lot of good. I went & dined on board the *Enchantress* last night and sat on the right of WC. He was absolutely
full out and talked hard about what he was going to do. Before
lunch he came up to my cabin to wash his hands & took a great
interest in the photos I have there, he asked me when it was coming off, & I said when I'd saved some money. We sent a machine
over to Whitstable for oysters for lunch, but they didn't arrive till
too late, so I took them on board as a birthday present from the
mess for WC, who is 39 today. I've never had such a day in my
life. I was quite tired when we did eventually get back to bed last
night. Courtney, Davis & Clark-Hall also were dining on board. I
hardly expected a letter from you....

The same day that Lushington wrote to his fiancée the First Lord
wrote to him:

WSC to Captain G. W-Lushington
(Airlie Madden Papers)

30 November 1913   Admiralty

Dear Captain Lushington,
    I wish you would clear up the question of the steering control
and let me know what was the real difficulty I had in making the
rudder act. Probably the explanation is that I was pushing against
myself, though I am not quite sure about this. It may be that
they are very stiff and hard to work. Certainly the feeling I had
was that I was being repeatedly over-ridden, and I thought you
were controlling the steering the whole time. Could you not go
up with another flying officer and, sitting yourself in the back seat,
see whether there is great stiffness and difficulty in steering, or
whether it was all my clumsiness.

                                        Yours sincerely
                                        WINSTON S. CHURCHILL

At the same time he instructed Sueter to fit one of the Sopwith biplanes at Eastchurch with dual controls of exact equality, without overriding power, which would be "useful for long-distance flying and enable one pilot to relieve the other."

Lushington replied on December 2 that he had flown No 2 from the passenger seat, and had found the rudders slightly heavy, which was generally considered "a good fault for a purely instructional machine, as the pupil is not so likely to get into difficulties." But Lushington felt that the main cause of the First Lord's difficulties came from "pushing against yourself," a fault which, he explained, was "a very common error of beginners, even of experienced pilots too." Lushington felt that with practice these faults would rectify themselves, and that such mistakes "are really all part of the instruction." "As an instructor," he concluded, "I prefer to find out these difficulties myself."

Before this letter reached the First Lord, Lushington was dead. Coming in to land at Eastchurch on December 2, he side-slipped and crashed into the ground. The First Lord wrote to Miss Hynes:

WSC to Miss Airlie Hynes
(Airlie Madden Papers)

7 December 1913   Admiralty
Private

Dear Miss Hynes,
    This letter was written to me by Captain Wildman-Lushington on the morning of the second of December. Before it reached me he was dead.
    I think you ought to have it; and may I ask you also to accept my deepest sympathy in the blow wh has fallen upon you.
    To be killed instantly without pain or fear in the necessary service of the country when one is quite happy and life is full of success & hope, cannot be reckoned the worst of fortune. But to some who are left behind the loss is terrible.

Yours vy tly
WINSTON S. CHURCHILL

Miss Airlie Hynes to WSC

9 December 1913   8 Helena Road
                                                   Southsea

Dear Mr Churchill,

I want to thank you very much for sending me Gilbert Lushington's last letter, it was kind of you & I am so glad to have it. In his
last to me he mentioned that he was writing to you & I wondered
if he had. Thank you also for the lovely wreath you sent. I felt so
proud when I saw that it was laurel, & most of all I would like
to thank you for helping to make Gilbert's last days absolutely
happy. He was so pleased at having given you your first instruction and his last letters were all about it and he was so happy. I
certainly can't grudge him the splendid end he had, it was a death
any man would wish & I am only proud to think that I always encouraged him to fly. I was just as keen on aviation as he was himself & in the future I shall like to think that I have helped to give
something towards it. Life seems a blank just now but it is a great
comfort to have a perfect past to look back on. With very sincere
thanks for being so kind.

                                                   Yours very truly
                                                   AIRLIE HYNES

This nobility of spirit and acceptance of sacrifice was to prove
indispensable to the salvation of our country in the terrible war
which was to come within nine months, and which was to command
supreme sacrifice from all that was finest in the British race. Miss
Hynes and her friends were to typify the exalted spirit with which
the challenge of war would be met. That spirit of sacrifice was to be
perpetuated through her. Miss Hynes married in 1918 Major J. G.
Madden, DSO. Two of their sons were killed in the Second War,
one of them gaining the Military Cross. Thus this strong strain of
patriotism and sacrifice was carried through for another generation
and another war, even more menacing to Britain's freedom. Lushington's younger brother, Godfrey, joined the Royal Marines in 1914,
served as a pilot in the Royal Naval Air Service throughout the First
War and as Assistant Chief of Staff to Lord Mountbatten in the Far
East in the Second War and ended his service as Chief of Combined
Operations 1947–50.

Churchill's own flying experience was soon to be interrupted. At the end of May Gustav Hamel disappeared while crossing the Channel by air. Churchill was among those who awaited his landing in vain: he was flying from Paris on the First Lord's invitation to give a demonstration to the Royal Naval Air Force pilots at an Air Station near Portsmouth. Lushington's death pricked the anxiety of Churchill's friends. F. E. Smith wrote to him on December 6:

Dear Winston

Why do you do such a foolish thing as fly repeatedly? Surely it is unfair to your family your career + your friends.

Yours ever

FE

WSC to his wife

EXTRACT

29 May 1914   Portsmouth

My darling one,

   I have been at the Central Flying School for a couple of days —
flying a little in good & careful hands & under perfect conditions.
So I did not write you from there as I know you wd be vexed. But

now that I am back on board & am off to Portland, I hasten to tell
you how much & how often you & the babies were in my thoughts
during these happy & interesting days. I was delighted to get your
telegram altho' I read it with an uneasy conscience: but I wd not
answer from such an address! — fearing it wd make you anxious
— where there was vy little occasion.

We had the false hopes of Hamel's safe arrival and the sombre
dispersal of them with the morning newspapers. What a cruel
brute the man must have been who invented that plausible lie! I
did not wholly accept it; but it seems to have caused an immense
wave of interest everywhere; & Masterton tells me that the people
in the streets formed little crowds round the newspaper boys in
their haste to get the special editions.

I went (by air) over to see the Yeomanry in their camp eleven
miles away and found them delighted to see me. We had a gt
reception — the men all running out in a mob, as if they had
never seen an aeroplane before. I saw also Cecil Grenfell in command of the Bucks & his young Rothschild officers etc. Today I
came on here: & find Masterton & Hood and a good deal of work.
As I have been up at 4 am each morning I am a little short of
sleep, & have been picking some up this afternoon. Goonie & Jack
have just arrived on board with A. Sinclair — & that is all our
party. . . .

WSC to his wife

6 June 1914   Admiralty Yacht

My darling one,

I will not fly any more until at any rate you have recovered from
your kitten: & by then or perhaps later the risks may have been
greatly reduced.

This is a wrench, because I was on the verge of taking my pilot's
certificate. It only needed a couple of calm mornings; & I am confident of my ability to achieve it vy respectably. I shd greatly have
liked to reach this point wh wd have made a suitable moment for
breaking off. But I must admit that the numerous fatalities of this
year wd justify you in complaining if I continued to share the
risks — as I am proud to do — of these good fellows. So I give it
up decidedly for many months & perhaps for ever. This is a gift —

so stupidly am I made — wh costs me more than anything wh cd be bought with money. So I am vy glad to lay it at your feet, because I know it will rejoice & relieve your heart.

Anyhow I can feel I know a good deal about this fascinating new art. I can manage a machine with ease in the air, even with high winds, & only a little more practice in landings wd have enabled me to go up with reasonable safety alone. I have been up nearly 140 times, with many pilots, & all kinds of machines, so I know the difficulties the dangers & the joys of the air — well enough to appreciate them, & to understand all the questions of policy wh will arise in the near future.

It is curious that while I have been lucky, accidents have happened to others who have flown with me out of the natural proportion. This poor Lieutenant whose loss has disturbed your anxieties again, took me up only last week in this vy machine!

You will give me some kisses and forgive me for past distresses — I am sure. Though I had no need & perhaps no right to do it — it was an important part of my life during the last 7 months, & I am sure my nerve, my spirits & my virtue were all improved by it. But at your expense my poor pussy cat! I am so sorry.

I thought of coming for you at Dieppe, but on second thoughts it is better not to repeat that voyage. If you telegraph to me I will meet you in the yacht at Newhaven & take you to Portsmouth. Then we can go up together the next day.

Always your loving & devoted
WINSTON

Churchill was not to resume flying until his official business at the Ministry of Munitions in 1917 compelled him to make frequent visits to France.

*

As part of the economies which the First Lord sought while preparing the 1914 Naval Estimates, the usual summer manœuvres were abandoned. In their place Churchill substituted the test mobilization of the Third Fleet. This change in customary naval practice was announced in Parliament on 18 March 1914. The First Lord described the coming mobilization to King Alfonso of Spain, who had

been invited to attend but was unable to do so because of political
troubles in Madrid:

WSC to King Alfonso

9 July 1914   Admiralty Yacht
                                                          at Sea

Copy

Sir,

I am very sorry that YM will not be able to come this year, as I
had hoped, to see a Fleet firing, but I followed with concern the
debates in the Cortes & can appreciate the reasons wh make it undesirable at the present time. I hope however that I shall have
the honour of seeing YM during yr visit in Sept in the seclusion of
the polo world. We have all greatly rejoiced at the victory & we
recognise how much it was due to the generous aid YM gave to our
players & to their practice at Madrid. The Irish question now
moves steadily forward to its culminating point, & I am more than
ever hopeful — tho' everyone lies under the stroke of chance —
that a good settlement will be effected.

At the Admy. we are vy busy with the mobilisation of the Fleet
wh takes place next week & is a considerable affair. The King himself is coming to inspect the Fleet & afterwards will lead it to sea
— 53 Battleships & nearly 400 pennants of all classes. Then there
will be 3 or 4 days of exercises, tactical & strategic, wh I am looking forward vy much to following.

I learn with gt interest that YM's new ships are to be armed
with the 15″ gun. All our results with that weapon are so far
excellent.

With sincere wishes for YM's health & prosperity,

I remain Sir, YM's humble servant
WSC

The orders for the test mobilization of the Third Fleet were issued
on July 10 and the mobilization began five days later. The grand
review of the whole fleet was held at Spithead on July 17–18. "It
constituted," as Churchill wrote in *The World Crisis,* "incomparably
the greatest assemblage of naval power ever witnessed in the history
of the world."

The assassination of Archduke Franz-Ferdinand of Austria-Hungary in Sarajevo on June 28 did not disturb the political or diplomatic situation unduly during the first three weeks of July. Balkan problems seemed irrelevant to European peace. Public opinion was hardened to bloody outrages in the Balkans. But on July 24 the Austrian Government sent an ultimatum to Serbia which among other severe demands urged Serbian acceptance of an Austrian-controlled search for "plotters" who might have planned the Archduke's murder from inside Serbia.

The arrogant and threatening tone of the Austrian ultimatum at once alarmed the Governments of Europe. The British Cabinet was in session that afternoon. They were discussing Ireland when Sir Edward Grey read out the terms of the Austrian ultimatum. It was on that day, and presumably immediately after this Cabinet meeting, that Churchill wrote his first reaction to the ultimatum, in a letter to his wife: "Europe is trembling on the verge of a general war, the Austrian ultimatum to Servia being the most insolent document of its kind ever devised."

The ships of the Third Fleet had completed their test mobilization as planned on July 23. They were about to disperse to their home ports when it was learnt at the Admiralty, on July 26, that Austria had curtly rejected Serbia's conciliatory reply to her ultimatum. Prince Louis immediately issued orders that the demobilization should be halted. Churchill, who was at Cromer with his family, at once approved of this measure and returned to London:

As Churchill was to write in *The World Crisis:*

Prince Louis awaited me at the Admiralty. The situation was evidently degenerating. Special editions of the Sunday papers showed intense excitement in nearly every European capital. The First Sea Lord told me that in accordance with our conversation he had told the Fleet not to disperse. I took occasion to refer to this four months later in my letter accepting his resignation. I was very glad publicly to testify at that moment of great grief and pain for him that his loyal hand had set the first order which began our vast naval mobilisation.

The Cabinet met two days later:

H. H. Asquith to The King
(Royal Archives)

EXTRACT

28 July 1914   10 Downing Street

... The action of the First Lord in postponing the dispersal of the first and second [and third] fleets was approved. . . .

The First Lord was alert to the needs of the crisis. He signalled to C-in-C Mediterranean:

WSC to Admiral Sir Berkeley Milne

Sent 27 July 1914   Admiralty

Secret. European political situation makes war between Triple Alliance and Triple Entente Powers by no means impossible. This is *not* the Warning Telegram, but be prepared to shadow possible hostile men-of-war. Return to Malta as arranged at ordinary speed and remain there with all your ships completing with coal and stores. Warn "Defence" to be ready to join with despatch.
  Measure is purely precautionary. The utmost secrecy is to be observed, and no unnecessary person is to be informed.

The First Lord described the preparations which he had initiated to the King:

WSC to The King
(Royal Archives)

28 July 1914   Admiralty
Secret

Sir,
  During the last few days the Navy has been placed upon a preparatory & precautionary basis. The First Fleet will sail secretly tomorrow for its preliminary Northern station. The Second Fleet will assemble at Portland as soon as its men return in the ordinary course from leave on Friday. The Patrol flotillas have been raised to full strength and are moving in succession to their war stations. The two

Irish blockades have been abandoned and all vessels engaged in them will conform to the general dispositions. The aircraft are collected at and around the estuary of the Thames to guard against airship attack. All vulnerable points such as oil tanks & magazines were last night guarded by the army against aerial attack (the air guns being manned) & against *sabotage*. It is possible that all East coast lights & guns will be manned tomorrow.

The reserves of oil & the coal arrangements are satisfactory. The reserves of ammunition show large surpluses. The torpedo reserve is complete. There will be no deficiency of officers on a complete mobilisation & we shall have at least 20,000 Reservists for whom no room can be found in any ship fit to send to sea.

A variety of other precautions & measures have been taken with wh I will not trouble Your Majesty.

It is needless to emphasize that these measures in no way prejudge an intervention or take for granted that the peace of the great powers will not be preserved.

I understand from Prince Louis that Your Majesty will desire to hear from me, & with my humble duty remain

Your Majesty's faithful & devoted servant

WINSTON S. CHURCHILL

Although diplomatic activity was intense at this time, it could not mask the dangerous situation. As the crisis developed it became clear that Germany was encouraging Austria to challenge Serbia, and that the German General Staff envisaged a war against both France and Russia.

Churchill was clear in his own mind where the responsibility for the crisis lay. He later wrote in *The World Crisis*:

Justice to France requires the explicit statement that the conduct of her Government at this awful juncture was faultless. She assented instantly to every proposal that could make for peace. She abstained from every form of provocative action. She even compromised her own safety, holding back her covering troops at a considerable distance behind her frontier, and delaying her mobilisation in the face of continually gathering German forces till the latest moment. Not until she was confronted with the direct demand of Germany to break her Treaty and abandon Russia, did France take up the challenge; and even had she acceded to the German demand, she would only, as we now know, have been faced with a further ultimatum to surrender to German military occupation as a guarantee for her neutrality the fortresses of Toul and Verdun. Thus there never was any chance of France being allowed to escape the ordeal. Even cowardice and dishonour would not have saved her. The Germans had resolved that if war came from any cause, they would take and break France forthwith as its first operation. The German military chiefs burned to give the signal, and were sure of the result. She would have begged for mercy in vain. She did not beg.

The more I reflect upon this situation, the more convinced I am that we took the only practical course that was open to us or to any British Cabinet; and that the objections which may be urged against it were less than those which would have attended any other sequence of action.

On July 28 the First Lord put further preparatory measures into operation. After consulting with Asquith, he arranged for the guarding of magazines and oil tanks "against evilly-disposed persons and attacks by aircraft." At midnight he wrote to his wife:

WSC to his wife
(CSC Papers)

28 July 1914   Admiralty
Midnight

My darling one & beautiful,

Everything tends towards catastrophe & collapse. I am interested, geared up & happy. Is it not horrible to be built like that? The preparations have a hideous fascination for me. I pray to God to forgive me for such fearful moods of levity. Yet I wd do my best for peace, & nothing wd induce me wrongfully to strike the blow. I cannot feel that we in this island are in any serious degree responsible for the wave of madness wh has swept the mind of Christendom. No one can measure the consequences. I wondered whether those stupid Kings & Emperors cd not assemble together & revivify kingship by saving the nations from hell but we all drift on in a kind of dull cataleptic trance. As if it was somebody else's operation!

The two black swans on St James's Park lake have a darling cygnet — grey, fluffy, precious & unique. I watched them this evening for

some time as a relief from all the plans & schemes. We are putting
the whole Navy into fighting trim (bar the reserve). And all seems
quite sound & thorough. The sailors are thrilled and confident.
Every supply is up to the prescribed standard. Everything is ready as
it has never been before. And we are awake to the tips of our fingers.
But war is the Unknown & the Unexpected! God guard us and our
long accumulated inheritance. You know how willingly & proudly
I wd risk — or give — if need be — my period of existence to keep
this country great & famous & prosperous & free. But the problems
are vy difficult. One has to try to measure the indefinite & weigh the
imponderable.

I feel sure however that if war comes we shall give them a good
drubbing.

My darling one — this is a vy good plan of ours on the telephone.
You remember the Grand Guignol play! Ring me up at fixed times.
But talk in parables — for they all listen.

Kiss those kittens & be loved for ever only by me
Your own
w

On July 29 the Cabinet authorized Churchill to put into force the
"precautionary period" regulations. "All over the country," he wrote
in *The World Crisis,* "emergency measures began to astonish the
public. Naval harbours were cleared, bridges were guarded, steamers
were boarded and examined, watchers lined the coasts."

On the night of July 29–30 the First Lord obtained Asquith's
approval to send the First Fleet from Portland to the North Sea. It
passed the straits of Dover swiftly and unobserved, without lights.
On July 31 it was at its battle stations, the battleships at Scapa Flow
and Cromarty, the battle-cruisers at Rosyth.

On July 30 the First Lord decided to replace Sir George Callaghan
as Commander-in-Chief of the Home Fleet by Sir John Jellicoe.
Callaghan was on the eve of his sixty-second birthday. Although he
was apparently in excellent health, the First Lord felt that he was not
equal to the strains which war would impose upon him. The change
caused a bitter controversy among the Admirals. Beatty telegraphed
to the First Lord that the proposed change, of which he had heard
rumours, "would cause unprecedented disaster. . . . Moral effect upon

Fleet at such a moment would be worse than a defeat at sea." Jellicoe
himself sent six telegrams to the First Lord in three days, urging that
Callaghan should be retained because of his experience and because
the Fleet was "imbued with feelings of extreme admiration and
loyalty for him." But Churchill was not to be deflected from what
he considered to be a necessary measure.

The decision to make Jellicoe Commander-in-Chief of the Home
Fleet had been in Churchill's mind since he arrived at the Admiralty.
Lord Fisher had in many letters urged the importance of Jellicoe's
ultimate promotion to this command. Sir George Callaghan would,
in the normal course of duty, have been relieved of his command in
October 1914. In November 1911 Fisher had written to a friend:

> My two private visits to Winston were fruitful. I'll tell you . . . the
> whole secret of the changes! To get Jellicoe Commander-in-Chief
> of the Home Fleet prior to October 21, 1914, which is the date of the
> Battle of Armageddon. He will succeed Callaghan automatically in
> two years from December 19, 1911, so will have all well in hand by
> the before-mentioned date! *"Nunc dimittis"!* Everything revolved
> round Jellicoe!

The First Lord kept his wife and the King informed of the
sombre developments:

WSC to The King
(Royal Archives)

31 July 1914   Admiralty
12.30 a.m.
Secret

Sir,
   Your Majesty is informed of the diplomatic, so I confine myself to
the military aspect.
   The First Fleet is now in the open seas. The Second Fleet will assemble tomorrow at Portland. All "precautionary" measures have
(so far) behaved magnificently. The four old battleships will reach
the Humber tomorrow. All the flotillas have reached their stations.

Guns and ammunition are being supplied to fast Merchant ships wh will be taken up & commissioned. I have taken the responsibility of forbidding the departure of the Turkish battleship *Osman* (late *Rio*) with the Prime Minister's approval. If war comes she will be called & shd Your Majesty approve the Agreement, will convey Sir Henry Jackson to reinforce, & at the regular date assume command of the Mediterranean.

Shd War come I shall have to submit to Your Majesty the name of Sir John Jellicoe for the supreme command. I have reached with regret the conclusion that Sir George Callaghan is not equal to the strains wh it wd entail upon the C in C. These are not times when personal feelings can be considered unduly. We must have a younger man. Your Majesty knows well the purely physical exertion wh the command of a gt fleet demands.

This however can remain in suspense till the situation becomes definite.

Arrangements are being made for some form of National indemnity for British traders at sea, & I shall bring proposals before the Cabinet tomorrow morning.

With my humble duty I remain

Your Majesty's faithful & devoted servant & subject
WINSTON S. CHURCHILL

WSC to The King
(Royal Archives)

1 August 1914   Admiralty
Secret

Mr Churchill with his humble duty submits to Your Majesty that the present situation renders a change in the supreme command of the Fleet imperative. Sir John Jellicoe has now arrived at Scapa, and Mr Churchill proposes, either tomorrow or the next day to relieve Sir George Callaghan & to appoint Sir John Jellicoe, with the acting rank of Admiral, to be Commander in Chief. Mr Churchill would respectfully and most earnestly ask Your Majesty's approval to the course proposed.

Mr Churchill last night found it necessary to send out summonses to the Reservists for a complete mobilisation of the Fleet, and it is expected that a proclamation regularizing and enforcing these summonses will, after submission to Your Majesty in the course of today, be made public soon after the meeting of Parliament tomorrow afternoon.

Mr Churchill has authorized the First Sea Lord & the Chief of the War Staff to confer with the French Naval Attaché on the naval measures which should be taken in common, should the Cabinet & Parliament decide that France and England are to be allies in the present war.

The general position and strength of the British Fleets Squadrons & Flotillas is regarded as satisfactory by the Board of Admiralty.

WINSTON S. CHURCHILL

WSC to his wife
(CSC Papers)

31 July 1914   Admiralty
Secret.
not to be left about but locked up or burned.

My darling,

There is still hope although the clouds are blacker & blacker. Germany is realising I think how great are the forces against her & is trying tardily to restrain her idiot ally. We are working to soothe Russia. But everybody is preparing swiftly for war and at any moment now the stroke may fall. We are ready.

I cd not tell you all the things I have done & the responsibilities I have taken in the last few days: but all is working well: & everyone has responded. The newspapers have observed an admirable reticence. The Baron de Forest was startled to receive a telegram that his yacht had been ordered out of Dover Harbour. He hurriedly left for Dover. As he journeyed down the line he found every bridge & tunnel guarded & became increasingly terrified. He telegraphed frantically clamouring for debates & questions in Parliament. But not a man moved — not a question nor so far any mention in the papers. The country will be united when the issue is joined. Be sure of it.

Germany has sent a proposal to us to be neutral if she promises not to take French territory nor to invade Holland. She must take French colonies & she cannot promise not to invade Belgium — wh she is by treaty bound not merely to respect but to defend. Grey has replied that these proposals are impossible & disgraceful. Everything points therefore to a collision on these issues. Still hope is not dead.

The city has simply broken into chaos. The world's credit system is virtually suspended. You cannot sell stocks & shares. You cannot borrow. Quite soon it will not perhaps be possible to cash a cheque. Prices of goods are rising to panic levels.

Scores of poor people are made bankrupts. These nice Derenburgs have been reduced from affluence to bankruptcy. Nelke has lost half his fortune.

But I expect the apprehension of war hurts these interests more or as much as war itself. I look for victory if it comes.

I have resolved to remove Callaghan & place Jellicoe in supreme command as soon as it becomes certain that war will be declared.

I dined last night again with the PM. Serene as ever. But he backs me well in all the necessary measures.

All the *Enchantress* officers on mobilisation go *en bloc* to *Invincible*. I am forcibly detaining the 2 Turkish Dreadnoughts wh are ready. Ireland I think is going to be settled.

I am perturbed at the expense for this month being £175. Please send me the bills for Pear Tree [Cottage] & Admiralty separately. Rigorous measures will have to be taken. I will pay the bills direct myself, & Jack can check the housekeeping here in your absence.

I am sending you the cheque for Pear Tree. I am so glad you find rest & contentment there.

Fondest love my darling one — your devoted husband

W

Churchill's opinion of the diplomatic crisis was clear: he considered that Britain must intervene against Germany if France or Belgium were attacked. When Arthur Ponsonby, a Liberal MP, wrote to ask his opinion of the crisis Churchill replied:

WSC to Arthur Ponsonby
(Ponsonby Papers)

31 July 1914   Admiralty
Private

My dear Ponsonby,

So long as no treaty obligation or true British interest is involved I am of your opinion that we shd remain neutral. Balkan quarrels are no vital concern of ours. We have done our best to keep the peace

& shall continue so to do to the end. But the march of events is sinister. The extension of the conflict by a German attack upon France or Belgium wd raise other issues than those which now exist, and it wd be wrong at this moment to pronounce finally one way or the other as to our duty or our interests.

I think you have shown much discretion & I quite understand your feelings & views.

Yours sincerely
WINSTON S. CHURCHILL

And on the following day Churchill made his position equally clear to Lord Robert Cecil, a Unionist MP and a brother of Lord Hugh Cecil:

WSC to Lord Robert Cecil
(Cecil Papers)

1 August 1914   Admiralty
Copy

Dear Cecil,

I thought you would not mind my sending yr letter to the Prime Minister.

The news tonight opens again hope. There seems to be a prospect of Austria & Russia resuming negotiations on a formula wh Germany has proposed: and every exertion will be made to that end.

But a collision between the armies may arise at any moment out of an incident or an accident. And I hold that in all the circumstances if we allowed Belgian neutrality to be trampled down by Germany without exerting ourselves to aid France we shd be in a very melancholy position both in regard to our interests & our honour.

I am grateful to you for your letter.

Yours sincerely
WINSTON S. CHURCHILL

In the Cabinet opinion was divided and, as Churchill later described it, "overwhelmingly pacific." Lord Morley was particularly reluctant to see Britain involved in a European war. On August 1 he seemed to have enlisted the support of Lloyd George, as well as of a number of more junior ministers. A set of Cabinet notes survives in the Lloyd George papers which give a glimpse of the arguments used by Churchill to bring the Chancellor of the Exchequer to his view:

Cabinet Notes
(Lloyd George Papers)

David Lloyd George to WSC

[1 August 1914]

Would you *commit* yourself in public *now* (Monday) to war if Belgium is invaded whether Belgium asks for our protection or not.

WSC to David Lloyd George

No

David Lloyd George to WSC

If patience prevails & you do not press us too hard tonight we [personally] might come together.

WSC to David Lloyd George

Please God — It is our whole future — comrades — or opponents. The march of events will be dominating.

David Lloyd George to WSC

What is your policy?

WSC to David Lloyd George

At the present moment I would act in such a way as to impress Germany with our intention to preserve the neutrality of Belgium. So much is still unknown as to the definite purpose that I would not go beyond this. Moreover public opinion might veer round at any moment if Belgium is invaded & we must be ready to meet this opinion.

WSC to David Lloyd George

I am most profoundly anxious that our long cooperation may not be severed. Remember your part at Agadir. I implore you to come and bring your mighty aid to the discharge of our duty. Afterwards by participating in the peace we can regulate the settlement & prevent a renewal of 1870 conditions.

WSC to David Lloyd George

All the rest of our lives we shall be opposed. I am deeply attached to you & have followed your instinct & guidance for nearly 10 years.

WSC to David Lloyd George

Together we can carry a wide social policy — *on the conference basis
your idea* — wh you taught me. The naval war will be cheap — not
more than 25 millions a year.

You *alone* can take the measures wh will assure food being kept
abundant & cheap to the people.

WSC to David Lloyd George

[3 Aug 1914]

The Welsh miners who had gone on their holidays after denouncing
the war are returning in full force tomorrow — having apparently
satisfied themselves of the justice of the war — and will cut all the
coal we need. This relieves a dangerous situation. I want you to send
them a strong Welsh message about small nations etc.

WSC to David Lloyd George

Turkish ships not to leave the country pending situation being determined.

David Lloyd George to WSC

He is summing up much too unfavourably to our own friends.

WSC to David Lloyd George

Yes.

David Lloyd George to WSC

Ready to defend ourselves. Whilst others fighting our business confined to starving the women and children including our own. What
will be the effect on Italy, Belgium and Holland.

WSC to David Lloyd George

Please study the question before you make up your mind. There are
all sorts of vital & precise facts — wh you *cannot* have at your fingers'
ends.

WSC to David Lloyd George

I am so glad you are turning your mind to the *vital* question of safe-guarding the credit & food supply of this country.

These notes which passed at Cabinet between Churchill and Lloyd George were mostly torn up by Lloyd George. The pieces were gathered together and preserved by his devoted Private Secretary, Miss Stevenson. Such a prolonged interchange by notes at Cabinet meetings is a rarity. They show how Churchill was wrestling with the conscience of Lloyd George for his soul.

In his *Great Contemporaries* Churchill wrote sympathetically of Lord Morley's opposition to war. For a week Morley had argued with his colleagues for leaving France and Germany to fight it out without British intervention.

Morley found himself looked to as leader by a gathering band . . . when later on he told me he must resign, I said in effect that if he would wait for two or three days more, everything would be clear, and we should be in full agreement. The Germans would make everyone easy in his conscience. They would accept all responsibilities and sweep away all doubts. Already their vanguards pouring through Luxembourg approached the Belgian frontier. Nothing could recall or deflect them. They were launched; and the catastrophe now imminent and certain would convince and unite the British Empire as it had never been convinced and united before. "They cannot stop now. If they tried, they would be thrown into utter confusion. They must go on in spite of frontiers, treaties, threats, appeals, through cruelties and horrors, trampling on until they meet the main French Armies and the largest battles of history are fought. Remember all the others are marching too. . . ."

I offered to illustrate the position on the map. But he took another line. "You may be right — perhaps you are — but I should be no use in a War Cabinet. I should only hamper you. If we have to fight, we must fight with single-hearted conviction. There is no place for me in such affairs." To this I could find no answer, except to repeat that all would speedily be made plain, and that in forty-eight hours what was going to happen in Belgium, and perhaps in the North Sea, would make him feel quite differently about things. But he persisted.

Gently, gaily almost, he withdrew from among us, never by word or sign to hinder old friends or add to the nation's burden.

On August 2 German intentions became even clearer:

WSC to Lord Robert Cecil
(Cecil Papers)

2 August 1914   Admiralty
Copy

Dear Cecil,
   I am sorry to say that since I wrote to you we have learned officially that Germany has declared war on Russia. I cannot think that the rupture with France can be long delayed. And the course of events is likely to be very serious as regards Belgium.

Yours sincerely
WINSTON S. CHURCHILL

The Cabinet now discussed certain measures to support France; measures which Churchill strongly urged on his colleagues, and with success:

Admiralty to Commander-in-Chief, Home Fleet, Vice Admirals,
2nd and 3rd Fleet. Commander-in-Chief, Home Ports

2 August 1914

At 2.20 today, 2nd August, the following note was handed to the French and German Ambassadors. The British Government would not allow the passage of German ships through the English Channel or the North Sea in order to attack the coasts or shipping of France.
   Be prepared to meet surprise attacks.

On August 3 the German armies crossed into France and Belgium. The doubts of some Cabinet members were at once ended. Lord Morley had already resigned in protest against a British involvement in the European war. Burns and Trevelyan were to follow. The British ultimatum to Germany demanding the maintenance of Belgian neutrality expired unheeded at midnight on August 4 (11 p.m. British time):

Admiralty to all HM ships and Naval
Establishments

SIGNAL

4 August 1914   Admiralty
11 pm

COMMENCE HOSTILITIES AGAINST GERMANY

*

Churchill was a romantic. Tears easily came to his eyes when he talked of the long story of Britain's achievement in the world and the many deeds of heroism which had adorned it. We have seen how deeply moved he had been by the untimely end of his flying instructor Lushington and the noble fortitude of his fiancée. Such fortitude in distress warmed and comforted his heart in all that he was doing to keep Britain and her Empire safe and glorious. If his life had ended in 1914 in his fortieth year we can be sure that he would not have been denied a page in history and that his epitaph would have been

When War Came

The Fleet was Ready

Index

Index

COMPILED BY G. NORMAN KNIGHT, M.A.

VICE-PRESIDENT OF THE SOCIETY OF INDEXERS

The entry under the name of Winston Churchill has been confined to those subheadings which cannot be readily found under other entries.

Throughout the index his name has been abbreviated to WSC, that of his wife to CC and that of his son, the author, to RSC. Similarly, LG stands for Lloyd George and BL for Bonar Law.

Other abbreviations used are: *q.* for "quoted"; *qv* for *quod vide* ("which see").

Large and small CAPITALS for a surname indicate that it is the subject of a short biography between pages xxiii and xxxii.

Subheadings have been arranged mainly in chronological order.

Page reference numbers in **bold type** indicate that more than a few lines are devoted to the subject in the text. Reference numbers in *italics* denote illustrations or their captions, or maps.

bis after a reference number denotes that the item is quite separately mentioned on the same page of the text, and *ter* three times. *Passim* after a group of reference numbers (e.g. 16–20) indicates that the item is not referred to continuously but is scattered throughout those pages.

The method of alphabetical arrangement is word-by-word.

Agadir (Morocco), German gunboat incident (1911), 371, **503–7**, 511, 513, 702
WSC warned by, 503, 541, 579
Aircraft carriers, development of, **679–81**
Airlie, 10th Earl of (1856–1900), 240
Airships, naval controversy over, **679**
Aitken, Sir Max (later 1st Baron Beaverbrook, *qv*) (1879–1966):
introduced to WSC (1911), 554; his career, **554, 555**; BL a "pliant tool" of, 445, 554; invites WSC to Canada to seek naval contribution (1912), **554–6**, 646
Akers-Douglas, Aretas (later 1st Viscount Chilston) (1851–1926), 329
Aliens Bill introduced by (1904), 80
Albert, Prince (later Edward VIII, now Duke of Windsor) (b. 1894), 552
Albert, Prince Consort (1819–61), 405
Albu, Sir George, 1st Bt (1857–1935), 170
Alexander the Great (356–23 BC), WSC quotes, 389
Alfonso XIII, King of Spain (1866–1941), prevented from attending British Fleet mobilization (July 1914), **689–90**
Alice, Grand-duchess of Hesse-Darmstadt (1843–78), 533
Aliens Act (1906), 84, 249
George V favours amendment of (1911), 395, 416
Aliens Bill (1904):
WSC's attitude to, **80–4**; Government abandon, 82
Aliens Bill drafted by WSC (1911), 394, **395–6**, 416
Althorp, Viscount (later 6th Earl Spencer) (1857–1922), Lord Chamberlain (1905–12), 326
Alverstone, Richard Webster, Viscount (LCJ) (1842–1915), writes to WSC, 397
American Civil War (1861–5), 436
Amery, Leopold (1873–1955):
on WSC's fleet movements off Ulster,

(1914), 482; *My Political Life* (1953–5), *q.*, **205–6**, 484
Anglo-Persian (now Anglo-Iranian) Oil Co., 593
Anglo-Persian Oil Convention (1913), 593
Anne, Queen (1665–1714), creation of 12 peers by (1712), 328
Annual Register, the:
calls WSC's argument "unanswerable" (1901), 14; on Education Act (1902), 40; on Deceased Wife's Sister Bill (1902), 41, 42; on Colonial Conference (1907), 207; on Daylight Saving Bill (1909), 280; on General Election (Jan. 1910), 321; on Royal inspection of Fleet (1912), 552; on equipping Ulster volunteers (1914), **485**
Anson, Sir William, 3rd Bt (1843–1914), on the Milner debate (1906), WSC "pompous and impertinent," 179–80
Antrim, HMS, 369
"Appeasement," WSC on, **491–2**
Arbitration courts, industrial, instituted by WSC (1909), **278**
Argyll, 9th Duke of (1845–1914), 306
Ark Royal, George V objects to name for warship (1913), **631–5**
Armadale Castle, RMS, 558
Armstrong-Vickers group, Turkish contract (1913), **625–6**
Army, the:
abolition of purchase of commissions (1871), 306; Brodrick's scheme for reform of, **16–20, 37**, 75, 84; "an adjunct to the navy" — WSC (1901), 17, 19; Arnold-Forster's reform scheme (1904), **84–5**; use of, in strikes (1910 and 1911), 358–62 *passim;* **368–72**; use of, in Ulster (1914), 474, **474–9**; General Staff distinguished from Naval War Staff, **524**
Army (Annual) Act, 4, 470
Army League, the, 17
ARNOLD-FORSTER, Hugh O.,
succeeds Brodrick as Secretary for

Churchill, Winston Leonard Spencer, *cont'd*

(*qv*), 21–2; attacks Government's handling of S. African War, 25–7; seeks a "Middle Party," 32, 34–5, 45–6; member of select committee on control of public expenditure (1902), 38; his Memorandum on this subject, 38–9

Is not offered office by Balfour on becoming Premier (1902), 50; his transformation from Tory to Liberal, **68–71**, 75–6; crosses the floor (1904 and 1924), 5, **78**, 427; serves on Standing Committee on Aliens Bill, 82; his motion against Preference (1905), 93, **98–101**; is offered by C-B the Financial Secretaryship to Treasury, but secures Under-Secretaryship for Colonies, 104–5, 232; reports for duty to Lord Elgin, 106–7; congratulatory messages on his appointment, **107–8**

Wins N-W Manchester as Liberal (1906), **111–23**; and conciliation of S. Africa, 142, **144–61**; all S. African business left entirely to him (1906), 155, 187–8, 196; his "terminological inexactitude" description of Chinese slavery, 163, 164 *bis;* results of his first year's work in office, **187–8**; appointed Privy Councillor (1907), 204, 205; enters Cabinet as President of Board of Trade (1908), **237**, 311, 428

Loses by-election, N-W Manchester, **249**, 435; wins at Dundee, *following 222*, **256**, 321; his Labour Exchanges Act (1909), **297–303**; Home Secretary (1910–11), 275, **352–79**, **391–411**; First Lord of Admiralty (1911–15), **518–26**, **531–5**, **543–706**; likelihood of his resignation over 1914 Estimates, 641 *ter*, 643, **648–9**, 649, 658, 670; "When War Came the Fleet was Ready," 706

POLITICAL MEMORANDA by, *see* Memoranda

POLITICAL SPEECHES by, *see* Speeches

WORKS by:

Edward Marsh "corrected the orthography" of some of, 110

(*see also* under following titles): *Savrola* (1900); *Mr Brodrick's Army* (1903); *Lord Randolph Churchill* (1906); "Smooth Way with the Peers, A" (1907); *My African Journey* (1908); "Untrodden Field in Politics, The" (1908); *People's Rights, The* (1910); *World Crisis, The* (1923–9); *My Early Life* (1930); *Thoughts and Adventures* (1932); *Great Contemporaries* (1934)

Churchill, Mrs Winston (née Clementine Hozier, *qv*) (b. 1885) (now Baroness Spencer-Churchill):

photos of, *following 222, 478;* honeymoon of, **266**; WSC's concern for her, 283–4, 284–5; birth of Diana (1909), 284; listened to LG's Limehouse speech (1909), 295; birth of RSC (1911), **337–8**; agrees that Winterton's conduct was "detestable," 339; sees Coronation from the King's box, **343**; she and WSC visit Asquith (1911), 514

And RSC's godparents, 345; WSC warned not to take her to Belfast (1912), 450; WSC writes to (1914) about "Ulster pogrom," 484 *bis;* dislikes WSC's flying — WSC writes that he "was on verge of taking" his air pilot's certificate (June 1914), **687–9**; WSC writes to, about imminence of War, **694–5**, **698–9**

LETTERS:

from WSC: (1909, March–April), 283 *bis*, 283–4, 289, 297, 312; (1909, May–Aug), 218, 283 *bis*, 284, 314–5; 317 *bis;* (1909, Sept–Nov), 217, 219, 301, 315, 316; (1910), 334; (1911, April), 332, 338; (June–July), 339, 340, 343, 344, 346, 347; (1909, Aug–Sept), 347 *bis*, 510, 511 *bis;* (1910), 334; (1911, April), 332, 338; (1911, June–July), 339, 340, 346, 347; (1911,